Quantitative Business Valuation

Other Titles in the Irwin Library of Investment and Finance

Convertible Securities
by John P. Calamos

Pricing and Managing Exotic and Hybrid Options
by Vineer Bhansali

Risk Management and Financial Derivatives
by Satyajit Das

Valuing Intangible Assets
by Robert F. Reilly and Robert P. Schweihs

Managing Financial Risk
by Charles W. Smithson

High-Yield Bonds
by Theodore Barnhill, William Maxwell, and Mark Shenkman

Valuing Small Business and Professional Practices, 3rd edition
by Shannon Pratt, Robert F. Reilly, and Robert P. Schweihs

Implementing Credit Derivatives
by Israel Nelken

The Handbook of Credit Derivatives
by Jack Clark Francis, Joyce Frost, and J. Gregg Whittaker

The Handbook of Advanced Business Valuation
by Robert F. Reilly and Robert P. Schweihs

Global Investment Risk Management
by Ezra Zask

Active Portfolio Management 2nd edition
by Richard Grinold and Ronald Kahn

The Hedge Fund Handbook
by Stefano Lavinio

Pricing, Hedging, and Trading Exotic Options
by Israel Nelken

Equity Management
by Bruce Jacobs and Kenneth Levy

Asset Allocation, 3rd edition
by Roger Gibson

Valuing a Business, 4th edition
by Shannon P. Pratt, Robert F. Reilly, and Robert Schweihs

The Relative Strength Index Advantage
by Andrew Cardwell and John Hayden

Quantitative Business Valuation

A Mathematical Approach for Today's Professional

JAY B. ABRAMS, ASA, CPA, MBA

McGRAW-HILL

New York   San Francisco   Washington, D.C.   Auckland   Bogotá
Caracas   Lisbon   London   Madrid   Mexico City   Milan
Montreal   New Delhi   San Juan   Singapore
Sydney   Tokyo   Toronto

Library of Congress Cataloging-in-Publication Data

Abrams, Jay B.
    Quantitative business valuation : a mathematical approach for today's professionals / by
Jay B. Abrams.
      p. cm.
    Includes bibliographical references and index.
    ISBN 0-07-000215-0
    1. Business enterprises—Valuation—Mathematical models.   I. Title.

HF5681.V3 A28 2000
657'.73—dc21

00-055092

McGraw-Hill

A Division of The **McGraw·Hill** Companies

1 2 3 4 5 6 7 8 9 0   BKM/BKM 9 0 9 8 7 6 5 4 3 2 1 0

ISBN 0-07-000215-0

It was set in Palatino by Pro-Image Corporation.

Printed and bound by BookMart Press.

This publication is designed to provide accurate and authoritative information in regard to the subject matter covered. It is sold with the understanding that neither the author nor the publisher is engaged in rendering legal, accounting, or other professional service. If legal advice or other expert assistance is required, the services of a competent professional person should be sought.

—From a declaration of Principles jointly adopted by a Committee of the American Bar Association and a Committee of Publishers.

McGraw-Hill books are available at special quantity discounts to use as premiums and sales promotions, or for use in corporate training programs. For more information, please write to the Director of Special Sales, Professional Publishing, McGraw-Hill, 2 Penn Plaza, New York, NY 10121-2298. Or contact your local bookstore.

This book is printed on recycled, acid-free paper containing a minimum of 50% recycled de-inked fiber.

To my father, Leonard Abrams, who taught me how to write. To my mother, Marilyn Abrams, who taught me mathematics. To my wife, Cindy, who believes in me. To my children, Yonatan, Binyamin, Miriam, and Nechamah Leah, who gave up countless Sundays with Abba (Dad) for this book. To my youngest child, Rivkah Sarah, who wasn't yet on the outside to miss the Sundays with me, but who has brought us peace. To my parents and my brother, Mark, for their tremendous support under difficult circumstances.

To my great teachers, Mr. Oshima and Christopher Hunt, who brought me to my power to make this happen. And finally, to R. K. Hiatt, who has caught my mistakes and made significant contributions to the thought that permeates this book.

Contents

Introduction *xiii*

Acknowledgments *xvii*

List of Figures *xix*

List of Tables *xxi*

PART I
FORECASTING CASH FLOWS

1. Cash Flow: A Mathematical Derivation *3*

Introduction. The Mathematical Model. *A Preliminary Explanation of Cash Flows. Analyzing Property, Plant, and Equipment Transactions. An Explanation of Cash Flows with More Detail for Equity Transactions. Considering the Components of Required Working Capital. Adjusting for Required Cash.* Comparison to Other Cash Flow Definitions. Conclusion.

2. Using Regression Analysis *21*

Introduction. Forecasting Costs and Expenses. *Adjustments to Expenses. Table 2-1A: Calculating Adjusted Costs and Expenses.* Performing Regression Analysis. Use of Regression Statistics to Test the Robustness of the Relationship. *Standard Error of the* y *Estimate. The Mean of* a *and* b*. The Variance of* a *and* b*. Selecting the Data Set and Regression Equation.* Problems with Using Regression Analysis for Forecasting Costs. *Insufficient Data. Substantial Changes in Competition or Product/Service.* Using Regression Analysis to Forecast Sales. *Spreadsheet Procedures to Perform Regression. Examining the Regression Statistics. Adding Industry-Specific Independent Variables. Try All Combinations of Potential Independent Variables.* Application of Regression Analysis to the Guideline Company Method. *Table 2-5: Regression Analysis of Guideline Companies.* Summary. Appendix: The ANOVA table.

3. Annuity Discount Factors and the Gordon Model *57*

Introduction. *Definitions.* Denoting Time. ADF with End-of-Year Cash Flows. *Behavior of the ADF with Growth. Special Case of ADF* when g = 0: *The Ordinary Annuity. Special Case when* n → ∞ *and* r > g: *The Gordon Model. Intuitively Understanding Equations (3-6) and (3-6a). Relationship between the ADF and the Gordon Model.* Table 3-1: *Proof of ADF Equations (3-6) through (3-6b). A Brief Summary.* Midyear Cash Flows. *Table 3-2: Example of Equations (3-10) through (3-10b). Special Cases for Midyear Cash Flows: No Growth,* g = 0. *Gordon Model. Starting Periods Other than Year 1. End-of-Year Formulas. Valuation Date* ≠ 0. *Table 3-3: Example of Equation (3-11). Tables 3-4 through 3-6: Variations of Table 3-3 with* S < 0, *Negative Growth, and* r < g. *Special Case: No Growth,* g = 0. *Generalized Gordon Model. Midyear Formula.* Periodic Perpetuity Factors (PPFs): Perpetuities for Periodic Cash Flows. *The Mathematical Formulas. Tables 3-7 and 3-8: Examples of Equations (3-18) and (3-19). Other Starting Years. New versus Used Equipment Decisions.* ADFs in Loan Mathematics. *Calculating Loan Payments. Present Value of a Loan.* Relationship of the Gordon Model to the Price/Earnings Ratio. *Definitions. Mathematical Derivation.* Conclusions.

PART II
CALCULATING DISCOUNT RATES

4. Discount Rates as a Function of Log Size   117

Prior Research. Table 4-1: Analysis of Historical Stock Returns. *Regression #1: Return versus Standard Deviation of Returns. Regression #2: Return versus Log Size. Regression #3: Return versus Beta. Market Performance. Which Data to Choose? Recalculation of the Log Size Model Based on 60 Years.* Application of the Log Size Model. *Discount Rates Based on the Log Size Model. Practical Illustration of the Log Size Model: Discounted Cash Flow Valuations. Total Return versus Equity Premium. Adjustments to the Discount Rate. Discounted Cash Flow or Net Income?* Discussion of Models and Size Effects. *CAPM. The Fama–French Cost of Equity Model. Log Size Models. Heteroscedasticity.* Industry Effects. Satisfying Revenue Ruling 59-60 without a Guideline Public Company Method. Summary and Conclusions. Appendix A: Automating Iteration Using Newton's Method. Appendix B: Mathematical Appendix. Appendix C: Abbreviated Review and Use.

5. Arithmetic versus Geometric Means: Empirical Evidence and Theoretical Issues   169

Introduction. Theoretical Superiority of Arithmetic Mean. *Table 5-1: Comparison of Two Stock Portfolios.* Empirical Evidence of the Superiority of the Arithmetic Mean. *Table 5-2: Regressions of Geometric and Arthmetic Returns for 1927–1997. Table 5-3: Regressions of Geometric Returns for 1938–1997. The Size Effect on the Arithmetic versus Geometric Means. Table 5-4: Log Size Comparison of Discount Rates and Gordon Model Multiples Using AM versus GM.* Indro and Lee Article.

6. An Iterative Valuation Approach   179

Introduction. Equity Valuation Method. *Table 6-1A: The First Iteration. Table 6-1B: Subsequent Iterations of the First Scenario. Table*

6-1C: Initial Choice of Equity Doesn't Matter. Convergence of the Equity Valuation Method. Invested Capital Approach. *Table 6-2A: Iterations Beginning with Book Equity. Table 6-2B: Initial Choice of Equity Doesn't Matter. Convergence of the Invested Capital Approach.* Log Size. Summary. Bibliography.

PART III
ADJUSTING FOR CONTROL AND MARKETABILITY

7. Adjusting for Levels of Control and Marketability   *195*

Introduction. The Value of Control and Adjusting for Level of Control. *Prior Research—Qualitative Professional. Prior Research—Academic. My Synthesis and Analysis.* Discount for Lack of Marketability (DLOM). *Mercer's Quantitative Marketability Discount Model. Kasper's BAS Model. Restricted Stock Discounts. Abrams' Economic Components Model. Mercer's Rebuttal. Conclusion.* Mathematical Appendix.

8. Sample Restricted Stock Discount Study   *293*

Introduction. *Background. Stock Ownership. Purpose of the Appraisal. No Economic Outlook Section. Sources of Data.* Valuation. *Commentary to Table 8-1: Regression Analysis of Management Planning Data. Commentary to Table 8-1A: Revenue and Earnings Stability. Commentary to Table 8-1B: Price Stability. Valuation Using Options Pricing Theory. Conclusion of Discount for Lack of Marketability.* Assumptions and Limiting Conditions. Appraiser's Qualifications.

9. Sample Appraisal Report   *315*

Introduction. *Purpose of the Report. Valuation of Considerations. Sources of Data.* History and Description of the LLC. *Significant Terms and Legal Issues. Conclusion.* Economic Outlook. *Economic Growth. Inflation. Interest Rates. State and Local Economics. Summary.* Financial Review. *Commentary to Table 9-2: FMV Balance Sheets. Commentary to Table 9-3: Income Statements. Commentary to Table 9-4: Cash Distributions.* Valuation. *Valuation Approaches. Selection of Valuation Approach. Economic Components Approach. Commentary to Table 9-5: Calculations of Combined Discounts. Commentary to Table 9-5A: Delay-to-Sale. Commentary to Table 9-5C: Calculation of DLOM. Commentary to Table 9-6: Partnership Profiles Approach—1999. Commentary to Table 9-7: Private Fractional Interest Sales. Commentary to Table 9-8: Final Calculation of Fractional Interest Discounts. Conclusion.* Statement of Limiting Conditions. Appraiser's Qualifications. Appendix: Tax Court's Opinion for Discount for Lack of Marketability. Introduction. The Court's 10 Factors. Application of the Court's 10 Factors to the Valuation.

PART IV
PUTTING IT ALL TOGETHER

10. Empirical Testing of Abrams' Valuation Theory   *357*

Introduction. *Steps in the Valuation Process. Applying a Valuation Model to the Steps. Table 10-1: Log Size for 1938–1986. Table 10-2:*

Reconciliation to the IBA Database. *Part 1: IBA P/CF Multiples.*
Part 2: Log Size P/CF Multiples. Conclusion. Calculation of DLOM.
Table 10-4: Computation of the Delay-to-Sale Component–$25,000 Firm.
Table 10-5: Calculation of Transactions Costs. Table 10-6: Calculation of
DLOM. Table 10-6A–10-6F: Calculations of DLOM for Larger Firms.
Calculation of DLOM for Large Firms. Interpretation of the Error.
Conclusion.

11. Measuring Valuation Uncertainty and Error   *383*

Introduction. *Differences Between Uncertainty and Error. Sources of*
Uncertainty and Error. Measuring Valuation Uncertainty. *Table 11-1:*
95% Confidence Intervals. Summary of Valuation Implications of
Statistical Uncertainty in the Discount Rate. Measuring the Effects of
Valuation Error. *Defining Absolute and Relative Error. The Valuation*
Model. Dollar Effects of Absolute Errors in Forecastng Year 1 Cash Flow.
Relative Effects of Absolute Errors in Forecasting Year 1 Cash Flow.
Absolute and Relative Effects of Relative Errors in Forecasting Year 1
Cash Flow. Absolute Errors in Forecasting Growth and the Discount
Rate. Table 11-5: Summary of Effects of Valuation Errors. Summary and
Conclusions.

PART V
SPECIAL TOPICS

12. Valuing Startups   *407*

Issues Unique to Startups. Organization of the Chapter. First
Chicago Approach. *Discounting Cash Flow Is Preferable to Net Income.*
Capital Structure Changes. Venture Capital Rates of Return. Table 12-1:
Example of the First Chicago Approach. Advantages of the First Chicago
Approach. Discounts for Lack of Marketability and Control. Venture
Capital Valuation Approach. *Venture Capital Rates of Return.*
Summary of the VC Approach. Debt Restructuring Study. *Backgound.*
Key Events. Decision Trees and Spreadsheet Calculations. Table 12-3:
Statistical Calculation of FMV. Conclusion. Exponentially Declining
Sales Growth Model.

13. ESOPs: Measuring and Apportioning Dilution   *433*

Introduction. *What Can Be Skipped.* Definitions of Dilution. *Dilution*
to the ESOP (Type 1 Dilution). Dilution to the Selling Owner (Type 2
Dilution). Defining Terms. Table 13-1: Calculation of Lifetime ESOP
Costs. The Direct Approach. *FMV Equations—All Dilution to the*
ESOP (Type 1 Dilution; No Type 2 Dilution). Table 13-2, Sections 1 and
2: Post-transaction FMV with All Dilution to the ESOP. The Post-
transaction Value Is a Parabola. FMV Equations—All Dilution to the
Owner (Type 2 Dilution). Table 13-2, Section 3: FMV Calculations—All
Dilution to the Seller. Sharing the Dilution. Equation to Calculate Type 2
Dilution. Tables 13-3 and 13-3A: Adjusting Dilution to Desired Levels.
Table 13-3B: Summary of Dilution Tradeoffs. The Iterative Approach.
Iteration #1. Iteration #2. Iteration #3. Iteration #n. Summary.
Advantages of Results. Function of ESOP Loan. Common Sense Is
Required. To Whom Should the Dilution Belong? Appendix A:

Mathematical Appendix. Appendix B: Shorter Version of Chapter 13.

14. Buyouts of Partners and Shareholders   *471*

Introduction. An Example of a Buyout. *The Solution*. Evaluating the Benchmarks.

Glossary   *475*
Index   *479*

Introduction

NATURE OF THE BOOK

This is an advanced book in the science and art of valuing privately held businesses. In order to read this book, you must already have read at least one introductory book such as *Valuing A Business* (Pratt, Reilly, and Schweihs 1996). Without such a background, you will be lost.

I have written this book with the professional business appraiser as my primary intended audience, though I think this book is also appropriate for attorneys who are very experienced in valuation matters, investment bankers, venture capitalists, financial analysts, and MBA students.

Uniqueness of This Book

This is a rigorous book, and it is not easy reading. However, the following unique attributes of this book make reading it worth the effort:

1. It emphasizes regression analysis of empirical data. Chapter 7, adjusting for control and marketability, contains the first regression analysis of the data related to restricted stock discounts. Chapter 9, a sample fractional interest discount study, contains a regression analysis of the Partnership Profiles database related to secondary limited partnership market trades. In both cases we found very significant results. We now know much of what drives (a) restricted stock discounts and (b) discounts from net asset values of the publicly registered/ privately traded limited partnerships. You will also see much empirical work in Chapter 4, "Discount Rates as a Function of Log Size," and Chapter 11, "Empirical Testing of Abrams' Valuation Theory."

2. It emphasizes quantitative skills. Chapter 2 focuses on using regression analysis in business valuation. Chapter 3, "Annuity Discount Factors and the Gordon Model," is the most comprehensive treatment of ADFs in print. For anyone wishing to use the Mercer quantitative marketability discount model,

Chapter 4 contains the ADF with constant growth not included in the Mercer text. ADFs crop up in many valuation contexts. I invented several new ADFs that appear in Chapter 3 that are useful in many valuation contexts. Chapter 11 contains the first treatise on how much statistical uncertainty we have in our valuations and how value is affected when the appraiser makes various errors.

3. It emphasizes putting all the pieces of the puzzle together to present a comprehensive, unified approach to valuation that can be empirically tested and whose principles work for the valuation of billion-dollar firms and ma and pa firms alike. While this book contains more mathematics—a worm's eye view, if you will—than other valuation texts, it also has more of a bird's eye view as well.

HOW TO READ THIS BOOK

I have tried to provide paths through this book to make it easier to follow. Chapters 4 and 13 both contain a shortcut version of the chapter at the end for those who want the bottom line without all the detail. In general, I have moved most of the heaviest mathematics to appendices in order to leave the bodies of the chapters more readable. Where that was not optimal, I have given instructions on which material can be safely skipped.

How to read this book depends on your quantitative skills and how much time you have available. For the reader with strong quantitative skills and abundant time, the ideal path is to read the book in its exact order, as there is a logical sequence. The first three parts to this book follow the chronological sequence of performing a valuation: (1) forecast cash flows, (2) discount to present value, and (3) adjust for control and marketability. The fourth part is a bird's eye view in order to test empirically whether my methodology works. Additionally, we explore (1) confidence intervals around valuation estimates and (2) what happens to the valuation when appraisers make mistakes. Part 5, on special topics, is the place for everything else. Each of parts of the book has an introduction preceding it that will preview the upcoming material in greater depth than we cover here.

Because most professionals do not have abundant time, I want to suggest another path geared for the maximum benefit from the least investment in time. The heart of the book is Chapters 4 and 7, on log size and on adjusting for control and marketability, respectively. I recommend the time-pressed reader follow this order:

1. Chapter 7 (discounts for lack of control and lack of marketability)
2. Chapter 8 (this is an application of Chapter 7—a sample restricted stock report)
3. Chapter 9 (this is an application of Chapter 7—a sample fractional ownership interest discount report)

4. Chapter 4 (the log size model for calculating discount rates)

5. Chapter 3—the following sections: from the beginning through the section titled "A Brief Summary"; "Periodic Perpetuity Factors: Perpetuities for Periodic Cash Flows"; and "Relationship of Gordon Model Multiple to the Price/Earnings Ratio." Some readers may want to read this chapter after Chapter 7, though it will be somewhat helpful, but definitely not necessary, to have read Chapter 3 before 4 and 7.

6. Chapter 10 (this empirically tests Chapters 4 and 7, the heart of the book)

7. Chapter 2 (some readers may want to start with Chapter 2 first, as the material on using regression analysis may help reading all of the other chapters).

After these chapters, you can read the remainder of the book in any order, though it is best to read Chapter 14 immediately after Chapter 13.

This book has close to 125 tables, many of them being two or three pages long. To facilitate your reading, it will help you to copy tables whose commentary in the text is extensive and sit with the separate tables next to you. Otherwise, you will spend an inordinate amount of time flipping pages back and forth. Note: readers with low blood pressure may wish to ignore that advice.

BIBLIOGRAPHY

Mercer, Z. Christopher. 1997. *Quantifying Marketability Discounts: Developing and Supporting Marketability Discounts in the Appraisal of Closely Held Business Interests.* Memphis, Tenn.: Peabody.

Pratt, Shannon P., Robert F. Reilly, and Robert P. Schweihs. 1996. *Valuing a Business: The Analysis and Appraisal of Closely Held Companies,* 3d ed. New York: McGraw-Hill.

Acknowledgments

I gratefully acknowledge help beyond the call of duty from my parents, Leonard and Marilyn Abrams. Professionally, R. K. Hiatt has been the ideal internal editor. Without his help, this book would have suffered greatly. He also contributed important insights throughout the book.

Robert Reilly edited the original manuscript cover-to-cover. I thank Robert very much for the huge time commitment for someone else's book. Larry Kasper gave me a surprise detailed edit of the first eight chapters. I benefited much from his input and thank him profusely.

Chris Mercer also read much or all of the book and gave me many corrections and very useful feedback. I thank Chris very much for his valuable time, of which he gave me much.

Michael Bolotsky and Eric Nath were very helpful to me in editing my summary of their work.

I thank Rob Oliver and Roy Meyers of Management Planning, Inc. for providing me with their restricted stock data. I also thank Bob Jones of Jones, Roach & Caringella for providing me with private fractional interest sales of real estate.

Chaim Borevitz provided important help on Chapters 8 and 9. Mark Shayne provided me with dozens of insightful comments. Professor William Megginson gave me considerable feedback on Chapter 7. I thank him for his wisdom, patience, and good humor. His colleague, Professor Lance Nail, also was very helpful to me.

I also appreciate the following people who gave me good feedback on individual chapters (or their predecessor articles): Don Wisehart, Betsy Cotter, Robert Wietzke, Abdul Walji, Jim Plummer, Mike Annin, Ed Murray, Greg Gilbert, Jared Kaplan, Esq., Robert Gross, Raymond Miles, and Steven Stamp.

I thank the following people who provided me with useful information that appears in the book: John Watson, Jr., Esq., David Boatwright, Esq., Douglas Obenshain, and Gordon Gregory.

I thank the following people who reviewed this book for McGraw-Hill: Shannon Pratt, Robert Reilly, Jay Fishman, Larry Kasper, Bob Grossman, Terry Isom, Herb Spiro, Don Shannon, Chris Mercer, Dave Bishop, Jim Rigby, and Kent Osborne.

I thank my editor at McGraw-Hill, Ela Aktay, for her encouragement and enthusiasm. I thank my publisher, Jeff Krames, for his patience and apologize for testing it so much due to my passion for perfection and the huge life-changes that occurred to me while writing this book.

All the people who have helped make this book a reality have my profound gratitude. In fact, there have been so many that it is almost impossible to remember every single person, and I apologize to anyone who should be in this acknowledgment section and who is not due to my human failings.

Acknowledgments

List of Figures

2-1	Z-distribution vs t-distribution	*34*
2-2	t-distribution of B around the Estimate b	*35*
3-1	Timeline of the ADF and Gordon Model	*65*
A3-1	Timeline of Cash Flows	*91*
A3-2	Payment Schedule	*100*
4-1	1926–1998 Arithmetic Mean Returns as a Function of Standard Deviation	*125*
4-2	1926–1998 Arithmetic Mean Returns as a Function of Ln(FMV)	*127*
4-3	Decade Standard Deviation of Returns versus Decade Average FMV per Company on NYSE 1935–1995	*128*
4-4	Decade Standard Deviation of Returns versus Decade Average FMV per Company on NYSE 1945–1995	*129*
4-5	Average Returns Each Decade	*130*
4-6	The Natural Logarithm	*137*
4-7	Discount Rates as a Function of FMV	*137*
4-8	1939–1998 Decile Standard Deviations as a Function of Ln(FMV)	*138*
7-1	Traditional Levels of Value Chart	*197*
7-2	Two-Tiered Levels of Value Chart	*198*
7-3	3×2 Levels of Value Chart	*230*
10-1	P/E Ratio as a Function of Size (From the IBA Database)	*363*
12-1	Decision Tree for Venture Capital Funding	*421*
12-2	Decision Tree for Bootstrapping Assuming Debt Restructure and No Venture Capital	*425*
12-3	Sales Forecast (Decay Rate = 0.5)	*430*
12-3A	Sales Forecast (Decay Rate = 0.3)	*431*
13-1	Post-Transaction Value of the ESOP Vs. % Sold	*442*

List of Tables

1-1	Abbreviated Balance Sheets	7
1-2	Income Statement	8
1-3	Analysis of Property, Plant, and Equipment	9
1-4	Statement of Stockholders' Equity	12
1-5	Abbreviated Statement of Cash Flows	13
1-6	Balance Sheets	15
1-7	Statement of Cash Flows	16
2-1A	Adjustments to Historical Costs and Expenses	24
2-1B	Regression Analysis 1988–1997	27
2-1B	Calculation of 95% Confidence Intervals for Forecast 1998 Costs	28
2-2	OLS Regression: Example of Deviation from Mean	31
2-3	Abbreviated Table of T-Statistics	36
2-4	Regression Analysis 1993–1997	40
2-5	Regression Analysis of Sales as a Function of GDP [1]	43
2-6	Regression Analysis of Guideline Companies	47
A2-1	Regression Analysis 1988–1997	54
3-1	ADF: End-of-Year Formula	66
3-2	ADF: Midyear Formula	69
3-3	ADF with Cash Flows Starting in Year 3.25: End-of-Year Formula	72
3-4	ADF with Cash Flows Starting in Year −2.00: End-of-Year Formula	74
3-5	ADF with Cash Flows Starting in Year −2.00 with Negative Growth: End-of-Year Formula	75
3-6	ADF with Cash Flows Starting in Year −2.00 with $g > r$: End-of-Year Formula	76
3-7	Periodic Perpetuity Factor (PPF): End-of-Year Formula	80
3-8	Periodic Perpetuity Factor (PPF): Midyear Formula	80
3-9	Periodic Perpetuity Factor (PPF): End-of-Year—Cash Flows Begin Year 6	83
3-10	PV of Loan with Market Rate > Nominal Rate: ADF, End-of-Year	86

3-11	ADF Equation Numbers	90
A3-1	ADF with Fractional Year: Midyear Formula	95
A3-2	ADF with Fractional Year: Midyear Formula	96
A3-3	Amortization of Principal with Irregular Starting Point	103
A3-4	PV of Principal Amortization	107
A3-5	Present Value of a Loan at Discount Rate Different than Nominal Rate	110
4-1	NYSE Data by Decile and Statistical Analysis: 1926–1998	121
4-2	Regressions of Returns over Standard Deviation and Log of Fair Market Value	132
4-2A	Regression Comparison [1]	133
4-3	Table of Stock Market Returns Based on FMV—60-Year Model	136
4-4A	Discounted Cash Flow Analysis Using 60-Year Model—First Iteration	141
4-4B	Discounted Cash Flow Analysis Using 60-Year Model—Second Iteration	142
4-4C	Discounted Cash Flow Analysis Using 60-Year Model—Final Valuation	143
A4-5	Gordon Model Valuation Using Newton's Iterative Process	157
5-1	Geometric versus Arithmetic Returns	171
5-2	Geometric versus Arithmetic Returns: NYSE Data by Decile & Statistical Analysis: 1926–1997	172
5-3	Geometric Mean versus AFMV: 60 Years	174
5-4	Comparison of Discount Rates Derived from the Log Size Model Using 60-Year Arithmetic and Geometric Means	176
6-1A	Equity Valuation Approach with Iterations Beginning with Book Equity: Iteration #1	182
6-1B	Equity Valuation Approach with Iterations Beginning with Book Equity	184
6-1C	Equity Valuation Approach with Iterations Beginning with Arbitrary Equity	185
6-2A	WACC Approach with Iterations Beginning with Book Equity	187
6-2B	WACC Approach with Iterations Beginning with Arbitrary Guess of Equity Value	189
7-1	Synergies as Measured by Acquisition Minus Going-Private Premiums	199
7-1A	Acquisition and Going-Private Transactions Premiums	200
7-2	Acquisition Premiums by SIC Code	206
7-3	Analysis of Megginson Results	215
7-3A	Analysis of American VRP Results	218
7-4	Mergerstat Mean Premiums: Control versus Minority Purchases	225
7-5	Abrams Regression of Management Planning Study Data	237
7-6	Calculation of Continuously Compounded Standard Deviation Chantal Pharmaceutical, Inc.—CHTL	242
7-7	Black–Scholes Put Option—CHTL	244
7-8	Put Model Results	245

7-9	Calculation of Restricted Stock Discounts for 13 Stocks Using Regression from Table 7-5	247
7-10	Calculation of Component #1—Delay To Sale [1]	254
7-11	Estimates of Transaction Costs [1]	259
7-12	Proof of Equation (7-9)	267
7-13	Proof of Equation (7-9a)	270
7-14	Sample Calculation of DLOM	272
7-15[a]	QMDM Baseline Data—30% MPI Discount	275
7-16[a]	Implied Returns for Holding Period—30% Discount	275
7-17[a]	Implied Returns for Holding Period—20% Discount	276
7-18	Summary of Results of Applying the QMDM in 10 Example Appraisals	277
7-19	QMDM Comparison of Restricted Stock Discount Rate versus Mercer Example 1	279
8-1	Abrams Valuation Group Regression of Management Planning, Inc. Data	300
8-1A	Calculation of Revenue and Earnings Stability (R^2)	304
8-1B	Calculation of Price Stability	305
8-2	Black–Scholes Call and Put Options	307
8-2A	Standard Deviation of Continuously Compounded Returns	309
8-3	Final Calculation of Discount	310
9-1	Member Interests at Inception on 1/6/96	322
9-2	Balance Sheets 12/25/99 [1]	324
9-3	Income Statements [1]	325
9-4	Cash Distributions	326
9-5	Economic Components Approach: 2.80% Member Interest	328
9-5A	Calculation of Component #1: Delay to Sale [1]	330
9-5B	Earnings and Revenue Stability	332
9-5C	Calculation of DLOM: 2.80% Member Interest	334
9-6	Regression Analysis of Partnership Profiles Database—1999 [1]	339
9-6A	Correlation Matrix	341
9-6B	Partnership Profiles Database: Price-to-Value Discounts—1999	342
9-7	Private Fractional Interest Sales	346
9-8	Final Calculation of Fractional Interest Discount	347
10-1	Log Size Equation for 1938–1986 NYSE Data by Decile and Statistical Analysis: 1938–1986	360
10-2	Reconciliation to IBA Database	362
10-3	Proof of Discount Calculation	364
10-4	Calculation of Component #1—Delay to Sale—$25,000 Firm	367
10-5	Calculation of Transaction Costs for Firms of All Sizes in the IBA Study	369
10-6	Calculation of DLOM—$25,000 Firm	370
10-4A	Calculation of Component #1—Delay to Sale—$75,000 Firm	371
10-4B	Calculation of Component #1—Delay to Sale—$125,000 Firm	371

10-4C	Calculation of Component #1—Delay to Sale—$175,000 Firm	372
10-4D	Calculation of Component #1—Delay to Sale—$225,000 Firm	372
10-4E	Calculation of Component #1—Delay to Sale—$375,000 Firm	373
10-4F	Calculation of Component #1—Delay to Sale—$750,000 Firm	373
10-4G	Calculation of Component #1—Delay to Sale—$10 Million Firm	374
10-6A	Calculation of DLOM—$75,000 Firm	374
10-6B	Calculation of DLOM—$125,000 Firm	375
10-6C	Calculation of DLOM—$175,000 Firm	375
10-6D	Calculation of DLOM—$225,000 Firm	376
10-6E	Calculation of DLOM—$375,000 Firm	376
10-6F	Calculation of DLOM—$750,000 Firm	377
10-6G	Calculation of DLOM—$10,000,000 Firm	377
11-1	95% Confidence Intervals	389
11-2	95% Confidence Intervals—60-Year Log Size Model	391
11-3	Absolute Errors in Forecasting Growth Rates	398
11-4	Percent Valuation Error for 10% Relative Error in Growth	400
11-4A	Percent Valuation Error for −10% Relative Error in Growth	401
11-4B	Percent Valuation Error for 10% Relative Error in Discount Rate	402
11-5	Summary of Effects of Valuation Errors	403
12-1	First Chicago Method	412
12-2	VC Pricing Approach	414
12-3	Statistical Calculation of Fair Market Value	418
12-4	Sales Model with Exponentially Declining Growth Rate Assumption	430
13-1	Calculation of Lifetime ESOP Costs	438
13-2	FMV Calculations: Firm, ESOP, and Dilution	441
13-3	Adjusting Dilution to Desired Levels	446
13-3A	Adjusting Dilution to Desired Levels—All Dilution to Owner	447
13-3B	Summary of Dilution Tradeoffs	447

Forecasting Cash Flows

Part 1 of this book focuses on forecasting cash flows, the initial step in the valuation process. In order to forecast cash flows, it is important to:

- Precisely define the components of cash flow.
- Develop statistical tools to aid in forecasting cash flows.
- Analyze different types of annuities, which are structured series of cash flows.

In Chapter 1, we mathematically derive the cash flow statement as the result of creating and manipulating a series of accounting equations and identities. This should give the appraiser a much greater depth of understanding of how cash flows derive from and relate to the balance sheet and income statement. It may help eliminate errors made by appraisers who perform discounted cash flow analysis using shortcut or even incorrect definitions of cash flow.

In Chapter 2, we demonstrate in detail:

- How appraisers can use regression analysis to forecast sales and expenses, the latter by far being the more important use of regression.
- When and why the common practice of not using more than five years of historical data to prevent using stale data may be wrong.
- How to use regression analysis in valuation using publicly traded guideline companies information. While this is not related to forecasting sales and expenses, it fits in with our other discussions about using regression analysis.

When using publicly traded guideline companies of widely varying sizes, ordinary least squares (OLS) regression will usually fail, as statistical error is generally proportional to the market value (size) of the guideline company. However, there are simple transformations the appraiser can make to the data that will (1) enable him or her to minimize the negative impact of differences in size and (2) still preserve the very important benefit we derive from the variation in size of the publicly traded guideline companies, as we discuss in the chapter. The final result is valuations that are more reliable, realistic, and objective.

Most electronic spreadsheets provide a least squares regression that is adequate for most appraisal needs. I am familiar with the regression tools in both Microsoft Excel and Lotus 123. Excel does a better job of presentation and offers much more comprehensive statistical feedback. Lotus has one significant advantage: it can provide multiple regression analysis for a virtually unlimited number of variables, while Excel is limited to 16 independent variables.

In Chapter 3, we discuss annuity discount factors (ADFs). Historically, ADFs have not been used much in business valuation and thus, have had relatively little importance. Their importance is growing, however, for several reasons. They can be used in:

- Calculating the present value of annuities, including those with constant growth. This application has become far more important since the Mercer Quantitative Marketability Discount Model requires an ADF with growth.
- Valuing periodic expenses such as moving expenses, losses from lawsuits, etc.
- Calculating the present value of periodic capital expenditures with growth, e.g., what is the PV of keeping one airplane of a certain class in service perpetually.
- Calculating loan payments.
- Calculating loan principal amortization.
- Calculating the present value of a loan. This is important in calculating the cash equivalency selling price of a business, as seller financing typically takes place at less-than-market rates. The present value of a loan is also important in ESOP valuations.

Among my colleagues in the office, I unofficially titled Chapter 3, "The Chapter That Would Not Die!!!" I edited and rewrote this chapter close to 40 times striving for perfection, the elusive and unattainable goal. It was quite a task to decide what belongs in the body of the chapter and what should be relegated to the appendix. In an effort to maximize readability, the most practical formulas appear in the body of chapter 3 and the least useful and most mathematical work appears in the appendix.

CHAPTER 1

Cash Flow: A Mathematical Derivation[1]

INTRODUCTION

THE MATHEMATICAL MODEL

    A Preliminary Explanation of Cash Flows

    Analyzing Property, Plant, and Equipment Transactions

    An Explanation of Cash Flows with More Detail for Equity Transactions

    Considering the Components of Required Working Capital

    Adjusting for Required Cash

COMPARISON TO OTHER CASH FLOW DEFINITIONS

CONCLUSION

---

1. This chapter was coauthored with Donald Shannon, School of Accountancy, DePaul University. The mathematical model was published in Abrams (1997).

INTRODUCTION

In 1987, the Financial Accounting Standards Board (FASB) issued Statement of Financial Accounting Standards No. 95, "Statement of Cash Flows." This standard stipulates that a statement of cash flows is required as part of a full set of financial statements for almost all business enterprises.

This chapter, which discusses the Statement of Cash Flows, is intended for readers who already have a basic knowledge of accounting. Much of what follows will involve alternating between accrual and cash reporting, which can be very challenging material. Also, a parsimonious style has been used to keep the chapter to a reasonable length. Accordingly, certain sections and derivations may require more than one reading.

The primary purpose of a statement of cash flows is to provide relevant information about the cash receipts and cash payments of an enterprise. These receipts and payments must be classified according to three basic types of activities: operating, investing, and financing.

Operating activities involve those transactions that enter into the determination of net income. Examples of these activities are sales of goods or services, purchases of component materials, and compensation of employees. *Net income* reports these activities when they are earned or incurred. *Cash flows from operations* reports these activities only when they are collected or paid. For example, net income is increased when a sale is made even though no cash is collected. Cash flows from operations would reflect the increase only at the time the cash is collected. Also, net income is decreased when, say, insurance expense is incurred even though no payment is made. Cash flows from operations would reflect the decrease only at the time the payment is made.

Of course, companies engage in numerous transactions involving cash but having no impact on the income statement. These transactions are classified as investing or financing activities. Investing activities include the acquisition of long-lived assets as well as their disposition when no gains or losses are involved.[2] Financing activities include obtaining and repaying funds from debt and equity holders and providing the owners with a return on their investment.

Either the direct or the indirect method may be used as a basis for reporting cash flows from operating activities. Under the direct method the enterprise lists its major categories of cash receipts from operations (such as receipts from product sales and receipts from consulting services) and cash disbursements for operations (such as payments for inventory, wages, interest, and taxes). The difference between these receipts and disbursements is the net cash flow from operations.

Under the indirect method, net cash flow from operations is found by adjusting net income for changes in related asset and liability accounts. For example, an increase in accounts receivable indicates that *cash receipts* from sales are less than reported *revenues*. Receivables increase as a result

---

2. This introductory comment presumes the long-lived assets are sold for their net book values. Of course, when gains or losses on disposition are involved they *do* appear in the income statement. The treatment of these gains and losses is addressed later in the chapter.

of failing to collect all revenues reported. Therefore, the amount of the increase in accounts receivable would have to be subtracted from net income to arrive at net cash flow from operations. Likewise, a decrease in wages payable would indicate that *cash payments* for wages were greater than the *expenses* shown in the income statement. Payables decrease when payments exceed the amount of expenses reported. Therefore, the amount of the decrease in wages payable also would have to be subtracted from net income to arrive at net cash flow from operations.

Usually it is easy to follow the logic of the adjustment required to infer the cash flow associated with *any single* reported revenue or expense. However, most statements of cash flows require a number of such adjustments, which often result in confusing entanglements.

Many business and real estate appraisers spend a significant part of their careers forecasting cash flows. The objective of this chapter is to improve their understanding of the cash flow statement and its interrelationship with the balance sheet and the income statement. Appraisers who read this chapter will, we hope, be able to understand better the cash flow logic and distinguish true cash flows from shortcut approximations thereof.

To achieve this result, this chapter provides a mathematical derivation of the cash flow statement using the indirect method. A realistic numerical example and an intuitive explanation accompany the mathematical derivation.[3]

THE MATHEMATICAL MODEL

In what follows, be careful to distinguish between equations and tables, as they both have the same numbering system to describe them. Equations always have some algebraic expression at the top, even if there are numbers below that serve as specific examples of the equations.

A Preliminary Explanation of Cash Flows

The following is a list of the symbols that will be used in this chapter.

Balance Sheet
    C = cash
  OCA = other current assets
 GPPE = gross property, plant, and equipment
   AD = accumulated depreciation
 NPPE = net property, plant, and equipment
    A = total assets
   CL = current liabilities
  LTD = long-term debt

---

3. Surely it would be possible to examine in detail every conceivable type of accounting transaction and its relation to cash flow. Here, certain transactions such as recapitalizations, the effects of accounting changes, and inventory write-downs have not been considered. The authors feel the additional complication of their inclusion would more than offset any benefits.

L = total liabilities
CAP = total stockholder's equity

Property, plant, and Equipment
CAPEX = capital expenditures
DEPR = depreciation expense
RETGBV = gross book value of retired property, plant and equipment
RETAD = accumulated depreciation on retired assets
SALESFA = selling price of property, plant and equipment disposed of or retired

Stockholders' Equity
NI = net income
DIV = dividends paid
SALSTK = sale of stock
TRSTK = purchase of stock
OET = other equity transactions
AET = additional equity transactions

Required Working Capital
RWC = required working capital
C_{Req} = required cash

The balance sheets for Feathers R Us for 1999 and 2000 are presented in Table 1-1. The changes in the balance sheet accounts from one year to the next are shown in the right column. On the far left the symbols used later to refer to these accounts in mathematical expressions have been repeated.

The balance sheet for the current year (t = 2000) is in balance. The total assets equal \$3,150,000, total liabilities equal \$1,085,000, and the total liabilities and equity also equal \$3,150,000. This can be shown as:

$$A_t = L_t + CAP_t \qquad (1-1)$$

$$3,150,000 = 1,085,000 + 2,065,000$$

Likewise, the balance sheet for the preceding year ($t - 1$ = 1999) is in balance.

$$A_{t-1} = L_{t-1} + CAP_{t-1} \qquad (1-2)$$

$$2,800,000 = 1,075,000 + 1,725,000$$

Subtracting the beginning balance sheet from the ending balance sheet shows *that the changes from one year to the next are also in balance.*

$$\Delta A = \Delta L + \Delta CAP \qquad (1-3)$$

$$350,000 = 10,000 + 340,000$$

Greater detail can be shown for each of the terms in equation (1-3). The change in total assets (ΔA) consists of the change in cash (ΔC), the change in other current assets (ΔOCA), and the change in net property, plant, and equipment. Net property, plant, and equipment (NPPE) is gross property, plant, and equipment (GPPE) less the accumulated depreciation (AD) on these assets. As shown in Table 1-3 below, the change

Symbols	ASSETS:	Feathers R Us ABBREVIATED BALANCE SHEETS For Calendar Years		
		1999	2000	Increase (Decrease)
C	Cash	1,125,000	1,500,000	375,000
OCA	Other current assets	875,000	790,000	(85,000)
	Total current assets	2,000,000	2,290,000	290,000
GPPE	Gross property, plant, & equipment	830,000	900,000	70,000
AD	Accumulated depreciation	30,000	40,000	10,000
NPPE	Net property, plant, & equipment	800,000	860,000	60,000
A	Total assets	2,800,000	3,150,000	350,000
	LIABILITIES			
	Current liabilities	325,000	360,000	35,000
LTD	Long-term debt	750,000	725,000	(25,000)
L	Total liabilities	1,075,000	1,085,000	10,000
	STOCKHOLDERS' EQUITY			
	Capital stock	100,000	150,000	50,000
	Additional paid in capital	200,000	500,000	300,000
	Retained earnings	1,425,000	1,465,000	40,000
	Treasury stock	0	50,000	50,000
CAP	Total stockholders' equity	1,725,000	2,065,000	340,000
	Total liabilities & equity	2,800,000	3,150,000	350,000

in net property, plant, and equipment (ΔNPPE) can be found by subtracting the change in accumulated depreciation from the change in gross property, plant, and equipment (ΔGPPE $-$ ΔAD).[4]

$$\Delta A = \Delta C + \Delta OCA + (\Delta GPPE - \Delta AD) \qquad (1\text{-}4)$$

$$350{,}000 = 375{,}000 + (85{,}000) + (70{,}000 - 10{,}000)$$

The change in total liabilities (ΔL) consists of the change in current liabilities (ΔCL) and the change in long-term debt (ΔLTD).

$$\Delta L = \Delta CL + \Delta LTD \qquad (1\text{-}5)$$

$$10{,}000 = 35{,}000 + (25{,}000)$$

To explain the change in stockholder's equity, the analyst would have to know the company's net income, provided in Table 1-2.

This income statement shows that Feathers R Us had net income after tax (NI) of $90,000. This explains only a portion of the change in the

---

4. Other long-lived assets, such as intangibles and certain investments, are treated the same as property, plant, and equipment.

TABLE 1-2

	Feathers R Us INCOME STATEMENT For Calendar Year 2000
Sales	1,000,000
Cost of sales	600,000
Gross profit	400,000
Sales expense	100,000
General & administrative expense	150,000
Depreciation	30,000
Total expense	280,000
Operating income	120,000
Gain on sale of assets	30,000
Net income before taxes	150,000
	60,000
Net Income	90,000

stockholder's equity. The total change in stockholder's equity (ΔCAP) is equal to net income (NI) *and* other equity transactions (OET) (definition is given below equation [1-6]).

$$\Delta CAP = NI + OET \tag{1-6}$$

$$340,000 = 90,000 + 250,000$$

The other equity transactions consist of the purchase and sale of the company's stock and the payment of cash dividends.[5] A detailed description of these transactions will be provided later in the chapter (refer to Table 1-4).

Substituting equations (1-4), (1-5), and (1-6) into equation (1-3) results in:[6]

$$\Delta C + \Delta OCA + (\Delta GPPE - \Delta AD)$$
$$= \Delta CL + \Delta LTD + NI + OET \tag{1-7}$$

$$375,000 + (85,000) + (70,000 - 10,000)$$
$$= 35,000 + (25,000) + 90,000 + 250,000$$

Equation (1-7) can be rearranged to satisfy the objective of the statement of cash flows—providing an explanation of the change in the cash balance.

---

5. Here it is assumed that all dividends declared are paid.
6. For the reader's convenience certain equations are repeated in the footnotes.
    Equation (1-3): $\Delta A = \Delta L + \Delta CAP$
    Equation (1-4): $\Delta A = \Delta C + \Delta OCA + (\Delta GPPE - \Delta AD)$
    Equation (1-5): $\Delta L = \Delta CL + \Delta LTD$
    Equation (1-6): $\Delta CAP = NI + \Delta OET$

$$\Delta C = NI - \Delta OCA + \Delta CL$$
$$- (\Delta GPPE - \Delta AD)$$
$$+ \Delta LTD + OET \qquad (1\text{-}8)$$
$$375{,}000 = 90{,}000 - (85{,}000) + 35{,}000$$
$$- (70{,}000 - 10{,}000)$$
$$+ (25{,}000) + 250{,}000$$

Equation (1-8) does provide an explanation of the $375,000 increase in the cash balance from 1999 to 2000, but it is still somewhat preliminary. Discussion of this explanation is best deferred until more details have been incorporated into the model.

Analyzing Property, Plant, and Equipment Transactions

The balance sheets in Table 1-1 show that the *net* property, plant, and equipment increased by $60,000. The analyst will want to obtain a more detailed understanding of this change. This can be accomplished by reviewing an analysis of property, plant, and equipment such as the one shown in Table 1-3.

This analysis shows that gross property, plant, and equipment are increased by capital expenditures (CAPEXP) and decreased by original book value of any assets retired (RETGBV). This relationship is restated as equation (1-9).

$$\Delta GPPE = CAPEXP - RETGBV \qquad (1\text{-}9)$$
$$70{,}000 = 175{,}000 - 105{,}000$$

Likewise, accumulated depreciation is increased by depreciation expense and decreased by the accumulated depreciation on any assets retired. This relationship is restated as equation (1-10).

TABLE 1-3

Symbols		Feathers R Us ANALYSIS OF PROPERTY, PLANT, & EQUIPMENT For Calendar Year 2000		
		GPPE	AD	NPPE
		Gross Prop, Plant & Equip	Accumulated Depreciation	Net Prop, Plant & Equp
	Balance, 1999	830,000	30,000	800,000
CAPEXP	Capital expenditures	175,000		175,000
DEPR	Depreciation expense		30,000	30,000
	Retirements			
RETGBV	Gross book value	105,000		105,000
RETAD	Accumulated depreciation		20,000	20,000
	Balance, 2000	900,000	40,000	860,000
	Change in the balance	70,000	10,000	60,000

$$\Delta AD = DEPR - RETAD \tag{1-10}$$

$$10,000 = 30,000 - 20,000$$

Substituting equations (1-9) and (1-10) into equation (1-8) and rearranging the terms results in equation (1-11):[7]

$$\Delta C = NI + \textbf{DEPR} - \Delta OCA + \Delta CL$$
$$- \textbf{CAPEXP} + \textbf{RETGBV} - \textbf{RETAD}$$
$$+ \Delta LTD + OET \tag{1-11}$$

$$375,000 = 90,000 + \textbf{30,000} - (85,000) + 35,000$$
$$- \textbf{175,000} + \textbf{105,000} - \textbf{20,000}$$
$$+ (25,000) + 250,000$$

The bold symbols in equation (1-11) are the symbols that have been changed by the substitutions described. For example DEPR, CAPEXP, RETGBV, and RETAD in equation (1-11) did not appear in equation (1-8).

To this point, only the book value of any assets retired has been considered. Most often, the retirement or disposition of assets involves a gain or a loss (a "negative" gain). This gain is the difference between the selling price of the property, plant, and equipment (SALESFA) and their net book values (RETGBV − RETAD). The assets in this illustration were sold for \$115,000, producing a gain of \$30,000. This is shown in equation (1-12).

$$GAIN = SALESFA - (RETGBV - RETAD) \tag{1-12}$$

$$30,000 = 115,000 - (105,000 - 20,000)$$

Equation (1-13) below is simply a rearrangement of equation (1-12).

$$RETGBV = SALESFA - GAIN + RETAD \tag{1-13}$$

$$105,000 = 115,000 - 30,000 + 20,000$$

Substituting equation (1-13) into equation (1-11) results in:[8]

$$\Delta C = NI + DEPR - \Delta OCA + \Delta CL$$
$$- CAPEXP + \textbf{SALESFA} - \textbf{GAIN} + \textbf{RETAD} - RETAD$$
$$+ \Delta LTD + OET$$

$$375,000 = 90,000 + 30,000 - (85,000) + 35,000$$
$$- 175,000 + \textbf{115,000} - \textbf{30,000} + \textbf{20,000} - 20,000$$
$$+ (25,000) + 250,000$$

$$\tag{1-14}$$

---

7. Equation (1-8): $\Delta C = NI - \Delta OCA + \Delta CL - (\Delta GPPE - \Delta AD) + \Delta LTD + OET$
   Equation (1-9): $\Delta GPPE = CAPEXP - RETGBV$
8. Equation (1-11): $\Delta C = NI + DEPR - \Delta OCA + \Delta CL - CAPEXP + RETGBV - RETAD + \Delta LTD + OET$

After canceling the $+$ RETAD and $-$ RETAD terms and rearranging, equation (1-14) simplifies to Equation (1-15):[9]

$$\Delta C = NI - GAIN + DEPR - \Delta OCA + \Delta CL$$
$$- CAPEXP + SALESFA$$
$$+ \Delta LTD + OET \qquad (1\text{-}15)$$

$$375{,}000 = 90{,}000 - 30{,}000 + 30{,}000 - (85{,}000) + 35{,}000$$
$$- 175{,}000 + 115{,}000$$
$$+ (25{,}000) + 250{,}000$$

The first line of equation (1-15) represents cash flows from operating activities, which is found by making certain adjustments to net income such as adding back depreciation and other noncash expenses, subtracting changes in other current assets, and adding changes in current liabilities. These adjustments will be explained in more detail later in the chapter. The second line in the equation represents cash flows from investing activities, and the third line represents a preliminary version of cash flows from financing activities.

An Explanation of Cash Flows with More Detail for Equity Transactions

Frequently the details of the other equity transactions (OET), referred to in equation (1-6), are also important. In this example the statement of stockholder equity included three common types of equity transactions: (DIV) issuing cash dividends, (SALSTK) selling stock, and (TRSTK) purchasing treasury stock. These are shown in Table 1-4 below.

During the year the company paid cash dividends of $50,000, sold some additional shares of stock for $350,000, and bought back some stock for $50,000. The net effect of these three transactions (OET) is a $250,000 increase in stockholder's equity. This is summarized in equation (1-16). The term AET has been added to equation (1-16) to represent *additional* equity transactions.[10]

$$OET = SALSTK - TRSTK - DIV + AET \qquad (1\text{-}16)$$

$$250{,}000 = 350{,}000 - 50{,}000 - 50{,}000 + 0$$

Substituting this last expression into equation (1-15) results in equation (1-17) below.[11]

---

9. Equation (1-14): $\Delta C = NI + DEPR - \Delta OCA + \Delta CL - CAPEXP + SALESFA - GAIN + RETAD - RETAD + \Delta LTD + OET$

10. The term *additional* equity transactions was used to describe equity transactions other than the sale or purchase of the company's stock and the payment of dividends. One example of an additional equity transaction would be the contribution of property to the company in exchange for an equity interest. For analytical purposes, the increase in equity could be treated as a source of cash from financing activities. The corresponding increase in assets could be treated as a use of cash from investing activities. The net result would be overall zero effect on cash. Normally, *noncash* transactions of this nature are not incorporated in formal statements of cash flows but are appended in a separate schedule.

11. Equation (1-15): $\Delta C = NI - GAIN + DEPR - \Delta OCA + \Delta CL - CAPEXP + SALESFA + \Delta LTD + OET$
    Equation (1-16): $OET = SALESTK - TRSTK - DIV + AET$

Symbols		Capital Stock	Additional Paid in Capital	Retained Earnings	Treasury Stock	Total Shareholder Equity
	Feathers R Us **STATEMENT OF STOCKHOLDERS' EQUITY** **For Calendar Year 2000**					
	Balance, 1999	100,000	200,000	1,425,000	0	1,725,000
NI	Net income			90,000		90,000
	Other equity transactions					
DIV	Dividends			50,000		50,000
SALSTK	Sales of stock	50,000	300,000			350,000
TRSTK	Purchase of stock				50,000	50,000
	Subtotal OET	50,000	300,000	50,000	50,000	*250,000*
	Balance, 2000	150,000	500,000	1,465,000	50,000	2,065,000

$$\Delta C = NI - GAIN + DEPR - \Delta OCA + \Delta CL$$
$$- CAPEXP + SALESFA$$
$$\Delta LTD + \textbf{SALSTK} - \textbf{TRSTK} - \textbf{DIV} + \textbf{AET} \qquad (1\text{-}17)$$

$$375,000 = 90,000 - 30,000 + 30,000 - (85,000) + 35,000$$
$$- 175,000 + 115,000$$
$$+ (25,000) + \textbf{350,000} - \textbf{50,000} - \textbf{50,000} + \textbf{0}$$

Equation (1-17) can be simplified to the more familiar form:

$$\Delta C = \text{Cash flows from operating activities}$$
$$+ \text{Cash flows from investing activities}$$
$$+ \text{Cash flows from financing activities} \qquad (1\text{-}18)$$

$$375,000 = 210,000$$
$$+ (60,000)$$
$$+ 225,000$$

Equations (1-17) and (1-18) describe the conventional Statement of Cash Flows shown in Table 1-5.

For the moment we will define the *required* change in working capital as the change in current assets other than cash, less the change in current liabilities, as shown in equation (1-19).[12]

$$\Delta RWC = \Delta OCA - \Delta CL \qquad (1\text{-}19)$$
$$(120,000) = (85,000) - 35,000$$

This illustration is somewhat unusual. Here working capital is being *reduced*. This reduction is a *source* of the cash from operating activities.

---

12. The definition in equation (1-19) will be modified later in the chapter.

Symbols		Feathers R Us ABBREVIATED STATEMENT OF CASH FLOWS For Calendar Year 2000	
	Cash flows from operating activities		
NI	Net income		90,000
	Adjustments to reconcile net income to net cash provided by operating activities:		
GAIN	Gain on sale of property, plant, & equipment	(30,000)	
DEPR	Depreciation expense	30,000	
ΔOCA	Decrease in current assets	85,000	
ΔCL	Increase in current liabilities	35,000	120,000
	Net cash provided by operating activities		210,000
	Cash flows from investing activities		
CAPEXP	Purchase of property, plant, & equipment	(175,000)	
SALESFA	Sale of property, plant, & equipment	115,000	
	Net cash used by investing activities		(60,000)
	Cash flows from financing activities		
ΔLTD	Increase in long term debt	(25,000)	
SALSTK	Sale of stock	350,000	
TRSTK	Purchase of treasury stock	(50,000)	
DIV	Payment of dividends	(50,000)	
	Net cash provided by financing activities		225,000
	Net increase in cash		**375,000**
	Cash, January 1, 2000		1,125,000
	Cash, December 31, 2000		1,500,000

(In the typical case working capital is being *increased*. This is usually true when sales are growing. In these cases, the increase in working capital represents a *use* of cash.)

Substituting equation (1-19) into equation (1-17) shows that [13]

$$\Delta C = NI - GAIN + DEPR - \Delta RWC$$
$$- CAPEXP + SALESFA$$
$$+ \Delta LTD + SALSTK - TRSTK - DIV + AET \quad (1\text{-}20)$$

$$375,000 = 90,000 - 30,000 + 30,000 - \textbf{(120,000)}$$
$$- 175,000 + 115,000$$
$$+ (25,000) + 350,000 - 50,000 - 50,000 + 0$$

The *first* line of equation (1-20) can be rephrased in the following way:

---

13. Equation (1-17): $\Delta C = NI - GAIN + DEPR - \Delta OCA + \Delta CL - CAPEXP + SALESFA + \Delta LTD + SALSTK - TRSTK - DIV + AET$
    Equation (1-19): $\Delta RWC = \Delta OCA - \Delta CL$

Activity	Symbol	Description
Operating	NI	+ Net income
	GAIN	− Gains (+ losses) on the sale of property, plant, and equipment
	DEPR	+ Depreciation and other noncash charges
	ΔRWC	− Increases (+ decreases) in required working capital

When deriving the cash flows from operating activities, we subtract the gain (or add the loss) on the sale of property, plant, and equipment for several reasons. First, these gains and losses simply are *not* the result of "operating" activities. They are the result of "investing" activities. These gains and losses arise when property, plant, and equipment are sold for more or less than their net book value. Furthermore, the *full* amount received for such sales (SALESFA) is included as part of the cash flows from investing activities. To show these gains or losses *again* as part of cash flows from operating activities would erroneously double count their impact.

Depreciation and other noncash expenses *do* reduce net income, but they *do not* involve any payments during the current period. Therefore, when the indirect method is used and net income is the starting point for arriving at a firm's net cash flow, these noncash expenses must be added back.

The rationale for subtracting required increases (or adding decreases) in working capital will be discussed at some length in the next section after introducing the components of the other current assets (ΔOCA) and the current liabilities (ΔCL).

To complete the summary of equations (1-17), (1-18), and (1-20), the *second* and *third* lines consist of [14]

Activity	Symbol	Description
Investing	CAPEXP	− Capital expenditures
	SALESFA	+ Selling price of property, plant, and equipment disposed of or retired
Financing	ΔLTD	+ Increases (− decreases) in long-term debt
	SALSTK	+ Proceeds received from the sale of stock
	TRSTK	− Payments for treasury stock
	DIV	− Dividends
	AET	+ Additional equity transactions

Considering the Components of Required Working Capital

Before discussing required working capital further, it will be helpful to break down changes in (ΔOCA) other current assets and (ΔCL) current liabilities into some typical component parts. Table 1-6 is a restatement of Table 1-1 with this additional detail provided in the boxed sections.

---

14. The second line of both equations (1-17) and (1-20) is: − CAPEXP + SALESFA
    The third line of both equations (1-17) and (1-20) is: ΔLTD + SALSTK − TRSTK − DIV + AET

TABLE 1-6

Symbols	ASSETS:	1999	2000	Increase (Decrease)
		Feathers R Us		
		BALANCE SHEETS		
		For Calendar Years		
C	Cash	1,125,000	1,500,000	375,000
	Accounts receivable	100,000	150,000	50,000
	Inventory	750,000	600,000	(150,000)
	Additional current assets	25,000	40,000	15,000
	Total current assets	2,000,000	2,290,000	290,000
GPPE	Gross property, plant, & equipment	830,000	900,000	70,000
AD	Accumulated depreciation	30,000	40,000	10,000
NPPE	Net property, plant, & equipment	800,000	860,000	60,000
A	Total assets	**2,800,000**	**3,150,000**	**350,000**
	LIABILITIES			
	Accounts payable	200,000	225,000	25,000
	Short-term notes payable	50,000	35,000	(15,000)
	Accrued expenses	75,000	100,000	25,000
CL	Current liabilities	325,000	360,000	35,000
LTD	Long-term debt	750,000	725,000	(25,000)
L	Total liabilities	**1,075,000**	**1,085,000**	**10,000**
	STOCKHOLDERS' EQUITY			
	Capital stock	100,000	150,000	50,000
	Additional paid in capital	200,000	500,000	300,000
	Retained earnings	1,425,000	1,465,000	40,000
	Treasury stock	0	50,000	50,000
CAP	Total stockholders' equity	**1,725,000**	**2,065,000**	**340,000**
	Total liabilities & equity	2,800,000	3,150,000	350,000

Here, other current assets consist of accounts receivable, inventory, and additional current assets. Current liabilities include accounts payable, short-term notes payable, and accrued expenses.

Accounts receivable, inventory, and additional current assets should all be treated in the same way that other current assets was treated. When using the indirect method, increases (decreases) in these component accounts should be subtracted from (added to) net income to arrive at net cash provided by operating activities.

Likewise, accounts payable, short-term notes payable, and accrued expenses should all be treated in the same way that current liabilities was treated. When using the indirect method, increases (decreases) in these component accounts should be added to (subtracted from) net income to arrive at net cash provided by operating activities.

Applying the procedures outlined in the two preceding paragraphs results in the Statement of Cash Flows shown in Table 1-7 which is simply a restatement of Table 1-5 with the boxed detail added.

TABLE 1-7

Symbols		Feathers R Us STATEMENT OF CASH FLOWS For Calendar Year 2000	
	Cash flows from operating activities		
NI	Net Income		90,000
	Adjustments to reconcile net income to net cash provided by operating activities:		
GAIN	Gain on sale of property, plant, & equipment	(30,000)	
DEPR	Depreciation expense	30,000	
Δ	Increase in accounts receivable	(50,000)	
Δ	Decrease in inventory	150,000	
Δ	Increase in additional current assets	(15,000)	
Δ	Increase in accounts payable	25,000	
Δ	Decrease in short-term notes payable	(15,000)	
Δ	Increase in accrued expenses	25,000	120,000
	Net cash provided by operating activities		210,000
	Cash flows from investing activities		
CAPEXP	Purchase of property, plant, & equipment	(175,000)	
SALESFA	Sale of property, plant, & equipment	115,000	
	Net cash used by investing activities		(60,000)
	Cash flows from financing activities		
ΔLTD	Decrease in long term debt	(25,000)	
SALSTK	Sale of stock	350,000	
TRSTK	Purchase of treasury stock	(50,000)	
DIV	Payment of dividends	(50,000)	
	Net cash provided by financing activities		225,000
	Net increase in cash		375,000
	Cash, January 1, 2000		1,125,000
	Cash, December 31, 2000		1,500,000

In many cases it is quite apparent why increases in current assets should be subtracted from net income to arrive at net cash provided by operating activities. Increases in inventories and other current assets (such as supplies) do require the use of cash.

However, accounts receivable can be troublesome to think through. Why should an increase in accounts receivable be subtracted from net income to arrive at net cash provided by operating activities? Before answering this question, it is helpful to consider why accounts receivable increase in the first place. They increase because the company has *failed* to collect cash. Its collections have been less than its reported revenues.

When applying the indirect method, the first source of cash from operating activities is net income. This implies that *each of the components of net income* represents a cash flow. The full amount of reported sales, for example, is implicitly being treated as a cash inflow. When net accounts receivable have increased over the period, collections must have been less than reported revenues. Therefore, it is necessary to subtract the increase in accounts receivable from net income to arrive at the true figure for cash provided from operations.

Also, it is usually apparent why increases in current liabilities should be added to net income to arrive at net cash provided by operating activities. Increases (decreases) in short-term notes payable do provide (use) cash.

To understand the treatment of accounts payable, again it is helpful to begin by considering why accounts payable increase. They increase because the company has not paid these bills yet. Its disbursements have been less than its reported expenses.

Again, under the indirect method, the full amount of a reported expense is implicitly being treated as a cash outflow. When accounts payable has increased over the period, payments must have been less than that reported expense. Therefore, it is necessary to add the increase in accounts payable back to net income when trying to arrive at the true figure for cash provided from operations.

Likewise, when accrued expenses increase, it means the company has disbursed less cash than indicated by one of its reported expenses. Again it is necessary to add the increase in accrued expenses back to net income when trying to arrive at the true figure for cash provided from operations.

This discussion of the treatment of the components of working capital calls to mind a major difference between the income statement and the statement of cash flows. Both do serve as a reconciling link between the beginning and ending balance sheets. However, the income statement in an accrual-based partial reconciliation between the beginning and ending balances in retained earnings. (The complete reconciliation requires consideration of dividends, and occasionally certain other items.) The statement of cash flows is a cash-based reconciliation between the beginning and ending cash balances. Much of the immediate discussion has simply been a recital of the differences between accrual and cash accounting.

Recall that cash flows from operating activities are the cash equivalent of the accrual-based income statement. Again, to complete the reconciliation between the beginning and ending cash balances, the statement of cash flows (as illustrated above) must also include cash from investing or financing activities.

Adjusting for Required Cash

For valuation purposes, it is important to recognize that all firms require a certain amount of cash be kept on hand; otherwise checks would constantly bounce. Therefore, the amount of required cash (C_{Req}) will not be available for dividend payments.

In equation (1-19), the required change in working capital was defined simply as the change in current assets other than cash, less the change in current liabilities. We will now modify that definition, as shown in equation (1-21) below, to include the changes in the cash balance the firm will be required to keep on hand ($20,000 in this illustration).[15]

$$\Delta RWC = \Delta OCA - \Delta CL + \Delta C_{Req} \qquad (1\text{-}21)$$

$$(100,000) = (85,000) - 35,000 + 20,000$$

---

15. Typically appraisers forecast required cash as a percentage of sales. Required cash increases (decreases) by that percentage multiplied by the increase (decrease) in sales.

Previously (in equation [1-19]), the $85,000 decrease in other current assets and the $35,000 increase in current liabilities gave rise to a reduction in required working capital of $120,000. After taking into consideration the $20,000 additional cash which will be required, the reduction in required working capital falls to $100,000, i.e., the net addition to cash flow from the reduction in required net working capital is $20,000 less.

Using this modified definition for ΔRWC lowers the resulting cash flow to $355,000 (from the $375,000 originally shown in equation [1-20]).[16]

$$\Delta C^* = NI - GAIN + DEPR - \Delta RWC$$
$$- CAPEXP + SALESFA$$
$$+ \Delta LTD + SALSTK - TRSTK - DIV + AET \quad \text{(1-20a)}$$
$$\mathbf{355,000} = 90,000 - 30,000 + 30,000 - \mathbf{(100,000)}$$
$$- 175,000 + 115,000$$
$$+ (25,000) + 350,000 - 50,000 - 50,000 + 0$$

This $355,000 amount represents the *net cash flow available for dividend payments in excess of the dividends already considered* ($50,000).

Alternatively, DIV could be added to both sides of equation (1-20a) to show the *total amount of net cash flow available for distribution to stockholders*. That amount is $405,000, as shown in equation (1-20b).

$$\Delta C^* + \mathbf{DIV} = NI - GAIN + DEPR - \Delta RWC$$
$$- CAPEXP + SALESFA$$
$$+ \Delta LTD + SALSTK - TRSTK + AET \quad \text{(1-20b)}$$
$$\mathbf{405,000} = 90,000 - 30,000 + 30,000 - (100,000)$$
$$- 175,000 + 115,000$$
$$+ (25,000) + 350,000 - 50,000 + 0$$

COMPARISON TO OTHER CASH FLOW DEFINITIONS

The definition of net cash flow available for distribution to stockholders in equation (1-20b) can be summarized in the following way:

Activity	Symbol	Description
Operating	NI	+ Net income
	GAIN	− Gains (+ losses) on the sale of property, plant, and equipment
	DEPR	+ Depreciation and other noncash charges
	ΔRWC	− Increases (+ decreases) in required working capital*
Investing	CAPEXP	− Capital expenditures
	SALESFA	+ Selling price of property, plant, and equipment disposed of or retired
Financing	ΔLTD	+ Increases (− decreases) in long-term debt
	SALSTK	+ Proceeds received from the sale of stock
	TRSTK	− Payments for treasury stock
	AET	+ Additional equity transactions

*After adjusting for required cash.

This is easily compared to other definitions that have been provided in the authoritative literature. For example, one group of authors (Pratt,

16. $\Delta C^* = \Delta C - \Delta C_{Req}$

Reilly, and Schweihs 1996) have proposed the following definition of net cash flow available for distribution to stockholders in their Formula 9-3 (at 156–157):

Description

+ Net income
+ Depreciation and other non-cash charges
− Increases (+ decreases) in required working capital
− Capital expenditures
+ Selling price of property, plant, and equipment disposed of or retired
+ Increases (− decreases) in long term debt

Implicitly, this definition assumes that gains and losses on the sale of property, plant, and equipment and the selling price of property, plant, and equipment disposed of or retired are immaterial. Likewise, this definition assumes that the proceeds from the sale of stock, payments made for treasury stock, and additional equity transactions are also immaterial.

These assumptions are quite reasonable and can safely be made in a large number of cases.[17] However, it is important for the analyst to realize that these assumptions are being made.

It is well known that when calculating value by capitalizing a single initial cash flow, the consequences of making adjustments to the initial cash flow are magnified considerably. It is important for the analyst to understand how these hidden assumptions might influence the amount of initial cash flow being capitalized. Perhaps it is even more important for the analyst to take into account how these assumptions might impact the *future* cash flows available for distribution to stockholders.

For example, if a company were to routinely to sell its equipment for significant sums, the analyst would be remiss if he or she overlooked the cash flows from these sales.

CONCLUSION

Careful consideration of mathematics in this chapter should enhance the analyst's understanding of important accounting relationships and the "whys" of the Statement of Cash Flows. It should also make the analyst aware of the simplifying assumptions embedded in abbreviated definitions of cash flow available for distribution to stockholders. Hopefully, this awareness will result in superior valuations in those instances where the making of these simplifying assumptions is unwarranted.

BIBLIOGRAPHY

Abrams, Jay B. 1997. "Cash Flow: A Mathematical Derivation." *Valuation* (March 1994): 64–71.
Pratt, Shannon P., Robert F. Reilly, and Robert P. Schweihs. 1996. *Valuing a Business: The Analysis and Appraisal of Closely Held Companies,* 3rd ed. New York: McGraw-Hill.

---

17. With respect to the proceeds from the sale of stock, it is unlikely that a firm would sell its stock in order to obtain cash for distribution to its stockholders. However, sometimes large sales of stock do occur.

CHAPTER 2

Using Regression Analysis

INTRODUCTION

FORECASTING COSTS AND EXPENSES

   Adjustments to Expenses

   Table 2-1A: Calculating Adjusted Costs and Expenses

PERFORMING REGRESSION ANALYSIS

USE OF REGRESSION STATISTICS TO TEST THE ROBUSTNESS OF
THE RELATIONSHIP

   Standard Error of the y Estimate

   The Mean of a and b

   The Variance of a and b

      Precise Confidence Intervals

   Selecting the Data Set and Regression Equation

PROBLEMS WITH USING REGRESSION ANALYSIS FOR
FORECASTING COSTS

   Insufficient Data

   Substantial Changes in Competition or Product / Service

USING REGRESSION ANALYSIS TO FORECAST SALES

   Spreadsheet Procedures to Perform Regression

   Examining the Regression Statistics

   Adding Industry-Specific Independent Variables

   Try All Combinations of Potential Independent Variables

APPLICATION OF REGRESSION ANALYSIS TO THE GUIDELINE
COMPANY METHOD

   Table 2-6: Regression Analysis of Guideline Companies

      95% Confidence Intervals

SUMMARY

APPENDIX: The ANOVA table

INTRODUCTION

Regression analysis is a statistical technique that estimates the mathematical relationship between causal variables, known as independent variables, and a dependent variable. The most common uses of regression analysis in business valuation are:

1. Forecasting sales in a discounted cash flow analysis
2. Forecasting costs and expenses in a discounted cash flow analysis
3. Measuring the relationship between market capitalization (fair market value) as the dependent variable and several possible independent variables for a publicly traded guideline company valuation approach. Typical independent variables that are candidates to affect the fair market value are net income (including nonlinear transformations such as its square, square root, and logarithm), book value, the debt-to-equity ratio, and so on.

This chapter is written to provide the appraiser with some statistical theory, but it is primarily focused on how to apply regression analysis to real-life appraisal assignments using standard spreadsheet regression tools. We have not attempted to provide a rigorous, exhaustive treatment on statistics and have put as much of the technical background discussion as possible in the appendix to keep the body of the chapter as simple as possible. Those who want a comprehensive refresher should consult a statistics text, such as Bhattacharyya and Johnson (1977) and Wonnacott and Wonnacott (1981). We present only bits and pieces of statistics that are necessary to facilitate our discussion of the important practical issues.

Even though you may not be familiar with using regression analysis at all, let alone with nonlinear transformations of the data, the material in this chapter is not that difficult and can be very useful in your day-to-day valuation practice. We will explain all the basics you need to use this very important tool on a daily basis and will lead you step-by-step through an example, so you can use this chapter as a guide to get "hands-on" experience.

For those who are unfamiliar with the mechanical procedures to perform regression analysis using spreadsheets, we explain that step-by-step in the section on using regression to forecast sales.

FORECASTING COSTS AND EXPENSES

In performing a discounted cash flow analysis, an analyst should forecast sales, expenses, and changes in balance sheet accounts that affect cash flows. Frequently analysts base their forecasts of future costs on historical averages of, or trends in, the ratio of costs as a percentage of sales.

One significant weakness of this methodology is that it ignores fixed costs, leading to undervaluation in good times and possible overvaluation in bad times. If the analyst treats all costs as variable, in good times when he or she forecasts rapid sales growth, the fixed costs should stay constant (or possibly increase with inflation, depending on the nature of the costs), but the analyst will forecast those fixed costs to rise in proportion to sales.

That leads to forecasting expenses too high and income too low in good times, which ultimately causes an undervaluation of the firm. In bad times, if sales are forecasted flat, then costs will be accidentally forecasted correctly. If sales are expected to decline, then treating all costs as variable will lead to forecasting expenses too low and net income too high, leading to overvaluation.

Ordinary least squares (OLS) regression analysis is an excellent tool to forecast adjusted costs and expenses (which for simplicity we will call "adjusted costs" or "costs") based on their historical relationship to sales. OLS produces a statistical estimate of both fixed and variable costs, which is useful in planning as well as in forecasting. Furthermore, the regression statistics produce feedback used to judge the robustness of the relationship between sales and costs.

Adjustments to Expenses

Prior to performing regression analysis, we should analyze historical income statements to ascertain if various expenses have maintained a consistent pattern or if there has been a shift in the structure of a particular expense. When past data is not likely to be representative of future expectations, we make *pro forma* adjustments to historical results to model how the Company would have looked if its operations in the past had conformed to the way we expect them to behave in the future. The purpose of these adjustments is to examine longstanding financial trends without the interference of obsolete information from the past. For example, if the cost of advertising was 10% of sales for the first two years of our historical analysis, decreased to 5% for the next five years, and is expected to remain at 5% in the future, we may add back the excess 5% to net income in the first two years to reflect our future expectations. We may make similar adjustments to other expenses that have changed during the historical period or that we expect to change in the future to arrive at adjusted net income.

Table 2-1A: Calculating Adjusted Costs and Expenses

Table 2-1A shows summary income statements for the years 1988 to 1997. Adjustments to pretax net income appear in Rows 15–20. The first adjustment, which appears in Rows 15–18, converts actual salary paid—along with bonuses and pension payments—to an arm's length salary. This type of adjustment is standard in all valuations of privately held companies.

The second type of adjustment is for a one-time event that is unlikely to repeat in the future. In our example, the Company wrote off a discontinued operation in 1994. As such, we add back the write-off to income (H19) because it is not expected to recur in the future.

The third type of adjustment is for a periodic expense. We use a company move as an example, since we expect a move to occur about every 10 years.[1] In our example, the company moved in 1993, 4 years

---

1. Losses from litigation are another type of expense that often has a periodic pattern.

T A B L E 2-1A

Adjustments to Historical Costs and Expenses

	A	B	C	D	E	F	G	H	I	J	K
4						Summary Income Statements					
6		1988	1989	1990	1991	1992	1993	1994	1995	1996	1997
7	Sales	$250,000	$500,000	$750,000	$1,000,000	$1,060,000	$1,123,600	$1,191,016	$1,262,477	$1,338,226	$1,415,000
8	Cost of sales	100,000	250,000	375,000	500,000	490,000	505,000	520,000	535,000	550,000	600,000
9	S, G & A expenses	100,000	150,000	250,000	335,000	335,000	360,000	370,000	405,000	435,000	450,000
10	Operating expenses	58,000	68,000	78,000	88,000	83,000	110,000	112,000	117,000	122,000	132,000
11	Other expense	5,000	15,000	20,000	25,000	20,000	43,000	100,000	50,000	50,000	50,000
12	Pretax income	−$13,000	$17,000	$27,000	$52,000	$132,000	$105,600	$89,016	$155,477	$181,226	$183,000
13	Pre-tax profit margin	−5.20%	3.40%	3.60%	5.20%	12.45%	9.40%	7.47%	12.32%	13.54%	12.93%
14	Adjustments:										
15	+ Actual salary	75,000	80,000	85,000	130,000	100,000	100,000	105,000	107,000	109,000	111,000
16	+ Bonus	3,000	4,000	4,000	20,000	5,000	5,000	5,000	7,000	9,000	10,000
17	+ Pension	1,000	1,000	1,500	2,000	2,000	2,000	2,000	2,000	2,000	2,000
18	− Arms length salary [1]	(58,015)	(60,916)	(63,961)	(67,159)	(70,517)	(74,043)	(77,745)	(81,633)	(85,714)	(90,000)
19	Discontinued operations [2]							55,000			
20	Moving expense [3]						20,000				
21	Adjusted pretax income	$7,985	$41,084	$53,539	$136,841	$168,483	$158,557	$178,271	$189,844	$215,511	$216,000
22	Adjusted pretax profit margin	3.19%	8.22%	7.14%	13.68%	15.89%	14.11%	14.97%	15.04%	16.10%	15.27%
23/24	Calculation of adjusted costs and expenses										
25	Sales	$250,000	$500,000	$750,000	$1,000,000	$1,060,000	$1,123,600	$1,191,016	$1,262,477	$1,338,226	$1,415,000
26	Adjusted pretax net income	$7,985	$41,084	$53,539	$136,841	$168,483	$158,557	$178,271	$189,844	$215,511	$216,000
27	Adjusted costs and expenses	$242,015	$458,916	$696,461	$863,159	$891,517	$965,043	$1,012,745	$1,072,633	$1,122,714	$1,199,000

[1] Arms length salary includes bonus and pension

[2] A write-off for discontinued operations was an unusual a one-time expense already included in other expense. We reverse it our here.

[3] Moving expense is a periodic expense which occurs approximately every 10 years. For the 1993 move, we add back the $20,000 cost to pre-tax income, and use a Periodic Perpetuity Factor to calculate an adjustment to FMV, which we apply later in the valuation process (see Chapter 3).

ago. We add back the $20,000 cost of the move in the adjustment section (G20) and treat the cost separately as a periodic perpetuity.

In Chapter 3, we develop two periodic perpetuity factors (PPFs)[2] for periodic cash flows occurring every j years, growing at a constant rate of g, discounted to present value at the rate r, where the last cash flow occurred b years ago. Those formulas are:

$$\text{PPF} = \frac{(1 + r)^b}{(1 + r)^j - (1 - g)^j} \quad \text{PPF—end-of-year} \qquad \text{(3-18a)}$$

$$\text{PPF} = \frac{\sqrt{1 + r}\,(1 + r)^b}{(1 + r)^j - (1 + g)^j} \quad \text{PPF—midyear} \qquad \text{(3-19a)}$$

We assume the move occurs at the end of the year and use equation (3-18a), the end-of-year PPF. We also assume a discount rate of $r = 20\%$, moves occur every $j = 10$ years, the last move occurred $b = 4$ years ago, and the cost of moving grows at $g = 5\%$ per year. The cost of the next move, which is forecast in Year 6, is $\$20,000 \times 1.2^{10} = \$20,000 \times 1.62889 = \$32,577.89$. We multiply this by the PPF, which is:

$$\text{PPF} = \frac{1.2^4}{1.2^{10} - 1.05^{10}} = 0.45445$$

(see Table 3-9, cell A20), which results in a present value of $14,805.14.

Assuming a 40% tax rate, the after-tax present value of moving costs is $\$14,805.14 \times (1 - 40\%) = \$8,883$. Since this is an expense, we must remember to subtract it from—not add it to—the FMV of the firm before moving expenses. For example, if we calculate a marketable minority interest FMV of $1,008,883 before moving expenses, then the marketable minority FMV would be $1 million after moving expenses.

The other possible treatment for the periodic expense, which is slightly less accurate but avoids the complex PPF, is to allocate the periodic expense over the applicable years—10 in this example. The appraiser who chooses this method must allocate expenses from the prior move to the years before 1993. This approach causes the regression R^2 to be artificially high, as the appraiser has created what appears to be a perfect fixed cost. For example, suppose we allocated $2,000 per year moving costs to the years 1993–1998. If we run a regression on those years only, R^2 will be overstated, as the perfect fixed cost of $2,000 per year is merely an allocation, not the real cash flow. Other regression measures will also be exaggerated. If the numbers being allocated are small, however, the overstatement is also likely to be small.

Adjusted pretax income appears in Row 21. Note that as a result of these adjustments, the adjusted pretax profit margin in Row 22 is substantially higher than the unadjusted pretax margin in Row 13.

---

2. This is a term to describe the present value of a periodic cash flow that runs in perpetuity. To my knowledge, these formulas are my own invention and PPF is my own name for it. As mentioned in Chapter 3, where we develop this, it is in essence the same as a Gordon model, but for a periodic, noncontiguous cash flow. As noted in Chapter 3, when sales occur every year, $j = 1$ and formulas (3-18a) and (3-19a) simplify to the familiar Gordon model multiples.

We repeat sales (Row 7) in Row 25 and adjusted pretax income (Row 21) in Row 26. Subtracting Row 26 from Row 25, we arrive at adjusted costs and expenses in Row 27. These adjusted costs and expenses are what is used in forecasting future costs and expenses regression analysis.

PERFORMING REGRESSION ANALYSIS

Ordinary least squares regression analysis measures the linear relationship between a dependent variable and an independent variable. Its mathematical form is $y = \alpha + \beta x$, where:

y = the dependent variable (in this case, adjusted costs).
x = the independent variable (in this case, sales).
α = the true (and unobservable) y-intercept value, i.e., fixed costs.
β = the true (and unobservable) slope of the line, i.e., variable costs.

Both α and β, the true fixed and variable costs of the Company, are unobservable. In performing the regression, we are estimating α and β from our historical analysis, and we will call our estimates:

a = the estimated y-intercept value (estimated fixed costs).
b = the estimated slope of the line (estimated variable costs).[3]

OLS estimates fixed and variable costs (the y-intercept and slope) by calculating the best fit line through the data points.[4] In our case, the dependent variable (y) is adjusted costs and the independent variable (x) is sales. Sales, which is in Table 2-1A, Row 7, appears in Table 2-1B as B6 to B15. Adjusted costs and expenses, Table 2-1A, Row 27, appears in Table 2-1B as C6 to C15. Table 2-1B shows the regression analysis of these variables using all 10 years of data. The resulting regression yields an intercept value of $56,770 (B33) and a (rounded) slope coefficient of $0.80 (B34). Using these results, the equation of the line becomes:

Adjusted Costs and Expenses = $56,770 + ($0.80 × Sales)

The y-intercept, $56,770, represents the fixed costs of operation, or the cost of operating the business at a zero sales volume. The slope coefficient, $0.80, is the variable cost per dollar of sales. This means that for every dollar of sales, there are directly related costs and expenses of $0.80. We show this relationship graphically at the bottom of the table. The diamonds are actual data points, and the line passing through them is the regression estimate. Note how close all of the data points are to the regression line, which indicates there is a strong relationship between sales and costs.[5]

---

3. The regression parameters a and b are often shown in statistical literature as α and β with a circumflex ($\hat{}$) over each letter.
4. The interested reader should consult a statistics text for the multivariate calculus involved in calculating a and b. Mathematically, OLS calculates the line that minimizes the sum of the squared deviations between the actual data points and the regression estimate.
5. We will discuss the second page of Table 2-1B later in the chapter.

Regression Analysis 1988–1997

	A	B	C	D	E	F	G
4		**Actual**					
5	**Year**	**Sales = X [1]**	**Adj. Costs = Y [2]**				
6	1988	$250,000	$242,015				
7	1989	$500,000	$458,916				
8	1990	$750,000	$696,461				
9	1991	$1,000,000	$863,159				
10	1992	$1,060,000	$891,517				
11	1993	$1,123,600	$965,043				
12	1994	$1,191,016	$1,012,745				
13	1995	$1,262,477	$1,072,633				
14	1996	$1,338,226	$1,122,714				
15	1997	$1,415,000	$1,199,000				
17	SUMMARY OUTPUT						
19	**Regression Statistics**						
20	Multiple R	99.88%					
21	R square	99.75%					
22	Adjusted R square	99.72%					
23	Standard error	16,014					
24	Observations	10					
26	ANOVA						
27		df	SS	MS	F	Significance F	
28	Regression	1	8.31E+11	8.31E+11	3.24E+03	1.00E−11	
29	Residual	8	2.05E+09	2.56E+08			
30	Total	9	8.33E+11				
32		Coefficients	Standard Error	t Stat	P-value	Lower 95%	Upper 95%
33	Intercept [3]	56,770	14,863	3.82	5.09E-03	22,496	91,045
34	Sales [4]	0.80	0.01	56.94	1.00E-11	0.77	0.84

[1] From Table 2-1A, Row 7
[2] From Table 2-1A, Row 27
[3] Regression estimate of fixed costs
[4] Regression estimate of variable costs

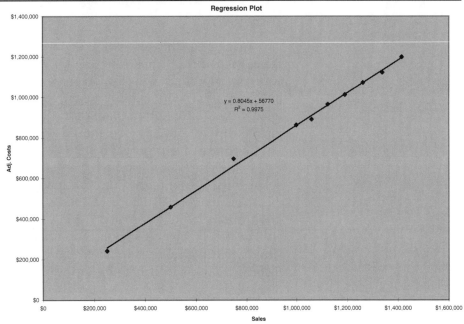

Regression Plot

$y = 0.8045x + 56770$
$R^2 = 0.9975$

Calculation of 95% Confidence Intervals for Forecast 1998 Costs

	A	B	C	D	E	F
4			Actual			
5	Year	Sales = X [1]	Adj. Costs = Y [2]	x	x^2	x^2_{1998}/Sum x^2
6	1988	$250,000	$242,015	−739,032	5.5E+11	
7	1989	$500,000	$458,916	−489,032	2.4E+11	
8	1990	$750,000	$696,461	−239,032	5.7E+10	
9	1991	$1,000,000	$863,159	10,968	1.2E+08	
10	1992	$1,060,000	$891,517	70,968	5.0E+09	
11	1993	$1,123,600	$965,043	134,568	1.8E+10	
12	1994	$1,191,016	$1,012,745	201,984	4.1E+10	
13	1995	$1,262,477	$1,072,633	273,445	7.5E+10	
14	1996	$1,338,226	$1,122,714	349,194	1.2E+11	
15	1997	$1,415,000	$1,199,000	425,968	1.8E+11	
16	Average/Total	**$989,032**		$ 0	1.28E+12	
17	Forecast 1998	$1,600,000	$1,343,928	610,968	3.7E+11	0.2905650

21	Confidence Interval =	$\pm t_{0.025}s\sqrt{\dfrac{1}{n}+\dfrac{x_o^2}{\sum x_i^2}}$	$\pm t_{0.025}s\sqrt{\dfrac{1}{n}+\dfrac{x_o^2}{\sum x_i^2}+1}$

	Confidence Intervals For:	Mean	Specific Year
24			
25	$t_{0.025}$ = [t-statistic for 8 degrees of freedom]	2.306	2.306
26	s = [From Table 2-1B, B23]	$16,014	$16,014
27	1/n =	0.1	0.1
28	x_o^2 / Sum (X_i^2) = [F17]	0.2905650	0.2905650
29	Add 0 for mean, 1 for specific year's exp.	0.0000000	1.0000000
30	Add rows 27 To 29	0.3905650	1.3905650
31	Square root of row 30	0.6249520	1.1792222
32	Confid interval = row 25 * row 26 * row 31	**$23,078**	**$43,547**
33	Confid interval/forecast 1998 costs row 32 / C17	1.7%	3.2%
35	**Regression Coefficients**	**Coefficients**	
36	Intercept [From Table 2-1B, B33]	56,770	
37	Sales [From Table 2-1B, B34]	0.80	

We can use this regression equation to calculate future costs once we generate a future sales forecast. Of course, to be useful, the regression equation should make common sense. For example, a negative y-intercept in this context would imply negative fixed costs, which makes no sense whatsoever (although in regressions involving other variables it may well make sense). Normally one should not use a result like that, despite otherwise impressive regression statistics.

If the regression forecasts variable costs above $1.00, one should be suspicious. If true, either the Company must anticipate a significant decrease in its cost structure in the near future—which would invalidate applicability of the regression analysis to the future—or the Company will be out of business soon. The analyst should also consider the possibility that the regression failed, perhaps because of either insufficient or incorrect data, and it may be unwise to use the results in the valuation.

USE OF REGRESSION STATISTICS TO TEST THE ROBUSTNESS OF THE RELATIONSHIP

Having determined the equation of the line, we use regression statistics to determine the strength of the relationship between the dependent and independent variable(s). We give only a brief verbal description of regression statistics below. For a more in-depth explanation, the reader should refer to a book on statistics.

In an OLS regression, the "goodness of fit" of the line is measured by the degree of correlation between the dependent and independent variable, referred to as the r value. An r value of 1 indicates a perfect direct relationship, where the independent variable explains all of the variation of the dependent variable. A value of -1 indicates a perfect inverse relationship. Most r values fall between 1 and -1, but the closer to 1 (or -1), the better the relationship. An r value of zero indicates no relationship between the variables.

In a multivariable regression equation, the multiple R measures how well the dependent variable is correlated to all of the independent variables in the regression equation. Multiple R measures the total amount of variation in the dependent variable that is explained by the independent variables. In our case, the value of 99.88% (B20) is very close to 1, indicating that almost all of the variation in adjusted costs is explained by sales.[6]

The square of the single or multiple R value, referred to as R-square (or R^2), measures the percentage of the variation in the dependent variable explained by the independent variable. It is the main measure of the goodness of fit. We obtain an R^2 of 99.75% (B21), which means that sales explains 99.75% of the variation in adjusted costs.

Adding more independent variables to the regression equation usually adds to R^2, even when there is no true causality. In statistics, this is called "spurious correlation." The adjusted R^2, which is 99.72% in our example (B22), removes the expected spurious correlation in the "gross" R^2.

$$\text{Adj } R^2 = \left(R^2 - \frac{k}{n-1} \right) \left(\frac{n-1}{n-k-1} \right)$$

where n is the number of observations and k is the number of independent variables (also known as regressors).

Although the data in Table 2-1A are fictitious, in practice I have found that regressions of adjusted costs versus sales usually give rise to R^2 values of 98% or better.[7]

Standard Error of the *y*-Estimate

The standard error of the *y*-estimate is another important regression statistic that gives us information about the reliability of the regression es-

---

6. Although the spreadsheet labels this statistic Multiple R, because our example is an OLS regression, it is simply R.
7. This obviously does not apply to start-ups.

timate. We can multiply the standard error of $16,014 (B23) by two to calculate an approximate 95% confidence interval for the regression estimate. Thus, we are 95% sure that the true adjusted costs are within ±$32,028 of the regression estimate of total adjusted costs.[8] Dividing $64,000 by the mean of adjusted costs (approximately $1 million) leads to a 95% confidence interval that varies by about ±3%, or 6% total. Later in the chapter we will calculate precise confidence intervals.

The Mean of a and b

Because a and b are specific numbers that we calculate in a regression analysis, it is easy to lose sight of the fact that they are not simply numbers, but rather random variables. Remember that we are trying to estimate α and β, the true fixed and variable cost, which we will never know. If we had 20 years of financial history for our Subject Company, we could take any number of combinations of years for our regression analysis. Suppose we had data for 1978–1997. We could use only the last five years, 1993–1997, or choose 1992–1995 and 1997, still keeping five years of data, but excluding 1996—although there is no good reason to do so. We could use 5, 6, 7, or more years of data. There are a large number of different samples we can draw out of 20 years of data. Each different sample would lead to a different calculation of a and b in our attempt to estimate α and β, which is why a and b are random variables. Of course, we will never be exactly correct in our estimate, and even if we were, there would be no way to know it!

Equations (2-1) and (2-2) state that a and b are unbiased estimators of α and β, which means that their expected values equal α and β. The capital E is the expected value operator.

$$E\,(a) = \alpha \qquad \text{the mean of } a \text{ is alpha} \qquad (2\text{-}1)$$

$$E\,(b) = \beta \qquad \text{the mean of } b \text{ is beta} \qquad (2\text{-}2)$$

The Variance of a and b

We want to do everything we can to minimize the variances of a and b in order to improve their reliability as estimators of α and β. If their variances are high, we cannot place much reliability on our regression estimate of costs—something we would like to avoid.

Equations (2-3) and (2-4) below for the variance of a and b give us important insights into deciding how many years of financial data to gather and analyze. Common practice is that an appraisal should encompass five years of data. Most appraisers consider anything older than five years to be stale data, and anything less than five years insufficient. You will see that the common practice may be wrong.

The mathematical definition for the variance of a is:

---

8. This is true at the sample mean of X, and the confidence interval widens as we move away from that.

PART 1   Forecasting Cash Flows

$$\text{Var}(a) = \frac{\sigma^2}{n} \tag{2-3}$$

where σ^2 is the true and unobservable population variance around the true regression line and n = number of observations.[9] Therefore, the variance of our estimate of fixed costs decreases with n, the number of years of data. If $n = 10$, the variance of our estimate of α is ½ of its variance if we use a sample of five years of data. The standard deviation of a, which is the square root of its variance, decreases somewhat less dramatically than the variance, but significantly nonetheless. Having 10 years of data reduces the standard deviation of our estimate of fixed costs by 29% vis-à-vis five years of data. Thus, having more years of data may increase the reliability of our statistical estimate of fixed costs if the data are not "stale," that is, out of date due to changes in the business, all else being constant.

The variance of b is equal to the population variance divided by the sum of the squared deviations from the mean of the independent variable, or:

$$\text{Var}(b) = \frac{\sigma^2}{\displaystyle\sum_{i=1}^{n} x_i^2} \tag{2-4}$$

where $x_i = X_i - \overline{X}$, the deviation of the independent variable of each observation, X_i, from the mean, $\overline{X}$, of all its observations. In this context, it is each year's sales minus the average of sales in the period of analysis. Since we have no control over the numerator—indeed, we cannot even know it—the denominator is the only portion where we can affect the variance of b. Let's take a further look at the denominator.

Table 2-2 is a simple example to illustrate the meaning of x versus X. Expenses (Column C) is our Y (dependent) variable, and sales (Column

TABLE 2-2

OLS Regression: Example of Deviation from Mean

	A	B	C	D	E	F
5				Variable		
6			Y	X	x	x²
7 8	Observation	Year	Expenses	Sales	Deviation From Mean	Squared Dev. From Mean
9	1	1994	$ 80,000	$100,000	$(66,667)	4,444,444,444
10	2	1996	$115,000	$150,000	$(16,667)	277,777,778
11	3	1997	$195,000	$250,000	$ 83,333	6,9444,444,444
12		Total		$500,000	$ -	11,666,666,667
13		Average		$166,667		

---

9. Technically this is true only when the y-axis is placed through the mean of x. The following arguments are valid, however, in either case.

D) is our X (independent) variable. The three years sales total $500,000 (cell D12), which averages to $166,667 (D13) per year, which is $\overline{X}$. Column E shows x, the deviation of each X observation from the sample mean, $\overline{X}$, of $166,667. In 1995, $x_1 = \$100,000 - \$166,667 = -\$66,667$. In 1996, $x_2 = \$150,000 - \$166,667 = -\$16,667$. Finally in 1997, $x_3 = \$250,000 - \$166,667 = \$83,333$. The sum of all deviations is always zero, or

$$\sum_{i=1}^{3} x_i = 0$$

Finally, Column F shows x^2, the square of Column E. The sum of the squared deviations,

$$\sum_{i=1}^{3} x_i^2 = \$11,666,666,667.$$

This squared term appears in several OLS formulas and is particularly important in calculating the variance of b.

When we use relatively fewer years of data, there tends to be less variation in sales. If sales are confined to a fairly narrow range, the squared deviations in the denominator are relatively small, which makes the variance of b large. The opposite is true when we use more years of data. A countervailing consideration is that using more years of data may lead to a higher sample variance, which is the regression estimate of σ^2. Thus, it is difficult to say in advance how many years of data are optimal.

This means that the common practice in the industry of using only five years of data so as not to corrupt our analysis with stale data may be incorrect if there are no significant structural changes in the competitive environment. The number of years of available data that gives the best overall statistical output for the regression equation is the most desirable. Ideally, the analyst should experiment with different numbers of years of data and let the regression statistics—the adjusted R^2, t-statistics, and standard error of the y-estimate—provide the feedback to making the optimal choice of how many years of data to use.

Sometimes prior data can truly be stale. For example, if the number of competitors in the Company's geographic area doubled, this would tend to drive down prices relative to costs, resulting in a decreased contribution margin and an increase in variable costs per dollar of sales. In this case, using the old data without adjustment would distort the regression results. Nevertheless, it may be advisable in some circumstances to use some of the old data—with adjustments—in order to have enough data points for analysis. In the example of more competition in later years, it is possible to reduce the sales in the years prior to the competitive change on a pro forma basis, keeping the costs the same. The regression on this adjusted data is often likely to be more accurate than "winging it" with only two or three years of fresh data.

Of course, the company's management has its view of the future. It is important for the appraiser to understand that view and consider it in his or her statistical work.

Confidence Intervals

Constructing confidence intervals around the regression estimates a and b is another important step in using regression analysis. We would like to be able to make a statement that we are 95% sure that the true variable (either α or β) is within a specific range of numbers, with our regression estimate (a or b) at the midpoint. To calculate the range, we must use the Student's t-distribution, which we define in equation (2-6).

We begin with a standardized normal (Z) distribution. A standardized normal distribution of b—our estimate of β—is constructed by subtracting the mean of b, which is β, and dividing by its standard deviation.

$$Z = \frac{b - \beta}{\sigma / \sqrt{\sum_i x_i^2}} \tag{2-5}$$

Since we do not know σ, the population standard deviation, the best we can do is estimate it with s, the sample standard deviation. The result is the Student's t-distribution, or simply the t-distribution. Figure 2-1 shows a z-distribution and a t-distribution. The t-distribution is very similar to the normal (Z) distribution, with t being slightly more spread out. The equation for the t-distribution is:

$$t = \frac{b - \beta}{s / \sqrt{\sum_i x_i^2}} \tag{2-6}$$

where the denominator is the standard error of b, commonly denoted as s_b (the standard error of a is s_a).

Since β is unobservable, we have to make an assumption about it in order to calculate a t-distribution for it. The usual procedure is to test for the probability that, regardless of the regression's estimate of β—which is our b—the true β is really zero. In statistics, this is known as the "null hypothesis." The magnitude of the t-statistic is indicative of our ability to reject the null hypothesis for an individual variable in the regression equation. When we reject the null hypothesis, we are saying that our regression estimate of β is statistically significant.

We can construct 95% confidence intervals around our estimate, b, of the unknown β. This means that we are 95% sure the correct value of β is in the interval described in equation (2-7).

$$\beta = b \pm t_{0.025} \, s_b \tag{2-7}$$

Formula for 95% confidence interval for the slope

Figure 2-2 shows a graph of the confidence interval. The graph is a t-distribution, with its center at b, our regression estimate of β. The markings on the x-axis are the number of standard errors below or above b. As mentioned before, we denote the standard error of b as s_b. The lower boundary of the 95% confidence interval is $b - t_{0.025} \, s_b$, and the upper boundary of boundary of the 95% confidence interval is $b + t_{0.025} \, s_b$. The

FIGURE 2-1

Z-distribution vs t-distribution

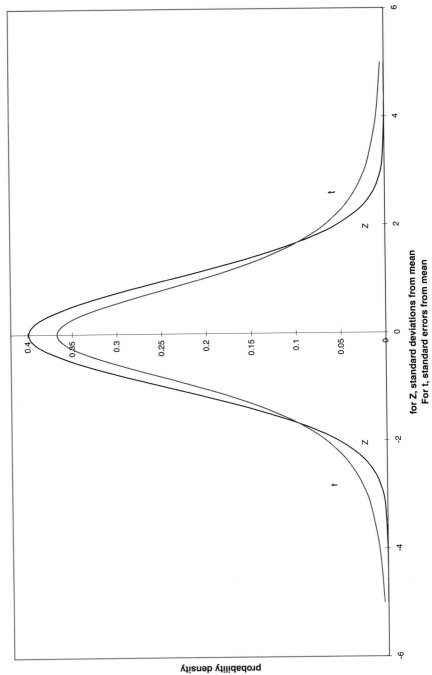

t-distribution of *B* around the Estimate *b*

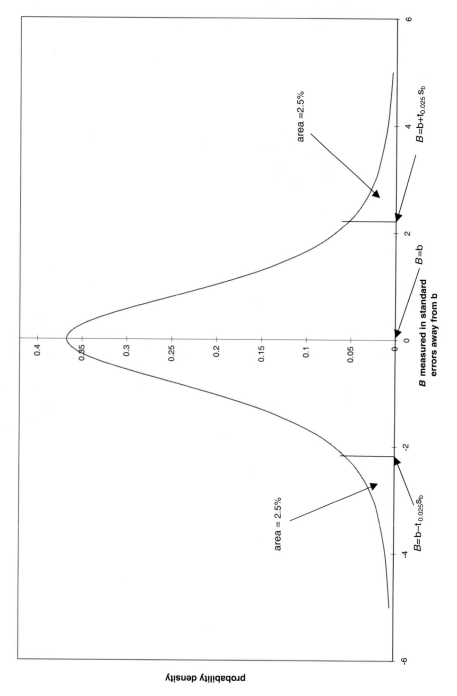

area under the curve for any given interval is the probability that β will be in that interval.

The t-distribution values are found in standard tables in most statistics books. It is very important to use the 0.025 probability column in the tables for a 95% confidence interval, not the 0.05 column. The 0.025 column tells us that for the given degrees of freedom there is a 2½% probability that the true and unobservable β is higher than the upper end of the 95% confidence interval and a 2½% probability that the true and unobservable β is lower than the lower end of the 95% confidence interval (see Figure 2-2). The degrees of freedom is equal to $n - k - 1$, where n is the number of observations and k is the number of independent variables.

Table 2-3 is an excerpt from a t-distribution table. We use the 0.025 column for a 95% confidence interval. To select the appropriate row in the table, we need to know the number of degrees of freedom. Assuming $n = 10$ observations and $k =$ one independent variable, there are eight degrees of freedom ($10 - 1 - 1$). The t-statistic in Table 2-3 is 2.306 (C7). That means that we must go 2.306 standard errors below and above our regression estimate to achieve a 95% confidence interval for β. The regression itself will provide us with the standard error of β. As n, the number of observations, goes to infinity, the t-distribution becomes a z-distribution. When n is large—over 100—the t-distribution is very close to a standardized normal distribution. You can see this in Table 2-3 in that the standard errors in Row 9 are very close to those in Row 10, the latter of which is equivalent to a standardized normal distribution.

The t-statistics for our regression in Table 2-1B are 3.82 (D33) and 56.94 (D34). The P-value, also known as the probability (or prob) value, represents the level at which we can reject the null hypothesis. One minus the P-value is the level of statistical significance of the y-intercept and independent variable(s). The P-values of 0.005 (E33) and 10^{-11} (E34) mean that the y-intercept and slope coefficients are significant at the 99.5% and 99.9%+ levels, respectively, which means we are 99.5% sure that the true y-intercept is not zero and 99.9% sure that the true slope is not zero.[10]

T A B L E   2-3

Abbreviated Table of *T*-Statistics

	A	B	C	D
4			**Selected *t* Statistics**	
5	d.f.\Pr.	0.050	0.025	0.010
6	3	2.353	3.182	4.541
7	8	1.860	**2.306**	2.896
8	12	1.782	2.179	2.681
9	120	1.658	1.980	2.358
10	Infinity	1.645	1.960	2.326

10. For spreadsheets that do not provide *P*-values, another way of calculating the statistical significance is to look up the *t*-statistics in a Student's *t*-distribution table and find the level of statistical significance that corresponds to the *t*-statistic obtained in the regression.

PART 1   Forecasting Cash Flows

The F test is another method of testing the null hypothesis. In multivariable regressions, the F-statistic measures whether the independent variables as a group explain a statistically significant portion of the variation in Y.

We interpret the confidence intervals as follows: there is a 95% probability that true fixed costs (the y-intercept) fall between \$22,496 (F33) and \$91,045 (G33); similarly, there is a 95% probability that the true variable cost (the slope coefficient) falls between \$0.77 (F34) and \$0.84 (G34).

The denominator of equation (2-6) is called the standard error of b, or s_b. The standard error of the Y-estimate, which is defined as

$$s = \sqrt{\frac{1}{n-2} \sum_{i=1}^{n} (Y_i - \hat{Y}_i)^2}$$

is \$16,014 (B23). The larger the amount of scatter of the points around the regression line, the greater the standard error.[11]

Precise Confidence Intervals[12]

Earlier in the chapter, we estimated 95% confidence intervals by subtracting and adding two standard errors of the y-estimate around the regression estimate. In this section, we demonstrate how to calculate precise 95% confidence intervals around the regression estimate using the equations:

$$\pm t_{0.25} s \sqrt{\frac{1}{n} + \frac{x_o^2}{\sum x_i^2}} \qquad (2\text{-}8)$$

95% confidence interval for the mean forecast

$$\pm t_{0.025} s \sqrt{\frac{1}{n} + \frac{x_o^2}{\sum x_i^2} + 1} \qquad (2\text{-}9)$$

95% confidence interval for a specific year's forecast

In the context of forecasting adjusted costs as a function of sales, equation (2-8) is the formula for the 95% confidence interval for the mean adjusted cost, while equation (2-9) is the 95% confidence interval for the costs in a particular year. We will explain what that means at the end of this section, after we present some material that illustrates this in Table 2-1B, page 2.

Note that these confidence intervals are different than those in equation (2-7), which was around the forecast slope only, i.e., b. In this section,

---

11. This standard error of the Y-estimate applies to the mean of our estimate of costs, i.e., the average error if we estimate adjusted costs and expenses many times. This is appropriate in valuation, as a valuation is a forecast of net income and / or cash flows for an infinite number of years. The standard error—and hence 95% confidence interval—for a single year's costs is higher.
12. This section is optional, as the material is somewhat advanced, and it is not necessary to understand this in order to be able to use regression analysis in business valuation. Nevertheless, it will enhance your understanding should you choose to read it.

we are calculating confidence intervals around the entire regression forecast.

The first 15 rows of Table 2-1B, page 2, are identical to the first page and require no explanation. The $989,032 in B16 is the average of the 10 years of sales in B6–B15.

Column D is the deviation of each observation from the mean, which is the sales in Column B minus the mean sales in B16. For example, D6 (−$739,032) is equal to B6 ($250,000) minus B16 ($989,032). D7 (−$489,032) equals B7 ($500,000) minus B16 ($989,032). The total of all deviations from the mean must always equal zero, which it does (D16). Column E is the squared deviations, i.e., the square of Column D. In statistics, the independent variable(s) is known as X, while the deviations from the mean are known as x, which explains the column labels in B5 and D5. The sum of squared deviations,

$$\sum_{i=1988}^{1997} x_i^2$$

equals 1.28×10^{12} (E16).

The next step is to compute the squared deviations for our sample forecast year. We assume that forecast sales for 1997 is $1.6 million (B17). We repeat the coefficients from the regression formula from the first page of the table in B36 and B37. Applying the regression equation, we would then forecast expenses at $1,343,928 (C17).

In order to compute a 95% confidence interval around the expense forecast of $1,343,928, we apply equations (2-8) and (2-9). 1998 forecast sales are $610,968 (D17 = B17 − B16) above the mean of the historical period. That is the x_0 in (3-8) and (3-9). We square the term to get 3.73×10^{11} (E17). Then we divide that by the sum of the squared deviations in the historical period 1.28×10^{12} (E16) to get 0.2905650 (F17), which we repeat below in Row 28.

In Row 25, we insert the t-statistic of 2.306, which one can find in a table for a 95% confidence level (the 0.025 column in a two-tailed distribution) and eight degrees of freedom ($n = 10$ observations − 1 independent variable − 1). In Row 26 we show the standard error of the y-estimate of $16,014, which came from Table 2-1B, B23. Row 27 is $1/n = 1/10 = 0.1$, where n is the number of observations.

Row 28 is a repetition of F17, the ratio of the squared deviation of the forecast to the sum of the squared deviations of the independent variables from their mean.

In B29 we add zero, and in C29 we add 1, according to equations (2-8) and (2-9), respectively. We will explain the difference in the two formulas shortly.

In Row 30 we add Rows 27 to 29, which are the terms in the square root sign in the equations. Obviously, C30 = B30 + 1. In Row 31 we take the square root of Row 30.

Finally, we are able to calculate our 95% confidence intervals as Row 25 × Row 26 × Row 31. The 95% confidence interval for the mean is 2.306 × $16,014 × 0.6249520 = $23,078 (B32), approximately 1.44 times the size of the standard error of the y-estimate. The 95% confidence interval for the specific year's cost forecast is $43,547 (C32), approximately 2.72 times the size of the standard error of the y-estimate. The 95% confidence intervals are 1.7% (B33) and 3.2% (C33) of the forecast costs for the mean and the specific year's forecast, respectively.

You can see that both the calculation of 95% confidence interval for the mean and the specific year's forecast cost is roughly two times the standard error of the y-estimate. Statisticians often loosely approximate the 95% confidence intervals as two standard errors below and above the regression estimate. Equations (2-8) and (2-9) are more precise.

Now we will discuss the difference between equations (2-8) and (2-9). We forecast sales to be $1.6 million in 1998, which means that our forecast of adjusted costs for that year according to the regression equation is $1,343,928. Of course, the actual expenses will not equal that number, even if actual sales by some miracle will equal forecast sales. The 95% confidence interval for the mean tells us that if we add and subtract $23,078 to our forecast of $1,343,928, then we are 95% sure that the true regression line at sales of $1.6 million should have been between $1,320,850 and $1,367,006. If we would experience sales of $1.6 million many times—say 1,000 times—we would be 95% sure that the average cost would fall in our confidence interval.[13] Equation (2-8) is the equation describing this confidence interval.

That does not mean that we are 95% sure that costs would be between $1,320,850 and $1,367,006 in any particular year when sales is $1.6 million. We need a wider confidence interval to be 95% sure of costs in a particular year, given a particular level of sales. Equation (2-9) describes the confidence interval for a particular year.

Thus, the $23,078 confidence interval—meaning that we add and subtract that number from forecast costs—appropriately quantifies our long-run expectation of the confidence interval around forecast costs, given the level of sales. In business valuation we are not very concerned that every individual year conform to our forecasts. Rather, we are concerned with the long-run accuracy of the regression equation. Thus, equation (2-8) is the relevant equation for 95% confidence intervals for valuation analysts. Remember that the confidence interval expands the further we move away from the mean of the historical period. Therefore, if we forecast the costs to go with a forecast sales of, say, $5 million in the year 2005, the confidence interval around the cost estimate is wider than the 1.7% (B33) around 1998 forecast.

Selecting the Data Set and Regression Equation

Table 2-4 is otherwise identical to Table 2-1B, except that instead of all 10 years of data, it only contains the last 5 years. The regression equation for the 5 years of data is (Table 2-4, B27 and B28)

$$\text{Adjusted costs} = \$71,252 + (\$0.79 \times \text{Sales})$$

Examining the regression statistics, we find that the adjusted R^2 is

---

13. This ignores the need to recompute the regression equation with new data.

TABLE 2-4

Regression Analysis 1993–1997

	A	B	C	D	E	F	G
4	**Year**	**Sales**	**Adjusted Costs**				
5	1993	$1,123,600	$965,043				
6	1994	$1,191,016	$1,012,745				
7	1995	$1,262,477	$1,072,633				
8	1996	$1,338,226	$1,122,714				
9	1997	$1,415,000	$1,199,000				
11	SUMMARY OUTPUT						
13	**Regression Statistics**						
14	Multiple R	99.79%					
15	R square	99.58%					
16	Adjusted R square	99.44%					
17	Standard error	6,840					
18	Observations	5					
20	ANOVA						
21		df	SS	MS	F	Significance F	
22	Regression	1	3.35E+10	3.35E+10	716	1.15E−04	
23	Residual	3	1.40E+08	4.68E+07			
24	Total	4	3.36E+10				
26		Coefficients	Standard Error	t Stat	P-value	Lower 95%	Upper 95%
27	Intercept [1]	71,252	37,624	1.89	0.15	(48,485)	190,989
28	Sales [2]	0.79	0.03	26.75	0.00	0.70	0.89

[1] This is the regression estimate of fixed costs
[2] This is the regression estimate of variable costs

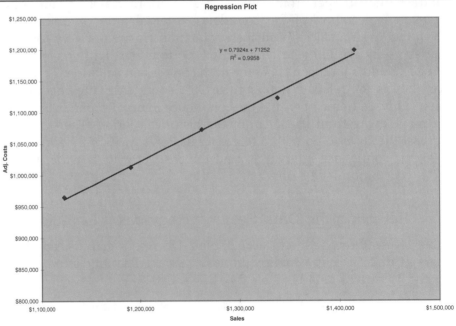

Regression Plot

$$y = 0.7924x + 71252$$
$$R^2 = 0.9958$$

99.44% (B16), still indicating an excellent relationship. We do see a difference in the t-statistics for the two regressions.

The t-statistic for the intercept is now 1.89 (D27), indicating it is no longer significant at the 95% level, whereas it was 3.82 in Table 2-1B. Another effect of fewer data is that the 95% confidence interval for the intercept value is −$48,485 (F27) to $190,989 (G27), a range of $239,475. In addition, the t-statistic for the slope coefficient, while still significant, has fallen from 56.94 (Table 2-1B, D34) to 26.75 (D28). The 95% confidence interval for the slope now becomes $0.70 (F28) to $0.89 (G28), a range that is 3½ times greater than that in Table 2-1B and indicates much more uncertainty in the variable cost than we obtain using 10 years of data.

The standard error of the Y-estimate, however, decreases from $16,014 (Table 2-1B, B23) to $6,840. This indicates that decreasing the number of data points improves the Y-estimate, an opposite result from all of the preceding. Why?

Earlier, we pointed out that using only a small range for the independent variable leads to a small denominator in the variance of b, i.e.,

$$\frac{\sigma^2}{\displaystyle\sum_{i=1}^{n} x_i^2}$$

which leads to larger confidence intervals. However, larger data sets (using more years of data) tend to lead to a larger standard error of the y-estimate, s. As we mentioned earlier,

$$s = \sqrt{\frac{1}{n-2}\sum_{i=1}^{n}(Y_i - \hat{Y}_i)^2}$$

where $\hat{Y}_i$ are the forecast (regression fitted) costs, Y_i are the historical costs, and n is the number of observations.[14] Thus, we often have a trade-off in deciding how many years of data to include in the regression. More years of data leads to better confidence intervals, but fewer years may lead to smaller standard errors of the y-estimate.

Table 2-4 was constructed to demonstrate that you should evaluate all of the regression statistics carefully to determine if the relationship is sufficiently strong to merit using it and which data set is best to use. Simply looking at the adjusted R^2 value is insufficient; all the regression statistics should be evaluated in their entirety, as an improvement in one may be counterbalanced by a deterioration in another. Therefore, it is best to test different data sets and compare all of the regression statistics to select the regression equation that represents the best overall relationship between the variables.

---

14. We divide by $n - 2$ instead of n because it takes two points to determine a line. If we only had two years of historical data, we could determine a regression line, but we would know absolutely nothing about the variance around the line. It takes a minimum of three years of data to be able to say anything at all about how well the regression line fits the data, and three years is usually insufficient. It is much better to have at least five years of data, though four years can often suffice.

PROBLEMS WITH USING REGRESSION ANALYSIS FOR FORECASTING COSTS

Although regression analysis is a powerful tool, its blind application can lead to serious errors. Various problems can be encountered, and one should be cognizant of the limitations of this technique. Aside from the obvious problems of poor fit and insufficient data, structural changes in the company can also invalidate the historical relationship of sales and costs.

Insufficient Data

Insufficient data leads to increased error in the regression, which in turn will lead to increased error in the forecast data. As mentioned previously, to optimize the regression equation it is best to examine overlapping data sets to determine which gives the best results.

Substantial Changes in Competition or Product/Service

Although regression analysis is applicable in most situations, substantial structural changes in a business may render it inappropriate. As mentioned previously, the appraiser can often compensate for changes in the competitive environment by making pro forma adjustments to historical sales, keeping costs the same. However, when a company changes its business, the past is less likely to be a good indicator of what may occur in the future, depending on the significance of the change.

USING REGRESSION ANALYSIS TO FORECAST SALES

Table 2-5 is an example of using regression techniques to forecast sales. In order to do this, it must be reasonable to assume that past performance is a reasonable indicator of future expectations. If there are fundamental changes in the industry that render the past a poor indicator of the future, then regression may useless and even quite misleading. As cautioned by Pratt, Reilly, and, Schweihs (1996), blind application of regression, where past performance is the sole indicator of future sales, can be misleading and incorrect. Instead, careful analysis is required to determine whether past income generating forces will be duplicated in the future. Nevertheless, regression analysis is often useful as a benchmark in forecasting.

In our example in Table 2-5, the primary independent variable is gross domestic product (GDP), which we show for the years 1988–1998 in billions of dollars in cells B5:B15 (the cell references separated by a colon will be our way to indicate contiguous spreadsheet ranges). In C5: C15, we show the square of GDP in billions of dollars, which is our second potential independent variable.[15] Our dependent variable is sales, which appears in D5:D15.

---

15. Another variation of this procedure is to substitute the square root of GDP for its square.

T A B L E 2-5

Regression Analysis of Sales as a Function of GDP [1]

	A	B	C	D	E	F	G	H	I
4	**Year**	**GDP**	**GDP²**	**Sales**					
5	1988	5,049.6	25,498,460.2	$1,000,000					
6	1989	5,438.7	29,579,457.7	$1,090,000					
7	1990	5,743.0	32,982,049.0	$1,177,200					
8	1991	5,916.7	35,007,338.9	$1,259,604					
9	1992	6,244.4	38,992,531.4	$1,341,478					
10	1993	6,558.1	43,008,675.6	$1,442,089					
11	1994	6,947.0	48,260,809.0	$1,528,614					
12	1995	7,269.6	52,847,084.2	$1,617,274					
13	1996	7,661.6	58,700,114.6	$1,706,224					
14	1997	8,110.9	65,786,698.8	$1,812,010					
15	1998	8,510.7	72,432,014.5	$1,929,791					
17	SUMMARY OUTPUT								
19	**Regression Statistics**								
20	Multiple R	0.999156207							
21	R square	0.998313125							
22	Adjusted R square	0.997891407							
23	Standard error	13893.80997							
24	Observations	11							
26	ANOVA								
27		**df**	**SS**	**MS**	**F**	**Significance F**			
28	Regression	2	9.13938E+11	4.5697E+11	2367.24925	8.0971E−12			
29	Residual	8	1544303643	193037955.4					
30	Total	10	9.15482E+11						
32		**Coefficients**	**Standard Error**	**t Stat**	**P-value**	**Lower 95%**	**Upper 95%**	**Lower 95.0%**	**Upper 95.0%**
33	Intercept	−824833.1304	182213.8131	−4.526732175	0.001932674	−1245019.209	−404647.0522	−1245019.209	−404647.0522
34	GDP	412.8368996	54.65310215	7.553768832	6.5848E−05	286.8065386	538.8672622	286.8065386	538.8672607
35	GDP²	−0.010625314	0.004016833	−2.64519663	0.029474667	−0.019888154	−0.001362473	−0.019888154	−0.001362473

[1] GDP, Gross Domestic Product, is in billions of dollars. GDP is a proxy for the overall economy.

Spreadsheet Procedures to Perform Regression

It is mandatory to put the variables in columns and the time periods in rows. Electronic spreadsheets will not permit you to perform regression analysis with time in columns and the variables in rows. In other words, we cannot transpose the data in Table 2-5, cells A4:D15 and still perform a regression analysis.

Another requirement is that all cells must contain numeric data. You cannot perform regression with blank cells or cells with alphanumeric data in them. Also, you will receive an error message if one of your independent variables is a multiple of another. For example, if each cell in C5:C15 is three times the corresponding cell in B5:B15, then the x variables are perfectly collinear and the regression produce an error message.

We will explain regression procedures in Microsoft Excel first, then in Lotus 123.

In Excel, the procedure to perform the regression analysis is as follows:

1. Select Tools|Data Analysis|Regression. This will bring up a dialog box and automatically places the cursor in Input Y Range.[16]

2. For the Y range (which is the dependent variable, sales in our example), click on the range icon with the red arrow immediately to the right. Doing so minimizes the dialog box and enables you to highlight the cell range D4:D15 with your mouse.[17] Note that we have included the label Sales in D4 in this range. Click again on the range icon again to return to the dialog box.

3. For the X range, which are the independent variables GDP and GDP^2 in our case, repeat the procedure in (2) and highlight the range B4:C15.

4. Click on the box Labels, which will put a check mark in the box.

5. Click on Output Range. Click on the box to the right, click on the range icon with the red arrow, and then click on cell A17. This tells the spreadsheet to begin the regression output at that cell.

6. Click OK.

Excel now calculates the regression and outputs the data as shown in the bottom half of Table 2-5.

The instructions for Lotus 123 are almost identical. The only differences are:

1. The command is Range|Analyze|Regression.

2. The ranges for the dependent and independent variables should not include the label in Row 4. Thus they are D5:D15 and B5:C15, respectively.

---

16. If Data Analysis is not yet enabled in Excel, you must select add-ins and then select Analysis|ToolPak.

17. Excel actually shows the range with dollar signs, e.g., $D$4:$D$15

3. Lotus 123 does not compute t-statistics for you.[18] You will have to do that manually by creating a formula. Divide the regression coefficient by its standard error. Unfortunately, Lotus 123 does not calculate the p-values either. You will have to look up your results in a standard table of t-statistics. We will cover that later.

Examining the Regression Statistics

Once again, we look at the statistical measures resulting from the regression to determine how strong is the relationship between sales and time. Adjusted R^2 is 99.8% (B22), a near-perfect relationship. The t-statistics for the independent variables, GDP and GDP^2, are 7.55 (D34) and –2.65 (D35), both statistically significant. The easiest way to determine the level of statistical significance is through the p-value. One minus the p-value is the level of statistical significance. For GDP, the p-value is 6.5848×10^{-5} (E34), which is much less than 0.1%. Thus GNP is statistically significant at a level greater than $100\% - 0.1\% = 99.9\%$. The square of GDP has a p-value of 0.029 (E35), which indicates statistical significance at the 97.1% level. We normally accept any regressor with significance greater than or equal to 95%, and we may consider accepting a regressor that is significant at the 90% to 95% level.

The standard error of the y-estimate, i.e., sales, is \$13,894 (B23). Our approximate 95% confidence interval is $\pm$ two standard errors $= \pm$ \$27,788, which is less than $\pm$ 2% of the mean of sales.

In actual practice, adjusted R^2 for a regression of sales of mature firms is often above 90% and frequently around 98%.

Adding Industry-Specific Independent Variables

One should also consider adding industry-specific independent variables. For example, when valuing a jeweler, we should try adding the price of gold and silver (and the nonlinear transformations, i.e., squares, square roots, and logarithms) as independent variables. When valuing a firm in the oil industry, we should try using the price of a barrel of oil (and its nonlinear transformations).

When valuing a coffee producer, we would want to have not only the average price of coffee as an independent variable, but also the price of tea and perhaps even sugar. The analyst should look to the prices of the product itself, complements, and substitutes.

Once again, it is important to examine the statistical validity of the relationship and use professional judgment to determine the usefulness of the equation. Sales forecasts obtained from regression analysis can serve as a benchmark from which adjustments can be made based on qualitative factors that may influence future sales.

One should also keep in mind that just because a less quantitative method of forecasting sales does not have an embarrassingly low R^2 staring the analyst in the face does not mean that it is superior to the re-

---

18. That is true of version 5, which is already at least four years old. If Lotus has added that feature in a later version, I would not be aware of that.

gression. It means we have no clue as to the reliability of the forecast. We should always be uncomfortable with our ignorance.

Try All Combinations of Potential Independent Variables

It is important to try all combinations of independent variables. With a statistics package, this is done automatically in using automated forward or backward regression. However, statistics packages have their drawbacks. They are not very user friendly in communicating with spreadsheet programs, which most appraisers use in valuation analysis. Most appraisers will find the spreadsheet regression capabilities more than adequate.

Therefore, it is important to try all combinations of potential independent variables in the regression process. For example, in regressing sales against both GDP and GDP^2, it is not at all unusual to find both independent variables statistically insignificant when regressed together, i.e., p-values greater than 0.05. However, they still may be statistically significant when regressed individually. So it is important to regress sales against GDP and perform a second regression against GDP^2. This process becomes more complicated with additional candidates for independent variables.

APPLICATION OF REGRESSION ANALYSIS TO THE GUIDELINE COMPANY METHOD

Valuation using the guideline company method involves the use of ratios of stock price to: earnings (P/E multiples), cash flow (P/CF or $P/EBIT$ multiples), book value (P/BV multiples), sales ($P/Sales$), or other measures of income, cash flow, or value. The stock prices typically are those of public companies in the same or similar business as the company. Consideration is therefore given to the opinion of the informed investor and what he or she is willing to pay for the stock of comparative public companies adjusted for the specific circumstances of the company being valued. While the use of ratios is common in valuation, regression analysis is more sophisticated and informative because it provides us with statistical feedback on the strength of the relationship. Pratt, Reilly, and Schweihs (1996) present a comprehensive chapter on use of the guideline company method, so we will only discuss it within the context of regression analysis.

Table 2-6: Regression Analysis of Guideline Companies

Table 2-6 shows data from an actual guideline company analysis, with the company names disguised in Column A. Column B contains the fair market values (FMVs) (market capitalization) for 11 companies, ranging from slightly over $3 million (B5) to over $150 million (B15). The average FMV is $41.3 million (B16), with a standard deviation of $44.6 million (B17). Net income (Column C) averages about $5.1 million (C16), with a range of $600,000 to $16.9 million. We had to exclude companies A and B, which were outliers with price earnings (PE) ratios over 60.

T A B L E   2-6

Regression Analysis of Guideline Companies

	A	B	C	D	E	F	G	H	I
4	**Company**	**FMV**	**Net Income**	**ln FMV**	**ln NI**	**1/g**	**g**	**PE Ratio**	
5	C	3,165,958	602,465	14.9680	13.3088	20.0000	0.0500	5.2550	
6	D	6,250,000	659,931	15.6481	13.3999	10.0000	0.1000	9.4707	
7	E	12,698,131	1,375,000	16.3570	14.1340	10.5263	0.0950	9.2350	
8	F	24,062,948	2,325,000	16.9962	14.6592	9.0909	0.1100	10.3497	
9	G	23,210,578	2,673,415	16.9601	14.7989	12.1951	0.0820	8.6820	
10	H	16,683,567	2,982,582	16.6299	14.9083	20.0000	0.0500	5.5937	
11	I	37,545,523	4,369,808	17.4411	15.2902	12.5000	0.0800	8.5920	
12	J	46,314,262	4,438,000	17.6510	15.3057	9.3023	0.1075	10.4358	
13	K	36,068,550	7,384,000	17.4009	15.8148	20.8333	0.0480	4.8847	
14	L	97,482,000	12,679,000	18.3952	16.3555	9.5238	0.1050	7.6885	
15	M	150,388,518	16,865,443	18.8287	16.6408	9.0909	0.1100	8.9170	
16	Average	**41,260,912**	**5,123,149**	**17.0251**	**14.9651**	**13.0057**	**0.0852**	**8.1004**	
17	Standard deviation	**44,558,275**	**5,233,919**	**1.1212**	**1.0814**	**4.8135**	**0.0252**	**1.9954**	

20	SUMMARY OUTPUT

22	Regression Statistics	
23	Multiple R	0.997820486
24	R square	0.995645723
25	Adjusted R square	0.994557153
26	Standard error	0.082720079
27	Observations	11

29	ANOVA				
30		df	SS	MS	F	Significance F
31	Regression	2	12.51701011	6.258505055	914.6369206	3.59471E-10
32	Residual	8	0.054740892	0.006842611		
33	Total	10	12.571751			

35		Coefficients	Standard Error	t Stat	P-value	Lower 95%	Upper 95%	Lower 95.0%	Upper 95.0%
36	Intercept	3.430881701	0.390158993	8.79354767	2.19714E-05	2.531172869	4.330590533	2.531172869	4.330590533
37	ln NI	0.957081978	0.024655341	38.81844378	2.13125E-10	0.900226622	1.013937333	0.900226622	1.013937333
38	1/g	-0.056021702	0.005538834	-10.1143497	7.79687E-06	-0.068794284	-0.04324912	-0.068794284	-0.04324912

T A B L E 2-6 *(continued)*

Regression Analysis of Guideline Companies

	A	B	C	D	E	F	G	H	I
40	**Valuation**								
41	NI	100,000	200,000	300,000	400,000	500,000	1,000,000		
42	ln NI	11.5129	12.2061	12.6115	12.8992	13.1224	13.8155		
43	X coefficient-NI	0.957081978	0.957081978	0.957081978	0.957081978	0.957081978	0.957081978		
44	ln NI × X coefficient	11.01881347	11.68221215	12.07027549	12.34561082	12.55917749	13.22257672		
45	g	0.05	0.055	0.06	0.065	0.07	0.075		
46	1/g	20	18.18181818	16.66666667	15.38461538	14.28571429	13.33333333		
47	X coefficient-1/g	-0.056021702	-0.056021702	-0.056021702	-0.056021702	-0.056021702	-0.056021702		
48	1/g × X coefficient	-1.120434033	-1.018576394	-0.933695028	-0.861872333	-0.800310024	-0.746956022		
49	Add intercept	3.430881701	3.430881701	3.430881701	3.430881701	3.430881701	3.430881702		
50	Total = ln FMV	13.32926101	14.09451745	14.56746217	14.91462019	15.18974917	15.90650185		
51	FMV	$614,928	$1,321,816	$2,121,136	$3,001,492	$3,952,067	$8,092,934		
52	PE Ratio	6.149284138	6.609082291	7.070452024	7.50373099	7.904133036	8.09293361		
54	**95% Confidence Intervals**								
55	2 Standard errors	0.165440158							
56	e^2 Std Err	1.179912352							
57	e^{-2} Std Err	0.847520579							

First we will briefly describe the regression results for the regression of FMV against net income. The regression yields an adjusted R^2 of 94.6% and a t-statistic for the x-coefficient of 12.4, which seems to indicate a successful regression. The regression equation obtained for the complete data set is:

$$\text{FMV} = -\$1,272,335 + (8.3 \times \text{Net Income})$$

If we were to use to value a firm with net income of $100,000, the regression would produce a value of $-\$442,000$. Something is wrong!

The problem is that the full regression equation is:

$$\text{FMV} = a + b \times \text{Net Income} + u_i \qquad (2\text{-}10)$$

where u_i is an error term, assumed to be normally distributed with an expected value of zero. Our specific regression equation is:

$$-\$1,272,335 + (8.3 \times \text{Net Income}) + u_i \qquad (2\text{-}11)$$

The problem is that this error term is additive and likely to be correlated to the size of the firm. When that occurs, we have a problem called "heteroscedasticity."

There are two possible solutions to the problem. The first is to use weighted least squares (WLS) instead of ordinary least squares regression. In WLS, we weight the extreme values less than the more mainstream values. This usually will not produce a usable solution for a privately held firm that is much smaller than the publicly traded guideline companies.

The second possible solution is to use a log–log specification. In doing so, we regress the natural logarithm of market capitalization as a function of the natural logarithm of net income. Its form is:

$$\ln \text{FMV}_i = a + b_i \ln \text{NI} + u_i, \ i = \text{guideline company } 1, 2, 3, \ldots n \qquad (2\text{-}12)$$

When we take antilogs, the original equation is:

$$\text{FMV}_i = A \, \text{NI}_i^b \, v_i \qquad (2\text{-}13)$$

where $A = e^a$, $v_i = e^{u_i}$ is Euler's constant, and the expected value of $v_i = 1$.

In equation (2-13), the regression equation x-coefficient, b_i, from equation (2-12) for net income thus becomes an exponent to net income. If $b = 1$, then size has no scaling effect on the FMV, and we would expect price earnings ratios to be uncorrelated to size, all other things being constant. If $b > 1$, then the price earnings multiple should rise with net income, and the opposite is true of $b < 1$. Relating this to the log size model in Chapter 4, we would thus expect to find $b > 1$ because over long periods of time large firms have lower discount rates than small firms, which means larger values relative to earnings.

Using equation (2-13), consider two identical errors of 20% for firms i and j, where firm i has net income of $100,000 and firm j has net income of $200,000. In other words, the error terms v_i and v_j are both 1.2.[19] For

---

19. This means the error terms u_i and u_j in equation (2-12) are equal to $\ln (1.2) = 0.182$.

simplicity, suppose that $b = 1$ for both firms. The same statistical error in the log of the fair market value of both firms produces an error in fair market value that is twice as large in firm j as in firm i. This is a desirable property, as it corresponds to our intuition that large firms will tend to have larger absolute deviations from the regression determined values. Thus, this form of regression is likely to be more successful than equation (2-10) for valuing small firms.

Equation (2-10) is probably fine for valuing firms of the same size as the guideline companies. When we apply equation (2–10) to various levels of net income, we find the forecast FMVs are −$442,000, $0 (rounded), $2.9 million, and $7.0 million for net incomes of $100,000, $154,000, $500,000, and $1 million. Obviously equation (3-10) works poorly at the low end. We would also have a similar, but opposite, scaling problem forecasting value for a firm with net income of $5 billion. The additive error term restricts the applicability of equation (2-10) to subject companies of similar size to the guideline companies.

There is an important possible enhancement to the regression equation, and that is the introduction of forecast growth as an independent variable. The emergence of the Internet makes it easier to obtain growth forecasts, although frequently there are no such estimates for smaller publicly traded firms.

For a firm with constant forecast growth, a midyear Gordon model is its proper valuation equation.

$$\text{FMV} = \text{CF}_{t+1} \frac{\sqrt{1 + r}}{r - g} \tag{2-14}$$

In Chapter 4, we show that New York Stock Exchange returns are negatively related to the natural logarithm of market capitalization (which can also be referred to as fair market value or size), which means that there is a nonlinear relationship between return and size. Therefore, the discount rate, r, in equation (2-14) impounds a nonlinear size effect. To the extent that there is a nonlinear size effect in equation (2-13), we should hopefully pick that up in the b coefficient.

Note that in equation (2-14) there is a growth term, g, which appears in the denominator of the Gordon model multiple. Thus, it is reasonable to try $1/g$ as an additional independent variable in equation (2-13).

Continuing our description of Table 2-6, Column C is net income and Columns D and E are the natural logarithms of FMV and net income. These are actual data from a real valuation. Column G shows a growth rate, and it is not actual data (which were unavailable). Column F is the inverse of Column G, i.e., $1/g$. Thus, Column D is our dependent variable and Columns E and F are our independent variables.[20]

Adjusted R^2 is 99.5% (B25), an excellent result. The standard error of the y-estimate is 0.08272 (B26). The y-intercept is 3.43 (B36) and the x-coefficients for ln NI and $1/g$ are 0.95708 and −0.05602 (B37, B38), respectively.

---

20. Electronic spreadsheets require that the independent variables be in contiguous columns.

On page 2 of Table 2-6, we show valuations for subject companies with differing levels of net income and expected growth. Row 41 shows firms with net incomes ranging from $100,000 to $1 million. Row 42 is the natural log of net income.[21] We multiply that by the x-coefficient for net income in Row 43, which produces a subtotal in Row 44.

Row 45 contains our forecast of constant growth for the various subject companies. We are assuming growth of 5% per year for the $100,000 net income firm in Column B, and we increase the growth estimate by 0.5% for each firm. Row 46 is one divided by forecast growth.

In Row 47 we repeat the x-coefficient for $1/g$ from the regression, and we multiply Row 46 × Row 47 = Row 48, which is another subtotal.

In Row 49 we repeat the y-intercept from the regression. In Row 50 we add Rows 44, 48, and 49, which is the natural logarithm of the forecast FMV (at the marketable minority interest level). We must then exponentiate that result, i.e., take the antilog. The Excel formula for B51 is = EXP(B50).[22] Finally, we calculate the P/E ratio in Row 52 as Row 51 divided by Row 41.

The P/E ratio rises because of the increase in the forecast growth rate across the columns. If all cells in Row 45 were equal to 0.05, then the PE ratios in Row 52 would actually decline going to the right across the columns. The reason for this is that the x-coefficient for ln NI is 0.95708 (page 1, B37) < 1. This is contrary to our expectations. If B38 were greater than 1, then P/E ratios would rise with firm size, holding forecast growth constant. Does this disprove the log size model? No. While all the rest of the data are real, these growth rates are not actual. They are made up. Also, one small sample of one industry at one point in time does not generalize to all firms at all times.

In the absence of the made-up growth rates, the actual regression yielded an adjusted R^2 of 93.3% and a standard error of 0.2896 (not shown).

95% Confidence Intervals

We multiply the standard error in B26 by 2 = 0.16544 (B55). To convert the standard error of ln FMV to the standard error of FMV, we have to exponentiate the two standard errors. In B56 we raise e, Euler's constant, to the power of B55. Thus, $e^{0.16544} = 1.1799$, which means the high side of our 95% confidence interval is 18% higher than our estimate.[23] To calculate the low side of our 95% confidence interval, we raise e to the power of two standard errors below the regression estimate. Thus B57 = $e^{-0.16544}$ = 0.8475, which is approximately 15% below the regression estimate. Thus our 95% confidence interval is the regression estimate +18% and −15%. Using only the actual data that were available at the time, the same regression without $1/g$ yielded confidence intervals of the regres-

---

21. The Excel formula for cell B42, for example, is = ln(B41). The Lotus 123 formula would be @ln(B41).

22. In Lotus 123 the formula would be @exp(B50)

23. The Excel formula for cell B56 is =EXP(B55) and the Lotus 123 formula is @EXP(B55). Similarly, the Excel formula for B57 is =EXP(−B55), and the Lotus 123 formula is @EXP(−B55).

sion estimate +78% and −56%. Obviously, growth can make a huge difference. Also, without growth, the x-coefficient for ln NI was slightly above one, indicating increasing P/E multiples with size.

SUMMARY

Regression analysis is a powerful tool for use in forecasting future costs, expenses, and sales and estimating fair market value. We should take care in evaluating and selecting the input data, however, to arrive at meaningful answer. Similarly, we should carefully scrutinize the regression output to determine the significance of the variables and the amount of error in the Y-estimate to determine if the overall relationship is meaningful.

BIBLIOGRAPHY

Bhattacharyya, Gouri K., and Richard A. Johnson. 1977. *Statistical Concepts and Methods.* New York: John Wiley & Sons.

Pratt, Shannon P., Robert F. Reilly, and Robert P. Schweihs. 1996. *Valuing a Business: The Analysis and Appraisal of Closely Held Companies;* 3d ed. New York: McGraw-Hill.

Wonnacott, Thomas H., and Ronald J. Wonnacott. 1981. *Regression: A Second Course in Statistics.* New York: John Wiley & Sons.

APPENDIX
The ANOVA table (Rows 28–32)

We have already discussed the importance of variance in regression analysis. The center section of Table A2-1, which is an extension of Table 2-1B, contains an analysis of variance (ANOVA) automatically generated by the spreadsheet. We calculate the components of ANOVA in the top portion of the table to "open up the black box" and show the reader where the numbers come from.

First, we calculate the regression estimate of adjusted costs in Column D using the regression equation:

$$\text{Costs} = \$56{,}770 + (0.80 \times \text{Sales}) \ (\text{B35, B36})$$

Next, we subtract the average actual adjusted cost of \$852,420 (C18) from the calculated costs in Column D to arrive at the deviation from the mean in Column E. Note that the sum of the deviations is zero in cell E17, as expected.

In Column F we square each deviation term in Column E and total them in F17. The total, 831,414,202,481, is known as the sum of squares and measures the amount of variation explained by the regression. In the absence of a regression, our best estimate of costs for any year during the 1988–1997 period would be $\overline{Y}$, the mean costs. Therefore, the difference between the historical mean and the regression estimate (Column E) is the absolute deviation explained by the regression. The square of that (Column F) is the variance explained by the regression. This term appears in the ANOVA table in C30 under SS (sum of squares).

The next term to the right in the ANOVA table is the mean squared error (MS), which measures the variance explained by the regression. In our case, the number is identical to the SS term (D30 = C30). This occurs because we have only one independent variable, sales, and thus one degree of freedom (B30) in the regression.

In Column G we calculate the difference between the each actual cost and the calculated cost (the regression estimate) by subtracting the values in Column D from Column C. Again, the sum of the deviations is zero. We square the deviations and sum them to arrive at a value of 2,051,637,107 (H17). This second sum of squares, which appears in the ANOVA table in cell C31, is the unexplained variation. We calculate the corresponding mean square error term in Column I by dividing the values in Column H by 8, the number of degrees of freedom (B30). The sum is 256,454,638 (I17), which appears in the ANOVA table in D31. This number represents the unexplained variance. Finally, we calculate the *F*-statistic of 3,241 (E30) by dividing the explained variance (D30) by the unexplained variance (D31).

The explained variation plus the unexplained equals the total variation. The correlation coefficient is

$$R^2 = \frac{\text{Explained Variation of } Y}{\text{Total Variation of } Y}$$

In our case, the explained variation (C30) divided by the total variation (C32) is equal to 99.75%, as seen in B23.

T A B L E   A2-1

Regression Analysis 1988–1997

	Actual							
	A	B	C	D	E	F	G	H	I
Year	Sales = X [1]	Adj. Costs = Y [2]	Calculated Costs = $\hat{Y}$ [3]	Deviation of Calc. from Mean [4] $= \hat{Y} - \bar{Y}$	Sum of Squares [5] $= (\hat{Y} - \bar{Y})^2$	Deviation of Actual from Calc. [6] $= Y - \hat{Y}$	Deviation from Actual Squared [5] $= (Y - \hat{Y})^2$	Mean Square [7] $= (Y - \hat{Y})^2/8$
1988	$250,000	$242,015	$257,889	−$594,532	353,467,822,773.69	−$15,874	251,983,658	31,497,957
1989	$500,000	$458,916	$459,007	−$393,413	154,773,949,895.09	−$92	8,399	1,050
1990	$750,000	$696,461	$660,126	−$192,295	36,977,294,181.16	$36,336	1,320,285,654	165,035,707
1991	$1,000,000	$863,159	$861,244	$8,824	77,855,631.91	$1,915	3,668,783	458,598
1992	$1,060,000	$891,517	$909,512	$57,092	3,259,496,294.19	−$17,995	323,821,415	40,477,677
1993	$1,123,600	$965,043	$960,677	$108,257	11,719,473,702.15	$4,366	19,064,659	2,383,082
1994	$1,191,016	$1,012,745	$1,014,911	$162,491	26,403,295,435.15	−$2,166	4,691,209	586,401
1995	$1,262,477	$1,072,633	$1,072,400	$219,979	48,390,920,118.80	$233	54,240	6,780
1996	$1,338,226	$1,122,714	$1,133,338	$280,917	78,914,430,752.87	−$10,623	112,853,095	14,106,637
1997	$1,415,000	$1,199,000	$1,195,101	$342,680	117,429,663,696.32	$3,899	15,205,993	1,900,749
Total				$0	831,414,202,481	$0	2,051,637,107	256,454,638

$852,420 = Average Actual Adjusted Costs ($\bar{Y}$)

SUMMARY OUTPUT

Regression Statistics

Multiple R	0.998768455
R square	0.997538427
Adjusted R square	0.99723073
Standard error	16014.20115
Observations	10

54

28	ANOVA				
29		df	SS	MS	F	Significance F
30	Regression	1	8.31414E+11	8.31414E+11	3241.954241	1.00493E-11
31	Residual	8	2051637107	256454638.3		
32	Total	9	8.33466E+11			

34		Coefficients	Standard Error	t Stat	P-value	Lower 95%	Upper 95%	Lower 95.0%	Upper 95.0%
35	Intercept	56770.40117	14863.25124	3.819514334	0.005093239	22495.66018	91045.14216	22495.66018	91045.14216
36	Sales = X [1]	0.804473578	0.0141289	56.93816156	1.00493E-11	0.771892255	0.8370549	0.771892255	0.8370549

[a] This sheet is an extension of Table 2-1B.
[1] from Table 2-1A, Row 7
[2] from Table 2-1A, Row 27
[3] Calculated costs using Costs = 0.80 × Sales + $56,806 with sales figures in Column B
[4] Deviation of calculated costs from average actual costs (Column D − C17) = $\hat{Y} - \bar{Y}$
[5] Deviations squared
[6] Deviation of actual costs from calculated costs (Column C − Column D)
[7] Deviations squared / 8 (degrees of freedom)
[8] Regression estimate of fixed costs
[9] Regression estimate of variable costs

55

Annuity Discount Factors and the Gordon Model

INTRODUCTION
   Definitions
   Denoting Time
ADF WITH END-OF-YEAR CASH FLOWS
   Behavior of the ADF with Growth
   Special Case of ADF when $g = 0$: The Ordinary Annuity
   Special Case when $n \to \infty$ and $r > g$: The Gordon Model
   Intuitively Understanding Equations (3-6) and (3-6a)
   Relationship between the ADF and the Gordon Model
   Table 3-1: Proof of ADF Equations (3-6) through (3-6b)
   A Brief Summary
MIDYEAR CASH FLOWS
   Table 3-2: Example of Equations (3-10) through (3-10b)
   Special Cases for Midyear Cash Flows: No Growth, $g = 0$
   Gordon Model
STARTING PERIODS OTHER THAN YEAR 1
   End-of-Year Formulas
   Valuation Date $\neq 0$
   Table 3-3: Example of Equation (3-11)
   Tables 3-4 through 3-6: Variations of Table 3-3 with $S < 0$, Negative
     Growth, and $r < g$
   Special Case: No Growth, $g = 0$
   Generalized Gordon Model
   Midyear Formula
PERIODIC PERPETUITY FACTORS (PPFs): PERPETUITIES FOR
  PERIODIC CASH FLOWS
   The Mathematical Formulas
   Tables 3-7 and 3-8: Examples of Equations (3-18) and (3-19)
   Other Starting Years
   New versus Used Equipment Decisions

ADFs IN LOAN MATHEMATICS

    Calculating Loan Payments

    Present Value of a Loan

        Table 3-10: Example of Equation (3-23)

RELATIONSHIP OF THE GORDON MODEL TO THE
PRICE/EARNINGS RATIO

    Definitions

    Mathematical Derivation

CONCLUSIONS

INTRODUCTION

This chapter describes the derivation of annuity discount factors (ADFs) and the Gordon model (Gordon and Shapiro 1956).[1] The ADF is the present value of a finite stream of cash flows (CF) with constant or zero growth, assuming the first cash flow $1.00. Thus, the actual first year's cash flow times the ADF is the present value as of time zero of the stream of cash flows from years 1 to n. Growth rates in cash flows may be positive, zero, or negative, the latter being a decline in cash flows.

The Gordon model is identical to the ADF, except that it produces the present value of a perpetuity for each $1.00 of initial cash flow. The resulting present value is known as the Gordon model multiple. When using the Gordon model multiple, the discount rate must be larger than the constant growth rate, which is not true of the ADF.

There are several varieties of ADFs, depending on whether the cash flows:

- Are constant or grow/decline.
- Occur midyear or at the end of the year.
- Begin in the first year or at some other time.
- Occur every year or at regular, skipped intervals.
- Finish on a whole year or a fractional year.

This chapter begins with the derivation of the ADF and later shows that the Gordon model, which is the present value of a perpetual annuity with constant growth, is simply a special case of the ADF. We will demonstrate that an ADF is actually the difference of two perpetuities.

There are several uses of ADFs, including:

- Calculating the present value of annuities. This application has become far more important since the quantitative marketability discount model (Mercer 1997) requires an ADF with growth (see Chapter 8). While Mercer's book has an approximation of the ADF (at 276) that appears to be fairly accurate, this chapter contains the exact formulas.
- Valuing periodic cash flows such as moving expenses, losses from lawsuits, etc. This requires a specialized ADF called a periodic perpetuity factor (PPF), which we develop later in the chapter. Additionally, PPFs are useful for decisions in buying new versus used income-producing equipment (such as CAT scans, ships, or taxicabs) and for calculating the value of used equipment.
- Calculating loan payments.
- Calculating loan principal amortization.
- Calculating the present value of a loan. This is important in calculating the correct selling price of a business, as seller financing typically takes place at less-than-market rates. The present value of a loan is also important in ESOP valuation.

---

1. Gordon and Shapiro were preceded by Williams (1938). See also Gordon (1962).

At first glance this chapter appears mathematically very intensive and daunting in its use of geometric sequences. However, because the primary concepts appear in equations (3-1) through (3-9), once you understand those equations, the remainder are merely special cases or slight variations on the original theme and can easily be comprehended. While the formulas look complex, we decompose them into units that behave as modular building blocks, each of which has an intuitive explanation. You will benefit from understanding the math in the body of the chapter, as this material is useful in several areas of business valuation. Additionally, you will also gain a much better understanding of the Gordon model, which appraisers often use in discounted future net income or discounted cash flow valuation.

ADFs are an area that many practitioners find difficult, leading to many mistakes. Timing errors in ADFs frequently result from the fact that the guideline company method uses the most recent *historical* earnings for calculating *P/E* multiples, whereas the Gordon model uses the first *future* period (forecast) cash flow as its earnings base. Many practitioners confuse the two and use historical rather than forecast earnings as their base in a discounted cash flow or discounted future net income approach. Another common error is the use of end-of-year multiples when midyear Gordon model multiples are appropriate.

The ADF formulas given within the chapter apply only to cash flow streams that have a whole number of years associated with them. If the cash flow stream ends in a fractional year, you should use the formulas in the appendix for ADFs with stub periods.

Unless otherwise specified, all ADF formulas are for cash flows with constant growth. At specific points in the chapter, we make the simplifying assumption that growth is zero and clearly state when that is the case. Otherwise the reader may assume growth is constant and non-zero.

Definitions

Let us initially consider an ADF with constant growth in cash flows, where the last cash flow occurs in period n. We will use the following definitions:

r = discount rate
g = annual growth rate in cash flows
ADF = annuity discount factor
PV = present value
CF = cash flow
LHS = left-hand side of the equation
RHS = right-hand side of the equation
n = terminal year of the cash flows
t = time (which can refer to a point in time or a year)

Denoting Time

Timing is frequently a source of confusion. Time t denotes the time period under discussion. It generally refers to a specific year.[2] Time t refers to

---

2. In the context of loan amortization, periods are usually months.

the entire year, except for two contexts that we discuss in the paragraph below. Thus, time t is a span of time, not a point in time.

There are two contexts in which time t means a point in time. The first occurs with the statement $t = 0$, which means the beginning of the period $t = 1$, i.e., usually the beginning of the first year of cash flows. For example, if $t = 1$ represents the calendar year 2000, then $t = 0$ means January 1, 2000, the first day of $t = 1$. Usually, but not always, $t = 0$ is the valuation date. The other context in which t means a point in time is when we specify either the beginning, midpoint, or end of t.

In business valuation, we generally assume that cash flows occur approximately evenly throughout time t. In present value terms, that is equivalent to assuming they occur at the midpoint of time t. Occasionally it is appropriate to assume that cash flows occur at the end of the year, which can be the case with annuities, royalties, etc. The former is commonly known as *the midyear assumption*, while the latter is known as *the end-of-year* (or *end year*) *assumption*.

Another important concept related to time that can be confusing is the valuation date, the point in time to which we discount the cash flows. The valuation date is rarely the same as the first cash flow. The most common valuation date in this chapter is as of time zero, i.e., $t = 0$. The cash flows usually, but not always, either begin during Year 1 or occur at the end of Year 1.

ADF WITH END-OF-YEAR CASH FLOWS

The ADF is the present value of a series of cash flows over n years with constant growth, beginning with \$1 of cash flow in Year 1. We multiply by the first year's forecast cash flow by the ADF to arrive at the PV of the cash flow stream. For example, if the ADF is 9.367 and the first year's cash flow is \$10,000, then the PV of the annuity is $9.367 \times \$10,000 = \$93,670$.

We begin the calculation of the ADF by defining the cash flows and discounting them to their present value. Initially, for simplicity, we assume end-of-year cash flows. The PV of an annuity of \$1, paid at the end of the year for each of n years, is:

$$PV = \frac{\$1}{(1 + r)^1} + \frac{\$1 \times (1 + g)}{(1 + r)^2} + \cdots + \frac{\$1 \times (1 + g)^{n-1}}{(1 + r)^n} \quad (3\text{-}1)$$

Factoring out the \$1:

$$PV = \$1 \times \left[\frac{1}{(1 + r)^1} + \frac{(1 + g)}{(1 + r)^2} + \cdots + \frac{(1 + g)^{n-1}}{(1 + r)^n} \right] \quad (3\text{-}1a)$$

The ADF is the PV of the constant growth cash flows per \$1 of starting year cash flow. Dividing both sides of equation (3-1a) by \$1, the left-hand side becomes PV/\$1, which equals the ADF. Thus, equation (3-1a) simplifies to:

$$ADF = \frac{1}{(1 + r)^1} + \frac{(1 + g)}{(1 + r)^2} + \cdots + \frac{(1 + g)^{n-1}}{(1 + r)^n} \quad (3\text{-}1b)$$

The numerators in equation (3-1b) are the forecast cash flows themselves, and the denominators are the present value factors for each cash flow. As mentioned previously, the first year's cash flow in an ADF calculation is always defined as $1. With constant growth in cash flow, each successive year is $(1 + g)$ times the previous year's cash flow, which means that the cash flow in period n is $(1 + g)^{n-1}$. The cash flow is not $(1 + g)^n$, because the first year's cash flow is $1.00, not $1 + g$. For example, if $g = 10\%$, the first year's cash flow is, by definition, $1.00. The second year's cash flow is $1.1 \times \$1.00 = \$1.10$. The third year's cash flow is $1.1 \times \$1.10 = 1.1^2 \times \$1.00 = 1.21$. The fourth year's cash flow is $1.1^3 \times \$1.00 = \$1.331$, etc. The denominators in equation (3-1b) discount the cash flows in the numerator to their present value.

Next, we begin a series of algebraic manipulations which will ultimately enable us to solve for the ADF and specify it in a formula. Multiplying equation (3-1b) by $(1 + g)/(1 + r)$, we get:

$$\frac{(1 + g)}{(1 + r)} \text{ADF} = \frac{(1 + g)}{(1 + r)^2} + \cdots + \frac{(1 + g)^{n-1}}{(1 + r)_n} + \frac{(1 + g)^n}{(1 + r)^{n+1}} \quad (3\text{-}2)$$

Notice that most of the terms in equation (3-2) are identical to equation (3-1b). We next subtract equation (3-2) from equation (3-1b). All of the terms in the middle of the equation are identical and thus drop out. The only terms that remain on the RHS after the subtraction are the first term on the RHS of equation (3-1b) and the last term on the RHS of equation (3-2).

$$\text{ADF} - \frac{1 + g}{1 + r} \text{ADF} = \frac{1}{1 + r} - \frac{(1 + g)^n}{(1 + r)^{n+1}} \quad (3\text{-}3)$$

Next, we wish to simplify only the left-hand side of equation (3-3):

$$\text{ADF} - \frac{1 + g}{1 + r} \text{ADF} = \text{ADF} \left[1 - \frac{1 + g}{1 + r} \right] \quad (3\text{-}3a)$$

Multiplying the 1 in the square brackets on the RHS of the equation by $(1 + r)/(1 + r)$, we get:

$$\text{ADF} \left[1 - \frac{1 + g}{1 + r} \right] = \text{ADF} \left[\frac{1 + r}{1 + r} - \frac{1 + g}{1 + r} \right]$$

$$= \text{ADF} \frac{(1 + r) - (1 + g)}{1 + r} = \text{ADF} \frac{r - g}{1 + r} \quad (3\text{-}3b)$$

Substituting the last expression of equation (3-3b) into the left-hand side of equation (3-3), we get:

$$\text{ADF} \frac{(r - g)}{(1 + r)} = \left[\frac{1}{(1 + r)} - \frac{(1 + g)^n}{(1 + r)^{n+1}} \right] \quad (3\text{-}4)$$

Multiplying both sides of the equation by $(1 + r)/(r - g)$, we obtain:

$$\text{ADF} = \frac{(1 + r)}{(r - g)} \left[\frac{1}{(1 + r)} - \frac{(1 + g)^n}{(1 + r)^{n+1}} \right] \quad (3\text{-}5)$$

After canceling out the $(1 + r)$, this simplifies to:

$$\text{ADF} = \frac{1}{r-g}\left[\left(\frac{1+g}{1+r}\right)^n \frac{1}{r-g}\right] \qquad (3\text{-}6)$$

ADF with growth and end-of-year cash flows

There are three alternative ways to regroup the terms in equation (3-6) that will prove useful, which we label as equations (3-6a), (3-6b), and (3-6c). In the first alternative expression for equation (3-6), we split up the first term in the square brackets into two separate terms, placing the denominator at the far right.

$$\text{ADF} = \frac{1}{r-g}\left[(1+g)^n \frac{1}{r-g}\frac{1}{(1+r)^n}\right] \qquad (3\text{-}6a)$$

first alternative expression for (3-6)

We derive the second alternative expression by simply factoring out the $1/(r-g)$ from equation (3-6) and restate the equation as equation (3-6b). It has the advantage of being more compact than equation (3-6).

$$\text{ADF} = \frac{1}{r-g}\left[1 - \left(\frac{1+g}{1+r}\right)^n\right] \qquad (3\text{-}6b)$$

second alternative expression for (3-6)

After we develop some additional results, we will be able to explain equations (3-6) through (3-6b) intuitively. In the meantime, we will make some substitutions in equation (3-6b) that will greatly simplify its form and eventually make the ADF much more intuitive.

Note that the first term on the right-hand-side of equation (3-6b) is the classical Gordon model multiple, $1/(r-g)$. Let's denote it GM. The next substitution that will simplify the expression is to let $x = (1+g)/(1+r)$. Then we can restate equation (3-6b) as:

$$\text{ADF} = \text{GM}\ (1 - x^n) \quad \text{third alternative expression for (3-6)} \quad (3\text{-}6c)$$

Behavior of the ADF with Growth

The ADF is inversely related to r and directly related to g, i.e., an increase in the discount rate decreases the ADF and vice-versa, while an increase in the growth rate causes an increase in the ADF, and vice-versa.

Special Case of ADF when $g = 0$: The Ordinary Annuity

When $g = 0$, there is no growth in cash flows, and equation (3-6) simplifies to equation (3-6d), the formula for an ordinary annuity.

$$\text{ADF} = \frac{1}{r} - \frac{1}{(1+r)^n}\frac{1}{r}, \quad \text{or} \quad \text{ADF} = \frac{1 - \dfrac{1}{(1+r)^n}}{r} \qquad (3\text{-}6d)$$

$1/r$ is the PV of a perpetuity that is constant in nominal dollars, or a Gordon model with $g = 0$.

Special Case when $n \to \infty$ and $r > g$: The Gordon Model

The Gordon model is a financial formula that every business appraiser knows—at least in the end-of-year form. It is the formula necessary to calculate the present value of the perpetuity with constant growth in cash flows in the terminal period (also known as the residual or reversion period), i.e., from years $n + 1$ to infinity (after discounting the first n years of cash flows or net income). To be valid, the growth rate must be less than the discount rate.

What few practitioners know, however, is that the Gordon model is merely a special case of the ADF. The Gordon model contains two additional assumptions that the ADF in equation (3-6) does not have.

- The time horizon is infinite, which means that we assume cash flows will grow at the constant rate of g forever. This means that n, the terminal year of the cash flows, equals infinity.
- The discount rate is greater than the growth rate, i.e., $r > g$.

Since $r > g$,

$$\left(\frac{1 + g}{1 + r} \right)^n$$

goes to zero as n goes to infinity. Therefore, the entire term in square brackets in equation (3-6) goes to zero, which simplifies to:

$$\text{ADF} = \frac{1}{r - g} \quad \text{Gordon model multiple, end-of-year cash flows} \quad (3\text{-}7)$$

Equation (3-7) is the end-of-year Gordon model multiple. In other words, the Gordon model multiple is just a special case of the ADF when n equals infinity. Using this multiple, we obtain the Gordon model, with end-of-year cash flows:

$$\text{PV} = \frac{\text{CF}}{(r - g)} \quad (3\text{-}8)$$

Another way of expressing equation (3-8) is rewriting it as:

$$\text{PV} = \text{CF} \times \left[\frac{1}{(r - g)} \right] \quad (3\text{-}9)$$

Thus, the present value of a perpetuity with growth contains two terms conceptually:

- CF, the starting year's *forecast* cash flow.[3]
- $1/(r - g)$, the Gordon model multiple, which when multiplied by the first year's forecast cash flow gives us the present value of the perpetuity.

---

3. Note that you do not use *historical* cash flow (or earnings).

Intuitively Understanding Equations (3-6) and (3-6a)

Now that we understand the Gordon model, we can gain deeper insight into equation (3-6). The ADF is the difference of two perpetuities. The first term, $1/(r - g)$, is the PV as of $t = 0$ of a perpetuity with cash flows going from $t = 1$ to infinity. The second term is the PV as of $t = 0$ of a perpetuity going from $t = n + 1$ to infinity, which is explained in the next paragraph. The difference of the two is the PV as of $t = 0$ of the annuity from $t = 1$ to n.

Let's give an intuitive explanation of equation (3-6a). The $(1 + g)^n$ is the forecast cash flow[4] for Year $(n + 1)$, which we then multiply by $1/(r - g)$, our familiar Gordon model multiple. The result is the PV as of $t = n$ of the forecast cash flows from $n + 1$ to infinity. Dividing by $(1 + r)^n$ transforms the PV as of $t = n$ to the PV as of $t = 0$.

Relationship between the ADF and the Gordon Model

The relationship between the ADF and Gordon model is so intimate that we can derive the Gordon model from the ADF and vice-versa. The ADF is the difference of two Gordon models, as illustrated graphically below in Figure 3-1.

In graphical terms, the top line represents the Gordon model with cash flows from $t = 1$ to infinity (our valuation date is actually time zero, which is not shown on the graph). The cash flows in the second Gordon model begin at $t = n + 1$ and continue to infinity. The difference between these two Gordon models is simply the ADF from $t = 1$ to n.

FIGURE 3-1

Timeline of the ADF and Gordon Model

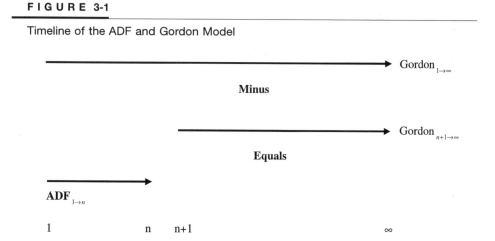

Table 3-1: Proof of ADF Equations (3-6) through (3-6b)

Table 3-1 is the valuation of a 10-year annuity, with a discount rate of 15% and an annual growth rate of 5.1%. All assumptions appear in cells

---

4. The first year's cash flow is 1, or $(1 + g)^0$. The second year's cash flow is $(1 + g)^1$. In general, cash flow in Year t $(1 + g)^{t-1}$.

TABLE 3-1

ADF: End-of-Year Formula

	A	B	C	D	E	F
4	t (Yrs)	Cash Flow (CF)	Growth in CF	$(1 + g)^{t-1}$	PV Factor	NPV
5	1	1.00000	0.00000	1.00000	0.86957	0.86957
6	2	1.05100	0.05100	1.05100	0.75614	0.79471
7	3	1.10460	0.05360	1.10460	0.65752	0.72629
8	4	1.16094	0.05633	1.16094	0.57175	0.66377
9	5	1.22014	0.05921	1.22014	0.49718	0.60663
10	6	1.28237	0.06223	1.28237	0.43233	0.55440
11	7	1.34777	0.06540	1.34777	0.37594	0.50668
12	8	1.41651	0.06874	1.41651	0.32690	0.46306
13	9	1.48875	0.07224	1.48875	0.28426	0.42320
14	10	1.56468	0.07593	1.56468	0.24718	0.38676
15	Totals					5.99506
17	Calculation of NPV by formulas:					
18					Grand	
19	Time	1 to Infinity	−(n + 1) to Infinity	=1 to n	Total	
20	NPV	10.10101	−4.10595	5.99506	5.99506	
22	Assumptions:					
24	n = Number of years of cash flows					10
24	r = Discount rate					15.0%
26	g = Growth rate in net inc/cash flow					5.1%
27	x = (1 + g)/(1 + r)					0.9139
28	Gordon model multiple = GM = 1/(r − g)					10.101010
30	Spreadsheet formulas:					
32	B20:	GM = 1/(r − g)				
33	C20:	− GM*x^n				
34	D20	B20 + C20				
35	E20	GM * (1 − x^n) This is equation (3-6c)				

F24 to F28. Recall that we define $x = (1 + g)/(1 - r) = 0.9139$ (F27).[5] If this were a perpetuity, the Gordon model multiple would be 10.101010 (F28).

We begin with a cash flow of $1.00 at the end of Year 1 (B5). Column C shows the annual growth in cash flows at 5.1%.[6] The cash flow in Column B is always equal to the previous cash flow plus the growth in the current period, where Cash Flow$_t$ = Cash Flow$_{t-1}$ + Growth$_t$. Column D replicates the cash flow in Column C using the formula Cash Flow = $(1+g)^{t-1}$, which thus provides us with a general formula for the cash flows. We multiply the cash flows in Column C by the end-of-year present value factor in Column E to arrive at the present value of the cash flows

---

5. As mentioned in a previous footnote, we use i synonymously with r.
6. We can use the same formulas for other time periods, e.g., months instead of years. Then we must use the monthly growth rate of 5.1%/12 = 0.4267% instead of the annual.

in Column F. The sum of the present values of the 10 years of cash flows is 5.99506 in F15. This is the "brute force" method of calculating the annuity.

As we will demonstrate, equation (3-6) is a more compact and elegant solution. Cell B20 contains the end-of-year Gordon multiple results of the first term in equation (3-6), which equals F28. This is the present value of the perpetuity of $1.00 growing at a constant 5.1% from Year 1 to infinity. In C20 we subtract the present value of the perpetuity from Year $n + 1$ to infinity, which equals 4.10595 and is the term in equation (3-6) in square brackets. The difference of the two perpetuities is 5.99506, which equals F15, our brute force solution. Finally, E20 is the formula for the entire equation, which equals the same 5.99506 calculated in D20 and F15, proving the validity of equation (3-6), including its components. We show the formulas for Row 20 at the bottom of Table 3-1. Note that the formula in E20 is equation (3-6c).

A Brief Summary

To help you decide if you should read on, let's take a look at what we have covered so far, what we will cover in the remainder of the chapter, and how difficult the material will be. We have thus far derived the end-of-year ADF, examined its special cases (the Gordon model and the no-growth formula), explained the intimate relationship of the ADF and the Gordon model, explained the intuition behind the components of the ADF model, and proved the model with an example.

The reader now should understand the principles of ADFs and Gordon models. If you are having difficulty with the mathematics, you may wish to skip to the sections on Periodic Perpetuity Factors (PPFs) and Relationship of the Gordon Model to the Price/Earnings Ratio, which are of practical significance to most readers. However, you now should understand almost everything you will need to easily comprehend the rest of the chapter. The rest of the chapter is primarily simple variations of the derivations we have done thus far.

In the remainder of the chapter, we will cover:

- The midyear version of the ADF (with the same special cases of the Gordon model and $g = 0$).
- Starting periods for the cash flows that are different than Year 1, which is of practical significance in discounted cash flow analysis in the calculation of the PV of the reversion.
- Calculating periodic perpetuity factors (PPFs), which are a variation of the Gordon model for periodic expenses such as moving expense and losses from lawsuits. Additionally, PPFs are useful for decisions in buying new versus used income-producing equipment (such as CAT scans, ships, or taxicabs) and for calculating the value of used equipment.
- Calculating loan payments.
- Calculating the present value of loans.

- The relationship of the Gordon model to the PE multiple, the misunderstanding of which may well be the single most common source of technical error in business valuation.

MIDYEAR CASH FLOWS

Most businesses have cash flows that more or less occur evenly throughout the year. In a present value sense, this is approximately equivalent to having all cash flows occur midway through the year. Thus, in valuing most businesses, it is appropriate to use midyear cash flows rather than end-of-year cash flows.

Midyear cash flows occur six months (one half-year) earlier than end-of-year cash flows. We derive this formula in exactly the same fashion as equation (3-6). We start with equation (3-1b); however, the denominators, which are the time periods by which we discount the cash flows, are one half-year less than those in equation (3-1b). We adjust for this difference by multiplying every numerator by $\sqrt{1 + r}$, which has the same effect as reducing the denominators by 0.5 years. We then factor the $\sqrt{1 + r}$ out of the sequence, resulting in a the midyear ADF that equals $\sqrt{1 + r}$ times the end-of-year ADF.

$$\text{ADF} = \frac{\sqrt{1 + r}}{r - g} - \left(\frac{1 + g}{1 + r}\right)^n \frac{\sqrt{1 + r}}{r - g} \quad \text{midyear ADF} \quad (3\text{-}10)$$

We interpret equation (3-10) in exactly the same fashion as equation (3-6). We can factor out the Gordon model multiple as before and restate equation (3-10) as equations (3-10a) and (3-10b) below. Note that equations (3-10a) and (3-10b) are identical to equations (3-6b) and (3-6c), respectively, except that the Gordon model multiple is midyear instead of end-of-year.

$$\text{ADF} = \frac{\sqrt{1 + r}}{r - g} \left[1 - \left(\frac{1 + g}{1 + r}\right)^n\right] \quad \text{alternative expression for (3-10)}$$
$$(3\text{-}10a)$$

$$\text{ADF} = \text{GM} (1 - x^n) \quad \text{second alternative expression for (3-10)} \quad (3\text{-}10b)$$

Table 3-2: Example of Equation (3-10) through (3-10b)

Table 3-2 is identical to Table 3-1, except that here we use the midyear rather than end-of-year ADF. Note that the Gordon model multiple (GM) in B20 and F28 is 10.83213 versus 10.101010 in Table 3-1. The GM in Table 3-2 is exactly $\sqrt{1 + r}$ times the GM in Table 3-1, i.e., $10.1010 \sqrt{1.15} = 10.83213$. This demonstrates the validity of equations (3-10) through (3-10b), the midyear ADF.

Special Cases for Midyear Cash Flows: No Growth, $g = 0$

Letting $g = 0$ in the equation above, we obtain the following ADF for midyear cash flows with no growth:

ADF: Midyear Formula

	A	B	C	D	E	F
4	t (Yrs)	Cash Flow (CF)	Growth in CF	$(1 + g)^{t-1}$	PV Factor	NPV
5	1	1.00000	0.00000	1.00000	0.93250	0.93250
6	2	1.05100	0.05100	1.05100	0.81087	0.85223
7	3	1.10460	0.05360	1.10460	0.70511	0.77886
8	4	1.16094	0.05633	1.16094	0.61314	0.71181
9	5	1.22014	0.05921	1.22014	0.53316	0.65053
10	6	1.28237	0.06223	1.28237	0.46362	0.59453
11	7	1.34777	0.06540	1.34777	0.40315	0.54335
12	8	1.41651	0.06874	1.41651	0.35056	0.49658
13	9	1.48875	0.07224	1.48875	0.30484	0.45383
14	10	1.56468	0.07593	1.56468	0.26508	0.41476
15	Totals					**6.42899**
17	Calculation of NPV by formulas:					
18					Grand	
19	Time	1 to Infinity	−(n + 1) to Infinity	=1 to n	Total	
20	NPV	10.83213	−4.40314	**6.42899**	**6.42899**	
22	Assumptions:					
24	n = Number of years of cash flows					10
25	r = Discount rate					15.0%
26	g = Growth rate in net inc/cash flow					5.1%
27	x = (1 + g)/(1 + r)					0.9139
28	Gordon model multiple = GM = SQRT(1 + r)/(r − g)					10.83213
30	Spreadsheet formulas:					
32	B20:	GM = SQRT(1 + r)/(r − G)				
33	C20:	− GM*x^n				
34	D20	B20 + C20				
35	E20	GM * (1 − x^n) This is equation (3-10b)				

$$\text{ADF} = \frac{\sqrt{1 + r}}{r} - \frac{1}{(1 + r)^n} \frac{\sqrt{1 + r}}{r} \quad \text{midyear ADF, no growth} \quad (3\text{-}10c)$$

This follows the same type of logic as equation (3-6), with modification for growth being zero. The first and third terms on the RHS of equation (3-10c) are midyear Gordon models for a constant \$1 cash flow. Since there is no growth of cash flows in this special case, the $(1 + g)^n$ in equation (3-10) simplifies to 1 and drops out of the equation. The $1/(1 + r)^n$ discounts the second Gordon model term from $t = n$ back to $t = 0$, i.e., it reduces the PV of the perpetuity to time zero. Again, the ADF is the difference of two perpetuities: the first one with cash flows from 1 to infinity, less the second one with cash flows from $n + 1$ to infinity, the difference being cash flows from 1 to n.

We can rewrite equation (3-10c) as equation (3-10d) by factoring out the $\sqrt{1 + r}/r$.

$$\text{ADF} = \frac{\sqrt{1 + r}}{r}\left[1 - \frac{1}{(1 + r)^n}\right] \quad \text{alternate expression for (3-10c),}$$

midyear, no growth

$$(3\text{-}10d)$$

Gordon Model

Letting $n \rightarrow \infty$ in equation (3-10) leads us to the Gordon model.

$$PV = CF \frac{\sqrt{1 + r}}{(r - g)} \quad \text{Gordon model—midyear} \quad (3\text{-}10e)$$

This can be split into the following terms:

$$CF \times \left[\frac{\sqrt{1 + r}}{(r - g)} \right]$$

The first term is the forecast net income for the first year, and the second term is the Gordon model multiple for a midyear cash flow.

STARTING PERIODS OTHER THAN YEAR 1

When cash flows begin in any year other than 1, it is necessary to use a more general (and complicated) ADF formula. We will present formulas for both the end-of-year and midyear cash flows when this occurs.

End-of-Year Formulas

In the following equations, S is the starting year of the cash flows. The end-of-year ADF is:

$$ADF = \left[\frac{1}{r - g} - \left(\frac{1 + g}{1 + r} \right)^{n - S + 1} \frac{1}{r - g} \right] \frac{1}{(1 + r)^{S - 1}}$$

$$\text{generalized end-of-year ADF} \quad (3\text{-}11)$$

Note that when $S = 1$, $n - S + 1 = n$, and equation (3-11) reduces to equation (3-6).

The intuition behind this formula is that if we are standing at point $t = S - 1$ looking at the cash flows that begin at S and end at n, they would appear the same as if we were at $t = 0$ looking at a normal series of cash flows that begin at $t = 1$. The only difference is that there are n cash flows in the latter case and $n - (S - 1) = n - S + 1$ cash flows in the former case.

Therefore, the term in square brackets, which is the PV of the cash flows at $t = S - 1$, is the usual ADF formula, except that the exponent of the second term in square brackets changes from n in equation (3-6) to $n - S + 1$ in equation (3-11). If the cash flows begin in a year later than Year 1, $S > 1$ and there are fewer years of cash flows from S to n than there are from 1 to n.[7] From the end of Year $S - 1$ to the end of Year n, there are $n - (S - 1) = n - S + 1$ years.

In order to calculate the PV as of $t = 0$, it is necessary to discount the cash flows $S - 1$ years using the term $1/(1 + r)^{S-1}$. Note that at $S = 1$, the term at the right—outside the brackets—becomes 1 and effectively

---

7. The converse is true for cash flows beginning in the past, where S is less than 1.

drops out of the equation. The exponent within the square brackets, $n - S + 1$, simplifies to n, and (3-11) simplifies to (3-6).

An alternative form of (3-11) with the Gordon model specifically factored out is:

$$\text{ADF} = \frac{1}{r-g}\left[1 - \left(\frac{1+g}{1+t}\right)^{n-S+1}\right]\frac{1}{(1+r)^{S-1}}$$

generalized end-of-year ADF—alternative form   (3-11a)

Valuation Date ≠ 0

If the valuation date is different than $t = 0$, then we do not discount by the entire $S - 1$ years. Letting the valuation date $= v$, then we discount back to $t = S - v - 1$, the reason being that normally we discount $S - 1$ years, but in this case we will discount only to v, not to zero. Therefore, we discount $S - 1 - v$ years, which we restate as $S - v - 1$. For example, if we want to value cash flows from $t = 23$ months to 34 months as of $t = 10$ months,[8] then we discount $23 - 10 - 1 = 12$ months, or 1 year. This formula is important in calculating the reduction in principal for an amortizing loan. The formula is:

$$\text{ADF} = \left[\frac{1}{r-g} - \left(\frac{1+g}{1+r}\right)^{n-S+1}\frac{1}{r-g}\right]\frac{1}{(1+r)^{S-v-1}} \quad \text{generalized ADF:}$$

end-of-year   (3-11b)

where v = valuation date. We will demonstrate the accuracy of this formula in Sections 2 and 3 of Table A3-3 in the Appendix.

Table 3-3: Example of Equation (3-11)

In Table 3-3, we begin with $1 of cash flows (C7) at $t = 3.25$ years, i.e., $S = 3.25$ (G40). The discount rate is 15% (G42), and cash flows grow at 5.1% (G43). In Year 4.25, cash flow grows $5.1\% \times \$1.00 = \$0.051$ (B8), which is equal to the prior year cash flow of $1.00 in C7 plus the growth in the current year, for a total of $1.051 in C8. We continue in the same fashion to calculate growth in cash flows and the actual cash flows through the last year $n = 22.25$.

In Column D, we use the formula Cash Flow $= (1 + g)^{t-S}$, which duplicates the results in Column C. Thus, the formula in Column D is a general formula for cash flow in any period.[9]

Next, we discount the cash flows to present value. In this table we show both a two-step and a single-step discounting process.

---

8. We actually do this in Table A3-3 in the Appendix. In the context of loan payments, cash flows are fixed, which means $g = 0$. Also, with loan payments we generally deal with time measured in months, not years. To remain consistent, the discount rates must also be monthly, not annual.

9. Note that when cash flows begin at $t = 1$, then $(1 + g)^{t-S} = (1 + g)^{t-1}$, which is the formula that describes the cash flows in Column D in Tables 3-1 and 3-2. Thus, $(1 + g)^{t-S}$ is truly a general formula for the cash flow.

TABLE 3-3

ADF with Cash Flows Starting in Year 3.25: End-of-Year Formula

	A	B	C	D	E	F	G	H
5		**Cash Flow**				**t = S − 1**		**t = 0**	
6	t (Yrs)	Growth	Cash Flow	$(1 + g)^{t-s}$	PV Factor	PV	PV Factor	PV
7	3.25	NA	1.00000	1.00000	0.86957	0.86957	0.63494	0.63494
8	4.25	0.05100	1.05100	1.05100	0.75614	0.79471	0.55212	0.58028
9	5.25	0.05360	1.10460	1.10460	0.65752	0.72629	0.48011	0.53032
10	6.25	0.05633	1.16094	1.16094	0.57175	0.66377	0.41748	0.48467
11	7.25	0.05921	1.22014	1.22014	0.49718	0.60663	0.36303	0.44295
12	8.25	0.06223	1.28237	1.28237	0.43233	0.55440	0.31568	0.40481
13	9.25	0.06540	1.34777	1.34777	0.37594	0.50668	0.27450	0.36997
14	10.25	0.06874	1.41651	1.41651	0.32690	0.46306	0.23870	0.33812
15	11.25	0.07224	1.48875	1.48875	0.28426	0.42320	0.20756	0.30901
16	12.25	0.07593	1.56468	1.56468	0.24718	0.38676	0.18049	0.28241
17	13.25	0.07980	1.64447	1.64447	0.21494	0.35347	0.15695	0.25810
18	14.25	0.08387	1.72834	1.72834	0.18691	0.32304	0.13648	0.23588
19	15.25	0.08815	1.81649	1.81649	0.16253	0.29523	0.11867	0.21557
20	16.25	0.09264	1.90913	1.90913	0.14133	0.26981	0.10320	0.19701
21	17.25	0.09737	2.00649	2.00649	0.12289	0.24659	0.08974	0.18005
22	18.25	0.10233	2.10883	2.10883	0.10686	0.22536	0.07803	0.16455
23	19.25	0.10755	2.21638	2.21638	0.09293	0.20596	0.06785	0.15039
24	20.25	0.11304	2.32941	2.32941	0.08081	0.18823	0.05900	0.13744
25	21.25	0.11880	2.44821	2.44821	0.07027	0.17202	0.05131	0.12561
26	22.25	0.12486	2.57307	2.57307	0.06110	0.15722	0.04461	0.11480
27	Pres. value (t = 2.25 for column F, t = 0 for column H)					8.43199		6.15687
28	Pres. value factor-discount from S − 1 (t = 2.25) to 0					0.73018		
29	Present value (t = 0)					6.15687		

31	Calculation of PV by formulas:				
32					Grand
33	Time	S to Infinity	−(n + 1) to Infinity	=S to n	Total
34	t = S − 1	10.10101	−1.66902	8.43199	**8.43199**
35	PV Factor	0.73018	0.73018	0.73018	**0.73018**
36	t = 0	7.37555	−1.21869	6.15687	**6.15687**

38	Assumptions:	
40	S = Beginning year of cash flows (valuation at t = 2.25)	**3.25**
41	n = Ending year of cash flows	**22.25**
42	r = Discount rate	**15.0%**
43	g = Growth rate in net inc/cash flow	**5.1%**
44	x = (1 + g)/(1 + r)	**0.913913**
45	Gordon model multiple = GM = [1/(r − g)]	**10.101010**

47	Spreadsheet formulas:
49	B34: GM Gordon model for years 3.25 to infinity as of t = 2.25
50	C34: −GM*(x^(n − S + 1)) Gordon model for years 23.25 to infinity as of t = 2.25
51	D34: B34 + C34
52	E34: GM*(1 − x^(n − S + 1)) grand total as of t = S − 1 = 2.25 years
53	Row 35: 1/(1 + r)^(S − 1) present value factor from t = S − 1 back to t = 0
54	Row 36: Row 34 * Row 35

First, we demonstrate two-step discounting in Columns E and F. Column E contains the present value (PV) factors to discount the cash flows to $t = S - 1$, the formula for which is $1/(1 + r)^{t-S+1}$. Column F is the PV as of $t = 2.25$ Years. The present value of the cash flows total \$8.43199 (F27). F28 is the PV factor, 0.73018, to discount that result back to $t = 0$ by multiplying it by F27, or \$8.43199 $\times$ 0.73018 = \$6.15687 (F29).

In Columns G and H, we perform the same procedures, the only difference being that Column G contains the PV factors to discount back to $t = 0$. Column H is the PV of the cash flows, which totals the same \$6.15687 (H27), which is the same result as F29. This demonstrates that the two-step and the one-step present value calculation lead to the same results, as long as they are done properly.

Cell B34 contains the Gordon model multiple 10.10101 for cash flows from $t = S$ (3.25) to infinity, which we can see calculated in G45. C34 is the Gordon model multiple for $t = n + 1$ to infinity, discounted to $t = S - 1$. Subtracting C34 from B34, we get the cash flows from S to n in D34, or \$8.43199, which also equals F27. Row 35 is the PV factor 0.73018, and Row 34 $\times$ Row 35 = Row 36, the PV as of $t = 0$. The total for cash flows from $S = 3.25$ to n appears in D36 as \$6.15687.

In E34 we show the grand total cash flows, as per equation (3-11). The spreadsheet formula for E34 is in A52, where GM is the Gordon model multiple. The \$8.43199 is the total of the cash flows from 3.25 to 22.25 as of $t = 2.25$ and corresponds to the term in equation (3-11) in square brackets. The PV factor 0.73018 is the term in equation (3-11) to the right of the square brackets, and the one multiplied by the other is the entirety of equation (3-11). Note that E36 = D36 = F29 = H27, which demonstrates the validity of equation (3-11).

Tables 3-4 through 3-6: Variations of Table 3-3 with $S < 0$, Negative Growth, and $r < g$

Tables 3-4 through 3-6 are identical to Table 3-3. The only difference is that Tables 3-4 through 3-6 have cash flows that begin in Year -2, ($S = -2.00$ in G40). Additionally, in Table 3-5 growth is a *negative* 5.1% (G43), instead of the usual positive 5.1% in the other tables.

In Table 3-6, $r < g$, so the discount rate is less than the growth rate, which is impossible for a perpetuity but acceptable for a finite annuity. Note that the Gordon model multiple is -20 (B34 and G45), which by itself would be a nonsense result. Nevertheless, it still works for a finite annuity, as the term for the cash flows from $n + 1$ to infinity is positive and greater than the negative Gordon model multiple.[10]

In all cases, equation (3-11) performs perfectly, with D36 = E36 = F29 = H27.

---

10. This is so because $[(1 + g)/(1 + r)]^n > 1$, so when we multiply that term by the GM—which is negative—the resulting term is negative and of greater magnitude than the GM itself. Since we are subtracting a larger negative from the negative GM, the overall result is a positive number.

ADF with Cash Flows Starting in Year −2.00: End-of-Year Formula

	A	B	C	D	E	F	G	H
5			Cash Flow		t = S − 1		t = 0	
6	t (Yrs)	Growth	Cash Flow	$(1 + g)^{t-s}$	PV Factor	PV	PV Factor	PV
7	−2.00	NA	1.00000	1.00000	0.86957	0.86957	1.32250	1.32250
8	−1.00	0.05100	1.05100	1.05100	0.75614	0.79471	0.15000	1.20865
9	0.00	0.05360	1.10460	1.10460	0.65752	0.72629	1.00000	1.10460
10	1.00	0.05633	1.16094	1.16094	0.57175	0.66377	0.86957	1.00951
11	2.00	0.05921	1.22014	1.22014	0.49718	0.60663	0.75614	0.92260
12	3.00	0.06223	1.28237	1.28237	0.43233	0.55440	0.65752	0.84318
13	4.00	0.06540	1.34777	1.34777	0.37594	0.50668	0.57175	0.77059
14	5.00	0.06874	1.41651	1.41651	0.32690	0.46306	0.49718	0.70425
15	6.00	0.07224	1.48875	1.48875	0.28426	0.42320	0.43233	0.64363
16	7.00	0.07593	1.56468	1.56468	0.24718	0.38676	0.37594	0.58822
17	8.00	0.07980	1.64447	1.64447	0.21494	0.35347	0.32690	0.53758
18	9.00	0.08387	1.72834	1.72834	0.18691	0.32304	0.28426	0.49130
19	10.00	0.08815	1.81649	1.81649	0.16253	0.29523	0.24718	0.44901
20	11.00	0.09264	1.90913	1.90913	0.14133	0.26981	0.21494	0.41035
21	12.00	0.09737	2.00649	2.00649	0.12289	0.24659	0.18691	0.37503
22	13.00	0.10233	2.10883	2.10883	0.10686	0.22536	0.16253	0.34274
23	14.00	0.10755	2.21638	2.21638	0.09293	0.20596	0.14133	0.31324
24	15.00	0.11304	2.32941	2.32941	0.08081	0.18823	0.12289	0.28627
25	16.00	0.11880	2.44821	2.44821	0.07027	0.17202	0.10686	0.26163
26	17.00	0.12486	2.57307	2.57307	0.06110	0.15722	0.09293	0.23910
27	Pres. value (t = 2.25 for column F, t = 0 for column H)					8.43199		12.8240
28	Pres. value factor-from S − 1 (t = −3.00) to 0					1.52088		
29	Present value (t = 0)					12.82400		
31	Calculation of PV by formulas:							
32					Grand			
33	Time	S to Infinity	−(n + 1) to Infinity	=S to n	Total			
34	t = S − 1	10.10101	−1.66902	8.43199	8.43199			
35	PV factor	1.52088	1.52088	1.52088	0.73018			
36	t = 0	15.36237	−2.53838	12.82400	12.82400			
38	Assumptions:							
40	S = Beginning year of cash flows (valuation at t = −3.00)						−2.00	
41	n = Ending year of cash flows						17.00	
42	r = Discount rate						15.0%	
43	g = Growth rate in net inc/cash flow						5.1%	
44	x = (1 + g)/(1 + r)						0.913913	
45	Gordon model multiple = GM = [1/(r − g)]						10.101010	
47	Spreadsheet formulas:							
49	B34: GM Gordon model for years −2.00 to infinity as of t = −3.00							
50	C34: −GM*(x^(n − S + 1)) Gordon model for years 18.00 to infinity as of t = −3.00							
51	D34: B34 + C34							
52	E34: GM*(1 − x^(n − S + 1)) grand total as of t = S − 1 = −3.00 years							
53	Row 35: 1/(1 + r)^(S − 1) present value factor from t = S − 1 back to t = 0							
54	Row 36: Row 34 * Row 35							

TABLE 3-5

ADF with Cash Flows Starting in Year −2.00 with Negative Growth: End-of-Year Formula

	A	B	C	D	E	F	G	H
			Cash Flow		**t = S − 1**		**t = 0**	
5								
6	**t (Yrs)**	**Growth**	**Cash Flow**	**$(1 + g)^{t-s}$**	**PV Factor**	**PV**	**PV Factor**	**PV**
7	−2.00	NA	1.00000	1.00000	0.86957	0.86957	1.32250	1.32250
8	−1.00	−0.05100	0.94900	0.94900	0.75614	0.71758	0.15000	1.09135
9	0.00	−0.04840	0.90060	0.90060	0.65752	0.59216	1.00000	1.90060
10	1.00	−0.04593	0.85467	0.85467	0.57175	0.48866	0.86957	0.74319
11	2.00	−0.04359	0.81108	0.81108	0.49718	0.40325	0.75614	0.61329
12	3.00	−0.04137	0.76972	0.76972	0.43233	0.33277	0.65752	0.50610
13	4.00	−0.03926	0.73046	0.73046	0.37594	0.27461	0.57175	0.41764
14	5.00	−0.03725	0.69321	0.69321	0.32690	0.22661	0.49718	0.34465
15	6.00	−0.03535	0.65785	0.65785	0.28426	0.18700	0.43233	0.28441
16	7.00	−0.03355	0.62430	0.62430	0.24718	0.15432	0.37594	0.23470
17	8.00	−0.03184	0.59246	0.59246	0.21494	0.12735	0.32690	0.19368
18	9.00	−0.03022	0.56225	0.56225	0.18691	0.10509	0.28426	0.15983
19	10.00	−0.02867	0.53357	0.53357	0.16253	0.08672	0.24718	0.13189
20	11.00	−0.02721	0.50636	0.50636	0.14133	0.07156	0.21494	0.10884
21	12.00	−0.02582	0.48054	0.48054	0.12289	0.05906	0.18691	0.08982
22	13.00	−0.02451	0.45603	0.45603	0.10686	0.04873	0.16253	0.07412
23	14.00	−0.02326	0.43277	0.43277	0.09293	0.04022	0.14133	0.06116
24	15.00	−0.02207	0.41070	0.41070	0.08081	0.03319	0.12289	0.05047
25	16.00	−0.02095	0.38976	0.38976	0.07027	0.02739	0.10686	0.04165
26	17.00	−0.01988	0.36988	0.36988	0.06110	0.02260	0.09293	0.03437
27	Pres. value (t = 2.25 for column F, t = 0 for column H)					**4.86842**		**7.40426**
28	Pres. value factor-from S − 1 (t = −3.00) to 0					**1.52088**		
29	Present value (t = 0)					**7.40426**		
31	Calculation of PV by formulas:							
32					**Grand**			
33	**Time**	**S to Infinity**	**−(n + 1) to Infinity**	**=S to n**	**Total**			
34	t = S − 1	4.97512	−0.10670	4.86842	**4.86842**			
35	PV Factor	1.52088	1.52088	1.52088	**1.52088**			
36	t = 0	7.56654	−0.16228	7.40426	**7.40426**			
38	Assumptions:							
40	S = Beginning year of cash flows (valuation at t = −3.00)							**−2.00**
41	n = Ending year of cash flows							**17.00**
42	r = Discount rate							**15.0%**
43	g = Growth rate in net inc/cash flow							**−5.1%**
44	x = (1 + g)/(1 + r)							**0.825217**
45	Gordon model multiple = GM = [1/(r − g)]							**4.975124**
47	Spreadsheet formulas:							
49	B34: GM Gordon model for years −2.00 to infinity as of t = −3.00							
50	C34: −GM*(x^(n − S + 1)) Gordon model for years 18.00 to infinity as of t = −3.00							
51	D34: B34 + C34							
52	E34: GM*(1 − x^(n − S + 1)) grand total as of t = S − 1 = −3.00 years							
53	Row 35: 1/(1 + r)^(S − 1) present value factor from t = S − 1 back to t = 0							
54	Row 36: Row 34 * Row 35							

TABLE 3-6

ADF with Cash Flows Starting in Year −2.00 with $g > r$: End-of-Year Formula

	A	B	C	D	E	F	G	H
5			Cash Flow			t = S − 1		t = 0	
6	t (Yrs)	Growth	Cash Flow	$(1 + g)^{t-s}$	PV Factor	PV	PV Factor	PV
7	−2.00	NA	1.00000	1.00000	0.86957	0.86957	1.32250	1.32250
8	−1.00	−0.20000	1.20000	1.20000	0.75614	0.90737	0.15000	1.38000
9	0.00	0.24000	1.44000	1.44000	0.65752	0.94682	1.00000	1.44000
10	1.00	0.28800	1.72800	1.72800	0.57175	0.98799	0.86957	1.50261
11	2.00	−0.34560	2.07360	2.07360	0.49718	1.03095	0.75614	1.56794
12	3.00	−0.41472	2.48832	2.48832	0.43233	0.07577	0.65752	1.63611
13	4.00	0.49766	2.98598	2.98598	0.37594	1.12254	0.57175	1.70725
14	5.00	0.59720	3.58318	3.58318	0.32690	1.17135	0.49718	1.78147
15	6.00	0.71664	4.29982	4.29982	0.28426	1.22228	0.43233	1.85893
16	7.00	0.85996	5.15978	5.15978	0.24718	1.27542	0.37594	1.93975
17	8.00	1.03196	6.19174	6.19174	0.21494	1.33087	0.32690	2.02409
18	9.00	1.23835	7.43008	7.43008	0.18691	1.38874	0.28426	2.11209
19	10.00	1.48602	8.91610	8.91610	0.16253	1.44912	0.24718	2.20392
20	11.00	1.78322	10.69932	10.69932	0.14133	1.51212	0.21494	2.29974
21	12.00	2.13986	12.83918	12.83918	0.12289	1.57786	0.18691	2.39974
22	13.00	2.56784	15.40702	15.40702	0.10686	1.64647	0.16253	2.50407
23	14.00	3.08140	18.48843	18.48843	0.09293	1.71805	0.14133	2.61294
24	15.00	3.69769	22.18611	22.18611	0.08081	1.79275	0.12289	2.72655
25	16.00	4.43722	26.62333	26.62333	0.07027	1.87070	0.10686	2.84510
26	17.00	5.32467	31.94800	31.94800	0.06110	1.95203	0.09293	2.96880
27	Pres. value (t = −3.00 for column F, t = 0 for column H)					26.84876		40.83361
28	Pres. value factor-From S − 1 (t = −3.00) to 0					1.52088		
29	Present Value (t = 0)					40.83361		

31	Calculation of PV by formulas:				
32					Grand
33	Time	S to Infinity	−(n + 1) to Infinity	=S to n	Total
34	t = S − 1	−20.00000	46.84876	26.84876	26.84876
35	PV Factor	1.52088	1.52088	1.52088	1.52088
36	t = 0	−30.41750	71.25111	40.83361	40.83361

38	Assumptions:	
40	S = Beginning year of cash flows (valuation at t = −3.00)	−2.00
41	n = Ending year of cash flows	17.00
42	r = Discount rate	15.0%
43	g = Growth rate in net inc/cash flow	20.0%
44	x = (1 + g)/(1 + r)	1.043478
45	Gordon model multiple = GM = [1/(r − g)]	−20.000000

47	Spreadsheet formulas:
49	B34: GM Gordon model for years −2.00 to infinity as of t = −3.00
50	C34: −GM*(x^(n − S + 1)) Gordon model for years 18.00 to infinity as of t = −3.00
51	D34: B34 + C34
52	E34: GM*(1 − x^(n − S + 1)) grand total as of t = S − 1 = −3.00 years
53	Row 35: 1/(1 + r)^(S − 1) present value factor from t = S − 1 back to t = 0
54	Row 36: Row 34 * Row 35

PART 1   Forecasting Cash Flows

Special Case: No Growth, $g = 0$

Setting $g = 0$, equation (3-11) reduces to:

$$\text{ADF} = \left[\frac{1}{r} - \frac{1}{(1+r)^{n-S+1}}\frac{1}{r}\right]\frac{1}{(1+r)^{S-1}}$$

$$= \frac{1}{r}\left[1 - \frac{1}{(1+r)^{n-S+1}}\right]\frac{1}{(1+r)^{S-1}} \qquad \text{ADF: no growth} \qquad (3\text{-}11c)$$

This formula is useful in calculating loan amortization, as the reader can see in the loan amortization section of the Appendix to this chapter.

Generalized Gordon Model

If we start with cash flows at any year other than Year 1, then we have to use a generalized Gordon model. Letting $n \to \infty$ in equation (3-11), the end-of-year formula is:

$$\text{PV} = \text{CF}\,\frac{1}{(r-g)}\frac{1}{(1+r)^{S-1}} \qquad (3\text{-}11d)$$

This is the formula for the PV of the reversion (the cash flows from $t = n + 1$ to infinity) that every appraiser uses in every discounted cash flow analysis. This is exactly what appraisers do in calculating the PV of the reversion, i.e., the infinity of time that follows the discounted cash flow forecasts for the first n years. For example, suppose we do a five-year forecast of cash flows in a discounted cash flow analysis and calculate its PV. We must then calculate the PV of the reversion, which is the sixth-year cash flow multiplied by the Gordon model and then discounted five years to $t = 0$, or:

$$\text{PV} = \text{CF}_6\,\frac{1}{r-g}\frac{1}{(1+r)^5} \qquad (3\text{-}11e)$$

The reason we discount five years and not six is that after discounting the first five years' cash flows to PV, we are standing at the end of Year 5 looking at the infinity of cash flows that we forecast to occur beginning with Year 6. The Gordon model requires us to use the first forecast year's cash flow, which is why we use CF_6 and not CF_5, but we still must discount the cash flows from the end of Year 5, or five years. The first two terms on the right-hand side of equation (3-11d) give us the formula for the PV of the cash flows from Years 6 to infinity as of the end of Year 5, and the final term on the right discounts that back to $t = 0$.

Midyear Formula

When the starting period is not in Year 1, the midyear ADF formula is:

$$\text{ADF} = \left[\frac{\sqrt{1+r}}{r-g} - \left(\frac{1+g}{1+r}\right)^{n-S+1}\frac{\sqrt{1+r}}{r-g}\right]\frac{1}{(1+r)^{S-1}}$$

$$= \frac{\sqrt{1+r}}{r-g}\left[1 - \left(\frac{1+g}{1+r}\right)^{n-S+1}\right]\frac{1}{(1+r)^{S-1}} \qquad (3\text{-}12)$$

Note that at $S = 1$, the term at the right—outside the brackets—becomes

1 and effectively drops out of the equation, which renders equation (3-12) equivalent to equation (3-10). The midyear ADF in equation (3-12) is identical to the end-of-year ADF in equation (3-11), except that we replace the two Gordon model $\sqrt{1 + r}$ terms with the value 1 in the latter.

PERIODIC PERPETUITY FACTORS (PPFs): PERPETUITIES FOR PERIODIC CASH FLOWS

Thus far, all ADFs and Gordon model perpetuities have been for contiguous cash flows. In this section we develop perpetuities for periodic cash flows that occur only at regular intervals or cycles. To my knowledge, these formulas are my own creation, and I call them periodic perpetuity factors (PPFs). PPFs are really Gordon model multiples for periodic (noncontiguous) cash flows and for contiguous cash flows that have repeating patterns.

The example we use here arose in Chapter 2 in dealing with moving expenses. Every small to midsize company that is growing in real terms moves periodically. We will assume a move occurs every 10 years, although we will derive formulas that can handle any periodicity. To further simplify the initial mathematics, we will assume the last move occurred in the last historical year of analysis. Later we will relax that assumption to handle different timing of the cash flows.

Suppose our subject company moved last year, and the move cost $20,000. We expect to move every 10 years, and moving costs increase at $g = 5\%$ per year. The PPFs are the present values of these periodic cash flows for both midyear and end-of-year assumptions.

The Mathematical Formulas

For every $1.00 of *forecast* moving costs in Year 10, the PV of the lifetime expected moving costs would be as follows in equation (3-13):

$$\text{PV} = \frac{1}{(1 + r)^{10}} + \frac{(1 + g)^{10}}{(1 + r)^{20}} + \cdots + \frac{(1 + g)^{\infty}}{(1 + r)^{\infty}} \qquad (3\text{-}13)$$

The $1.00 grows at rate g for 10 years, and we discount it back to PV for 10 years. We follow the same pattern at 20 years, 30 years, etc. to infinity. Multiplying equation (3-13) by $[(1 + g)/(1 + r)]^{10}$, we get:

$$\left(\frac{1 + g}{1 + r}\right)^{10} \text{PV} = \frac{(1 + g)^{10}}{(1 + r)^{20}} + \frac{(1 + g)^{20}}{(1 + r)^{30}} + \cdots + \frac{(1 + g)^{\infty}}{(1 + r)^{\infty}} \qquad (3\text{-}14)$$

Subtracting equation (3-14) from equation (3-13), we get:

$$\left[1 - \left(\frac{1 + g}{1 + r}\right)^{10}\right] \text{PV} = \frac{1}{(1 + r)^{10}} \qquad (3\text{-}15)$$

The left-hand side of equation (3-15) simplifies to

$$\frac{(1 + r)^{10} - (1 + g)^{10}}{(1 + r)^{10}} \text{PV}$$

Multiplying both sides of equation (3-15) by the inverse,

$$\frac{(1 + r)^{10}}{(1 + r)^{10} - (1 + g)^{10}}$$

we come to:

$$PV = \frac{(1 + r)^{10}}{(1 + r)^{10} - (1 + g)^{10}} \frac{1}{(1 + r)^{10}} \qquad (3\text{-}16)$$

Canceling out $(1 + r)^{10}$ in the numerator and denominator, the solution is:

$$PV = \frac{1}{(1 + r)^{10} - (1 + g)^{10}} \qquad (3\text{-}17)$$

We can generalize this formula to other periods of cash flows by letting cash flows occur every j years. The PV of the cash flows is the same, except that we replace each 10 in equation (3-17) with a j in equation (3-18). Additionally, we rename the term PV as PPF, the periodic perpetuity factor. Therefore, the PPF for \$1 of payment, first occurring in year j, is:

$$PPF = \frac{1}{(1 + r)^j - (1 + g)^j} \qquad PPF\text{—end-of-year} \qquad (3\text{-}18)$$

The midyear PPF is again our familiar result of $\sqrt{1 + r}$ times the end-of-year PPF, or:

$$PPF = \frac{\sqrt{1 + r}}{(1 + r)^j - (1 + g)^j} \qquad PPF\text{—midyear} \qquad (3\text{-}19)$$

Note that for $j = 1$, equations (3-18) and (3-19) reduce to the Gordon model. As you will see further below, the above two formulas only work if the last cash flow occurred in the immediate prior year, i.e., $t = -1$. In the section on other starting years, we generalize these two formulas to equations (3-18a) and (3-18b) to be able to handle different starting times.

Tables 3-7 and 3-8: Examples of Equations (3-18) and (3-19)

We begin in Table 3-7 with \$1.00 (B5) of moving expenses[11] that we forecast to occur in the next move, 10 years from now. The second move, which we expect to occur in 20 years, should cost $(1 + g)^{10} = \$1.62889$ (B6), assuming a 5% (D26) constant growth rate (g) in the cost. We discount cash flows at a 20% discount rate (D25).

Column A shows time in 10-year increments going up to 100 years. Cells B5 to B14 contain the forecast cash flows and are equal to $(1 + g)^{t-j}$, where $t = 10, 20, 30, \ldots, 100$ years and $j = 10$. Actually, time should continue to $t = \infty$, but at a 20% discount rate and 5% growth rate, the

---

11. Another common periodic expense that is less predictable than moving expenses is losses from lawsuits. Rather than use the actual loss from the last lawsuit, one should use a base-level, long-run average loss, which will grow at a rate of g.

T A B L E 3-7

Periodic Perpetuity Factor (PPF): End-of-Year Formula

	A	B	C	D	E	F
		Cash Flow	PV Factor			
4	t(Yrs)	$= (1 + g)^{t-j}$	$= 1/(1 + r)^t$	PV	% PV	Cum % PV
5	10	1.00000	0.16151	0.16151	74%	74%
6	20	1.62889	0.02608	0.04249	19%	93%
7	30	2.65330	0.00421	0.01118	5%	98%
8	40	4.32194	0.00068	0.00294	1%	100%
9	50	7.03999	0.00011	0.00077	0%	100%
10	60	11.46740	0.00002	0.00020	0%	100%
11	70	18.67919	0.00000	0.00005	0%	100%
12	80	30.42643	0.00000	0.00001	0%	100%
13	90	49.56144	0.00000	0.00000	0%	100%
14	100	80.73037	0.00000	0.00000	0%	100%
15	Totals			**0.21916**	**100%**	
17	Calculation of PPF by formula:					
19	PPF					
20	0.21916					
22	Assumptions:					
24	j = Number of years between moves			10		
25	r = Discount rate			20.0%		
26	g = Growth rate in moving costs			5.0%		
28	Spreadsheet formulas:					
30	A20: $= 1/((1 + r)^{\wedge}j - (1 + g)^{\wedge}j)$		Equation (3-18)			

T A B L E 3-8

Periodic Perpetuity Factor (PPF): Midyear Formula

	A	B	C	D	E	F
		Cash Flow	V Factor			
4	t (Yrs)	$= (1 + g)^{t-j}$	$= 1/(1 + r)^{t-0.5}$	PV	% PV	Cum % PV
5	10	1.00000	0.17692	0.17692	74%	74%
6	20	1.62889	0.02857	0.04654	19%	93%
7	30	2.65330	0.00461	0.01224	5%	98%
8	40	4.32194	0.00075	0.00322	1%	100%
9	50	7.03999	0.00012	0.00085	0%	100%
10	60	11.46740	0.00002	0.00022	0%	100%
11	70	18.67919	0.00000	0.00006	0%	100%
12	80	30.42643	0.00000	0.00002	0%	100%
13	90	49.56144	0.00000	0.00000	0%	100%
14	100	80.73037	0.00000	0.00000	0%	100%
15	Totals			**0.24008**	**100%**	
17	Calculation of PPF by formula:					
19	PPF					
20	0.24008					
22	Assumptions:					
24	j = Number of years between moves			10		
25	r = Discount rate			20.0%		
26	g = Growth rate in moving costs			5.0%		
28	Spreadsheet formulas:					
30	A20: $= SQRT(1 + r)/((1 + r)^{\wedge}j - (1 + g)^{\wedge}j)$		Equation (3-19)			

present value factors nullify all cash flows after year 40.[12] Column C contains a standard present value factor, where

$$PV = \frac{1}{(1 + r)^t}$$

Column D, the present value of the cash flows, equals Column B × Column C. Cell D15, the total PV, equals $0.21916 for every $1.00 of moving expenses in the next move. This is the final result using the "brute force" method of scheduling all the cash flows and discounting them to PV. Cell A20 contains the formula for equation (3-18), and the result is $0.21916, which demonstrates the accuracy of the formula. Note that the formula for A20 appears at A30.

To calculate the PV of $20,000 of the previous year's moving expense growing at 5% per year and occurring every 10 years, we forecast the cost of the next move by multiplying the $20,000 by 1.05^{10} = $32,577.89. We then multiply the cost of the next move by the PPF, i.e., $32,577.89 × 0.21916 (A20) = $7,139.83 before corporate taxes. Assuming a 40% tax rate, that rounds to $4,284 after tax. Since this is an expense, we must remember to subtract it from—not add it to—the value we calculated before moving expenses.[13] For example, suppose we calculated a marketable minority interest FMV of $1,004,284 before moving expenses. The final marketable minority FMV would be $1 million.

Column E shows the percentage of the PV contributed by each move. Seventy-four percent (E5) of the PV comes from the first move (Year 10), and 19% from the second move (Year 20, at E6). Column F shows the cumulative PV. The first two moves cumulatively account for 93% (F6) of the entire PV generated by all moves, and the first three moves account for 98% (F7) of the PV. Thus, in most circumstances we need not worry about the argument that after attaining a certain size a company tends to not move anymore. As long as it moves at least twice, the PPF will be accurate.

Table 3-8 is identical to Table 3-7, except that it is testing equation (3-19), the midyear formula, instead of the end-of-year formula, equation (3-18). Again C20 = D15, which verifies the formula.

Other Starting Years

Another question to address is what happens when the periodic expense occurred before the prior year. Using our moving expense every 10 years example, suppose the subject company last moved 4 years ago. It will be another 6 years, not 10 years, to the next move. The easiest way to handle this situation is first to value the cash flows from a point in time where

---

12. Of course, at a higher growth rate and the same discount rate, it will take longer for the present value factors to nullify the growth. The converse is also true.
13. We accomplish this by removing moving expenses from historical costs before developing our forecast of expenses (see Chapter 2).

we can use the ADF equations in (3-18) and (3-19) and then adjust. Thus, if we choose $t = -4$ as our temporary valuation date, all cash flows will be spaced every 10 years, and the ADF formulas (3-18) and (3-19) apply. We then roll forward to $t = 0$ by multiplying the preliminary PPF by $(1 + r)^b$.

The generalized PPF formulas are:

$$\text{PPF} = \frac{(1 + r)^b}{(1 + r)^j - (1 + g)^j} \quad \text{generalized PPF—end-of-year} \quad (3\text{-}18\text{a})$$

The midyear generalized PPF is again our familiar result of $\sqrt{1 + r}$ times the end-of-year PPF, or:

$$\text{PPF} = \frac{\sqrt{1 + r}\,(1 + r)^b}{(1 + r)^j - (1 + g)^j} \quad \text{generalized PPF—midyear} \quad (3\text{-}19\text{a})$$

Note that for $j = 1$ and $b = 0$, equations (3-18a) and (3-19a) reduce to the Gordon model.

It is important to roll forward the cash flow properly. With the $20,000 move occurring 4 years ago, our forecast of the next move is still $20,000 \times 1.05^{10} = \$32,577.89$. Whether the last move occurred 4 years ago or yesterday, the forecast cost of the next move is the same 10 years growth. The present value, and therefore the PPF, is different for the two different moves, and that is captured in the numerator of the PPF, as we have already discussed.

It is also important to recognize that the valuation date is at $t = 0$, which is the end of the prior year. Thus, if the valuation date is January 1, 1998, the end of the prior year is December 31, 1997. If the move occurred, for example, in December 1995, then that is 2 years ago and $b = 2$. We would use an end-of-year assumption, which means using the formula in equation (3-18a). If the move occurred in June 1995, we use the formula in equation (3-19a), and b still equals 2.

Table 3-9 is identical to Table 3-7, except that the expenses occur in Years 6, 16, . . . instead of 10, 20, ... The nominal cash flows are identical to Table 3-7, but the formula that generates them is different. In Table 3-7 the cash flows are equal to $(1 + g)^{t-j}$. In Table 3-9 the cash flows are equal to $(1 + g)^{t-j+b}$ because the cash flows still grow at the rate g for 10 years from the last move, not just the 6 years to the next move. However, the cash flows in Table 3-9 are discounted 6 years instead of 10 years. The PPF is $0.45445. The calculation by formula in A20 matches the brute force calculation in D15, which demonstrates the validity of equation (3-18a).

Modifying the moving expense example in Table 3-7, the PV of all moving costs throughout time equals $20,000 \times 1.62889 \times \$0.45445 = \$14,805.14$. Assuming a 40% tax rate, the after-tax present value of the perpetuity of moving costs is $8,883, compared to the $4,284 we calculated in the discussion of Table 3-7. The present value of moving costs is higher in this example, because the first cash flow occurs in Year 6 instead of Year 10.

TABLE 3-9

Periodic Perpetuity Factor (PPF): End-of-Year—Cash Flows Begin Year 6

	A	B	C	D	E	F
		Cash Flow	**PV Factor**			
4	**t (Yrs)**	**= $(1 + g)^{t-j+b}$**	**= $1/(1 + r)^t$**	**PV**	**% PV**	**Cum % PV**
5	6	1.00000	0.33490	0.33490	74%	74%
6	16	1.62889	0.05409	0.08810	19%	93%
7	26	2.65330	0.00874	0.02318	5%	98%
8	36	4.32194	0.00141	0.00610	1%	100%
9	46	7.03999	0.00023	0.00160	0%	100%
10	56	11.46740	0.00004	0.00042	0%	100%
11	66	18.67919	0.00001	0.00011	0%	100%
12	76	30.42643	0.00000	0.00003	0%	100%
13	86	49.56144	0.00000	0.00001	0%	100%
14	96	80.73037	0.00000	0.00000	0%	100%
15	Totals			**0.45445**	**100%**	
17	Calculation of PPF by formula:					
19	PPF					
20	0.45445					
22	Assumptions:					
24	j = Number of years between moves [1]			10		
25	r = Discount rate			20.0%		
26	g = Growth rate in net inc/cash flow			5.0%		
27	b = Number of years from last cash flow			4		
29	Spreadsheet formulas:					
31	A20: = $(1 + r)^b/((1 + r)^j - (1 + g)^j)$		Equation (3-18a)			

[1] As j decreases, the PV Factors and the PV increase. It is possible that you will have to add additional rows above Row 15 to capture all the PV of the cash flows. Otherwise, the PV in C20 will appear to be higher than the total of the cash flows in D15.

PPFs in New versus Used Equipment Decisions

Another important use of PPFs is in new versus used equipment decisions and in valuing used income-producing equipment. Let's use a taxicab as an example. The cab company can buy a new car or a used car. Suppose a new car would last six years. It costs $20,000 to buy a new one today, and we can model the cash flows for its six-year expected life.

The cash flows will consist of the purchase of the cab, income, gasoline, maintenance, insurance, etc. Each expense category has its own pattern. Gas consumption is a variable expense that increases in dollars over time with the rate of increase in gas prices. Maintenance is probably low for the first two years and then begins increasing rapidly in Year 3 or 4.

We can then take the NPV of the cash flows, and that represents the NPV of operating a new cab for six years. It would be nice to compare that with the NPV of operating a one-year-old cab for five years (or any other term desired). The problem is that these are different time periods. We could use the lowest common multiple of 30 years (6 years × 5 years) and run the new cab cash flows five times and the used cab cycle six times, but that is a lot of work. It is a far more elegant solution to use a PPF for the new and the used equipment. The result of those computations will be the present value of keeping one new cab and one used cab in service forever. We can then choose the one with the superior NPV.

Even though the cash flows are contiguous, which is not true in the periodic expense example, the cycle and the NPV of the cash flows are periodic. Every six years the operator buys a new cab. We can measure the NPV of the first cab as of $t = 0$. The operator buys the second cab and uses it from Years 7–12. Its NPV as of the end of Year 6 ($t = 6$) should be the same as the NPV at $t = 0$ of the first six years' cash flows, with a growth rate for the rise in prices. If there are substantial difference in the growth rates of income versus expenses or of the different categories of expenses, then we can break the expenses into two or more subcategories and apply a PPF to each subcategory, then add the NPVs together. Buying a new cab every six years would then generate a series of NPVs with constant growth at $t = 0, 6, 12, \ldots$. That repeating pattern is what enables us to use a PPF to value the cash flows.

We could perform this procedure for each different vintage of used equipment, e.g., buying one-year-old cabs, two-year old cabs, etc. Our final comparison would be the NPV of buying and operating a single cab of each age (a new cab, one year old, two years old, etc.) forever. We then simply choose the cab life with the highest NPV.

If equipment is not income producing, we can still the PPF to value the periodic costs in perpetuity. Then the NPV would be negative.

ADFs IN LOAN MATHEMATICS

There are four related topics that should ideally all be together dealing with the use of ADFs in loan mathematics to create formulas to calculate: loan payments, principal amortization, the after-tax cost of a loan, and the PV of a loan when the nominal and market rates differ. We will deal with the first and the last topics in this section. Calculating the amortization of principal is mathematically very complex. To maintain readability, it will be explained, along with the related problem of calculating the after-tax cost of a loan, in the Appendix.

Calculating Loan Payments

We can use our earlier ADF results to easily create a formula to calculate loan payments. We know that in the case of a fixed rate amortizing loan, the principal must be equal to the PV of the payments when discounted by the *nominal* rate of the loan. We can calculate the PV of the payments using equation (3-6d) and the following definitions:

$\text{ADF}_{\text{Nominal}}$ = ADF at the nominal interest rate of the loan
ADF_{Mkt} = ADF at the market interest rate of the loan

The nominal ADF is simply an end-of-year ADF with no growth. Repeating equation (3-6d), the ADF is:

$$\text{ADF}_{\text{Nominal}} = \frac{1 - \dfrac{1}{(1 + r)^n}}{r}$$

where r in this case is the nominal interest of the loan. If we use the market interest rate instead of the nominal rate, we get ADF_{Mkt}. We know that the loan payment multiplied by the nominal ADF equals the principal of the loan. Stating that as an equation:

$$\text{Loan Payment} \times ADF_{Nominal} = \text{Principal} \qquad (3\text{-}20)$$

Dividing both sides of the equation by $ADF_{Nominal}$, we get:

$$\text{Loan Payment} = \frac{\text{Principal}}{ADF_{Nominal}} = \text{Principal} \times \frac{1}{ADF_{Nominal}} \qquad (3\text{-}21)$$

Present Value of a Loan

The PV of a loan is the loan payment multiplied by the market rate ADF, or:

$$PV = \text{Loan Payment} \times ADF_{Mkt} \qquad (3\text{-}22)$$

From equation (3-21), the loan payment is the principal divided by the nominal ADF. Substituting this into equation (3-22) gives us:

$$PV \text{ of Loan} = \text{Principal} \times \frac{ADF_{Mkt}}{ADF_{Nominal}} \qquad (3\text{-}23)$$

The intuition behind this is the Principal $\times\ 1/ADF_{Nominal}$ is the amount of the loan payment. When we then multiply that by the ADF_{Mkt}, this gives us the PV of the loan.

Table 3-10: Example of Equation (3-23)

Table 3-10 is an example of calculating the present value of a loan. The assumptions appear in Table 3-10 in E77 to E82. We assume a $1 million principal on a five-year loan. The loan payment, calculated using Excel's spreadsheet function, is $20,276.39 (E78) for 60 months. The annual loan rate is 8% (E79), and the monthly rate is 0.667% (E80 = E79/12). The annual market rate of interest (the discount rate) on this loan is assumed at 14% (I81), and the monthly market interest rate is 1.167% (I82 = I81/12).

Column A shows the 60 months of payments. Column B shows the monthly payment of $20,276.39 for 60 months. Columns C and D show the PV factor and the PV of each month's payment at the nominal 8% annual interest rate (0.667% monthly rate), while Columns E and F show the same calculations at the market rate of 14% (1.167% monthly rate).

The present value factors in C6 to C65 total 49.31843, and present value factors in E6 to E65 total 42.97702. Note also that the PV of the loan at the nominal interest rate adds to the $1 million principal (D66), as it should.

E70 is the ADF at 8% according to equation (3-6d). We show the spreadsheet formula for E70 in A86. E71 is $1/ADF_{Nominal} = \$0.02027639$, the amount of loan payment for each $1 of principal. We multiply that by the $1 million principal to obtain the loan payment of $20,276.39 in F71, which matches E78, as it should. In E72 we calculate the ADF at the market rate of interest, the formula for which is also equation (3-6d), merely using the 1.167% monthly interest rate in the formula, which we show in A88. In E73 we calculate the ratio of the market ADF to the

T A B L E 3-10

PV of Loan with Market Rate > Nominal Rate: ADF, End-of-Year

	A	B	C	D	E	F
4				r = 8%		r = 14%
5	Month	Cash Flow	PV Factor	Present Value	PV Factor	Present Value
6	1	$20,276.39	0.99338	$ 20,142	0.98847	$ 20,043
7	2	$20,276.39	0.98680	$ 20,009	0.97707	$ 19,811
8	3	$20,276.39	0.98026	$ 19,876	0.96580	$ 19,583
9	4	$20,276.39	0.97377	$ 19,745	0.95466	$ 19,357
10	5	$20,276.39	0.96732	$ 19,614	0.94365	$ 19,134
11	6	$20,276.39	0.96092	$ 19,484	0.93277	$ 18,913
12	7	$20,276.39	0.95455	$ 19,355	0.92201	$ 18,695
13	8	$20,276.39	0.94823	$ 19,227	0.91138	$ 18,480
14	9	$20,276.39	0.94195	$ 19,099	0.90087	$ 18,266
15	10	$20,276.39	0.93571	$ 18,973	0.89048	$ 18,056
16	11	$20,276.39	0.92952	$ 18,847	0.88021	$ 17,848
17	12	$20,276.39	0.92336	$ 18,722	0.87006	$ 17,642
18	13	$20,276.39	0.91725	$ 18,598	0.86003	$ 17,438
19	14	$20,276.39	0.91117	$ 18,475	0.85011	$ 17,237
20	15	$20,276.39	0.90514	$ 18,353	0.84031	$ 17,038
21	16	$20,276.39	0.89914	$ 18,231	0.83062	$ 16,842
22	17	$20,276.39	0.89319	$ 18,111	0.82104	$ 16,648
23	18	$20,276.39	0.88727	$ 17,991	0.81157	$ 16,456
24	19	$20,276.39	0.88140	$ 17,872	0.80221	$ 16,266
25	20	$20,276.39	0.87556	$ 17,753	0.79296	$ 16,078
26	21	$20,276.39	0.86976	$ 17,636	0.78382	$ 15,893
27	22	$20,276.39	0.86400	$ 17,519	0.77478	$ 15,710
28	23	$20,276.39	0.85828	$ 17,403	0.76584	$ 15,529
29	24	$20,276.39	0.85260	$ 17,288	0.75701	$ 15,349
30	25	$20,276.39	0.84695	$ 17,173	0.74828	$ 15,172
31	26	$20,276.39	0.84134	$ 17,059	0.73965	$ 14,997
32	27	$20,276.39	0.83577	$ 16,946	0.73112	$ 14,824
33	28	$20,276.39	0.83023	$ 16,834	0.72269	$ 14,654
34	29	$20,276.39	0.82474	$ 16,723	0.71436	$ 14,485
35	30	$20,276.39	0.81927	$ 16,612	0.70612	$ 14,318
36	31	$20,276.39	0.81385	$ 16,502	0.69797	$ 14,152
37	32	$20,276.39	0.80846	$ 16,393	0.68993	$ 13,989
38	33	$20,276.39	0.80310	$ 16,284	0.68197	$ 13,828
39	34	$20,276.39	0.79779	$ 16,176	0.67410	$ 13,668
40	35	$20,276.39	0.79250	$ 16,069	0.66633	$ 13,511
41	36	$20,276.39	0.78725	$ 15,963	0.65865	$ 13,355
42	37	$20,276.39	0.78204	$ 15,857	0.65105	$ 13,201
43	38	$20,276.39	0.77686	$ 15,752	0.64354	$ 13,049
44	39	$20,276.39	0.77172	$ 15,648	0.63612	$ 12,898
45	40	$20,276.39	0.76661	$ 15,544	0.62879	$ 12,749
46	41	$20,276.39	0.76153	$ 15,441	0.62153	$ 12,602
47	42	$20,276.39	0.75649	$ 15,339	0.61437	$ 12,457
48	43	$20,276.39	0.75148	$ 15,237	0.60728	$ 12,313
49	44	$20,276.39	0.74650	$ 15,136	0.60028	$ 12,171
50	45	$20,276.39	0.74156	$ 15,036	0.59336	$ 12,031
51	46	$20,276.39	0.73665	$ 14,937	0.58651	$ 11,892
52	47	$20,276.39	0.73177	$ 14,838	0.57975	$ 11,755
53	48	$20,276.39	0.72692	$ 14,739	0.57306	$ 11,620
54	49	$20,276.39	0.72211	$ 14,642	0.56645	$ 11,486
55	50	$20,276.39	0.71732	$ 14,545	0.55992	$ 11,353
56	51	$20,276.39	0.71257	$ 14,448	0.55347	$ 11,222
57	52	$20,276.39	0.70785	$ 14,353	0.54708	$ 11,093
58	53	$20,276.39	0.70317	$ 14,258	0.54077	$ 10,965
59	54	$20,276.39	0.69851	$ 14,163	0.53454	$ 10,838
60	55	$20,276.39	0.69388	$ 14,069	0.52837	$ 10,714
61	56	$20,276.39	0.68929	$ 13,976	0.52228	$ 10,590

PV of Loan with Market Rate > Nominal Rate: ADF, End-of-Year

	A	B	C	D	E	F
4				r = 8%		r = 14%
5	Month	Cash Flow	PV Factor	Present Value	PV Factor	Present Value
62	57	$20,276.39	0.68472	$ 13,884	0.51626	$ 10,468
63	58	$20,276.39	0.68019	$ 13,792	0.51030	$ 10,347
64	59	$20,276.39	0.67569	$ 13,700	0.50442	$ 10,228
65	60	$20,276.39	0.67121	$ 13,610	0.49860	$ 10,110
66	Totals	$1,216,584	49.31843	$1,000,000	42.97702	$871,419
68						X Principal
69					Per $1	of $1 Million
70	ADF @ 8% = C66				49.318433	
71	Formula for payment = 1/ADF				0.02027639	$20,276.39
72	ADF @ 14% = E66				42.977016	
73	ADF @ 14%/ADF @ 8% = F66				0.871419	$871,419
75	Assumptions:					
77	Principal				$1,000,000	
78	Loan payment				$20,276.39	
79	r = Nominal discount rate-annual				8.0%	
80	r_1 = Nominal discount rate-monthly				0.667%	
81	r_2 = Market discount rate				14.0%	
82	r_3 = Market discount rate				1.167%	
84	Spreadsheet formulas:					
86	E70: =(1 − 1/(1 + E80)^60)/E80					
87	E71: =1/E70					
88	E72: =(1 − 1/(1 + E82)^60)/E82					
89	E73: =E72/E70					

nominal ADF, which is E72 divided by E70 and equals 0.871419. In F73 we multiply E73 by the $1 million principal to obtain the present value of the loan of $871,419. Note that this matches our brute force calculation in F66, as it should.

RELATIONSHIP OF THE GORDON MODEL TO THE PRICE/EARNINGS RATIO

In this section, we will mathematically derive the relationship between the price/earnings (PE) ratio and the Gordon model. The confusion between the two leads to possibly more mistakes by appraisers than any other single source of mistakes—I have seen numerous reports in which the appraiser used the wrong earnings base. Understanding this section should clear the potential confusion that exists. First, we will begin with some definitions that will aid in developing the mathematics. All other definitions retain their same meaning as in the rest of the chapter.

Definitions

P_t = stock price at time t

E_t = *historical* earnings in the *prior* year (usually the prior 12 months)

E_{t+1} = *forecast* earnings in the *upcoming* year

b = earnings retention rate. Thus, cash flow to shareholders equals $(1 - b) \times$ earnings.

g_1 = one-year forecast growth rate in earnings, i.e., $E_{t+1}/E_t - 1$

PE = price/earnings ratio = P_t/E_t

Mathematical Derivation

We begin with the statement that the market capitalization of a publicly held firm is its fair market value, and that is equal to its PE ratio times the previous year's *historical* earnings:

$$\text{FMV} = \frac{P_t}{E_t} * E_t \qquad (3\text{-}24)$$

We repeat equation (3-10e) below as equation (3-25), with one change. We will assume that forecast cash flow to shareholders, CF_{t+1}, is equal to $(1 - b) \times E_{t+1}$, where b is the earnings retention rate.[14] The earnings retention rate is the sum total of all the reconciling items between net income and cash flow (see Chapter 1). Now we have an expression for the FMV of the firm[15] according to the midyear Gordon model.

$$\text{FMV} = (1 - b)\, E_{t+1}\, \frac{\sqrt{1 + r}}{(r - g)} \quad \text{midyear Gordon model} \qquad (3\text{-}25)$$

Substituting $E_{t+1} = E_t\,(1 + g_1)$ into equation (3-25), we come to:

$$\text{FMV} = (1 - b)\, E_t\,(1 + g_1)\, \frac{\sqrt{1 + r}}{(r - g)} \qquad (3\text{-}26)$$

The left-hand sides of equations (3-24) and (3-26) are the same. Therefore, we can equate the right-hand sides of those equations.

$$\frac{P_t}{E_t} * E_t = (1 - b)\, E_t\,(1 + g_1)\, \frac{\sqrt{1 + r}}{(r - g)} \qquad (3\text{-}27)$$

E_t cancels out on both sides of the equation. Additionally, we use the simpler notation PE for the price-earnings multiple. Thus, equation (3-27) reduces to:

$$\text{PE} = (1 - b)\,(1 + g_1)\, \frac{\sqrt{1 + r}}{r - g}$$

relationship of PE to Gordon model multiple $\qquad (3\text{-}28)$

The left-hand term is the price-earnings multiple and the right-hand term is one minus the earnings retention rate times one plus the one-year growth rate times the midyear Gordon model multiple. In reality, inves-

---

14. I wish to thank Larry Kasper for pointing out the need for this.
15. Assuming the present value of the cash flows of the firm is its FMV. This ignores valuation discounts, an acceptable simplification in this limited context.

tors do not expect constant growth to perpetuity. They usually have expectations of uneven growth for a few years and a vague, long-run expectation of growth thereafter that they approximate as being constant. Therefore, we should look at g, the perpetual growth rate in cash flow, as an average growth rate over the infinite period of time that we are modeling.

We should be very clear that the earnings base in the PE multiple and the Gordon model are different. The former is the immediate prior year and the latter is the first forecast year. When an appraiser develops PE multiples from guideline companies, whether publicly or privately owned, he should multiply the PE multiple from the guideline companies (after appropriate adjustments) by the subject company's *prior* year earnings. When using a discounted cash flow approach, the appraiser should multiply the Gordon model by the first *forecast* year's earnings. Using the wrong earnings will cause an error in the valuation by a factor of one plus the forecast one-year growth rate.

CONCLUSIONS

We can see that there is a family of annuity discount factors (ADFs), from the simplest case of an ordinary annuity to the most complicated case of an annuity with stub periods (fractional years), as discussed in the Appendix. The elements that determine which formula to use are:

- Whether the cash flows are midyear versus end-of-year.
- When the cash flows begin (Year 1 versus any other time).
- If they occur every year or at regular, skipped intervals (or have repeating cycles).
- Whether or not the constant growth is zero.
- Whether there is a stub period.

For cash flows without a stub period, the ADF is the difference of two Gordon model perpetuities. The first term is the perpetuity from S to infinity, where S is the starting year of the cash flow. The second term is the perpetuity starting at $n + 1$ (where n is the final cash flow in the annuity) going to infinity. For cash flows with a stub period, the preceding statement is true with the addition of a third term for the single cash flow of the stub period itself, discounted to PV.

While this chapter contains some complex algebra, the focus has been on the intuitive explanation of each ADF. The most difficult mathematics have been moved to the Appendix, which contains the formulas for ADF with stub periods and some advanced material on the use of ADFs in calculating loan amortization. ADFs are also used for practical applications in Chris Mercer's quantitative marketability discount model (see Chapter 7), periodic expenses such as moving costs and losses from lawsuits, ESOP valuation, in reducing a seller-subsidized loan to its cash equivalent price in Chapter 10, and to calculate loan payments.

We have performed a rigorous derivation of the PE multiple and the Gordon model. This derivation demonstrates that the PE multiple equals one minus the earnings retention rate times one plus the one-year growth

ADF Equation Numbers

Formulas in the Chapter	With Growth		No Growth	
	End-of-Year	**Midyear**	**End-of-Year**	**Midyear**
Ordinary ADF	(3-6) to (3-6b)	(3-10) to (3-10b)	(3-6d)	(3-10c) & (3-10d)
Gordon model	(3-7)	(3-10e)		
Starting cash flow not t = 1	(3-11) & (3-11a)	(3-12)	(3-11c)	
Valuation date = v	(3-11b)			
Gordon model for starting CF not = 1	(3-11d)			
Periodic expenses	(3-18)	(3-19)		
Periodic expenses-flexible timing	(3-18a)	(3-19a)		
Loan payment			(3-21)	
Relationship of Gordon model to PE		(3-28)		
Formulas in the Appendix				
ADF with stub period	(A3-3)	(A3-4)		
Amortization of loan principal			(A3-10)	
PV of loan after-tax			(A3-24) & (A3-25)	

rate times the midyear Gordon model multiple. Furthermore, we showed how the former uses the *prior* year's earnings, while the latter uses the first *forecast* year's earnings. Many appraisers have found that confusing, and hopefully this section of the chapter will do much to eliminate that confusion.

Because there are so many ADFs for different purposes and assumptions, we include Table 3-11 to point the reader to the correct ADF equation.

BIBLIOGRAPHY

Gordon, M. J., and E. Shapiro. 1956. "Capital Equipment Analysis: The Required Rate of Profit," *Management Science* 3: 102–110.

Gordon, M. J. 1962. *The Investment, Financing, and Valuation of the Corporation*, 2d ed. Homewood, Ill.: R. D. Irwin.

Mercer, Z. Christopher. 1997. *Quantifying Marketability Discounts: Developing and Supporting Marketability Discounts in the Appraisal of Closely Held Business Interests.* Memphis, Tenn.: Peabody.

Williams, J. B. *The Theory of Investment Value.* 1938. Cambridge, Mass.: Harvard University Press.

APPENDIX
INTRODUCTION

This appendix is an extension of the material developed in the chapter. The topics that we cover are:

- Developing ADFs for cash flows that end on a fractional year (stub period).
- Developing ADFs for loan mathematics, consisting of calculating the amortization of principal in loans and the net after-tax cost of a loan.

This appendix is truly for the mathematically brave. The topics covered and formulas developed are esoteric and less practically useful than the formulas in the chapter, though the formula for the after-tax cost of a loan may be useful to some practitioners. The material in this appendix is included primarily for reference. Nevertheless, even those not completely comfortable with the difficult mathematics can benefit from focusing on the verbal explanations before the equations and the development of the first one or two equations in the derivation of each of the formulas. The rest is just the tedious math, which can be skipped.

THE ADF WITH STUB PERIODS (FRACTIONAL YEARS)

We will now develop a formula to handle annuities that have stub periods, constant growth in cash flows, and cash flows that start at any time. To the best of my knowledge, I invented this formula. In this section we will assume midyear cash flows and later present the formula for end-of-year cash flows.

Let's begin with constructing a timeline of the cash flows in Figure A3-1, using the following definitions and assumptions:

Definitions

S = time (in years) of the first cash flow for end-of-year cash flows. For midyear cash flows, S = end of the year in which the first cash flow occurs = 3.25 years in this example, which means the cash flow for that year begins at $t = 2.25$ years and we assume the cash flow occurs in the middle of the year, or $S - 0.5 = 3.25 - 0.5 = 2.75$ years.

n = end of the last whole year's cash flows = 12.25 years in this example

z = end of the stub period = 12.60 years.

p = proportion of a full year represented by the stub period = $z - n = 12.60 - 12.25 = 0.35$ years

g = constant growth rate in cash flows = 5.1%

t = point in time, measured in years

The Cash Flows

We assume the first cash flow of $1.00 (Figure A3-1, cell C4) occurs during year S (S is for starting cash flow), where $t = 2.25$ to $t = 3.25$ years. For

Timeline of Cash Flows

Row \ Col.	B	C	D	E	F	G	H
1	Year (numeric)	3.25	4.25	5.25	...	12.25	12.60
2	Year (symbolic)	S	S+1	S+2	...	n	z
3	Growth (in $)	0	g	g(1+g)	...	$g(1+g)^{n-S-1}$	NA
4	Cash Flow	1	1+g	$(1+g)^2$	...	$(1+g)^{n-S}$	$p(1+g)^{n-S+1}$

simplicity, we denote that the cash flow is for the year ending at $t = 3.25$ years (cell C1). Note that for Year 3.25, there is no growth in the cash flow, i.e., cell B3 = 0.

The following year is 4.25 (cell D1), or $S + 1$ (cell D2). The $1.00 grows at a rate of g (cell D3), so the ending cash flow is $1 + g$ (cell D4). Note that the ending cash flow is equal to $(1 + g)^{t-S} = (1 + g)^{4.25-3.25}$.

For Year 5.25, or $S + 2$ (cell E2), growth in cash flows is g times the prior year's cash flow of $(1 + g)$, or $g(1 + g)$ (cell E3), which leads to a cash flow equal to the prior year's cash flow plus this year's growth, or $(1 + g) + g(1 + g) = (1 + g)(1 + g) = (1 + g)^2$ [cell E4]. Again, the cash flow equals $(1 + g)^{t-S} = (1 + g)^{5.25-3.25}$.

For the year 6.25, or $S + 3$, which is not shown in Figure A3-1, cash flows grow $g(1 + g)^2$, so cash flows are $(1 + g)^2 + g(1 + g)^2 = (1 + g)^2(1 + g) = (1 + g)^3 = (1 + g)^{t-S} = (1 + g)^{6.25-3.25}$.

We continue in this fashion through the last whole year of cash flows, which we call Year n (Column G). In our example, $n = 12.25$ years (cell G1). The cash flows during Year n are equal to $(1 + g)^{n-S}$ [cell G4].

Had we completed one more full year, the cash flows would have extended to Year 13.25, or Year $n + 1$. If so, the cash flow would have been $(1 + g)^{n-S+1}$. However, since the stub year's cash flow is only for a partial year, the ending cash flow is multiplied by p—the fractional portion of the year—leading to an ending cash flow of $p(1 + g)^{n-S+1}$.

It is important to recognize that there may be other ways of specifying how the partial year affects the cash flows. For example, it is possible, but very unlikely, that the cash flows can be based on a legal document that specifies that only the growth rate itself will be fractional, but the corpus of the cash flow will not diminish for the partial year. We could calculate a solution to this ADF, but we will not, as it is very unlikely to be of any practical use and we have already demonstrated how to model the most likely method of splitting the cash flows in the fractional year. The point is that modeling the fractional year cash flows depends on the agreement and/or the underlying scenario, and one should not blindly charge off into the sunset applying a formula developed under an assumption that does not apply in another case.

Discounting Periods

The first cash flow occurs during the year that spans from $t = 2.25$ to $t = 3.25$. We assume the cash flows occur evenly throughout the year, which is tantamount to assuming all cash flows occur on average halfway through the year, i.e., at Year 2.75. Therefore as of time zero, defined as $t = 0$, the first $1 cash flow has a present value of

$$\frac{1}{(1 + r)^{2.75}} = \frac{1}{(1 + r)^{S-0.5}}$$

We will be discounting the cash flows in two stages because that will later enable us to provide a more intuitive explanation of our results. Our first discounting of cash flows will be to $t = S - 1$, the beginning of the first year of cash flows. The first year's cash flow then receives a dis-

PART 1 Forecasting Cash Flows

count of $1/(1 + r)^{0.5}$, the second year's cash flows receive a discount of $1/(1 + r)^{1.5}$, etc. Thus, the denominators here are identical to those for cash flows that would begin in Year 1 instead of S.

The Equations

The PV of our series of cash flows as of $t = S - 1$ is:

$$PV = \frac{1}{(1 + r)^{0.5}} + \frac{(1 + g)}{(1 + r)^{1.5}}$$

$$+ \ldots + \frac{(1 + g)^{n-S}}{(1 + r)^{n-S+0.5}} + \frac{p(1 + g)^{n-S+1}}{(1 + r)^{n-S+1+0.5p}} \qquad \text{(A3-1)}$$

Note that the exponent in the denominator of the last term (the fractional year) is equal to the one before it (the last whole year) plus ½ year to bring us to the end of Year n, plus ½ of the fractional year, thus maintaining a midyear assumption.

We already have a solution to the PV of the whole years in the body of the chapter—equation (3-10). Thus, the PV of the entire series of cash flows as of $t = S - 1$ is equation (3-10) plus the final term in equation (A3-1), or:

$$NPV = \frac{\sqrt{1 + r}}{r - g} - \left(\frac{1 + g}{1 + r}\right)^{n-S+1} \frac{\sqrt{1 + r}}{r - g} + \frac{p(1 + g)^{n-S+1}}{(1 + r)^{n-S+1+0.5p}} \qquad \text{(A3-2)}$$

The next step is to discount the PV from $t = S - 1$ to $t = 0$. We do this by multiplying by $1/(1 + r)^{S-1}$. The result is our annuity discount factor for midyear cash flows with a stub period.

$$NPV = \left\{ \frac{\sqrt{1 + r}}{r - g} - \left(\frac{1 + g}{1 + r}\right)^{n-S+1} \frac{\sqrt{1 + r}}{r - g} \right.$$

$$\left. + \frac{p(1 + g)^{n-S+1}}{(1 + r)^{n-S+1+0.5p}} \right\} \frac{1}{(1 + r)^{S-1}} \qquad \text{(A3-3)}$$

The ADF formula for end-of-year cash flows with a stub period is:

$$ADF = \left\{ \frac{1}{r - g} - \left(\frac{1 + g}{1 + r}\right)^{n-S+1} \frac{1}{r - g} \right.$$

$$\left. + \frac{p(1 + g)^{n-S+1}}{(1 + r)^{(z-S+1)}} \right\} \frac{1}{(1 + r)^{S-1}} \qquad \text{(A3-4)}$$

The individual terms in equation (A3-4) have the same meaning as in the midyear cash flows of equation (A3-3). To easily see the derivation of the end-of-year (EOY) model from the midyear, note that an EOY model in equation (A3-1) would require the exponent in each denominator to be 0.5 years larger, which changes the $\sqrt{1 + r}$ term in equation (A3-3) to 1. $1/(r - g)$ is the EOY Gordon model formula. The only other difference is the discount factor in the rightmost term in the braces of equations (A3-3) and (A3-4). In the former, we discount the stub period cash flow by $(1 + r)^{n-S+1+0.5p}$, while in the latter we discount by $(1 + r)^{(z-S+1)}$.

Tables A3-1 and A3-2: Example of Equations [A3-3] and [A3-4]

Table A3-1 is an example of the midyear ADF with a fractional year cash flow, and Table A3-2 is an example using end-of-year cash flows. Table A3-2 has the identical structure and meaning as Table A3-1—merely using end-of-year formulas rather than midyear. Therefore, we will explain only Table A3-1.

In the first part of Table A3-1, we will use a "brute force" method of scheduling out the cash flows, calculating their present values, and then summing them. Later we will directly test the formulas and demonstrate they produce the same result as the brute force method.

Brute Force Method of Calculating PV of Cash Flows

Rows 7 through 17 in Table A3-1 are a detailed listing of the cash flows and their present values each year. The first cash flows begin in Row 7 at Year 2.25 and finish at $t = 3.25$, with Year 2.75 as the midpoint from which we discount. We will refer to the years by the ending year, i.e., the cash flow in Row 7 is for the year ending at $t = 3.25$. Assumptions of the model begin in Row 33.

We begin with $1.00 of cash flow for the year ending at $t = 3.25$ (C7). Column B shows the growth in cash flows and is equal to $g = 5.1\%$ multiplied by the previous period's cash flow. In B8 the calculation is $1.00 \times 5.1\% = \$0.051$. The cash flow in C8 is C7 + B8, or $1.00 + \$.051 = \$1.051$. We repeat this pattern through Row 16, the last whole year's cash flow.

Column D replicates Column C using the formula cash flow $= (1 + g)^{t-S}$ for all cells except D17, which is the fractional year cash flow. The formula for that cell is $p(1 + g)^{n-S+1}$, where multiplying by $p = 0.35$ years converts what would have been the cash flow for the whole year $n + 1$ (and would have been 1.64447) into the fractional year cash flow of 0.57557.[16] Note that in that formula, $n = 12.25$ years, the last whole year.

We show the present values of the cash flows as of $t = S - 1$ in Columns E and F and the present values as of $t = 0$ in Columns G and H. The discount rate is 15% (G36).

Column E contains the present value factors (PVFs), and its formula is[17]

$$PVF = \frac{1}{(1 + r)^{t-S+0.5}}$$

Column F is Column C (or Column D, as the results are identical) times

---

16. See cell A45 for the formula in the spreadsheet.

17. The intuition behind the exponent is that we are discounting from t to $S - 1$, which is equal to $t - (S - 1) = t - S + 1$ years. Using a midyear convention, we always discount from ½ year earlier than end-of-year, which reduces the exponent to $t - S + 0.5$. The 0.5 reverts to 1 in the end-of-year formula.

TABLE A3-1

ADF with Fractional Year: Midyear Formula

	A	B	C	D	E	F	G	H
5		**Cash Flows**			**t = S − 1**		**t = 0**	
6	t (Yrs)	Growth	Cash Flow	$(1 + g)^{t-S}$	$PVF = 1/(1 + r)^{t-S+0.5}$	PV	$PVF = 1/(1 + r)^{t-0.5}$	PV
7	3.25	NA	1.00000	1.00000	0.93250	0.93250	0.68090	0.68090
8	4.25	0.05100	1.05100	1.05100	0.81087	0.85223	0.59208	0.62228
9	5.25	0.05360	1.10460	1.10460	0.70511	0.77886	0.51486	0.56871
10	6.25	0.05633	1.16094	1.16094	0.61314	0.71181	0.44770	0.51975
11	7.25	0.05921	1.22014	1.22014	0.53316	0.65053	0.38930	0.47501
12	8.25	0.06223	1.28237	1.28237	0.46362	0.59453	0.33853	0.43412
13	9.25	0.06540	1.34777	1.34777	0.40315	0.54335	0.29437	0.39674
14	10.25	0.06874	1.41651	1.41651	0.35056	0.49658	0.25597	0.36259
15	11.25	0.07224	1.48875	1.48875	0.30484	0.45383	0.22259	0.33138
16	12.25	0.07593	1.56468	1.56468	0.26508	0.41476	0.19355	0.30285
17	12.60	NA	0.57557	0.57557	0.24121	0.13883	0.17613	0.10137

18	Totals for whole years = 3.25 − 12.25					6.42899		4.69432
19	Add fractional year = 12.60					0.13833		0.10137
20	Grand total (t = S − 1 in Column G and t = 0 in Column I)					6.56782		4.79469
21	Present value factor-discount from S − 1 (t = 2.25) to 0					0.73018		
22	Grand total (t = 0)					4.79569		

24	Calculation of PV by formulas:				

		Whole Yrs	**Frac Yr**	**Total**	**Grand Total**
25/26					
27	t = S − 1	6.42899	0.13883	6.56782	
28	PV Factor	0.73018	0.73018		
29	t = 0	4.69432	0.10137	**4.79469**	4.79569

31	Assumptions:

33	S = Beginning year of cash flows (valuation at t = 2.25)	3.25
34	n = Ending year of cash flows-whole year	12.25
35	z = Ending year of cash flows-stub year	12.60
36	r = Discount rate	15.0%
37	g = growth rate in cash flow	5.1%
38	p = proportion of year in the stub period	0.35
39	Midpoint = n + 0.5 p = midpoint of the fractional year	12.425
40	x = (1 + g)/(1 + r)	0.913913
41	Gordon model multiple = GM = Sqrt (1 + r)/(r − g)	10.832127

43	Spreadsheet Formulas:

45	C17, D17: $p*(1 + g)^{(n - s + 1)}$ stub period cash flow
46	E17: $1/(1 + r)^{(n - S + 1 + 0.5*p)}$ stub period present value factor at t = 2.25
47	G17: $1/(1 + r)^{(n + 0.5*p)}$ stub period present value factor for t = 0
48	B27: $GM*(1 - x^{(n - S + 1)})$ ADF for years 3.25 to 32.25 at t = 2.25
49	C27: $p*(1 + g)^{(n - S + 1)}/(1 + r)^{(n - S + 1 + 0.5*p)}$ PV of stub period CF at t = 2.25
50	B28, C28: $1/(1 + r)^{(S - 1)}$ present value factor at t = S − 1 = 2.25
51	E29: $(GM*(1 - x^{(n - S + 1)})) + p*(1 + G)^{(n - S + 1)}/(1 + r)^{(n - S + 1 + 0.5*p)})*(1/(1 + r)^{(S - 1)})$

Note: E29 is the formula for the Grand Total

CHAPTER 3 Annuity Discount Factors and the Gordon Model   95

T A B L E A3-2

ADF with Fractional Year: Midyear Formula

	A	B	C	D	E	F	G	H
5			**Cash Flows**		**t = S − 1**		**t = 0**	
6	**t (Yrs)**	**Growth**	**Cash Flow**	**(1 + g)$^{t-S}$**	**PVF = 1/(1 + r)$^{t-S+1}$**	**PV**	**PVF = 1/(1 + r)^t**	**PV**
7	3.25	NA	1.00000	1.00000	0.86957	0.86957	0.63494	0.63494
8	4.25	0.05100	1.05100	1.05100	0.75614	0.79471	0.55212	0.58028
9	5.25	0.05360	1.10460	1.10460	0.65752	0.72629	0.48011	0.53032
10	6.25	0.05633	1.16094	1.16094	0.57175	0.66377	0.41748	0.48467
11	7.25	0.05921	1.22014	1.22014	0.49718	0.60663	0.36303	0.44295
12	8.25	0.06223	1.28237	1.28237	0.43233	0.55440	0.31568	0.40481
13	9.25	0.06540	1.34777	1.34777	0.37594	0.50668	0.27450	0.36997
14	10.25	0.06874	1.41651	1.41651	0.32690	0.46306	0.23870	0.33812
15	11.25	0.07224	1.48875	1.48875	0.28426	0.42320	0.20756	0.30901
16	12.25	0.07593	1.56468	1.56468	0.24718	0.38676	0.18049	0.28241
17	12.60	NA	0.57557	0.57557	0.23538	0.13548	0.17187	0.09892
18	Totals for whole years = 3.25 − 22.25					5.99506		4.37747
19	Add fractional year = 22.60					0.13548		0.09892
20	Grand total (t = S − 1 in Column G and t = 0 in Column H)					6.13054		4.47640
21	Present value factor-discount from S − 1 (t = 2.25) to 0					0.73018		
22	Grand total (t = 0)					4.47640		
24	Calculation of PV by formulas:							
25					**Grand**			
26		**Whole Yrs**	**Frac Yr**	**Total**	**Total**			
27	t = S − 1	5.99506	0.13548	6.13054				
28	PV Factor	0.73018	0.73018					
29	t = 0	4.33747	0.09892	**4.447640**	**4.47640**			
31	Assumptions:							
33	S = Beginning year of cash flows (valuation at t = 2.25)							**3.25**
34	n = Ending year of cash flows-whole year							**12.25**
35	z = Ending year of cash flows-stub year							**12.60**
36	r = Discount rate							**15.0%**
37	g = Growth rate in cash flow							**5.1%**
38	p = Proportion of year in the stub period							**0.35**
39	This row is not used							
40	x = (1 + g)/(1 + r)							**0.913913**
41	Gordon model multiple = GM = 1/(r − g)							**10.101010**
43	Spreadsheet formulas:							
45	C17, D17: p*(1 + g)$^{\wedge}$(n − s + 1) stub period cash flow							
46	E17: 1/(1 + r)$^{\wedge}$(z − S + 1) stub period present value factor at t = 2.25							
47	G17: 1/(1 + r)$^{\wedge}$z stub period present value factor for t = 0							
48	B27: GM*(1 − x$^{\wedge}$(n − S + 1)) ADF for years 3.25 to 32.25 at t = 2.25							
49	C27: p*(1 + g)$^{\wedge}$(n − S + 1)/(1 + r)$^{\wedge}$(z − S + 1) PV of stub period CF at t = 2.25							
50	B28, C28: 1/(1 + r)$^{\wedge}$(S − 1) present value factor at t = S − 1 = 2.25							
51	E29: (GM*(1 − x$^{\wedge}$(n − S + 1)) + p*(1 + g)$^{\wedge}$(n − S + 1)/(1 + r)$^{\wedge}$(z − S + 1))/(1 + r)$^{\wedge}$(S − 1)							

Note: E29 is the formula for the Grand Total

Column E. The only exception to the PVF formula is cell E17, the fractional year. Its formula is

$$PVF = \frac{1}{(1 + r)^{n-S+1+0.5p}}$$

(in the EOY formula, the exponent is $z - S + 1$). This formula appears in the spreadsheet at A46. The total present value at $t = 2.25$ of the cash flows from $t = 3.25$ through $t = 12.25$ is $6.42899 (F18). The present value of the fractional year cash flow is $0.13883 (F19), for a total of $6.56782 (F20). In F21 we show the present value factor of 0.73018 to discount from $t = 2.25$ to $t = 0$.[18] Multiplying G20 by G21, we come to the PV of the cash flows in F22 at $t = 0$ of $4.79569 for each $1.00 of starting cash flows. Thus, if our annuity were actually $100,000 at the beginning, with all other assumptions remaining the same, the PV would be $479,569.

Column G contains the present value factors for $t = 0$, the formula of which is the more usual

$$PVF = \frac{1}{(1 + r)^{t-0.5}}$$

When we multiply Column D by Column G to get Column H, the latter is the PV of the cash flows as of time zero. Note that the final sum in H20 is identical to F22, as it should be.

So far we have come to the PV of the cash flows using the brute force method. In the next section we will test the formulas in the preceding pages to see if they produce the same result.

Testing Equations (A3-3) and (A3-4)

Cell B27 contains the formula for the PV of the first 10 whole years of cash flows (see A48 for the spreadsheet formula). It is the same as equation (A3-2) without the rightmost term.[19] The result of $6.42899 in B27 matches F18, thereby demonstrating the accuracy of that portion of equation (A3-2).

Cell C27 is calculated using the rightmost term in equation (A3-2) and comes to $0.13883 (see A49 for the spreadsheet formula), which matches F19, thus proving that portion of the formula. The sum of the two is $6.56782 (D27), which matches F20.

Row 29 is the result of multiplying Row 27 by Row 28, the latter of which is the present value factor to discount the cash flows from $t = 2.25$ to $t = 0$ (it is the same as F21). We total B29 and C29 to $4.79569 (D29), which matches F22 and H20. Finally, in E29 we use the complete formula in equation (A3-3) to produce the same result of $4.79569 (see cell A51 for the spreadsheet formula). Thus, we have demonstrated the accuracy

---

18. This is $1/(1 + r)^{S-1} = 1/1.15^{2.25} = 0.73018$ (see formulas in cell A50).
19. The formulas are the same; however, in the spreadsheet we have substituted GM (Gordon multiple) for $\sqrt{1 + r}/(r - g)$ and x for $(1 + g)/(1 + r)$. Additionally, we have factored out the GM.

of equation (A3-3) as a whole as well as showing how we can calculate the parts.

Table A3-2 is identical to Table A3-1, except that we use end-of-year present values, and equation (A3-4) is the relevant ADF formula. The end-of-year formula gives a grand total of 4.47640 (F22, H20, D29, and E29).

TABLE A3-3: LOAN AMORTIZATION

In the chapter we demonstrated how ADFs are useful in calculating loan payments and the present value of a loan. This section on loan amortization complements the material we presented in the chapter.

The amortization of loan principal in any time period is the PV of the loan at the beginning of the period, less the PV at the end of the period. While this is conceptually easy, it is a cumbersome procedure. Let's develop some preliminary results that will lead us to a more efficient way to calculate loan amortization.

Section 1: Traditional Loan Amortization Schedule

Table A3-3 is a loan amortization schedule that is divided into three sections. Section 1 is a traditional amortization schedule for a $1 million loan at 10% for 5 years. The loan begins on February 28, 1998 (B7), and the first payment is on March 31, 1998 (B8). During the calendar year 1998 there will be 10 payments, leaving 50 more. There will be 12 monthly payments in each of the years 1999–2002, and the final two payments are in the beginning of 2003, with February 28, 2003 (B67), being the final payment.

Column A is the payment number. There are 60 months of the loan, hence 60 payments. Columns D and E are the interest and principal for the particular payment, while columns G and H are interest and principal cumulated in calendar year totals. Because the loan payments begin on March 31, 1998, the first year's totals in columns G and H are totals for the first 10 payments only. Column I is the present value factor (PVF) at 10%, and column J is the present value of each loan payment. Column K is the sum of the present values of the loan payments by calendar year. Note that the PV of the loan payments sum to $1 million (J68).

Section 2: Present Values of Yearly Loan Payment

In Section 2 we calculate the present value of each year's loan payment using the ADF equation for no growth, no stub period, and end-of-year cash flows. We could use equation (3-11b) from the chapter, but first we will simplify it further by setting $g = 0$, so equation (3-11b) reduces to:

$$\text{ADF} = \left[\frac{1}{r} - \frac{1}{(1+r)^{n-S+1}}\frac{1}{r}\right]\frac{1}{(1+r)^{S-v-1}}$$

$$= \frac{1}{r}\left[1 - \frac{1}{(1+r)^{n-S+1}}\right]\frac{1}{(1+r)^{S-v-1}} \tag{A3-5}$$

Cells D77 through D82 list the PV of the various calendar years' cash flows discounted to the inception of the loan, February 28, 1998. Note that these amounts exactly match those in column K of Section 1, and the total is exactly $1 million—the principal of the loan—as it should be. This demonstrates the accuracy of equation (A3-5), as all amounts calculated in D77 through D82 use that equation (note that v, the valuation date in months, appears in Row 86).

In Column E we are viewing the cash flows from January 1, 1999, i.e., immediately after the last payment in 1998 and one month before the first payment in 1999. Therefore, the 1998 cash flows drop out entirely and the PV of the 1999–2003 cash flows increase relative to column D because we discount the cash flows 10 months less. The difference between the sum of the 1998 PVs discounted to February 28, 1998, and the 1999 payments discounted to January 1, 1999,[20] is $1 million (D84) − $865,911 (E84) = $134,089 (E85). We follow the same procedure each year to calculate the difference in the PVs (Row 85), and finally we come to a total of the reductions in PV of $1 million, in K85, which is identical with the original principal of the loan.

There are some significant numbers that repeat in southeasterly-sloped diagonals in Section 2. The PV $241,675 appears in cells E78, F79, G80, and H81. This means that the 1999 payments as seen from the beginning of 1999 have the same PV as the 2000 payments as seen from the beginning of 2000, etc. through 2002. Similarly, the PV of $218,767 repeats in cells E79, F80, and G81. The interpretation of this series is the same as before, except everything is moved back one year, i.e., the 2000 payments as seen from the beginning of 1999 have the same PV as the 2001 payments as seen from the beginning of 2000 and the 2002 payments as seen from the beginning of 2001.

This downward-sloping pattern gives us a clue to a more direct formula for loan amortization. At the start of the loan, we have 60 payments of $21,247. In the first calendar year, 10 payments will be made, for a total of $212,470. At the end of the first year, which effectively is the same as January 1, 1999, 50 payments will remain. The PV of the final 50 payments discounted to January 1, 1999, is the same as the PV of the first 50 payments discounted to March 1, 1998 (using March 1 synonymously with February 28 in a present value sense), because the entire time line will have shifted by 10 months (10 payments). Therefore, the first calendar year's loan amortization can be represented by the PV of the final 10 payments discounted to March 1, 1998, as that would make up the only difference in the two series of cash flows as perceived from their different points in time. This is illustrated graphically in Figure A3-2.

Figure A3-2 is a time line of payments on the five-year (60-month) loan. The top portion of the figure, labeled A, graphically represents the entire payment schedule. In the bottom figure the loan is split into several pieces: payments 1–10, which are not labeled;[21] payments 1–50, labeled

20. Technically, we discount to the end of December 31, 1998, but in PV terms it is easier to think of January 1, 1999.
21. In all cases the zero is there only as a valuation date. There are no loan payments (cash flows) that occur at zero.

Payment Schedule

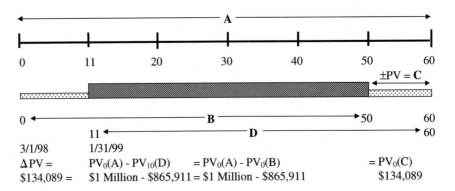

3/1/98   1/31/99

$\Delta PV =$

$\$134,089 =$ $PV_0(A) - PV_{10}(D)$ $= PV_0(A) - PV_0(B)$ $= PV_0(C)$

         $\$1$ Million $- \$865,911 = \$1$ Million $- \$865,911$ $\$134,089$

B; payments 11–60, labeled D; and payments 51–60, labeled C ($t = 50$ is the end of B, not the beginning of C).

The equation at the bottom of Figure A3-2, which we explain below in 1–3, is: $\Delta PV = PV_0(A) - PV_{10}(D) = PV_0(A) - PV_0(B) = PV_0(C)$. The amortization of the loan principal during any year is the change in the present value of the loan between years. That is equal to each of the following three expressions:

1. $PV_0(A) - PV_{10}(D)$: The PV at $t = 0$ of A (all 60 months of the loan) minus the PV at $t = 10$ of D, the last 50 payments of the loan. Notice that the valuation dates are different, $t = 0$ versus $t = 10$. The PV at $t = 0$ of A is the principal, $\$1$ million (Table A3-3, Section 2, D84). The PV at $t = 10$ of D is $\$865,911$ (E84). The difference of the two is the amortization of $\$134,089$ (E85).

2. $PV_0(A) - PV_0(B)$: The PV at $t = 0$ of A (all 60 months of the loan), which is $\$1$ million, minus the PV at $t = 0$ of the first 50 months of the loan. The latter calculation does not appear directly in Table A3-3. However, using equation (3-6d) from the chapter with $g = 0$, $r = 0.83333\%$, and $n = 50$ periods leads to the ADF of 40.75442. Multiplying the ADF by the monthly payment of $\$21,247.04$ gives us the PV of B, which is $\$865,911$. The difference of the two PVs is $\$134,089$, the same as above.

3. $PV_0(C)$: The PV at $t = 0$ of C, payments 51–60. This is the most important of the expressions because it is the most compact and the easiest to use. The other expressions are the difference of two formulas, while this one requires only a single formula. It is stated in mathematical terms below in equation (A3-10). The reduction in the principal is the PV of the opposite or mirror-image series of cash flows working backward from the end of the loan.

Section 3: A Better Way to Calculate Loan Amortization

In Section 3 we calculate the principal reduction using equation (A3-10). Let's look first at the 1998 cash flows in Row 93. The amortization of principal in 1998 is equal to the PV of the *last* 10 payments of the loan.

Letting n (the final payment period) = 60, we want to calculate the PV of payments 51–60, discounted to month 0. If we let F = finishing month = 10, the formula $n - F + 1$ describes S, the starting month in C93 through C98. The formula $n - S + 1$ describes F, the finishing month in D93 through D98. For 1998, $S = 60 - 10$ (D93) $+ 1 = 51$, and $F = 60 - 1$ (C93) $+ 1 = 60$. Thus, our formulas give us the result that in calendar 1998 the amortization of principal is equal to the PV at $t = 0$ of payments 51–60, which is correct.

For calendar 1999, $S = 60 - 22$ (D94) $+ 1 = 39$, and $F = 60 - 11$ (C94) $+ 1 = 50$. The amortization of principal in calendar 1999 is the PV at $t = 0$ of payments 39–50, which is also correct. Thus, the amortization of principal in any year is equal to an ADF with no growth and end-of-year cash flows that run from $n - F + 1$ to $n - S + 1$. We begin the calculation of this loan amortization ADF in equation (A3-6).

$$\text{ADF} = \frac{1}{(1 + r)^{n-F+1}} + \frac{1}{(1 + r)^{n-F+2}} + \ldots + \frac{1}{(1 + r)^{n-S+1}} \quad \text{(A3-6)}$$

Multiplying equation (A3-6) by $1/(1 + r)$, we get:

$$\frac{1}{1 + r} \text{ADF} = \frac{1}{(1 + r)^{n-F+2}} + \frac{1}{(1 + r)^{n-F+3}}$$

$$+ \ldots + \frac{1}{(1 + r)^{n-S+1}} + \frac{1}{(1 + r)^{n-S+2}} \quad \text{(A3-7)}$$

Subtracting equation (A3-7) from equation (A3-6), we get:

$$\left(1 - \frac{1}{1 + r}\right) \text{ADF} = \frac{1}{(1 + r)^{n-F+1}} - \frac{1}{(1 + r)^{n-S+2}} \quad \text{(A3-8)}$$

The left-hand side of equation (A3-8) simplifies to $r/(1 + r)$ ADF. Multiplying both sides of equation (A3-8) by $(1 + r)/r$, we come to:

$$\text{ADF} = \frac{1 + r}{r} \left[\frac{1}{(1 + r)^{n-F+1}} - \frac{1}{(1 + r)^{n-S+2}} \right] \quad \text{(A3-9)}$$

Canceling out the $1 + r$ in the numerator and denominator, we arrive at our final solution:

$$\text{ADF} = \frac{1}{r} \left[\frac{1}{(1 + r)^{n-F}} - \frac{1}{(1 + r)^{n-S+1}} \right]$$

ADF formula for loan amortization   (A3-10)

The spreadsheet formulas begin in column F of Rows 93 through 98. Note that we multiply the ADF in equation (A3-10) by the monthly payment in F93 through F98 to calculate the PV of the loan. I is the monthly interest rate = 10%/12 months = 0.833%, which is equivalent to r in equation (A3-10).

The amortization in 1998 is \$134,089 (E93), which equals:

$$\text{ADF} = \frac{1}{0.008333} \left[\frac{1}{1.008333^{60-10}} - \frac{1}{1.008333^{60-1+1}} \right] \quad \text{(A3-10a)}$$

The amortization in 1999 is \$176,309, as per E94, which equals:

$$ADF = \frac{1}{0.008333} \left[\frac{1}{1.008333^{60-22}} - \frac{1}{1.008333^{60-11+1}} \right] \quad (A3\text{-}10b)$$

The principal amortization in cells E93 through E98 is equal to that in column H of Section 1, which demonstrates the accuracy of equation (A3-10).

The After-Tax Cost of a Loan

In our discussion in Table A3-3, Sections 2 and 3, we came to the insight that principal amortizes in mirror image, and we used that understanding to develop equation (A3-10) to calculate the principal amortization over any given block of time. Now it is appropriate to present month-by-month amortization of principal, as it will enable us to develop formulas to calculate the PV of principal and interest of a loan. The primary practical application is to calculate the after-tax cost of a loan.

We begin with a month-by-month amortization. In the first month, amortization equals the PVF for the last month. In the second month, amortization equals the PVF for the second-to-last month, and we continue in that fashion. Mathematically, amortization is thus equal to:

$$\text{Amort} = \left[\frac{1}{(1+r)^n} + \frac{1}{(1+r)^{n-1}} + \frac{1}{(1+r)^{n-2}} + \dots + \frac{1}{1+r} \right] \times \text{Pymt}$$

$$(A3\text{-}11)$$

Note that this expression is the exact reverse of a simple series of cash flows that solves to an end-of-year ADF with no growth, i.e., equation (3-6d) in the body of the chapter. Thus, the total amortization equals equation (3-6d) $\times$ Loan Payment = Principal of the Loan. This is a rearrangement of equation (3-21). Note that one should use the nominal interest rate in this calculation.

Next we take the PV of equation (A3-11) at the nominal rate of interest (when valuing a loan at a discount rate other than the nominal rate of interest, see that discussion at the end of this chapter).

$$\text{PV (Amort)} = \left[\frac{\frac{1}{(1+r)^n}}{1+r} + \frac{\frac{1}{(1+r)^{n-1}}}{(1+r)^2} + \frac{\frac{1}{(1+r)^{n-2}}}{(1+r)^3} \right. $$
$$\left. + \dots + \frac{\frac{1}{1+r}}{(1+r)^n} \right] \times \text{Pymt} \quad (A3\text{-}12)$$

We can move the second denominator into the first denominator, and equation (A3-12) simplifies to:

$$\text{PV (Amort)} = \left[\frac{1}{(1+r)^{n+1}} + \frac{1}{(1+r)^{n+1}} + \frac{1}{(1+r)^{n+1}} \right.$$
$$\left. + \dots + \frac{1}{(1+r)^{n+1}} \right] \times \text{Pymt} \ [n \text{ terms}] \quad (A3\text{-}13)$$

T A B L E   A3-3

Amortization of Principal with Irregular Starting Point

	A	B	C	D	E	F	G	H	I	J	K	L	M	N	O
4						SECTION 1: LOAN AMORTIZATION SCHEDULE									
5/6	Pmt #	Date	Pmt	Int	Prin	Bal	Int	Prin	PVF	NPV Pymt	Annual NPV	Aft-Tax Cost-Loan			
7	0	02/28/98				1,000,000			1.0000						
8	1	03/31/98	21,247	8,333	12,914	987,086			0.9917	21,071		17,766	12807	4959	
9	2	04/30/98	21,247	8,226	13,021	974,065			0.9835	20,897		17,661	12807	4854	
10	3	05/31/98	21,247	8,117	13,130	960,935			0.9754	20,725		17,558	12807	4751	
11	4	06/30/98	21,247	8,008	13,239	947,696			0.9673	20,553		17,455	12807	4648	
12	5	07/31/98	21,247	7,897	13,350	934,346			0.9594	20,383		17,353	12807	4546	
13	6	08/31/98	21,247	7,786	13,461	920,885			0.9514	20,215		17,252	12807	4445	
14	7	09/30/98	21,247	7,674	13,573	907,312			0.9436	20,048		17,152	12807	4345	
15	8	10/31/98	21,247	7,561	13,686	893,626			0.9358	19,882		17,052	12807	4245	
16	9	11/30/98	21,247	7,447	13,800	879,826			0.9280	19,718		16,954	12807	4147	
17	10	12/31/98	21,247	7,332	13,915	865,911	78,381	134,089	0.9204	19,555	203,048	16,856	12807	4049	
18	11	01/31/99	21,247	7,216	14,031	851,880			0.9128	19,393		16,759	12807	3952	
19	12	02/28/99	21,247	7,099	14,148	837,732			0.9052	19,233		16,663	12807	3856	
20	13	03/31/99	21,247	6,981	14,266	823,466			0.8977	19,074		16,567	12807	3760	
21	14	04/30/99	21,247	6,862	14,385	809,081			0.8903	18,917		16,473	12807	3666	
22	15	05/31/99	21,247	6,742	14,505	794,576			0.8830	18,760		16,379	12807	3572	
23	16	06/30/99	21,247	6,621	14,626	779,951			0.8757	18,605		16,286	12807	3479	
24	17	07/31/99	21,247	6,500	14,747	765,203			0.8684	18,451		16,194	12807	3387	
25	18	08/31/99	21,247	6,377	14,870	750,333			0.8612	18,299		16,102	12807	3295	
26	19	09/30/99	21,247	6,253	14,994	735,339			0.8541	18,148		16,011	12807	3204	
27	20	10/31/99	21,247	6,128	15,119	720,220			0.8471	17,998		15,921	12807	3114	
28	21	11/30/99	21,247	6,002	15,245	704,974			0.8401	17,849		15,832	12807	3025	
29	22	12/31/99	21,247	5,875	15,372	689,602	78,656	176,309	0.8331	17,701	222,428	15,744	12807	2937	
30	23	01/31/00	21,247	5,747	15,500	674,102			0.8262	17,555		15,656	12807	2849	
31	24	02/28/00	21,247	5,618	15,630	658,472			0.8194	17,410		15,569	12807	2762	
32	25	03/31/00	21,247	5,487	15,760	642,712			0.8126	17,266		15,482	12807	2675	
33	26	04/30/00	21,247	5,356	15,891	626,821			0.8059	17,123		15,397	12807	2590	
34	27	05/31/00	21,247	5,224	16,024	610,798			0.7993	16,982		15,312	12807	2505	
35	28	06/30/00	21,247	5,090	16,157	594,641			0.7927	16,842		15,228	12807	2421	
36	29	07/31/00	21,247	4,955	16,292	578,349			0.7861	16,702		15,144	12807	2337	
37	30	08/31/00	21,247	4,820	16,427	561,922			0.7796	16,564		15,061	12807	2254	

T A B L E A3-3 (continued)

Amortization of Principal with Irregular Starting Point

	A	B	C	D	E	F	G	H	I	J	K	L	M	N	O
4							SECTION 1: LOAN AMORTIZATION SCHEDULE								
5/6	Pmt #	Date	Pmt	Int	Prin	Bal	Int	Prin	PVF	NPV Pymt	Annual NPV	Aft-Tax Cost-Loan			
38	31	09/30/00	21,247	4,683	16,564	545,357			0.7732	16,427		14,979	12807	2172	
39	32	10/31/00	21,247	4,545	16,702	528,655			0.7668	16,292		14,898	12807	2091	
40	33	11/30/00	21,247	4,405	16,842	511,813			0.7604	16,157		14,817	12807	2010	
41	34	12/31/00	21,247	4,265	16,982	494,831	60,194	194,771	0.7542	16,024	201,345	14,737	12807	1930	
42	35	01/31/01	21,247	4,124	17,123	477,708			0.7479	15,891		14,657	12807	1850	
43	36	02/28/01	21,247	3,981	17,266	460,442			0.7417	15,760		14,579	12807	1772	
44	37	03/31/01	21,247	3,837	17,410	443,032			0.7356	15,630		14,501	12807	1694	
45	38	04/30/01	21,247	3,692	17,555	425,476			0.7295	15,500		14,423	12807	1616	
46	39	05/31/01	21,247	3,546	17,701	407,775			0.7235	15,372		14,346	12807	1539	
47	40	06/30/01	21,247	3,398	17,849	389,926			0.7175	15,245		14,270	12807	1463	
48	41	07/31/01	21,247	3,249	17,998	371,928			0.7116	15,119		14,194	12807	1387	
49	42	08/31/01	21,247	3,099	18,148	353,781			0.7057	14,994		14,119	12807	1312	
50	43	09/30/01	21,247	2,948	18,299	335,482			0.6999	14,870		14,045	12807	1238	
51	44	10/31/01	21,247	2,796	18,451	317,031			0.6941	14,747		13,971	12807	1164	
52	45	11/30/01	21,247	2,642	18,605	298,425			0.6884	14,626		13,898	12807	1091	
53	46	12/31/01	21,247	2,487	18,760	279,665	39,799	215,166	0.6827	14,505	182,260	13,826	12807	1019	
54	47	01/31/02	21,247	2,331	18,917	260,749			0.6770	14,385		13,754	12807	947	
55	48	02/28/02	21,247	2,173	19,074	241,675			0.6714	14,266		13,682	12807	875	
56	49	03/31/02	21,247	2,014	19,233	222,442			0.6659	14,148		13,612	12807	805	
57	50	04/30/02	21,247	1,854	19,393	203,048			0.6604	14,031		13,541	12807	734	
58	51	05/31/02	21,247	1,692	19,555	183,493			0.6549	13,915		13,472	12807	665	
59	52	06/30/02	21,247	1,529	19,718	163,775			0.6495	13,800		13,403	12807	596	
60	53	07/31/02	21,247	1,365	19,882	143,893			0.6441	13,686		13,334	12807	527	
61	54	08/31/02	21,247	1,199	20,048	123,845			0.6388	13,573		13,267	12807	460	
62	55	09/30/02	21,247	1,032	20,215	103,630			0.6335	13,461		13,199	12807	392	
63	56	10/31/02	21,247	864	20,383	83,247			0.6283	13,350		13,133	12807	326	
64	57	11/30/02	21,247	694	20,553	62,693			0.6231	13,239		13,066	12807	259	
65	58	12/31/02	21,247	522	20,725	41,969	17,268	237,697	0.6180	13,130	164,984	13,001	12807	194	
66	59	01/31/03	21,247	350	20,897	21,071			0.6129	13,021		12,936	12807	129	
67	60	02/28/03	21,247	176	21,071	0	525	41,969	0.6078	12,914	25,935	12,871	12807	64	
68	Totals		1,274,823	274,823	1,000,000		274,823	1,000,000		1,000,000	1,000,000	907,368			

T A B L E A3-3 (continued)

Amortization of Principal with Irregular Starting Point

SECTION 2: SCHEDULE OF PRESENT VALUES CALCULATED BY ADF EQUATION (A3-5)

As Seen From The Beginning of Year

	1998	1999	2000	2001	2002	2003	2004	Total
NPV 1998 payments [1]	203,048							
NPV 1999 payments	222,428	241,675						
NPV 2000 payments	201,345	218,767	241,675					
NPV 2001 payments	182,260	198,031	218,767	241,675				
NPV 2002 payments	164,984	179,260	198,031	218,767	241,675			
NPV 2003 payments	25,935	28,179	31,130	34,390	37,991	41,969		
NPV 2004 payments							0	
Sum NPVs-all pymts	1,000,000	865,911	689,602	494,831	279,665	41,969	0	
Reduction in NPV		134,089	176,309	194,771	215,166	237,697	41,969	1,000,000
Valuation date = v	10	22	34	46	58			

0

SECTION 3: AMORTIZATION CALCULATED AS THE PYMT * THE ADF in (A3-16)

Formulas For Principal Amortization, where:
I = Monthly Interest = 0.833%, n = 60 Months,
Pymt = $21,247/Month

	Starting Month	Finishing Month	Prin Amort	
Calendar 1998	1	10	134,089	PYMT*(1/r)*((1/(1 + r)^(N − $D93) − (1/(1 + r)^(N − $C93 + 1))))
Calendar 1999	11	22	176,309	PYMT*(1/r)*((1/(1 + r)^(N − $D94) − (1/(1 + r)^(N − $C94 + 1))))
Calendar 2000	23	34	194,771	PYMT*(1/r)*((1/(1 + r)^(N − $D95) − (1/(1 + r)^(N − $C95 + 1))))
Calendar 2001	35	46	215,166	PYMT*(1/r)*((1/(1 + r)^(N − $D96) − (1/(1 + r)^(N − $C96 + 1))))
Calendar 2002	47	58	237,697	PYMT*(1/r)*((1/(1 + r)^(N − $D97) − (1/(1 + r)^(N − $C97 + 1))))
Calendar 2003	59	60	41,969	PYMT*(1/r)*((1/(1 + r)^(N − $D98) − (1/(1 + r)^(N − $C98 + 1))))
Total			1,000,000	

T A B L E A3-3 *(continued)*

Amortization of Principal with Irregular Starting Point

	A	B	C	D	E	F	G	H	I	J	K	L	M	N	O
102	Assumptions:					After-Tax Cost of the Loan									
104	Prin		1,000,000			(1 – t) * Prin		0.600000	600,000						
105	Int		10.0000%			t*n/(1 + r)^(n + 1)*PYMT		0.307368	307,368						
106	Int-Mo		0.8333%			Total = L68		**0.907368**	**907,368**						
107	Years		5												
108	Months = n		60			**H106: (1 – t) + [t*N/(1 + r)^(N + 1)*PYMT/P] Equation (A3-24a)**									
109	Pymt		21,247			**I106: (1 – t)*P + [t*N/(1 + r)^(N + 1)*PYMT] Equation (A3-23a)**									
110	Form-Prin		1,000,000												
111	Start month = S		3												
112	x = (1 + g)/(1 + r)		0.9917												
113	y = 1/(1 + r)		0.9917												
114	GM = 1/r		120												

Notes:

[1] Formula for D77 according to (A3-5): GM*(1 – x^($D93 – $C93 + 1))y ($C93 – A$86 – 1)*PYMT

n = # months of cash flow = $D93 – $C93 + 1, which is the ending month - beginning month +1. The exponent of y is the ending month - the valuation date); thus it is the discounting period. This formula copies both down and across, i.e., it is the formula for all cells from D77 to I82. D78 > D77 because there are 10 payments in 1998 and 12 in 1999–2002.

All the bracketed terms in equation (A3-13) are identical. Thus, the PV of the amortization of principal, which we denote below as PV(P), is equal to $n \times$ any one of these terms $\times$ the loan payment.

$$\text{PV (Amort)} \equiv \text{PV }(P) = \frac{n}{(1 + r)^{n+1}} \times \text{Pymt}$$

PV of principal payments   (A3-14)

Restating equation (3-21) as equation (A3-15),

$$\text{Pymt} = \frac{P}{\text{ADF}},$$ (A3-15)

where ADF is defined by equation (3-6d). Substituting equation (A3-15) into equation (A3-14), we get:

$$\text{PV}(P) = \frac{n}{(1 + r)^{n+1}} \times \frac{P}{\text{ADF}}$$ (A3-16)

The next section, in which we develop equations (3-16a) and (3-16b), is somewhat of a digression from the previous and the subsequent discussion. We do not use equations (A3-16a) and (A3-16b) in our subsequent work. However, these formulas can be useful alternative forms of (A3-16). Substituting in the definition of the ADF, dividing through by the principal, and solving the equation,[22] another form of equation (A3-16) is:

$$\frac{\text{PV}(P)}{P} = \frac{n}{[(1 + r)^n - 1](1 + r)}$$ (A3-16a)

Table A3-4 verifies the accuracy of this formula, which is my own formula, to the best of my knowledge. For a five-year (60-month) loan at 12% per year, or 1% per month (A5 and A4, respectively), the present

T A B L E A3-4

PV of Principal Amortization

	A	B
4	r	1%
5	n	60
6	PV(P)/Pmt	32.69997718
7	Pmt/P	$0.0222444
8	PV(P)/P	$0.7273929
9	PV(P)/P	$0.7273929
11	Cell Formulas:	
13	B6: $= n/(1 + r)\wedge(n + 1)$	
14	B7: $= \text{PMT}(.01,60,-1)$	
15	B9: $= \text{B7}*\text{B8}$	
16	B10: $= (n*r)/(((1 + r)\wedge n - 1)*(1 + r))$	

---

22. We do not show the steps to the solution, as we are not using this equation in our subsequent work.

value of the principal divided by the loan payment is 32.69997718 (B6). The formula for that cell appears in cell A13, and that formula is equation (A3-14) after dividing both sides of the equation by the payment. In B7 we show the monthly payment per dollar of loan principal, which we calculate using a standard spreadsheet financial function for a $1 loan with 60 monthly payments at 1% interest (see cell A14 for the formula). In B8 we multiply B6 × B7. In B9 we test equation (A3-16a), and it comes to the same answer as B8, i.e., the present value of the principal is $0.7273929 per $1 of principal. That the two answers are identical demonstrates the accuracy of equation (A3-16a). Of course, the present value of the interest on a pretax basis is one minus that, or approximately $0.273 per $1 of principal.

In algebraic terms, the present value of the interest portion of a loan per dollar of principal on a pretax basis is one minus (A3-16a), or:

$$\frac{PV(Int)}{P} = 1 - \frac{n}{[(1 + r)^n - 1](1 + r)} \qquad \text{(A3-16b)}$$

Resuming our discussion after the digression in the last several paragraphs, the PV of the interest portion of the payments is simply the PV of the loan payments—which is the principal—minus the PV of the principal portion, or:

$$PV(Int) = P - PV(P) \qquad \text{(A3-17)}$$

Substituting equation (A3-16) into equation (A3-17), we get:

$$PV(Int) = P - \frac{n}{(1 + r)^{n+1}} \frac{P}{ADF} = P\left[1 - \frac{n}{(1 + r)^{n+1}} \frac{1}{ADF}\right] \qquad \text{(A3-18)}$$

The PV of the after-tax cost of the interest portion is $(1 - t) * $ (A3-18), where t is the tax rate, or:

$$PV(Int)_{After-Tax} = (1 - t) P\left[1 - \frac{n}{(1 + r)^{n+1}} \frac{1}{ADF}\right] \qquad \text{(A3-19)}$$

Thus, the after-tax cost of the loan, L, is (A3-16) plus (A3-19), or:

$$L = \frac{n}{(1 + r)^{n+1}} \frac{P}{ADF} + (1 - t)P\left[1 - \frac{n}{(1 + r)^{n+1}} \frac{1}{ADF}\right] \qquad \text{(A3-20)}$$

Factoring terms, we get:

$$L = \frac{n}{(1 + r)^{n+1}} \frac{P}{ADF} [1 - (1 - t)] + (1 - t)P \qquad \text{(A3-21)}$$

which simplifies to:

$$L = t \frac{n}{(1 + r)^{n+1}} \frac{P}{ADF} + (1 - t)P \qquad \text{(A3-22)}$$

Switching terms, our final equation for the after-tax cost of a loan is:

$$L = (1 - t)P + \left[t \frac{n}{(1 + r)^{n+1}} \frac{P}{ADF}\right] \quad \text{after-tax cost of a loan} \quad \text{(A3-23)}$$

Alternatively, using

$$\text{Loan Payment} = \frac{P}{\text{ADF}}$$

we can restate equation (A3-23) as:

$$L = (1 - t)P + \left[t \frac{n}{(1 + r)^{n+1}} \text{Pymt} \right]$$

(A3-23a)

alternative expression—after-tax cost of loan

Equation (A3-23) gives us the equation for the after-tax cost of a loan in dollars. We can restate equation (A3-23) to give us the after-tax cost of the loan for each \$1.00 of loan principal by dividing through by P.

$$\frac{L}{P} = (1 - t) + \left[t \frac{n}{(1 + r)^{n+1}} \frac{1}{\text{ADF}} \right]$$

after-tax cost of loan per each \$1.00 of principal   (A3-24)

Analyzing equation (A3-24), we can see the after-tax cost of the loan is made up of two parts:

1. The after-tax cost of the principal, as if the entire loan payment was tax-deductible, plus

2. The tax rate times the PV of the principal payments on the loan.

In item 1 we temporarily assume that principal and interest are tax-deductible. This is actually true for ESOP loans, and the PV of an ESOP loan is item 1. To adjust item 1 upwards for the lack of tax shield on the principal of ordinary loans, in item 2 we add back the tax shield included in item 1 that we do not really get. Of course, we can substitute the exact expression for ADF in equation (A3-24) to keep the solution strictly in terms of the variables t, n, and r.

We can derive an alternative expression for equation (A3-24) by dividing equation (A3-23a) by P:

$$\frac{L}{P} = (1 - t) + \left[t \frac{n}{(1 + r)^{n+1}} \frac{\text{Pymt}}{P} \right]$$

alternative expression—after-tax cost of loan/\$1 of principal

(A3-24a)

We demonstrate the accuracy of equations (A3-23a) and (A3-24a) in Table A3-3. In Section 1, Column L is the after-tax cost of each loan payment. It is equal to the sum of [Principal (Column E) + (1 − Tax Rate) × Interest (Column D)] × Present Value Factor (Column I). We assume a 40% tax rate in this table. Thus cell L8, the after-tax cost of the first month's loan payment, is equal to [\$12,914 (E8) + (1 − 40%) × \$8,333 (D8)] × 0.9917 (I8) = \$17,766. The sum of the after-tax cost of the loan payments is \$907,368 (L68).

We now move to Section 3, F102 to J109. Here we use equation (A3-24a) to test if we get the same answer as the brute force approach in L68. In I104 we show the PV of the principal after tax, corresponding to item 1 above, as \$600,000 (H104 is the same, but for each \$1.00 of principal). In I105 we show the tax shield on the principal that we do not get at

$307,368. The sum of the two is $907,368 (I106), which matches L68 and thus proves equation (A3-24a). Note that I106, which we calculate according to equation (A3-23a), equals $0.907368, which is the correct after-tax cost of the loan per each dollar of principal. When we multiply that by the $1 million principal, we get the correct after-tax cost of the loan in dollars, as per cell I106 and equation (A3-23a).

TABLE A3-5

Present Value of a Loan at Discount Rate Different than Nominal Rate

	A	B	C	D	E	F	G
5	Pmt						
6	#	Pmt	Int	Prin	Bal	PVF (r_1)	PV(P)
7	0				1,000,000	1.0000	
8	1	21,247	8,333	12,914	987,086	0.9901	12,786
9	2	21,247	8,226	13,021	974,065	0.9803	12,765
10	3	21,247	8,117	13,130	960,935	0.9706	12,744
11	4	21,247	8,008	13,239	947,696	0.9610	12,723
12	5	21,247	7,897	13,350	934,346	0.9515	12,702
13	6	21,247	7,786	13,461	920,885	0.9420	12,681
14	7	21,247	7,674	13,573	907,312	0.9327	12,660
15	8	21,247	7,561	13,686	893,626	0.9235	12,639
16	9	21,247	7,447	13,800	879,826	0.9143	12,618
17	10	21,247	7,332	13,915	865,911	0.9053	12,597
18	11	21,247	7,216	14,031	851,880	0.8963	12,576
19	12	21,247	7,099	14,148	837,732	0.8874	12,556
20	13	21,247	6,981	14,266	823,466	0.8787	12,535
21	14	21,247	6,862	14,385	809,081	0.8700	12,514
22	15	21,247	6,742	14,505	794,576	0.8613	12,494
23	16	21,247	6,621	14,626	779,951	0.8528	12,473
24	17	21,247	6,500	14,747	765,203	0.8444	12,452
25	18	21,247	6,377	14,870	750,333	0.8360	12,432
26	19	21,247	6,253	14,994	735,339	0.8277	12,411
27	20	21,247	6,128	15,119	720,220	0.8195	12,391
28	21	21,247	6,002	15,245	704,974	0.8114	12,370
29	22	21,247	5,875	15,372	689,602	0.8034	12,350
30	23	21,247	5,747	15,500	674,102	0.7954	12,330
31	24	21,247	5,618	15,630	658,472	0.7876	12,309
32	25	21,247	5,487	15,760	642,712	0.7798	12,289
33	26	21,247	5,356	15,891	626,821	0.7720	12,269
34	27	21,247	5,224	16,024	610,798	0.7644	12,248
35	28	21,247	5,090	16,157	594,641	0.7568	12,228
36	29	21,247	4,955	16,292	578,349	0.7493	12,208
37	30	21,247	4,820	16,427	561,922	0.7419	12,188
38	31	21,247	4,683	16,564	545,357	0.7346	12,168
39	32	21,247	4,545	16,702	528,655	0.7273	12,148
40	33	21,247	4,405	16,842	511,813	0.7201	12,128
41	34	21,247	4,265	16,982	494,831	0.7130	12,108
42	35	21,247	4,124	17,123	477,708	0.7059	12,088
43	36	21,247	3,981	17,266	460,442	0.6989	12,068
44	37	21,247	3,837	17,410	443,032	0.6920	12,048
45	38	21,247	3,692	17,555	425,476	0.6852	12,028
46	39	21,247	3,546	17,701	407,775	0.6784	12,008
47	40	21,247	3,398	17,849	389,926	0.6717	11,988
48	41	21,247	3,249	17,998	371,928	0.6650	11,968
49	42	21,247	3,099	18,148	353,781	0.6584	11,949

Present Value of a Loan at Discount Rate Different than Nominal Rate

	A	B	C	D	E	F	G
5	**Pmt**						
6	**#**	**Pmt**	**Int**	**Prin**	**Bal**	**PVF (r₁)**	**PV(P)**
50	43	21,247	2,948	18,299	335,482	0.6519	11,929
51	44	21,247	2,796	18,451	317,031	0.6454	11,909
52	45	21,247	2,642	18,605	298,425	0.6391	11,890
53	46	21,247	2,487	18,760	279,665	0.6327	11,870
54	47	21,247	2,331	18,917	260,749	0.6265	11,850
55	48	21,247	2,173	19,074	241,675	0.6203	11,831
56	49	21,247	2,014	19,233	222,442	0.6141	11,811
57	50	21,247	1,854	19,393	203,048	0.6080	11,792
58	51	21,247	1,692	19,555	183,493	0.6020	11,772
59	52	21,247	1,529	19,718	163,775	0.5961	11,753
60	53	21,247	1,365	19,882	143,893	0.5902	11,734
61	54	21,247	1,199	20,048	123,845	0.5843	11,714
62	55	21,247	1,032	20,215	103,630	0.5785	11,695
63	56	21,247	864	20,383	83,247	0.5728	11,676
64	57	21,247	694	20,553	62,693	0.5671	11,656
65	58	21,247	522	20,725	41,969	0.5615	11,637
66	59	21,247	350	20,897	21,071	0.5560	11,618
67	60	21,247	176	21,071	0	0.5504	11,599
68	Total	1,274,823	274,823	1,000,000			730,970
70	**Assumptions:**						
72	Prin	1,000,000					
73	Int	10.0000%					
74	Int − Mo = r	0.8333%					
75	Int	12.0000%					
76	Int − Mo = r₁	1.0000%					
77	Years	5					
78	Months = n	60					
79	Pymt	21,247					
80	Start month = S	3					
81	(1/(r₁ − r))*((1/(1 + r)^n) − (1/(1 + r₁)^n))*PYMT						730,970

Present Value of the Principal when the Discount Rate is Different than the Nominal Rate

When valuing a loan at a discount rate, r_1, that is different than the nominal rate of interest, r, the present value of principal is as follows:

$$PV\ (Amort) = \left[\frac{\frac{1}{(1 + r)^n}}{1 + r_1} + \frac{\frac{1}{(1 + r)^{n-1}}}{(1 + r_1)^2} + \frac{\frac{1}{(1 + r)^{n-2}}}{(1 + r_1)^3} \right.$$

$$\left. + \ldots + \frac{\frac{1}{1 + r}}{(1 + r_1)^n} \right] \times Pymt \qquad (A3\text{-}25)$$

We can move the second denominator into the first to simplify the equation:

$$PV \text{ (Amort)} = \frac{1}{(1 + r)^n(1 + r_1)} + \frac{1}{(1 + r)^{n-1}(1 + r_1)^2}$$

$$+ \ldots + \frac{1}{(1 + r)(1 + r_1)^n} \times Pymt \qquad \text{(A3-26)}$$

Multiplying both sides by $(1 + r)/(1 + r_1)$, we get:

$$\frac{1 + r}{1 + r_1} PV \text{ (Amort)} = \left[\frac{1}{(1 + r)^{n-1}(1 + r_1)^2} + \frac{1}{(1 + r)^{n-2}(1 + r_1)^3} \right.$$

$$\left. + \ldots + \frac{1}{(1 + r)(1 + r_1)^n} \right] \times Pymt \qquad \text{(A3-27)}$$

Subtracting equation (A3-27) from equation (A3-26) and simplifying, we get:

$$\frac{r_1 - r}{1 + r_1} PV \text{ (Amort)} = \left[\frac{1}{(1 + r)^n(1 + r_1)} - \frac{1}{(1 + r)(1 + r_1)^n} \right] \times Pymt$$

$$\text{(A3-28)}$$

This simplifies to:

$$PV \text{ (Amort)} = \frac{1}{r_1 - r} \left[\frac{1}{(1 + r)^n} - \frac{1}{(1 + r_1)^n} \right] \times Pymt \qquad \text{(A3-29)}$$

Table A3-5 is almost identical to Section 1 of Table A3-3. We use a nominal interest rate of 10% per year (B73), which is 0.8333% per month (B74), and a discount rate of 12% per year (B75), or 1% per month (B76).

We discount the principal amortization at r_1, the discount rate of 1%, in Column F, so that Column G gives us the present value of the principal, which totals $730,970 (G68). The Excel formula equivalent for equation (A3-29) appears in cell A81, and the result of that formula appears in G81, which matches the brute force calculation in G68, thus demonstrating the accuracy of the formula.

CONCLUSION

In this mathematical appendix to the ADF chapter, we have presented:

- ADFs with stub periods (partial years) for both midyear and end-of-year.
- Tables to demonstrate their accuracy.
- ADFs to calculate the amortization of principal on a loan.
- A formula for the after-tax PV of a loan.

Calculating Discount Rates

Part 2 of this book, Chapters 4, 5, and 6, deals with calculating discount rates; discounting cash flows is the second of the four steps in business valuation.

Chapter 4 is a long chapter, with a significant amount of empirical analysis of stock market returns. Our primary finding is that returns are negatively related to the logarithm of the size of the firm. The most successful measure of size in explaining returns of publicly held stocks is market capitalization, though research by Grabowski and King shows that many other measures of size also do a fairly good job of explaining stock market returns.

In their 1999 article, Grabowski and King found the relationship of return to three underlying variables: operating margin, the logarithm of the coefficient of variation of operating margin, and the logarithm of the coefficient of variation of return on equity. This is a very important research result, and it is very important that professionals read and understand their article. Even so, their methodology is based on Compustat data, which leaves out the first 37 years of the New York Stock Exchange data. As a consequence, their standard errors are higher than my log size model, and appraisers should be familiar with both.

In this chapter, we:

- Develop the mathematics of potential log size equations.
- Analyze the statistical error in the log size equation for different time periods and determine that the last 60 years, i.e., 1939–1998, is the optimal time frame.
- Present research by Harrison that shows that the distribution of stock market returns in the 18th century is the same as it is in the 20th century and discuss its implications for which 20th century data we should use.
- Give practical examples of using the log size equation.
- Compare log size to the capital asset pricing model (CAPM) for accuracy.
- Discuss industry effects.

- Discuss industry effects.
- Present a claim that, with rare exceptions, valuations of small and medium-sized privately held businesses do not require a public guideline companies method (developing PE and other types of multiples), as the log size model satisfies the intent behind the Revenue Ruling 59-60 requirement to use that approach when it is relevant.

The last bullet point is very important; in my opinion, it frees appraisers from wasting countless hours on an approach that is worse than useless for valuing small firms.[1] The log size model itself saves much time compared to using CAPM. The former literally takes one minute, while the latter often requires one to two days of research. Log size is also much more accurate for smaller firms than is either CAPM or the buildup approach. Using 1939–1998 data, the log size standard error of the valuation estimate is only 41% as large as CAPM standard error. This means that the CAPM 95% confidence intervals are approximately two and one half times larger than the log size confidence intervals.[2]

Summarizing, log size has two advantages:

- It saves much time and money for the appraiser.
- It is far more accurate.

For those who prefer not to read through the research that leads to our conclusions and simply want to learn how to use the log size model, Appendix C presents a much shorter version of Chapter 4. It also serves as a useful refresher for those who read Chapter 4 in its entirety but periodically wish to refresh their skills and understanding.

Chapter 5 discusses arithmetic versus geometric mean returns. There have been many articles in the professional literature arguing whether arithmetic or geometric mean returns are most appropriate. For valuing small businesses, the two measures can easily make a 100% difference in the valuation, as geometric returns are always lower than arithmetic returns (as long as returns are not identical in every period, which, of course, they are not). Most of the arguments have centered around Professor Ibbotson's famous two-period example.

The majority of Chapter 5 consists of empirical evidence that arithmetic mean returns do a better job than geometric means of explaining log size results. Additionally, we spend some time discussing a very mathematical article by Indro and Lee that argues for using a time horizon-weighted average of the arithmetic and geometric means.

For those who use CAPM, whether in a direct equity approach or in an invested capital approach, there is a trap into which many appraisers fall, which is producing an answer that is internally inconsistent.

Common practice is to assume a degree of leverage—usually equal to the subject company's existing or industry average leverage—

---

1. When the subject company is close to the size of publicly traded firms, say one half their size, then the public guideline company approach is reasonable.
2. Using 1938–1997 data, the log size standard error was only 6% as large as CAPM's standard error. 1998 was a bad year for the log size model.

assuming book value for equity. This implies an equity for the firm, which is an ex-ante value of equity. The problem comes when the appraiser stops after obtaining his or her valuation estimate. This is because the calculated value of equity will almost always be inconsistent with the value of equity that is implied in the leverage assumed in the calculation of the CAPM discount rate.

In Chapter 6 we present an iterative method that solves the problem by repeating the valuation calculations until the assumed and the calculated equity are equal.

CHAPTER 4

Discount Rates as a Function of Log Size[1]

PRIOR RESEARCH

TABLE 4-1: ANALYSIS OF HISTORICAL STOCK RETURNS

   Regression #1: Return versus Standard Deviation of Returns

   Regression #2: Return versus Log Size

   Regression #3: Return versus Beta

   Market Performance

   Which Data to Choose?

      Tables 4-2 and 4-2A: Regression Results for Different Time Periods

      18th Century Stock Market Returns

      Conclusion on Data Set

   Recalculation of the Log Size Model Based on 60 Years

APPLICATION OF THE LOG SIZE MODEL

   Discount Rates Based on the Log Size Model

      Need for Annual Updating

      Computation of Discount Rate Is an Iterative Process

   Practical Illustration of the Log Size Model: Discounted Cash Flow Valuations

      The Second Iteration: Table 4-4B

      Consistency in Levels of Value

      Adding Specific Company Adjustments to the DCF Analysis: Table 4-4C

   Total Return versus Equity Premium

   Adjustments to the Discount Rate

   Discounted Cash Flow or Net Income?

DISCUSSION OF MODELS AND SIZE EFFECTS

   CAPM

---

1. Adapted and reprinted with permission from *Valuation* (August 1994): 8–24 and *The Valuation Examiner* (February/March 1997): 19–21.

Sum Beta

The Fama–French Cost of Equity Model

Log Size Models

Heteroscedasticity

INDUSTRY EFFECTS

SATISFYING REVENUE RULING 59-60 WITHOUT A GUIDELINE
PUBLIC COMPANY METHOD

SUMMARY AND CONCLUSIONS

APPENDIX A: AUTOMATING ITERATION USING
NEWTON'S METHOD

APPENDIX B: MATHEMATICAL APPENDIX

APPENDIX C: ABBREVIATED REVIEW AND USE

PRIOR RESEARCH

Historically, small companies have shown higher rates of return when compared to large ones, as evidenced by data for the New York Stock Exchange (NYSE) over the past 73 years of its existence (Ibbotson Associates 1999). The relationship between firm size and rate of return was first published by Rolf Banz in 1981 and is now universally recognized. Accordingly, company size has been included as a variable in several models used to determine stock market returns.

Jacobs and Levy (1988) examined small firm size as one of 25 variables associated with anomalous rates of return on stocks. They found that small size was statistically significant both in single-variable and multivariate form, although size effects appear to change over time, i.e., they are nonstationary. They found that the natural logarithm (log) of market capitalization was negatively related to the rate of return.

Fama and French (1993) found they could explain historical market returns well with a three-factor multiple regression model using firm size, the ratio of book equity to market equity (BE/ME), and the overall market factor $R_m - R_f$, i.e., the equity premium. The latter factor explained overall returns to stocks across the board, but it did not explain differences from one stock to another, or more precisely, from one portfolio to another.[2]

The entire variation in portfolio returns was explained by the first two factors. Fama and French found BE/ME to be the more significant factor in explaining the cross-sectional difference in returns, with firm size next; however, they consider both factors as proxies for risk. Furthermore, they state, "Without a theory that specifies the exact form of the state variables or common factors in returns, the choice of any particular version of the factors is somewhat arbitrary. Thus detailed stories for the slopes and average premiums associated with particular versions of the factors are suggestive, but never definitive."

Abrams (1994) showed strong statistical evidence that returns are linearly related to the natural logarithm of the value of the firm, as measured by market capitalization. He used this relationship to determine the appropriate discount rate for privately held firms. In a follow-up article, Abrams (1997) further simplified the calculations by relating the natural log of size to total return without splitting the result into the risk-free rate plus the equity premium.

Grabowski and King (1995) also described the logarithmic relationship between firm size and market return. They later (Grabowski and King 1996) demonstrated that a similar, but weaker, logarithmic relationship exists for other measures of firm size, including the book value of common equity, five-year average net income, market value of invested capital, five-year average EBITDA, sales, and number of employees. Their latest research (Grabowski and King 1999) demonstrates a negative logarithmic relationship between returns and operating margin and a posi-

---

2. The regression coefficient is essentially beta controlled for size and BE/ME. After controlling for the other two systematic variables, this beta is very close to 1 and explains only the market premium overall. It does not explain any differentials in premiums across firms or portfolios, as the variation was insignificant.

tive logarithmic relationship between returns and the coefficient of variation of operating margin and accounting return on equity.

The discovery that return (the discount rate) has a negative linear relationship to the natural logarithm of the value of the firm means that the value of the firm decays exponentially with increasing rates of return. We will also show that firm value decays exponentially with the standard deviation of returns.

TABLE 4-1: ANALYSIS OF HISTORICAL STOCK RETURNS

Columns A–F in Table 4-1 contain the input data from the *Stocks, Bonds, Bills and Inflation 1999 Yearbook* (Ibbotson Associates 1999) for all of the regression analyses as well as the regression results. We use the 73-year average arithmetic returns in both regressions, from 1926 to 1998. For simplicity, we have collapsed 730 data points (73 years × 10 deciles) into 73 data points by using averages. Thus, the regressions are cross-sectional rather than time series. Column A lists the entire NYSE divided into different groups (known as deciles) based on market capitalization as a proxy for size, with the largest firms in decile #1 and the smallest in decile 10.[3] Columns B through F contain market data for each decile which is described below.

Note that the 73-year average market return in Column B rises with each decile. The standard deviation of returns (Column C) also rises with each decile. Column D shows the 1998 market capitalization of each decile, with decile #1 containing 189 firms (Column F) with a market capitalization of $5.986 trillion (D8). Market capitalization is the price per share times the number of shares. We use it as a proxy for the fair market value (FMV).

Dividing Column D (FMV) by Column F (the number of firms in the decile), we obtain Column G, the average capitalization, or the average fair market value of the firms in each decile. For example, the average company in decile #1 has an FMV of $31.670 billion (G8, rounded), while the average firm in decile #10 has an FMV of $56.654 million (G17, rounded).

Column H shows the percentage difference between each successive decile. For example, the average firm size in decile #9 ($146.3 million; G16) is 158.2% (H16) larger than the average firm size in decile #10 ($56.7 million; G17). The average firm size in decile #8 is 92.5% larger (H15) than that of decile #9, and so on.

The largest gap in absolute dollars and in percentages is between decile #1 and decile #2, a difference of $26.1 billion (G8–G9), or 468.9% (H8). Deciles #9 and #10 have the second-largest difference between them in percentage terms (158.2%, per H16). Most deciles are only 45% to 70% larger than the next-smaller one.

The difference in return (Column B) between deciles #1 and #2 is 1.6% and between deciles #9 and #10 is 3.2%, while the difference between

---

[3]All of the underlying decile data in Ibbotson originate with the University of Chicago's Center for Research in Security Prices (CRSP), which also determines the composition of the deciles.

TABLE 4-1

NYSE Data by Decile and Statistical Analysis: 1926–1998

	A	B	C	D	E	F	G	H	I
		Note [1] Y	Note [1] $X1$	Note [2]	Note [2]	Note [2]	= D/F		$X2$
	Decile	Mean Arith Return	Std Dev	Recent Mkt Capitalization	% Cap	# Co.s	Avg Cap = FMV	% Change in Avg FMV	Ln(FMV)
8	1	12.11%	18.90%	5,985,553,146,000	72.60%	189	31,669,593,365	468.9%	24.1786
9	2	13.66%	22.17%	1,052,131,226,000	12.76%	189	5,566,831,884	121.8%	22.4401
10	3	14.11%	23.95%	476,920,534,000	5.78%	190	2,510,108,074	73.2%	21.6436
11	4	14.76%	26.40%	273,895,749,000	3.32%	189	1,449,183,857	60.3%	21.0943
12	5	15.52%	27.24%	170,846,605,000	2.07%	189	903,950,291	49.2%	20.6223
13	6	15.60%	28.23%	114,517,587,000	1.39%	189	605,913,159	46.5%	20.2222
14	7	15.99%	30.58%	78,601,405,000	0.95%	190	413,691,605	46.9%	19.8406
15	8	17.05%	34.36%	53,218,441,000	0.65%	189	281,579,053	92.5%	19.4559
16	9	17.85%	37.02%	27,647,937,000	0.34%	189	146,285,381	158.2%	18.8011
17	10	21.03%	45.84%	10,764,268,000	0.13%	190	56,654,042	N/A	17.8525
18	Std deviation	2.48%							
19	Value wtd index	12.73%	NA	8,244,096,898,000	100.00%	1,893			

	1st Regression: Return = F(Std Dev. of Returns)		
23			
25		1926–1998	1939–1998
26	Constant	6.56%	8.90%
27	72/60 year mean T-bond yield [Note 3]	5.28%	5.70%
28	Std err of Y est	0.27%	0.42%
29	R squared	98.95%	95.84%
30	Adjusted R squared	98.82%	95.31%
31	No. of observations	10	10
32	Degrees of freedom	8	8
33	X coefficient(s)	31.24%	30.79%
34	Std err of coef.	1.14%	2.27%
35	T	27.4	13.6
36	P	< .01%	< .01%

T A B L E 4-1 *(continued)*

NYSE Data by Decile and Statistical Analysis: 1926–1998

	A	B	C	D	E	F	G	H	I
39			**2nd Regression: Return = F[LN(Mkt Capitalization)]**						
41				1926–1998	1939–1998				
42			Constant	42.24%	37.50%				
43			Std err of Y est.	0.82%	0.34%				
44			R squared	90.37%	97.29%				
45			Adjusted R squared	89.17%	96.95%				
46			No. of observations	10	10				
47			Degrees of freedom	8	8				
48			X coefficient(s)	−1.284%	−1.039%				
49			Std err of coef.	0.148%	0.061%				
50			T	−8.7	−16.9				
51			P	<.01%	<.01%				
53			**3rd Regression: Return = F[Decile Beta]**						
54					Note [4]				
55				1926–1998	1939–1998				
56			Constant	−2.78%	NA				
57			Std err of Y est	0.57%	NA				
58			R squared	95.30%	NA				
59			Adjusted R squared	94.71%	NA				
60			No. of observations	10	NA				
61			Degrees of freedom	8	NA				
62			X coefficient(s)	15.75%	NA				
63			Std err of coef.	1.24%	NA				
64			T	12.7	NA				
65			P	<.01%	NA				
68			**Assumptions:**						
69			Long-term gov't bonds arithmetic mean income return	1926–1998 [1] 5.20%					
70			Long horizon equity premium [2]	8.0%					

Notes:
[1] SBBI-1999, p. 140
[2] SBBI-1999, p. 164

T A B L E 4-1 (*continued*)

NYSE Data by Decile and Statistical Analysis: 1926–1998

	J	K	L	M	N	O	P	Q
4		Note [1]	Note [5]	= B – L	= M²		= B – O	= P²
6						Regr #2	Regr #2	
7	Decile	Beta	CAPM E(R)	CAPM Error	Sq Error	Estimate	Error	Sq Error
8	1	0.90	12.40%	–0.29%	0.0008%	11.19%	0.92%	0.0085%
9	2	1.04	13.52%	0.14%	0.0002%	13.42%	0.24%	0.0006%
10	3	1.09	13.92%	0.19%	0.0004%	14.45%	–0.34%	0.0011%
11	4	1.13	14.24%	0.52%	0.0027%	15.15%	–0.39%	0.0015%
12	5	1.16	14.48%	1.04%	0.0107%	15.76%	–0.24%	0.0006%
13	6	1.18	14.64%	0.96%	0.0092%	16.27%	–0.68%	0.0046%
14	7	1.23	15.04%	0.95%	0.0091%	16.76%	–0.77%	0.0060%
15	8	1.27	15.36%	1.69%	0.0285%	17.26%	–0.21%	0.0004%
16	9	1.34	15.92%	1.93%	0.0373%	18.10%	–0.25%	0.0006%
17	10	1.44	16.72%	4.31%	0.1859%	19.32%	1.72%	0.0294%
19			Totals →		0.2848%			0.0533%
20			Standard error →		1.89%			0.82%
21			Std error-CAPM/std error-log size model					231.11%
23			Std error—60 year model					0.34%

Notes

[1] Derived from SBBI-1999 pages 130, 131.*

[2] SBBI-1999, page 138**

[3] These averages derived from SBBI-1999, pages 200–201.* Beginning of year 1926 yield was not available.

[4] Betas were not available for the 1939–1998 time period.

[5] SBBI-1999, page 140*

[6] CAPM Equation: R_f + (Beta × Equity Premium) = 5.2% + (Beta × 8.0%). The equity premium is the simple difference of historical arithmetic mean returns for large company stocks and the risk free rate per SBBI 1999 p. 164. The risk free rate of 5.2% is the 73 year arithmetic mean income return component of 20 year government bonds per SBBI-1999, page 140.*

all other deciles is less than 1%. Thus, it seems that for fairly regular percentage increases in size we see a reasonably constant drop in the average returns. This suggests a logarithmic relationship between size and return, which we investigate later and confirm.

Column I, the last column in the table, is the natural logarithm of the average FMV. The natural logarithm of FMV is the number, which when used as an exponent to Euler's constant, e (the natural exponent from calculus), results in the FMV. Thus, $e^{\ln \text{ FMV}} = \text{FMV}$. The number e, like pi, is an irrational, transcendental number. Its first digits begin 2.718 . . . .

The natural logarithm operates in the same way as the Richter scale used to measure earthquakes, except that the latter works in base 10 logarithms. The principle, however, is the same. An earthquake of 7 on the Richter scale is 10 times stronger than an earthquake of 6, 100 times more powerful than an earthquake of 5, 1,000 times more powerful than an earthquake of 4, and so on. The difference in power between two earthquakes whose Richter scale measurement varies by Δx is $10^{\Delta x}$. Thus, the latter example comparing two earthquakes with a rating of 7 and 4 is a difference of 3 on the Richter scale, which means the former is $10^3 = 1,000$ times more powerful than the latter. Similarly, the difference in value between firms whose natural logs of average value differ by Δx is $2.718^{\Delta x}$. An increase in the natural log by 1 means the resulting value (from taking the antilog) will be 2.718 times larger than the value whose natural log is one less. Similarly, an increase in natural log by 2 is a value $2.718^2 = 7.4$ times larger, and an increase of 3 is $2.718^3 = 20.1$ times larger than the base value.

For example, the average market capitalization for decile #10 of $56.7 million (G17) $= e^{17.8525} \cong 2.718^{17.8525}$, where the exponent is the natural log in cell I17. Similarly, $e^{24.1786} = \$31.7$ billion (G8), where 24.1786 (I8) is the natural log of the decile #1 market capitalization.

Let's go through an example of how to generate a natural logarithm on a spreadsheet. In Microsoft Excel, the formula in cell I8 is = ln(G8). In Lotus 123, the formula would be: @ln(G8). To take the antilog, i.e., exponentiating, use the formulas: =exp(I8) in Excel and @exp(I8) in Lotus 123.

Regression #1: Return versus Standard Deviation of Returns

Figure 4-1 is a graph of stock market returns as a function of standard deviation of returns. The nodes numbered 1–10 are the actual data points, with the number being the decile, and the straight line running through the points is the regression estimate. Note the strong linear relationship of the two. The deciles are in numerical order, and each successive decile is northeast of the other except for #5 and #6, which are almost parallel. The graph tells us that as the decile number goes up—which means as size goes down—returns and risk both increase.

Of course, it is an axiom of finance that as risk increases, so does return. Logically, investors would never deliberately invest in one firm

FIGURE 4-1

1926–1998 Arithmetic Mean Returns as a Function of Standard Deviation

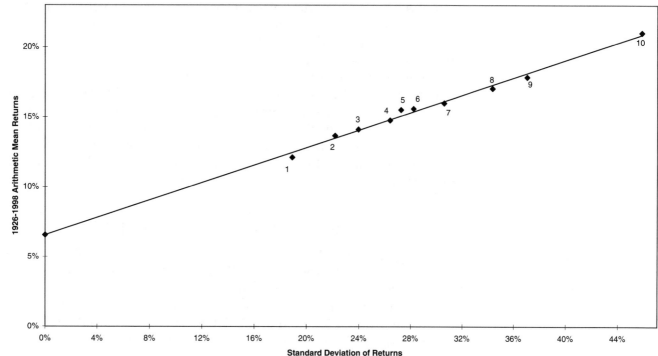

Standard Deviation of Returns
These are arithmetic mean returns for the CRSP deciles. Data labels are decile numbers.
Y intercept is regression data, not actual
Regression #1: r = 6.56% + (31.24% x Std Dev of Decile)

(or portfolio) with higher risk than another unless the expected return is also higher. It is still a relatively new observation that we can see this relationship in the size of the firms. Figure 4-1 shows this relationship graphically, and the regressions in Table 4-1 that follow demonstrate that relationship mathematically.

Regression #1 in Table 4-1 (Rows 23–36) is a statistical measurement of return as a function of standard deviation of returns. The results for the period 1926–1998 (D26–D36) confirm that a very strong relationship exists between historical returns and standard deviation. The regression equation is:

$$r = 6.56\% + (31.24\% \times S) \qquad (4\text{-}1)$$

where r = return and S = standard deviation of returns.

The adjusted R^2 for equation (4-1) is 98.82% (D30), and the t-statistic of the slope is 27.4 (D35). The p-value is less than 0.01% (D36), which means the slope coefficient is statistically significant at the 99.9%+ level. The standard error of the estimate is 0.27% (D28), also indicating a high degree of confidence in the results obtained. Another important result is that the constant of 6.56% (D26) is the regression estimate of the long-term risk-free rate, i.e., the rate of return for a no-risk (zero standard deviation) asset. The 73-year arithmetic mean income return from 1926–

1998 on long-term Treasury Bonds is 5.20%.[4] Therefore, in addition to the other robust results, the regression equation does a reasonable job of estimating the risk-free rate. In prior years the regression estimate was much closer to the historical average risk-free rate, but very strong performance of large cap stocks in 1995–1998 has weakened this relationship. We will temporarily ignore the 1938–1998 data in Column E and address that later on in the chapter.

The major problem with direct application of this relationship to the valuation of privately held businesses is coming up with a reliable standard deviation of returns. Appraisers cannot directly measure the standard deviation of returns for privately held firms, since there is no objective stock price. We can measure the standard deviation of income, and we cover that later in the chapter in our discussion of Grabowski and King (1999).

Regression #2: Return versus Log Size

Fortunately, there is a much more practical relationship. Notice that the returns are negatively correlated with the market capitalization, that is, the fair market value of the firm. The second regression in Table 4-1 (D42–D51) is the more useful one for valuing privately held firms. Regression #2 shows return as a function of the natural logarithm of the FMV of the firm. The regression equation for the period 1926–1998, which comes from cells D42 and D48, is as follows:

$$r = 42.24\% - [1.284\% \times \ln (FMV)] \qquad (4\text{-}2)$$

The adjusted R^2 is 89.2% (D45), the t-statistic is -8.7 (D50), and the p-value is less than 0.01% (D51), meaning that these results are statistically robust. The standard error of the Y-estimate is 0.82% (D43). As discussed in Chapters 2 and 11, we can form an approximate 95% confidence interval around the regression estimate by adding and subtracting two standard errors. Thus, we can be 95% confident that the regression forecast is approximately $2 \times 0.82\% \cong 1.6\%$.[5]

Figure 4-2 is a graph of arithmetic mean returns over the past 73 years (1926–1998) versus the natural log of FMV. As in Figure 4-1, the numbered nodes are the actual data for each decile, while the straight line is the regression estimate. While Figure 4-1 shows that returns are positively related to risk, Figure 4-2 shows they are negatively related to size.

Regression #3: Return versus Beta

The third regression in Table 4-1 shows the relationship between the decile returns and the decile betas for the period 1926–1998 (D56–D65). According to the capital asset pricing model (CAPM) equation, the y-

---

4. SBBI-1999, p. 140 uses this measure as the risk-free rate for CAPM. Arguably, the average bond yield is a better measure of the risk-free rate, but the difference is immaterial.

5. This is true near the mean value of our data. Uncertainty increases gradually as we move from the mean.

PART 2   Calculating Discount Rates

1926–1998 Arithmetic Mean Returns as a Function of Ln(FMV)

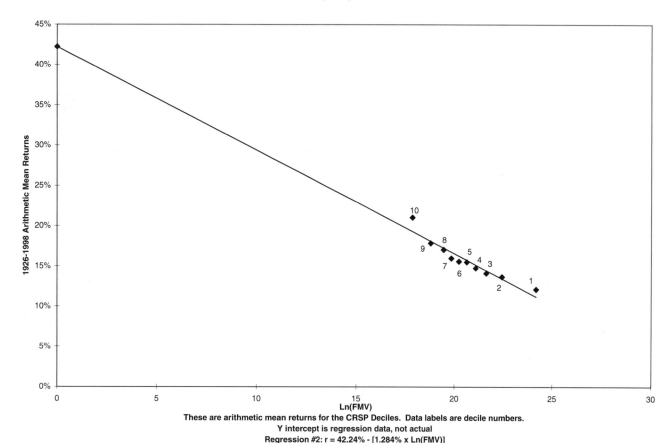

These are arithmetic mean returns for the CRSP Deciles. Data labels are decile numbers.
Y intercept is regression data, not actual
Regression #2: r = 42.24% - [1.284% x Ln(FMV)]

intercept should be the risk-free rate and the *x*-coefficient should be the long-run equity premium of 8.0%.[6] Instead, the *y*-intercept at −2.78% (D56) is a country mile from the historical risk-free rate of 5.20%, as is the *x*-coefficient at 15.75% from the equity premium of 8.0%, demonstrating the inaccuracy of CAPM.

While the equation we obtain is contrary to the theoretical CAPM, it does constitute an empirical CAPM, which could be used for a firm whose capitalization is at least as large as a decile #10 firm. Merely select the appropriate decile, use the beta of that decile, possibly with some adjustment, and use regression equation #3 to generate a discount rate. While it is possible to do this, it is far better to use regression #2.

The second page of Table 4-1 compares the log size model to CAPM. Columns L and O show the regression estimated return for each decile using both models—Column L for CAPM and O for log size. The CAPM expected return was calculated using the CAPM equation: $r = R_F + (\beta \times \text{Equity Premium}) = 5.20\% + (\beta \times 8.0\%)$.

Columns M and N show the error and squared error for CAPM, whereas columns P and Q contain the same information for the log size

---

6. SBBI-1999, p. 164.

model. Note that the CAPM standard error of 1.89% (N20) is 230% larger than the log size standard error of 0.82% (Q20). Later in this chapter we use only the last 60 years of NYSE data, and its standard error for the log size model is 0.34% (Q23), only 18% of the CAPM error.

The differences in the log size versus CAPM calculations for the 60 years of stock market data ending in 1997 were far more pronounced. The reason is that for 1995–1998, returns to large cap stocks were higher than small cap stocks, with 1998 being the most extreme example. For the four years, the arithmetic mean return to decile #1 firms was 31.2%, and for decile #10 firms it was 11.1%—contrary to long-term trends. In 1998, returns to decile #1 firms were 28.5%, and returns to decile #10 firms were −15.4%. Thus, the regression equation was much better at the end of 1997 than at the end of 1998. The 1938–1997 adjusted R^2 was 99.5% (versus 97.0% for 1939–1998), and the standard error of the y-estimate was 0.14% (versus 0.34% for 1939–1998).

Market Performance

Regression #1 shows that return is a linear function of risk, as measured by the standard deviation of returns. Regression #2 shows that return declines linearly with the logarithm of firm size. The logic behind this is that investors demand and receive higher returns for higher risk. Smaller firms have more volatile (risky) returns, so return is therefore negatively related to size.

Figure 4-3 shows the relationship between volatility and size, with the y-axis being the standard deviation of returns for the value-weighted

FIGURE 4-3

Decade Standard Deviation of Returns versus Decade Average FMV per Company on NYSE 1935–1995

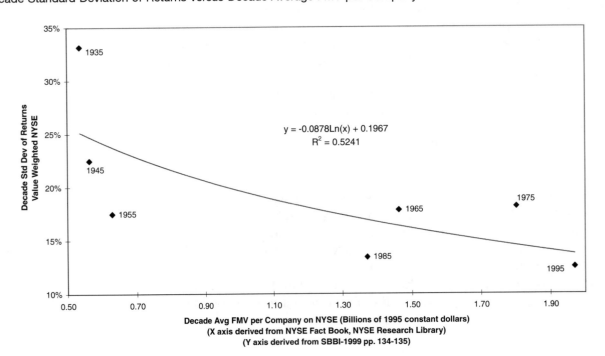

PART 2   Calculating Discount Rates

NYSE and the *x*-axis being the average FMV per NYSE company in 1995 constant dollars in successive decades.[7] The year adjacent to each data point is the final year of the decade, e.g., 1935 encompasses 1926 to 1935. The decade average FMV (in 1995 constant dollars) has increased from slightly over $0.5 billion to over $1.9 billion. Therefore, we might predict from a theoretical standpoint that the standard deviation of returns should decline over time—and it has.

As you can see, the standard deviation of returns per decade declines exponentially from about 33% for the decade ending in 1935 to 13% in the decade ending in 1995, for a range of 20%. If we examine the major historical events that took place over time, the decade ending 1935 includes some of the Roaring Twenties and the Depression. It is no surprise that it has such a high standard deviation. Figure 4-4 is identical to Figure 4-3, except that we have eliminated the decade ending 1935 in Figure 4-4. Eliminating the most volatile decade results in a flattening out of the regression curve. The fitted curve in Figure 4-4 appears about half as steep as Figure 4-3 (the standard deviation ranges from 13–22%, or a range of 9%, versus the 20% range of Figure 4-3) and much less curved.

The relationship between volatility and size when viewing the market as a whole is somewhat loose, as the data points vary considerably from the fitted curve in Figure 4-3. The $R^2 = 52\%$ (45% in Figure 4-4).

FIGURE 4-4

Decade Standard Deviation of Returns versus Decade Average FMV per Company on NYSE 1945–1995

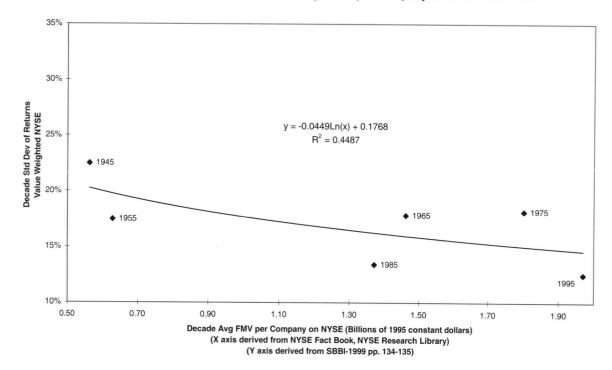

7. Though 1996–1998 data are available, we choose to stop at 1995 in this graph to maintain 10 years of data in each node on the graph.

For the decade ending 1945, standard deviation of returns is about one-third lower than the previous decade (approximately 22% versus 33%), while average firm size is about the same. Standard deviation of returns dropped again in the decade ending 1955, with only a small increase in size. In the decade ending 1965, average firm size more than doubled in real terms, yet volatility was almost identical (we would have expected a decrease). In the decade ending 1975, firm size and volatility increased. In the decade ending 1985, both average firm size and volatility decreased significantly, which is counterintuitive, while in the final decade firm size increased from over $1.3 billion to almost $2 billion, while volatility decreased slightly.

Figure 4-5 shows the relationship of average NYSE return and time, with each data point being a decade. The relationship is a very loose one, with $R^2 = 0.09$. The decade ending 1975 appears an outlier in this regression, with average returns at half or less of the other decades (except the one ending 1935). The regression equation is return = $-1.0242 +$ ($0.0006 \times$ Year). Since every decade is 10 years, this equation implies returns increase 0.6% every 10 years. However, the relationship is not statistically significant.

In summary, there appears to be increasing efficiency of investment over time. The market as a whole seems to deliver the same or better

FIGURE 4-5

Average Returns Each Decade

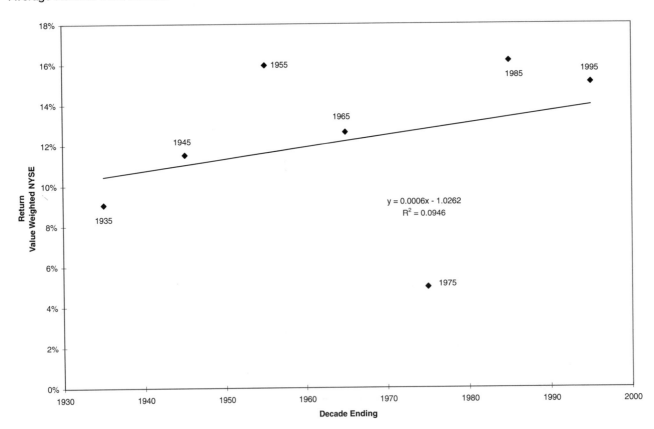

PART 2 Calculating Discount Rates

performance as measured by return experienced for risk undertaken. We can speculate on explanations for this phenomenon: increases in the size of the NYSE firms, greater investor sophistication, professional money management, and the proliferation of mutual funds. In any case, the risk of investing in one portfolio (or firm) relative to others still matters very much. This may possibly be the phenomenon underlying the observations of the nonstationarity of the data.

Which Data to Choose?

With a total of 73 years of data on the NYSE, we must decide whether to use all of the data or some subset, and if so, which subset. In making this choice, we will consider three sources of information:

1. Tables 4-2 and 4-2A, the statistical results of regression analyses of the different time periods of the NYSE.
2. A study (Harrison 1998) that explores the distribution of 18th century European stock market returns.
3. Figures 4-3 and 4-4.

Tables 4-2 and 4-2A: Regression Results for Different Time Periods

Nonstationary data require us to consider the possibility of removing some of the older NYSE data. In Table 4-2 we repeat regressions #1 and #2 from Table 4-1 for the most recent 30, 40, 50, 60, and 73 years of NYSE data. The upper table in each time period is regression #1 and the lower table is regression #2. For example, the data for regression #1 for the last 30 years appear in Rows 7–9, 40 years in Rows 17–19, and so on. Similarly, the data for regression #2 for 30 years appear in Rows 12–14, 40 years in Rows 22–24, and so on.

Table 4-2, Rows 8–14, shows regressions #1 and #2 using only the past 30 years of data, i.e., from 1969–1998.[8] Regression equation #1 for this period is: $r = 14.64\% - (2.37\% \times S)$ (B8, B9), and regression equation #2 is $r = 14.14\% - [0.001\% \times \ln (FMV)]$ (B13 and B14). Note that both the slope coefficient and the intercept of these equations are different from those obtained for 73 years of data.

Rows 47–49 repeat regression #1 for the same 73 years as Table 4-1. The y-intercept of 6.56% (B48) and the x-coefficient of 31.24% (B49) in Table 4-2 are identical to those appearing in Table 4-1 (D26 and D33, respectively). Rows 52–54 repeat regression #2 for the same period. Once again, the y-intercept in Table 4-2 of 42.24% (B53) and the coefficient of $\ln (FMV)$ of -1.284% (B54) match those found in Table 4-1 (D42 and D48, respectively).

Table 4-2A summarizes the key regression feedback from Table 4-2. For the five different time periods we consider, the 60-year period is sta-

---

8. The time sequence in Table 4-2 differs by two years from that in Figures 4-3 to 4-6. Whereas the latter show decades ending in 19X5 (e.g., 1945, 1955, etc.), Table 4-2's terminal year is 1998.

TABLE 4-2

Regressions of Returns over Standard Deviation and Log of Fair Market Value

	A	B	C	D	E	F	G	H	I
		Coefficients	Standard Error	t Stat	P-value	Lower 95%	Upper 95%		
6				30 Year					
7								R square	1.35%
8	Intercept	14.64%	1.62%	9.06	0.00%	10.92%	18.37%	Adjusted R square	−10.98%
9	Std Dev	−2.37%	7.18%	−0.33	74.92%	−18.92%	14.17%	Standard error	0.90%
12								R square	0.00%
13	Intercept	14.14%	3.39%	4.17	0.31%	6.32%	21.95%	Adjusted R square	−12.50%
14	Ln(FMV)	−0.001%	0.164%	−0.01	99.54%	−0.38%	0.38%	Standard error	0.90%
16				40 Year					
17								R square	67.84%
18	Intercept	10.13%	1.17%	8.66	0.00%	7.43%	12.82%	Adjusted R square	63.82%
19	Std Dev	21.74%	5.29%	4.11	0.34%	9.53%	33.94%	Standard error	0.75%
22								R square	78.94%
23	Intercept	27.30%	2.28%	11.95	0.00%	22.03%	32.57%	Adjusted R square	76.31%
24	Ln FMV	−0.605%	0.110%	−5.48	0.06%	−0.86%	−0.35%	Standard error	0.61%
26				50 Year					
27								R square	77.28%
28	Intercept	11.54%	0.89%	13.00	0.00%	9.49%	13.58%	Adjusted R square	74.44%
29	Std Dev	20.61%	3.95%	5.22	0.08%	11.50%	29.72%	Standard error	0.54%
32								R square	89.60%
33	Intercept	27.35%	1.36%	20.08	0.00%	24.21%	30.49%	Adjusted R square	88.30%
34	Ln(FMV)	−0.546%	0.066%	−8.30	0.00%	−0.70%	−0.39%	Standard error	0.36%
36				60 Year					
37								R square	95.84%
38	Intercept	8.90%	0.55%	16.30	0.00%	7.64%	10.16%	Adjusted R square	95.31%
39	Std Dev	30.79%	2.27%	13.57	0.00%	25.56%	36.03%	Standard error	0.42%
42								R square	97.29%
43	Intercept	**37.50%**	1.27%	29.57	0.00%	34.58%	40.43%	Adjusted R square	**96.95%**
44	Ln(FMV)	**−1.039%**	0.061%	−16.94	0.00%	−1.18%	−0.90%	Standard error	0.34%
46				73 Year					
47								R square	98.95%
48	Intercept	6.56%	0.35%	18.94	0.00%	5.76%	7.36%	Adjusted R square	98.82%
49	Std Dev	31.24%	1.14%	27.42	0.00%	28.61%	33.87%	Standard error	0.27%
52								R square	90.37%
53	Intercept	**42.24%**	3.07%	13.78	0.00%	35.17%	49.32%	Adjusted R square	**89.17%**
54	Ln(FMV)	**−1.284%**	0.148%	−8.66	0.00%	−1.63%	−0.94%	Standard error	0.82%

tistically a solid winner. Regression #2 is the more important regression for valuing privately held firms, and the 60-year standard error at 0.34% (C9) is the lowest among the five listed. The standard error of the y-estimate using all 73 years of data (1.09%, D10) is larger than the 60-year standard error (0.82%; C10). The next-lowest standard error is 0.90% (D8) for 50 years of data, which is still larger than the 60-year regression. The 60-year regression also has the highest R^2—97% (E9)—and it has a low standard error for regression #1, second only to the full 73 years.

The 95% confidence intervals for the 60 years of data are smaller than they are for the other candidates. For regression #2 they are between

TABLE 4-2A

Regression Comparison [1]

	A	B	C	D	E
4		Standard Errors			
5	Years	Regr #1 [2]	Regr #2 [3]	Total	Adj R² (Regr #2) [4]
6	30	0.90%	0.90%	1.80%	−12.50%
7	40	0.75%	0.61%	1.36%	76.31%
8	50	0.54%	0.36%	0.90%	88.30%
9	60	0.42%	0.34%	0.76%	96.95%
10	73	0.27%	0.82%	1.09%	89.17%

[1] Summary Regression Statistics from Table 4-2
[2] Table 4-2: I9, I19, ...
[3] Table 4-2: I14, I24, ...
[4] Table 4-2: I13, I23, ...

34.58% and 40.43% (Table 4-2, F43, G43) for the y-intercept—a range of 5.8%—and −1.18% to −0.90% (F44, G44) for the slope—a range of 0.28%. For 73 years of data, the range is 14% for the y-intercept (G53–F53) and 0.69% (G54–F54) for the slope, which is 2½ times larger than the 60-year data. Thus, the past 60 years data are a more efficient estimator of stock market returns than other time periods, as measured by the size of confidence intervals around the regression estimates for the log size approach.

18th Century Stock Market Returns

Paul Harrison's article (Harrison 1998) is a fascinating econometric study which is very advanced and extremely mathematical. The data for this study came primarily from biweekly Amsterdam stock prices published from July 1723 to December 1794 for the Dutch East India Company and a select group of English stocks that were traded in Amsterdam: the Bank of England, the English East India Company, and the South Sea Company. Harrison also examined stock prices from London spanning the 18th century.

Harrison found the shape of the distribution of stock price returns in the 18th and 20th centuries to be very similar, although their means and standard deviations are different. The 18th century returns were lower—but less volatile—than 20th century returns. He found the distributions to be symmetric, like a normal curve, but leptokurtic (fat tailed), which means there are more extreme events occurring than would be predicted by a normal curve. The same fundamental pattern exists in both 1725 and 1995.

Harrison remarks that clearly much has changed over the last 300 years, but, interestingly, such changes do not seem to matter in his analysis. He comments that the distribution of prices is not driven by information technology, regulatory oversight, or by the specialist—none of these existed in the 18th century markets. However, what did exist in the 18th century bears resemblance to what exists today.

Harrison describes the following as some of the evidence for similarities in the market:

- Stock traders in the 18th century reacted to and affected market prices like traders today. They competed vigorously for information,[9] and the 18th century markets followed a near random walk—so much so that an entire pamphlet literature sprang up in the early 18th century lamenting the unpredictability of the market. Harrison says that unpredictability is a theoretical result of competition in the market.
- Eighteenth century stock markets were informationally efficient, as shown econometrically by Neal (1990).
- The practices of 18th century brokers were sophisticated. Investors early in the 18th century valued stocks according to their discounted stream of future dividends. Tables were published (such as Hayes 1726) showing the appropriate discount for different interest rates and time horizons. Traders engaged in cash contracts, futures contracts, and options; they sold short, issued credit, and used "modern" investment strategies, such as forming portfolios, diversification, and hedging.

To all of the foregoing, I would add an observation by King Solomon, who said, "There is nothing new under the sun." (Ecclesiastes 1:9) Also in keeping with the theme in our chapter, King Solomon became the inventor of portfolio theory when he wrote, "Divide your wealth into seven, even eight parts, for you cannot know what misfortune may occur on earth" (Ecclesiastes, 11:2).

Conclusion on Data Set

To return to the 20th century, Ibbotson (Ibbotson Associates 1998, p. 27) enunciated the principle that over the very long run there are very few events that are truly outliers. Paul Harrison's research seems to corroborate this. It is in the nature of the stock market for there to be periodic booms and crashes, indicating that we should use all 73 years of the NYSE data. On the other hand, the statistical feedback in Table 4-2A shows that eliminating the 1926–1938 data provides the most statistically reliable log size relationship. Similarly, Figure 4-4 shows a flattening of the regression curve when the decade ending 1935 is eliminated. Paul Harrison said that even with 300 years of history showing similarity in the distribution of returns, he would be inclined to label the years in question as an outlier that should probably be excluded from the regres-

---

9. A fascinating story that I remember from an economic history course is that Baron Rothschild, having placed men with carrier pigeons at the Battle of Waterloo, was the first nonparticipant to know the results of the battle. He first paid a visit to inform the King of the British victory, and then he proceeded to the stock market to make 100 million pounds—many billions of dollars in today's money—a tidy sum for having insider information. He struck a blow for market efficiency. Even his method of making a fortune in the market that day is a paradigm of the extent of market efficiency then. He knew that he was being observed. He began selling, and others followed him in a panic. Later, he sent his employees to do a huge amount of buying anonymously. The markets were indeed efficient—at least they were by the end of the day!

sion.[10] Thus, we eliminate the years 1926–1937 from the final regression. The superior adjusted R^2 and 95% confidence intervals of the past 60 years, coupled with Harrison's results and Ibbotson's general principle of using more rather than less data, lead us to conclude that the past 60 years provide the best guide for the future.

Recalculation of the Log Size Model Based on 60 Years

Based on our previous discussion, NYSE data from the past 60 years are likely to be the most relevant for use in forecasting the future. This time frame contains numerous data points but excludes the decade of highest volatility, attributed to nonrecurring historical events, i.e., the Roaring Twenties and the Depression years. Therefore, we repeat all three regressions for the 60-year time period from 1939–1998, as shown in Column E of Table 4-1. Regression #1 for this time period is:

$$r = 8.90\% + (30.79\% \times S) \qquad (4\text{-}3)$$

where S is the standard deviation. The adjusted R^2 in this case falls to 95.31% (E30) from the 98.82% (D30) obtained from the 73-year equation, but is still indicative of a strong relationship. On average, returns were exceptionally high and volatile during the first 13 years of the NYSE, especially in the small firms. It appears that including those years improves the relationship of returns to standard deviation of returns, even as it worsens the relationship between returns and log size.

The log size equation (regression #2) for the 60-year period is:

$$r = 37.50\% - [1.039\% \times \ln (\text{FMV})] \quad (\text{E42, E48}) \qquad (4\text{-}4)$$

The regression statistics indicate an excellent fit, with an adjusted R^2 of 96.95% (E45).[11]

APPLICATION OF THE LOG SIZE MODEL

Equation (4-4) is the most appropriate for calculating current discount rates and will be used for the remainder of the book. In the next sections we will use it to calculate discount rates for various firm sizes and demonstrate its use in a simplified discounted cash flow analysis.

Discount Rates Based on the Log Size Model

Table 4-3 shows the implied equity discount rate for firms of various sizes using the log size model (regression equation #2) for the past 60 years. The implied equity discount rate for a $10 billion firm is 13.6% (B7), and for a $50 million firm it is 19.1% (B10), based on 60-year average market returns for deciles #1–#10. While those values and all values in between are interpolations based on the model, the discount rates for firm val-

---

10. Related in a personal conversation.
11. For 1938–1997 data, adjusted R^2 was 99.54%. The "perverse" results of 1998 caused a deterioration in the relationship.

TABLE 4-3

Table of Stock Market Returns Based on FMV—60-Year Model

	A	B
5	**Regression Results**	**Implied Discount**
6	**Mktable Min FMV**	**Rate (R)**
7	$10,000,000,000	13.6%
8	$1,000,000,000	16.0%
9	$100,000,000	18.4%
10	$50,000,000	19.1%
11	$10,000,000	20.8%
12	$5,000,000	21.5%
13	$3,000,000	22.0%
14	$1,000,000	23.2%
15	$750,000	23.5%
16	$500,000	23.9%
17	$400,000	24.1%
18	$300,000	24.4%
19	$200,000	24.8%
20	$150,000	25.1%
21	$100,000	25.5%
22	$50,000	26.3%
23	$30,000	26.8%
24	$10,000	27.9%
25	$1,000	30.3%
26	$1	37.5%

ues below that are extrapolations because they lie outside the original data set.

Using equation (4-4), the Excel formula for cell B7 is: = 0.3750 − (0.01039 * ln(A7)). In Lotus 123, the formula would be: + 0.3750 − (0.01039 * @ ln(A7)).

Regression #2 (equation [4-4]) tells us that the discount rate is a constant minus another constant multiplied by ln (FMV). Since ln (FMV) has a characteristic upwardly sloping shape, as seen in Figure 4-6, subtracting a curve of that shape from a constant leads to a discount rate function that is a mirror image of Figure 4-6. Figure 4-7 is the graph of that relationship, and the reader can see that the result is a downward sloping curve. Again, this curve depicts the rate of return, i.e., the discount rate, as a function of the absolute dollar value of the firm. Note that this is not on a log scale. Since the regression equation is $r = 37.50\% − [1.0309\% \times$ ln (FMV)], we begin at the extreme left with a return of 37.5% for a firm worth $1 and subtract the fraction of the ln FMV dictated by the equation.

An important property of logarithms is that ln xy = ln x + ln y.[12] Since regression equation #2 has the form $r = a + b$ ln FMV, where $a = 0.3750$ and $b = −0.01039$, we can ask how the discount rate varies with differing orders of magnitude in value. First, however, we will work

---

12. That is because $e^x \times e^y = e^{x+y}$. Taking logs of both sides of that equation is the proof.

PART 2   Calculating Discount Rates

FIGURE 4-6

The Natural Logarithm

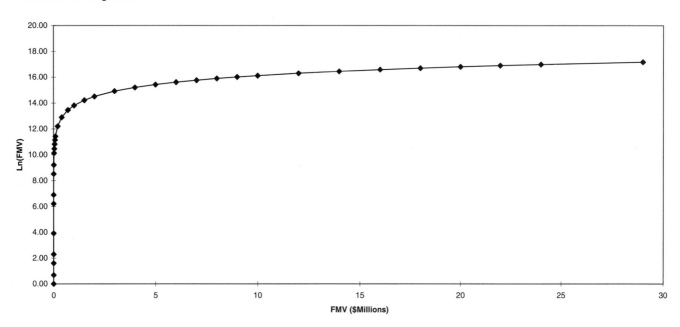

through some general equations where we vary the value of the firm by a factor of K.

Let r_1 = the discount rate for Firm #1, whose value = FMV_1

FIGURE 4-7

Discount Rates as a Function of FMV

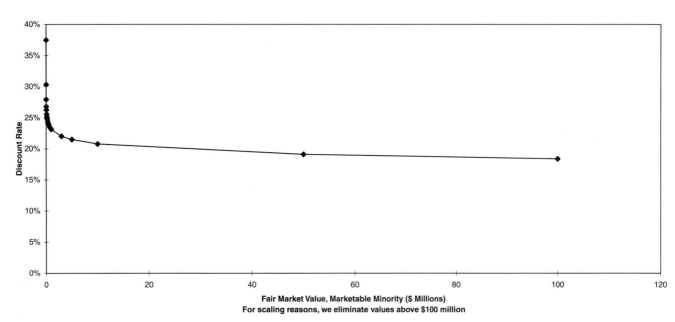

1939–1998 Decile Standard Deviations as a Function of Ln(FMV)

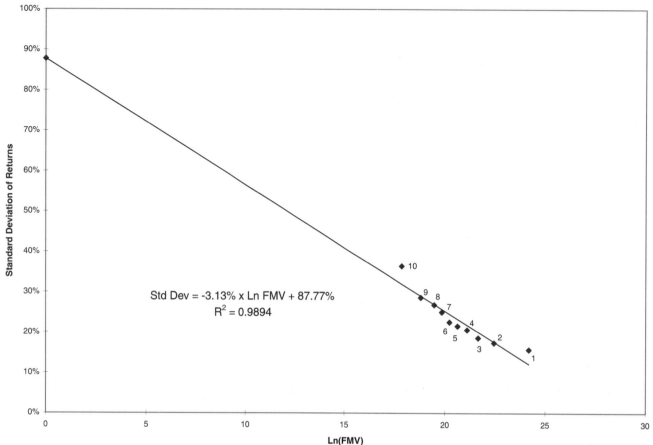

Std Dev = -3.13% x Ln FMV + 87.77%
R^2 = 0.9894

Ln(FMV)

Standard deviations of yearly returns are derived from the CRSP Deciles. Data labels are decile numbers. The Y intercept is the regression intercept, not an actual data point.

r_2 = the discount rate for Firm #2, whose value = FMV_2 = K FMV_1

$$r_1 = a + b \ln FMV_1 \tag{4-6}$$

regression equation #2 applied to Firm #1

$$r_2 = a + b \ln (K\ FMV_1) \tag{4-7}$$

regression equation #2 applied to Firm #2

$$r_2 = a + b [\ln K + \ln FMV_1] \tag{4-8}$$

$$r_2 = a + b \ln FMV_1 + b \ln K \tag{4-9}$$

$$r_2 = r_1 + b \ln K \tag{4-10}$$

In words, the discount rate of a firm K times larger (smaller) than Firm #1 is always $b \ln K$ smaller (larger) than r_1.

Let's illustrate the nature of this relationship with some specific examples. First, let's examine what happens with orders of magnitude of

10. Ln 10 = 2.302535, so $b \times$ ln 10 = $-0.01039 \times 2.302585 = -.02391$, or -2.4%. This means that if Firm #2 is 10 times larger (smaller) than Firm #1, its discount rate should be 2.4% lower (higher) than the Firm #1 discount rate. This result can be seen in Table 4-3. The $10 billion firm has a discount rate of 13.6%, while the $1 billion firm has a discount rate of 16.0%, which is 2.4% higher. The $100 million firm has a discount rate of 18.4%, which is 2.4% higher than the $1 billion firm. Because of the mathematical properties of logarithms, the same *percentage* change in FMV will always result in the same *absolute* change in the discount rate. This phenomenon is also seen in graphs containing log scales. Equal distances on a log scale are equal percentage changes, not absolute changes.

Let's try one more useful calculation—an order of magnitude 2. Ln 2 = 0.6931, so that $b \times$ ln $K = -0.01039 \times 0.6931 = -0.72\%$. Doubling (halving) the value of the firm reduces (increases) the discount rate by 0.72%. You can see that in going from a $10 million firm to a $5 million firm, the discount rate has increased from 20.8% to 21.5%, a 0.7% difference (see Table 4-3).

Now it is possible to construct your own table. All you need to know is your starting FMV and discount rate. The rest follows easily from the above formulas. Also, we can easily interpolate the table. Suppose you wanted to know the discount rate for a $25 million firm. Simply start with the $50 million firm, where $r = 19.1\%$, and add 0.7% = 19.8%.

Need for Annual Updating

Tables 4-1 through 4-3 should be updated annually, as the Ibbotson averages change, and new regression equations should be generated. This becomes more crucial when shorter historical time periods are used, because changes will have a greater impact on the average values.

Additionally, it is important to be careful to match the regression equation to the year of the valuation. If the valuation assignment is retroactive and the valuation date is 1994, then one should use a regression equation for 1939–1994.[13]

Computation of Discount Rate Is an Iterative Process

In spite of the straightforwardness of these relationships, we have a problem of circular reasoning when it comes to computing of the discount rate. We need FMV to obtain the discount rate, which is in turn used to discount cash flows or income to calculate the FMV! Hence, it is necessary to make sure that our initial estimate of FMV is consistent with the final result. If it is not, then we have to use the calculated FMV from the end of iteration #1 as our new assumed FMV in iteration #2. Using either equation (4-4) or Table 4-3, that will imply a new discount rate, which we use to value the firm. We keep repeating the process until the results are consistent.

It is extremely rare to require more than two iterations to achieve consistency in the ex ante and ex post values. The reason is that even if

---

13. Alternatively, one could either use the regression equation in the original article, run one's own regression on the Ibbotson data, or contact the author to provide the right equation.

we guess the value of the firm incorrectly by a factor of 10, we will only be 2.4% off in our discount rate. By the time we come to the second iteration, we usually are consistent. The reason behind this is that the discount rate is based on the logarithm of the value. As we saw earlier, there is not much difference between the log of $10 billion and the log of $10 million, and multiplying that by the x-coefficient of −0.01039 further reduces the effects of an initial incorrect estimate of value. This is a convergent system 99% of the time with any kind of reasonable initial guess of value and even most unreasonable guesses.

The need for iteration arises because of the mathematical properties of the equations we use in valuing a firm. The simplest type of valuation is that of a firm with constant growth to perpetuity, where we simply apply the Gordon growth model ("Gordon model") to our forecast of cash flow for the coming year. For simplicity, we will use the end-year Gordon model formula, although it is not as accurate as the midyear formula.

We use the following definitions:

CF = cash flow (available to equity) in year $t + 1$ (the first forecast year)

$a = 0.3750$, the regression constant from regression #2

$b = -0.01039$, the x-coefficient from regression #2

V = fair market value (FMV) of the firm

r = the discount rate

Using the Gordon model and ignoring valuation discounts and premiums, the FMV of the firm is:

$$V = \frac{CF}{r - g} \tag{4-11}$$

Per equation (4-6), our log size equation for the discount rate is:

$$r = a + b \ln V \tag{4-12}$$

Substituting (4-12) into (4-11), we get:

$$V = \frac{CF}{a + b \ln V - g} \tag{4-13}$$

Equation (4-13) is a transcendental equation with no analytic solution.[14] Therefore, successive approximation is the only method of determining an answer. The simple iterative procedure in Tables 4-4A, 4-4B, and 4-4C is very easy to use and works in almost all situations.

Practical Illustration of the Log Size Model: Discounted Cash Flow Valuations

Let's illustrate how the iterative process works with a specific example. The assumptions in Tables 4-4A, 4-4B and 4-4C are identical, except for the discount rate. Table 4-4A is a very simple discounted cash flow (DCF)

---

14. I thank my friend William Scott, Jr., a physicist, for the terminology and the definitive word that there is no analytic solution.

TABLE 4-4A

Discounted Cash Flow Analysis Using 60-Year Model—First Iteration

	A	B	C	D	E	F	G
5	**Description:**	**1999**	**2000**	**2001**	**2002**	**2003**	**Total**
6	**Assumptions:**						
7	Base adjusted cash flow	$100,000					
8	Growth rate in adj cash flow	12%	10%	9%	8%	7%	
9	Discount rate = R	20%					
10	Growth rate to perpetuity = G	6%					
11	Control premium	40%					
12	Discount-lack of marketability	35%					
14	**5 Year Forecasts**						
16	Forecast cash flow	$112,000	$123,200	$134,288	$145,031	$155,183	
17	Present value factor	0.9129	0.7607	0.6339	0.5283	0.4402	
18	PV of cash flow	**$102,242**	**$93,721**	**$85,130**	**$76,617**	**$68,317**	**$426,028**
20	**Calculation of Fair Market Value:**						
21			**Formula**				
22	Forecast cash flow 2003	$164,494	(1 + G) * F16				
23	Gordon model cap rate	7.8246	SQRT (1 + R) / (R − G)				
24	FMV 2003-infinity as of 1/1/2003	$1,287,103	B22 × B23				
25	Present value factor-5 Yrs	0.4019	1/(1 + R)^5 [Where 5 is # yrs from 1/1/98 to 1/1/2003]				
26	PV of 2003-infinity cash flow	$517,258	B24 × B25				
27	Add PV of 1998–2002 cash flow	426,028	Total of row 18				
28	FMV-marketable minority	**$943,285**	B26 + B27				
29	Control premium	377,314	B11 × B28				
30	FMV-marketable control interest	1,320,599	B28 + B29				
31	Disc-lack of marketability	(462,210)	− B12 × B30				
32	Fair market − illiquid control	**$858,390**	B30 + B31				
33	**Calc of Disc Rate-Regr Eq #2**						
34	Ln (FMV-marketable minority)	13.7571	Ln(B28)				
35	* X coefficient of −.01039	−0.1429	B34 * X coefficient-regr #2				
36	Constant	0.3750	Constant-regression #2				
37	Discount rate (rounded)	**23%**	B35 + B36				

analysis of a hypothetical firm. The basic assumptions appear in B7–B12. We assume the firm had $100,000 cash flow in 1998. We forecast annual growth through the year 2003 in B8 through F8 and perpetual growth at 6% thereafter in B10. In B9 we assume a 20% discount rate.

The DCF analysis in B22–B32 is standard and requires little explanation. The present value factors are midyear, and the value in B28 is a marketable minority interest.[15] It is this value ($943,285) that we use to compare the consistency between the assumed discount rate of 20% (B9) and the calculated discount rate according to the log size model.

We begin calculating the discount rate using the log size model in B34, where we compute ln (943,285) = 13.7571. This is the natural log of the marketable minority value of the firm. In B35 we multiply that result

---

15. See Chapter 7 for explanation of the levels of value and valuation discounts and premiums.

TABLE 4-4B

Discounted Cash Flow Analysis Using 60-Year Model—Second Iteration

	A	B	C	D	E	F	G
5	Description:	1999	2000	2001	2002	2003	Total
6	Assumptions:						
7	Base adjusted cash flow	$100,000					
8	Growth rate in adj cash flow	12%	10%	9%	8%	7%	
9	Disc rate = R (Table 4-4A, row 37)	23%					
10	Growth rate to perpetuity = G	6%					
11	Control premium	40%					
12	Discount-lack of marketability	35%					
14	5 Year Forecasts						
16	Forecast cash flow	$112,000	$123,200	$134,288	$145,031	$155,183	
17	Present value factor	0.9017	0.7331	0.5960	0.4845	0.3939	
18	PV of cash flow	$100,987	$90,314	$80,034	$70,274	$61,132	$402,741
20	Calculation of Fair Market Value:						
21			Formula				
22	Forecast cash flow 2003	$164,494	(1 + G) * F16				
23	Gordon model cap rate	6.5238	SQRT (1 + R)/(R − G)				
24	FMV 2003-infinity as of 1/1/2003	$1,073,135	B22 × B23				
25	Present value factor-5 yrs	0.3552	1/(1 + R)^5 [where 5 is # yrs from 1/1/98 to 1/1/2003]				
26	PV of 2003-infinity cash flow	$381,179	B24 × B25				
27	Add PV of 1998-2002 cash flow	402,741	Total of row 18				
28	FMV-marketable minority	$783,919	B26 + B27				
29	Control premium	313,568	B11 × B28				
30	FMV-marketable control interest	1,097,487	B28 + B29				
31	Disc-lack of marketability	(384,121)	− B12 × B30				
32	Fair market value − illiquid control	$713,367	B30 + B31				
33	Calc of Disc Rate-Regr Eq #2						
34	Ln (FMV-marketable minority)	13.5721	Ln(B28)				
35	* X coefficient of −.01039	−0.1410	B34 * X coefficient-regr #2				
36	Constant	0.3750	Constant-regression #2				
37	Discount rate (rounded)	23%	B35 + B36				

Note: We have achieved consistency in the discount rate assumed (Row 9) and the implied discount rate (Row 37). Also the discount rates match Table 4-3 as we interpolate between $500k and $750k.

by the x-coefficient from the regression, or -0.01039, to come to -0.1429. We then add that product to the regression constant of 0.3750, which appears in B36, to obtain an implied discount rate of 23% (rounded, B37).

Comparison of the two discount rates (assumed and calculated) reveals that we initially assumed too high a discount rate, meaning that we undervalued the firm. B29–B31 contain the control premium and discount for lack of marketability. Because the discount rate is not yet consistent, ignore these numbers in this table, as they are irrelevant. These topics are explained in depth in Chapter 7. While the magnitude of the control premium has been the subject of hot debate, it is merely a parameter in the spreadsheet and does not affect the logic of the analysis.

Discounted Cash Flow Analysis Using 60-Year Model—Final Valuation

	A	B	C	D	E	F	G
5	**Description:**	**1999**	**2000**	**2001**	**2002**	**2003**	**Total**
6	**Assumptions:**						
7	Base adjusted cash flow	$100,000					
8	Growth rate in adj cash flow	12%	10%	9%	8%	7%	
9	Disc rate = R [1]	25%					
10	Growth rate to perpetuity = G	16%					
11	Control premium	40%					
12	Discount-lack of marketability	35%					
14	**5 Year Forecasts**						
16	Forecast cash flow	$112,000	$123,200	$134,288	$145,031	$155,183	
17	Present value factor	0.8944	0.7155	0.5724	0.4579	0.3664	
18	PV of cash flows	**$100,176**	**$88,155**	**$76,871**	**$66,416**	**$56,853**	**$388,471**
20	**Calculation of Fair Market Value:**						
21			**Formula**				
22	Forecast cash flow 2003	$164,494	(1 + G) * F16				
23	Gordon model cap rate	5.8844	SQRT (1 + R)/(R − G)				
24	FMV 2003-infinity as of 1/1/2003	$967,948	B22 × B23				
25	Present value factor-5 yrs	0.3277	1/(1 + R)^5 [where 5 is # yrs from 1/1/98 to 1/1/2003]				
26	PV of 2003-infinity cash flow	$317,177	B24 × B25				
27	Add PV of 1998–2002 cash flow	388,471	Total of row 18				
28	FMV-marketable minority	**$705,648**	B26 + B27				
29	Control premium	282,259	B11 × B28				
30	FMV-marketable control interest	987,907	B28 + B29				
31	Disc-lack of marketability	(345,767)	− B12 × B30				
32	Fair market value − illiquid control	**$642,139**	B30 + B31				

[1] Disc Rate = 23% (from Table 4-4B, B37) + 2% for Specific Company Adjustments = 25%

The Second Iteration: Table 4-4B

Having determined that a 20% discount rate is too low, we revise our assumption to a 23% discount rate (B9) in Table 4-4B. In this case, we arrive at a marketable minority FMV of $ 783,919 (B28). When we perform the discount rate calculation with this value (B34–B37), we obtain a matching discount rate of 23%, indicating that no further iterations are necessary.

Consistency in Levels of Value

In calculating discount rates, it is important to be consistent in the level of fair market value that we are using. Since the log size model is based on returns from the NYSE, the corresponding values generated are on a marketable minority basis. Consequently, it is this level of value that is we should use for the discount rate calculations.

Frequently, however, the marketable minority value is not the ultimate level of fair market value that we are calculating. Therefore, it is crucial to be aware of the differing levels of FMV that occur as a result of valuation adjustments. For example, if our valuation assignment is to calculate an illiquid control interest, we will add a control premium and subtract a discount for lack of marketability from the marketable minority value. Nevertheless, we use only the marketable minority level of FMV in iterating to the proper discount rate.

Adding Specific Company Adjustments to the DCF Analysis: Table 4-4C

The final step in our DCF analysis is performing specific company adjustments. Let's suppose for illustrative purposes that there is only one owner of this firm. She is 62 years old and had a heart attack three years ago. The success of the firm depends to a great extent on her personal relationships with customers, which may not be easily duplicated by a new owner. Therefore, we decide to add a 2% specific company adjustment to the discount rate to reflect this situation.[16] If there is no specific company adjustment, then we would proceed with the calculations in B22–B32.

Prior to adding a specific company adjustment, it is important to achieve internal consistency in the ex ante and ex post marketable minority values, as we did in Table 4-4B. Next, we merely add the 2% to get a 25% discount rate, which we place in B9. The remainder of the table is identical to its predecessors, except that we eliminate the ex post calculation of the discount rate in B34–B37, since we have already achieved consistency.

It is at this point in the valuation process that we make adjustments for the control premium and discount for lack of marketability, which appear in B29 and B31. Our final fair market value of $642,139 (B32) is on an illiquid control basis.

In a valuation report, it would be unnecessary to show Table 4-4A. One should show Tables 4-4B and 4-4C only.

Total Return versus Equity Premium

CAPM uses an equity risk premium as one component for calculating return. The discount rate is calculated by multiplying the equity premium by beta and adding the risk free rate. In my first article on the log size model (Abrams 1994), I also used an equity premium in the calculation of the discount rate. Similarly, Grabowski and King (1995) used an equity risk premium in the computation of the discount rate.

---

16. A different approach would be to take a discount from the final value, which would be consistent with key person discount literature appearing in a number of articles in *Business Valuation Review* (see the BVR index for cites). Another approach is to lower our estimate of earnings to reflect our weighted average estimate of decline in earnings that would follow from a change in ownership or the decreased capacity of the existing owner, whichever is more appropriate, depending on the context of the valuation. In this example I have already assumed that we have done that. There are opinions that one should lower earnings estimates and not increase the discount rate. It is my opinion that we should definitely increase the discount rate in such a situation, and we should also decrease the earnings estimates if that has not already been done.

The equity premium form of the log size model is:

$$r = R_F + \text{size-based equity premium} \qquad (4\text{-}14)$$

The size-based equity premium is equal to the return, as calculated by the log size model, minus the historical average risk-free rate.[17]

$$\text{Equity Premium} = a + b \ln \text{FMV} - \overline{R}_F \qquad (4\text{-}15)$$

where $\overline{R}_F$ is the historical average risk-free rate. Substituting equation (4-15) into (4-14), we get:

$$r = R_F + a + b \ln \text{FMV} - \overline{R}_F \qquad (4\text{-}16)$$

Rearranging terms, we get:

$$r = a + b \ln \text{FMV} + (R_F - \overline{R}_F) \qquad (4\text{-}17)$$

Note that the first two terms in equation (4-17) are the sole terms included in the total return version of the log size model. Therefore, the only difference in calculation of discount rates between the two models is $R_F - \overline{R}_F$, the last two terms appearing in equation [4-17]. Consequently, the total return of the log size model will exceed the equity premium version of the model whenever current bond yields exceed historical average yields and vice versa.

The equity premium term was eliminated in Abrams' second article (1997) in favor of total return because of the low correlation between stock returns and bond yields for the past 60 years. The actual correlation was 6.3%—an amount small enough to ignore.

Bond yields were in the 2–3% range before 1960, under 5% until 1968, and over 7% from 1975–1993; in 1982 they were as high as 13%. During the 60-year period from 1939–1998, the low bond yields prevalent in the 1950s and 1960s are balanced by higher subsequent rates, resulting in little difference in the results obtained using the two models. The 60-year mean bond yield is 5.64%, as compared with 1998 yields that have ranged from 5.5% to 6.0%. Thus, current yields are comparable with the 60 year average yields.

Therefore, it is reasonable to simplify the procedure of calculating discount rates and eliminate the bifurcation of the discount rate into the risk-free rate and equity premium components.

---

17. In CAPM, the latter term is a beta-adjusted equity risk premium, equal to ($\beta \times$ equity risk premium). The equity risk premium (ERP) itself is the arithmetic average of the annual market returns in excess of the risk-free rate. Mathematically, that is ERP $= \sum\limits_{t=1926}^{1998} [r_{mt} - r_{Ft})/73]$, where r = return and the subscripts m = market and F = risk-free rate. However, we can rearrange the equation to ERP $= \sum\limits_{t=1926}^{1998} [(r_{mt}/73) - (r_{Ft}/73)] = \overline{r}_m - \overline{r}_F$. This is appropriate for the market as a whole. To calculate a discount rate for a particular firm, in CAPM we scale the ERP up or down according to the systematic risk as measured by beta. In log size, we replace the average return on the market with the size-based return for the firm. There is no algebraic scaling, as the log size equation accomplishes the adjustment of the ERP directly by size.

Adjustments to the Discount Rate

Is Table 4-3 the last word in calculating discount rates? No, but it is the best starting point based on the available data. Table 4-3 is an extrapolation of NYSE data to privately held firms. While the results appear very reasonable to me, it would be preferable to perform a similar regression for NASD data. Unfortunately, the data are not readily obtainable.

Privately held firms are generally owned by people who are not well diversified. Table 4-3 was derived from portfolios of stocks that were diversified in every sense except for size, as size itself was the method of sorting the deciles. In contrast, the owner of the local bar is probably not well diversified, nor is the probable buyer. The appraiser may want to add a specific company adjustment of, say, 2% to 5% to the discount rate implied by Table 4-3 to account for that. On the other hand, a $100 million FMV firm is likely to be bought by a well diversified buyer and may not merit increasing the discount rate.

Another common adjustment to Table 4-3 discount rates would be for the depth and breadth of management of the subject company compared to other firms of the same size. In general, Table 4-3 already incorporates the size effect. No one expects a $100,000 FMV firm to have three Harvard MBAs running it, but there is still a difference between a complete one-man show and a firm with two talented people. In general, this methodology of calculating discount rates will increase the importance of comparing the subject company to its peers via RMA Associates or similar data. Differences in leverage between the subject company and its RMA peers could well be another common adjustment.

Discounted Cash Flow or Net Income?

Since the market returns are based on the cash dividends and the market price at which one can sell one's stock, the discount rates obtained with the log size model should be properly applied to cash flow, not to net income. We appraisers, however, sometimes work with clients who want a "quick and dirty valuation," and we often don't want to bother estimating cash flow. I have seen suggestions in *Business Valuation Review* (Gilbert 1990, for example) that we can increase the discount rate and thereby apply it to net income, and that will often lead to reasonable results. Nevertheless, it is better to make an adjustment from net income based on judgment to estimate cash flow to preserve the accuracy of the discount rate.

DISCUSSION OF MODELS AND SIZE EFFECTS

The size effects described by Fama and French (1993), Abrams (1994, 1997), and Grabowski and King (1995) strongly suggest that the traditional one-factor CAPM model is obsolete. As Fama and French (1993, p. 54) say, "Many continue to use the one-factor Sharpe–Lintner model to evaluate portfolio performance and to estimate the cost of capital, despite the lack of evidence that it is relevant. At a minimum, these results here and in Fama and French (1992) should help to break this common habit."

CAPM

Consider the usual way we calculate discount rates using CAPM. We average the betas of many different firms in the industry, which vary considerably in size, and apply the resulting beta to a firm that is probably 0.1% to 1% of the industry average, without correction for size, and hence risk. Ignoring the size effect corrupts the CAPM results.

This flaw also applies to the guideline public company method. The usual approach is to average price earnings multiples (and/or price cash flow multiples, etc.) for the various firms in the industry without correcting for size and apply the multiple to a small private firm. A better method is to perform a regression analysis of market capitalization (value) as a function of earnings (or cash flow) and forecast growth, when available. I also recommend using another form of the regression with P/E or P/CF as the dependent variable and market capitalization and forecast growth as the independent variables.

The beta used in CAPM is usually calculated by running a regression of the equity premium for an individual company versus the market premium. As previously discussed, the inability of the resulting beta to explain the size effect has called into question the validity of CAPM. An alternative method of calculating beta has been proposed which attempts to capture the size effect and better correlate with market equity returns, possibly ameliorating this problem.

Sum Beta

Ibbotson et al. (Peterson, Kaplan, and Ibbotson 1997) postulated that conventional estimates of beta are too low for small stocks due to the higher degree of auto-correlation in returns exhibited by smaller firms. They calculated a beta using a multiple regression model for both the current and the prior period, which they call "sum beta." These adjusted estimates of beta helped to account for the size effect and showed positive correlation with future returns.

This improved method of calculating betas will reduce will reduce some of the downward bias in CAPM discount rates, but it still will not account for the size effect differences between the large firms in the NYSE—where even the smallest firms are large—and the smaller privately held firms that many appraisers are called upon to value. Size should be an explicit variable in the model to accomplish that.

It may be possible to combine the models. One could use the log size model to calculate a size premium over the average market return and add that to a CAPM calculation of the discount rate using Ibbotson's sum betas. It will take more research to determine whether than is a worthwhile improvement in methodology.

The Fama–French Cost of Equity Model[18]

The Fama–French cost of equity model is a multivariable regression model that uses size ("small minus big" premium $\equiv$ SMB) and book to

---

18. The precise method of calculating beta, SMB, and HML using the three-factor model, along with the regression equation, is more fully explained in Ibbotson Associates' *Beta Book*.

market equity ("high minus low" premium ≡ HML) in addition to beta as variables that affect market returns. Michael Annin (1997) examined the model in detail and found that it does appear to correct for size, both in the long term and short term, over the 30-year time period tested.

The cost of equity model, however, is neither generally accepted nor easy to use (Annin 1997), and using it to determine discount rates for privately held firms is particularly problematic. Market returns are not available for these firms, rendering direct use of the model impossible.[19] Discount rates based on using the three-factor model are published by Ibbotson Associates in the *Cost of Capital Quarterly* by industry SIC code, with companies in each industry sorted from highest to lowest. Determining the appropriate percentile grouping for a privately held firm is a major obstacle, however. The Fama–French model is a superior model for calculating discount rates of publicly held firms. It is not practical for privately held firms.

Log Size Models

The log size model is a superior approach because it better correlates with historical equity returns. Therefore, it enables business appraisers to dispense with CAPM altogether and use firm size as the basis for deriving a discount rate before adjustments for qualitative factors different from the norm for similarly sized companies.

In another study on stock market returns, analysts at an investment banking firm regressed P/E ratios against long-term growth rate and market capitalization. The R^2 values produced by the regressions were 89% for the December 1989 data and 73% for the November 1990 data. Substituting the natural logarithm of market capitalization in place of market capitalization, the same data yields an R^2 value of 91% for each data set, a marginal increase in explanatory power for the first regression but a significant increase in explanatory power for the second regression.

From Chapter 3, equation (3-28), the PE multiple is equal to

$$PE = (1 - b)(1 + g_1) \frac{\sqrt{1 + r}}{r - g}$$

Using a log size model to determine r, the PE multiple is equal to:

$$PE = (1 - RR)(1 + g_1) \frac{\sqrt{1 + a + b \ln (FMV)}}{a + b \ln(FMV) - g} \qquad (4-18)$$

where g_1 is expected growth in the first forecast year, RR is the retention ratio,[20] a and b are the log size regression coefficients, and g is the long-term growth rate. Looking at equation (4-18), it is clear why using the log of market capitalization improved the R^2 of the above regression.

Grabowski and King (1995) applied a finer breakdown of portfolio returns than was previously used to relate size to equity premiums. When

---

19. Based on a conversation with Michael Annin.
20. Equation (3-28) uses the more conventional term b instead of RR to denote the retention ratio. Here we have changed the notation in order to eliminate confusion, as we use the term b for the regression x-coefficient.

they performed regressions with 31-year data for 25 and 100 portfolios (as compared to our 10), they found results similar to the equity premium form of log size model, i.e., the equity premium is a function of the negative of the log of the average market value of equity, further supporting this relationship.[21]

Grabowski and King (1996) in an update article also used other proxies for firm size in their log size discount rate model, including sales, five-year average net income, and EBITDA. Following is a summary of their regression results sorted first by R^2 in descending order, then by the standard error of the y-estimate in ascending order. Overall, we are attempting to present their best results first.

Measure of Size	R^2	Standard Error of Y-Estimate
1. Mkt cap—common equity	93%	0.862%
2. Five-year average net income	90%	0.868%
3. Market value of invested capital	90%	1.000%
4. Five-year average EBITDA	87%	0.928%
5. Book value—invested capital	87%	0.989%
6. Book value—equity	87%	0.954%
7. Number of employees	83%	0.726%
8. Sales	73%	1.166%

Note that the market value of common equity, i.e., market capitalization of common equity, has the highest R^2 of all the measures. This is the measure that we have used in our log size model. The five-year average net income, with an R^2 of 90%, is the next-best independent variable, superior to the market value of invested capital by virtue of its lower standard error.

This is a very important result. It tells us that the majority of the information conveyed in the market price of the stock is contained in net income. When we use a log size model based on equity in valuing a privately held firm, we do not have the benefit of using a market-determined equity. The value will be determined primarily by the magnitude and timing of the forecast cash flows, the primary component of which is forecast net income. If we did not know that the log of net income was the primary causative variable of the log size effect, it is possible that other variables such as leverage, sales, book value, etc. significantly impact the log size effect. If we failed to take those variables into account and our subject company's leverage varied materially from the average of the market (in each decile) as it is impounded into the log size equation, our model would be inaccurate. Grabowski and King's research eliminates this problem. Thus, we can be reasonably confident that the log size model as presented is accurate and is not missing any significant variable.

Of Grabowski and King's eight different measures of size, only market capitalization (#1) and the market value of invested capital (#3) have

---

21. Grabowski and King actually used base 10 logarithms.

the circular reasoning problem of our log size model. The other measures of size have the advantage in a log size model of eliminating the need for iteration since the discount rate equation does not depend on the market value of equity, the determination of which is the ultimate purpose of the discount rate calculation. For example, if we were to use #2, net income, we would simply insert the subject company's five-year average net income into Grabowski and King's regression equation and it would determine the discount rate. This is problematic, however, for determining discount rates for high-growth firms, due to the inability to adequately capture significant future growth in sales, net income, and so on. Start-up firms in high technology industries frequently have negative net income for the first several years due to their investment in research and development. Sales may subsequently rise dramatically once products reach the market. Therefore, five-year averages are not suitable in this situation.

Another problem with Grabowski and King's results is that their data only encompass 1963–1994, 31 years—the years for which Compustat data were available for all companies. Thus, their equations suffer from the same wide confidence intervals that our 30-year regressions have. Their standard error of the y-estimate is 0.862% (Exhibit A, p. 106), which is six times larger than our 1938–1997 confidence intervals.[22] Thus, their 95% confidence intervals will also be approximately six times wider around the regression estimate.

As mentioned in the introduction, in their latest article (Grabowski and King 1999) they demonstrate a negative logarithmic relationship between returns and operating margin and a positive logarithmic relationship between returns and the coefficient of variation of operating margin and accounting return on equity.

This is their most important result so far because it relates returns to fundamental measures of risk. Actually, it appears to me that operating margin in itself works because of its strong correlation of 0.97 to market capitalization, i.e., value. However, the coefficient of variations (CV) of operating margin and return on equity seem to be more fundamental measures of risk than size itself. In other words, it appears that size itself is a proxy for the volatility of operating margin, return on equity, and possibly other measures. Thus, we must pay serious attention to their results.

Below is a summary of their statistical results.

Measure of Risk	R^2	Standard Error of Y-Estimate
1. Log of five-year operating margin	76%	1.185%
2. Log CV(operating margin)	54%	0.957%
3. Log CV (return on equity)	54%	0.957%

---

22. Our standard error increased after incorporating the 1998 stock market results because it was such a perverse year, with decile #1 performing fabulously and decile #10 losing. Thus, both our results and Grabowski and King's would be worse with 1998 included, and the relative difference between the two would be less.

In conclusion, Grabowski and King's (1996) work is very important in that it demonstrates that other measures of size can serve as effective proxies for our regression equation. It is noteworthy that the finer breakdown into 25 portfolios versus Ibbotson's 10 has a significant impact on the reliability of the regression equation. Our 30-year results show a negative R^2 (Table 4-2, I13), while their R^2 was 93%.[23] It did not seem to improve the standard error of the y-estimate. Overall, our log size results using 60-year data are superior to Grabowski and King's results because of the significantly smaller standard error of the y-estimate, which means the 95% confidence intervals around the estimate are correspondingly smaller using the 60 years of data.[24]

Grabowski and King's (1999) work is even more important. It is the first finding of the underlying variables for which size is a proxy. If Compustat data went back to 1926, as do the CRSP data, then I would recommend abandoning log size entirely in favor of their variables. However, there are several reasons why I do not recommend abandoning log size:

1. Because the Compustat database begins in 1963, it misses 1926–1962 data.[25] Because of this, their R^2's are lower and their standard error of y-estimates are significantly higher than ours, leading to larger confidence intervals.

2. Their sample universe consists of publicly traded firms that are all subject to Securities Exchange Commission scrutiny. There is much greater uniformity of accounting treatment in the public firms than in the private firms to which professional appraisers will be applying their results. This would greatly increase confidence intervals around the valuation estimates.

3. The lower R^2's of Grabowski and King's results may mean that size still proxies for other currently unknown variables or that size itself has a pure effect on returns that must be accounted for in an asset pricing model. Thus, log size is still important, and Grabowski and King themselves said that was still the case.

Heteroscedasticity

Schwert and Seguin (1990) also found that stock market returns for small firms are higher than predicted by CAPM by using a weighted least squares estimation procedure. They suggest that the inability of beta to correctly predict market returns for small stocks is partially due to heteroscedasticity in stock returns.

Heteroscedasticity is the term used to describe the statistical condition that the variance of the error term is not constant. The standard assumption in an ordinary least squares (OLS) regression is that the errors

---

23. Again, the 1998 anomalous stock market results had a large impact on this measure. For the 30 years ending 1997, the R^2 was 53%.

24. Again, the difference would be less after including 1998 results.

25. While we have eliminated the first 12 or 13 years of stock market data—a choice that is reasonable, but arguable—that still means the Grabowski and King results eliminate 1938–1962.

are normally distributed, have constant variance, and are independent of the x-variable(s). When that is not true, it can bias the results. In the simplest case of heteroscedasticity, the variance of the error term is linearly related to the independent variable. This means that observations with the largest x-values are generating the largest errors and causing bias to the results. Using weighted least squares (WLS) instead of OLS will correct for that problem by weighting the largest observations the least.

In the case of CAPM, the regression is usually done in the form of excess returns to the firm as a function of excess returns in the market, or: $(r_i - r_F) = \hat{\alpha} + \hat{\beta}(R_m - R_F)$. Here we are using the historical market returns as our estimate of future returns. If everything works properly, $\hat{\alpha}$ should be equal to zero. If there is heteroscedasticity, then when excess market returns are high, the errors will tend to be high. That is what Schwert and Seguin found.

Schwert and Seguin also discovered that after taking heteroscedasticity into account, the relationship between firm size and risk-adjusted returns is *stronger* than previously reported. They also found that the spread between the risk of small and large stocks was greater during periods of heavier market volatility, e.g., 1929–1933.

INDUSTRY EFFECTS

Jacobs and Levy (1988) examined rates of return in 38 different industries by including industry as a dummy variable in their regression analyses. Only one industry (media) showed (excess) returns different from zero that were significant at the $p = 1\%$ level,[26] which the authors speculate was possibly related to the then recent wave of takeovers. The higher returns to media would only be relevant to a subject company if it was a serious candidate for a takeover.

There were seven industries where (excess) returns were different from zero at the $p = 10\%$ level, but this is not persuasive, as the usual level for rejecting the null hypothesis that industry does not matter in investor returns is $p = 5\%$ or less. Thus, Jacobs and Levy's results lead to the general conclusion that industry does not matter in investor returns.[27]

SATISFYING REVENUE RULING 59-60 WITHOUT A GUIDELINE PUBLIC COMPANY METHOD

Revenue Ruling 59-60 requires that we look at publicly traded stocks in the same industry as the subject company. I claim that our excellent re-

---

26. This means that, given the data, there is only a 1% probability that the media industry returns were the same as all other industries.
27. Jacobs and Levy also found an interest rate-sensitive financial sector. They also found that macroeconomic events appear to explain some industry returns. Their example was that precious metals was the most volatile industry and its returns were closely related to gold prices. Thus, there may be some—but not many—exceptions to the general rule of industry insignificance.

sults with the log size model[28] combined with Jacobs and Levy's general finding of industry insignificance satisfies the intent of Revenue Ruling 59-60 for small and medium firms without the need actually to perform a publicly traded guideline company method. Some in our profession may view this as heresy, but I stick to my guns on this point.

We repeat equation (3-28) from Chapter 3 to show the relationship of the PE multiple to the Gordon model.

$$PE = (1 + g_1)(1 - b) \frac{\sqrt{1 + r}}{r - g}$$

relationship of the PE multiple to the Gordon model multiple

(3-28)

The PE multiple[29] of a publicly traded firm gives us information on the one-year and long-run expected growth rates and the discount rate of that firm—and nothing else. The PE multiple only gives us a combined relationship of r and g. In order to derive either r or g, we would have to assume a value for the other variable or calculate it according to a model.

For example, suppose we use the log size model (or any other model) to determine r. Then the only new information to come out of a guideline public company method (GPCM) is the market's estimate of g,[30] the growth rate of the public firm. There are much easier and less expensive ways to estimate g than to do a GPCM. When all the market research is finished, the appraiser still must modify g to be appropriate for the subject company, and its g is often quite different than the public companies'. So the GPCM wastes much time and accomplishes little.

Because discount rates appropriate for the publicly traded firms are much lower than are appropriate for smaller, privately held firms, using public PE multiples will lead to gross overvaluations of small and medium privately held firms. This is true even after applying a discount, which many appraisers do, typically in the 20–40% range—and rarely with any empirical justification.

If the appraiser is set on using a GPCM, then he or she should use regression analysis and include the logarithm of market capitalization as an independent variable. This will control for size. In the absence of that, it is critical to only use public guideline companies that are approximately the same size as the subject company, which is rarely possible.

This does not mean that we should ignore privately held guideline company transactions, as those are far more likely to be truly comparable. Also, when valuing a very large privately held company, where the size effect will not confound the results, it is more likely to be worthwhile to do a guideline public company method, though there is a potential problem with statistical error from looking at only one industry.

---

28. In the context of performing a discounted cash flow method.
29. Included in this discussion are the variations of PE, e.g., P/CF, etc.
30. This is under the simplest assumption that $g_1 = g$.

SUMMARY AND CONCLUSIONS

The log size model is not only far more accurate than CAPM for valuing privately held businesses, but it is much faster and easier to use. It requires no research,[31] whereas CAPM often requires considerable research of the appropriate comparables (guideline companies).

Moreover, it is very inaccurate to apply the betas for IBM, Compaq, Apple Computer, etc. to a small startup computer firm with $2 million in sales. The size effect drowns out any real information contained in betas, especially applying betas of large firms to small firms. The almost six-fold improvement that we found in the 0.34% standard error in the 60-year log size equation versus the 1.89% standard error from the 73-year CAPM applies only to firms of the same magnitude. When applied to small firms, CAPM yields even more erroneous results, unless the appraiser compensates by blindly adding another 5–10% beyond the typical Ibbotson "small firm premium" and calling that a specific company adjustment (SCA). I suspect this practice is common, but then it is not really an SCA; rather, it is an outright attempt to compensate for a model that has no place being used to value small and medium firms.

Several years ago, in the process of valuing a midsize firm with $25 million in sales, $2 million in net income after taxes, and very fast growth, I used a guideline public company method—among others. I found 16 guideline companies with positive earnings in the same SIC Code. I regressed the value of the firm against net income, with "great" results—99.5% R^2 and high t-statistics. When I applied the regression equation to the subject company, the value came to −$91 million![32] I suspect that much of this scaling problem goes on with CAPM as well, i.e., many appraisers seriously overvalue small companies using discount rates appropriate for large firms only.

When using the log size model, we extrapolate the discount rate to the appropriate level for each firm that we value. There is no further need for a size adjustment. We merely need to compare our subject company to other companies of its size, not to IBM. Using Robert Morris Associates data to compare the subject company to other firms of its size is appropriate, as those companies are often far more comparable than NYSE firms.

Since we have already extrapolated the rate of return through the regression equation in a manner that appropriately considers the average risk of being any particular size, the relevant comparison when considering specific company adjustments is to other companies of the same size. There is a difference between two firms that each do $2 million in sales volume when one is a one-man show and the other has two Harvard MBAs running it. If the former is closer to average management, you should probably subtract 1% or 2% from the discount rate for the latter;

---

31. One needs only a single regression equation for all valuations performed within a single year.
32. The magnitude problem was solved by regressing the natural log of value against the natural log of net income. That eliminated the scaling problem and led to reasonable results. That particular technique is not always the best solution, but it sometimes works beautifully. We cover this topic in more detail near the end of Chapter 2.

if the latter is the norm, it is appropriate to add that much to the discount rate of the former. Although specific company adjustments are subjective, they serve to further refine the discount rate obtained from discount rate calculations.

BIBLIOGRAPHY

Abrams, Jay B. 1994. "A Breakthrough in Calculating Reliable Discount Rates." *Business Valuation Review* (August): 8–24.

Abrams, Jay B. 1997. "Discount Rates as a Function of Log Size and Valuation Error Measurement." *The Valuation Examiner* (Feb./March): 19–21.

Annin, Michael. 1997. "Fama-French and Small Company Cost of Equity Calculations." *Business Valuation Review* (March 1997): 3–12.

Banz, Rolf W. 1981. "The Relationship Between Returns and Market Value of Common Stocks." *Journal of Financial Economics* 9: 3–18.

Fama, Eugene F., and Kenneth R. French. 1992. "The Cross-Section of Expected Stock Returns." *Journal of Finance* 47: 427–65.

———. 1993. "Common Risk Factors in the Returns on Stocks and Bonds." *Journal of Financial Economics* 33: 3–56.

Gilbert, Gregory A. 1990. "Discount Rates and Capitalization Rates: Where are We?" *Business Valuation Review* (December): 108–13.

Grabowski, Roger, and David King. 1995. "The Size Effect and Equity Returns." *Business Valuation Review* (June): 69–74.

———. 1996. "New Evidence on Size Effects and Rates of Return." *Business Valuation Review* (September): 103–15.

———. 1999. "New Evidence on Size Effects and Rates of Return." *Business Valuation Review* (September): 112–30.

Harrison, Paul. 1998. "Similarities in the Distribution of Stock Market Price Changes between the Eighteenth and Twentieth Centuries." *Journal of Business* 71, no. 1 (January).

Hayes, Richard. 1726. *The Money'd Man's Guide: or, the Purchaser's Pocket-Companion.* London: W. Meadows.

Ibbotson & Associates. 1999. *Stocks, Bonds, Bills and Inflation: 1999 Yearbook.* Chicago: The Associates.

Jacobs, Bruce I., and Kenneth N. Levy. 1988. "Disentangling Equity Return Regularities: New Insights and Investment Opportunities." *Financial Analysts Journal* (May–June): 18–42.

Neal, L. 1990. *The Rise of Financial Capitalism: International Capital Markets in the Age of Reason.* Cambridge: Cambridge University Press.

Peterson, James D., Paul D. Kaplan, and Roger G. Ibbotson. 1997. "Estimates of Small Stock Betas Are Much Too Low." *Journal of Portfolio Management* 23 (Summer): 104–11.

Schwert, G. William, and Paul J. Seguin. 1990. "Heteroscedasticity in Stock Returns." *Journal of Finance* 45: 1129–56.

Thomas, George B., Jr. 1972. *Calculus and Analytic Geometry.* Reading, Mass: Addison-Wesley.

APPENDIX A

Automating Iteration using Newton's Method

This appendix is optional. It is mathematically difficult and is more analytically interesting than practical.

In this section we present a numerical method for automatically iterating to the correct log size discount rate. Isaac Newton invented an iterative procedure using calculus to provide numerical solutions to equations with no analytic solution. Most calculus texts will have a section on his method (for example, see Thomas 1972). His procedure involves making an initial guess of the solution, then subtracting the equation itself divided by its own first derivative to provide a second guess. We repeat the process until we converge to a single answer.

The benefit of Newton's method is that it will enable us to simply enter assumptions for the cash flow base and the perpetual growth, and the spreadsheet will automatically calculate the value of the firm without our having to manually go through the iterations as we did in Tables 4-4A, B, and C. Remember, some iteration process is necessary when using log size discount rates because the discount rate is not independent of size, as it is using other discount rate models.

To use Newton's procedure, we rewrite equation (4-13) as:

$$\text{Let } f(V) = V - \left[\frac{CF}{(a + b \ln V - g)} \right] = 0 \qquad (A4-1)$$

$$f'(V) = 1 + \left[\frac{bCF}{V(a + b \ln V - g)^2} \right] \qquad (A4-2)$$

Assuming our initial guess of value is V_0, the formula that defines our next iteration of value, V_1, is:

$$V_1 = V_0 - \frac{V_0 - \dfrac{CF}{(a + b \ln V_0 - g)}}{1 + \dfrac{bCF}{V_0(a + b \ln V_0 - g)^2}} \qquad (A4-3)$$

Table A4-5 shows Newton's iterative process for the simplest valuation. In B22–B26 we enter our initial guess of value of an arbitrary $2 trillion (B22), our forecast cash flow base of $100,000 (B23), perpetual growth $g = 7\%$ (B24), and our regression coefficients a and b (B25 and B26, which come from Table 4-1, E42 and E48, respectively).

In B7 we see our initial guess of $2 trillion. The iteration #2 value of $280,530 (B8) is the result of the formula in the note immediately below Table A4-5, which is equation (A4-3).[33] B9 to B12 are simply the formula in B8 copied to the remaining spreadsheet cells.

Once we have the formula, we can value any firm with constant growth in its cash flows by simply changing the parameters in B23 to B24.

---

33. Cell B7, our initial guess, is V_0 in equation (A4-3).

Gordon Model Valuation Using Newton's Iterative Process

	A	B
5	**Iteration**	**Value**
6	**t**	**V(t)**
	0	2,000,000,000,000
8	1	280,530
9	2	612,879
10	3	599,634
11	4	599,625
12	5	599,625
14	**Proof of Calculation:**	
16	Discount rate	23.68%
17	Gordon multiple	5.9963
18	× CF = FMV	$599,625
30	**Parameters**	
22	V(0)	2,000,000,000,000
23	CF	100,000
24	g	7%
25	a	37.50%
26	b	−1.039%
29	**Model Sensitivity**	
30	**FMV**	**Initial Guess = V(0)**
31	Explodes	3,000,000,000,000
32	599,625	2,000,000,000,000
33	599,625	27,000
34	Explodes	26,000

Formula in Cell B8:

= B7 − ((B7 − (CF/(A + B * LN(B7) − G)))/(1 + (B * CF)/(B7 * (A + B * LN(B7) −G)^2)))

Note: The above formula assumes an End-Year Gordon Model. Newton's Method converges for the midyear Gordon Model, but too slowly to be of practical use.

B31 to B34 show the sensitivity of the model to the initial guess. If we guess poorly enough, the model will explode instead of converging to the right answer. For this particular set of assumptions, an initial guess of anywhere between $27,000 and $2 trillion will converge to the right answer. Assumptions above $3 trillion or below $26,000 explode the model.

Unfortunately, the midyear Gordon model, which is more accurate, has a much more complex formula. The iterative process does converge, but much too slowly to be of any practical use. One can use the end-of-year Gordon model and multiply the result by the square root of $(1 + r)$.

Mathematical Appendix

This appendix provides the mathematics behind the log size model, as well as some philosophical analysis of the mathematics—specifically on the nature of exponential decay function and how that relates to phenomena in physics as well as our log size model. This is intended more as intellectual observation than as required information.

We will begin with two definitions:

r = return of a portfolio
S = standard deviation of returns of the portfolio

Equation (B4-1) states that the return on a portfolio of securities (each decile is a portfolio) varies positively with the risk of the portfolio, or:

$$r = a_1 + b_1 S \qquad \text{(B4-1)}$$

This is a generalization of equation (4-1) in the chapter. This relationship is not directly observable for privately held firms. Therefore, we use the next equation, which is a generalization of equation (4-2) from the chapter, to calculate expected return.

The parameter a_1 is the regression estimate of the risk-free rate,[34] while the parameter b_1 is the regression estimate of the slope, which is the return for each unit increase of risk undertaken, i.e., the standard deviation of returns. Thus, b_1 is the regression estimate of the price of or the reward for taking on risk.

$$r = a_2 + b_2 \ln \text{FMV}, \quad b_2 < 0 \qquad \text{(B4-2)}$$

Equation (B4-2) states that return decreases in a linear fashion with the natural logarithm of firm value. The parameter a_2 is the regression estimate of the return for a \$1 firm[35]—the valueless firm—while the parameter b_2 is the regression estimate of the slope, which is the return for each increase in ln FMV. Thus, b_2 is the regression estimate of the reduction in return investors accept for investing in smaller firms. The terms a_1, a_2, b_1, and b_2 are all parameters determined in regression equations (4-1) and (4-2).

Using all 73 years of stock market data, our regression estimate of $a_1 = 6.56\%$ (Table 4-1, D26), which compares well with the 73-year mean Treasury Bond yield of 5.28%. It would initially appear that the log size regression does a reasonable job of also providing an estimate of the risk-free return. Unfortunately, it is not all that simple, as the log size estimate using 60 years of data fares worse. The log size 60-year estimate of a_1 is 8.90% (Table 4-1, E26), which is a long way off from the 60-year mean treasury bond yield of 5.70% (Table 4-1, E27). Thus, eliminating the first

---

34. A zero risk asset would have no standard deviation of returns. Thus, $S = 0$ and $r = a_1$.
35. A firm worth \$1 would have ln FMV = ln \$1 = 0. Thus in equation (B4-2), for FMV = \$1,
$r = a_2$.

13 years of data had the effect of shifting the regression line upwards and flattening it slightly.

We already knew from our analysis of Table 4-2 in the chapter that using 60 years of data was the overall best choice because of its superiority in the log size equation estimates, but it was not the best choice for estimating equation (4-1). Its R^2 is lower and standard error is higher than the 73-year results.

Focusing now on equation (B5-2), the log size equation, the 60-year regression estimate of $b_1 = -1.0309\%$ (Table 4-1, E48), which is significantly lower in absolute value than the 73-year estimate of -1.284% (D48). The parameter b_2 is the reduction in return that comes about from each unit increase in company value (in natural logarithms). The parameter a_2 is the y-intercept. It is the return (discount rate) for a valueless firm—more specifically, a \$1 firm in value—as $\ln(\$1) = 0$.

Equating the right-hand sides of equation (B4-1) and (B4-2) and solving for S, we see how we are implicitly using the size of the firm as a proxy for risk.

$$S = \frac{a_2 - a_1}{b_1} + \frac{b_2}{b_1} \ln \text{FMV} \qquad (\text{B4-3})$$

Since a_2 is the rate of return for the valueless firm and a_1 is the regression estimate of the risk-free rate—flawed as it is—the difference between them, $a_2 - a_1$ is the equity premium for a \$1.00 firm, i.e., the valueless firm. Dividing by b_1, the price of risk (or reward) for each increment of standard deviation, we get $(a_2 - a_1)/b_1$, the standard deviation of a \$1 firm. We then reduce our estimate of the standard deviation by the ratio of the relative prices of risk in size divided by the price of risk in standard deviation, and multiply that ratio by the log of the size of the firm. In other words, we start with the maximum risk, a \$1 firm, and reduce the standard deviation by the appropriate price times the log of the value of the firm in order to calculate the standard deviation of the firm.

Rearranging equation (B4-3), we get

$$\ln \text{FMV} = \frac{(a_1 - a_2) + b_1 S}{b_2} \qquad (\text{B4-4})$$

Raising both sides of the equation as powers of e, the natural exponent, we get:

$$\text{FMV} = e^{\frac{(a_1 - a_2) + b_1 S}{b_2}} = e^{\frac{(a_1 - a_2)}{b_2}} e^{\frac{b_1 S}{b_2}}, \quad \text{or} \qquad (\text{B4-5})$$

$$\text{FMV} = A e^{kS}, \quad \text{where } A = e^{\frac{(a_1 - a_2)}{b_2}}, \quad k = \frac{b_1}{b_2} < 0 \qquad (\text{B4-6})$$

Here we see that the value of the firm or portfolio declines exponentially with risk, i.e., the standard deviation.

Unfortunately, the standard deviation of most private firms is unobservable since there are no reliable market prices. Therefore, we must solve for the value of a private firm another way. Restating equation (B4-2),

$$r = a_2 + b_2 \ln(\text{FMV}) \qquad (B4\text{-}7)$$

Rearranging the equation, we get:

$$\ln \text{FMV} = \frac{(r - a_2)}{b_2} \qquad (B4\text{-}8)$$

Raising both sides by e, i.e., taking the antilog, we get:

$$\text{FMV} = e^{\frac{(r-a_2)}{b_2}} \qquad (B4\text{-}9)$$

or $\qquad\qquad\qquad\qquad\qquad\qquad\qquad\qquad\qquad\qquad\qquad (B4\text{-}10)$

$$\text{FMV} = Ce^{mr}, \quad \text{where } C = e^{-\frac{a_2}{b_2}} \text{ and } m = \frac{1}{b_2}$$

This shows the FMV of a firm or portfolio declines exponentially with the discount rate. This is reminiscent of a continuous time present value formula; in this case, though, instead of traveling through time we are traveling though expected rates of return. The same is true of equation (B4-6), where we are traveling through degree of risk.

What Does the Exponential Relationship Mean?

Let's try to get an intuitive feel for what an exponential relationship means and why that makes intuitive sense. Equation (B4-6) shows that the fair market value of the firm is an exponentially declining function of risk, as measured by the standard deviation of returns. Repeating equation (B4-6), $\text{FMV} = Ae^{kS}$, $k < 0$. Because we find that risk itself is primarily related to the size of the firm, we come to a similar equation for size. Repeating equation (B4-10), we see that $\text{FMV} = Ce^{mr}$, $m < 0$.

In physics, radioactive minerals such as uranium decay exponentially. That means that a constant proportion of uranium decays at every moment. As the remaining portion of uranium is constantly less over time due to the radioactive decay, the amount of decay at any moment in time or during any finite time period is always less than the previous period. A graph of the amount of uranium remaining over time would be a downward sloping curve, steep at first and increasing shallow over time. Figure 4-3 shows an exponential decay curve.

It appears the same is true of the value of firms. Instead of decaying over time, their value decays over risk. Because it turns out that risk is so closely related to size and the rate of return is so closely related to size, the value also decays exponentially with the market rate of return, i.e., the discount rate. The graph of exponential decay in value over risk has the same general shape as the uranium decay curve.

Imagine the largest ship in the world sailing on a moderately stormy ocean. You as a passenger hardly feel the effects of the storm. If instead you sailed on a slightly smaller ship, you would feel the storm a bit more. As we keep switching to increasingly smaller ships, the storm feels increasingly powerful. The smallest ship on the NYSE might be akin to a 35-foot cabin cruiser, while appraisers often have to value little paddle-boats, the passengers of which would be in danger of their lives while the passengers of the General Electric boat would hardly feel the turbulence.

That is my understanding of the principle underlying the size effect. Size offers diversification of product and service. Size reduces transaction costs in proportion to the entity, e.g., the proceeds of floating a $1 million stock issue after flotation costs are far less in percentage terms than floating a $100 million stock issue. Large firms have greater depth and breadth of management, and greater staying power. Even the chances of beating a bankruptcy exist for the largest businesses. Remember Chrysler? If it were not a very big business, the government would never have jumped in to rescue it. The same is true of the S&Ls. For these and other reasons, the returns of big businesses fluctuate less than small businesses, which means that the smaller the business, the greater the risk, the greater the return.

The FMV of a firm or portfolio declining exponentially with the discount rate/risk is reminiscent of a continuous time present value formula, where Present Value = Principal $\times e^{-rt}$; in this case, though, instead of traveling through time we are traveling though expected rates of return/risk.

APPENDIX C

Abbreviated Review and Use

This abbreviated version of the chapter is intended for those who simply wish to learn the model without the benefit of additional background and explanation, or wish to use it as a quick reference for review.

INTRODUCTION

Historically, small companies have shown higher rates of return than large ones, as evidenced by New York Stock Exchange (NYSE) data over the past 73 years (Ibbotson Associates 1999). Further investigation into this phenomenon has led to the discovery that return (the discount rate) strongly correlates with the natural logarithm of the value of the firm (firm size), which has the following implications:

- The discount rate is a linear function negatively related to the natural logarithm of the value of the firm.
- The value of the firm is an exponential decay function, decaying with the investment rate of return (the discount rate). Consequently, the value also decays in the same fashion with the standard deviation of returns.

As we have already described regression analysis in Chapter 3, we now apply these techniques to examine the statistical relationship between market returns, risk (measured by the standard deviation of returns) and company size.

REGRESSION #1: RETURN VERSUS STANDARD DEVIATION OF RETURNS

Columns A–F in Table 4-1 contain the input data from the *Stocks, Bonds, Bills and Inflation 1999 Yearbook* (Ibbotson Associates 1999) for all of the regression analyses as well as the regression results. We use 73-year average returns in both regressions. For simplicity, we have collapsed 730 data points (73 years × 10 deciles) into 73 data points by using averages. Thus, the regressions are cross-sectional rather than time series. In Column A we list Ibbotson Associates' (1999) division of the entire NYSE into 10 different divisions—known as deciles—based on size, with the largest firms in decile 1 and the smallest in decile 10.[36] Columns B through F contain market data for each decile which is described below.

Note that the 73-year average market return in Column B rises with each decile, as does the standard deviation of returns (Column C). Column D shows the 1998 market capitalization of each decile, which is the price per share times the number of shares. It is also the fair market value (FMV).

Dividing Column D (FMV) by Column F (the number of firms in the decile), we obtain Column G, the average capitalization, or the average

---

36. All of the underlying decile data in Ibbotson originate with the University of Chicago's Center for Research in Security Prices (CRSP), which also determines the composition of the deciles.

fair market value of the firms in each decile. Column H, the last column in the table titled ln (FMV), is the natural logarithm of the average FMV.

Regression of ln (FMV) against standard deviation of returns for the period 1926–1998 (D26 to D36, Table 4-1), gives rise to the equation:

$$r = 6.56\% + (31.24\% \times S) \tag{4-1}$$

where r = return and S = standard deviation of returns.

The regression statistics of adjusted R^2 of 98.82% (D30) a t-statistic of the slope of 27.4 (D35), a p-value of less than 0.01% (D36), and the standard error of the estimate of 0.27% (D28), all indicate a high degree of confidence in the results obtained. Also, the constant of 6.56% (D26) is the regression estimate of the long-term risk-free rate, which compares favorably with the 73-year arithmetic mean income return from 1926–1998 on long-term Treasury Bonds of 5.20%.[37]

The major problem with direct application of this relationship to the valuation of small businesses is coming up with a reliable standard deviation of returns. Appraisers cannot directly measure the standard deviation of returns for privately held firms, since there is no objective stock price. We can measure the standard deviation of income, and we covered that in our discussion in the chapter of Grabowski and King (1999).

REGRESSION #2: RETURN VERSUS LOG SIZE

Fortunately, there is a much more practical relationship. Notice that the returns are negatively related to the market capitalization, i.e., the fair market value of the firm. The second regression in Table 4-1 (D42–D51) is the more useful one for valuing privately held firms. Regression #2 shows return as a function of the natural logarithm of the FMV of the firm. The regression equation for the period 1926–1998 is:

$$r = 42.24\% - [1.284\% \times \ln (FMV)] \tag{4-2}$$

The adjusted R^2 is 92.3% (D45), the t-statistic is -10.4 (D50), and the p-value is less than 0.01% (D51), meaning that these results are statistically robust. The standard error for the Y-estimate is 0.82% (D43), which means that we can be 95% confident that the regression forecast is accurate within approximately $2 \times 0.82\% \cong 1.6$.

Recalculation of the Log Size Model Based on 60 Years

NYSE data from the past 60 years are likely to be the most relevant for use in forecasting the future (see chapter for discussion). This time frame still contains numerous data points, but it excludes the decade of highest volatility, attributed to nonrecurring historical events, i.e., the Roaring Twenties and Depression years. Also, Table 4-2A shows that the 60-year regression equation has the highest adjusted R^2 and lowest standard error

---

37. SBBI-1999, p. 140 uses this measure as the risk-free rate for CAPM. Arguably, the average bond yield is a better measure of the risk-free rate, but the difference is immaterial.

when compared to the other four examined. Therefore, we repeat all three regressions for the 60-year time period from 1939–1998, as shown in Table 4-1, Column E. Regression #1 for this time period for is:

$$r = 8.90\% + (30.79\% \times S) \tag{4-3}$$

where S is the standard deviation.

The adjusted R^2 in this case falls to 95.31% (E30) from the 98.82% (D30) obtained from the 73-year equation, but is still indicative of a strong relationship.

The corresponding log size equation (regression #2) for the 60-year period is:

$$r = 37.50\% - [1.039\% \times \ln (FMV)] \tag{4-4}$$

The regression statistics indicate a good fit, with an adjusted R^2 of 96.95% (E45).[38] Equation (4-4) will be used for the remainder of the book to calculate interest rates, as this time period is the most appropriate for calculating current discount rates.

Need for Annual Updating

Table 4-1 should be updated annually, as the Ibbotson averages change, and new regression equations should be generated. This becomes more crucial when shorter time periods are used, because changes will have a greater impact on the average values. Additionally, it is important to be careful to match the regression equation to the year of the valuation. If the valuation assignment is retroactive and the valuation date is 1994, then don't use the regression equation for 1939–1998. Instead, either use the regression equation in the original article, run your own regression on the Ibbotson data, or contact the author to provide the right equation.

Computation of Discount Rate Is an Iterative Process

In spite of the straightforwardness of these relationships, we have a problem of circular reasoning when it comes to computing of the discount rate. We need FMV to obtain the discount rate, which is in turn used to discount cash flows or income to calculate the FMV! Hence, it is necessary to make sure that our initial estimate of FMV is consistent with the final result. If it is not, then we have to keep repeating the process until the results are consistent. Fortunately, discount rates remain virtually constant over large ranges of values, so this should not be much of a problem.

Practical Illustration of the Log Size Model: Discounted Cash Flow Valuations

Let's illustrate how the iterative process works with a specific example. The assumptions in Tables 4-4A, 4-4B, and 4-4C are identical, except for the discount rate. Table 4-4A is a very simple discounted cash flow (DCF) analysis of a hypothetical firm. The basic assumptions appear in Rows B7 through B12. We assume the firm had $100,000 cash flow in 1998. We

---

38. For 1938–1997 data, adjusted R^2 was 99.54%. The "perverse" results of 1998 caused a deterioration in the relationship.

PART 2 Calculating Discount Rates

forecast annual growth through the year 2003 in B8 through F8 and perpetual growth at 6% thereafter in B10. In B9 we assume a 20% discount rate.

The DCF analysis in Rows B22 through B32 is standard and requires little explanation other than that the present value factors are midyear, and the value in B28 is a marketable minority interest. It is this value ($943,285) that we use to compare the consistency between the assumed discount rate (in Row 4) and calculated discount rate according to the log size model.

We begin calculating the of discount rate using the log size model in B34, where we compute ln (943,285) = 13.7571. This is the natural log of the marketable minority value of the firm. In B35 we multiply that result by the x-coefficient from the regression, or −0.01039, to come to −0.1429. We then add that product to the regression constant of 0.3750, which appears in B36, to obtain an implied discount rate of 23% (rounded, B37).

Comparison of the two discount rates (assumed and calculated) reveals that we initially assumed too high a discount rate, meaning that we undervalued the firm. B29–B31 contain the control premium and discount for lack of marketability. Because the discount rate is not yet consistent, ignore these numbers in this table, as they are irrelevant.

In Chapter 7, we discuss the considerable controversy over the appropriate magnitude of control premiums. Nevertheless, it is merely a parameter in the spreadsheet, and its magnitude does not affect the logic of the analysis.

The Second Iteration: Table 4-4B

Having determined that a 20% discount rate is too low, we revise our assumption to a 23% discount rate (B9) in Table 4-4B. In this case, we arrive at a marketable minority FMV of $ 783,919 (B28). When we perform the discount rate calculation with this value (B34–B37), we obtain a matching discount rate of 23%, indicating that no further iterations are necessary.

Consistency in Levels of Value

In calculating discount rates, it is important to be consistent in the level of fair market value that we are using. Since the log size model is based on returns from the NYSE, the corresponding values generated are on a marketable minority basis. Consequently, it is this level of value that we should use for the discount rate calculations.

Frequently, however, the marketable minority value is not the ultimate level of fair market value that we are calculating. Therefore, it is crucial to be aware of the differing levels of FMV that occur as a result of valuation adjustments. For example, if our valuation assignment is to calculate an illiquid control interest, we will add a control premium and subtract a discount for lack of marketability from the marketable minority value.[39] Nevertheless, we use only the marketable minority level of FMV in iterating to the proper discount rate.

---

39. Not all authorities would agree with this statement. There is considerable disagreement on the levels of value. We cover those controversies in Chapter 7.

Adding Specific Company Adjustments to the DCF Analysis: Table 4-4C

The final step in our DCF analysis is performing specific company adjustments. Let's suppose for illustrative purposes that there is only one owner of this firm. She is 62 years old and had a heart attack three years ago. The success of the firm depends to a great extent on her personal relationships with customers, which may not be easily duplicated by a new owner. Therefore, we decide to add a 2% specific company adjustment to the discount rate to reflect this situation.[40] If there are no specific company adjustments, then we would proceed with the calculations in B22–B32.

Prior to adding specific company adjustments, it is important to achieve internal consistency in the ex ante and ex post marketable minority values, as we did in Table 4-4B. Next, we merely add the 2% to get a 25% discount rate, which we place in B9. The remainder of the table is identical to its predecessors, except that we eliminate the ex post calculation of the discount rate in B34–B37, since we have already achieved consistency.

It is at this point in the valuation process that we make adjustments for the control premium and discount for lack of marketability, which appear in B29 and B31. Our final fair market value of $642,139 (B32) is on an illiquid control basis.

In a valuation report, it would be unnecessary to show Table 4-4A. One should show Tables 4-4B and 4-4C only.

Total Return versus Equity Premium

CAPM uses an equity risk premium as one component for calculating return. The discount rate is calculated by multiplying the equity premium by beta and adding the risk free rate. In my first article on the log size model (Abrams 1994), I used an equity premium in the calculation of discount rate. Similarly, Grabowski and King (1995) used an equity risk premium in the computation of discount rate.

The equity premium term was eliminated in my second article (Abrams 1997) in favor of total return because of the low correlation between stock returns and bond yields for the past 60 years. The actual correlation is 6.3%—an amount small enough to ignore.

Adjustments to the Discount Rate

Privately held firms are generally owned by people who are not well diversified. The NYSE decile data were derived from portfolios of stocks

---

40. A different approach would be to take a discount from the final value, which would be consistent with key person discount literature appearing in a number of articles in *Business Valuation Review* (see the BVR index for cites). Another approach is to lower our estimate of earnings to reflect our weighted average estimate of decline in earnings that would follow from a change in ownership or the decreased capacity of the existing owner, whichever is more appropriate, depending on the context of the valuation. In this example I have already assumed that we have done that. There are opinions that one should lower earnings estimates and not increase the discount rate. It is my opinion that we should definitely increase the discount rate in such a situation, and we should also decrease the earnings estimates if that has not already been done.

that were diversified in every sense except for size, as size itself was the method of sorting the deciles. In contrast, the owner of the local bar is probably not well diversified, nor is the probable buyer. The appraiser may want to add 2% to 5% to the discount rate to account for that. On the other hand, a $1 million FMV firm is likely to be bought by a well-diversified buyer and may not merit increasing the discount rate.

Another common adjustment to discount rates would be for the depth and breadth of management of the subject company compared to other firms of the same size. In general, the regression equation already incorporates the size effect. No one expects a $100,000 FMV firm to have three Harvard MBAs running it, but there is still a difference between a complete one-man show and a firm with two talented people. In general, this methodology of calculating discount rates will increase the importance of comparing the subject company to its peers via RMA Associates or similar data. Differences in leverage between the subject company and its RMA peers could well be another common adjustment.

Discounted Cash Flow or Net Income?

Since the market returns are based on the cash dividends and the market price at which one can sell one's stock, the discount rates obtained with the log size model should be properly applied to cash flow, not to net income. We appraisers, however, sometimes work with clients who want a "quick and dirty valuation," and we often don't want to bother estimating cash flow. I have seen suggestions in *Business Valuation Review* (Gilbert 1990, for example) that we can increase the discount rate and thereby apply it to net income, and that will often lead to reasonable results. Nevertheless, it is better to make an adjustment from net income based on judgment to estimate cash flow to preserve the accuracy of the discount rate.

SATISFYING REVENUE RULING 59-60

As discussed in more detail in the body of this chapter, a study (Jacobs and Levy 1988) found that, in general, industry was insignificant in determining rates of return.[41] Revenue ruling 59-60 requires that we look at publicly traded stocks in the same industry as the subject company. I claim that our excellent results with the log size model,[42] combined with Jacobs and Levy's general finding of industry insignificance, satisfy the intent of Revenue Ruling 59-60 without the need to actually perform a guideline publicly traded company method (GPCM).

The PE multiple[43] of a publicly traded firm gives us information on the one-year and long-run expected growth rates and the discount rate of that firm—and nothing else. Then the only new information to come

---

41. For the appraiser who wants to use the rationale in this section as a valid reason to eliminate the GPCM from an appraisal, there are some possible exceptions to the "industry doesn't matter conclusion" that one should read in the body of the chapter.
42. In the context of performing a discounted cash flow approach.
43. Included in this discussion are the variations of PE, e.g., P/CF, etc.

out of a GPCM is the market's estimate of g,[44] the growth rate of the public firm. There are much easier and less expensive ways to estimate g than doing a GPCM. When all the market research is finished, the appraiser still must modify g to be appropriate for the subject company, and its g is often quite different than the public companies. So the GPCM wastes much time and accomplishes little.

Because discount rates appropriate for the publicly traded firms are much lower than are appropriate for smaller, privately held firms, using public PE multiples will lead to gross overvaluations of small and medium privately held firms. This is true even after applying a discount, which many appraisers do, typically in the 20–40% range—and rarely with any empirical justification.

If the appraiser is set on using a GPCM, then he or she should use regression analysis and include the logarithm of market capitalization as an independent variable. This will control for size. In the absence of that, it is critical to only use public guideline companies that are approximately the same size as the subject company, which is rarely possible.

This does not mean that we should ignore privately held guideline company transactions, as those are far more likely to be truly comparable. Also, when valuing a very large privately held company, where the size effect will not confound the results, it is more likely to be worthwhile to do a guideline public company method, though there is a potential problem with statistical error from looking at only one industry.

---

44. This is under the simplest assumption that $g_1 = g$.

CHAPTER 5

Arithmetic versus Geometric Means: Empirical Evidence and Theoretical Issues

INTRODUCTION

THEORETICAL SUPERIORITY OF ARITHMETIC MEAN

    Table 5-1: Comparison of Two Stock Portfolios

EMPIRICAL EVIDENCE OF THE SUPERIORITY OF THE
ARITHMETIC MEAN

    Table 5-2: Regressions of Geometric and Arithmetic Returns for
    1927–1997

    Table 5-3: Regressions of Geometric Returns for 1938–1997

    The Size Effect on the Arithmetic versus Geometric Means

    Table 5-4: Log Size Comparison of Discount Rates and Gordon Model
    Multiples Using AM versus GM

INDRO AND LEE ARTICLE

This chapter compares the attributes of the arithmetic and geometric mean returns and presents theoretical and empirical evidence why the arithmetic mean is the proper one for use in valuation.

INTRODUCTION

There has been a flurry of articles about the relative merits of using the arithmetic mean (AM) versus the geometric mean (GM) in valuing businesses. The SBBI Yearbook (see Ibbotson Associates 1998) for many years has taken the position that the arithmetic mean is the correct mean to use in valuation. Conversely, Allyn Joyce (1995) initiated arguments for the GM as the correct mean. Previous articles have centered around Professor Ibbotson's famous example using a binomial distribution with 50%–50% probabilities of a +30% and −10% return. His example is an important theoretical reason why the AM is the correct mean. The articles critical of Ibbotson are interesting but largely incorrect and off on a tangent. There are both theoretical and empirical reasons why the arithmetic mean is the correct one.

THEORETICAL SUPERIORITY OF ARITHMETIC MEAN

We begin with a quote from Ibbotson: "Since the arithmetic mean equates the expected future value with the present value, it is the discount rate" (Ibbotson Associates 1998, p. 159). This is a fundamental theoretical reason for the superiority of AM.

Rather than argue about Ibbotson's much-debated above example, let's cite and elucidate a different quote from his book (Ibbotson Associates 1998, p. 108). "In general, the geometric mean for any time period is less than or equal to the arithmetic mean. The two means are equal only for a return series that is constant (i.e., the same return in every period). For a non-constant series, the difference between the two is positively related to the variability or standard deviation of the returns. For example, in Table 6-7 [the SBBI table number], the difference between the arithmetic and geometric mean is much larger for risky large company stocks than it is for nearly riskless Treasury bills."

The GM measures the magnitude of the returns as the investor starts with one portfolio value and ends with another. It does not measure the variability (volatility) of the journey, as does the AM.[1] The GM is backward looking, while the AM is forward looking (Ibbotson Associates 1997). As Mark Twain said, "Forecasting is difficult—especially into the future."

Table 5-1: Comparison of Two Stock Portfolios

Table 5-1 contains an illustration of two differing stock series. The first is highly volatile, with a standard deviation of returns of 65% (C17), while the second has a zero standard deviation. Although the arithmetic mean

---

1. Technically it is the *difference* of the AM and GM that measures the volatility. Put another way, the AM consists of two components: the GM plus the volatility.

TABLE 5-1

Geometric versus Arithmetic Returns

	A	B	C	D	E
4		(Stock (or Portfolio) #1		Stock (or Portfolio) #2	
5	Year	Price	Annual Return	Price	Annual Return
6	0	$100.00	NA	$100.00	NA
7	1	$150.00	50.0000%	$111.61	11.6123%
8	2	$68.00	−54.6667%	$124.57	11.6123%
9	3	$135.00	98.5294%	$139.04	11.6123%
10	4	$192.00	42.2222%	$155.18	11.6123%
11	5	$130.00	−32.2917%	$173.21	11.6123%
12	6	$79.00	−39.2308%	$193.32	11.6123%
13	7	$200.00	153.1646%	$215.77	11.6123%
14	8	$180.00	−10.0000%	$240.82	11.6123%
15	9	$250.00	38.8889%	$268.79	11.6123%
16	10	$300.00	20.0000%	$300.00	11.6123%
17	Standard deviation		64.9139%		0.0000%
18	Arithmetic mean		26.6616%		11.6123%
19	Geometric mean		11.6123%		11.6123%

differs significantly for the two, both give rise to an identical geometric mean return. It makes no sense intuitively that the GM is the correct one. That would imply that both stocks are equally risky since they have the same GM; yet no one would *really* consider stock #2 equally as risky as #1. A risk-averse investor will always pay less for #1 than for #2.

EMPIRICAL EVIDENCE OF THE SUPERIORITY OF THE ARITHMETIC MEAN

Much of the remainder of this chapter is focused on empirical evidence of the superiority of the AM using the log size model. The heart of the evidence in favor of the AM can be found in Chapter 4, Table 4-1, which demonstrates that the arithmetic mean of stock market portfolio returns correlate very well (98% R^2) with the standard deviation of returns, i.e., risk as well as the logarithm of firm size, which is related to risk. We show that the AM correlates better with risk than the GM. Also, the dependent variable (AM returns) is consistent with the independent variable (standard deviation of returns) in the regression. The latter *is* risk, and the former is the fully risk-impounded rate of return. In contrast, the GM does not fully impound risk.

Table 5-2: Regressions of Geometric and Arithmetic Returns for 1927–1997

Table 5-2 contains both the geometric and arithmetic means for the Ibbotson deciles for 1926–1997 data[2] and regressions of those returns

---

2. Note that this will not match Table 4-1, because the latter contains data through 1998. While both chapters were originally written in the same year, we chose to update all of the regressions in Chapter 4 to include 1998 stock market data, while we did not do so in this and other chapters.

T A B L E 5-2

Geometric versus Arithmetic Returns: NYSE Data by Decile & Statistical Analysis: 1926–1997

	A	B	C	D	E	F
5		Geometric	Arithmetic		Avg Cap	
6	Decile	Mean	Mean Return	Std Dev	= FMV [1]	Ln(FMV)
7	1	10.17%	**11.89%**	**18.93%**	$28,650,613,989	24.0784
8	2	11.30%	**13.68%**	**22.33%**	$5,987,835,737	22.5130
9	3	11.67%	**14.29%**	**24.08%**	$3,066,356,194	21.8438
10	4	11.86%	**14.99%**	**26.54%**	$1,785,917,011	21.3032
11	5	12.33%	**15.75%**	**27.29%**	$1,126,473,849	20.8424
12	6	12.08%	**15.82%**	**28.38%**	$796,602,581	20.4959
13	7	12.17%	**16.39%**	**30.84%**	$543,164,462	20.1129
14	8	12.40%	**17.46%**	**35.57%**	$339,165,962	19.6420
15	9	12.54%	**18.21%**	**37.11%**	$209,737,489	19.1614
16	10	13.85%	**21.83%**	**46.14%**	$68,389,789	18.0407
17	Std dev	0.94%	2.7%			
18	Value wtd index	10.7%	12.6%			

20		Regression #1: Return = f(Std Dev. of Returns)		
22			**Arithmetic**	**Geometric**
23			**Mean**	**Mean**
24	Constant		5.90%	8.76%
25	Std err of *Y* est		**0.32%**	**0.36%**
26	*R* squared		98.76%	86.93%
27	Adjusted *R* squared		**98.60%**	**85.29%**
28	No. of observations		10	10
29	Degrees of freedom		8	8
30	*X* coefficient(s)		34.19%	11.05%
31	Std err of coef.		1.35%	1.52%
32	*T*		25.2	7.2
33	*P*		<.01%	0.01%

35		Regression #2: Return = f [Ln(FMV)]		
37			**Arithmetic**	**Geometric**
38			**Mean**	**Mean**
39	Constant		47.62%	22.90%
40	Std err of *Y* est		**0.76%**	**0.27%**
41	*R* squared		93.16%	92.79%
42	Adjusted *R* squared		**92.30%**	**91.89%**
43	No. of observations		10	10
44	Degrees of freedom		8	8
45	*X* coefficient(s)		−1.52%	−0.52
46	Std err of coef.		0.15%	0.05%
47	*T*		−10.4	−10.1
48	*P*		<0.01%	<0.01%

[1] See Table 4-1 of Chapter 4 for specific inputs and method of calcuation

against the standard deviation of returns and the natural logarithm of the average market capitalization of the firms in the decile. It is a repetition of Table 4-1, with the addition of the GM data.

The arithmetic mean outperforms[3] the geometric mean in regression #1, with adjusted R^2 of 98.60% (C27) versus 85.29% (D27) and t-statistic of 25.2 (C32) versus 7.2 (D32). In regression #2, which regresses the return as a function of log size, the arithmetic mean slightly outperforms the geometric mean in terms of goodness of fit with the data. Its adjusted R^2 is 92.3% (C42), compared to 91.9% (D42) for the geometric mean. The absolute value of its t-statistic is 10.4 (C47), compared to 10.1 (D47) for the geometric mean. However, the geometric mean does have a lower standard error of the estimate.

Table 5-3: Regressions of Geometric Returns for 1938–1997

In Chapter 4 we discussed the relative merits of using the log size model based on the past 60 years of NYSE return data rather than 73 years. Table 5-3 shows the regression of ln (FMV) against the geometric mean for the 61-year period 1937–1997.

Comparing the results in Table 5-3 to Table 4-1, the arithmetic mean significantly outperforms the geometric mean. Looking at Regression #2, the Adjusted R^2 in Table 4-1, cell E45 for the arithmetic mean is 99.54%, while the geometric mean adjusted R^2 in Table 5-3, B22 is 81.69%. The t-statistic for the AM is −44.1 (Table 4-1, E50), while it is −6.41 (D34) for the GM. The standard error of the estimate is 0.34% (Table 4-1, E43) for the AM versus 0.47% for the GM.[4] Looking at Regression #1, in Table 4-1, E30, Adjusted R^2 for the AM is 95.31%, while it is 51.52% (B41) for the GM. T-statistics are 13.6 for the AM (Table 4-1, E35) and 3.3 (D53) for the GM. The standard error of the estimate is 0.42% (Table 4-1, E28) for the AM and 0.76% (B42) for the GM. Using the past 60 years of data, the AM significantly outperforms the GM by all measures.

GM does correlate to risk. Its R^2 value in the various regressions is reasonable, but it is just not as good a measure of risk as the AM.

Eliminating the volatile period of 1926–1936 reduces the difference between the geometric and arithmetic means in the calculation of discount rates. We illustrate this at the bottom of Table 4-3, where discount rates are compared for a $20 million and $300,000 FMV firm using both regression equations. For the $20 million firm, the difference in discount rate decreases from 7.9% (E57) using the 72-year equations to 4.9% (E58) for the 60-year equations. We see a larger difference for smaller firms, as shown in Rows 59–60 for the $300,000 FMV firm. In this case, the difference in discount rates falls from 12.1% (E59) to 7.5% (E60), or almost by half.

---

3. In other words, the AM is more highly correlated with risk than the GM.
4. The standard error was 0.14% for the AM for the years 1938–1997.

TABLE 5-3

Geometric Mean versus FMV: 60 Years

	A	B	C	D	E	F	G
4		**Year End Index Value [1]**					
5	**Decile**	1937	1997	GM 1937–1997 [2]	Ln FMV	Std Dev.	
6	1	1.369	1064.570	11.732%	24.0784	15.687%	
7	2	1.345	2232.833	13.154%	22.5130	17.612%	
8	3	1.182	2834.406	13.849%	21.8438	18.758%	
9	4	1.154	3193.072	14.121%	21.3032	20.704%	
10	5	1.141	4324.787	14.721%	20.8424	21.829%	
11	6	0.983	3686.234	14.701%	20.4959	22.750%	
12	7	0.957	3906.82	14.863%	20.1129	24.909%	
13	8	0.894	4509.832	15.269%	19.6420	26.859%	
14	9	1.093	4958.931	15.066%	19.1614	28.415%	
15	10	2.647	11398.583	14.966%	18.0407	36.081%	
17	SUMMARY OUTPUT: GM vs Ln FMV, 60 years						
19	**Regression Statistics**						
20	Multiple R	91.50%					
21	R square	83.73%					
22	Adjusted R square	81.69%					
23	Standard error	0.47%					
24	Observations	10					
26	ANOVA						
27		df	SS	MS	F	Significance F	
28	Regression	1	0.0009	0.0009	41.1611	0.0002	
29	Residual	8	0.0002	0.0000			
30	Total	9	0.0011				
32		Coefficients	Standard Error	t Stat	P-value	Lower 95%	Upper 95%
33	Intercept	26.20%	1.87%	14.0	0.00%	21.89%	30.51%
34	Ln (FMV)	−0.57%	0.09%	−6.4	0.02%	−0.78%	−0.37%
36	SUMMARY OUTPUT: GM vs. Std. Dev., 60 Years						
38	**Regression Statistics**						
39	Multiple R	75.44%					
40	R square	56.91%					
41	Adjusted R square	51.52%					
42	Standard error	0.76%					
43	Observations	1000.00%					

The Size Effect on the Arithmetic versus Geometric Means

It is useful to note that the greater divergence between the AM and GM as firm size decreases and volatility increases means that using the GM results in overvaluation that is inversely related to size, i.e., using the GM on a small firm will cause a greater percentage overvaluation than using the GM on a large firm.

Geometric Mean versus AFMV: 60 Years

	A	B	C	D	E	F	G
45	ANOVA						
46		*df*	*SS*	*MS*	*F*	Significance *F*	
47	Regression	1	0.0006	0.0006	10.5650	0.0117	
48	Residual	8	0.0005	0.0001			
49	Total	9	0.0011				
51		Coefficients	Standard Error	*t* Stat	*P*-value	Lower 95%	Upper 95%
52	Intercept	11.04%	1.01%	10.9	0.00%	8.70%	13.38%
53	Std dev.	13.71%	4.22%	3.3	1.17%	3.98%	23.44%
55	Comparison of Discount Rates Using 60 and 72 Year Models						
56	FMV	Regression Model	Geometric Mean	Arithmetic Mean	Difference		
57	$20,000,000	72 year	14.2%	22.1%	7.9%		
58		60 year	16.6%	21.5%	4.9%		
59	$300,000	72 year	16.3%	28.5%	12.1%		
60		60 year	19.0%	26.5%	7.5%		

[1] Values from Ibbotson's 1998 SBBI Yearbook, Table 7-3
[2] Geometric mean for 1937-1997 was calculated using Year End Index Values for 1937 (for year starting 1938) and 1997 according to the formula $r_g = [v_n/v_o]^{1/n} - 1$
[3] From Table 4-1, Chapter 4

Table 5-4: Log Size Comparison of Discount Rates and Gordon Model Multiples Using AM versus GM

Table 5-4 illustrates this, where discount rates are calculated using the log size model, with both the arithmetic and geometric mean regression equations derived from Tables 4-1 and 5-3, respectively. There is a dramatic difference in discount rates, especially with small firms. The log size discount rate for a $250,000 firm is 26.76% using the AM (B7) and 19.12% using the GM (C7). The resulting midyear Gordon model multiples are 5.42 (D7) using the AM and 8.32 (E7) using the GM.

Column F is the ratio of the Gordon model multiples using the geometric mean to the Gordon model multiples using the arithmetic mean. Dividing the 8.32 GM multiple by the 5.42 AM multiple gives us a ratio of 153.41%, i.e., the GM leads to a valuation that is 53.41% higher than the AM for such a small firm (this is assuming a firm with 6% constant growth). Notice that the ratio declines continuously as we move down Column F. The overvaluation of a $10 billion firm using the GM is 12.57%—far less than the overvaluation of the $250,000 firm. The differences are significantly greater when using the 72-year log size models, as including the most volatile years in the regression makes for a greater difference in the AM versus GM Gordon model multiples. These numerical examples underscore the importance of using the arithmetic mean when valuing expected future earnings or cash flow.

INDRO AND LEE ARTICLE

This article (Indro and Lee 1997) is extremely mathematical, exceedingly difficult reading. The authors begin by citing (Brealey and Myers 1991),

TABLE 5-4

Comparison of Discount Rates Derived from the Log Size Model Using 60-Year Arithmetic and Geometric Means

	A	B	C	D	E	F
5				**Gordon Model Multiples Using**		**Ratio**
6	**Firm Size**	**AM [1]**	**GM [2]**	**AM [3]**	**GM [3]**	**GG/AG [4]**
7	$250,000	26.76%	19.12%	5.42	8.32	153.41%
8	$1,000,000	25.09%	18.33%	5.86	8.83	150.61%
9	$25,000,000	21.21%	16.49%	7.24	10.29	142.14%
10	$50,000,000	20.38%	16.10%	7.63	10.67	139.85%
11	$100,000,000	19.54%	15.70%	8.07	11.09	137.34%
12	$500,000,000	17.60%	14.78%	9.35	12.20	130.52%
13	$10,000,000,000	14.00%	13.08%	13.35	15.03	112.57%

Conclusion: The ratio of Gordon Model Multiples decreases with firm size (Column F)

Notes:

[1] Arithmetic Mean (AM) Regression Equation, 60 year model $r = 41.72\% - 0.01204 \times$ Ln (FMV)

[2] Geometric Mean (GM) Regression Equation, 60 year model. $r = 26.2\% - 0.0057 \times$ Ln (FMV)

[3] Gordon Model Multiple calculated assuming 6% growth in earnings-midyear assumption. Discount rates are not rounded in these calculations.

[4] Geometric Gordon Model Multiple / Arithmetic Gordon Model Multiple

who say that if monthly returns are identically and independently distributed, then the arithmetic average of monthly returns should be used to estimate the long-run expected return. They then cite empirical evidence that there is significant negative autocorrelation in long-term equity returns and that historical monthly returns are not independent draws from a stationery distribution. This means that high returns in one time period will tend to mean that on average there will be low returns in the next period, and vice-versa. Based on this, Copeland, Koller, and Murrin (1994) argue that the geometric average is a better estimate of the long-run expected returns.

Indro and Lee show that the arithmetic and geometric means have upward and downward biases, respectively, and that a horizon-weighted average of the two is the least biased and most efficient estimator.

If the authors are correct, it would mean that there would no longer be a single discount rate. Every year would have its own unique weighted-average discount rate. That would also add complexity to the use of the Gordon model to calculate a residual value.

Because of the extremely difficult mathematics in the article, it was necessary to speak to academic sources to evaluate it. Professor Myers, cited above, did agree that long-term (five-year) returns are negatively autocorrelated but that there are "very few data points." He had not fully read the article, is not sure of its significance, and did not have an opinion of it. Ibbotson Associates does not feel the evidence for mean reversion is that strong, and on that basis is not moved to change its opinion that the AM is the correct mean. It seems that it will take some time before this article gets enough academic attention to cause the valuation profession to make any changes in the way it operates.

BIBLIOGRAPHY

Brealey, R. A., and Stewart C. Myers. 1991. *Principles of Corporate Finance*. New York: McGraw-Hill.

Copeland, Tom, Tim Koller, and Jack Murrin. 1994. Valuation: Measuring and Managing the Value of Companies. John Wiley & Sons, Inc. New York, NY.

Ibbotson Associates. 1998. *Stocks, Bills, Bonds and Inflation: 1998 Yearbook*. Chicago: The Associates. 107–08; 153–155.

Indro, Daniel C., and Wayne Y. Lee. 1997. "Biases in Arithmetic and Geometric Averages as Estimates of Long-Run Expected Returns and Risk Premia." *Financial Management* 26, no. 4 (Winter): 81–90.

Joyce, Allyn A. 1995. "Arithmetic Mean vs. Geometric Mean: The Issue in Rate of Return." *Business Valuation Review* (June): 62–68.

CHAPTER 6

An Iterative Valuation Approach

INTRODUCTION
EQUITY VALUATION METHOD
   Table 6-1A: The First Iteration
   Table 6-1B: Subsequent Iterations of the First Scenario
   Table 6-1C: Initial Choice of Equity Doesn't Matter
   Convergence of the Equity Valuation Method
INVESTED CAPITAL APPROACH
   Table 6-2A: Iterations Beginning with Book Equity
   Table 6-2B: Initial Choice of Equity Doesn't Matter
   Convergence of the Invested Capital Approach
LOG SIZE
SUMMARY
BIBLIOGRAPHY

INTRODUCTION

The capital asset pricing model (CAPM) is probably the most common model appraisers use to calculate discount rates, even though in my opinion it is generally inferior to the log size model for valuing privately held businesses.

At the 1993 ASA summer conference, one of the most controversial and enjoyable sessions was titled "Invested Capital Versus Equity Valuation Methods (or Direct Capital Approaches)." The proponents of the equity valuation methods—primarily using CAPM—for valuing firms argued that the weakness of the invested capital approach (ICA) is that we appraisers are not smart enough to determine the appropriate debt to equity ratio to use in the calculation of the weighted average cost of capital (WACC). They also argued that the wide swings in WACC caused by changes in the assumed debt/equity mix can drastically affect the calculation of fair market value (FMV). While those arguments are sound, the direct capital approach also suffers from a similar deficiency since the appraiser must choose a debt to equity ratio in order to relever beta for the subject company. In other words, both methods suffer from essentially the same problem.

In this chapter, based on Abrams (1995), we show how using an iterative approach eliminates this deficiency in both models. After determining the market value of debt, we can assume any value for equity to get our initial debt to equity ratio. We calculate the first iteration of equity value using this initial ratio. After several iterations, we eventually obtain a unique solution for equity that is consistent with the last iteration of the debt to equity ratio and is independent of our initial choice of equity.

EQUITY VALUATION METHOD

For the equity valuation method, the iterative procedure involves the following steps:

1. Determine forecast after tax earnings (or, preferably, the cash flow equivalent).[1] This should be normalized, i.e., with owners' salaries adjusted to arm's length, etc.

2. Determine the discount rate for the Company's debt and the risk-free rate of interest.

3. Determine the fair market value of interest-bearing debt. This is easy to do, and the FMV of debt will remain constant through all iterations.

4. Derive an unlevered beta using publicly traded guideline Company data.

5. Determine the equity premium and small company premium.

6. Specify an initial capital structure, consisting of the FMV of debt and an initial arbitrary choice of equity. You may use either

---

1. Note: While cash flow is the preferable measure, in this chapter we discount earnings for simplicity of presentation. This is also true for the invested capital approach.

your best guess of the FMV of equity or you can use the net book value of equity. Eventually your initial guess will make no difference.

Steps 1–6 are not repeated. The following steps are iterative.

7. Calculate a relevered beta and equity discount rate using your initial capital structure and use it to value the firm.

8. Substitute the first calculated fair market value of equity into a new capital structure and use the new weights to calculate the next iteration of beta, equity discount rate, and FMV of equity.

9. Keep repeating 7 and 8 until you reach a steady state value for beta, equity discount rate, and FMV of equity.

Let's illustrate this with a couple of examples.

Table 6-1A: The First Iteration

We use a deliberately simple discounted future earnings approach in Table 6-1A to illustrate how this process works. Starting with a firm whose net income before taxes (NIBT) in 1997, the previous year, was $400,000 (cell D28), we assume a declining growth rate in income: 15% (B7) in 1998, 13% (C7) in 1999, finishing with 8% (F7) in 2002. We use these growth rates to forecast income in 1998–2002. Subtracting 40% for income taxes, we arrive at net income after taxes (NIAT) of $276,000 in 1998 (B9), rising to $407,531 in 2002 (F9). The bottom row of the top section is the present value of NIAT, using the calculated equity discount rate and a midyear assumption.

The valuation section begins in cell D17 with the sum of the present value of NIAT for the first five years. The next seven rows are intermediate calculations using a Gordon model with an 8% constant growth rate and the midyear assumption (D17–D23). Forecast income in 2003 is the 2002 net income times one plus the growth rate [F9 × (1 + D18) = D19 = $440,134]. The midyear Gordon model multiple, D20, is equal to SQRT(1 + $r)/(r − g)$ = SQRT(1 + D36)/(D36 − D18) = 8.1456. Multiplying $440,134 × 8.1456 = $3,585,135 (D21), which is the present value of net income after year 2002 as of December 31, 2002. The present value factor for five years is 0.377146 (D22). Multiplying $3,585,135 × 0.377146 = $1,352,121 (D23), which is the present value of income after 2002 as of the valuation date, January 1, 1998.

Adding the present value of the first five years' net income of $1,055,852 (D17) to the present value of the net income after five years of $1,352,121 (D23), we arrive at our first approximation of the FMV of the equity of $2,407,973 (D24).

Rows 28 through 35 contain the assumptions of the model and the data necessary to lever and unlever industry average betas and calculate equity discount rates. The discount rate is in cell D36, though it is calculated in G54 and transferred from there.

Rows 42 through 46 detail the calculation of an unlevered beta of 0.91 (F46) from an average of publicly traded guideline companies. In the capital structure and iterations section, Row 54 shows the market value of debt and

TABLE 6-1A

Equity Valuation Approach with Iterations Beginning with Book Equity: Iteration #1

	A	B	C	D	E	F	G	H
5		**1998**	**1999**	**2000**	**2001**	**2002**		
6	Net inc before taxes	460,000	519,800	576,978	628,906	679,219		
7	Growth rate in NIBT	15%	13%	11%	9%	8%		
8	Income taxes	(184,000)	(207,920)	(230,791)	(251,562)	(271,687)		
9	Net inc after taxes	276,000	311,880	346,187	377,344	407,531		
10	Present value factor	0.9071	0.7464	0.6141	0.5053	0.4158		
11	Pres value NIAT	**$250,357**	**$232,777**	**$212,601**	**$190,675**	**$169,441**		
16	**Final Valuation:**							
17	PV 1998–2002 net income			$1,055,852				
18	Constant growth rate in income = G			8%				
19	Forecast net income-2003			440,134				
20	Gordon model mult = SQRT(1 + R)/(R − G)			8.1456				
21	Present value-net inc after 2002 as of 12/31/2002			3,585,135				
22	Present value factor-5 years			0.377146				
23	Present value of net income after 2002 as of 1/1/98			1,352,121				
24	FMV of equity-100% interest			$2,407,973				
27	**Assumptions:**							
28	Net income before tax-1997			400,000				
29	Income tax rate			40%				
30	Discount rate-debt: pre-tax			10%				
31	Discount rate-debt: after-tax			6%				
32	Unlevered beta (from F46)			0.91				
33	Risk free rate			6%				
34	Equity premium			8%				
35	Small company premium			3%				
36	Equity discount rate = R			**21.534%**				
38	**Calculation of Equity Discount Rate Using Comparables**							
40		**Equity**				**Unlevered**		
41		**Beta**	**Debt**	**Equity**	**D/E**	**Beta**		
42	Guideline Company #1	1.15	454,646	874,464	52.0%	0.88		
43	Guideline Company #2	1.20	146,464	546,454	26.8%	1.03		
44	Guideline Company #3	0.95	46,464	705,464	6.6%	0.91		
45	Guideline Company #4	0.85	52,646	846,467	6.2%	0.82		
46	Totals or averages	1.04	700,220	2,972,849	23.55%	0.91		
49	**Capital Structure & Iterations**							
51			**Interest-**					
52			**Bearing**	**Equity Before**		**Relevered**	**Equity**	**FMV**
53		**t**	**Debt**	**Iteration**	**D/E**	**Beta**	**Disc. Rate**	**Equity**
54	FMV debt, eqty at t − 1	1	900,000	750,000	1.20	1.5668	21.534%	2,407,973
55	FMV debt, eqty at t − 1	2	900,000	2,407,973	0.37	1.1152	17.921%	2,407,973
56	FMV debt, eqty at t − 1	3	900,000	2,407,973	0.37	1.1152	17.921%	2,407,973
57	FMV debt, eqty at t − 1	4	900,000	2,407,973	0.37	1.1152	17.921%	2,407,973
58	FMV debt, eqty at t − 1	5	900,000	2,407,973	0.37	1.1152	17.921%	2,407,973
59	FMV debt, eqty at t − 1	6	900,000	2,407,973	0.37	1.1152	17.921%	2,407,973
60	FMV debt, eqty at t − 1	7	900,000	2,407,973	0.37	1.1152	17.921%	2,407,973
61	FMV debt, eqty at t − 1	8	900,000	2,407,973	0.37	1.1152	17.921%	2,407,973
62	FMV debt, eqty at t − 1	9	900,000	2,407,973	0.37	1.1152	17.921%	2,407,973
63	FMV debt, eqty at t − 1	10	900,000	2,407,973	0.37	1.1152	17.921%	2,407,973
64	FMV debt, eqty at t − 1	11	900,000	2,407,973	0.37	1.1152	17.921%	2,407,973
65	FMV debt, eqty at t − 1	12	900,000	2,407,973	0.37	1.1152	17.921%	2,407,973
66	FMV debt, eqty at t − 1	13	900,000	2,407,973	0.37	1.1152	17.921%	2,407,973
67	FMV debt, eqty at t − 1	14	900,000	2,407,973	0.37	1.1152	17.921%	2,407,973
68	FMV debt, eqty at t − 1	15	900,000	2,407,973	0.37	1.1152	17.921%	2,407,973
69	FMV debt, eqty at t − 1	16	900,000	2,407,973	0.37	1.1152	17.921%	2,407,973
70	FMV debt, eqty at t − 1	17	900,000	2,407,973	0.37	1.1152	17.921%	2,407,973
71	FMV debt, eqty at t − 1	18	900,000	2,407,973	0.37	1.1152	17.921%	2,407,973
72	FMV debt, eqty at t − 1	19	900,000	2,407,973	0.37	1.1152	17.921%	2,407,973
73	FMV debt, eqty at t − 1	20	900,000	2,407,973	0.37	1.1152	17.921%	2,407,973

the book value of equity (our initial guess of market value) as well as the implied debt/equity ratio and relevered beta according to Hamada's formula (Hamada 1972):[2]

$$\beta_{\text{levered}} = \beta_{\text{unlevered}} \times \left[1 + (1 - \text{Tax Rate}) \frac{\text{Debt}}{\text{Equity}} \right]$$

Cell G54 is the discount rate of 21.534% for the first iteration, calculated according to the formula

$$\text{Disc Rate} = \text{Risk Free Rate} + (\beta_{\text{levered}} \times \text{Equity Premium})$$
$$+ \text{Small Company Premium}$$

We use this discount rate to calculate the first iteration of FMV of equity in cell H54.

Table 6-1B: Subsequent Iterations of the First Scenario

Table 6-1B is identical to Table 6-1A, except that it contains nine iterations in the capital structure section instead of 1. Also, cell D36 contains the final equity discount rate from Row 62.[3] We denote the iteration number as t, which appears in Column B, Rows 54–62. When $t = 1$, we obtain an equity discount rate of 21.534% (G54) and a FMV of the equity of $2,407,973 (H54), as before. This tells us that our initial guess of the FMV of the equity, which was the book value of the equity of $750,000 (D54), is too low.

We substitute the $2,407,973 (H54) first iteration of equity into the new capital structure in D55 to get a debt/equity ratio of 0.37 (E55), as seen in the second iteration of Table 6-1B. This changes the discount rate to 17.921% (G55). This results in the second iteration of equity value of $3,245,701 (H55). We use the new equity as the basis for our third iteration, which we calculate in the same fashion as the previous iteration. We follow these steps until we reach a steady state, which in this case occurs in the eighth iteration, with a FMV of $3,404,686 (H61). We must carry out an additional iteration to know for sure that we have reached a steady state, which is the purpose of iteration #9.

Table 6-1C: Initial Choice of Equity Doesn't Matter

Tables 6-1B and 6-1C demonstrate that the initial choice of equity doesn't matter. Instead of choosing book equity as the starting point, in Table 6-1C we make an arbitrary guess of $5,000,000 (D54) as a starting point.[4]

---

2. This equation is most accurate when the firm's pretax discount rate for debt is close to the risk-free rate.
3. Actually, D36 takes on the value calculated in each iteration in G54 through G62, so the discount rate used in all the calculations changes in each iteration of the spreadsheet.
4. For those who buy the electronic spreadsheet from the author, which is not included with this book, the steps are: (1) input your initial guess of equity in D54; (2) initialize the spreadsheet by pressing Control-X; (3) press Control-Z for each iteration. Every time you press Control-Z, the spreadsheet will calculate one iteration of value, as in Rows 54 to 62. Repeat pressing Control-Z until you have reached a steady state, i.e., the value in Column H is the same twice in a row.

Equity Valuation Approach with Iterations Beginning with Book Equity

	A	B	C	D	E	F	G	H
5		1998	1999	2000	2001	2002		
6	Net inc before taxes	460,000	519,800	576,978	628,906	679,219		
7	Growth rate in NIBT	15%	13%	11%	9%	8%		
8	Income taxes	(184,000)	(207,920)	(230,791)	(251,562)	(271,687)		
9	Net inc after taxes	276,000	311,880	346,187	377,344	407,531		
10	Present value factor	0.9228	0.7857	0.6690	0.5696	0.4850		
11	Pres value NIAT	$254,680	$245,045	$231,602	$214,952	$197,669		
16	**Final Valuation:**							
17	PV 1998–2002 net income			$1,143,949				
18	Constant growth rate in net income = G			8%				
19	Forecast net income-2003			440,134				
20	Gordon model mult = SQRT(1 + R)/(R − G)			11.4763				
21	Present value-net inc after 20002 as of 12/31/2002			5,051,106				
22	Present value factor-5 years			0.447573				
23	Pres value of net income after 2002 as of 1/1/98			2,260,738				
24	FMV of equity-100% interest			$3,404,686				
27	**Assumptions:**							
28	Net income before tax-1997			400,000				
29	Income tax rate			40%				
30	Discount rate-debt: pre-tax			10%				
31	Discount rate-debt: after-tax			6%				
32	Unlevered beta (from F46)			0.91				
33	Risk free rate			6%				
34	Equity premium			8%				
35	Small company premium			3%				
36	Equity discount rate = R			**17.443%**				
38	**Calculation of Equity Discount Rate Using Comparables**							
40		Equity				Unlevered		
41		Beta	Debt	Equity	D/E	Beta		
42	Guideline Company #1	1.15	454,646	874,464	52.0%	0.88		
43	Guideline Company #2	1.20	146,464	546,454	26.8%	1.03		
44	Guideline Company #3	0.95	46,464	705,464	6.6%	0.91		
45	Guideline Company #4	0.85	52,646	846,467	6.2%	0.82		
46	Totals or averages	1.04	700,220	2,972,849	23.55%	0.91		
49	**Capital Structure & Iterations**							
51			Interest-					
52			Bearing	Equity Before		Relevered	Equity	FMV
53		t	Debt	Iteration	D/E	Beta	Disc. Rate	Equity
54	FMV debt, eqty at t − 1	1	900,000	750,000	1.20	1.5668	21.534%	2,407,973
55	FMV debt, eqty at t − 1	2	900,000	2,407,973	0.37	1.1152	17.921%	3,245,701
56	FMV debt, eqty at t − 1	3	900,000	3,245,701	0.28	1.0625	17.500%	3,385,037
57	FMV debt, eqty at t − 1	4	900,000	3,385,037	0.27	1.0562	17.450%	3,402,345
58	FMV debt, eqty at t − 1	5	900,000	3,402,345	0.26	1.0555	17.444%	3,404,409
59	FMV debt, eqty at t − 1	6	900,000	3,404,409	0.26	1.0554	17.443%	3,404,653
60	FMV debt, eqty at t − 1	7	900,000	3,404,653	0.26	1.0554	17.443%	3,404,682
61	FMV debt, eqty at t − 1	8	900,000	3,404,682	0.26	1.0554	17.443%	3,404,686
62	FMV debt, eqty at t − 1	9	900,000	3,404,686	0.26	1.0554	17.443%	3,404,686

Equity Valuation Approach with Iterations Beginning with Arbitrary Equity

	A	B	C	D	E	F	G	H
5		**1998**	**1999**	**2000**	**2001**	**2002**		
6	Net inc before taxes	460,000	519,800	576,978	628,906	679,219		
7	Growth rate in NIBT	15%	13%	11%	9%	8%		
8	Income taxes	(184,000)	(207,920)	(230,791)	(251,562)	(271,687)		
9	Net inc after taxes	276,000	311,880	346,187	377,344	407,531		
10	Present value factor	0.9228	0.7857	0.6690	0.5696	0.4850		
11	Pres value NIAT	**$254,680**	**$245,045**	**$231,602**	**$214,952**	**$197,669**		
16	**Final Valuation:**							
17	PV 1998–2002 net income			$1,143,949				
18	Constant growth rate in net income = G			8%				
19	Forecast net income-2003			440,134				
20	Gordon model mult = SQRT(1 + R)/(R − G)			11.4763				
21	Present value-net inc after 20002 as of 12/31/2002			5,051,106				
22	Present value factor-5 years			0.447573				
23	Pres value of net income after 2002 as of 1/1/98			2,260,738				
24	FMV of equity-100% interest			$3,404,686				
27	**Assumptions:**							
28	Net income before tax-1997			400,000				
29	Income tax rate			40%				
30	Discount rate-debt: pre-tax			10%				
31	Discount rate-debt: after-tax			6%				
32	Unlevered beta (from F46)			0.91				
33	Risk free rate			6%				
34	Equity premium			8%				
35	Small company premium			3%				
36	Equity discount rate = R			**17.443%**				
38	**Calculation of Equity Discount Rate Using Comparables**							
40		**Equity**				**Unlevered**		
41		**Beta**	**Debt**	**Equity**	**D/E**	**Beta**		
42	Guideline Company #1	1.15	454,646	874,464	52.0%	0.88		
43	Guideline Company #2	1.20	146,464	546,454	26.8%	1.03		
44	Guideline Company #3	0.95	46,464	705,464	6.6%	0.91		
45	Guideline Company #4	0.85	52,646	846,467	6.2%	0.82		
46	Totals or averages	1.04	700,220	2,972,849	23.55%	0.91		
49	**Capital Structure & Iterations**							
51			**Interest-**					
52			**Bearing**	**Equity Before**		**Relevered**	**Equity**	**FMV**
53		**t**	**Debt**	**Iteration**	**D/E**	**Beta**	**Disc. Rate**	**Equity**
54	FMV debt, eqty at t − 1	1	900,000	5,000,000	1.18	1.0093	17.074%	3,538,676
55	FMV debt, eqty at t − 1	2	900,000	3,538,676	0.25	1.0499	17.399%	3,420,038
56	FMV debt, eqty at t − 1	3	900,000	3,420,038	0.26	1.0547	17.438%	3,406,499
57	FMV debt, eqty at t − 1	4	900,000	3,406,499	0.26	1.0553	17.442%	3,404,901
58	FMV debt, eqty at t − 1	5	900,000	3,404,901	0.26	1.0554	17.443%	3,404,712
59	FMV debt, eqty at t − 1	6	900,000	3,404,712	0.26	1.0554	17.443%	3,404,689
60	FMV debt, eqty at t − 1	7	900,000	3,404,689	0.26	1.0554	17.443%	3,404,687
61	FMV debt, eqty at t − 1	8	900,000	3,404,687	0.26	1.0554	17.443%	3,404,686
62	FMV debt, eqty at t − 1	9	900,000	3,404,686	0.26	1.0554	17.443%	3,404,686

Table 6-1C is identical to Table 6-1B except in the initial choice of value of the equity and the intermediate iterations. The final FMV is identical. Note that it does not matter whether your initial guess is too low or too high: as Table 6-1B is too low and Table 6-1C is too high, but they both lead to the same FMV.

Convergence of the Equity Valuation Method

While rare, it can happen that the FMV diverges instead of converges. If the method described above does not converge, an alternative is to take the average of the resulting FMV of equity and the previously assumed value as your input into column D when starting the next iteration as opposed to using just the latest iteration of equity alone. This can be done by making a small alteration to the spreadsheet.[5]

INVESTED CAPITAL APPROACH

Tables 6-2A and 6-2B are examples of the invested capital approach. They are very similar to Table 6-1B for the equity valuation method, with the following exceptions:

1. We determine earnings before interest but after taxes (EBIBAT) as the income measure.[6] This should be normalized EBIBAT.[7]
2. We discount EBIBAT using the WACC.
3. We must subtract the market value of debt from the calculated market value of invested capital to get the market value of equity.
4. We must calculate a new WACC for every new iteration of FMV of equity.
5. We do not show the calculation of unlevered beta but will assume that it has already been calculated to be 1.05.

Let's illustrate this with a couple of examples.

Table 6-2A: Iterations Beginning with Book Equity

Earnings before interest and taxes (EBIT) in 1997, the previous year, was $600,000 (cell D28). We assume a declining growth rate in earnings as before: 15% (B6) in 1998, 13% (C6) in 1999, finishing with 8% (F6) in 2002. We use these growth rates to forecast EBIT in 1998–2002. Subtracting 40% for income taxes, we arrive at earnings before interest, but after taxes (EBIBAT) of $414,000 in 1998 (B8), rising to $611,297 in 2002 (F8). The growth rates in EBIBAT are identical to those for EBIT because we assume a constant 40% income tax (D29). The last row of the top section is the

---

5. Change the formula in D55, which previously was =H55, to =AVERAGE(D54,H54). Then copy the formula down Column D.
6. It is better to use cash flow (before interest but after taxes), but for simplicity we use EBIBAT.
7. This does not necessarily correspond to the NIBT in Tables 6-1A, 6-1B, and 6-1C, because we are dealing with a different hypothetical company.

WACC Approach with Iterations Beginning with Book Equity

	A	B	C	D	E	F	G	H	I	J
4		1998	1999	2000	2001	2002				
5	EBIT	690,000	779,700	865,467	943,359	1,018,828				
6	Growth rate in EBIT	15%	13%	11%	9%	8%				
7	Income taxes	(276,000)	(311,880)	(346,187)	(377,344)	(407,531)				
8	EBIBAT	414,000	467,820	519,280	566,015	611,297				
9	Growth rate-EBIBAT	15%	13%	11%	9%	8%				
10	Present value factor	0.9308	0.8064	0.6986	0.6052	0.5243				
11	Pres value-EBIBAT	$385,341	$377,237	$362,767	$342,566	$320,523				
14	**Final Valuation:**									
15	PV 1998–2002 EBIBAT			$1,788,434						
16	Constant growth rate in EBIBAT			8%						
17	Forecast EBIBAT-2003			660,200						
18	Gordon model mult = SQRT(1 + R)/(R − G)			14.4646						
19	PV-EBIBAT after 2002 as of 1-1-2003			9,549,547						
20	Present value factor-5 years			0.488036						
21	PV-EBIBAT after 2002			4,660,523						
22	Enterprise FMV-100% interest			$6,448,957						
23	Less FMV of debt			(2,000,000)						
24	FMV of equity-100% interest			$4,448,957						
27	**Assumptions:**									
28	EBIT-1997			600,000						
29	Income tax rate			40%						
30	Discount rate-debt: pre-tax			10%						
31	Discount rate-debt: after-tax			6%						
32	Unlevered beta			1.05						
33	Risk free rate			6%						
34	Equity premium			8%						
35	Small company premium			3%						
36	Wtd avg cost of capital (WACC)			15.428%						
38	**Capital Structure & Iterations**									

	A	t	Interest-Bearing Debt	Equity	Total	Interest-Bearing Debt	Equity	Equity Disc. Rate	WACC	FMV Equity
43	FMV debt, eqty at t − 1	1	2,000,000	800,000	2,800,000	71.4%	28.6%	30.000%	12.857%	7,776,091
44	FMV debt, eqty at t − 1	2	2,000,000	7,776,091	9,776,091	20.5%	79.5%	18.696%	16.099%	3,927,835
45	FMV debt, eqty at t − 1	3	2,000,000	3,927,835	5,927,835	33.7%	66.3%	19.966%	15.254%	4,599,240
46	FMV debt, eqty at t − 1	4	2,000,000	4,599,240	6,599,240	30.3%	69.7%	19.592%	15.473%	4,411,165
47	FMV debt, eqty at t − 1	5	2,000,000	4,411,165	6,411,165	31.2%	68.8%	19.685%	15.416%	4,458,814
48	FMV debt, eqty at t − 1	6	2,000,000	4,458,814	6,458,814	31.0%	69.0%	19.661%	15.431%	4,446,410
49	FMV debt, eqty at t − 1	7	2,000,000	4,446,410	6,446,410	31.0%	69.0%	19.667%	15.427%	4,449,617
50	FMV debt, eqty at t − 1	8	2,000,000	4,449,617	6,449,617	31.0%	69.0%	19.665%	15.428%	4,448,787
51	FMV debt, eqty at t − 1	9	2,000,000	4,448,787	6,448,787	31.0%	69.0%	19.666%	15.428%	4,449,002
52	FMV debt, eqty at t − 1	10	2,000,000	4,449,002	6,449,002	31.0%	69.0%	19.666%	15.428%	4,448,946
53	FMV debt, eqty at t − 1	11	2,000,000	4,448,946	6,448,946	31.0%	69.0%	19.666%	15.428%	4,448,960
54	FMV debt, eqty at t − 1	12	2,000,000	4,448,960	6,448,960	31.0%	69.0%	19.666%	15.428%	4,448,957
55	FMV debt, eqty at t − 1	13	2,000,000	4,448,957	6,448,957	31.0%	69.0%	19.666%	15.428%	4,448,957

present value of EBIBAT, using the calculated WACC as the discount rate and a midyear assumption.

The valuation section begins in cell D15 with the sum of the present value of the first five years of EBIBAT. The next seven rows are the same intermediate calculations as in Tables 6-1A, 6-1B, and 6-1C, using a Gordon model with an 8% constant growth rate and the midyear assumption (D16–D21). Our final iteration of the FMV of the equity plus debt (enterprise value, or enterprise FMV) is $6,448,957 (D22). From this we subtract the FMV of the debt of $2,000,000 to arrive at the final iteration of FMV of equity of $4,448,957 (D24).

Let's look at the calculation of WACC for the first iteration. For this firm, we assume the FMV of interest-bearing debt is $2,000,000 (C43). We further temporarily assume the FMV of the equity is its book value of $800,000 (D43). Using these two initial values as our first approximation, debt is 71.4% (F43) of the invested capital and equity is 28.6% (G43). We calculate the first iteration of equity discount rate of 30% in cell H43 in the same way as in the previous tables. We calculate the WACC to be:

$$\text{WACC} = [(1 - \text{Tax Rate}) \times \text{Debt Discount Rate} \times \% \text{ Debt}]$$
$$+ [\text{Equity Discount Rate} \times \% \text{ Equity}]$$

or

$$\text{WACC} = [(1 - 0.4) \times 0.10 \times 71.4\%] + (.30 \times 28.6\%]$$
$$= 12.857\% \text{ (I43)}[8]$$

We discount EBIBAT at this WACC to get the FMV of equity of $7,776,091 in cell J43. This iteration of equity is then transferred to cell D44, and the process is repeated. After 12 iterations we arrive at a FMV of equity of $4,448,957 (J54). We then confirm this value by iterating once more in Row 55.

Table 6-2B: Initial Choice of Equity Doesn't Matter

Tables 6-2A and 6-2B demonstrate that the initial choice of equity doesn't matter. Instead of choosing book equity as the starting point, in Table 6-2B we make an arbitrary guess of $10,000,000 (D43) as a starting point. Table 6-2B is identical to Table 6-2A, except in the initial choice of value of the equity and the intermediate iterations. The final result is identical. Note that it does not matter whether your initial guess is too low or too high: Table 6-2A is too low and Table 6-2B is too high, but they both lead to the same result.

Convergence of the Invested Capital Approach

As with the equity valuation method, if the method described above does not converge, an alternative is to take the average of the resulting FMV of equity and the previously assumed value as your input into column D

---

8. There is an apparent rounding error, as the percentages of debt and equity to six decimal places are 0.714286 and 0.285714.

WACC Approach with Iterations Beginning with Arbitrary Guess of Equity Value

	A	B	C	D	E	F	G	H	I	J
4		**1998**	**1999**	**2000**	**2001**	**2002**				
5	EBIT	690,000	779,700	865,467	943,359	1,018,828				
6	Growth rate in EBIT	15%	13%	11%	9%	8%				
7	Income taxes	(276,000)	(311,880)	(346,187)	(377,344)	(407,531)				
8	EBIBAT	414,000	467,820	519,280	566,015	611,297				
9	Growth rate-EBIBAT	15%	13%	11%	9%	8%				
10	Present value factor	0.9308	0.8064	0.6986	0.6052	0.5243				
11	Pres value-EBIBAT	**$385,341**	**$377,237**	**$362,767**	**$342,566**	**$320,523**				

14	**Final Valuation:**	
15	PV 1998–2002 EBIBAT	$1,788,434
16	Constant growth rate in EBIBAT	8%
17	Forecast EBIBAT-2003	660,200
18	Gordon model mult = SQRT(1 + R)/(R − G)	14.4646
19	PV-EBIBAT after 2002 as of 1-1-2003	9,549,547
20	Present value factor-5 years	0.488036
21	PV-EBIBAT after 2002	4,660,523
22	Enterprise FMV-100% interest	$6,448,957
23	Less FMV of debt	(2,000,000)
24	FMV of equity-100% interest	**$4,448,957**

27	**Assumptions:**	
28	EBIT-1997	600,000
29	Income tax rate	40%
30	Discount rate-debt: pre-tax	10%
31	Discount rate-debt: after-tax	6%
32	Unlevered beta	1.05
33	Risk free rate	6%
34	Equity premium	8%
35	Small company premium	3%
36	Wtd avg cost of capital (WACC)	**15.428%**

38	**Capital Structure & Iterations**									
40 41 42		t	Interest-Bearing Debt	Equity	Total	Interest-Bearing Debt	Equity	Equity Disc. Rate	WACC	FMV Equity
43	FMV debt, eqty at t − 1	1	2,000,000	10,000,000	12,000,000	16.7%	83.3%	18.408%	16.340%	3,761,117
44	FMV debt, eqty at t − 1	2	2,000,000	3,761,117	5,761,117	34.7%	65.3%	20.080%	15.192%	4,654,820
45	FMV debt, eqty at t − 1	3	2,000,000	4,654,820	6,654,820	30.1%	69.9%	19.565%	15.489%	4,397,731
46	FMV debt, eqty at t − 1	4	2,000,000	4,397,731	6,397,731	31.3%	68.7%	19.692%	15.412%	4,462,354
47	FMV debt, eqty at t − 1	5	2,000,000	4,462,354	6,462,354	30.9%	69.1%	19.659%	15.432%	4,445,498
48	FMV debt, eqty at t − 1	6	2,000,000	4,445,498	6,445,498	31.0%	69.0%	19.667%	15.427%	4,449,853
49	FMV debt, eqty at t − 1	7	2,000,000	4,449,853	6,449,853	31.0%	69.0%	19.665%	15.428%	4,448,725
50	FMV debt, eqty at t − 1	8	2,000,000	4,448,725	6,448,725	31.0%	69.0%	19.666%	15.428%	4,449,017
51	FMV debt, eqty at t − 1	9	2,000,000	4,449,017	6,449,017	31.0%	69.0%	19.666%	15.428%	4,448,942
52	FMV debt, eqty at t − 1	10	2,000,000	4,448,942	6,448,942	31.0%	69.0%	19.666%	15.428%	4,448,961
53	FMV debt, eqty at t − 1	11	2,000,000	4,448,961	6,448,961	31.0%	69.0%	19.666%	15.428%	4,448,956
54	FMV debt, eqty at t − 1	12	2,000,000	4,448,956	6,448,956	31.0%	69.0%	19.666%	15.428%	4,448,958
55	FMV debt, eqty at t − 1	13	2,000,000	4,448,958	6,448,958	31.0%	69.0%	19.666%	15.428%	4,448,957
56	FMV debt, eqty at t − 1	14	2,000,000	4,448,957	6,448,957	31.0%	69.0%	19.666%	15.428%	4,448,957

when starting the next iteration as opposed to just using the latest iteration of equity. This can be done by making a small alteration to the spreadsheet.

LOG SIZE

The log size model converges far faster than the CAPM versions of the invested capital approach or the equity valuation method. The reason is that when we use logarithms to calculate the discount rate, large absolute changes in equity value cause fairly small changes in the discount rate, which is not true of CAPM.

SUMMARY

When using CAPM, using this iterative approach will improve appraisal accuracy and eliminate arguments over the proper leverage. One look at the difference between the beginning guess of the FMV of equity and the final FMV will show how much more accuracy can be gained. While it is true that had we guessed a number based on industry average capitalization we would have been closer, the advantage of this approach is that it obviates the need for precise initial guesses.

The iterative approach should give us the ability to get much closer answers from both the invested capital and the direct capital approaches, as long as the subject firm is sufficiently profitable. The iterative approach does not seem to work for very small firms with little profitability, but those are the firms for which you are least likely to want to bother with the extra work involved in the iterations.

BIBLIOGRAPHY

Abrams, Jay B. 1995. "An Iterative Valuation Approach." *Business Valuation Review* (March): 26–35.
Hamada, R. S. 1972. "The Effects of the Firm's Capital Structure on the Systematic Risk of Common Stocks." *Journal of Finance* 27: 435–52.

Adjusting for Control and Marketability

INTRODUCTION

Part 3 of this book, consisting of Chapters 7, 8, and 9, deals with calculating control premiums, the discount for lack of control (DLOC), and discount for lack of marketability (DLOM). These topics correspond to the third and fourth steps in valuing businesses. These are practical, "how-to" chapters.

Adjusting for levels of control and marketability is probably the most controversial topic in business valuation. As such, Chapter 7 is almost a book unto itself. It is the longest chapter in this book, and it probably has the most startling research results of any chapter.

Chapter 7 is divided into two parts: the first part primarily dealing with control and the second primarily with marketability. I chose that order because of the one-way relationship—control affects marketability, but marketability does not affect control. The chapter begins with a comprehensive overview of the major professional articles on the topic and then proceeds to review a number of academic articles that provide insight into the issue of control.

In part 2 of Chapter 7 we review two quantitative models (other than my own): Mercer's quantitative marketability discount model (QMDM) and Kasper's bid-ask spread model. We then analyze restricted stock discounts with multiple regression analysis for two reasons. The first reason is that this is intrinsically useful in restricted stock discount studies. The second, more important, reason is that restricted stock discounts serve as one of the components of my economic components model of DLOM, which makes up the majority of part 2. At the end of the chapter, Z. Christopher Mercer provides a rebuttal to my critique of the quantitative marketability discount model, and we go back and forth with arguments that the profession should find interesting and enlightening, and possibly somewhat confusing and frustrating as well.

Economic Components Model

The heart of Chapter 7 is my own economic components model for DLOM, which consists of four components:

1. The economic consequences of the delay to sale experienced by all privately-held firms. I model this component using a regression analysis of restricted stock discount data published by Management Planning, Inc. in Mercer's book.[1]

2. Extra bargaining power ("monospony power") to the buyer arising from thin markets. The academic article by Schwert contains a key finding that enables us to estimate this component of DLOM reliably.

3. Buyer's transactions costs in excess of transactions costs for publicly held stocks.

4. Seller's transactions costs in excess of transactions costs for publicly held stocks.

We present research on the magnitude of transactions costs for both buyers and sellers with different business sizes as well as regression analyses of each. This enables us to calculate transactions costs for any business size for both buyer and seller.

Items 3 and 4 above, which we label components #3A and #3B in the chapter, occur every time the business is sold. Those fees and costs leave the system by being paid to outsiders such as business brokers, accountants, attorneys, and appraisers. Thus, we need to be able to calculate the present value effect of the infinite continuum of periodic transactions costs, which we do in the form of one formula for buyers' excess transactions costs and another formula for sellers' excess transactions costs.[2] This process is now vastly simplified over the process in my original *Business Valuation Review* article on the topic. We also give an example of how to calculate DLOM.

A very important test that we perform in Chapter 7 is a comparison of several models in their ability to explain the restricted stock discounts from the Management Planning, Inc. data: the Black–Scholes options pricing model (BSOPM) put formula using specifically calculated standard deviations of returns (volatility) of the public stocks, the BSOPM put using indirectly calculated (through log size equations) standard deviations, the quantitative marketability discount model (QMDM), a regression equation, and the mean discount. The regression equation was the best forecast of restricted stock discounts, with the BSOPM with directly calculated volatility a very close second. Both the BSOPM using indirectly calculated volatility and the QMDM were worse than the mean in forecasting discounts, with QMDM being farthest out of the money. This is significant because it is the first empirical test of any model to calculate restricted stock discounts.

Chapters 8 and 9 are practical applications of the work in Chapter 7 in the form of sample reports. Chapter 8 is a sample restricted stock discount report, and Chapter 9 is a sample fractional interest discount study for a Limited Liability Company interest in real property. Chapter 8 is

---

1. The data have been corrected since publication in Mercer's book, and Management Planning, Inc. provided us with additional data.

2. That is because the seller's costs on the first sale do not count in calculating DLOM, whereas buyer's costs do. In all subsequent sales of the business, both count.

purely an application of Chapter 7 and contains no research that is not already in Chapter 7, while Chapter 9 does contain two types of new research:

1. My own regression analysis of discounts from net asset value compiled by Partnership Profiles, Ltd.
2. My regression analysis of private fractional interest data.

Thus, in Chapter 10 we use three models for calculating the fractional interest discount: the economic components model, the partnership profiles database regression, and the private data regression.

If any chapter may have rough edges to it, Chapter 7 is it. I hope to be able to smooth those edges in future editions of this book. For now, however, this chapter will have to remain as it is.

The calculation of the discount for lack of control in Chapter 9 is also subject to further research and revision. Nevertheless, this is valuable and novel material well worth the struggle through the quantitative parts.

I caution the reader not to get bogged down in the quantitative parts of Chapter 7. Read it through lightly first for understanding the gist, and do not worry about understanding every statistic in the academic articles. The most important thing to get out of Chapter 7 in a first reading is an understanding of why the acquisition premium data that we have been using for the past 30 years tell us almost nothing useful about the value of control of a private firm and why we have to look elsewhere. It is then worth a second reading to master the technical details.

Adjusting for Levels of Control and Marketability

INTRODUCTION

THE VALUE OF CONTROL AND ADJUSTING FOR LEVEL OF
CONTROL

  Prior Research—Qualitative Professional

    Nath

    Mercer (1990)

    Bolotsky

    Jankowske

    Roach

    Mercer (1998) and (1999)

    Summary of Professional Research on Control Premiums

  Prior Research—Academic

    Schwert (1996)

    Lease, McConnell, and Mikkelson (1983)

    Megginson (1990)

      My Conclusions from the Megginson Results

      My Analysis of the Megginson Results

    The Houlihan Lokey Howard & Zukin (HLHZ) Study

    International Voting Rights Premia

    Bradley, Desai, and Kim (1988)

    Maquieira, Megginson, and Nail (1998)

    Other Corporate Control Research

    Menyah and Paudyal

  My Synthesis and Analysis

    Decomposing the Acquisition Premium

    Inferences from the Academic Articles

    The Disappearing Control Premium

    The Control Premium Reappears

    Estimating the Control Premium

    DLOC

DISCOUNT FOR LACK OF MARKETABILITY (DLOM)
  Mercer's Quantitative Marketability Discount Model
  Kasper's BAS Model
  Restricted Stock Discounts
    Regression of MPI Data
    Using the Put Option Model to Calculate DLOM of Restricted
    Stock
      Annualized Standard Deviation of Continuously Compounded
      Returns
      Calculation of the Discount
      Table 7-8: Black–Scholes Put Model Results
    Comparison of the Put Model and the Regression Model
      Empirical versus Theoretical Black–Scholes
    Comparison to the Quantitative Marketability Discount Model
    (QMDM)
  Abrams' Economic Components Model
    Component #1: The Delay to Sale
      Psychology
      Black–Scholes Options Pricing Model
      Other Models of Component #1
      Abrams Regression of the Management Planning, Inc. Data
      Limitations of the Regression
    Component #2: Buyer Monopsony Power
    Component #3: Transactions Costs
      Table 7-11: Quantifying Transactions Costs for Buyer and Seller
      Component #3 Is Different than #1 and #2
      Developing Formulas to Calculate DLOM Component #3
      A Simplified Example of Sellers' Transactions Costs
      Tables 7-12 and 7-13: Proving Formulas (7-9) and (7-9a)
      Value Remaining Formula and the Total Discount
    Table 7-14: Sample Calculation of DLOM
    Evidence from the Institute of Business Appraisers
  Mercer's Rebuttal
    Expected Growth and Expected Returns
    Conclusion
    My Counterpoints
    Mercer's Response
  Conclusion
MATHEMATICAL APPENDIX

INTRODUCTION

Adjusting for levels of control and marketability is a complicated and very important topic. We will be discussing control premiums (CP), their opposite, discount for lack of control (DLOC), and discount for lack of marketability (DLOM).

Historically, these valuation adjustments have accounted for substantial adjustments in appraisal reports—often 20–40% of the net present value of the cash flows—and yet valuation analysts may spend little to no time calculating and explaining these adjustments.

This is a long chapter, with much data and analysis. It will be helpful to break the discussion into two parts. The first part will deal with primarily with control and the second part primarily with marketability. I say primarily, because the two concepts are interrelated. The level of control of a business interest impacts its level of marketability. Therefore, it is logical to begin with a discussion of control. Because of the interrelationship, two academic articles that we will discuss in the section on control relate more to marketability, yet they fit in better in the control discussion.

THE VALUE OF CONTROL AND ADJUSTING FOR LEVEL OF CONTROL

We will begin our analysis of the effects of control on value by reviewing prior qualitative professional research and prior academic research. Then we will present some additional data and come to some conclusions about the magnitude of control premiums and DLOC.

The top portion of Figure 7-1 shows the traditional level of values chart.[3] The conventional wisdom represented in the traditional levels of value chart holds that it is appropriate to add a control premium to the

FIGURE 7-1

Traditional Levels of Value Chart

Level of Value	Adjustment up To	Adjustment Down To
Control interest	Control premium	NA
Marketable minority interest	Reverse out DLOM	DLOC
Private Minority Interest	NA	DLOM

Mercer's Mercer (1998) modified traditional levels of value chart

Strategic value	Value of synergies	NA
Control value	Control premium	Eliminate synergies
Marketable minority interest[a]	Reverse out DLOM	DLOC
Private minority interest	NA	DLOM

[a] Often referred to in the literature as the "as-if-freely-traded-value" for private firms.

---

3. The bottom portion shows Chris Mercer's modified traditional levels of value chart, which is identical to the one above, except with the addition of the strategic value. We will cover this later in the chapter.

marketable minority interest value. There are significant opinions to the contrary, i.e., that one should not add any control premium whatsoever. Additionally, there is controversy over the appropriate magnitude of the control premium among those who do add them to the marketable minority interest value. We will cover that in greater depth later in the chapter. Of course, if the valuation method is a guideline company approach using a database of sales of privately held firms, the starting value is a private control interest, and a control premium is inappropriate.

It is extremely important to understand that the valuation adjustments in Figure 7-1 be appropriate to the valuation method used. If we are valuing a control interest and we used a discounted cash flow analysis with discount rates calculated using New York Stock Exchange data, the resulting value is a marketable minority interest, and a control premium must be considered.[4]

The alternative levels of value chart is two tiered, i.e., it is a 2 × 2 chart (2 rows and 2 columns, versus the traditional chart, which is 3 × 1). It represents the four basic types of ownership interests, which are combinations of public versus private and control versus minority interest. Obviously, there are shades of gray in between the extremes. Bolotsky (1991) was the first to propound this chart, although he used it for slightly different purposes, which we discuss below. Much later in the chapter, we will discuss Figure 7-3, which is my own extension of Bolotsky's levels of value chart to a 3 × 2 chart.

The traditional sources of control premiums are the Mergerstat and the Houlihan Lokey Howard & Zukin (HLHZ) studies.[5] Table 7-1, columns B and C show Mergerstat's compilation of average (mean) and median five-day acquisition premiums from 1985–1997. The premiums were measured as $(P_{\text{Offer}}/P_{\text{5Day}}) - 1$, where the numerator is the offering price and the denominator is the minority trading price five days before the announcement of the offer. Mean acquisition premiums have ranged from 35–45%, with the average being 39.5% (B21), while median premiums have ranged from 27–35%, with an average of 30.5% (C21).

FIGURE 7-2

Two-Tiered Levels of Value Chart[a]

	Public	Private
Control	x	x
Minority	x	x

[a] Note: these are also the four basic types of ownership interests.

4. It is also important to make sure the measure of income is consistent with the interest valued. When valuing a control interest, it is appropriate to add back excess salaries of the owners. When valuing a minority interest that cannot force salaries lower, the add-back is inappropriate.
5. HLHZ now owns Mergerstat, although the latter was previously owned by Merrill Lynch and the W. T. Grimm Co.

TABLE 7-1

Synergies as Measured by Acquisition Minus Going-Private Premiums

	A	B	C	D	E	F	G
5		Acquisition Premiums [1]		Going Private Prem [2]		Difference = Synergy?	
6		Mean	Median	Mean	Median	Mean	Median
7	1985	37.1%	27.7%	30.9%	25.7%	6.2%	2.0%
8	1986	38.2%	29.9%	31.9%	26.1%	6.3%	3.8%
9	1987	38.3%	30.8%	34.8%	30.9%	3.5%	−0.1%
10	1988	41.9%	30.9%	33.8%	26.3%	8.1%	4.6%
11	1989	41.0%	29.0%	35.0%	22.7%	6.0%	6.3%
12	1990	42.0%	32.0%	34.3%	31.6%	7.7%	0.4%
13	1991	35.1%	29.4%	23.8%	20.0%	11.3%	9.4%
14	1992	41.0%	34.7%	24.8%	8.1%	16.2%	26.6%
15	1993	38.7%	33.0%	34.7%	20.0%	4.0%	13.0%
16	1994	41.9%	35.0%	41.9%	35.0%	0.0%	0.0%
17	1995	44.7%	29.2%	29.8%	19.2%	14.9%	10.0%
18	1996	36.6%	27.3%	34.8%	26.2%	1.8%	1.1%
19	1997	35.7%	27.5%	30.4%	24.5%	5.3%	3.0%
20	1998	40.7%	30.1%	29.1%	20.4%	11.6%	9.7%
21	Mean	39.5%	30.5%	32.1%	24.1%	7.4%	6.4%

[1] Mergerstat-1999, Chart 1-8, Page 23 (Mergerstat-1994, Figure 41, Page 98 for 1985-1988). Mergerstat is a division of Houlihan Lokey Howard & Zukin.

[2] Mergerstat-1999, Table 1-39, Page 42. For 1985-1988, Mergerstat-1994, Figure 39, Page 96.

Note that we deliberately use the term *acquisition premium* instead of the more common term *control premium*. Eventually we will distinguish between the amounts that are paid for control versus the amounts that are paid for synergies, as the latter are generally part of investment value and not fair market value.

The mean and median going-private premiums are 32.1% and 24.1% (D21 and E21), and the difference of means and medians of acquisition versus going private premiums are 7.4% and 6.4%, respectively. At a first glance, it would seem that the 7.4% mean or 6.4% median difference is a potential measure of synergies, as going private transactions do not have synergies. Also, the 32.1% mean or 24.1% median going private premium would be good candidates as a benchmark for measuring control premiums.

Table 7-1A shows additional detail of the premiums as measured by different points in time. An *n*-day acquisition premium is equal to $\frac{P_{Announcement}}{P_n} - 1$, where the denominator is the stock price *n* days before the announcement date. It is clear that acquisition premiums increase with an increase in *n*, as can be seen by moving to the right across any row. Rows 6 and 7 show median and mean acquisition premiums for ordinary acquisitions, while columns B through D in rows 10 and 11 show the same premiums with the potential 7.4% synergies from Table 7-1, F21 subtracted. These are a net acquisition premium for ordinary acquisitions

Acquisition and Going-Private Transactions Premiums

	A	B	C	D	F	G	H	J	K	L
4		**Ordinary Acquisitions**			**Going Private Transactions**			**Difference**		
5	**Gross Acquisition Premiums**	**1 Day**	**5 Days**	**30 Days**	**1 Day**	**5 Days**	**30 Days**	**1 Day**	**5 Days**	**30 Days**
6	Median	22.8%	28.4%	36.7%						
7	Mean (with max. of 100%) [1]	27.2%	32.9%	42.7%						
9	Premiums net of 7.4% synergies									
10	Median	15.4%	21.0%	29.3%	20.0%	23.0%	26.9%	−4.6%	−2.0%	2.4%
11	Mean (with max. of 100%) [1]	19.8%	25.5%	35.3%	25.7%	27.2%	31.7%	−5.9%	−1.7%	3.6%

[1] All premiums > 100% treated as 100%

Data Source: Mergerstat database. This contains going private premiums from 3/89 to 5/98 and ordinary acquisition premiums from 12/83 to 1/99. There are 46 to 69 going private premiums and 1,175 to 1,430 ordinary premiums.

that is a candidate for the control premium. Columns F through H in rows 10 and 11 are the going private transactions, and columns J through L are the difference of the net acquisition premiums for ordinary acquisitions and the going private premiums. Notice that only the one-day differences at −4.6% and −5.9% (J10 and J11) are significant in size, while the five-day and thirty-day differences are quite small. Again it seems that going private premiums are a strong contender for the measure of the value of control.

The traditional calculation of discount for lack of control (DLOC) is based on the control premium. If the marketable minority FMV is $100 per share and one buys control for $140 per share, the control premium (CP) is $40 per share. In percentages, the premium is $40 per share divided by the marketable minority price of $100 per share, or $40/$100 = 40%. Going in the other direction, DLOC is the $40 premium divided by the control price of $140, or 28.6%. Symbolically, DLOC = CP/(1 + CP).

The vast majority of valuation assignments for valuation professionals call for a fair market value standard of value. Unless a market is dominated by strategic buyers and the subject company is a reasonable candidate to be bought by a strategic buyer in the mergers & acquisitions (M&A) market, it is necessary to remove any synergistic element in acquisition premiums before applying a control premium. The data are confusing, and there are different ideological camps in the valuation profession. The goal of the control section of this chapter is to present a large body of professional and academic research, arrive at a coherent explanation of the diverse data, and provide guidance and quantitative benchmarks for use in the profession.

Prior Research—Qualitative Professional

As mentioned earlier, we examine two types of prior research: professional and academic. In this section we examine prior professional research on control premiums. The professional research itself is composed of a long series of articles that develop important valuation theory that

PART 3   Adjusting for Control and Marketability

is primarily qualitative. We will now review the main articles, which are written by Eric Nath, Chris Mercer, Michael Bolotsky, and Wayne Jankowske. Again, because control and marketability are so intertwined, these articles also contain material relevant to adjusting for marketability.

Nath

The original attack on the traditional position came from Eric Nath (1990). Nath later clarified and slightly modified his initial position (Nath 1994 and 1997). Nath argued:

- Fewer than 4% of all public firms are taken over each year. Using an efficient markets hypothesis argument, Nath said that the LBO funds, strategic buyers, and their bankers, who collectively represent hundreds of billions of dollars scouring the market for deals, keep the market clean. Any good takeover opportunity will not last long. If there were hidden premiums in the firms, their stock prices would rapidly be bid up to that level.

- Minority shares in publicly held firms are liquid. The existence of liquidity tends to eliminate nonstrategic acquisition premiums if the companies are well managed and management communicates effectively with investors (I would add that they must be benevolent to minority interests, which is the usual case in publicly held firms and is not usual in privately held firms).

- The previous points lead to the conclusion that the publicly traded prices are control values and not just minority values. His major conclusion, which contradicts conventional wisdom of the three-tiered levels of value chart, is that starting from a public market derived value, one must take both DLOM and DLOC to value a privately held minority interest. Apparently influenced by articles from Bolotsky and Jankowske, both discussed below, Nath later (1997) switched to the two-tiered levels of value structure. Doing so had no material effect on his conclusions, merely the presentation.

- Buyers are often strategically motivated, and therefore what they pay is not equivalent to FMV. Nath's evidence is that similar premiums are paid for minority interest acquisitions. More recently, his position has modified. Nath is concerned whether the market of relevant buyers for a subject company is likely to consist of many strategic buyers who would participate in an auction for the company. If so, then he contends that strategic value essentially becomes fair market value. If there are not many strategic buyers, then he is still concerned that the M&A multiples may contain a strategic element in the acquisition premium, leading to overvaluation of the company unless that element is removed. He determines this by an analysis of three entities: the company itself, the market for firms in that industry, and the M&A databases.

- Several problems with the computations of control premiums cause them to be misleading. Mergerstat's control premium statistics exclude acquisition discounts, i.e., some acquisitions occur at lower prices than the minority trading price. Other problems are that the range of premiums is enormous and Mergerstat uses simple averages instead of market weighted averages.

- There are at least two additional problems in using takeover prices as an indicator of value. The first is that transactions are unique and time-specific. Just because a specific buyer pays a specific premium for a particular firm, that does not mean that another buyer would pay a similar premium for a comparable firm, let alone for a much smaller and less exciting company. The second problem, Nath contends, is that some people overpay. These points are related to the comments above on the strategic element of acquisition premiums in the M&A market.

Mercer (1990)
In his initial article on the topic, Mercer (1990) disagreed with Nath.[6] Mercer was the most notable proponent of the traditional viewpoint and levels of value chart. He disagreed with Nath's belief that firms that are taken over are different than those that are not, which led him to disagree with Nath's conclusion that the public minority price is a control value. Bolotsky (1991) said that that is a matter of opinion and cannot be tested.

Mercer also contested Nath's statement that most takeovers are fully or partially motivated by strategic reasons and that this makes the transaction prices unsuitable measures of FMV. Essentially, Mercer said that buyer motivations are irrelevant and that it is not up to us to question their motivations—just to use the data generated by their actions.

He also wrote that premiums paid for minority interests are premiums paid for creeping control, not for synergies. Bolotsky agreed with Mercer on this point.

Mercer has since changed his views considerably, and we will cover his 1998 article separately in this professional review.

Bolotsky[7]
Michael Bolotsky (1991) and (1995) agrees with many of Nath's criticisms of conventional wisdom but disagrees with his conclusions. With regard to the results of his analysis, he represents a middle position between Mercer and Nath. With regard to the theoretical underpinnings, his work is unique in that it is the first article that abandons the linear levels of value concept entirely and replaces it with a multifactor, multidimension matrix of fundamental attributes. For example, he gets rid of the concept that 100% ownership value must always be somehow higher than or equal to minority ownership value. He contends that both Mercer and Nath are still arguing around a linear concept of going from "up here" to "down there."

Bolotsky has a comprehensive, logical framework of analysis that includes differences in ownership rights, liquidity, information access,

---

6. He has since changed his views considerably, and we will cover his 1998 article later.
7. I thank Michael Bolotsky for editing this section and helping me to interpret his work correctly.

and information reliability between the four types of ownership interests listed in Figure 7-2. Bolotsky's article is important theoretical work and obviously influenced subsequent articles by both Nath and Mercer. Bolotsky's article contains no empirical evidence nor any attempt to quantify the implications of his framework into an economic model. The practical significance of the article is that he disagrees with Nath's conclusion that valuing a private minority interest with reference to public minority interests as a starting point requires applying both a DLOM and a DLOC.

It is significant that Bolotsky did not attempt to squash four levels of value (public-control, public-minority, private-control, and private-minority) into three, as both Nath and Mercer did.[8] Bolotsky's assertion that the more the buy side knows about the seller and the more he or she can rely on it, the higher the price, is also significant and logical.

Bolotsky characterized the public markets as a consensus opinion of value that may occasionally experience an anomalous trade, but that trade will be quickly bid back to a rational, equilibrium consensus value. He says:

> [T]he purchase of an entire company is typically a one-time purchase of a unique item; the price that ultimately gets recorded is not the consensus opinion of the limited group of buyers and sellers for a particular entire company but is rather the winning bid, which is normally the highest bid. There is no "market" process going on here in the sense described above for public minority blocks. It is analogous to a situation where the single anomalous trade described earlier does not get rapidly bid down to a consensus price; instead, it gets memorialized in Mergerstat Review, to be relied upon by valuation consultants. Clearly, relative to fair market value, there is an upwards bias in prices that represent either the highest bid, the only bid, or the bid of a buyer bringing special attributes to the table.

Bolotsky takes a middle position on whether the takeovers are for typical or atypical public companies, the former position being taken by Mercer and the latter by Nath. Bolotsky says that it is inappropriate to insist that unless a subject company is in play, one must assume there is no control premium. He thus disagrees with Nath on that point.

Bolotsky's theoretical framework has no concept of sequential levels of value, with control value at the top, followed by minority marketable value, and nonmarketable minority value at the bottom. Rather, Bolotsky advances the concept that the value of various types of ownership interests is the result of building up the contribution to value of fundamental ownership attributes, to the degree that each attribute applies to the interest in question. In addition, Bolotsky's framework implies that rather than *discounts* and *premiums*, there are *adjustments* for differences in ownership attributes and that the adjustment can be positive, negative, or zero. In this framework there is nothing that mandates that a 100% own-

---

8. Nath stopped doing that in his December 1997 article. Until fairly recently, Mercer believed that there are only three levels of value, as he contends that there is no discount for lack of marketability (DLOM) for private control interests, as the private control interest has control over cash flows (I disagree that control over cash flows eliminates DLOM and will cover that later in the chapter). He has more recently added a strategic level of value, as shown in the lower section of Figure 7-1, but it is still linear, i.e., a single column of values.

ership position will be equal to or greater in value than a public minority price; indeed, Bolotsky's framework implies that if investors in a security value liquidity and the options that liquidity provides to a greater degree than they value power, then public minority pricing for that security will exceed 100% ownership pricing.

Thus, Bolotsky says that for those public companies where we would conclude that the per share 100% ownership value is the same amount as the public minority value, the two prices might be the same but for very different reasons. In effect, the same price for different ownership interests is resulting from the *net* of the differences in the impact of various ownership attributes on each interest. Since the concept is of the net of differences, there is no reason why the net difference in price between a 100% ownership position and a public minority position cannot be zero or even negative. Accordingly, when we state that the public minority value and the 100% ownership value are the same, we are really saying that we should apply a net value adjustment of zero. I agree with his position that there is a very important distinction in saying we are applying a net zero premium versus saying that by definition there is no premium.

Bolotsky also states that Nath's conclusion is internally flawed in that in valuing private minority interests with reference to public minority prices as a starting point we need to take both a DLOM and a DLOC. He argues that if a public minority block of shares happens to have the same per-share value as a 100% ownership interest, this does not affect the fact that the block in question is still a minority block of stock having no attributes of control over the company. He contends it would be illogical to subtract a DLOC from a block that has no attributes of control.[9] Rather, the oftentimes extreme price differentials between public and private minority interests must be explained by other ownership attributes besides control, including but not limited to differentials in relative liquidity, relative level of information availability, and relative information reliability.

Bolotsky claims—reasonably, in my opinion—that there are many public firms whose perceived 100% ownership value will be more than their minority value, but not enough more to make a tender offer worthwhile. In addition, Bolotsky's theoretical framework is the only one that can readily accommodate several market features that appear anomalous when relying on the linear levels of value framework, such as 100% ownership pricing at levels considerably below IPO pricing for many companies in today's markets.

Jankowske

Wayne Jankowske's article (Jankowske 1991) corrects certain key errors in the articles by Nath and Bolotsky. He says one does not have to accept Nath's assertion that the marketable minority value is a control value to accept the proposition that DLOC can differ between public and private

---

9. This is a very logical statement and appears to be self-evident. Nevertheless, I will disagree with this later in the chapter.

firms. He says differences in legal and contractual protection, agency costs, relative incentives, and differential economic benefits can account for differences in the public versus private DLOC.

Prevailing wisdom's assertion is that since public market prices are minority prices, we can use public guideline company prices to value private minority shares, with only DLOM necessary. Jankowske says that for that to be true, it implies that the economic disadvantages of lack of control associated with public minority shares is equal to that of private minority shares, which is unrealistic.

Conceptually, the magnitude of DLOC in guideline public prices makes no difference, whether it is 30%, or, as Nath contended in his first two articles, 0%. The difference between the public and subject company's DLOC must be recognized to avoid an overvaluation.

He developed the following formula to value a private minority interest:[10]

$$\text{Additional DLOC} = \left[\frac{\text{FMV}_{MM}}{1 - \text{DLOC}_{GC}} \right] \times (\text{DLOC}_{SC} - \text{DLOC}_{GC})$$

where

FMV_{MM} = the marketable minority fair market value
DLOC_{GC} = discount for lack of control in the public guideline companies
DLOC_{SC} = discount for lack of control in the subject company

He gave the following example: FMV_{MM}, the marketable minority interest value is $900; DLOC_{GC}, the discount for lack of control implicit in the public minority stock is 10%; and DLOC_{SC}, the discount for lack of control appropriate to the subject company, is 40%. His calculation of incremental discount is:

$$\frac{\$900}{1 - 10\%} \times (40\% - 10\%) = \$1,000 \times 30\% = \$300$$

He disagrees with Bolotsky that the guideline firms must have identical shareholder attributes.

In his second article on the topic (Jankowske 1995), he stressed that it is the economic benefits to which we must look as a justification for control premiums, not the powers that come with control. He cites the following economic benefits of control:

- Company level.
  - Performance improvements.
  - Synergy.
- Shareholder Level.
  - Wealth transfer opportunities—the Machiavellian ability to transfer wealth from the minority shareholders.
  - Protection of investment—the flip side of the above point is that control protects the shareholder from being exploited. This

---

10. I have changed his notation.

motivation is important because it relates to ambiguity avoidance in the academic literature reviewed in this chapter.

- Liquidity—control enhances liquidity in privately held businesses.

Of the company level advantages, the extent to which performance improvements on a standalone basis account for control premiums properly belongs in our calculations of fair market value. That portion accounted for by synergy is investment value and should not be included in fair market value.

Roach

George Roach (1998) summarized percentage acquisition premiums from a database of business sales. The premiums were measured as $(P_{Acq}/P_{5Day}) - 1$, where the numerator is the acquisition price and the denominator is the minority trading price five days before the announcement of the acquisition. He also provided the premium based on the price 30 days prior. We excerpt from his Exhibit IV to our Table 7-2.

There is no pattern to the first three premiums listed in Table 7-2. The 50+ SIC code difference level between buyers and sellers has the highest premium, which is counterintuitive. Roach found similar patterns in the results for median premiums. Additionally, while the 30-day premiums were higher than the 5-day premiums, the patterns were similar.

Under the assumption that acquisitions of firms in the same or almost the same SIC code are more likely to be strategic acquisitions than firms acquired in very different SIC codes, Roach's analysis appears to be strong evidence that premiums paid for strategic buys are no larger than premiums paid for financial buys. This leads to the conclusion that acquisition premiums are control premiums, not premiums for synergy.

This conclusion supports Mercer (1990) and Bolotsky in their opinion that the similarity of premiums for acquiring minority positions and control positions can be explained as acquiring "creeping control," because it appears to rule out synergy as an explanation. This is in contrast to Nath's position and Mercer (1998 and 1999).

Mercer (1998) and (1999)

Mercer (1998) represents a significant change in thinking since his 1990 article. He now believes that the majority of premiums for mergers and

TABLE 7-2

Acquisition Premiums by SIC Code

SIC Code Differences Between Buyer & Seller	5-Day Avg Prem
0	37.2%
1–9	41.0%
10–48	37.1%
50+	50.8%

Source: George P. Roach, "Control Premiums and Strategic Mergers," *Business Valuation Review* (June 1998), Table IV, p. 47.

PART 3 Adjusting for Control and Marketability

acquisitions recorded in Houlihan Lokey Howard & Zukin's Mergerstat represent strategic premiums for synergies, which do not qualify for fair market value. He has modified the traditional levels of value chart in the top of Figure 7-1 to the one in the middle. It is the same as the one above, with the addition of a strategic value above the control value.

For sake of discussion, let's look at an end-of-year Gordon model formula to calculate value.

$$\text{PV(Cash Flows)} = \frac{CF_{t+1}(1 - b)}{r - g}$$

where r is the discount rate, g is the constant growth rate, and b is the retention ratio for the company, i.e., it retains b (with $0 \leq b \leq 1$), leaving $(1 - b)$ times the next year's forecast cash flow as forecast dividends.

Mercer's position (Mercer 1999) is that the discount rate is the same at the marketable minority level as it is in all levels of value above that (though not the same as the private minority level, which almost always carries a higher discount rate). The main difference in the valuation comes from the numerator, not the denominator. Control buyers, whether financial or strategic, upwardly adjust forecast cash flows. He details the types of adjustments as follows:

1. *Normalizing adjustments:* these adjust private company earnings to well-run public company equivalent. Mercer classifies two types of normalizing adjustments. Type 1 is to eliminate nonrecurring items and adjust for non-operating assets. Type 2 is to adjust insider compensation to an arm's length level, including eliminating discretionary expenses that would not exist in a public company.

2. *Control adjustments:* Mercer lists two types of control adjustments. Type 1 are for what Jankowske calls performance improvements and apply to both financial buyers and strategic buyers. Mercer says these are adjustments for *improving* the (existing) earnings stream, i.e., running the company more efficiently. This could also include the volume discounts coming from the buying efficiencies achievable by being owned by a larger company that is a financial buyer. Type 2 are for *changing* the earnings stream, i.e., running the company differently, and apply only to strategic buyers. These include consolidating G&A expenses, eliminating duplicate operations, selling more product, and negotiating power with suppliers, distributors, or customers that is above and beyond that which can be achieved by a financial buyer.

Mercer is in very good company in this position. Consider (Pratt 1998, p. 134): "The exploitation of minority shareholders is far less prevalent in public companies than in private companies, at least in larger public companies. If company cash flows are already maximized and the returns are already distributed pro rata to all shareholders, then there may be no difference between a control value and a minority value."

Other similar opinions can be found in Ibbotson (1999), Zukin (1998), and Vander Linden (1998).

Actually, Mercer is not the originator of this position on control premiums, but he may be the person who has written the most about it. The original statement of this position came from Glass and McCarter (1995).

Summary of Professional Research on Control Premiums

Now we will summarize the past 10 years of professional research on control premiums. The primary research supporting the traditional control premiums of 35% to 40+% is Roach's. The other extreme—a zero control premium—is represented by Nath and Mercer. While the original gap between Nath's and Mercer's positions on control premiums was large, the current gap is much smaller and often may not even exist. The logic of how they arrived at their opinions is different, but they would probably come to similar calculations of control premiums in the majority of circumstances.

Nath does not ever use control premiums. Mercer, following Glass and McCarter, now agrees that after taking into consideration increases in forecast cash flows from performance improvements and arm's length salary adjustments for the control shareholder that are appropriate for a financial buyer, there are no control premiums. In the absence of information to do so, he says control premiums should be very small—no more than 10%, with the implication that it could still be as little as zero. That is essentially Nath's position, that the public minority value is a control value and therefore we should not apply control premiums to a discounted cash flow valuation. Mercer rarely assigns control premiums unless there are identifiable increases in forecast cash flows at the control level. In that case, he would simply increase the cash flow forecast and the control level value would increase vis-à-vis the marketable minority interest level. Nath would do the same thing, except he does not like the term *marketable minority level of value* (or its synonym, *as if freely traded*). Their terminology differs far more than their results, at least with regard to control premiums.

Regarding the discount for lack of marketability (DLOM), neither Mercer nor Nath believes in taking DLOM for a control interest—a position with which I disagree in the DLOM section of this chapter. Nath's reason for this position is that the M&A and business brokerage markets are very active, and that activity negates any tendency to a DLOM. He makes an analogy of the real estate market to the market for companies. Rather than apply DLOM, real estate appraisers put an "expected marketing time" on their values. Mercer's main reason for opposing DLOM for control interests is that they control cash flows until a sale.

Nath always begins with a controlling owner's value, which in his view is the greater of the values obtained by the M&A markets, the public markets (reduced by the restricted stock discount that one would experience in going public), and liquidation. It is extremely important to note that to the extent that the M&A market values contains synergies and whenever the M&A valuation dominates, Nath's fair market values will contain synergies.

His opinion is that that is what buyers will pay, and therefore that is fair market value. There is a question as to whether that is investment

PART 3   Adjusting for Control and Marketability

value rather than fair market value. I agree that it probably is not investment value, as it is not value to a particular buyer. It is value to an entire class of buyers. If all buyers in the M&A market are strategic—which is certainly not completely true, but may be largely true is some industries—then that is what buyers would pay. With this fine distinction, it is very important to make sure that if one follows Nath's method, one must be careful that the subject company fits with the assumptions underlying Nath's logic.

I do not believe that most small firms and many midsized firms are serious candidates for the M&A market. They are business broker material, and such buyers would rarely ever be synergistic. Therefore, it is imperative to be realistic about the market in which the subject company is likely to sell.

For a private minority interest, Nath takes both the discount for lack of marketability and lack of control. In conversation, he has revealed his own dissatisfaction with the lack of relevant information for calculating DLOC, since there is still nothing to use other than the traditional flip side of the control premiums that he personally demolished as being valid premiums to add to a "minority value."

Mercer comes to what probably amounts to a very similar result through a different path. He does not calculate a discount for lack of control for private minority interests. Instead, he uses his quantitative marketability discount model (QMDM) (which we cover in more detail later in this chapter) to subsume any DLOC, which he feels is automatically included in his DLOM. I agree with Mercer that the QMDM includes the impact of DLOC because, in the QMDM, one must forecast the specific cash flows to the minority shareholder and discount them to present value. Thus, by using the QMDM, Mercer does not need a DLOC. Mercer's position is internally consistent.

Prior Research—Academic

Now that we have summarized the professional literature, we will summarize the results of various academic studies relevant to our topic. The primary orientation of academic research in finance is on publicly traded stocks. It is generally not directly concerned with the issues of the valuation profession, which is focused on valuing private firms. Often a slightly interesting side point in an academic article is a golden nugget for the valuation profession—if not a diamond.

There are two types of evidence of the value of control. The first is the value of complete control. The second deals with the value of voting rights. Voting rights do not represent control, but they do represent some degree of influence or partial control.[11]

The academic research falls into the following categories:

1. The article by Schwert focuses primarily on analyzing returns in mergers and acquisitions during two periods: the runup period,

---

11. Mergerstat Review does track premiums for acquisitions of minority interests, which make up a third category of evidence. I am not aware of any academic literature dealing with this issue.

which is the time before announcement of the merger, and the markup period, which is the time period after the announcement. This is significant in the context of this book primarily as providing empirical evidence that is relevant in my economic components model for the discount for lack of marketability (DLOM). It could easily belong to the DLOM part of this chapter, but I include it here with the rest of the academic articles.

2. The articles by Lease, McConnell, and Mikkelson; Megginson; Houlihan Lokey Howard & Zukin (HLHZ); and the section on international voting rights premia all deal with the value of voting rights and provide insight on the value of control that fits in the definition of fair market value.[12]

3. The articles by Bradley, Desai, Kim and Maquieira, Megginson, and Nail are about the value of complete control. In particular, their focus is on measuring the synergies in acquisitions, which is a critical piece of evidence to understand in sorting through the apparently conflicting results and opinions in the professional literature.

4. The article by Menyah and Paudyal is an analysis of bid–ask spreads and is primarily related to DLOM, not control. It could also have been included in section on marketability.

Schwert (1996)

Since business appraisers calculate control premiums and discounts for lack of control from merger and acquisition (M&A) data of publicly traded firms, it is important to understand what variables drive control premiums in order to be able to properly apply them to privately held firms. Schwert's article has some important findings.

Schwert's main purpose is to examine the relationship between runups and markups in M&A pricing. (The runup period is that period of time before the announcement of a merger in which the target firm's price is increasing.) Schwert finds that cumulative abnormal returns (CARs)[13] begin rising around 42 days before an acquisition. Thus, he defines the runup period from day −42 to day −1, with day 0 being the announcement of the merger. The markup period is from day 1 to day 126 or delisting, whichever is first. The sum of the runup and markup period is the entire relevant timeline of an acquisition, and the sum of their CARs is the total acquisition premium.

Schwert finds that CARs during the runup period for successful acquisitions between 1975–1991 average 25%, with CARs for unsuccessful acquisitions, i.e., where the bidder ultimately fails to take over the target, averaging 19%.[14] After the announcement date, CARs for successful ac-

---

12. The HLHZ article is professional rather than academic, but its topic fits in better in our discussion of academic research.
13. These are the cumulative error terms for actual returns minus market returns calculated by CAPM.
14. One thousand, eight hundred and fourteen transactions in total, which are later reduced to 1,523 in his main sample.

quisitions increase to 37%, while for unsuccessful acquisitions they decrease to zero.

He discusses two opposite bidding strategies, the substitution hypothesis and the markup pricing hypothesis.

The substitution hypothesis states that each dollar of preannouncement runup reduces the post-bid markup dollar for dollar. The assumptions behind this hypothesis are that both the bidder and the target have private information that is not reflected in the market price of the stock and that no other bidder has valuable private information. Therefore, both the bidder and the target will ignore price movements that occur prior to and during the negotiations in setting the final deal price.

The markup pricing hypothesis is that each dollar of preannouncement runup has no impact on the post-bid markup. Thus, the preannouncement runup increases the ultimate acquisition premium dollar for dollar. The assumption behind this hypothesis is that both the bidder and the target are uncertain about whether movements in the market price of the target's shares reflect valuable private information of other traders. Therefore, runups in the stock price could cause both the bidder and the target to revise their valuations of the target's stock. Schwert used the example that if they suspect that another bidder may be acquiring shares, both the bidder and the target will probably revise their valuations of the target's stock upward.

The markup hypothesis reflects rational behavior of bidders and targets when they have incomplete information. A different explanation of the markup hypothesis is that of Roll (1986), who postulates that bidders are interested in taking over targets regardless of cost (the hubris hypothesis). This would reflect irrational behavior. Using regression analysis, Schwert finds strongly in favor of the markup hypothesis, while rejecting Roll's hubris explanation as well as the substitution hypothesis.

Had the substitution hypothesis been the winner, this would have implied that the acquisition premiums that occur in the market would require major adjustments for calculating fair market value. It would have meant that the post-bid markups are based on private information to a particular buyer and seller, who ignore the effects of the pre-bid runup because they both believe that no other bidder has valuable private information. This would then be investment value, not fair market value. With the markup hypothesis being the winner, at least we do not have that complication.

For professional appraisers, the most important finding in Schwert's paper is the impact of competitive bidding, i.e., when there is more than one bidder for a target, on the cumulative abnormal returns on the target's stock. Approximately 20% of the takeovers were competitive (312 out of 1,523), with 80% (1,211 out of 1,523) noncompetitive. Table 4 in the article shows that the presence of competitive bidding increases the premium paid by 12.2%.[15] This is significant evidence of the impact of competition that will have an important role to play in calculating D_2, the

---

15. That is, it adds an absolute 12.2% to the premium. It does not increase the premium by 12.2%. For example, if the average premium with only one bidder is 30%, with two or more bidders it is 42.2%.

component in Abrams' economic components model of the discount for lack of marketability due to the absence of competition in thin markets. We will cover that in detail later in this chapter.

Lease, McConnell, and Mikkelson (1983)

Lease, McConnell, and Mikkelson (LMM) examined all companies with two classes of common stock outstanding sometime between 1940 and 1978. Both classes of common shares were entitled to identical dividends and liquidation preferences. In total, 30 companies met the criteria, although never more than 11 companies in any one year. On average, there were only 7 companies in the population per year.

LMM found a statistically significant voting rights premium. They split their population into three categories. Category 1 firms had only voting and nonvoting common, with no voting preferred stock. Category 2 firms had two classes of voting common—one with superior voting rights and one with inferior voting rights. Category 3 firms had superior voting common, either nonvoting or inferior voting common, and voting preferred. Their results were as follows:

Category	Mean Voting Rights Premium
1	3.8%
2	7.0%
3	−1.1%

The mean voting premium of the Category 1 and 2 firms is 5.44%. There is no logical reason why Category 2 firms should have a higher voting rights premium than Category 1 firms, and the authors labeled this result "a puzzle." The relationship should have been the opposite. There was one large outlier in Category 2. Without it, the Category 2 premium is only 1.9%. However, the authors investigated this outlier thoroughly and found no reason to exclude it from the data. It had no distinguishing characteristics.

As to the other puzzling result of a voting rights discount to the superior common shares in the presence of voting preferred stock, the authors speculate that there might be some incremental costs borne by the superior rights shares that are not borne by the inferior rights shares. However, Megginson (1990) and the HLHZ articles did not find this result. Megginson found a 23% premium for Category 3.

Megginson (1990)

The author analyzes 152 British firms traded on the London Stock Exchange in the 28 years from 1955–1982 that have at least two classes of common stock, with one class possessing superior voting (SV) power to the other, for the purpose of explaining the underlying variables that explain the voting rights premium (VRP) to the SV shares. He labels the inferior common shares those with restricted voting (RV) power. While the article does not say so, in one of many telephone conversations that I had with Professor Megginson, he said that all of the RV shares are simply nonvoting, even though he was using a more generic terminology.

A minority of firms in his sample also had preferred shares. His work is a continuation of that of Lease, McConnell, and Mikkelson in a different environment.

Megginson was hoping for his regression analysis to shed light on which of three competing hypotheses explain the voting rights premium to SV shares. Ultimately, the regression results could not shed any light on the source of VRP. However, his article does provide some information to determine the magnitude of the control premium that is purely for control and not for anticipated higher cash flows.

Under the ownership structure hypothesis, there is an optimal amount of stock ownership for insiders—management and directors. If insiders hold too little SV stock, company performance can be improved by increasing insider ownership. However, if insiders own too much SV stock, they can become overly entrenched and immune to forced removal, lowering the value of all classes of stock in general and restricted voting (RV) stock in particular.

Under this hypothesis, the voting rights premium is positively related to insider holdings of SV shares and negatively related to RV shares. The reason for the former is the entrenchment effect, and the reason for the latter is that the larger the percentage of RV shares owned by insiders, the more incentive they have to maximize the value of RV shares.

Some of the more interesting summary statistics from Megginson are listed below. Pay particular attention to numbers 3 and 4—as they contain the main information for our analysis below.

1. SV shares represented 38.4% of total common equity but 94.3% of total voting power.

2. Insiders held 28.7% of SV shares (29.8% for companies with voting preferred) and 8.6% of RV shares (2.7% for companies with voting preferred).

3. The mean voting rights premium was 13.3% across all firms, 23% for firms with voting preferred, and 6% for firms that were subsidiaries of other companies.

4. Forty-three of the 152 firms (28.3%) were taken over during the sample period. In 37 out of the 43 cases, which is 86% of the 43 firms or 24.3% percent of the entire sample of 152 firms, the SV shares received higher prices than the RV shares by an average 27.6%.[16] The existence of significant tender offer premiums that go disproportionately to SV shares and whose timing is generally unknown could possibly explain the VRP, though Megginson feels the magnitudes of the VRP are too high to be explained by 28% premiums at unknown times.

5. His regression analysis in logarithmic form[17] with the ratio of the price of SV shares to the RV shares as the dependent variable found the percentage holdings of insiders of SV and RV

---

16. It is unclear whether the 27.6% refers to all 43 firms or just the 37 firms where the SV shares received a premium over the RV shares. Assuming the former instead of the latter changes the conclusion later in the chapter in Table 7-3, cell D24 from 1.4% to 1.5%.

17. The logarithm of the price variables most closely approximates a normal distribution.

shares as the only statistically significant variables. The former was positively related and the latter negatively related to the ratio of prices. Even then, the adjusted R^2 was only 11%.

My Conclusions from the Megginson Results.   The British VRP of 13.3% is significantly higher than the American VRP, which in the Lease, McConnell, and Mikkelson study is 5.4% and in the Houlihan Lokey Howard & Zukin study (which follows the section on Megginson) is 3.2%. The purpose of this section is to determine how much of the 13.3% VRP is for the power of the vote versus the higher expected cash flows to the SV shareholders.

The analysis that follows shows that of the 13.3% VRP, 11.9% is due to higher expected cash flows to the SV shareholders and 1.4% is being paid purely for the right to vote.

The rest of this section is a detailed explanation of Table 7-3, which is my quantitative analysis of the Megginson results. The reader who wants to save time can safely skip the rest of this section and continue with the Houlihan Lokey Howard & Zukin (Much and Fagan) study.

My Analysis of the Megginson Results.   We assume that the average holding period on the London Stock Exchange during the 1955–1982 period was five years. The table begins with expected cash flows to the shareholders in rows 6 to 13, which we show in two different scenarios. In scenario #1 (Columns A–F), the firm will not be acquired during the shareholder's tenure. In scenario #2 (Columns H–M), the firm will be acquired during the shareholder's tenure.

The assumptions of the model are as follows:

1. Using large capitalization NYSE firm data from the SBBI yearbooks,[18] for the years 1955–1982, total returns were 10.48% (B30), which we use as our discount rate. This broke down to a dividend yield of 3.94% (B27) and capital gains return of 6.54% (B29).

2. The voting rights premium is 13.3% (B28), per Megginson (1990).

3. When firms were acquired, we assume a 20% acquisition premium to the RV shares.[19] The final results are insensitive to the magnitude of this assumption.

4. The SV shares receive a premium that is 27.6% (B32) higher than the RV shares in the event of an acquisition.

The RV shareholder cash flows appear in cells C6 to C12. The shareholder invests $1.00 (C6) at time zero. In Year 1, he or she receives dividends of 3.94% × $1.00 = $0.0394 (C7). As the shares rise in price by 6.54% (B29) annually, applying the constant dividend yield is equivalent

---

18. London Stock Exchange data were unavailable to us. We use NYSE data as a proxy for the LSE data. According to Professor Megginson, the NYSE data should be a good proxy for the LSE.

19. These data did not appear in the article and are no longer available.

TABLE 7-3

Analysis of Megginson Results

	Scenario #1: SV Shares-No Acquisition						Scenario #2: SV Shares-Acquisition				
Yr	SV	RV	PV Factor [1]	NPV SV	NPV RV	Yr	SV	RV	PV Factor [1]	NPV SV	NPV RV
0	-1.1330	-1.0000	1.0000	-1.1330	-1.0000	0	-1.1330	-1.0000	1.0000	-1.1330	-1.0000
1	0.0394	0.0394	0.9051	0.0357	0.0357	1	0.0394	0.0394	0.9051	0.0357	0.0357
2	0.0420	0.0420	0.8193	0.0344	0.0344	2	0.0394	0.0394	0.8193	0.0323	0.0323
3	0.0447	0.0447	0.7416	0.0332	0.0332	3	0.0394	0.0394	0.7416	0.0292	0.0292
4	0.0476	0.0476	0.6712	0.0320	0.0320	4	0.0394	0.0394	0.6712	0.0264	0.0264
5	0.0508	0.0508	0.6075	0.0308	0.0308	5	0.0394	0.0394	0.6075	0.0239	0.0239
5	1.5552	1.3727	0.6075	0.9449	0.8340	5	2.101819	1.647194	0.6075	1.2770	1.0008
Total				**-0.0221**	**0.0000**	**Total**				**0.2915**	**0.1483**

Summary of NPVs

	No Acq	Acquisition	Total
SV	-0.0221	0.2915	
RV	0.0000	0.1483	
Probabilities [2]	94.95%	5.05%	100.00%
Probability Wtd NPVs			
SV	-0.0210	0.0147	-0.0062
RV	0.0000	0.0075	0.0075
RV-SV			0.0137
RV-SV (in percent)			1.4%

SENSITIVITY ANALYSIS: NPV of RV-SV

Capital Apprec	RV-SV
0.00%	0.0461
2.00%	0.0371
4.00%	0.0273
6.54%	0.0137
8.00%	0.0053
10.48%	-0.0100

Assumptions

Dividend yield [3]	3.94%
Voting rights prem	0.133
Cap apprec = g [3]	6.54%
Disc rate = r [3]	10.48%
Acq prem-RV [4]	20%
SV/RV acq prem	27.6%

[1] Present value factors are end-of-year. Using midyear factors makes no difference in the final result to four decimal places.
[2] Probability of acquisition 5 year holding period/[152 Firms/(43 Acquisitions/28 Years)], or 5 Years / 98.98 years
[3] Derived from SBBI-1999 for 1955-1982. We use the US data as a proxy for UK data, as the latter were unavailable.
[4] This is an assumption, as the data were unavailable. However, the final results are insensitive to the assumption.

to having dividends rise by the same capital appreciation percentage of 6.54%. Thus, $0.0394 \times (1 + 0.0654) = 0.0420 (C8). As we go down the column, each year's dividend is 6.54% higher than the previous year's. The final dividend is $0.0508 (C11). Finally, at the end of Year 5, the shareholder sells for $1.3727 (C12), which is the original investment of $1.00, with five years of compound growth at the 6.54% or $1.00 \times 1.0654^5 = 1.3727.

The SV share cash flows begin with a $1.133 investment (B6). The SV shareholders receive the same dividend stream as the RV shareholders, so B7 through B11 is the same as those rows in column C. At the end of Year 5, the SV shareholder sells at the voting rights premium of 13.3%, i.e., $1.3727 \times 1.133 = 1.5552 [C12 $\times$ (1 + B28) = B12].

We discount the forecast cash flows at the average return of 10.48% (B30). The end-of-year present value factors at 10.48% appear in D6 to D12. Multiplying the SV and RV forecast cash flows by the present value factors leads to present values of the SV and RV forecast cash flows in E6 through E12 and F6 through F12, respectively. The totals are the net present values of the investments, which are −$.0221 (E13) and 0 (F13) for SV and RV.

The analysis of scenario #2 is structured identically to that of scenario #1. The forecast cash flows in I6 through J11, which are the initial investments and the dividends, are identical to their counterparts in columns B and C. The only differences are in Year 5, where we assume the firms are acquired. The acquisition amount for the RV shares is composed of two parts. The first is the five years of growth at 6.54% (B29), or $1.0654^5 = 1.3727, which is the same as C12. We then multiply that by 1 plus the assumed acquisition premium for RV shares of 20% (B31), or $1.3727 \times 1.2 = 1.647194 (J12). The actual premium is unknown; however, a sensitivity analysis showed our final results are insensitive to this assumption within a fairly wide range around our assumption.

The SV buyout occurs at the SV-over-RV premium of 27.6% (B32), or $1.647194 \times 1.276 = 2.101819 (I12). The present values of the cash flows are $0.2915 (L13) and $0.1483 (M13) for SV and RV shares when there is an acquisition.[20]

We now proceed to the summary of the net present values (NPVs) and begin with the no-acquisition scenario. In B17 and B18, we transfer the NPVs of −$0.0221 and zero from E13 and F13 for the SV and RV shares. We then multiply those conditional FMVs by the probability of not being acquired in our assumed five-year holding period, which is 94.95% (B19) and is calculated in footnote [2] to Table 7-3. The probability-weighted NPVs for the SV and RV shares are −$0.0210 and 0 (B21, B22).

Next we transfer the acquisition scenario NPVs of $0.2915 and $0.1483 for SV and RV shares from L13 and M13 to C17 and C18, respectively. We multiply those NPVs by the probability of acquisition of 5.05% (C19), which is 1 minus the 94.95% in B19, to obtain the probability-

---

20. Actually, the present values are slightly higher, as the acquisitions could take place before Year 5. However, this simplification has no material impact on the outcome of the analysis.

weighted NPVs of $0.0147 (C21) and $0.0075 (C22) for the SV and RV shares.

We add columns B and C to obtain the probability-weighted NPVs of SV shares of −$0.0062 (D21) and $0.0075 (D22). The RV minus SV NPV difference is $0.0137 (D23), or approximately 1.4% (D24) of the RV share price.

Let's do a recap of this table, as it is very detailed. At the 10.48% (B30) discount rate, the RV shares are priced exactly right, assuming there will be no acquisition, i.e., they have a zero present value (F13), while they actually have a small, positive weighted average NPV of $0.0075 (D22) after including the 5% probability of an acquisition premium. Thus, RV shares are a good buy based on expected cash flows for one with a 10.48% hurdle rate.

The SV shares, on the other hand, are a bad buy on a pure discounted cash flow basis. In the absence of an acquisition, which is a 95% probability for a five-year holding period, the NPV is −$0.0221 (E13, transferred to B17). The positive NPV of $0.2915 (L13, transferred to C17) in the event of an acquisition, which is only a 5% probability, is insufficient to outweigh the negative NPV absent the acquisition. Overall, the SV shares have a negative NPV of −$0.0062 (D21). On a pure basis of NPV of forecast cash flows, the RV shares have a $0.0137 (D23) NPV differential over the SV shares. The investor in SV shares passed up $0.014 (rounded) of NPV to buy the vote, or 1.4% (D24) of the $1.00 RV price. We subtract this from the average SV price of $1.133, and $1.119, or 11.9% of the 13.3% voting rights premium is justified by higher expected cash flows, while 1.4% of it appears to be paid for the right to vote and the marginal power that goes with it.

In the middle-right section of the table, we present a sensitivity analysis of the SV-RV NPV differential. The SV-RV NPV differential rises as the fraction of the total return shifts more towards dividend yield and away from capital appreciation. For example, if capital appreciation accounted for none of the 10.48% yield, then the portion of the $0.133 voting rights premium attributable to the power of the vote rises to $0.0461 (I19) versus the base case.

The intuition for this result is that when returns are weighted more heavily towards dividends, the SV shares receive a lower effective dividend yield. This is because the SV shares receive the same absolute dividends as the RV shares but paid a higher price per share to receive them. Also, both SV and RV share prices grow more slowly, and the absolute cash value of the 27.6% SV-over-RV premium upon acquisition is less than when returns are primarily in the form of capital gains.

Table 7-3A is identical to Table 7-3, but it is for the Lease, McConnell, and Mikkelson study. The net VRP is 1.1% (D24).

The Houlihan Lokey Howard & Zukin (HLHZ) Study

Much and Fagan (2000), of HLHZ, describe their own update of the Lease, McConnell, and Mikkelson study. The HLHZ study consists of 18 dual-class firms with identical dividend rights and liquidity preference. While this is professional rather than academic research, we include it here because it is an update of academic research and fits in better topically.

T A B L E 7-3A

Analysis of American VRP Results

	A	B	C	D	E	F		H	I	J	K	L	M
4		Scenario #1: SV Shares-No Acquisition						Scenario #2: SV Shares-Acquisition					
5	Yr	SV	RV	PV Factor [1]	PV SV	NPV RV		Yr	SV	RV	PV Factor [1]	PV SV	NPV RV
6	0	-1.0544	-1.0000	1.0000	-1.0544	-1.0000		0	-1.0544	-1.0000	1.0000	-1.0544	-1.0000
7	1	0.0394	0.0394	0.9051	0.0357	0.0357		1	0.0394	0.0394	0.9051	0.0357	0.0357
8	2	0.0420	0.0420	0.8193	0.0344	0.0344		2	0.0394	0.0394	0.8193	0.0323	0.0323
9	3	0.0447	0.0447	0.7416	0.0332	0.0332		3	0.0394	0.0394	0.7416	0.0292	0.0292
10	4	0.0476	0.0476	0.6712	0.0320	0.0320		4	0.0394	0.0394	0.6712	0.0264	0.0264
11	5	0.0508	0.0508	0.6075	0.0308	0.0308		5	0.0394	0.0394	0.6075	0.0239	0.0239
12	5	1.4473	1.3727	0.6075	0.8793	0.8340		5	1.921726	1.921726	0.6075	1.1675	1.1675
13	Total				-0.0090	0.0000		Total				0.2607	0.3151

Summary of NPVs

	No Acq	Acquisition	Total
SV	-0.0090	0.2607	
RV	0.0000	0.3151	
Probabilities [2]	94.95%	5.05%	100.00%
Probability Wtd NPVs			
SV	-0.0086	0.0132	0.0046
RV	0.0000	0.0159	0.0159
RV-SV			00.0113
RV-SV (in percent)			1.1%

SENSITIVITY ANALYSIS: NPV of RV-SV

Discount Rate	RV-SV
8%	0.0061
10.48%	0.0113
12%	0.0142
14%	0.0176

Capital Apprec	RV-SV
0.00%	0.0230
2.00%	0.0230
4.00%	0.0162
6.54%	0.0113
8.00%	0.0083
10.48%	0.0027

Assumptions

Dividend yield [3]	3.94%
Voting rights prem [5]	0.0544
Cap apprec = g [3]	6.54%
Disc rate = r [3]	10.48%
Acq perm-both [4]	40%
SV/RV acq prem	0.0%

[1] Present value factors are end-of-year. Using midyear factors makes no difference in the final result to four decimal places.
[2] Probability of acquisition is from the British data. However, increasing cell C19 to 25% causes D24 to rise to only 2%.
[3] Derived from SBBI-1999 for 1955-1982.
[4] This is an assumption, as the data were unavailable. However, the final results are insensitive to the assumption.

The HLHZ study presents the VRP over a very short period of time ending with December 31, 1994.[21] In this respect it is very different than the two previous studies, which present VRP averages over many years. The Lease, McConnell, and Mikkelson VRP results are the averages over 38 years, while the Megginson results are averages over 28 years. In contrast, the HLHZ study covers a short snippet of time.

The 260-day moving average mean and median voting rights premiums were 3.2% and 2.7%, respectively, while they were 1.5% and 1.15% for 60-day moving averages. The longer the time period, the more reliable is the result, unless there are clear trends that render older data obsolete, which is not the case here. Therefore, the 260-day moving average of 3.2% is the best measure of the VRP in this study. These are lower premiums than those in the Lease, McConnell, and Mikkelson study, although the mean VRP was monotonically increasing with the length of the moving-average time period (the authors also presented data for 120- and 180-day moving averages. Given the reported results, it is possible that expanding the time horizon would have led to a larger VRP.

The authors point out anecdotally that the voting rights premium can be affected by other factors. They mentioned that until the fourth quarter of 1994, the Class A stock of Pacificare Health Systems, Inc. was included in the S&P 400 index. During this time, the Class A voting shares consistently traded at a 1.5–2.5% premium over the nonvoting shares. During the fourth quarter 1994, the Class B nonvoting stock replaced the Class A stock in the S&P 400 index. Since then, Class A traded at a 1.5% discount to the nonvoting shares. The authors conclude that the visibility of the stock, not its voting rights, accounted for its premium.

Another example they give is Playboy Enterprises, whose Class A voting shares also trade at a discount from the nonvoting shares. However, the company's largest shareholder owns over 70% of the Class A voting stock. Institutional investors are interested in liquidity and prefer to trade in the Class B stock, which has higher trading volume. The authors conclude that the liquidity difference appeared to account for the voting rights discount. Their final conclusion is that the 5.4% voting rights premium in Lease, McConnell, and Mikkelson is too high, given their more current data.

The anecdote about the liquidity difference depressing the voting rights premium is consistent with Megginson (1990), where it was far more obvious in the British markets. My conclusion from this is that the 3.2% voting rights premium would likely be higher after adjusting for liquidity differences.

International Voting Rights Premia

Maher and Andersson (1999) refer to a number of articles that deal with voting rights premia.[22] Zingales (1995) finds that while the voting rights premium in the US is normally small, it rises sharply in situations where

---

21. In their chapter, they say as of December 31, 1994. However, I assume their use of moving averages means that it is a span of time ending on that date.
22. I was unable to obtain those articles before this book went to press.

control is contested, from which he infers that control shareholders receive private benefits at the expense of minority shareholders.

The remaining evidence in this section is from other countries, where concentrated ownership is the norm. Rydqvist (1987) finds a 6.5% voting rights premium for Sweden. Levy (1982) finds a 45.5% VRP in Israel, Horner (1988) finds a 20% VRP for Switzerland, and Zingales (1994) finds an 82% VRP on the Milan Stock Exchange. The large voting premium in Italy suggests high private benefits of control, and Zingales (1994) and Barca (1995) suggest that managers in Italy divert profits to themselves at the expense of nonvoting shareholders. Zingales also measures the average proportion of private benefits to be around 30% of the firm value. Zingales (1994) conjectures that the private benefits of control in Italy are so large because the legal system is ineffective in preventing exploitation by controlling shareholders.

Bradley, Desai, and Kim (1988)

The authors document that successful tender offers increase the combined value of the target and acquiring firm by an average of 7.4% over the period 1963–1984. In this article the 7.4% remains stable over the entire 22 years of analysis, which the Maquieira, Megginson, and Nail results (in the next section) do, too. However, there was a constant movement over time for the target shareholders to capture the lion's share of synergies, with the acquirer faring worse over time. Also noteworthy is that the authors present theoretical arguments why multiple-bidder contests lead to larger payments to target stockholders.

The breakdown of the 7.4% overall synergy is very important to business appraisers. The targets, who are, on average, 20% of the combined entity (i.e., one-fourth of the size of the bidders), experienced an average 31.8% synergistic gain, as measured by cumulative abnormal returns (CARs), and the bidders experienced a 1% synergistic gain. However, the specific results in different subperiods varied and will be significant in my synthesis and analysis later in the chapter. The acquirers had CARs of 4.1%, 1.3%, and −2.9% for July 1963–June 1968, July 1968–December 1980, and January 1981–December 1984, respectively. There is a clear downward trend in the synergistic gains of the acquirers.

They also presented data showing that targets experience cumulative abnormal returns (CARs) of 9.8% from five trading days before the announcement of the first bid to five trading days after the announcement. A multiple bidding scenario increases the CARs by an absolute 13.0%, which is consistent with the result from Schwert discussed above, although not directly comparable in magnitude. Another interesting finding is that synergies were higher in multiple-bidder scenarios. As to the nature of the synergies, the authors cite work (Eckbo 1983, 1985 and Stillman 1983) that indicates that the corporate acquisitions have no measurable effect on the firm's degree of market power in the economy. This is consistent with Maquieira, Megginson, and Nail's results, discussed immediately below, that the synergies are operating and not financial.

Maquieira, Megginson, and Nail (1998)

The authors examine wealth changes for all 1,283 publicly traded debt and equity securities in 260 pure stock-for-stock mergers. They find nonconglomerate mergers create financial synergies. They define conglomerate mergers as those mergers in which the first two digits of the SIC code of the acquirer and the target are different. They determine the SIC code by examining the primary line of business listing for each company in the relevant edition of the *Moody's* manual. This data source differs from Roach (1998), described earlier, and the SIC code scheme is different, which may explain their different results.

To compute the synergy from the mergers, the authors used data from two months before the merger to predict what would have been the value of the two companies (and their individual classes of equity and debt) as separate entities two months after the merger. They then added the two separate company values together to form a "predicted value" of the merged entity. From this, they subtracted the actual market valuation of the merged entity at two months after the merger, and they call this difference the valuation prediction error (VPE), as well as the measure of synergy.

The mean and median VPEs for common and preferred stock were 8.58% and 8.55% for nonconglomerate mergers—and statistically significant at the 1% level—while they were 3.28% and 1.98% for conglomerate mergers—and statistically insignificant. For all classes of securities, which also include convertible and nonconvertible preferred stock and bonds, the mean and median net synergistic gains were 6.91% and 6.79% for nonconglomerate mergers—and statistically significant at the 1% level— while they were 3.91% and 1.25% for conglomerate mergers—and statistically insignificant. The positive VPEs in nonconglomerate mergers occur in a statistically significant 66.4% of the mergers, while a statistically insignificant 56.3% of the conglomerate mergers yield positive VPEs.

The breakdown between acquirers and targets is significant. In nonconglomerate mergers, the acquirers had mean and median VPEs of 6.14% and 4.64%, while the targets were at 38.08% and 24.33%. In conglomerate mergers, the acquirers were the only losers, with mean and median VPEs of −4.79% and −7.36%.

Maquieira, Megginson, and Nail also mention similar synergy figures provided by Lang et al. (1991), Eckbo (1992), and Berkovitch and Narayanan (1993). Another very significant conclusion of their analysis is that the stock-for-stock merger synergies are operating synergies, not financial.

The authors also report the time to complete each merger, which are interesting data and provide a benchmark for the delay-to-sale component of my economic components model, described later in the chapter. The time to complete the mergers ranged from a low of 11 months to a high of 31 months—roughly 1 to 2 1/2 years. This underestimates the time to complete a merger, as it starts from the announcement date rather than the date at which the parties first thought of the idea.

Other Corporate Control Research

This section is brief. Its purpose is to present summary findings of other researchers that will ultimately add to the discussion of what business appraisers need to know about corporate control.

Franks and Harris (1989) analyze 1,445 takeovers in British stock markets using the London Share Price Database. Their findings are very similar to those in the United States discussed in the previous sections, i.e., that targets capture the majority of the gains from acquisition.

Cumulative abnormal returns (CARs)[23] to the target shareholders in Month 0 for single bids for which there were no revisions and no contest were 20.6% and CARs for contested bids were 29.1%, for a differential of 8.5%. This is fairly similar, although somewhat lower than Schwert. The CARs for Months −4 to +1 are much higher: 27.4% for the single bids and 46.6% for contested bids, for a differential of 19.2%, which is higher than Schwert's result. There is an interesting intermediate category of revised, but uncontested, bids, which the authors say probably reflects results when the buyers are worried that another firm might compete with their initial lower bid. The CARs for this category are 28.7% in Month 0 and 40.5% for Months −4 to +1. These might provide interesting benchmarks for different levels of competition, both actual and potential. CARs to bidders are very low, which echo the US results.

In a cross-sectional analysis of total wealth gains, multiple bidders increase the control premium by an absolute 8.44%.[24] This is also similar to Schwert's result, although slightly lower.

Harris (1994) provides an explanation of why any firm would want to be the bidder rather than the target. If target shareholders are the big winners and bidders barely break even, then why bother being a bidder? Why not wait for the other firm to be the bidder and be the target instead? The answer is that while the target's shareholders are the winners, the target's management are losers. Harris cites another author who cites a *Wall Street Journal* article that reported 65% of a sample of 515 target CEOs left their firms shortly after the acquisitions (less so in mergers). The reward for the bidder is that management gets to keep their jobs. The reward for target management is that the bidder pays a high price for their stock, which gives many of them plenty of time to take life graciously while looking for their next job.

Menyah and Paudyal

This research provides a method of quantifying the bid–ask spread (BAS). Later in the chapter we review some of the work on DLOM by Larry Kasper, which involves using an econometric equation to determine the BAS to add to the CAPM-determined discount rate before DLOM. Those interested in using Kasper's method may want to understand this research. Otherwise, this work is not used in my own models and can be skipped.

The authors study stocks on the London Stock Exchange and find the security prices, volume of transactions, risk associated with security returns, and the degree of competition among market makers explain 91% of the cross-sectional variations in bid–ask spreads (BAS) (Menyah and Paudyaul 1996).

---

23. The authors actually use the term *total abnormal returns*.
24. See the *x*-coefficient for variable α_2 in their Table 9.

PART 3   Adjusting for Control and Marketability

The average inside spread[25] for liquid stocks was 0.83% before the October 1987 stock market crash. It increased to 2% but has since declined to 0.71% by the end of 1993. The average inside spread for less liquid stocks declined from 10% to 6% over the same period. Transactions over £2000 have lower BASs.[26]

The academic literature has identified three components to the BAS: order processing, inventory adjustment, and adverse information. The authors quote Stoll (Stoll 1978a, b), who says that because dealers must service their customers, they cannot maintain an optimal portfolio suitable to their risk–return strategy. Therefore, total risk, not just systematic risk—as measured by beta—is the relevant variable in determining the BAS.

Their regression equation is: $\ln \text{BAS} = -0.097 + 0.592 \ln \text{Price} + 0.649 \ln \sigma - 0.369 \ln \text{\# Market Makers} - 0.209 \ln \text{Volume}$. All coefficients were significant at the 5% level, except the y-intercept. $R^2 = 91\%$.

The BAS equation shows that in the public markets, an increase in volatility increases the BAS—and thus DLOM—while an increase in the number of market makers decreases BAS and DLOM. With privately held firms, there is no market maker, i.e., a dealer who is willing to buy and sell. Business brokers and investment bankers never take possession of the firm. This is an substantial intellectual problem for one wishing to use this model. Nevertheless, it may provide some useful benchmarks.

My Synthesis and Analysis

Trying to make sense of the oceans of research and opinions is like trying to put together a giant picture puzzle. For a long time it was difficult to see where some of the pieces fit, and some did not seem to fit at all. However, some coherence is beginning to form.

Decomposing the Acquisition Premium

Let's begin by decomposing the acquisition premium into its potential components:

1. Performance improvements.
2. Synergies.
3. Control premium, i.e., the pure value of control.

Performance improvements are the additional expected cash flows from the target when the bidder runs the target more efficiently. In valuation profession parlance, synergies mean the additional value that comes from combining the target with the bidder—let's call that pure synergy. Specifically, it is that portion of the pure synergy in the control

---

25. The best bid and offer prices at which market makers are prepared to deal in specified quantities are quoted on the yellow strip of the Stock Exchange Automated Quotation (SEAQ) screens.
26. Commission rates are also lower since 1986. In 1991 the commission rate for small trades was 2% of transaction value, while trades over £1 million incurred commissions of 0.15% and declined further in 1993 to 0.13%.

premium for which the bidder pays. We never see the portion that the bidder keeps in the Mergerstat acquisition premiums.[27] However, in the academic literature cited, synergy is used to mean the increase in value of the combined entity regardless of the source. It is the combination of the added value from performance improvements and pure synergy.[28]

Ideally, if we could quantify each component, we would want to apply only the pure control premium, item 3, to a marketable minority interest fair market value (FMV) to arrive at a marketable control FMV. We would not want to apply the average amount of performance improvements in the market to a subject company, as it is more appropriate to quantify the specific expected performance improvements for the subject company and add those to the forecast cash flows. This follows Mercer (1998) and McCarter and Glass (1995). Finally, synergies normally belong in investment value, not fair market value—unless the market is dominated by strategic buyers and the subject company is a serious candidate for the M&A market.

Inferences from the Academic Articles

The Bradley, Desai, and Kim results are very revealing. On average over 22 years, the acquirers actually gained, with a CAR of 1%. This means that the acquirers are not paying for control! They are paying for expected cash flows. There is no information in this article to tell us how to break down the CAR to the target between performance improvements and synergies. However, the Maquieira, Megginson, and Nail article provides some information to enable us to do that. The VPEs for the nonconglomerate acquirers were about 11% higher than they were for the conglomerate acquirers, which suggests that synergies account for the entire premium. Bidders are approximately four times the size of the targets in their study.[29] Multiplying the VPE differential of 11% × 4 = 44% attributable to synergies. Since acquisition premiums are rarely even that large, this is evidence that acquisition premiums are being paid exclusively for pure synergies and not for performance improvements.

The Roach article suggests the opposite—that the majority of the increase should be from performance improvements, since there was no pattern to the acquisition premiums by the difference in SIC codes. The two articles used different schemes for determining a potential synergistic merger. Maquieira, Megginson, and Nail only require that the two firms be in the same two-digit SIC code. A merger of SIC codes 3600 and 3699 would be nonconglomerate, while in Roach's work they would be a difference greater than 50 and presumably the equivalent of conglomerate, although he did not use that terminology. On the other hand, a merger

---

27. That also would be true about the portion of performance improvements that the bidder keeps.
28. We could add valuation corrections for underpricing errors to the previous list. To the extent that bidders spot undervalued firms and pay a premium for some or all of that undervaluation, that portion does not belong in the control premium applicable to private companies, as we already presume that the valuation before discounts and premiums was done correctly.
29. The book value of total assets of the bidding firms made up 81.2% of total assets of both firms combined, and the targets made up 18.8% of total assets.

of SIC codes 3599 and 3600 would be a conglomerate merger according to Maquieira, Megginson, and Nail, but a difference of one in the SIC code in Roach's work. It is logical that one can achieve synergies from combining two firms in similar but different businesses and that the two-digit SIC code scheme is better for that purpose. For our analysis, we will assume that the academic article is the more correct approach.[30]

Strong evidence supports this conclusion that acquirers are paying for synergies and not control in Table 7-4, which compiles Mergerstat acquisition premiums for control and minority interests. The average difference of control and minority purchase acquisition premiums was −0.16% (K7), and the average minority-to-control ratio was 99.11% (K8).[31] If acquisition premiums were really measuring the value of control, then minority interest acquisitions should have had a significantly lower premium. Instead, this is strong evidence that acquisition premiums are measuring synergies, not control.

Back to Bradley, Desai, and Kim, in the 1981–1984 subperiod, the acquirers did suffer a loss of 2.9%, as measured in CARs. This could mean that the acquiring firms were willing to suffer a net loss of 2.9% of market capitalization for the privilege of control over the target. Since targets were, on average, about one-fourth the size of the bidders, this translates to 11.6% of target value. However, 4 years out of 22 does not seem enough to assert strongly that this is a reliable control premium—let alone *the* control premium.[32]

The Maquieira, Megginson, and Nail article provides similar results. The only negative VPE was for the acquirers in conglomerate mergers, who had a mean and median VPE of −4.79% and −7.36%. Multiplying that mean VPE by four for the bidder-to-target size ratio leads to a pos-

TABLE 7-4

Mergerstat Mean Premiums: Control versus Minority Purchases

	A	B	C	D	E	F	G	H	I	J	K	L
4		1990	1991	1992	1993	1994	1995	1996	1997	1998	Average	
5	Control interest [1]	42.3%	35.4%	41.3%	38.7%	40.7%	44.1%	37.1%	35.9%	40.7%		
6	Minority interest [1]	39.6%	32.6%	38.3%	38.3%	54.5%	61.7%	29.4%	22.4%	39.5%		
7	Difference	2.7%	2.8%	3.0%	0.4%	−13.8%	−17.6%	7.7%	13.5%	1.2%	−0.16%	
8	Minority/control interest	93.6%	92.1%	92.7%	99.0%	133.9%	139.9%	79.2%	62.4%	97.1%	99.11%	
9	SYD weights	2.8%	5.6%	8.3%	11.1%	13.9%	16.7%	19.4%	22.2%	25.0%	100.00%	← Total
10	SYD difference	0.1%	0.2%	0.3%	0.0%	−1.9%	−2.9%	1.5%	3.0%	0.3%	0.17%	
11	SYD minority/control	2.6%	5.1%	7.7%	11.0%	18.6%	23.3%	15.4%	13.9%	24.3%	97.63%	
13	# Transactions											
14	Control interest	154	125	127	151	237	313	358	480	506		
15	Minority interest	21	12	15	22	23	11	16	7	6		

[1] Mergerstat 1999, Table 1-17, Page 25 (Mergerstat 1994, Figure 43, Page 100 for 1990-1993). Mergerstat is a division of Houlihan Lokey Howard & Zukin.

30. This is not to denigrate Roach's work, which was very creative and is still significant evidence.
    I made the same mistake in my own research.
31. In the data provided to me by Mergerstat, the average size of minority purchase was 38%.
32. Even though the regression coefficient was significant at the 0.01 level.

sible control premium of 19.2% of the target's pre-announcement value. Perhaps this is a subset of the market that is paying something for pure control, but it is not representative of the market as a whole.

Thus, it appears that our tentative conclusion, that the 7.4% difference between acquisition premiums in ordinary acquisitions and going private premiums represents synergies, appears to be incorrect. However, it is still possible that going private premiums might be the true control premium. We will come back to this question.

The Disappearing Control Premium

Let's consider the acquisition process. Conventional wisdom is that Company A buys control of Company B and pays, say, a 40% premium for B. Therefore, B is worth 40% more on a control basis than on a marketable minority basis. However, what happens after the acquisition? B no longer exists as an entity. It is absorbed into A, which itself is a public firm owned by a large number of minority shareholders.

How can one justify the 40% premium to the shareholders of A? Won't the minority shareholders of A lose? If it is true that A is paying purely for the control of B, then yes, they will lose, because the minority shareholders of A pay for control that they ultimately do not receive. Paying for control means that the buyer is willing to accept a lower rate of return in order to be in control of the seller, and the Bradley, Desai, and Kim results do not support that contention.[33] After the acquisition, who is in control of B? The management of A is in control, not the shareholders of A. For there to be a pure value of control, it must go to management, who may enhance their salaries and perquisites for running a larger organization. It makes sense that if firms are paying for control anywhere, it is in conglomerates. That only goes so far, though, before the shareholders revolt or another firm comes along and makes a hostile takeover, booting out the inefficient management team (or a team who looks after its own interests at the expense of the shareholders).

This seems to suggest that Mercer (1998) and McCarter and Glass (1995) are correct. There is no value to control in itself. The appraiser should simply try to quantify the performance improvements that one can implement in the subject company, if they are relevant to the purpose of the valuation, and proceed with the discounted cash flow or guideline company valuation. The difference in the marketable minority value and the "control value" comes from the changes in cash flows, not from a control premium.

The Control Premium Reappears

Does this mean there is no such thing as a value to control? No. It's just that we cannot find it directly in the U.S. M&A market or in the public markets, with the possible exception of the conglomerate mergers in the Maquieira, Megginson, and Nail article. The reason is that there has to be one individual or a small group of individuals[34] actually in control

---

33. Again, with the possible exception of the 1981–1984 period.
34. Henceforth, for ease of exposition, reference to one individual in this context will also include the possibility of meaning a small group of individuals.

who derive psychic benefits from it for there to be a pure control premium—and there is no such thing in the United States—almost.

Estimating the Control Premium

We begin the process of estimating the control premium by starting with the voting rights premium (VRP) data, which show that there is a value of the vote to individual shareholders. If the vote has value, then logically control must have more value—but again only to an individual who is really in control.

Our VRP analysis shows two levels of voting rights premium. The gross premiums were 5.4% and 3.2% in the United States from the Lease, McConnell, and Mikkelson study and the HLHZ study, and 13.3% in England, per Megginson (1990). The net premiums—meaning those above and beyond expected higher cash flows to the voting stock—were 1–1.4%. For the valuation of most small and medium-size businesses, the gross VRP is the more relevant measure, for reasons we will discuss shortly.

The U.S. gross VRPs average 4.3%, i.e., the average of the 5.44% and 3.2% gross VRPs from Lease, McConnell, and Mikkelson and HLHZ articles. According to Professor Megginson, we then need to add another 2% to 3%, say 2.5%, for the depressing effect on the VRP of the illiquidity of the voting shares, which brings us to 6.8%, which we round to 7%.

Control must be worth at least three to four times the value of the vote. That would place the value of control to an individual at at least 21–28%. It could easily be more. Currently, the only possible direct evidence in the United States is the conglomerate control premium of 19.2% in the Maquieira, Megginson, and Nail article, which is very close to the above estimate. The VRP in Switzerland, Israel, and Milan of 20%, 45.5%, and 82%, respectively, is another indication of the value of control when minority shareholders are not well protected, again keeping in mind that those were the value of the vote, not control.

Another piece of data indicating the value of control is the one outlier in the Lease, McConnell, and Mikkelson study, which had a 42% VRP. Such a high VRP in the United States is probably indicative of control battles taking place and could rapidly reduce to a more normal VRP. Thus, the voting shareholders probably could not rely on being able to resell their shares at a similar premium at which they buy. That 42% premium is evidence of the value of the vote in an extreme situation when small blocks of shares would have a large impact on who has control.

The reason why the gross VRP is relevant for most businesses in the process of inferring the value of control is that as long as the buyer of a business can turn around and sell the business for the same control premium as he or she bought it, there is no loss in net present value of cash flows, other than the pure control portion, which derives from the net VRP.[35] The buyer will eventually recoup the control premium later on as a seller. That works as long as the business is small enough that its buyers

---

35. There is actually a second-order effect where this is not literally true. To the extent that the owner is taking implicit dividends in the form of excess salary, there is some loss in present value from this.

will be either private individuals or private firms. If the business grows large enough to be bought by a public firm or undergoes its own IPO, then instead of recouping a private control premium, the owner may receive an acquisition premium with synergies in the case of a buyout. In the case of an IPO, the company will experience an increase in value from increased marketability.[36] Also, while the control premium will be smaller, DLOM may also be smaller.

The best source of data for control premiums and DLOC for private firms in the United States will probably come from a thorough analysis of the international literature. The publicly traded firms overseas are probably better guidelines to use to understand the value of control than United States firms for two reasons. The first reason is that in most foreign countries—especially those outside the United Kingdom—ownership of public firms is far more concentrated than it is in the United States. The second reason is that the minority shareholders there are far more vulnerable to abuse by the control interests, which is closer to the case in privately held firms in the United States.

Unfortunately, that will have to remain as future research. In the meantime, I would suggest that the 21–28% control premium based on the gross VRP is probably reasonable to add to a marketable minority FMV—at least for small and medium firms. For large private firms, that range may still be right if a synergistic buy is likely in the future. Otherwise, it is probably more appropriate to use a smaller control premium based on the net VRP, which would be in the 3–6% range.

At this point, we need to compare our control premium inferred by VRPs with going private premiums, as the latter is also a candidate for our measure of the value of control. The median going private premium of 24.1% (Table 7-1, E21) is right in the middle of our 21–28% range for control calculated by VRPs. However, the mean going private premium of 32.1% (Table 7-1, D21) is above our VRP-calculated range. Which is more likely to be right?

The going private premiums have the advantage of being directly calculated rather than indirectly inferred, so that is one point in their favor. There is no consensus in the valuation profession in general whether medians or means are better measures. All other things being equal, then, it would make sense to use the median, as it is consistent with the VRP-calculated control premium. I more often use means than medians, which leaves me a little dissatisfied relying solely on the consistency of the two measures.

There is other logic that convinces me that the lower measure of control is more correct. What are the motivations for going private? The management team may believe:

(1) The company is underpriced in the market.
(2) Removing the burdens of SEC reporting will increase profitability.

---

36. The appraiser must consider the issue of restricted stock discounts in this case.

(3) If the going private transaction is a division of a public company, it can operate more efficiently without interference and the burden of overhead from the corporate people.

(4) The management group and the buyout group want to be in control of the company.

Item (1) implies that the universe of going private transactions may have a sample bias with respect to the valuation of privately held firms. However, to the extent that (1) is true, that portion of the control premium is inapplicable to the valuation of private firms, as we presume that the valuation is done correctly up to this point. Item (2) is also inapplicable to the valuation of private firms, as this represents a performance improvement to the going private firm that is unavailable to the firm that has always been private. Therefore, that portion of the going private premium represented by the economic efficiencies of being private also does not belong in our calculation of the value of control.

Item (3) is a performance improvement and not really a value of control itself. It represents improvements in cash flow, and thus could be considered a control premium to the extent that we believe that the average going private firm would achieve the same amount of performance improvements that an already private firm could expect with new management, but I find that very speculative.

A direct measurement of the premium associated with item (4) would be the closest to our VRP approach to calculating the value of control. However, I find it hard to believe that there is a single shareholder who is in control in the large going private transactions recorded in Mergerstat. Who is in control of the buyout group? Management?

I think that the composition of the observed going private premium is a mixture of all four items above and probably others of which I am unaware. It is likely that some of the going private premium is irrelevant to the valuation of private firms, some of it is for performance improvements that might be applicable to private firms, and some is for the value of control itself, although the latter certainly is less for going private transactions than it is for true control of a firm by a single individual.

Let's make a wild guess as to how the four components comprise the going private premium. Suppose each item is one-fourth of the premium, i.e.:

(1) Company underpriced	8%
(2) Remove SEC reporting	8%
(3) Eliminate corporate overhead	8%
(4) Control	8%
Total—Mean	32%

If this were the true breakdown of the going private premium, then the value of pure control would be only 8%. But, perhaps that is reasonable in a situation where control is not concentrated in a single individual but rather is spread among a few people in the buyout group and a few people in management. This would tell us fairly little about how to apply it to an already private company.

Ultimately, I am more comfortable with the VRP inference of the value of control than the going private premium, as it makes a clean separation of performance improvements from control. In any case, it seems clear that the mean going private premium is probably too high as a measure of the value of control, and we should stick with the 21–28% control premium.

DLOC

It is my opinion that Nath is correct in his assertion that both DLOM and DLOC are needed from the marketable minority interest.[37] Bolotsky disagrees with this more in form than in substance. He asks—logically enough—how one can subtract a DLOC from an interest that has no control attributes to it. The answer is that control matters much less in publicly held firms in the United States than it does in privately held firms. The public minority shareholder has little fear of control shareholders ruining the company or abusing the minority shareholders. Even if he or she does, there are remedies such as class action lawsuits, takeovers, shareholder meetings, etc. that the private minority shareholder can only wish for.

I suggest that Bolotsky's 2 × 2 levels of value chart, as depicted in Figure 7-2, is still too simple.[38] Using his own very innovative and perceptive framework of differing shareholder attributes, it is possible to see why it may still be appropriate to subtract an incremental DLOC in valuing a private minority interest. Figure 7-3 is my own expansion of Bolotsky's 2 × 2 levels of value chart. Here I have split minority interests into well treated and exploited. Most U.S. public minority interests are well treated, and the values are in row 2, column 2 of Figure 7-3. Most private minorities in the United States are poorly treated or, if not, may have to fear being poorly treated with a change in control ownership or a change in attitude of the existing owners. Thus, most U.S. private minorities are in row 3, column 2. The DLOC calculated as the flip side of the control premium going from a well-treated minority to control is insufficient to measure the lower position of an exploited minority. You will

FIGURE 7-3

3 × 2 Levels of Value Chart

	Public	Private
Control	x	x
Minority (well treated)	x	x
Minority (exploited)	x	x

37. This distinction is more important vis-à-vis Mercer's original position than it is in using his quantitative marketability discount model.
38. In fairness, his 2 × 2 levels of value chart is his own simplification of his more complicated system.

PART 3 Adjusting for Control and Marketability

see this later in the chapter in the section on international voting rights premia, where we examine the difference in market value of voting versus nonvoting stock in international public markets. When minority rights are poorly protected, the voting rights premium is as high as 82%, i.e., voting stock sells for an 82% higher price than nonvoting stock. Control must be very valuable in Milan!

It often may be appropriate to use control premia from other countries to calculate a DLOC that is appropriate for U.S. minorities. Then one can use Jankowske's formula to make the incremental adjustment. Thus, it is my opinion that we should subtract both an incremental DLOC and DLOM from the marketable minority value to arrive at a private minority value. However, this is an area that requires further research.

It is important to understand that those are not six unique and discrete cells in the figure. While public or private is an either/or concept, both the degree of control and how well treated are the minority interests are continuums. Thus, there are not only six values that one could calculate as DLOM, but an infinity of values, depending on the magnitudes.

In my correspondence with Mike Bolotsky, he agrees in substance with this view. He prefers to think in a multidimensional matrix of factors, labeled something like "SEC oversight and enforcement power," instead of a control issue. Even so, I will quote from his letter to me. "In valuing private minority interests that are either poorly treated, which is typical of most, or even have reason to fear being poorly treated, I think it is reasonable to subtract DLOC. However, we cannot learn what that is from the American public stock markets, where minority interests are well protected administratively and legally." I agree completely.

That is a research task to be done in the future. In the meantime, the above simplification works and is easier than a multifactor matrix.

What measure of control premium should we use to calculate DLOC? Starting with a marketable minority FMV, we have to decide whether we are coming down to a well-treated private minority or an exploited private minority interest. Additionally, even a well-treated private minority today may turn into a poorly treated minority tomorrow, and the fear of that alone should create a positive DLOC from the marketable minority level. I would suggest again that the 40% range for the foreign VRPs and the American outlier in the Lease, McConnell, and Mikkelson study (which, by coincidence, are similar to American acquisition premiums) plus some additional amount for control being more valuable than the vote, is a reasonable range from which to calculate DLOC. One caveat: if you are valuing an "exploited" minority interest and have not added back excessive salaries taken by the control shareholders, the 40+% range control premium would translate to a 28.6% DLOC, which might be excessive, depending on the magnitude of excessive salary. The reason for this is that the 40+% VRP may, to some extent, represent excess salaries to holders of voting shares. Therefore, if we have already accounted for it in the discounted cash flow, we do not want to double-count and take the full discount.

It is important to note that, given the previous analysis, I do not consider the decrease in value from a public "control" value to a marketable minority level to be DLOC. It tells us nothing about control. It only tells us the magnitude of synergies in acquisitions. I would not use it go from a private control interest to a private minority interest.

DISCOUNT FOR LACK OF MARKETABILITY (DLOM)

Three quantitative models for calculating DLOM have appeared in the professional literature: Jay Abrams' economic components model (Abrams 1994a),[39] Z. Christopher Mercer's quantitative marketability discount model (Mercer 1997), and Larry Kasper's discounted time to market model (Kasper 1997). In this section we will review Mercer's and Kasper's work. In the next section we will cover Abrams' model in greater depth.

Mercer's Quantitative Marketability Discount Model

Mercer presents the quantitative marketability discount model (QMDM) in his impressive volume devoted entirely to the topic of discount for lack of marketability. His book contains much important research in the field and does an excellent job of summarizing prior research and identifying and discussing many of the important issues involved in quantifying DLOM. I consider his book mandatory reading in the field, even though I will present my own competing model that I contend is superior to the QMDM. I will not attempt to give more than a bare summary of his work—not because it is not important, but for the opposite reason: it is too important to be adequately represented by a summary.

With that caveat in mind, the QMDM is based on calculating the net present value of forecast cash flows to shareholders in a business entity. His key concept is that one can evaluate the additional risk of minority ownership in an illiquid business entity compared to ownership of publicly traded stock and quantify it. The appraiser evaluates a list of various factors that affect risk (Mercer 1997, p. 323) and quantifies the differential risk of minority ownership of the private firm compared to the public firm or direct ownership of the underlying assets—whichever is appropriate—and discounts forecast cash flows to present value at the higher risk-adjusted rate of return to calculate the discount.

To simplify the calculations, Mercer usually assumes a growing annuity. He presents an approximate formula for the present value of an annuity with growth (p. 276). In using the QMDM, one improvement the appraiser can make is to use the exact annuity discount factors (ADFs) with growth that we developed in Chapter 3 and that we repeat below.

$$\text{ADF} = \frac{1}{r - g}\left[1 - \left(\frac{1 + g}{1 + r}\right)^n\right]$$

ADF with perpetual growth: End-of-year formula   (3-6b)

$$\text{ADF} = \frac{\sqrt{1 + r}}{r - g}\left[1 - \left(\frac{1 + g}{1 + r}\right)^n\right]$$

ADF with perpetual growth: midyear formula   (3-10a)

---

39. There is no name for the model in the article cited. I have named it since.

Note that the first terms on the right-hand-side of equations (3-6b) and (3-10a) are the end-of-year and midyear Gordon models. As

$$n \to \infty, \ \left(\frac{1 + g}{1 + r}\right)^n \to 0$$

and the ADF reduces to the Gordon model with which we are all familiar.

In his Chapter 12, Mercer reiterates his opposition to a DLOM for controlling interests from his original article (Mercer 1994). His primary objection seems to be that the control owner has control of cash flows until he or she sells the business, at which time there is no longer DLOM. I disagree, as the ability to enjoy cash flows one day at a time and to instantaneously actualize the present value of all cash flow to perpetuity are quite different, the difference being measured by the DLOM that Mr. Mercer suggests does not exist.

In support of his belief that a DLOM is inappropriate for a controlling interests, Mercer (p. 340) cites an article (Phillips and Freeman 1995) that finds that after controlling for size, margin, and industry, privately held firms do not sell for lower multiples than publicly held firms when the buyer is another publicly held firm. There are a few problems with this study:

1. Since the buyers are all publicly held firms, once the sellers' businesses are absorbed into the buyers', there is no DLOM that applies anymore. When a privately held firm sells to a publicly held firm, ignoring any other differences such as potential synergies, there are at least two FMVs for the seller: a "floor FMV," which is the FMV of the standalone business, including DLOM, and a "ceiling FMV," which is the FMV without DLOM. The seller should not be willing to sell below the floor FMV, and the buyer should not be willing to pay more than the ceiling FMV. An actual transaction can take place anywhere between the two, and Mergerstat will record that as the FMV. The articles by Schwert (1996) and Bradley, Desai, and Kim (1988) cited earlier in this chapter show that the lion's share of excess returns in acquisitions go to the seller. Thus, it is normal that the buyer pays top dollar, which would mean that the seller would insist that the buyer forgo the DLOM, which disappears in any case after the transaction. Therefore, at a minimum, the Phillips/Freeman article's applicability is limited to privately held firms that are large enough to attract the attention of and be acquired by publicly held buyers.

2. In both regressions—the Mergerstat and the SDC database— banks show up as having different valuations than all other industries. However, the signs of the regression coefficients for banks are opposite in the two regressions. The regression of the Mergerstat database demonstrates at the 99.99% significance level that buyers pay lower multiples of sales for banks than for other industries, and the regression of the SDC database demonstrates at the 99.99% significance level that buyers pay higher multiples of sales for banks than other industries! There

were several other inconsistencies in the results of the two regressions.

3. The log–log form of regression that Phillips and Freeman used can have the effect of making large variations look small. The standard errors of their regressions were very high. The standard error of the Mergerstat regression was 0.925. Two standard errors is 1.85. Exponentiating, the 95% confidence interval is approximately equal to multiplying the (value/sales) estimate by two standard errors on either side of the regression estimate. The high side of the 95% confidence interval is $e^{1.85} = 6.36$ times the regression estimate, and the low side is $e^{-1.85} = 0.157$ times the regression estimate. Let's put some specific numbers into their equation to see what the confidence intervals look like. Let's assume we are forecasting the value of the common stock as a percentage of sales for a firm over $100 million in value that is neither a bank, a private placement, nor a subsidiary. Their regression equation is ln(Value/Sales) = 3.242 + 0.56 ln net margin + 0.45 ln (1/PE of the S&P 500). Let's assume a 5% after-tax margin and an average PE for the S&P 500 of 15, so 1/PE = 0.067. Then, ln(Value/Sales) = 3.242 + (0.56 × ln 0.05) + (0.45 × ln 0.067) = 3.242 − 1.678 − 1.219 = 0.345. Thus, the regression estimate of (Value/Sales) = $e^{0.345}$ = 1.413, or value is approximately 1.4 times sales, which seems high. If sales are $100, then net income after taxes is $5, which when multiplied by a PE ratio of 15 leads to a value of $75, which implies value should be 0.75 × Sales, not 1.4. The reliability of the forecast is low. The 95% confidence interval is approximately: 0.22 × Sales < Value < 8.99 × Sales.

4. There were fairly few transactions with a private seller. In the Mergerstat database, private targets were 18 out of 416 transactions, and in the SDC database, private targets were 33 out of 445 targets. In total, private targets were approximately 6% of the combined databases.

The small number of transactions with privately held sellers is not necessarily worrisome in itself, but combined with the limitations of the results in 1, the inconsistent results in 2, and the very wide confidence intervals in 3, the results of this study are insufficient to reject DLOM for control interests of privately held firms.

Kasper's BAS Model

Larry Kasper (Kasper 1997, p. 106) uses an econometric equation developed by Amihud and Mendelson (Amihud and Mendelson 1991) to calculate the bid-ask spread (BAS). Their equation is: $r = 0.006477 + 0.01012 \beta + 0.002144 \ln BAS$, where r is the *excess* monthly returns on a stock portfolio over the 90-day Treasury Bill rate and the BAS is multiplied by 100, i.e., a BAS of 25% is denominated as 25, not 0.25.

Kasper says that most business brokers would not list a business that had to be discounted more than 25%. Substituting 25 into the above equation, the excess return required for a BAS of 25% is 0.0069 per month, or approximately 8.28% per year. One would then seek out business brokers (or through IBA, Pratt's Stats, BIZCOMPS, etc.) for actual BASs. Anyone interested in using Kasper's model must read his outstanding book, as this summary is inadequate for understanding his work.

A number of differences in the environment of NASDAQ and privately held business can weaken the applicability of this regression equation from the former to the latter:

1. The BAS in NASDAQ compensates the dealer for actually taking possession of the stock. The dealer actually stands to gain or lose money, whereas business brokers do not.

2. It takes much longer to sell a private business than stock on Nasdaq.

3. The market for privately held firms is much thinner than it is with Nasdaq.

4. Transactions costs are far higher in privately held business than in Nasdaq.

Note that items 2 through 4 are the components of the economic components approach, which we will cover shortly in my model. Also, the reservation in 1 also applied in the Menyah and Paudyal results earlier in the chapter, where the BAS depends on the number of market makers. Again, business brokers are not market makers in the same sense that dealers are. Additionally, as Kasper points out, the regression coefficients will change over time. Kasper also presents a different model, the discounted time to market model (Kasper 1997, pp. 103;–04) that is worth reading. Neither of his models considers transactions costs or the effects of thin markets.[40]

Restricted Stock Discounts

We will now discuss DLOM for restricted stocks as a preparation for our general model for DLOM. We use two valuation methodologies in calculating the restricted stock discount. The first is based on my own multiple regression analysis of data collected by Management Planning, Inc. (MPI),[41] an independent valuation firm in Princeton, New Jersey. The second method involves using a Black–Scholes put option as a proxy for the discount.

Regression of MPI Data
Ten studies of sales of restricted stocks have been published.[42] The first nine appear in Pratt, Reilly, Schweihs (1996, chap. 15) and Mercer (1997);

---

40. That is not to say that I downgrade his book. It is brilliant and a must read for anyone in the profession.

41. Published in Chapter 12 of Mercer (1997). I wish to thank MPI for being gracious and helpful in providing us with its data and consulting with us. In particular, Roy H. Meyers, Vice President, was extremely helpful. MPI provided us with four additional data points and some data corrections.

42. See Mercer (1997, p. 69) for a summary of the results of the first nine studies.

in those studies, the authors did not publish the underlying data and merely presented their analysis and summary of the data. Additionally, only the Hall/Polacek study contains data beyond 1988 (through 1992). The Management Planning study, which Mercer justifiably accords a separate chapter and extensive commentary in his book, contains data on trades from 1980–1996 and thus is superior to the others in two ways: the detail of the data exists and the data are more current.

Table 7-5 is two pages long. The first page contains data on 53 sales of restricted stock between 1980–1996. Column A is numbered 1 through 53 to indicate the sale number. Column C, our dependent (Y) variable, is the restricted stock discount for each transaction. Columns D through J are our seven statistically significant independent variables, which I have labeled $X_1, X_2, \ldots, X_7$. Below is a description of the independent variables:

#	Independent Variable
1	Revenues squared.
2	Shares Sold—$: the discounted dollar value of the traded restricted shares.
3	Market capitalization = price per share times shares outstanding, summed for all classes of stock.
4	Earnings stability: the R^2 of the regression of net income as a function of time, with time measured as years 1, 2, 3, etc.
5	Revenue stability: the R^2 of the regression of revenue as a function of time, with time measured as years 1, 2, 3, etc.
6	Average years to sell: the weighted average years to sell by a nonaffiliate based on SEC Rule 144. I calculated the holding period for the last four issues (DPAC, UMED, NEDI, and ARCCA) based on changes in Rule 144, even though it was not effective yet, because the change was out for review at that time and was highly likely to be accepted.[43] These transactions occurred near the beginning of March 1996, well after the SEC issued the exposure draft on June 27, 1995. This was approximately 14 months before the rule change went into effect at the end of April 1997. The average time to resale for the shares in these four transactions was determined based on the rule change, resulting in a minimum and maximum average holding period of 14 months and 2 years, respectively.[44]
7	Price stability: This ratio is calculated by dividing the standard deviation of the stock price by the mean of the stock price—which is the coefficient of variation of price—then multiplying by 100. The end-of-month stock prices for the 12 months prior to the valuation date are used.

I regressed 30 other independent variables included in or derived from the Management Planning study, and all were statistically insignificant. I restrict our commentary to the seven independent variables that were statistically significant at the 95% level.

The third page of Table 7-5 contains the regression statistics. In regression #1 the adjusted R^2 is 59.47% (B9), a reasonable though not stunning result for such an analysis. This means that the regression model accounts for 59.47% of the variation in the restricted stock discounts. The

---

43. According to John Watson, Jr., Esq., of Latham & Watkins in Washington, D.C., the securities community knew the rule change would take place. In a telephone conversation with Mr. Watson, he said it was only a question of timing.

44. In other words, I assumed perfect foreknowledge of when the rule change would become effective.

TABLE 7-5

Abrams Regression of Management Planning Study Data

	A	B	C	D	E	F	G	H	I	J
4			Y	X_1	X_2	X_3	X_4	X_5	X_6	X_7
6			Discount	Rev^2	Shares Sold-$	Mkt Cap	Earn Stab	Rev Stab	AvgYrs2Sell	Price Stab
7	1	Air Express Int'l	0.0%	8.58E+16	$4,998,000	25,760,000	0.08	0.22	2.84	12.0
8	2	AirTran Corp	19.4%	1.55E+16	$9,998,000	63,477,000	0.90	0.94	2.64	12.0
9	3	Anaren Microwave, Inc.	34.2%	6.90E+13	$1,250,000	13,517,000	0.24	0.78	2.64	28.6
10	4	Angeles Corp	19.6%	7.99E+14	$1,800,000	16,242,000	0.08	0.82	2.13	8.4
11	5	AW Computer Systems, Inc.	57.3%	1.82E+13	$1,843,000	11,698,000	0.00	0.00	2.91	22.6
12	6	Besicorp Group, Inc.	57.6%	1.57E+13	$1,500,000	63,145,000	0.03	0.75	2.13	98.6
13	7	Bioplasty, Inc,	31.1%	6.20E+13	$11,550,000	43,478,000	0.38	0.62	2.85	44.9
14	8	Blyth Holdings, Inc.	31.4%	8.62E+13	$4,452,000	98,053,000	0.04	0.64	2.13	58.6
15	9	Byers Communications Systems, Inc.	22.5%	4.49E+14	$5,007,000	14,027,000	0.90	0.79	2.92	6.6
16	10	Centennial Technologies, Inc.	2.8%	6.75E+13	$656,000	27,045,000	0.94	0.87	2.13	35.0
17	11	Chantal Pharm. Corp.	44.8%	5.21E+13	$4,900,000	149,286,000	0.70	0.23	2.13	51.0
18	12	Choice Drug Delivery Systems, Inc.	28.8%	6.19E+14	$3,375,000	21,233,000	0.29	0.89	2.86	23.6
19	13	Crystal Oil Co.	24.1%	7.47E+16	$24,990,000	686,475,000	0.42	0.57	2.50	28.5
20	14	Cucos, Inc.	18.8%	4.63E+13	$2,003,000	12,579,000	0.77	0.87	2.84	20.4
21	15	Davox Corp.	46.3%	1.14E+15	$999,000	18,942,000	0.01	0.65	2.72	24.6
22	16	Del Electronics Corp.	41.0%	4.21E+13	$394,000	3,406,000	0.08	0.10	2.84	4.0
23	17	Edmark Corp	16.0%	3.56E+13	$2,000,000	12,275,000	0.57	0.92	2.84	10.5
24	18	Electro Nucleonics	24.8%	1.22E+15	$1,055,000	38,435,000	0.68	0.97	2.13	21.4
25	19	Esmor Correctional Svces, Inc.	32.6%	5.89E+14	$3,852,000	50,692,000	0.95	0.90	2.64	34.0
26	20	Gendex Corp	16.7%	2.97E+15	$5,000,000	55,005,000	0.99	0.71	2.69	11.5
27	21	Harken Oil & Gas, Inc.	30.4%	7.55E+13	$1,999,000	27,223,000	0.13	0.88	2.75	19.0
28	22	ICN Paramaceuticals, Inc.	10.5%	1.50E+15	$9,400,000	78,834,000	0.11	0.87	2.25	23.9
29	23	Ion Laser Technology, Inc.	41.1%	1.02E+13	$975,000	10,046,000	0.71	0.92	2.82	22.0
30	24	Max & Erma's Restaurants, Inc.	12.7%	1.87E+15	$1,192,000	31,080,000	0.87	0.87	2.25	18.8

TABLE 7-5 (*continued*)

Abrams Regression of Management Planning Study Data

	A	B	C	D	E	F	G	H	I	J
			Y	X_1	X_2	X_3	X_4	X_5	X_6	X_7
			Discount	Rev²	Shares Sold-$	Mkt Cap	Earn Stab	Rev Stab	AvgYrs2Sell	Price Stab
31	25	Medco Containment Svces, Inc.	15.5%	5.42E+15	$99,994,000	561,890,000	0.84	0.89	2.85	12.8
32	26	Newport Pharm. Int'l, Inc.	37.8%	1.10E+14	$5,950,000	101,259,000	0.00	0.87	2.00	30.2
33	27	Noble Roman's Inc.	17.2%	8.29E+13	$1,251,000	11,422,000	0.06	0.47	2.79	17.0
34	28	No. American Holding Corp.	30.4%	1.35E+15	$3,000,000	79,730,000	0.63	0.84	2.50	22.1
35	29	No. Hills Electronics, Inc.	36.6%	1.15E+13	$3,675,000	21,812,000	0.81	0.79	2.83	52.7
36	30	Photographic Sciences Corp	49.5%	2.70E+14	$5,000,000	44,113,000	0.06	0.76	2.86	27.2
37	31	Presidential Life Corp	15.9%	4.37E+16	$38,063,000	246,787,000	0.00	0.00	2.83	17.0
38	32	Pride Petroleum Svces, Inc.	24.5%	4.34E+15	$21,500,000	74,028,000	0.31	0.26	2.83	18.0
39	33	Quadrex Corp.	39.4%	1.10E+15	$5,000,000	71,016,000	0.41	0.66	2.50	44.2
40	34	Quality Care, Inc.	34.4%	7.97E+14	$3,150,000	19,689,000	0.68	0.74	2.88	7.0
41	35	Ragen Precision Industries, Inc.	15.3%	8.85E+14	$2,000,000	22,653,000	0.61	0.75	2.25	26.0
42	36	REN Corp-USA	17.9%	2.85E+15	$53,625,000	151,074,000	0.02	0.88	2.92	19.8
43	37	REN Corp-USA	29.3%	2.85E+15	$12,003,000	163,749,000	0.02	0.88	2.72	36.1
44	38	Rentrak Corp.	32.5%	1.15E+15	$20,650,000	61,482,000	0.60	0.70	2.92	30.0
45	39	Ryan's Family Steak Houses, Inc.	8.7%	1.02E+15	$5,250,000	159,390,000	0.90	0.87	2.13	13.6
46	40	Ryan's Family Steak Houses, Inc.	5.2%	1.02E+15	$7,250,000	110,160,000	0.90	0.87	2.58	14.4
47	41	Sahlen & Assoc., Inc.	27.5%	3.02E+15	$6,057,000	42,955,000	0.54	0.81	2.72	26.1
48	42	Starrett Housing Corp.	44.8%	1.11E+16	$3,000,000	95,291,000	0.02	0.01	2.50	12.4
49	43	Sudbury Holdings, Inc.	46.5%	1.39E+16	$22,325,000	33,431,000	0.65	0.17	2.96	26.6
50	44	Superior Care, Inc.	41.9%	1.32E+15	$5,660,000	50,403,000	0.21	0.93	2.77	42.2
51	45	Sym-Tek Systems, Inc.	31.6%	4.03E+14	$995,000	20,550,000	0.34	0.92	2.58	13.4
52	46	Telepictures Corp.	11.6%	5.50E+15	$15,250,000	106,849,000	0.81	0.86	2.72	6.6
53	47	Velo-Bind, Inc.	19.5%	5.51E+14	$2,325,000	18,509,000	0.65	0.85	2.81	14.5
54	48	Western Digital Corp.	47.3%	4.24E+14	$7,825,000	50,417,000	0.00	0.32	2.64	22.7
55	49	50-Off Stores, Inc.	12.5%	6.10E+15	$5,670,000	43,024,000	0.80	0.87	2.38	23.7
56	50	ARC Capital	18.8%	3.76E+14	$2,275,000	18,846,000	0.03	0.74	1.63	35.0
57	51	Dense Pac Microsystems, Inc.	23.1%	3.24E+14	$4,500,000	108,862,000	0.08	0.70	1.17	42.4
58	52	Nobel Education Dynamics, Inc.	19.3%	1.95E+15	$12,000,000	60,913,000	0.34	0.76	1.74	32.1
59	53	Unimed Pharmaceuticals	15.8%	5.49E+13	$8,400,000	44,681,000	0.09	0.74	1.90	21.0
60		Mean	27.1%	5.65E+15	$9,223,226	$78,621,472	0.42	0.69	2.54	25.4

Regression #1

Regression Statistics

Multiple R	0.8058
R square	0.6493
Adjusted R square	0.5947
Standard error	0.0873
Observations	53

ANOVA

	df	SS	MS	F	Significance F
Regression	7	0.6354	0.0908	11.9009	1.810E-08
Residual	45	0.3432	0.0076		
Total	52	0.9786			

	Coefficients	Standard Error	t Stat	P-value	Lower 95%	Upper 95%
Intercept	-0.0673	0.1082	-0.6221	0.5370	-0.2854	0.1507
Rev2	-4.629E-18	9.913E-19	-4.6698	0.0000	-6.626E-18	-2.633E-18
Shares sold-$	-3.619E-09	1.199E-09	-3.0169	0.0042	-6.035E-09	-1.203E-09
Mkt cap	4.789E-10	1.790E-10	2.6754	0.0104	1.184E-10	8.394E-10
Earn stab	-0.1038	0.0402	-2.5831	0.0131	-0.1848	-0.0229
Rev stab	-0.1824	0.0531	-3.4315	0.0013	-0.2894	-0.0753
AvgYrs2Sell	0.1722	0.0362	4.7569	0.0000	0.0993	0.2451
Price stab	0.0037	8.316E-04	4.3909	0.0001	0.0020	0.0053

Source: Management Planning, Inc. Princeton NJ (except for "AvgYrs2Sell" and "Rev2", which we derived from their data)

239

T A B L E 7-5 *(continued)*

Abrams Regression of Management Planning Study Data

	A	B	C	D	E	F	G
32	**Regression #2 (Without Price Stability)**						
34	**Regression Statistics**						
35	Multiple R	0.7064					
36	R square	0.4990					
37	Adjusted R square	0.4337					
38	Standard error	0.1032					
39	Observations	53					
41	ANOVA						
42		df	SS	MS	F	Significance F	
43	Regression	6	0.4883	0.0814	7.6365	0.0000	
44	Residual	46	0.4903	0.0107			
45	Total	52	0.9786				
47		Coefficients	Standard Error	t Stat	P-value	Lower 95%	Upper 95%
48	Intercept	0.1292	0.1165	1.1089	0.2732	−0.1053	0.3637
49	Rev^2	−5.39E-18	1.15E-18	−4.6740	0.0000	−7.71E-18	−3.07E-18
50	Shares sold-$	−4.39E-09	1.40E-09	−3.1287	0.0030	−7.21E-09	−1.57E-09
51	Mkt cap	6.10E-10	2.09E-10	2.9249	0.0053	1.90E-10	1.03E-09
52	Earn stab	−0.1381	0.0466	−2.9626	0.0048	−0.2319	−0.0443
53	Rev stab	−0.1800	0.0628	−2.8653	0.0063	−0.3065	−0.0536
54	AvgYrs2Sell	0.1368	0.0417	3.2790	0.0020	0.0528	0.2208

other 40.53% of variation in the discounts that remains unexplained is due to two possible sources: other significant independent variables of which I (and Management Planning, Inc.) do not know, and random variation. The standard error of the y-estimate is 8.7% (B10 rounded). We can form approximate 95% confidence intervals around the y-estimate by adding and subtracting two standard errors, or 17.4%.

Cell B20 contains the regression estimate of the y-intercept, and B21 through B27 contain the regression coefficients for the independent variables. The t-statistics are in D20 through D27. Only the y-intercept itself is not significant at the 95% confidence level. The market capitalization and earnings stability variables are significant at the 98% level,[45] and all the other variables are significant at the 99+% confidence level.

Note that several of the variables are similar to Grabowski and King's results (Grabowski and King 1999), discussed in Chapter 5. They found that the coefficient of variations (in log form) of operating margin and return on equity are statistically significant in explaining stock market returns. Here we find that the stability of revenues and earnings (as well as the coefficient of variation of stock market prices) explain restricted stock discounts. Thus, these variables are significant in determining the value of the underlying companies, assuming they are marketable, and in determining restricted stock discounts when restrictions exist.

I obtained regression #2 in Table 7-5 by regressing all the independent variables in the first regression except for price stability. The adjusted R^2 has dropped to 43.37% (B37), indicating that regression #1 is superior when price data are available, which generally it is for restricted stock studies and is not for calculating DLOM for privately held businesses. The second regression is not recommended for the calculation of restricted stock discounts, but it will be useful in other contexts.

Using the Put Option Model to Calculate DLOM of Restricted Stock

Chaffe (1993) wrote a brilliant article in which he reasoned that buying a hypothetical put option on Section 144 restricted stock would "buy" marketability and that the cost of that put option is an excellent measure of the discount for lack of marketability of the stock. For puts, the Black–Scholes option pricing model has the following formula:

$$P = E \, N(-d_2)e^{-R_f t} - S \, N(-d_1)$$

where:

S = stock price
$N(\ )$ = cumulative normal density function
E = exercise price
R_f = risk-free rate, i.e., treasury rate of the same term as the option
t = time remaining to expiration of the option
$d_1 = [\ln(S/E) + (R_f + 0.5 \times \text{variance}) \times t]/[\text{std dev} \times t^{0.5}]$
$d_2 = d_1 - [\text{std dev} \times t^{0.5}]$

We have sufficient daily price history on 13 of the stocks in Table

---

45. The statistical significance is one minus the P-value, which is in E20 through E27.

7-5 to derive the proper annualized standard deviation (std dev) of continuously compounded returns to test Chaffe's approach.

Annualized Standard Deviation of Continuously Compounded Returns. Table 7-6 is a sample calculation of the annualized standard deviation of continuously compounded returns for Chantal Pharmaceutical, Inc. (CHTL), which is one of the 13 stocks. The purpose of this table is to demonstrate how to calculate the standard deviation.

Column A shows the date, column B shows the closing price, and columns C and D show the continuously compounded returns. The sample period is just over 6 months and ends the day prior to the transaction date.

We calculate continuously compounded returns over 10-trading-day intervals for CHTL stock.[46] The reason for using 10-day intervals in our

TABLE 7-6

Calculation of Continuously Compounded Standard Deviation
Chantal Pharmaceutical, Inc.—CHTL

	A	B	C	D
6	**Date**	**Close**	**Interval Returns**	
7	1/31/95	$2.1650		
8	2/7/95	$2.2500		
9	2/14/95	$2.5660	0.169928	
10	2/22/95	$2.8440		0.234281
11	3/1/95	$2.6250	0.022733	
12	3/8/95	$2.9410		0.033538
13	3/15/95	$2.4480	−0.069810	
14	3/22/95	$2.5000		−0.162459
15	3/29/95	$2.2500	−0.084341	
16	4/5/95	$2.0360		−0.205304
17	4/12/95	$2.2220	−0.012523	
18	4/20/95	$2.1910		0.073371
19	4/27/95	$2.6950	0.192991	
20	5/4/95	$2.6600		0.193968
21	5/11/95	$2.5660	−0.049050	
22	5/18/95	$2.5620		−0.037538
23	5/25/95	$2.9740	0.147560	
24	6/2/95	$3.3120		0.256764
25	6/9/95	$5.1250	0.544223	
26	6/16/95	$6.0000		0.594207
27	6/23/95	$5.8135	0.126052	
28	6/30/95	$6.4440		0.071390
29	7/10/95	$6.5680	0.122027	
30	7/17/95	$6.6250		0.027701
31	7/24/95	$8.0000	0.197232	
32	7/31/95	$7.1250		0.072759
33	8/7/95	$7.8120	−0.023781	0.092051
34	**Interval standard deviation—CHTL**		**0.16900**	**0.20175**
35	**Annualized**		**0.84901**	**1.03298**
36	**Average of standard deviations**			**0.94099**

46. The only exception is the return from 7/31/95 to 8/7/95, which is in cell D33.

calculation instead of daily intervals is that the bid–ask spread on the stock may create apparent volatility that is not really present. This is because the quoted closing prices are from the last trade. In Nasdaq trading, one sells to a dealer at the bid price and buys at the ask price. If on successive days the last price of the day is switching randomly from a bid to an ask price and back, this can cause us to measure a considerable amount of apparent volatility that is not really there. By using 10-day intervals, we minimize this measurement error caused by the spread.

We start with the 1/31/95 closing price in column C and the 2/7/95 closing price in column D. For example, the 10-trading-day return from 1/31/95 (A7) to 2/14/95 (A9) is calculated as follows: return = Ln(B9/B7) = Ln(2.5660/2.1650) = 0.169928 (C9).

Using this methodology, we get two measures of standard deviation: 0.16900 (C34) and 0.20175 (D34). To convert to the annualized standard deviation, we must multiply each interval standard deviation by the square root of the number of intervals that would occur in a year. The equation is as follows:

$$\sigma_{\text{annualized}} = \sigma_{\text{interval returns}} \times \text{SQRT} \left(\begin{array}{l} \text{\# of interval returns in sample period} \\[6pt] \times \dfrac{365 \text{ days per year}}{\text{days in sample period}} \end{array} \right)$$

For example, the sample period in column C is the time period from the close of trading on January 31, 1995, to the close of trading on August 7, 1995, or 188 days, and there are 13 calculated returns. Therefore the annualized standard deviation of returns is:

$$\sigma_{\text{annualized}} = 0.1690 \times \text{SQRT}(13 \times 365/188)$$

$$= 0.1690 \times \text{SQRT}(25.2394) = 0.84901 \text{ (cell C35)}$$

The 13 trading periods that span 188 days would become 25.2394 trading periods in one year (25.2394 = 13 × 365/188). The square root of the 25.2394 trading periods is 5.0239. We multiply the sample standard deviation of 0.1690 by 5.0239 = 0.84901 to annualize the standard deviation. Similarly, the annualized standard deviation of returns in column D is 1.03298 (D35), and the average of the two is 0.94099 (D36).

Calculation of the Discount.   Table 7-7 is the Black–Scholes put option calculation of the restricted stock discount. We begin in cell B5 with *S*, the stock price on the valuation date of August 8, 1995, of $8.875. We then assume that *E*, the exercise price, is identical (B6).

B7 is the time in years from the valuation date to marketability. According to SEC Rule 144, the shares have a two-year period of restriction before the first portion of the block can be sold. At 2.25 years the rest can be sold. The weighted average time to sell is 2.125 years (B7, transferred from Table 7-5, I17) for this particular block of Chantal.

B8 shows the two-year Treasury rate, which was 5.90% as of the transaction date. B9 contains the annualized standard deviation of returns

TABLE 7-7

Black–Scholes Put Option—CHTL

	A	B
5	S = Stk price on valuation date	$8.875
6	E = Exercise price	$8.875
7	t = time to expiration in yrs (Table 7-5, I17)	2.125
8	r = risk-free rate [1]	5.90%
9	stdev = standard deviation (Table 7-6, D36)	0.941
10	var = variance	0.885
11	d_1 = 1st Black-Scholes parameter [2]	0.777
12	d_2 = 2nd Black-Scholes parameter 3]	(0.594)
13	$N(-d_1)$ = cum normal density function	0.219
14	$N(-d_2)$ = cum normal density function	0.724
15	$P = [E^*N(-d_2)^*e^{-rt}] - S^*N(-d_1)$	$3.73
16	P/S	**42.0%**

Note: Values are for European options. The put option formula can be found in Options Futures and Other Derivatives, 3rd Ed. by John C. Hull, Prentice Hall, 1997, pp. 241 and 242.
[1] 2 Year Treasury rate on transaction date, 8/8/95 (Source: Federal Reserve)
[2] d_1 = [ln (S/E) + (r + .5 * var) * t]/[stdev *$t^{0.5}$], where variance and standard deviation are expressed in annual terms.
[3] d_2 = d_1 − [std dev * $t^{0.5}$]

for CHTL of 0.941, transferred from Table 7-6, cell D36, while B10 is variance, merely the square of B9.

Cells B11 and B12 are the calculation of the two Black–Scholes parameters, d_1 and d_2. B13 and B14 are the cumulative normal density functions for $-d_1$ and $-d_2$. For example, look at cell B13, which is N(−0.777) = 0.219. This requires some explanation. The cumulative normal table from which the 0.219 came assumes the normal distribution has been standardized to a mean of zero and standard deviation of 1.[47] This means that there is a 21.9% probability that our variable is less than or equal to 0.777 standard deviations below the mean. In cell B14, $N(-d_2)$ = N(−0.594)) = N(0.594) = 0.724, which means there is a 72.4% probability of being less than or equal to 0.594 standard deviations above the mean. For perspective, it is useful to note that since the normal distribution is symmetric, N(0) = 0.5000, i.e., there is a 50% probability of being less than or equal to the mean, which implies there is a 50% probability of being above the mean.

In B15, we calculate the value of the put option, which is $3.73 (B15), or 42.0% (B16) of the stock price of $8.875 (B5). Thus, our calculation of the restricted stock discount for the Chantal block using the Black–Scholes model is 42.0% (B16).

Table 7-8: Black–Scholes Put Model Results. The stock symbols in Table 7-8, column A, relate to restricted stock sale numbers 8, 11, 15, 17, 23, 31, 32, 38, and 49–53 in Table 7-5, column A. Cells B6 through B18 show the discounts calculated using the Black–Scholes put model for the

---

47. One standardizes a normal distribution by subtracting the mean from each value and dividing by the standard deviation.

TABLE 7-8

Put Model Results

	A	B	C	D	E	F
4		**Black-Scholes**				
5	**Company**	**Put Calculation**	**Actual**	**Error**	**Error^2**	**Absolute Error**
6	BLYH	32.3%	31.4%	0.9%	0.0%	0.9%
7	CHTL	42.0%	44.8%	−2.8%	0.1%	2.8%
8	DAVX	47.5%	46.3%	1.2%	0.0%	1.2%
9	EDMK	11.9%	16.0%	−4.1%	0.2%	4.1%
10	ILT	38.3%	41.1%	−2.8%	0.1%	2.8%
11	PLFE	23.7%	15.9%	7.8%	0.6%	7.8%
12	PRDE	13.3%	24.5%	−11.2%	1.2%	11.2%
13	RENT	41.5%	32.5%	9.0%	0.8%	9.0%
14	FOFF	27.2%	12.5%	14.7%	2.2%	14.7%
15	ARCCA	36.1%	18.8%	17.3%	3.0%	17.3%
16	DPAC	18.3%	23.1%	−4.8%	0.2%	4.8%
17	NEDI	24.6%	19.3%	5.3%	0.3%	5.3%
18	UMED	12.9%	15.8%	−2.9%	0.1%	2.9%
19	**Mean**	**28.4%**	**26.3%**	**2.1%**	**0.67%**	**6.5%**
22			**Comparison with the Mean as the Discount**			
24	**Company**	**Mean Discount**	**Actual**	**Error**	**Error^2**	**Absolute Error**
25	BLYH	27.1%	31.4%	−4.3%	0.2%	4.3%
26	CHTL	27.1%	44.8%	−17.7%	3.1%	17.7%
27	DAVX	27.1%	46.3%	−19.2%	3.7%	19.2%
28	EDMK	27.1%	16.0%	11.1%	1.2%	11.1%
29	ILT	27.1%	41.1%	−14.0%	2.0%	14.0%
30	PLFE	27.1%	15.9%	11.2%	1.3%	11.2%
31	PRDE	27.1%	24.5%	2.6%	0.1%	2.6%
32	RENT	27.1%	32.5%	−5.4%	0.3%	5.4%
33	FOFF	27.1%	12.5%	14.6%	2.1%	14.6%
34	ARCCA	27.1%	18.8%	8.3%	0.7%	8.3%
35	DPAC	27.1%	23.1%	4.0%	0.2%	4.0%
36	NEDI	27.1%	19.3%	7.8%	0.6%	7.8%
37	UMED	27.1%	15.8%	11.3%	1.3%	11.3%
38	**Mean**	**27.1%**	**26.3%**	**0.8%**	**1.28%**	**10.1%**

13 stocks. The actual discounts are in column C, and the error in the put model estimate is in column D.[48] Columns E and F are the squared error and the absolute error. Row 19 is the mean of each column. The bottom half of the table is identical to the top half, except that we use the mean discount of 27.1% as the estimated discount instead of the Black–Scholes put model.

A comparison of the top and bottom of Table 7-8 reveals that the put option model performs much better than the mean discount of 27.1% for the 13 stocks. The put model's mean absolute error of 6.5% (F19) and mean squared error of 0.67% (E19) are much smaller than the mean absolute error of 10.1% (F38) and mean squared error of 1.28% (E38) using

---

48. The error is equal to the estimated discount minus the actual discount, or column B minus column C.

the MPI data mean discount as the forecast. The mean errors in cells D19 and D38 are not indicative of relative predictive power, since low values could be obtained even though the individual errors are high due to negative and positive errors canceling out.

Comparison of the Put Model and the Regression Model

In order to compare the put model discount results with the regression model, we will analyze Table 7-9, which shows the calculation of discounts, using regression #1 in Table 7-5, on the 13 stocks for which price data was available.

The intercept of the regression is in cell B6, and the coefficients for the independent variables are in cells B7 through B13. The variables for each stock are in columns C through O, Rows 7 through 13. Multiplying the variables for each stock by their respective coefficients and then adding them together with the y-intercept results in the regression estimated discounts in C14 through O14.

The errors in row 16 equal the actual discounts in row 15 minus the estimated discounts in Row 14. We then calculate the error squared and absolute error in Rows 17 and 18.

The mean squared error of 0.57% (C20) and the mean absolute error of 6.33% (C21) are comparable but slightly better than the put model results of 0.67% and 6.5% in Table 7-8, E19 and F19, respectively. Having only been able to test the put model on 13 stocks and not the entire database of 53 reduces our ability to distinguish which model is better. At this point it is probably best to use an average of the results of both models when determining a discount in a restricted stock valuation.

Empirical versus Theoretical Black–Scholes. It is important to understand that in using the BSOPM put for calculating restricted stock discounts, we are using it as an empirical model, not as a theoretical model. That is because buying a put on a publicly traded stock does not "buy marketability" for the restricted stock.[49] Rather, it locks in a minimum price for the restricted shares once they become marketable, while allowing for theoretically unlimited price appreciation. Therefore, issuing a hypothetical put on the freely tradable stock does not accomplish the same task as providing marketability for the restricted stock, but it does compensate for the downside risk on the restricted stock during its holding period.

BSOPM has some attributes that make it a successful predictor of restricted stock discounts, i.e., it is a better forecaster than the mean discount and did almost as well as the regression of the MPI data.

The reason for BSOPM's success is that its mathematics is compatible with the underlying variable—primarily volatility—that would tend to drive restricted stock discounts. It is logical that the more volatile the restricted stock, the larger the discount, and that volatility is the single most important determinant of BSOPM results. Therefore, BSOPM is a good candidate for empirically explaining restricted stock discounts, even

---

49. I thank R. K. Hiatt for this observation

T A B L E   7-9

Calculation of Restricted Stock Discounts for 13 Stocks Using Regression from Table 7-5

	A	B	C	D	E	F	G	H	I	J	K	L	M	N	O
5		Coefficients	BLYH	CHTL	DAVX	EDMK	ITL	PLFE	PRDE	RENT	FOFF	ARCCA	DPAC	NEDI	UMED
6	Intercept	-0.0673													
7	Rev^2	-4.629E - 18	8.62E + 13	5.21E + 13	1.14E + 15	3.56E + 13	1.02E + 13	4.37E + 16	4.34E + 15	1.15E + 15	6.10E + 15	3.76E + 14	3.24E + 14	1.95E + 15	5.49E + 13
8	Shares sold-$	-3.619E - 09	4,452,000	4,900,000	$999,000	$2,000,000	$975,000	$38,063,000	$21,500,000	$20,650,000	$5,670,000	$2,275,000	$4,500,000	$12,000,000	$8,400,000
9	Mkt cap	4.789E - 10	98,053,000	149,286,000	18,942,000	12,275,000	10,046,000	246,787,000	74,028,000	61,482,000	43,024,000	18,846,000	108,862,000	60,913,000	44,681,000
10	Earn stab	-0.1038	0.04	0.70	0.01	0.57	0.71	0.00	0.31	0.60	0.80	0.03	0.08	0.34	0.09
11	Rev stabil	-0.1824	0.64	0.23	0.65	0.92	0.92	0.00	0.26	0.70	0.87	0.74	0.70	0.76	0.74
12	Avg yrs to sell	0.1722	2.125	2.125	2.750	2.868	2.844	2.861	2.833	2.950	2.375	1.633	1.167	1.738	1.898
13	Price stability	0.0037	58.6	51.0	24.6	10.5	22.0	17.0	18.0	30.0	23.7	35.0	42.4	32.1	21.0
14	**Calculated discount**		**42.22%**	**42.37%**	**37.67%**	**23.65%**	**26.25%**	**26.57%**	**34.43%**	**30.97%**	**15.83%**	**20.27%**	**18.68%**	**15.20%**	**18.27%**
15	Actual discount		31.40%	44.80%	46.30%	16.00%	41.10%	15.90%	24.50%	32.50%	12.50%	18.80%	23.10%	19.30%	15.80%
16	Error (actual − calculated)		-10.82%	2.43%	8.63%	-7.65%	14.85%	-10.67%	-9.93%	1.53%	-3.33%	-1.47%	4.42%	4.10%	-2.47%
17	Error squared		1.17%	0.06%	0.75%	0.59%	2.21%	1.14%	0.99%	0.02%	0.11%	0.02%	0.20%	0.17%	0.06%
18	Absolute error		10.82%	2.43%	8.63%	7.65%	14.85%	10.67%	9.93%	1.53%	3.33%	1.47%	4.42%	4.10%	2.47%
19	Mean error		-0.80%												
20	Mean squared error		0.57%												
21	Mean absolute error		6.33%												

though that is not the original intended use of the model, nor is this scenario part of the assumptions of the model.

Comparison to the Quantitative Marketability Discount Model (QMDM)

Mercer shows various examples of investment risk premium calculations Mercer 1997, chapter 10). When he adds this premium to the required return on a marketable minority basis, he gets the required holding period return for a nonmarketable minority interest. Judging from his example calculations of the risk premium for other types of illiquid interests, the investment specific risk premium for restricted stocks should be somewhere in the range of 1.5–5% or less.[50] This is because restricted stocks have short and well-defined holding periods. Also, the payoff at the end of the holding period is almost sure to be at the marketable minority level.

To test the applicability of QMDM to restricted stocks, we first estimate a typical marketable minority level required return. The MPI database average market capitalization is approximately $78 million. This puts the MPI stocks in the mid-cap to small-cap category, given the dates of the transactions in the database. A reasonable expected rate of return for stocks of this size is 15% or so on a marketable minority basis.

We will assume that the stocks, given their size, were probably not paying any significant dividends. Therefore, the expected growth rate equals the expected rate of return at the marketable minority level of 15%. Given the average years to liquidity of approximately 2.5 years in the data set, we can calculate a typical restricted stock discount using QMDM.

Assuming a 1.5% investment risk premium, and therefore a required holding period return of 16.5%, QMDM would predict the following restricted stock discount:

$$\text{Min Discount} = 1 - (\text{FV} \times \text{PVF}) = 1 - \left(1.15^{2.5} \times \frac{1}{1.165^{2.5}}\right) = 3.2\%$$

where FV = future value of the investment and PVF = the present value factor. With a 5% investment risk premium, we have:

$$\text{Max Discount} = 1 - (\text{FV} \times \text{PVF}) = 1 - \left(1.15^{2.5} \times \frac{1}{1.20^{2.5}}\right) = 10.1\%$$

The QMDM forecast of restricted stock discounts thus range from 3–10%, with the lower end of the range appearing most appropriate, considering the examples in Mercer's Chapter 10.[51] These calculated discounts are

---

50. Actually, the lower end of the range—1.5%—appears most appropriate.
51. The QMDM restricted stock discount is insensitive to the absolute level of the discount rate. It is only sensitive to the premium above the discount rate. For example, changing the minimum discount formula to

$$(1 - 1.20^{2.5}) \times \frac{1}{1.215^{2.5}}$$

has little impact on the QMDM result. It is the 1.5% premium that is the difference between the 20% growth and the 21.5% required return that constitutes the bulk of the QMDM discount—and, of course, the holding period.

nowhere near the average discount of 27.1% in the MPI database. This sheds doubt on the applicability of QMDM for restricted stocks and the applicability of the model in general. At least it shows that the model does not work well for small holding periods.

I invited Chris Mercer to write a rebuttal to my analysis of the QMDM results. His rebuttal is at the end of this chapter, just before the conclusion, after which I provide my comments, as I disagree with some of his methodology.

Abrams' Economic Components Model

The remainder of this chapter will be spent on Abrams' economic components model (ECM). The origins of this model appear in Abrams (1994a) (the "original article"). While the basic structure of the model is the same, this chapter contains major revisions of that article. One of the revisions is that for greater clarity and ease of exposition, components #2 and #3 have switched places. In the original article, transactions costs was component #2 and monopsony power to the buyer due to thin markets was component #3, but in this chapter they are reversed.

We will be assuming that we are applying DLOM to a valuation determined either directly or indirectly by comparison to publicly traded firms. This could be a guideline company method or a discounted cash flow method, with discount rates determined by data on publicly traded firms. The ECM is not meant to be used as described on data coming from sales of privately held businesses.

Component #1: The Delay to Sale
The first component of DLOM is the economic disadvantage of the considerable time that it takes to sell a privately held business in excess of the near instantaneous ability to sell the publicly held stocks from which we calculate our discount rates.

Psychology. Investors don't like illiquidity. Medical and other emergencies arise in life, causing people to have to sell their assets, possibly including their businesses. Even without the pressure of a fire sale, it usually takes three to six months to sell a small business and one year or more to sell a business worth $1 million or more.

The selling process may entail dressing up the business, i.e., tidying up the accounting records, halting the standard operating procedures of charging personal expenses to the business, and getting an appraisal. Either during or after the dress-up stage, the seller needs to identify potential buyers or engage a business broker or investment banker to do so. This is also difficult, as the most likely buyers are often competitors. If the match doesn't work, the seller is worse off, having divulged confidential information to his competitors. The potential buyers need to go through their due diligence process, which is time consuming and expensive.

During this long process, the seller is exposed to the market. He or she would like to sell immediately, and having to wait when one wants to sell right away tries one's patience. The business environment may be better or worse when the transaction is close to consummation. It is well established in behavioral science—and it is the major principle on which the sale of insurance is based—that the fear of loss is stronger than the desire for gain (Tversky and Kahneman 1987). This creates pressure for the seller to accept a lower price in order to get on with life.

Another important finding in behavioral science that is relevant in explaining DLOM and DLOC is ambiguity aversion (Einhorn and Hogarth 1986). The authors cite a paradox proposed by the psychologist Daniel Ellsberg (Ellsberg 1961) (of Pentagon Papers fame), known as the Ellsberg paradox.

Ellsberg asked subjects which of two gambles they prefer. In gamble A the subject draws from an urn with 100 balls in it. They are red or black only, but we don't know how many of each. It could be 100 black and 0 red, 0 black and 100 red, or anything in between. The subject calls "red" or "black" before the draw and, if he or she calls it right, wins $100; otherwise, he or she gets nothing. In gamble B, the subject draws one ball from an urn that has 50 red balls and 50 black balls. Again, if the subject forecasts the correct draw, he or she wins $100 and otherwise wins nothing.

Most people are indifferent between choosing red or black in both gambles. When asked which gamble they prefer, the majority of people had an interesting response (before we proceed, ask yourself which gamble you would prefer and why). Most people prefer to draw from urn #2. This is contrary to risk-neutral logic. The finding of Ellsberg and Einhorn and Hogarth is that people dislike ambiguity and will pay to avoid it.

Ambiguity is a second-order uncertainty. It is "uncertainty about uncertainties," and it exists pervasively in our lives. Gamble B has uncertainty, but it does not have ambiguity. The return-generating process is well understood. It is a clear 50–50 gamble. Gamble A, on the other hand, is fuzzier. The return-generating process is not well understood. People feel uncomfortable with that and will pay to avoid it.

It is my opinion that ambiguity aversion probably explains much of shareholder level discounts. As mentioned earlier in the chapter, Jankowske mentions wealth transfer opportunities and the protection of investment as economic benefits of control. Many minority investors are exposed to the harsh reality of having their wealth transferred away. Many of those who do not experience that still have to worry about it occurring in the future. The minority investor is always in a more ambiguous position than a control shareholder.

In our regressions of the partnership profiles database that tracks the results of trading in the secondary limited partnership markets (see Chapter 9), we find that regular cash distributions are the primary determinant of discounts from net asset value. Why would this be so? After all, there have already been appraisals of the underlying properties, and those appraisals certainly included a discounted cash flow approach to valuation.[52] If the appraisal of the properties already considered cash flow, then

---

52. In the regression we included a dummy variable to determine whether the discount from net asset value depended on whether the properties were appraised by the general partner or by independent appraiser. The dummy variable was statistically insignificant, meaning that the market trusts the appraisals of the general partners as much as the independent appraisers.

why would we consider cash flow again in determining discounts? I would speculate the following reasons:

1. If the general partner (GP) takes greater than arm's-length fees for managing the property, that would not be included in the appraisal of the whole properties and would reduce the value of the limited partner (LP) interest. It is a transfer of wealth from the LP to the GP.

2. Even if the GP takes an arm's-length management fee, he or she still determines the magnitude and the timing of the distributions, which may or may not be convenient for the individual LPs.

3. LPs may fear potential actions of the GP, even if he or she never takes those actions. The LP only knows that information about the investment that the GP discloses and may fear what the GP does not divulge—which, of course, he or she won't know. The LPs may hear rumors of good or bad news and not know what to do with it or about it.

The bottom line is that investors don't like ignorance, and they will pay less for investments that are ambiguous than for ones that are not— or that are, at least, less ambiguous—even if both have the same expected value.

Our paradigm for valuation is the two-parameter normal distribution, where everything depends only on expected return and expected risk. Appraisers are used to thinking of risk only as either systematic risk, measured by β, or total risk in the form of σ, the historical standard deviation of returns. The research on ambiguity avoidance adds another dimension to our concept of risk, which makes our task more difficult but affords the possibility of being more realistic.

It is also noteworthy that the magnitude of special distributions, i.e., those coming from a sale or refinancing or property, was statistically insignificant. Investors care only about what they feel they can count on, the regular distributions.

Black–Scholes Options Pricing Model. One method of modeling the economic disadvantage of the period of illiquidity is to use the Black–Scholes options pricing model (BSOPM) to calculate the value of a put on the stock for the period of illiquidity. A European put, the simplest type, is the right to sell the stock at a specific price on a specific day. An American put is the right to sell the stock on or before the specific day. We will be using the European put.

The origins of using this method go back to David Chaffe (Chaffe 1993), who first proposed using the BSOPM for calculating restricted stock discounts for SEC Rule 144 restricted stock. The restricted stock discounts are for minority interests of publicly held firms. There is no admixture of minority interest discount in this number, as the restricted stock studies in Pratt's Chapter 15 (Pratt, Reilly, and Schweihs 1996) are minority interests both pre- and posttransaction.

Then Abrams (1994a) suggested that owning a privately held business is similar to owning restricted stock in that it is very difficult to sell a private firm in less than the normal due diligence time discussed above. The BSOPM is a reasonable model with which to calculate Component #1 of DLOM, the delay to sale discount.

There is disagreement in the profession about using BSOPM for this purpose. Chapter 14 of Mercer's book (Mercer 1997) is entitled, "Why Not the Black–Scholes Options Pricing Model Rather Than the QMDM?" Mercer's key objections to the BSOPM are:[53]

1. It requires the standard deviation of returns as an input to the model. This input is not observable in privately held companies.

2. It is too abstract and complex to meaningfully represent the thinking of the hypothetical willing investor.

Argument 2 does not matter, as the success of the model is an empirical question. Argument 1, however, turned out to be more true than I would have imagined. It is true that we cannot see or measure return volatility in privately held firms. However, there are two ways that we indirectly measured it. We combined the regression equations from regressions #1 and #2 in Table 4-1 to develop an expression for return volatility as a function of log size, and we performed a regression of the same data to directly develop an expression for the same. We tried using both indirect estimates of volatility as inputs to the BSOPM to forecast the restricted stock discounts in the Management Planning, Inc. data, and both approaches performed worse than using the average discount. Thus, argument 1 was an assertion that turned out to be correct.

When volatility can be directly calculated, the BSOPM is superior to using the mean and the QMDM. So, BSOPM is a competent model for forecasting when we have firm-specific volatility data, which we will not have for privately-held firms.

Other Models of Component #1. The regression equation developed from the Management Planning, Inc. data is superior to both the non-firm-specific BSOPM and the QMDM. Thus, it is, so far, the best model to measure component #1, the delay to sale component, as long as the expected delay to sale is one to five (or possibly as high as six) years.

The QMDM is pure present value analysis. It has no ability to quantify volatility—other than the analyst guessing at the premium to add to the discount rate. It also suffers from being highly subjective. None of the components of the risk premium at the shareholder level can be empirically measured in any way.

Is the QMDM useless? No. It may be the best model in some scenarios. As mentioned before, one of the limitations of my restricted stock discount regression is that because the restricted stocks had so little range in time to marketability, the regression equation performs poorly when the time to marketability is substantially outside that range—above five to six years. Not all models work in all situations. The QMDM has its place in the toolbox of the valuation professional. It is important to un-

---

53. Actually, Chapter 14 is co-authored by J. Michael Julius and Matthew R. Crow, employees at Mercer Capital.

derstand its limitations in addition to its strengths, which are flexibility and simplicity.

The BSOPM is based on present value analysis, but contains far more heavy-duty mathematics to quantify the probable effects of volatility on investor's potential gains or losses. While the general BSOPM did not perform well when volatility was measured indirectly, we can see by looking at the regression results that Black–Scholes has the essence of the right idea. Two of the variables in the regression analysis are earnings stability and revenue stability. They are the R^2 from regressions of earnings and revenues as dependent variables against time as the independent variable. In other words, the more stabile the growth of revenues and earnings throughout time, the higher the earnings and revenue stability. These are measures of volatility of earnings and revenues, which are the volatilities underlying the volatility of returns. Price stability is another of the independent variables, and that is the standard deviation of stock price divided by the mean of returns (which is the coefficient of variation of price) and then multiplied by 100.

Thus, the regression results demonstrate that using volatility to measure restricted stock discounts is empirically sound. The failure of the non-firm-specific BSOPM to quantify restricted stock discounts is a measurement problem, not a theoretical problem.[54]

An important observation regarding the MPI data is that MPI excluded startup and developmental firms from its study. There were no firms that had negative net income in the latest fiscal year. That may possibly explain the difference in results between the average 35% discounts in most of the other studies cited in Pratt's Chapter 15 (Pratt, Reilly, and Schweihs 1996) and MPI's results. When using my regression of the MPI data to calculate component #1 for a firm without positive earnings, I would make a subjective adjustment to increase the discount. As to magnitude, we have to make an assumption. If we assume that the other studies did contain restricted stock sales of firms with negative earnings in the latest fiscal year, then it would seem that those firms should have a higher discount than the average of that study. With the average of all of them being around 33–35%, let's say for the moment that the firms with losses may have averaged 38–40% discounts, all other things being equal (see the paragraph below for the rationale). Then 38–40% minus 27% in the MPI study would lead to an upward adjustment to component #1 of 11% to 13%. That all rests on an assumption that this is the only cause of the difference in the results of the two studies. Further research is needed on this topic.

We can see the reason that firms with losses would have averaged higher discounts than those who did not in the x-coefficient for earnings stability in Table 7-10, cell B9, which is -0.1381. This regression tells us the market does not like volatility in earnings, which implies that the

---

54. There is a significant difference between forecasting volatility and forecasting returns. Returns do not exhibit statistically significant trends over time, while volatility does (see Chapter 4). Therefore, it is not surprising that using long-term averages to forecast volatility fail in the BSOPM. The market is obviously more concerned about recent than historical volatility in pricing restricted stock. That is not true about returns.

market likes stability in earnings. Logically, the market would not like earnings to be stable and negative, so investors obviously prefer stable, positive earnings. Thus, we can infer from the regression in Table 7-10 that, all other things being equal, the discount for firms with negative earnings in the prior year must be higher than for firms with positive earnings. Ideally, we will eventually have restricted stock data on firms that have negative earnings, and we can control for that by including earnings as a regression variable.

It is also worth noting that the regression analysis results are based on the database of transactions from which we developed the regression, while the BSOPM did not have that advantage. Thus, the regression had an inherent advantage in this data set over all other models.

Abrams' Regression of the Management Planning, Inc. Data. As mentioned earlier in the chapter, there are two regression equations in our analysis of the MPI data. The first one includes price stability as an independent variable. This is fine for doing restricted stock studies. However, it does not work for calculating Component #1 in a DLOM calculation for the valuation of a privately held firm, whether a business or a family limited partnership with real estate. In both cases there is no objective market stock price with which to calculate the price stability. Therefore, in those types of assignments, we use the less accurate second regression equation that excludes price stability.

Table 7-10 is an example of using regression #2 to calculate component #1, the delay to sale of DLOM, for a privately held firm. Note that "Value of Block—Post Discount" (Table 7-10, A7) is analogous to "Shares Sold—$" (Table 7-5, A50), and "FMV–100% Marketable Minority Interest" (Table 7-10, B8) is analogous to "Market Capitalization" (Table 7-5, A51). The regression coefficients are in B5–B11. We insert the subject com-

TABLE 7-10

Calculation of Component #1—Delay To Sale [1]

	A	B	C	D
4		**Coefficients**	**Subject Co. Data**	**Discount**
5	Intercept	0.1292	NA	12.9%
6	Revenues^2 [2]	−5.39E − 18	3.600E + 13	0.0%
7	Value of block-post-discount [3]	−4.39E − 09	$4,331,435	−1.9%
8	FMV-100% marketable minority interest	6.10E − 10	$5,000,000	0.3%
9	Earnings stability	−0.1381	0.4500	−6.2%
10	Revenue stability	−0.1800	0.3000	−5.4%
11	Average years to sell	0.1368	1.0000	13.7%
12	**Total Discount**			**13.4%**
14	Value of block—pre-discount [4]	$5,000,000		

[1] Based on Abrams' Regression #2 of Management Planning, Inc. data
[2] Revenues^2 = $6,000,000^2 = (6 × 10^6)^2 = 3.6 × 10^{13}
[3] Equal to (value of block − pre-discount) * (1 − discount).
[4] Marketable minority interest FMV

pany data in C6–C11, except for row 7, which we will discuss below. Our subject company has $5 million in revenues (which, squared, equals 3.6 × 10^{13}, per (C6), 100% marketable minority interest FMV of $5 million (C8, analogous to market capitalization for the public companies in the Management Planning, Inc. data), and earnings and revenue stability of 0.45 (C9) and 0.30 (C10), respectively.[55] We estimate it will take one year to sell the interest (C11).

Since we are valuing 100% of the capital stock of the firm, the value of the block of stock also has an FMV of $5 million (B14) before DLOM.[56] The regression calls for the postdiscount FMV, which means we must subtract the discount. The formula in cell C7 is: =B14*(1 − D12), i.e., the postdiscount FMV equals the prediscount FMV × (1 − Discount). However, this is a simultaneous equation since the discount and the shares sold in dollars each depend on the other. In order to be able to calculate this, your spreadsheet should be set to allow recalculation with multiple iterations. Otherwise you will get an error message with a circular reference.[57] Column D is equal to column B × column C, except for the y-intercept in D5, which transfers directly from B5. Adding each of the components in column D, we obtain a forecast discount of 13.4% (D12).

Limitations of the Regression. There may be combinations of subject company data that can lead to strange results. This is especially true because:

1. The subject company data are near the end or outside of the ranges of data in the regression of the MPI data.
2. There is very little variation in the range of the "average time to sale" variable in our set. Most all of the restricted stock could be sold between two and three years from the transaction date, which is very little variation. Only 4 of the 53 sales were expected to take less than two years (see below).
3. The R^2 is low.
4. The standard error of the y-estimate is fairly high—10%.

Regarding number 1, 47 of the 53 restricted stock sales in the MPI database took place before the SEC circulated its Exposure Draft on June 27, 1995,[58] to amend Rule 144(d) and (k) to shorten the waiting period

---

55. We do not explicitly show the detail of the calculations of earnings and revenue stability. Our sample Restricted Stock Discount Study in Chapter 8, Table 8-1, shows these calculations.
56. Had we been valuing a 10% block of stock, B14 would have been $500,000.
57. If you create your own spreadsheet and make changes to the data, the simultaneous equation is fragile, and it can easily happen that you may get error messages. When that happens, you must put in a simple number in C7, e.g., $200,000, allow the spreadsheet to "recalibrate" and come back to equilibrium, then put in the correct formula. We do not have this iterative problem with the other components of DLOM.
58. Revision of Holding Period Requirements in Rule 144; Section 16(a) Reporting of Equity Swaps and Other Derivative Securities. File No. S7-17-95, SEC Release Nos. 33-7187; 34-35896; 17 CFR Parts 230 and 241; RIN 3235-AG53. The author expresses his gratitude to John Watson, Jr., Esq., of Latham & Watkins in Washington, D.C., for providing him with a copy of the exposure draft.

for selling restricted stock to one year from two years and for nonaffiliated shareholders to sell shares without restriction after two years instead of three.

Two sales took place in 1995 (Esmor Correctional Services, Inc. and Chantal Pharmaceuticals Corp.) after the SEC Exposure Draft, and four sales took place in 1996 (ARC Capital, Dense Pac Microsystems, Inc., Nobel Education Dynamics, Inc., and Unimed Pharmaceuticals). That means the market knew there was some probability that this would become law and might shorten the waiting period to sell the restricted stock it was issuing, and the later the sale, the more likely it was at the time that the Exposure Draft would become law and provide relief to the buyer of the restricted stock.

Thus, we should expect that those sales would carry lower discounts than earlier sales—and that is correct. The discounts on the 1996 sales were significantly lower than discounts on the earlier sales, all other things being equal. The discounts ranged from 16–23% on the 1996 sales. However, the two post-Exposure Draft 1995 sales had higher-than-average discounts, which is somewhat counterintuitive. It is true that the 1996 sales would be more affected because the relief from restrictions for the 1995 sales were more likely to have lapsed from the passage of time than the 1996 sales, if it would take a long time for the Exposure Draft to become law. Nevertheless, the two 1995 sales remain anomalies.

The average years needed to sell the stock ranged from a low of 1.2 years for Dense Pac Microsystems to 2.96 years for Sudbury Holdings, Inc., with the vast majority being between 2 and 3 years. Extrapolating this model to forecast a restricted stock discount for a sale with a restriction of 10 years, for example, leads to ridiculous results, and even more than 4 years is very questionable.

The coefficient for average years to sell is 0.1368 (B11), which means that for each year more (less) than the forecast we made for this subject company of 1 year, the discount increases (decreases) by 13.68%, holding all else constant. Thus, if we were to forecast for a 10-year restriction, we would get a discount of 136.8%—a nonsense result.

Thus, the appraiser must exercise good judgment and common sense in using these results. Mechanically using these regression formulas to all situations can be dangerous. It may be necessary to run other regressions with the same data, i.e., using different independent variables or different transformations of the data, to accommodate valuation assignments with facts that vary considerably with those underlying these data. Another possible solution is to assume, for example, that when a particular subject company's R^2 is beyond the maximum in the MPI database, that it is equal to the maximum in the MPI database. It may be necessary to use the other models, i.e., BSOPM with inferred rather than explicit standard deviations or the QMDM, for more extreme situations where the regression equation is strained by extreme data. Hopefully we will soon have much more data, as there will be increasingly more transactions subject to the relaxed Rule 144 restrictions.

Component #2: Buyer Monopsony Power

The control stockholder of a privately held firm has no guarantee at all that he or she can sell his or her firm. The market for privately held businesses is very thin. Most small and medium-size firms are unlikely to attract more than a small handful of buyers—and even then probably not more than one or two every several months—while the seller of publicly traded stock has millions of potential buyers. Just as a monopolist is a single seller who can drive up price by withholding production, a single buyer—a monopsonist—can drive price down by withholding purchase.

The presence of 100 or even 10 interested buyers is likely to drive the selling price of a business to its theoretical maximum, i.e., "the right price." The absence of enough buyers may confer monopsony power on the few who are interested. Therefore, a small, unexciting business will have an additional component of the discount for lack of marketability for the additional bargaining power accruing to the buyers in thin markets.

It is easy to think that component #2 may already be included in component #1, i.e., they both derive from the long time to sell an illiquid asset. To demonstrate that they are indeed distinct components and that we are not double counting, it is helpful to consider the hypothetical case of a very exciting privately held firm that has just discovered the cure for cancer. Such a firm would have no lack of interested buyers, yet it still is very unlikely to be sold in less than one year. In that year other things could happen. Congress could pass legislation regulating the medical breakthrough, and the value could decrease significantly. Therefore, it would still be necessary to have a significant discount for component #1, while component #2 would be zero. It may not take longer to sell the corner dry-cleaning store, but while the first firm is virtually guaranteed to be able to sell at the highest price after its required marketing time, the dry-cleaning store will have the additional uncertainty of sale, and its few buyers would have more negotiating power than the buyers of the firm with the cure for cancer.

The results from Schwert, described earlier in the chapter, are relevant here. He found that the presence of multiple bidders for control of publicly held companies on average led to increased premiums of 12.2% compared to takeovers without competitive bidding. Based on the regression in Table 4 of his article, we assumed a typical deal configuration that would apply to a privately held firm.[59] The premium without an auction was 21.5%. Adding 12.2%, the premium with an auction was 33.7%. To calculate the discount for lack of competition, we go in the other direction, i.e., 12.2% divided by one plus 33.7% = 0.122/1.337 = 9.1%, or approximately 9%. This is a useful benchmark for D_2.

However, it is quite possible that D_2 for any subject interest should be larger or smaller than 9%. It all depends on the facts and circumstances of the situation. Using Schwert's measure of the effect of multiple versus single bidders as our estimate of D_3 may possibly have a downward bias in that the markets for the underlying minority interests in the same firms is very deep. So it is only the market for control of publicly held firms that is thin. The market for privately held firms is thin for whole firms and razor thin for minority interests.

---

59. We assume a successful purchase, a tender offer, and a cash deal.

Component #3: Transactions Costs

Transactions costs in selling a privately held business are substantially more than they are for selling stock in publicly traded firms. Most stock in publicly traded firms can be sold with a broker's fee of 1–2%—or less.

Table 7-11: Quantifying Transactions Costs for Buyer and Seller. Table 7-11 shows estimates of transactions costs for both the buyer and the seller for the following categories: legal, accounting, and appraisal fees (the latter split into posttransaction, tax-based appraisal for allocation of purchase price and/or valuation of in-process R&D and the pretransaction "deal appraisal" to help buyer and/or seller establish the right price), the opportunity cost of internal management spending its time on the sale rather than on other company business, and investment banking (or, for small sales, business broker) fees. The first five of the categories appear in columns B through F, which we subtotal in column G, and the investment banking fees appear in column H. The reason for segregating between the investment banking fees and all the others is that the others are constantly increasing as the deal size (FMV) decreases, while investment banking fees reach a maximum of 10% and stop increasing as the deal size decreases.

Rows 6–9 are transactions costs estimates for the buyer, while rows 13–16 are for the seller. Note that the buyer does not pay the investment banking fees—only the seller pays. Rows 20–23 are total fees for both sides.

Note that the subtotal transactions costs (column G) are inversely related to the size of the transaction. For the buyer, they are as low as 0.23% (I6) for a $1 billion transaction and as high as 5.7% (I9) for a $1 million transaction. We summarize the total in Rows 27–30 and include the base 10 logarithm of the sales price as a variable for regression.[60] The purpose of the regression is to allow the reader to calculate an estimated transactions costs for any size transaction.

The buyer regression equation is:

$$\frac{\text{Buyer Subtotal Transaction Cost}}{\text{Price}} = 0.1531 - (0.0173 \times \log_{10} \text{Price})$$

The regression coefficients are in cells B48 and B49. The adjusted R^2 is 83% (B37), which is a good result. The standard error of the y-estimate is 0.9% (B38), so the 95% confidence interval around the estimate is approximately two standard errors, or $\pm 1.8\%$—a very good result.

The seller regression equation is:

$$\frac{\text{Seller Subtotal Transaction Cost}}{\text{Price}} = 0.1414 - (0.01599 \times \log_{10} \text{Price})$$

The regression coefficients are in cells B67 and B68. The adjusted R^2 is 82% (B56), which is a good result. The standard error of the y-estimate is

---

60. Normally we use the natural logarithm for regression. Here we chose base 10 because the logs are whole numbers and are easy to understand. Ultimately, it makes no difference which one we use in the regression. The results are identical either way.

PART 3   Adjusting for Control and Marketability

TABLE 7-11

Estimates of Transaction Costs [1]

	A	B	C	D	E	F	G	H	I
4	**Buyer**								
5	Deal Size	Legal [2]	Acctg	Tax Appraisal	Deal Appraisal [3]	Internal Mgt [4]	Subtotal	Inv Bank	Total
6	$1 billion	0.10%	0.02%	0.02%	0.00%	0.09%	0.23%	0.00%	0.23%
7	$100 million	1.00%	0.10%	0.06%	0.00%	0.16%	1.32%	0.00%	1.32%
8	$10 million	1.50%	0.23%	0.20%	0.00%	0.25%	2.18%	0.00%	2.18%
9	$1 million	4.00%	0.30%	0.70%	0.00%	0.70%	5.70%	0.00%	5.70%
11	**Seller**								
12	Deal Size	Legal [2]	Acctg	Tax Appraisal	Deal Appraisal [3]	Internal Mgt [4]	Subtotal	Inv Bank	Total
13	$1 billion	0.10%	0.01%	0.00%	0.02%	0.05%	0.18%	0.75%	0.93%
14	$100 million	1.00%	0.05%	0.00%	0.05%	0.10%	1.20%	1.10%	2.30%
15	$10 million	1.50%	0.08%	0.00%	0.20%	0.15%	1.93%	2.75%	4.68%
16	$1 million	4.00%	0.10%	0.00%	0.75%	0.42%	5.27%	10.00%	15.27%
18	**Total**								
19	Deal Size	Legal [2]	Acctg	Tax Appraisal	Deal Appraisal [3]	Internal Mgt [4]	Subtotal	Inv Bank	Total
20	$1 billion	0.20%	0.03%	0.02%	0.02%	0.14%	0.41%	0.75%	1.16%
21	$100 million	2.00%	0.15%	0.06%	0.05%	0.26%	2.52%	1.10%	3.62%
22	$10 million	3.00%	0.30%	0.20%	0.20%	0.40%	4.10%	2.75%	6.85%
23	$1 million	8.00%	0.40%	0.70%	0.75%	1.12%	10.97%	10.00%	20.97%

Summary For Regression Analysis–Buyer

Sales Price	Log$_{10}$ Price	Subtotal
$1,000,000,000	9.0	0.23%
$100,000,000	8.0	1.32%
$10,000,000	7.0	2.18%
$1,000,000	6.0	5.70%

Summary For Regression Analysis–Seller

Sales Price	Log$_{10}$ Price	Subtotal
$1,000,000,000	9.0	0.18%
$100,000,000	8.0	1.20%
$10,000,000	7.0	1.93%
$1,000,000	6.0	5.27%

TABLE 7-11 *(continued)*

Estimates of Transaction Costs [1]

	A	B	C	D	E	F	G	H
32	SUMMARY OUTPUT: Buyer Subtotal Fees as a Function of Log$_{10}$ FMV							
34	Regression Statistics							
35	Multiple R	0.9417624						
36	R square	0.88691642						
37	Adjusted R square	0.83037464						
38	Standard error	0.00975177						
39	Observations	4						
41	ANOVA							
42		df	SS	MS	F	Significance F		
43	Regression	1	0.001491696	0.0014917	15.68603437	0.058237596		
44	Residual	2	0.000190194	9.5097E − 05				
45	Total	3	0.00168189					
47		Coefficients	Standard Error	t Stat	P-value	Lower 95%	Upper 95%	
48	Intercept	**0.1531**	0.033069874	4.62959125	0.043626277	0.010811717	0.295388283	
49	Log$_{10}$ price	**−0.0172725**	0.004361126	−3.96055986	0.058237596	−0.036036923	0.001491923	
51	SUMMARY OUTPUT: Seller Subtotal Fees as a Function of Log$_{10}$ FMV							
53	Regression Statistics							
54	Multiple R	0.93697224						
55	R square	0.87791699						
56	Adjusted R square	0.81687548						
57	Standard error	0.00943065						
58	Observations	4						
60	ANOVA							
61		df	SS	MS	F	Significance F		
62	Regression	1	0.00127912	0.00127912	14.38229564	0.063027755		
63	Residual	2	0.000177874	8.8937E − 05				
64	Total	3	0.001456994					
66		Coefficients	Standard Error	t Stat	P-value	Lower 95%	Upper 95%	
67	Intercept	**0.14139**	0.031980886	4.42107833	0.04754262	0.00378726	0.27899274	
68	Log$_{10}$ price	**−0.0159945**	0.004217514	−3.79239972	0.063027755	−0.034141012	0.002152012	

also 0.9% (B57), which gives us the same confidence intervals around the *y*-estimate of ±1.8%.

Rows 73 and 74 show a sample calculation of transactions costs for the buyer and seller, respectively. We estimate FMV before discounts for our subject company of $5 million (B73, B74). The base 10 logarithm of 5 million is 6.69897 (C73, C74).[61] In D73 and D74, we insert the *x*-coefficient from the regression, which is −0.0172725 (from B49) for the buyer and −0.0159945 (from B68) for the seller. We multiply column C × column

---

61. In other words, $10^{6.69897}$ = 5 million.

T A B L E 7-11 *(continued)*

Estimates of Transaction Costs [1]

	A	B	C	D	E	F	G	H	I	J
70	**Sample Forecast of Transactions Costs For $5 Million Subject Company:**									
72		**FMV**	**log₁₀ FMV**	**X-Coeff.**	**log FMV × Coef**	**Regr. Constant**	**Forecast Subtotal**	**Inv Bank [5]**	**Forecast Total**	
73	Buyer	$5,000,000	6.698970004	−0.0172725	−0.115707959	0.1531	3.7%	0.0%	3.7%	
74	Seller	$5,000,000	6.698970004	−0.0159945	−0.107146676	0.14139	3.4%	5.0%	8.4%	

Notes:

[1] Based on interviews with investment banker Gordon Gregory, attorney David Boatwright, Esq; and Douglas Obenshain, CPA. Costs include buy and sell side. These are estimates of average costs. Actual costs vary with the complexity of the transaction.

[2] Legal fees will vary with the complexity of the transaction. An extremely complex $1 billion sale could have legal fees of as much as $5 million each for the buyer and the seller, though this is rare. Complexity increases with: stock deals (or asset deals with a very large number of assets), seller "carries paper", contingent payments, escrow, tax-free (which is treated as a pooling-of-interests), etc.

[3] We are assuming the seller pays for the deal appraisal. Individual sales may vary. Sometimes both sides hire a single appraiser and split the fees, and sometimes each side has its own appraiser.

[4] Internal management costs are the most speculative of all. We estimate 6,000 hours (3 people fulltime for 1 year) at an average $150/hr. internal cost for the $1 billion sale, 2,000 hours @ $80 for the $100 million sale, 500 hours at $50 for the $10 million sale, and 200 hours @$35 for the $1 million sale for the buyer, and 60% of that for the seller. Actual results may vary considerably from these estimates.

[5] Ideally calculated by another regression, but this is sight-estimated. Can often use the Lehman Bros. Formula—5% for 1st $1 million, 4%, for 2nd, etc., leveling off at 1% for each $1 million.

261

D = column E. F73 and F74 are repetitions of the regression constants from B48 and B67, respectively. We then add column E to column F to obtain the forecast subtotal transactions costs in G73 and G74. Finally, we add in investment banking fees of 5%[62] for the seller (the buyer doesn't pay for the investment banker or business broker) to arrive at totals of 3.7% (I73) and 8.4% (I74) for the buyer and seller, respectively.

Component #3 Is Different than #1 and #2. Component #3, transactions costs, is different than the first two components of DLOM. For component #3, we need to calculate explicitly the present value of the occurrence of transactions costs every time the company sells. The reason is that, unlike the first two components, transactions costs are actually out-of-pocket costs that leave the system.[63] They are paid to attorneys, accountants, appraisers, and investment bankers or business brokers. Additionally, internal management of both the buyer and the seller spend significant time on the sale to make it happen, and they often have to spend time on failed acquisitions before being successful.

We also need to distinguish between the buyer's transactions costs and the seller's costs. The reason for this is that the buyer's transactions costs are always relevant, whereas the seller's transactions costs for the immediate transaction reduce the net proceeds to the seller but do not reduce FMV. However, before the buyer is willing to buy, he or she should be saying, "It's true, I don't care about the seller's costs. That's his or her problem. However, 10 years or so down the road when it's my turn to be the seller, I do care about that. To the extent that seller's costs exceed the brokerage cost of selling publicly traded stock, in 10 years my buyer will pay me less because of those costs, and therefore I must pay my seller less because of my costs as a seller in Year 10. Additionally, the process goes on forever, because in Year 20, my buyer becomes a seller and faces the same problem." Thus, we need to quantify the present value of a periodic perpetuity of buyer's transactions costs beginning with the immediate sale and sellers' transactions costs that begin with the second sale of the business.[64] In the next section we will develop the mathematics necessary to do this.

Developing Formulas to Calculate DLOM Component #3. This section contains some difficult mathematics, but ultimately we will arrive at some very usable formulas that are not that difficult. It is not necessary to follow all of the mathematics that gets us there, but it is worthwhile to skim through the math to get a feel for what it means. In the Mathe-

---

62. We could run another regression to forecast investment banking fees. This was sight estimated. One could also use a formula such as the Lehman Brothers formula to forecast investment banking fees.
63. I thank R. K. Hiatt for the brilliant insight that the first two components of DLOM do not have this characteristic and thus do not require this additional present value calculation.
64. One might think that the buyers' transactions costs are not relevant the first time, because the buyer has to put in due diligence time whether or not a transaction results. In individual instances that is true, but in the aggregate, if buyers would not receive compensation for their due diligence time, they would cease to buy private firms until the prices declined enough to compensate them.

matical Appendix we develop the formulas below step by step. In order to avoid presenting volumes of burdensome math in the body of the chapter, we present only occasional snapshots of the math—just enough to present the conclusions and convey some of the logic behind it.

For simplicity, suppose that, on average, business owners hold the business for 10 years and then sell. Every time an owner sells, he or she incurs a transactions cost of z. The net present value (NPV) of the cash flows to the business owner is:[65]

$$NPV = NPV_{1-10} + (1 - z)NPV_{11-\infty} \qquad (7\text{-}1)$$

Equation (7-1) states that the NPV of cash flows at Year 0 to the owner is the sum of the NPV of the first 10 years' cash flows and $(1 - z)$ times the NPV of all cash flows from Year 11 to infinity. If transactions costs are 10% every time a business sells, then $z = 10\%$ and $1 - z = 90\%$.[66] The first owner would have 10 years of cash flows undiminished by transactions costs and then pay transactions costs of 10% of the NPV at Year 10 of all future cash flows.

The second owner operates the business for 10 years and then sells at Year 20. He or she pays transactions costs of z at Year 20. The NPV of cash flows to the second owner is:

$$NPV_{11-\infty} = NPV_{11-20} + (1 - z)NPV_{21-\infty} \qquad (7\text{-}2)$$

Substituting (7-2) into equation (7-1), the NPV of cash flows to the first owner is:

$$NPV = NPV_{1-10} + (1 - z)[NPV_{11-20} + (1 - z)NPV_{21-\infty}] \qquad (7\text{-}3)$$

This expression simplifies to:

$$NPV = NPV_{1-10} + (1 - z)NPV_{11-20} + (1 - z)^2 NPV_{21-\infty} \qquad (7\text{-}4)$$

We can continue on in this fashion *ad infinitum*. The final expression for NPV is:

$$NPV = \sum_{i=1}^{\infty} (1 - z)^{i-1} NPV_{[10(i-1)+1]-10i} \qquad (7\text{-}5)$$

The NPV is a geometric sequence. Using a Gordon model, i.e., assuming constant, perpetual growth, in the Mathematical Appendix, we show that equation (7-5) solves to:

$$NPV_{TC} = \frac{\sqrt{1 + r}}{r - g} \left\{ \frac{1 - \left(\dfrac{1 + g}{1 + r}\right)^{10}}{1 - \left[(1 - z)\left(\dfrac{1 + g}{1 + r}\right)^{10}\right]} \right\} \qquad (7\text{-}6)$$

where NPV_{TC} is the NPV of the cash flows with the NPV of the transactions costs that occur every 10 years removed, g is the constant growth

---

65. Read the hyphen in the following equation's subscript text as the word "to," i.e., the NPV from one time period to another.
66. z is actually an incremental transaction cost, as we will explain later in the chapter.

rate of cash flows, r is the discount rate, and cash flows are midyear.[67] The end-of-year formula is the same, replacing the $\sqrt{1 + r}$ in the numerator with the number 1.

The NPV of the cash flows without removing the NPV of transactions costs every 10 years is simply the Gordon model multiple of $(\sqrt{1 + r})/(r - g)$, which is identical with the first term on the right-hand side of equation (7-6). The discount for lack of marketability for transactions costs is equal to:

$$\text{DLOM} = 1 - \frac{NPV_{\text{TC}}}{NPV} \qquad (7\text{-}7)$$

The fraction in equation (7-7) is simply the term in the large braces in equation (7-6). Thus, DLOM simplifies to:

$$D = 1 - \left\{ \frac{1 - \left(\dfrac{1 + g}{1 + r}\right)^{10}}{1 - \left[(1 - z)\left(\dfrac{1 + g}{1 + r}\right)^{10}\right]} \right\} = 1 - \frac{1 - x^{10}}{1 - (1 - z)x^{10}} \qquad (7\text{-}8)$$

where $x = (1 + g)/(1 + r)$, D is the discount, and $g < r, \Rightarrow 0 < x < 1$.[68]

Equation (7-8) is the formula for the discount assuming a sale every 10 years. Instead of assuming a business sale every 10 years, now we let the average years between sale be a random variable, j, which leads to the generalized equation in (7-9) for sellers' transactions costs:[69]

$$D_{3B} = 1 - \left\{ \frac{1 - \left(\dfrac{1 + g}{1 + r}\right)^{j}}{1 - \left[(1 - z)\left(\dfrac{1 + g}{1 + r}\right)^{j}\right]} \right\} = 1 - \frac{1 - x^{j}}{1 - (1 - z)x^{j}}$$

DLOM formula—sellers' costs $\qquad (7\text{-}9)$

Using an end-of-year Gordon Model assumption instead of midyear cash flows leads to the identical equation, i.e., equation (7-9) holds for both.

Analysis of partial derivatives in the Mathematical Appendix shows that the discount, i.e., DLOM, is always increasing with increases in growth (g) and transactions costs (z) and is always decreasing with increases in the discount rate (r) and the average number of years between sales (j). The converse is true as well. Decreases in the independent variables have opposite effects on DLOM as increases do.

---

67. This appears as equation (A7-7) in the Mathematical Appendix.
68. This is identical with equation (A7-10) in the Mathematical Appendix.
69. This is identical with equation (A7-11) in the Mathematical Appendix. Note that we use the plural possessive here because we are speaking about an infinite continuum of sellers (and buyers).

PART 3   Adjusting for Control and Marketability

Equation (7-9) is the appropriate formula to use for quantifying the sellers' transactions costs, because it ignores the first sale, as discussed above.[70] The appropriate formula for quantifying the buyers' transactions costs incorporates an initial transaction cost at time zero instead of at $t = j$. With this assumption, we would modify the above analysis by changing the $(1 - z)^{i-1}$ to $(1 - z)^i$ in equation (7-5). The immediate transaction equivalent formula of equation (7-9) for buyers' transactions costs is:[71]

$$D_{3A} = 1 - \frac{(1 - z)(1 - x^j)}{1 - (1 - z)x^j}$$

generalized DLOM formula—buyers' transactions costs   7-9a

Obviously, equation (7-9a), which assumes an immediate sale, results in much larger discounts than equation (7-9), where the first sale occurs j years later. Equation (7-9) constitutes the discount appropriate for sellers' transactions costs, while equation (7-9a) constitutes the discount appropriate for buyers' transactions costs. Thus, component #3 splits into #3A and #3B because we must use different formulas to value them.[72,73]

A Simplified Example of Sellers' Transactions Costs.   Because appraisers are used to automatically assuming that all sellers' costs merely reduce the net proceeds to the seller but have no impact on the fair market value, the concept of periodic sellers' costs that do affect FMV is potentially very confusing. Let's look at a very simplified example to make the concept clear.

Consider a business that will sell once at $t = 0$ for $1,000 and once at $t = 10$ years for $1,500, after which the owner will run the company and eventually liquidate it. For simplicity, we will ignore buyers' transactions costs. We can model the thinking of the first buyer, i.e., at $t = 0$, as follows: "When I eventually sell in Year 10, I'll have to pay a business broker $150. If I were selling publicly traded stock, I would have paid a broker's fee of 2% on the $1,500, or $30, so the difference is $130. Assuming a 25% discount rate, the present value factor is 0.1074, and $130 × 0.1074 = $13.96 today. On a price of $1,000, the excess transactions costs from my eventual sale are 1.396%, or approximately 1.4%. Formulas (7-9) and (7-9a) extend this logic to cover the infinite continuum of transactions every 10 years (or every j years, allowing the average selling period to be a variable).

---

70. Note that we have shifted from speaking in the singular about the first seller to the plural in speaking about the entire continuum of sellers throughout infinite time. We will make the same shift in language with the buyers as well.
71. This is identical with equation (A7-11A) in the Mathematical Appendix.
72. An alternative approach is to use equation (7-9a) for both and subtract the first round seller's costs.
73. It is not that buyers and sellers sit around and develop equations like (7-9) and (7-9a) and run them on their spreadsheets before making deals. One might think this complexity is silly, because real-life buyers and sellers don't do this. However, we are merely attempting to model economically their combination of ideal rationality and intuition.

Tables 7-12 and 7-13: Proving Formulas (7-9) and (7-9a). Tables 7-12 and 7-13 prove equations (7-9) and (7-9a), respectively. The two tables have identical structure and logic, so we will cover both of them by explaining Table 7-12.

Column A shows 100 years of cash flow. While the formulas presume perpetuities, the present value effect is so small that there is no relevant present value after Year 100.

The assumptions of the model are: the discount rate is 20% (cell B112), the perpetual growth rate is 5% (B113), sellers' transactions costs = z = 12% (B114),

$$x = \frac{1 + g}{1 + r} = \frac{1.05}{1.2} = 0.875 \quad \text{(B115)}$$

and j, the average years between sales of the business, equals 10 years (B116).

In B7 we begin with $1.00 of forecast cash flow in Year 1. The cash flow grows at a rate of g = 5%. Thus, every cash flow in column B from rows 8–106 equals 1.05 times the number above it. Column C is the present value factor assuming midyear cash flows at a discount rate of 20%. Column D, the present value of cash flows, equals column B × column C.

Column E is the factor that tells us how much of the cash flows from each year remains with the original owner after removing the seller's transactions costs. The buyer does not care about the seller's transactions costs, so only future sellers' transactions costs count in this calculation. In other words, the buyer cares about the transactions costs that he or she will face in 10 years when he or she sells the business. In turn, he or she knows that his or her own buyer eventually becomes a seller. Therefore, each 10 years, or more generally, each j years, the cash flows that remains with the original owner declines by a multiple of $(1 - z)$. Its formula is $(1 - z)^{\text{Int}(\text{Yr}-1)}$.

Thus, the first 10 years, 100% = 1.0000 (E7–E16) of the cash flows with respect to sellers' transactions costs remain with the original owner. The next 10 years, Years 11–20, the original owner's cash flows are reduced to $(1 - z)$ = 88% (E17–E26) of the entire cash flow, with the 12% being lost as sellers' transactions costs to the second buyer. For Years 21–30, the original owner loses another 12% to transactions costs for the third buyer, so the value that remains is $(1 - z)^2 = (1 - 0.12)^2 = 0.88^2 = 0.7744$ (E27–E36). This continues in the same pattern *ad infinitum*.

Column F is the posttransactions costs present value of cash flows, which is column D × column E. Thus, D17 × E17 = 0.240154 × 0.8800 = 0.2113356 (F17). We sum the first 100 years' cash flows in F107, which equals $7.0030. In other words, the present value of posttransactions costs cash flows to the present owner of the business is $7.003. However, the present value of the cash flows without removing transactions costs is $7.3030 (D107). In F108 we calculate the discount as 1 − (F107/D108) = 1 − ($7.0030/$7.3030) = 4.1%.

In F109 we present the calculations according to equation (7-9), and it, too, equals 4.1%. Thus we have demonstrated that equation (7-9) is accurate.

Proof of Equation (7-9)

	A	B	C	D	E	F	G
					$(1 - z)^{\wedge}\text{Int}(Yr - 1)$	Post Tx	
		Cash		PV Cash	= Post-Trans	PV Cash	
	Year	Flow	PVF	Flow	Costs	Flow	
7	1	1.0000	0.912871	0.912871	1.0000	0.9128709	
8	2	1.0500	0.760726	0.798762	1.0000	0.7987621	
9	3	1.1025	0.633938	0.698917	1.0000	0.6989168	
10	4	1.1576	0.528282	0.611552	1.0000	0.6115522	
11	5	1.2155	0.440235	0.535108	1.0000	0.5351082	
12	6	1.2763	0.366862	0.468220	1.0000	0.4682197	
13	7	1.3401	0.305719	0.409692	1.0000	0.4096922	
14	8	1.4071	0.254766	0.358481	1.0000	0.3584807	
15	9	1.4775	0.212305	0.313671	1.0000	0.3136706	
16	10	1.5513	0.176921	0.274462	1.0000	0.2744618	
17	11	1.6289	0.147434	0.240154	0.8800	0.2113356	
18	12	1.7103	0.122861	0.210135	0.8800	0.1849186	
19	13	1.7959	0.102385	0.183868	0.8800	0.1618038	
20	14	1.8856	0.0852	0.160884	0.8800	0.1415783	
15	15	1.9799	0.0711	0.140774	0.8800	0.1238810	
22	16	2.0789	0.05925	0.123177	0.8800	0.1083959	
23	17	2.1829	0.049375	0.107780	0.8800	0.0948464	
24	18	2.2920	0.041146	0.094308	0.8800	0.0829906	
25	19	2.4066	0.034288	0.082519	0.8800	0.0726168	
26	20	2.5270	0.028574	0.072204	0.8800	0.0635397	
27	21	2.6533	0.023811	0.063179	0.7744	0.0489256	
28	22	2.7860	0.019843	0.055281	0.7744	0.0428099	
29	23	2.9253	0.016536	0.048371	0.7744	0.0374586	
30	24	3.0715	0.0138	0.042325	0.7744	0.0327763	
31	25	3.2251	0.011483	0.037034	0.7744	0.0286793	
32	26	3.3864	0.009569	0.032405	0.7744	0.0250944	
33	27	3.5557	0.007974	0.028354	0.7744	0.0219576	
34	28	3.7335	0.006645	0.024810	0.7744	0.0192129	
35	29	3.9201	0.005538	0.021709	0.7744	0.0168113	
36	30	4.1161	0.004615	0.018995	0.7744	0.0147099	
37	31	4.3219	0.003846	0.016621	0.6815	0.0113266	
38	32	4.5380	0.003205	0.014543	0.6815	0.0099108	
39	33	4.7649	0.002671	0.012725	0.6815	0.0086719	
40	34	5.0032	0.002226	0.011135	0.6815	0.0075879	
41	35	5.2533	0.001855	0.009743	0.6815	0.0066394	
42	36	5.5160	0.001545	0.008525	0.6815	0.0058095	
43	37	5.7918	0.001288	0.007459	0.6815	0.0050833	
44	38	6.0814	0.001073	0.006527	0.6815	0.0044479	
45	39	6.3855	0.000894	0.005711	0.6815	0.0038919	
46	40	6.7048	0.000745	0.004997	0.6815	0.0034054	
47	41	7.0400	0.000621	0.004373	0.5997	0.0026222	
48	42	7.3920	0.000518	0.003826	0.5997	0.0022944	
49	43	7.7616	0.000431	0.003348	0.5997	0.0020076	
50	44	8.1497	0.000359	0.002929	0.5997	0.0017567	
51	45	8.5572	0.0003	0.002563	0.5997	0.0015371	
52	46	8.9850	0.00025	0.002243	0.5997	0.0013449	
53	47	9.4343	0.000208	0.001962	0.5997	0.0011768	
54	48	9.9060	0.000173	0.001717	0.5997	0.0010297	
55	49	10.4013	0.000144	0.001502	0.5997	0.0009010	
56	50	10.9213	0.00012	0.001315	0.5997	0.0007884	
57	51	11.4674	0.0001	0.001150	0.5277	0.0006071	
58	52	12.0408	8.36E-05	0.001007	0.5277	0.0005312	
59	53	12.6428	6.97E-05	0.000881	0.5277	0.0004648	
59	54	13.2749	5.81E-05	0.000771	0.5277	0.0004067	
61	55	13.9387	4.84E-05	0.000674	0.5277	0.0003558	
62	56	14.6356	4.03E-05	0.000590	0.5277	0.0003114	

Proof of Equation (7-9)

	A	B	C	D	E	F	G
	Year	**Cash Flow**	**PVF**	**PV Cash Flow**	**(1 − z)^Int(Yr − 1) = Post-Trans Costs**	**Post Tx PV Cash Flow**	
63	57	15.3674	3.36E-05	0.000516	0.5277	0.0002724	
64	58	16.1358	2.8E-05	0.000452	0.5277	0.0002384	
65	59	16.9426	2.33E-05	0.000395	0.5277	0.0002086	
66	60	17.7897	1.94E-05	0.000346	0.5277	0.0001825	
67	61	18.6792	1.62E-05	0.000303	0.4644	0.0001405	
68	62	19.6131	1.35E-05	0.000265	0.4644	0.0001230	
69	63	20.5938	1.13E-05	0.000232	0.4644	0.0001076	
70	64	21.6235	9.38E-06	0.000203	0.4644	0.0000941	
71	65	22.7047	7.81E-06	0.000177	0.4644	0.0000824	
72	66	23.8399	6.51E-06	0.000155	0.4644	0.0000721	
73	67	25.0319	5.43E-06	0.000136	0.4644	0.0000631	
74	68	26.2835	4.52E-06	0.000119	0.4644	0.0000552	
75	69	27.5977	3.77E-06	0.000104	0.4644	0.0000483	
76	70	28.9775	3.14E-06	0.000091	0.4644	0.0000423	
77	71	30.4264	2.62E-06	0.000080	0.4087	0.0000325	
78	72	31.9477	2.18E-06	0.000070	0.4087	0.0000285	
79	73	33.5451	1.82E-06	0.000061	0.4087	0.0000249	
80	74	35.2224	1.51E-06	0.000053	0.4087	0.0000218	
81	75	36.9835	1.26E-06	0.000047	0.4087	0.0000191	
82	76	38.8327	1.05E-06	0.000041	0.4087	0.0000167	
83	77	40.7743	8.76E-07	0.000036	0.4087	0.0000146	
84	78	42.8130	7.3E-07	0.000031	0.4087	0.0000128	
85	79	44.9537	6.09E-07	0.000027	0.4087	0.0000112	
86	80	47.2014	5.07E-07	0.000024	0.4087	0.0000098	
87	81	49.5614	4.23E-07	0.000021	0.3596	0.0000075	
88	82	52.0395	3.52E-07	0.000018	0.3596 ·	0.0000066	
89	83	54.6415	2.93E-07	0.000016	0.3596	0.0000058	
90	84	57.3736	2.45E-07	0.000014	0.3596	0.0000050	
91	85	60.2422	2.04E-07	0.000012	0.3596	0.0000044	
92	86	63.2544	1.7E-07	0.000011	0.3596	0.0000039	
93	87	66.4171	1.42E-07	0.000009	0.3596	0.0000034	
94	88	69.7379	1.18E-07	0.000008	0.3596	0.0000030	
95	89	73.2248	9.83E-07	0.000007	0.3596	0.0000026	
96	90	76.8861	8.19E-08	0.000006	0.3596	0.0000023	
97	91	80.7304	6.82E-08	0.000006	0.3165	0.0000017	
98	92	84.7669	5.69E-08	0.000005	0.3165	0.0000015	
99	93	89.0052	4.74E-08	0.000004	0.3165	0.0000013	
100	94	93.4555	3.95E-08	0.000004	0.3165	0.0000012	
101	95	98.1283	3.29E-08	0.000003	0.3165	0.0000010	
102	96	103.0347	2.74E-08	0.000003	0.3165	0.0000009	
103	97	108.1864	2.29E-08	0.000002	0.3165	0.0000008	
104	98	113.5957	1.9E-08	0.000002	0.3165	0.0000007	
105	99	119.2755	1.59E-08	0.000002	0.3165	0.0000006	
106	100	125.2393	1.32E-08	0.000002	0.3165	0.0000005	
107	**Totals**			**$7.3030**		**$7.0030**	

108	Discount = 1 − (F107/D107)	4.1%
109	Discount-By Formula [1]	4.1%

111	**Parameters**	**Sensitivity Analysis**

			Avg Yrs Between Sales		
112	r	20%			
113	g	5%	**8**	**10**	**12**
114	z	12%	18%	7.2%	5.1%	3.8%
115	x = (1 + g)/ (1 + r)	87.50%	20%	5.9%	**4.1%**	2.9%
116	j = yrs to sale	10	22%	4.9%	3.3%	2.3%

[1] Formula For Discount: 1 − ((1 − x^j)/((1 − (1 − z)*x^j)))

Table 7-13 is identical to Table 7-12, except that it demonstrates the accuracy of equation (7-9a), which is the formula appropriate for buyers' transactions costs. Buyers care about their own transactions costs from the outset. Therefore, the continuum of buyers' transactions costs begins immediately. Thus, E7 to E16 equal 0.88 in Table 7-13, while they were equal to 1.00 in Table 7-12.

The discount in Table 7-13 is considerably larger—15.6%, which we calculate in F108 using the "brute force" method and in F109 using equation (7-9a). The spreadsheet formula appears in note [1] as it also does in Table 7-12. Table 7-13 thus demonstrates the accuracy of equation (7-9a).

Value Remaining Formula and the Total Discount. The fraction in (7-9) is the percentage of value that remains after removing the perpetuity of transactions costs. Equation (7-10) shows the equation for the value remaining, denoted as VR:

$$VR = \frac{1 - x^j}{1 - (1 - z)x^j} \quad \text{valuing remaining formula} \qquad (7\text{-}10)$$

We can multiply all three value remaining figures for each of the three components, and the result is the value remaining for the firm overall. The final discount is then one minus the value remaining for the firm overall.

Next we will demonstrate the final calculation of DLOM.

Table 7-14: Sample Calculation of DLOM

Table 7-14 is an example of calculating DLOM for a privately held firm with a $5 million FMV on a marketable minority basis. Column B is the pure discount of each component as calculated according to the methodology in the previous tables. Component #1, the discount due to the delay to sale, is equal to 13.4% (B9), which comes from Table 7-10, cell D12. Component #2, monopsony power to the buyer, equals 9% (B10), per our discussion of Schwert's article earlier in this chapter. Component #3A, buyers' transactions costs, equals 3.7% (Table 7-11, I73) for private buyers, minus the approximately 1% brokerage fee to buy a $5 million interest in publicly traded stocks = 2.7% (B11). Component #3B, sellers' transactions costs, equals 8.4% (Table 7-11, I74) for private buyers minus the approximate 1% brokerage fee to buy publicly traded stocks = 7.4% (B12). The reason that we subtract stock market transactions costs from the private market transactions costs is that we are using public market values as our basis of comparison, i.e., our point of reference.

Column C is the present value of the perpetual discount, which means that for Components #3A and #3B, we quantify the infinite periodic transactions costs. Using equations (7-9a) for the buyers and (7-9) for the sellers, the 2.7% (B11) pure discount for buyers results in a net present value of buyers' transactions costs of 3.6% (C11), and the 7.4% (B12) pure discount for sellers results in a net present value of sellers' transactions costs of 2.4% (C12). Again, that excludes the seller's costs on the assumed sale to the hypothetical buyer at $t = 0$. The first two

T A B L E 7-13

Proof of Equation (7-9a)

	A	B	C	D	E	F	G
4					(1 − z)^Int(Yr − 1)	Post Tx	
5		Cash		PV Cash	= Post-Trans	PV Cash	
6	Year	Flow	PVF	Flow	Costs	Flow	
7	1	1.0000	0.912871	0.912871	0.8800	0.8033264	
8	2	1.0500	0.760726	0.798762	0.8800	0.7029106	
9	3	1.1025	0.633938	0.698917	0.8800	0.6150468	
10	4	1.1576	0.528282	0.611552	0.8800	0.5381659	
11	5	1.2155	0.440235	0.535108	0.8800	0.4708952	
12	6	1.2763	0.366862	0.468220	0.8800	0.4120333	
13	7	1.3401	0.305719	0.409692	0.8800	0.3605291	
14	8	1.4071	0.254766	0.358481	0.8800	0.3154630	
15	9	1.4775	0.212305	0.313671	0.8800	0.2760301	
16	10	1.5513	0.176921	0.274462	0.8800	0.2415264	
17	11	1.6289	0.147434	0.240154	0.7744	0.1859753	
18	12	1.7103	0.122861	0.210135	0.7744	0.1627284	
19	13	1.7959	0.102385	0.183868	0.7744	0.1423873	
20	14	1.8856	0.08532	0.160884	0.7744	0.1245889	
21	15	1.9799	0.0711	0.140774	0.7744	0.1090153	
22	16	2.0789	0.05925	0.123177	0.7744	0.0953884	
23	17	2.1829	0.049375	0.107780	0.7744	0.0834648	
24	18	2.2920	0.041146	0.094308	0.7744	0.0730317	
25	19	2.4066	0.034288	0.082519	0.7744	0.0639028	
26	20	2.5270	0.028574	0.072204	0.7744	0.0559149	
27	21	2.6533	0.023811	0.063179	0.6815	0.0430545	
28	22	2.7860	0.019843	0.055281	0.6815	0.0376727	
29	23	2.9253	0.016536	0.048371	0.6815	0.0329636	
30	24	3.0715	0.0138	0.042325	0.6815	0.0288431	
31	25	3.2251	0.011483	0.037034	0.6815	0.0252378	
32	26	3.3864	0.009569	0.032405	0.6815	0.0220830	
33	27	3.5557	0.007974	0.028354	0.6815	0.0193227	
34	28	3.7335	0.006645	0.024810	0.6815	0.0169073	
35	29	3.9201	0.005538	0.021709	0.6815	0.0147939	
36	30	4.1161	0.004615	0.018995	0.6815	0.0129447	
37	31	4.3219	0.003846	0.016621	0.5997	0.0099674	
38	32	4.5380	0.003205	0.014543	0.5997	0.0087215	
39	33	4.7649	0.002671	0.012725	0.5997	0.0076313	
40	34	5.0032	0.002226	0.011135	0.5997	0.0066774	
41	35	5.2533	0.001855	0.009743	0.5997	0.0058427	
42	36	5.5160	0.001545	0.008525	0.5997	0.0051124	
43	37	5.7918	0.001288	0.007459	0.5997	0.0044733	
44	38	6.0814	0.001073	0.006527	0.5997	0.0039142	
45	39	6.3855	0.000894	0.005711	0.5997	0.0034249	
46	40	6.7048	0.000745	0.004997	0.5997	0.0029968	
47	41	7.0400	0.000621	0.004373	0.5277	0.0023075	
48	42	7.3920	0.000518	0.003826	0.5277	0.0020191	
49	43	7.7616	0.000431	0.003348	0.5277	0.0017667	
50	44	8.1497	0.000359	0.002929	0.5277	0.0015459	
51	45	8.5572	0.0003	0.002563	0.5277	0.0013526	
52	46	8.9850	0.00025	0.002243	0.5277	0.0011835	
53	47	9.4343	0.000208	0.001962	0.5277	0.0010356	
54	48	9.9060	0.000173	0.001717	0.5277	0.0009062	
55	49	10.4013	0.000144	0.001502	0.5277	0.0007929	
56	50	10.9213	0.00012	0.001315	0.5277	0.0006938	
57	51	11.4674	0.0001	0.001150	0.4644	0.0005342	
58	52	12.0408	8.36E-05	0.001007	0.4644	0.0004674	
59	53	12.6428	6.97E-05	0.000881	0.4644	0.0004090	
60	54	13.2749	5.81E-05	0.000771	0.4644	0.0003579	
61	55	13.9387	4.84E-05	0.000674	0.4644	0.0003131	
62	56	14.6356	4.03E-05	0.000590	0.4644	0.0002740	
63	57	15.3674	3.36E-05	0.000516	0.4644	0.0002397	

TABLE 7-13 (continued)

Proof of Equation (7-9a)

	A	B	C	D	E	F	G
					$(1 - z)^\wedge\text{Int}(Yr - 1)$	Post Tx	
		Cash		PV Cash	= Post-Trans	PV Cash	
	Year	Flow	PVF	Flow	Costs	Flow	
64	58	16.1358	2.8E-05	0.000452	0.4644	0.0002098	
65	59	16.9426	2.33E-05	0.000395	0.4644	0.0001836	
66	60	17.7897	1.94E-05	0.000346	0.4644	0.0001606	
67	61	18.6792	1.62E-05	0.000303	0.4087	0.0001237	
68	62	19.6131	1.35E-05	0.000265	0.4087	0.0001082	
69	63	20.5938	1.13E-05	0.000232	0.4087	0.0000947	
70	64	21.6235	9.38E-06	0.000203	0.4087	0.0000829	
71	65	22.7047	7.81E-06	0.000177	0.4087	0.0000725	
72	66	23.8399	6.51E-06	0.000155	0.4087	0.0000634	
73	67	25.0319	5.43E-06	0.000136	0.4087	0.0000555	
74	68	26.2835	4.52E-06	0.000119	0.4087	0.0000486	
75	69	27.5977	3.77E-06	0.000104	0.4087	0.0000425	
76	70	28.9775	3.14E-06	0.000091	0.4087	0.0000372	
77	71	30.4264	2.62E-06	0.000080	0.3596	0.0000286	
78	72	31.9477	2.18E-06	0.000070	0.3596	0.0000251	
79	73	33.5451	1.82E-06	0.000061	0.3596	0.0000219	
80	74	35.2224	1.51E-06	0.000053	0.3596	0.0000192	
81	75	36.9835	1.26E-06	0.000047	0.3596	0.0000168	
82	76	38.8327	1.05E-06	0.000041	0.3596	0.0000147	
83	77	40.7743	8.76E-07	0.000036	0.3596	0.0000128	
84	78	42.8130	7.3E-07	0.000031	0.3596	0.0000112	
85	79	44.9537	6.09E-07	0.000027	0.3596	0.0000098	
86	80	47.2014	5.07E-07	0.000024	0.3596	0.0000086	
87	81	49.5614	4.23E-07	0.000021	0.3165	0.0000066	
88	82	52.0395	3.52E-07	0.000018	0.3165	0.0000058	
89	83	54.6415	2.93E-07	0.000016	0.3165	0.0000051	
90	84	57.3736	2.45E-07	0.000014	0.3165	0.0000044	
91	85	60.2422	2.04E-07	0.000012	0.3165	0.0000039	
92	86	63.2544	1.7E-07	0.000011	0.3165	0.0000034	
93	87	66.4171	1.42E-07	0.000009	0.3165	0.0000030	
94	88	69.7379	1.18E-07	0.000008	0.3165	0.0000026	
95	89	73.2248	9.83E-07	0.000007	0.3165	0.0000023	
96	90	76.8861	8.19E-08	0.000006	0.3165	0.0000020	
97	91	80.7304	6.82E-08	0.000006	0.2785	0.0000015	
98	92	84.7669	5.69E-08	0.000005	0.2785	0.0000013	
99	93	89.0052	4.74E-08	0.000004	0.2785	0.0000012	
100	94	93.4555	3.95E-08	0.000004	0.2785	0.0000010	
101	95	98.1283	3.29E-08	0.000003	0.2785	0.0000009	
102	96	103.0347	2.74E-08	0.000003	0.2785	0.0000008	
103	97	108.1864	2.29E-08	0.000002	0.2785	0.0000007	
104	98	113.5957	1.9E-08	0.000002	0.2785	0.0000006	
105	99	119.2755	1.59E-08	0.000002	0.2785	0.0000005	
106	100	125.2393	1.32E-08	0.000002	0.2785	0.0000005	
107	Totals			$7.3030		$6.1626	
108	Discount = 1 − (F107/D107)					15.6%	
109	Discount-By Formula [1]					15.6%	

111	Parameters				Sensitivity Analysis		
112	r	20%			Avg Yrs Between Sales		
113	g	5%			8	10	12
114	z	12%		18%	18.3%	16.5%	15.3%
115	x = (1 + g)/	87.50%		20%	17.2%	15.6%	14.6%
	(1 + r)						
116	j = yrs to sale	10		22%	16.3%	14.9%	14.0%

[1] Formula For Discount: $1 - ((1 - x^\wedge j)/((1 - (1 - z)*x^\wedge j)))$

TABLE 7-14

Sample Calculation of DLOM

	A	B	C	D	E	F	G
4	Section 1: Calculation of the Discount for Lack of Marketability						
6				= 1 − Col. [C]			
7		**Pure Discount**	**PV of Perpetual**	**Remaining**			
8	Component	= z [1]	Discount [2]	Value			
9	1	13.4%	13.4%	86.6%	Delay To sale-1 yr (Table 7-10, D12)		
10	2	9.0%	9.0%	91.0%	Buyer's monopsony power—thin markets		
11	3A	2.7%	3.6%	96.4%	Transactions costs-buyers		
12	3B	7.4%	2.4%	97.6%	Transactions costs-sellers		
13	Percent remaining			76.9%	Total % remaining = components 1 × 2 × 3A × 3B		
14	**Final discount**			**23.1%**	Discount = 1 − Total % remaining		
16	Section 2: Assumptions and Intermediate Calculations:						
18	FMV-equity of co. (before discounts)			$5,000,000			
19	Discount rate = r [3]			23.0%			
20	Constant growth rate = g			7.0%			
21	Intermediate calculation: x = (1 + g)/(1 + r)			0.8699			
22	Avg # years between sales = j			10			
24	Section 3: Sensitivity Analysis						
26		j = Average Years Between Sales					
27	j =	5	10	15	20		
28	Discount	26.6%	23.1%	22.0%	21.6%		

[1] Pure discounts: for component #1, Table 7-10, cell D12; for component #2, 9% per Schwert article. For component #3A and #3B, Table 7-11, cells I73 and I74 − 1% for public brokerage costs.

[2] PV of perpetual discount formula: $1 − (1 − x^j)/((1 − (1 − z)*x^j))$, per equation (7-9), used for component #3B. PV of perpetual discount formula: $1 − (1 − z)*(1 − x^j)/((1 − (1 − z)*x^j))$, per equation (7-9a), used for component #3A. Components #1 and #2 simply transfer the pure discount.

[3] The formula is: 0.4172 − (.01204 ln FMV), based on Table 4-1

components, as mentioned earlier, do not repeat through time, so their perpetual discount is equal to their pure discount. Thus, C9 = B9 and C10 = B10.

Column D is the remaining value after subtracting the perpetual discount column from one, i.e., Column D = 1 − Column C. We multiply D9 × D10 × D11 × D12 = D13 = 76.9%. The Final Discount is 1 − Remaining Value = 1 − 76.9% (D13) = 23.1% (D14).

The sensitivity analysis in section 3, row 28 of the table shows how the final discount varies with different assumptions of j = the average number of years between sales. At j = 10 years, it appears that DLOM is more sensitive to reducing j than increasing it. At j = 5, the discount increased from 23.1% (at j = 10) to 26.6%, whereas it only dropped slightly for j = 15 and 20–22.0% and 21.6%, respectively.

Evidence from the Institute of Business Appraisers

In Chapter 10, we examine data published by Raymond Miles, founder of the Institute of Business Appraisers (IBA), and apply log size discount rates and the DLOM calculations in this chapter to determine how well the they explain price/earnings multiples of real world sales of small businesses. The evidence in Chapter 10 is that within an order of magnitude, the log size model and the economic components model of DLOM perform well. Unfortunately, there is much data in the IBA and other databases that we need in order to be more precise. The lack of these data, e.g., forecast or at least historical growth rates and the magnitude of personal expenses charged to the business, forces us to makes estimates. There is too much estimating due to missing data for us to claim forcefully that the combination of the log size model, control premiums, DLOM, and DLOC as presented in this book is *the* solution to all valuation problems. Also, one could achieve the great results in Chapter 10 with other valuation assumptions. So Chapter 10 is only evidence that we are in the ballpark.

Mercer's Rebuttal

I invited Chris Mercer to provide his rebuttal to my criticisms of the QMDM. His rebuttal follows immediately, after which I provide my counterpoints.

Is the Quantitative Marketability Discount Model Flawed?

Response by Z. Christopher Mercer, ASA, CFA.

Jay Abrams attempts to "test the applicability" of the quantitative marketability discount model in his new book. In so doing, he uses the approximate range of "investment specific risk premiums" used in *Quantifying Marketability Discounts* of 1.5–5.0% and calculates, using an assumed expected rate of return for a non-dividend paying stock, implied marketability discounts over an assumed 2.5-year holding period.

He refers to the Management Planning, Inc. restricted stock study (published as Chapter 12 of *Quantifying Marketability Discounts*) and assumes a "reasonable expected rate of return for stocks of this size" of about 15% on a marketable minority interest basis. The expected rate of return is then used as a proxy for the *expected growth rate in value* factor used in the QMDM. In Abrams' calculations there is, therefore, no differential between the required rate of return of potential investors and the expected growth rate in value.

His analysis then calculates minimum (3.2%) and maximum discounts (10.1%) based on investor specific risk premiums in the range of 1.5–5.0%. Since these discounts are lower than those developed in the appraisals summarized in Chapter 10 of *Quantifying Marketability Discounts* (summarized in Table 7-18 below) and with discounts generally developed by other appraisers, Mr. Abrams suggests that the QMDM is flawed. While he has some other criticisms of *Quantifying Marketability Discounts*, I will attempt to address the threshold question he raises in this reply.

In a recent article revisiting the QMDM (Mercer 2000), I addressed Mr. Abrams' question, along with several others that have been raised since the publication of *Quantifying Marketability Discounts* in 1997. The following is an excerpt from that article explaining why I believe Mr. Abrams' analysis is incorrect. I thank Mr. Abrams for this opportunity to address his criticisms.

Expected Growth and Expected Returns
In many real-life valuation situations there is a discrepancy between the

rate of return (discount rate) implied in the valuation *of an enterprise* and the expected returns attributable to minority investors of that enterprise. There can be many sources of these differentials, several of which were noted above [in the text of the article leading to this point].

In most cases in which the QMDM is applied, there is a differential between the expected growth rate in value assumed and the required holding period return (discount rate) applied. This differential is the primary source of discounting using the QMDM. Several of my colleagues have pointed to this aspect of the QMDM. Their comments range from: (1) Mercer's Bermuda Triangle of disappearing value; to (2) there should be no difference at all; to (3) using the range of specific illiquidity discounts used in Chapter 10 of *Quantifying Marketability Discounts* (roughly 1.5–5.0% or so), when applied to the base equity discount rate (as a proxy for the expected growth rate), should yield much smaller marketability discounts than implied by the QMDM. Note that the essence of this third criticism [which is Mr. Abrams' criticism] is that the *differential* between the expected growth rate in value and the discount rate used would be only 1.5–5.0% or so in this case.

The criticisms seem to reflect a lack of understanding of the conceptual workings of the QMDM and a lack of familiarity with its consistency with existing empirical research. We can rely on market evidence from the various restricted stock studies to support the need for a differential in the expected growth rate and the required holding period return (discount) rate. The implications of two recent restricted stock studies are illustrated next, followed by a similar analysis of actual appraisals using the QMDM.

The Management Planning Study, "Analysis of Restricted Stocks of Public Companies (1980–1995), was published, with permission of Management Planning, Inc. ("MPI"), as Chapter 12 of *Quantifying Marketability Discounts*. The median and average restricted stock discounts in the MPI study were 27.7% and 28.9%, respectively. For this analysis we will round the average to 30%.[74] We can further assume that the typical expected holding period before the restrictions of Rule 144 were lifted was on the order of 2.5 years, or 2 years plus a reasonable period to sell the shares into the market.

A recently published study by Bruce A. Johnson, ASA (Johnson 1999) focusing on transactions in the 1991–1995 timeframe yields a smaller average restricted stock discount of 20%. We will consider the implications of the Johnson study using a shorter two-year holding period (versus the MPI average of a 30% average discount and a 2.5-year holding period). Tables 7-15 and 7-16 use the MPI study and Table 7-17 uses the Johnson study to illustrate the differential between the expected growth of public companies and the discount rate embedded in their average restricted stock pricing.

---

74. The average of the averages of the 10 restricted stock studies discussed in Chapters 2 and 12 of *Quantifying Marketability Discounts* is 31%.

TABLE 7-15[a]

Assume market price of public entity		$1.00
Average management planning discount (rounded)	30.0%	($0.30)
Assumed purchase price of restricted shares		$0.70
Holding period until restricted shares are freely tradable (years)		2.5

[a] Using the MPI study 30% average discount.

Now we can examine a variety of assumptions about the "average" restricted stock transaction in the Management Planning study.[75] The average public price has been indexed to $1.00 per share. As a result, the average restricted stock transaction price, as indexed, is $0.70 per share.

We can estimate the implied returns that were required by investors in restricted stocks based on a variety of assumptions about the expected growth rates in value (or the expected returns of the publicly traded stocks). For purposes of this analysis we have assumed that the consensus expectations for the public stock returns were somewhere in the range of 0% (no expected appreciation) to 30% compounded. The most relevant portion of this range likely begins at about 10% since stocks expected to appreciate less than that were probably not attractive for investments in their restricted shares. See Table 7-16.

Note that the implied holding period returns for the restricted stock transactions, on average, ranged from about 27% per year compounded (with value growing at 10%) to 50% per year compounded (with expected growth of 30%). As noted in Chapter 8 of *Quantifying Marketability Dis-*

TABLE 7-16[a]

Assumed Expected Growth in Value (G)	Expected Future Value in 2.5 Years	Implied Return for Holding Period (R)	Annualized Incremental Return Attributable to Restricted Stock Discount (R − G)
0%	$1.00	15.3%	15.3%
5%	$1.13	21.1%	16.1%
10%	$1.27	26.9%	16.9%
15%	$1.42	32.7%	17.7%
20%	$1.58	38.5%	18.5%
25%	$1.75	44.3%	19.3%
30%	$1.93	50.0%	20.0%

[a] Using the MPI study 30% average discount and a 2.5 year holding period.

---

75. This analysis is for purposes of illustration only. Chapters 2 and 3 of *Quantifying Marketability Discounts* raise significant questions about reliance on averages of widely varying transactions indications for both the restricted stock and the pre-IPO studies.

TABLE 7-17[a]

Assumed Expected Growth in Value (G)	Expected Future Value in 2.0 Years	Implied Return for Holding Period (R)	Annualized Incremental Return Attributable to Restricted Stock Discount (R − G)
0%	$1.00	11.8%	11.8%
5%	$1.10	17.4%	12.4%
10%	$1.21	23.0%	13.0%
15%	$1.32	28.6%	13.6%
20%	$1.44	34.2%	14.2%
25%	$1.56	39.8%	14.8%
30%	$1.69	45.3%	15.3%

[a] Using the Johnson study 20% average discount and a 2 year holding period.

counts, the implied returns are in the range of expected venture capital returns for initial investments (not *average* venture capital returns, which include unsuccessful investments). Interestingly, the *differential* between the implied holding period returns above and the expected growth rate in values used are quite high, ranging from 15.3–20.0%.

This analysis is ex post. We do not know how the actual investment decisions were made in the transactions included in the Management Planning study or any of the restricted stock studies. But, ex post, it is clear that the investors in the "average" restricted stock transactions were, ex ante, either: (1) placing very high discount rates on their restricted stock transactions (ranging from 15–20% in excess of the expected returns of the public companies they were investing in; (2) questioning the consensus expectations for returns; or (3) some combination of 1 and 2.

The Johnson study cited above focused on transactions in the 1991–1995 timeframe when the Rule 144 restriction period was still two years in length. If we assume an index price of $0.80 per share ($1.00 per share freely tradable price less the 20% average discount) and a holding period of two years (and instant liquidity thereafter) and replicate our analysis of Table 7-16 we obtain the following result in Table 7-17.

Even with a shortened assumed holding period and a smaller average restricted stock discount, the implied required returns for the Johnson study are in the range of 23–45% for companies assumed to be growing at 10–30% per year. And the average differential between this calculated discount rate and the expected growth rate of the investment companies is in the range of 13.0–15.3%.

We can make several observations about the seemingly high differentials between the restricted stock investors' required returns and the expected value growth of the typical entity:

- The average discounts appear to be indicative of defensive pricing.
- The discounts would likely ensure at least a market return if the expected growth is not realized.
- Very high implied returns are seen as expected growth increases, suggesting that high growth is viewed with skepticism.

• The implied incremental returns of R over expected G are substantial at any level, suggesting that the base "cost" of 2.0 or 2.5 years of illiquidity is quite expensive.

Given varying assumptions about holding periods longer than 2.5 years and allowing for entities that pay regular dividends, we would expect some variation from the premium range found in appraisals of private company interests.

By way of comparison, we have made the same calculations for the example applications of the QMDM from Chapter 10 of *Quantifying Marketability Discounts.*

As noted in Table 7-18, the range of differences between the average required returns and the expected growth rates in value assumed in the 10 appraisals was from 8.5–21.4%, with an average of about 13%. The table also indicates the range of other assumptions that yielded the concluded marketability discounts in the illustrations. I believe that these results, which came from actual appraisals, are generally consistent with the market evidence gleaned from the restricted stock studies above. Indeed, the premium returns required by the restricted stock investors, on average, exceed those applied in the above examples, suggesting the conclusions yielded conservative (i.e., relatively low) marketability discounts on average. [section omitted]

Conclusion

The QMDM, which is used primarily in valuing (nonmarketable) minority interests of private companies, develops concrete estimates of expected growth in value of the enterprise and reasonable estimates of additional risk premia to account for risks faced by investors in nonmarketable minority interests of companies. In its fully developed form, it incorporates expectations regarding distributions to assist appraisers in reaching logical, supportable, and reasonable conclusions regarding the appropriate level of marketability discounts for specific valuations.

TABLE 7-18

Summary of Results of Applying the QMDM in 10 Example Appraisals

Example	Holding Period	Average Required Holding Period Return (R)	Expected Growth in Value Assumed (G)	(R − G) Difference	Dividend Yield	Concluded Marketability Discount
1	5–8 years	20.0%	10.0%	10.0%	0.0%	45.0%
2	5–9 years	20.5%	4.0%	16.5%	8.8%	25.0%
3	7–15 years	18.5%	7.0%	11.5%	8.0%	15.0%
4	1.5–5 years	19.5%	7.5%	12.0%	0.0%	20.0%
5	5–10 years	20.5%	9.8%	10.7%	3.2%	40.0%
6	5–10 years	18.5%	10.0%	8.5%	2.1%	25.0%
7	5–15 years	19.5%	6.0%	13.5%	0.0%	60.0%
8	10–15 years	19.5%	5.0%	14.5%	10.0%	25.0%
9	10 years	26.4%	5.0%	21.4%	0.6%	80.0%
10	3–5 years	22.5%	6.0%	16.5%	0.0%	35.0%
Averages		20.5%	7.0%	13.5%	3.3%	37.0%
Medians		19.8%	6.5%	12.8%	1.4%	30.0%

Source: Quantifying Marketability Discounts, Chapter 10

The unpublished [and Mr. Abrams'] criticisms of the QMDM outlined above are, I believe, not correct. They do not recognize the critical distinctions that appraisers must draw between their analyses in valuing companies and valuing minority interests in those companies. And they do not consider the implications of the market evidence of required returns provided by the familiar restricted stock studies.

Marketable minority (and controlling interest) appraisals are developed based on the capitalized expected cash flows of businesses, or enterprises. Minority interests in those businesses must be valued based on consideration of the cash flows expected to be available to minority investors. The QMDM allows the business appraiser to bridge the gap between these two cash flow concepts, enterprise and shareholder, to develop reasoned and reasonable valuation conclusions at the non-marketable minority interest level.

My Counterpoints

In responding to Mr. Mercer's rebuttal, it is clear that we will need a specific numerical example to make my criticism clear of the QMDM's inability to forecast restricted stock discounts.

Table 7-19, columns H and I, which we take from Mercer's Chapter 10, Example 1, show his calculation of the required holding period return of a minority stake for a private, closely held C corporation. The corporation is expected to grow in value by 10% each year mainly through an increase in earnings. It is not expected to pay dividends, and the majority owner is expected to retire and sell the business in five to eight years.

In columns K and L we show our own calculation of a restricted stock's required holding period return using Mercer's Example 1 as a guide. Our purpose is to show that the QMDM cannot even come close to forecasting ex ante the ex post discount rates of 27–50% from Table 7-16 that are necessary to explain restricted stock discounts using the QMDM.

We assume a non-dividend-paying stock with an equivalent base equity discount rate as the stock in Mercer's example of 16.7% (row 14). It is in the investment specific risk premiums where the restricted stock differs from the private minority shares. The restricted stock should be much easier to sell than a minority stake in a private closely held C corporation, since the ability to sell at the then-market rate in 2.5 years is guaranteed and public minority shareholder rights are generally better protected they are in private firms. We therefore reduce this premium for illiquidity from the premium in Mercer's example of between 1 and 2% (H18 and I18) to 0% (K18, L18) for the restricted stock. While it is possible that the restricted stocks should have a positive premium for this factor, they are nevertheless far more liquid than all of the private firms in Mercer's examples. If we should increase K18 and L18 to, say, 1%, then we should increase H18 and I18 to at least 2–3%, respectively, or probably higher yet.

Relative to the private C corporation shares, the expected holding period for the restricted stock is short and certain. We therefore reduce the premium for holding period uncertainty from between 0 and 1% (H19 and I19) for Example 1 to 0 (K19, L19) for the restricted shares. As both

QMDM Comparison of Restricted Stock Discount Rate versus Mercer Example 1

	A	B	C	D	E	F	G	Mercer Example 1			Restricted Stock	
								Range of Returns			Range of Returns	
								H	I	J	K	L
7	Components of the Required Holding Period Return							Lower	Higher		Lower	Higher
8	**Base equity discount rate (adjusted capital asset pricing model)**											
9	Current yield-to-maturity composite long term treasuries							6.7%	6.7%		6.7%	6.7%
10	+ Adjusted Ibbotson large stock premium						6.5%					
11	× applicable beta statistic						× 1					
12	= Beta adjusted large stock premium							6.5%	6.5%		6.5%	6.5%
13	+ Adjusted Ibbotson small stock premium							3.5%	3.5%		3.5%	3.5%
14	**Base equity discount rate**							16.7%	16.7%		16.7%	16.7%
17	**Investment Specific Risk Premiums**											
18	General illiquidity of the investment [1]							1.0%	2.0%		0.0%	0.0%
19	Uncertainties related to length of expected holding period [2]							0.0%	1.0%		0.0%	0.0%
20	Lack of expected interim cash flows [3]							0.5%	1.0%		0.5%	1.0%
21	Small shareholder base [4]							0.0%	1.0%		0.0%	0.0%
22	**Range of specific risk premiums for the investment**							1.5%	5.0%		0.5%	1.0%
24	**Initial range of required returns**							18.2%	21.7%		17.2%	17.7%
26	**Concluded range of required holding period returns (rounded)**							18.0%	22.0%		17.0%	18.0%

[1] The restricted stock should be much easier to sell than a minority stake in a private closely held C corporation, since public minority shareholder rights are generally better protected. While it is possible that the restricted stocks should have a positive premium for this factor, they are nevertheless far more liquid than all of the private firms in Mercer's examples. If we should increase K18 and L18 to 1%, then we should increase H18 and I18 to at least 2% to 3% or probably higher yet.

[2] Relative to the private shares, the expected holding period for the restricted stock is short and certain.

[3] We assume a non dividend paying restricted stock. The example also concerned a non dividend paying C corporation. We therefore assign the same risk premium for this factor.

[4] The restricted stock shares are shares of public corporations, which in general have large shareholder bases.

investments are expected to pay no dividends, there is no difference in the premium for lack of expected interim cash flows (Row 20), although the latter experiences that lack of dividends for a far shorter and much more certain time period, which could well justify a lower premium than the former.

At this point I can digress to pose my objections to the first two factors. *General illiquidity of the investment* is a very fuzzy term. It can mean almost anything. There is no empirical measure of it. Therefore, it can be almost anything that one wants it to be—which I admit has its advantages in practical application, but it's not good science. It is also unclear where general illiquidity stops and uncertainties in the holding period begin. Do they overlap? How does one prevent him- or herself from double-counting them? That is a problem with loosely-defined terms.

Returning to the main train of thought, the private, closely held C corporation would have a much smaller shareholder base than the restricted stock corporations. We therefore reduce the premium for a small shareholder base from between 0 and 1% (H21 and I21) for Example 1 to 0 (K21, L21) for the restricted stock. The total specific risk premium for the restricted stock comes to 0.5% (K22) to 1.0% (L22) versus the 1.5% (H22) to 5% (I22) for the private shares. After adding the base equity discount rates and rounding, we arrive at a concluded range of required holding period returns of 18–22% and 17–18% (Row 26) for Mercer's Example 1 and the restricted stock, respectively.

Next we need to determine the expected growth rate in value of the unrestricted marketable minority shares. Since there are no dividends, the expected growth rate must be equal to the discount rate—by definition.[76] In this example the equity discount rate of the unrestricted marketable shares or the "base equity discount rate" is 16.7%.

Let's now calculate the QMDM discount on the restricted stock with the following assumptions:

1. A midrange (of K26 and L26) required holding period return of 17.5%.
2. The 2.5-year average holding period.
3. The growth rate in value of 16.7%.

The calculation is as follows:

$$\text{DLOM} = 1 - (\text{FV} \times \text{PVF}) = 1 - \left(1.167^{2.5} \times \frac{1}{1.175^{2.5}} \right) = 1.7\%$$

Assuming the correct discount is 30%, the QMDM is almost 95% too low!

Mercer's Response

After reviewing Mr. Abrams' response to my rebuttal of his criticism of the QMDM, it is apparent that he and I continue to disagree over how the QMDM is applied in practice. The average marketability discounts in the 10 examples cited in my rebuttal of his criticism was 37%, and the median discount was 30%, not 1.7%. Mr. Abrams' mistake is in assuming that the discount rate embedded in the pricing of a publicly traded stock is the required return of restricted stock investors. The fact that the average restricted stock discount is 30% or so indicates that investors have extracted a significant premium in return relative to the expected returns of the counterpart publicly traded securities.

What may be true "by definition" in a perpetuity calculation may well not be true for shorter holding periods. The QMDM deals, not with perpetuity calculations, but with investor assessments of expected cash flows over finite time horizons. And it makes explicit the assumptions made about the relationship between the expected growth in value of investments and the required returns of investors in those investments. I maintain that the model does indeed provide an excellent tool for estimating marketability discounts (from an estimated freely traded value) for minority interests in closely held companies.

---

76. This is the discount rate applicable to marketable minority shares, not the higher discount rate applicable to illiquid shares, i.e., the required holding period return.

Conclusion

We have reviewed the professional and some of the academic literature dealing with control premiums and DLOM. My opinion is that with our current information set, we should use control premiums in the 21–28% range. We developed this as being three to four times the value of the voting rights premium adjusted to U.S. laws and for liquidity differences between voting and nonvoting stock. This measure is consistent with the median going private premium of 24.1% (Table 7-1, E21), although it is preferable to make a clean separation of expected performance improvements, which increase the "top line," i.e., cash flows, versus the pure value of control, which is represented by a reduction in the discount rate.

We reviewed three quantitative models of DLOM: Mercer's, Kasper's, and Abrams'. The QMDM was unable to provide any meaningful restricted stock discounts for the Management Planning, Inc. data, as discounting modest risk premiums for two to three years provides little variation in discount. Abrams' non-company-specific Black-Scholes options pricing model performed worse at explaining restricted stock discounts than the mean, while using BSOPM with firm-specific calculations of standard deviations was superior to the mean. While that makes Black–Scholes a viable candidate for restricted stock studies, it is not a possible model for valuing the delay-to-sale component of DLOM, and we must use the regression of the MPI data.

We quantified component #2, monopsony power to the buyer, as 9%, according to Schwert's findings of a 12.2% greater premium in takeovers when there are multiple buyers than when there is only one buyer.

Finally, we quantified transactions costs separately for the buyer and the seller. The premise of fair market value is such that we ask, "What would a hypothetical buyer be willing to pay for this interest," which means that we are presuming a first sale immediately. Buyers care about their own transactions costs, but they do not care about sellers' transactions cost on the immediate transaction. However, buyers do care that in 10 years or so they become the sellers. They therefore care about all subsequent sellers' (and buyers') transactions costs. We presented two discount formulas—equations (7-9) and (7-9a), which are appropriate for seller and buyer, respectively, to translate the pure discount that applies to each transaction into a discount based on the present value of the infinite continuum of periodic transactions.

In Table 7-14 we applied our DLOM model to a control interest in a hypothetical private company. The result was a DLOM of 23.1%, which is a reasonable result.

Of course, the economic components model is merely a model. It is certainly imperfect, and it must be used with common sense. It is possible to obtain strange or nonsensical results, and if the appraiser is asleep at the wheel, he or she may not realize it. There is plenty of room for additional research to improve our modeling and results. Nevertheless, in my opinion this is the most realistic and comprehensive model to date for calculating DLOM.

BIBLIOGRAPHY

Abrams, Jay B. 1994a. "Discount for Lack of Marketability: A Theoretical Model." *Business Valuation Review* (September): 132–39.

———. 1994b. "A Breakthrough in Calculating Reliable Discount Rates." *Valuation* (August): 8–24.

Amihud, Y., and H. Mendelson. 1991. "Liquidity, Asset Prices, and Financial Policy." *Financial Analysts Journal* (November–December): 56–66.

Barca, F. 1995. "On Corporate Governance in Italy: Issues, Facts, and Agency." Mimeo, Bank of Italy.

Bergstrom, C., and K. Rydqvist. 1990. "Ownership of Equity in Dual-Class Firms." *Journal of Banking and Finance* 14:237–53.

Berkovitch, E., and M. P. Narayanan. 1993. "Motives for Takeovers: An Empirical Investigation. *Journal of Financial and Quantitative Analysis* 28:347–62.

Bolotsky, Michael J. 1991. "Adjustments for Differences in Ownership Rights, Liquidity, Information Access, and Information Reliability: An Assessment of 'Prevailing Wisdom' versus the 'Nath Hypothesis'." *Business Valuation Review* (September): 94–110.

———. 1995. "Is the 'Levels of Value' Concept Still Viable? Bolotsky's Response." *Business Valuation Education Sessions from the American Society of Appraisers Convention,* June, Denver, Col. 21–34.

Bradley, M., A. Desai, and E. H. Kim. 1988. "Synergistic Gains from Corporate Acquisitions and Their Division between the Stockholders of Target and Acquiring Firms." *Journal of Financial Economics* 39:3–40.

Chaffe, David B. H. 1993. "Option Pricing as a Proxy for Discount for Lack of Marketability in Private Company Valuations—A Working Paper." *Business Valuation Review* (December): 182–188.

Eckbo, B. E. 1983. "Horizontal Mergers, Collusion, and Stockholder Wealth." *Journal of Financial Economics* 11:241–74.

———. 1985. "Mergers and the Market Concentration Doctrine: Evidence from the Capital Market." *Journal of Business* 58:325–49.

———. 1992. "Mergers and the Value of Antitrust Deterrence." *Journal of Finance* 47:1005–30.

Einhorn, Hillel J., and Robin M. Hogarth. 1987. "Decision Making under Ambiguity." In *Rational Choice*, ed. Robin M. Hogarth and Melvin W. Reder. Chicago: University of Chicago Press, pp. 41–66.

Ellsberg, D. 1961. "Risk, Ambiguity, and the Savage Axioms." *Quarterly Journal of Economics* 75:643–69.

Franks, J. R., and Julian R. Harris. 1989. "Shareholder Wealth Effects of Corporate Takeovers: The U.K. Experience 1955–1985." *Journal of Financial Economics* 23:225–49.

Glass, Carla, and Mary M. McCarter. 1995. "The Foundations for Minority and Control Position Adjustments." Paper presented at American Society of Appraisers' 14th Annual Advanced Business Valuation Conference., November 3, Boston, Mass.

Grabowski, Roger, and David King. 1999. "New Evidence on Size Effects and Rates of Return." *Business Valuation Review* (September): 112–30.

Harris, Ellie G. 1994. "Why One Firm Is the Target and the Other the Bidder in Single-Bidder, Synergistic Takeovers." *Journal of Business* 67:263–80.

Horner, M. R. 1988. "The Value of the corporate voting right: Evidence from Switzerland." *Journal of Banking and Finance* 12:69–83.

Ibbotson Associates. 1999. *Stocks, Bonds, Bills, and Inflation: 1999 Yearbook—Valuation Edition.* Chicago: The Associates, p. 119.

Jankowske, Wayne C. 1991. "Valuing Minority Interests in Relation to Guideline Firms," *Business Valuation Review* (December 1991): 139–43.

———. 1995. "Frameworks for Analysis of Control Premiums." *Business Valuation Review* (March): 3–10.

Johnson, Bruce A. 1999. "Quantitative Support for Discounts for Lack of Marketability." *Business Valuation Review* (December 1999): 152–55.

Kasper, Larry, J. 1997. *Business Valuations: Advanced Topics.* Westport, Conn.: Quorum Books.

Lang, L. H. P., R. Stulz, R. A. Walkling. 1991. "A Test of the Free Cash Flow Hypothesis: The Case of Bidder Returns." *Journal of Financial Economics* 29:315–36.

Lease, Ronald C., John J. McConnell, and Wayne H. Mikkelson. 1983. "The Market Value of Control in Publicly-Traded Corporations." *Journal of Financial Economics* 11.

Lerch, Mary Ann. 1991. "Quantitative Measures of Minority Interest Discounts." *Business Valuation Review* (March): 14–20.

———. 1997. "Yet Another Discount for Lack of Marketability Study." *Business Valuation Review* (June): 70–106.

Levy, H. 1982. "Economic Evaluation of Voting Power of Common Stock." *Journal of Finance* 38:79–93.

Maher, Maria, and Thomas Andersson. 1999. "Corporate Governance: Effects on Firm Performance and Economic Growth." Organization for Economic Co-operation and Development. Downloadable from www.OECD.org.

Maquieira, Carlos P., William L. Megginson, and Lance Nail. 1998. "Wealth Creation versus Wealth Redistributions in Pure Stock-for-Stock Mergers." *Journal of Financial Economics* 48:3–33.

Megginson, William L. 1990. "Restricted Voting Stock, Acquisition Premiums, and the Market Value of Corporate Control." *The Financial Review* 25(May): 175–98.

Menyah, Kojo, and Krishna Paudyal. 1996. "The Determinants and Dynamics of Bid–Ask Spreads on the London Stock Exchange." *Journal of Financial Research* 19:377–94.

Mercer, Z. Christopher. 1990. "Do Public Company (Minority) Transactions Yield Controlling Interest or Minority Interest Pricing Data?" *Business Valuation Review* (December): 123–26.

———. 1994. "Should 'Marketability Discounts' Be Applied to Controlling Interests of Private Companies?" *Business Valuation Review* (June): 55–65.

———. *Quantifying Marketability Discounts: Developing and Supporting Marketability Discounts in the Appraisal of Closely Held Business Interests*. Memphis, Tenn.: Peabody.

———. 1998. *The 1999 Journal of Business Valuation: Proceedings of the Fourth Joint Business Valuation Conference of The Canadian Institute of Chartered Business Valuators and the American Society of Appraisers*, September 24 and 25, Montreal, Que., Canada.

———. 1999. "Theoretical Determinants of Value in the Context of 'Levels of Value.'" Presentation to the American Society of Appraisers, August 23. Memphis: Tenn.: Mercer Capital. [See especially slides 17–28 and 46a–46d.]

———. 2000. "Revisiting, the Quantitative Marketability Discount Model." *Valuation Strategies* (March–April).

Much, Paul J., and Timothy J. Fagan. 2000. "The Value of Voting Rights." In *Financial Valuation: Business and Business Interests*, ed. James H. Zukin. 2000 Update with Cumulative Index prepared by Richard C. May and Loren B. Garruto. New York: Warren, Gorham & Lamont/RIA Group, pp. U9B-1–U9B-7.

Nath, Eric. 1990. Control Premiums and Minority Interest Discounts in Private Companies." *Business Valuation Review* (June): 39–46.

———. 1994. "A Tale of Two Markets." *Business Valuation Review* (September): 107–12.

———. 1997. "How Public Guideline Companies Represent Control Value for a Private Company." *Business Valuation Review* (December): 167–71.

Phillips, John R., and Neill Freeman. 1995. "Do Privately-Held Controlling Interests Sell for Less?" *Business Valuation Review* (September): 102–13.

Pratt, Shannon P. 1998. *Cost of Capital: Estimations and Applications*. New York: John Wiley & Sons.

Pratt, Shannon P., Robert F. Reilly, and Robert P. Schweihs. 1996. *Valuing a Business: The Analysis and Appraisal of Closely Held Companies*, 3d ed. New York: McGraw-Hill.

Roach, George P. 1998. "Control Premiums and Strategic Mergers." *Business Valuation Review* (December): 42–49.

Roll, Richard. 1986. "The Hubris Hypothesis of Corporate Takeovers." *Journal of Business* 59:197–216.

Rydqvst, K. 1987. "Empirical Investigation of the Voting Premium." Northwestern University. Working Paper No. 35.

Schilt, James H. 1996. "Discounts for Minority Interests." *Business Valuation Review* (December): 161.

Schwert, G. William. 1996. "Markup Pricing in Mergers and Acquisitions." *Journal of Financial Economics* 41:153–92.

Simpson, David W. 1991. "Minority Interest and Marketability Discounts: A Perspective." *Business Valuation Review* (March): 7–13.

Stern, Joel. 1993. "A Discussion of Mergers and Acquisitions." *Midland Corporate Finance Journal* (Summer) [cited in Jankowske 1995].

Stillman, R. 1983. "Examining Antitrust Policy Towards Horizontal Mergers." *Journal of Financial Economics* 11:225–40.

Stoll, H. R., 1978a. "The Supply of Dealer Services in Securities Markets." *Journal of Finance* 33:1133–51.

———. 1978b. "The Pricing of Security Dealer Services: An Empirical Study of NASDAQ Stocks." *Journal of Finance* 33:1153–72.

Tversky, Amos, and Daniel Kahneman. 1987. "Rational Choice and the Framing of Decisions." In *Rational Choice*, ed. Robin M. Hogarth and Melvin W. Reder. Chicago: University of Chicago Press, pp. 67–94.

Vander Linder, Eric. 1998. "Cost of Capital Derived from Ibbotson Data Equals Minority Value?" *Business Valuation Review* (December): 123–27.

Zingales, L. 1994. "The Value of the Voting Right: A Study of the Milan Stock Exchange. *Review of Financial Studies* 7:125–48.

Zukin, James H., ed. 1998. *Financial Valuation: Businesses and Business Interests*. 1998 Update with Cumulative Index prepared by Martin D. Hanan and Ray A. Sheeler. New York: Warren, Gorham & Lamont/RIA Group, p. U9A-12.

MATHEMATICAL APPENDIX
DEVELOPING THE DISCOUNT FORMULAS

Initially we assume the current business owner will operate the business for 10 years, sell it, and pay transaction costs of z.[77] The next owner will run the business another 10 years, sell it, and pay transaction costs. We assume this pattern occurs *ad infinitum*. Of course, there will be variations from the sale every 10 years—some will sell after 1 year, others after 30 years. In the meantime, in the absence of prior knowledge, we assume every 10 years to be a reasonable estimate of the average of what will occur.

NPV of Cash Flows with Periodic Transaction Costs Removed

The net present value (NPV) of cash flows to the existing business owner with periodic transaction costs removed is the full amount of the first 10 years' cash flows, plus $(1 - z)$ times the next 10 years' cash flows, where z is the periodic transaction cost, plus $(1 - z)^2$ times the next 10 years' cash flows, etc. We will denote the NPV net of transaction costs, i.e., with transaction costs removed from the stream of cash flows, as NPV_{TC}.

$$
\begin{aligned}
\text{NPV}_{\text{TC}} = &\left[\frac{1}{(1 + r)^{0.5}} + \frac{(1 + g)}{(1 + r)^{1.5}} + \cdots + \frac{(1 + g)^9}{(1 + r)^{9.5}} \right] \\
&+ (1 - z) \left[\frac{(1 + g)^{10}}{(1 + r)^{10.5}} + \cdots + \frac{(1 + g)^{19}}{(1 + r)^{19.5}} \right] \\
&+ (1 - z)^2 \left[\frac{(1 + g)^{20}}{(1 + r)^{20.5}} + \cdots + \frac{(1 + g)^{29}}{(1 + r)^{29.5}} \right] + \cdots \quad \text{(A7-1)}
\end{aligned}
$$

Multiplying each term in equation (A7-1) by $(1 + g)/(1 + r)$, we get:

---

77. As explained in the body of the chapter, z is an incremental transaction cost. For example, when we value a small fractional ownership in a privately owned business, often our preliminary value is on a marketable minority basis. In this case z would be the difference in transaction cost (expressed as a percentage) between selling a private business interest and selling publicly traded stock through a stockbroker.

$$\frac{1+g}{1+r}\,\mathrm{NPV_{TC}} = \left[\frac{1+g}{(1+r)^{1.5}} + \cdots + \frac{(1+g)^{10}}{(1+r)^{10.5}}\right]$$

$$+ (1-z)\left[\frac{(1+g)^{11}}{(1+r)^{11.5}} + \cdots + \frac{(1+g)^{20}}{(1+r)^{20.5}}\right]$$

$$+ (1-z)^2\left[\frac{(1+g)^{21}}{(1+r)^{21.5}} + \cdots + \frac{(1+g)^{20}}{(1+r)^{30.5}}\right]$$

$$+ \cdots \tag{A7-2}$$

Subtracting equation (A7-2) from equation (A7-1), we get:

$$\left[1 - \frac{1+g}{1+r}\right]\mathrm{NPV} = \left[\frac{1}{(1+r)^{0.5}} - \frac{(1+g)^{10}}{(1+r)^{10.5}}\right]$$

$$+ (1-z)\left[\frac{(1+g)^{10}}{(1+r)^{10.5}} - \frac{(1+g)^{20}}{(1+r)^{20.5}}\right]$$

$$+ (1-z)^2\left[\frac{(1+g)^{20}}{(1+r)^{20.5}} - \frac{(1+g)^{30}}{(1+r)^{30.5}}\right] \tag{A7-3}$$

Note that all terms in each sequence drop out except for the first terms in equation (A7-1) and the last terms in equation (A7-2). In equation (A7-4), we collect the positive terms from equation (A7-3) in the first set of square brackets and the negative terms from equation (A7-3) in the second one. Additionally, the left-hand side of equation (A7-3) reduces to $(r+g)/(1+r)\mathrm{NPV_{TC}}$. Multiplying through by $(1+r)/(r-g)$, we get:

$$\mathrm{NPV_{TC}} = \frac{1+r}{r-g}$$

$$\left\{\left[\frac{1}{(1+r)^{0.5}} + (1-z)\frac{(1+g)^{10}}{(1+r)^{10.5}} + (1-z)^2\frac{(1+g)^{20}}{(1+r)^{20.5}} + \cdots\right]\right.$$

$$\left. - \left[\frac{(1+g)^{10}}{(1+r)^{10.5}} + (1-z)\frac{(1+g)^{20}}{(1-r)^{20.5}} + (1-z)^2\frac{(1+g)^{30}}{(1+r)^{30.5}} + \cdots\right]\right\} \tag{A7-4}$$

Next we will manipulate the right-hand side of the equation only. We divide the term $(1+r)/(r+g)$ by $\sqrt{1+r}$, which leaves that term as $(\sqrt{1+r})/(r-g)$ and we multiply all terms inside the brackets by $\sqrt{1+r}$. The latter action has the effect of reducing the exponents in the denominators by 0.5 years. Thus, we get:

$$\mathrm{NPV_{TC}} = \frac{\sqrt{1+r}}{r-g}$$

$$\left\{\left[1 + (1-z)\left(\frac{1+g}{1+r}\right)^{10} + (1-z)^2\left(\frac{1+g}{1+r}\right)^{20} + \cdots\right]\right.$$

$$\left. - \left[\left(\frac{1+g}{1+r}\right)^{10} + (1-z)\left(\frac{1+g}{1+r}\right)^{20} + (1-z)^2\left(\frac{1+g}{1+r}\right)^{30} + \cdots\right]\right\} \tag{A7-5}$$

Recognizing that each term in brackets is an infinite geometric sequence, this solves to:

$$\text{NPV}_{\text{TC}} = \frac{\sqrt{1 + r}}{r - g}$$

$$\left[\frac{1}{1 - \dfrac{(1 - z)(1 + g)^{10}}{(1 + r)^{10}}} - \frac{\left(\dfrac{1 + g}{1 + r}\right)^{10}}{1 - \dfrac{(1 - z)(1 + g)^{10}}{(1 + r)^{10}}} \right] \qquad \text{(A7-6)}$$

Since the denominators are identical, we can combine both terms in the brackets into a single term by adding the numerators.

$$\text{NPV}_{\text{TC}} = \frac{\sqrt{1 + r}}{r - g} \left[\frac{1 - \left(\dfrac{1 + g}{1 + r}\right)^{10}}{1 - (1 - z)\left(\dfrac{1 + g}{1 + r}\right)^{10}} \right] \qquad \text{(A7-7)}$$

Letting $x = (1 + g)/(1 + r)$, this simplifies to:

$$\text{NPV}_{\text{TC}} = \frac{\sqrt{1 + r}}{r - g} \left\{ \frac{1 - x^{10}}{1 - (1 - z)x^{10}} \right\} \qquad \text{(A7-8)}$$

The Discount Formula

D, the component of the discount for lack of marketability that measures the periodic transaction costs, is one minus the ratio of the NPV of the cash flows net of transaction costs (NPV_{TC}) to the NPV without removing transaction costs (NPV). Using a midyear Gordon model formula of $(\sqrt{1 + r})/(r - g)$ as the NPV, we come to:

$$D = 1 - \frac{\text{NPV}_{\text{TC}}}{\text{NPV}} = 1 - \frac{\dfrac{\sqrt{1 + r}}{r - g} \left\{ \dfrac{1 - x^{10}}{1 - (1 - z)x^{10}} \right\}}{\dfrac{\sqrt{1 + r}}{r - g}} \qquad \text{(A7-9)}$$

The term $(\sqrt{1 + r})/(r - g)$ cancels out, and the expression simplifies to:

$$D = 1 - \frac{1 - x^{10}}{1 - (1 - z)x^{10}}, \text{ where } x = \frac{1 + g}{1 + r} \text{ and } g < r, \Rightarrow 0 < x < 1 \qquad \text{(A7-10)}$$

Equation (A7-10) is the formula for the discount assuming a sale every 10 years. Instead of assuming a business sale every 10 years, now we let the average years between sale be a random variable, j, which leads to the generalized equation in equation (A7-11):

$$D = 1 - \frac{1 - x^j}{1 - (1 - z)x^j}$$

generalized discount formula–sellers' transaction costs   (A7-11)

In determining fair market value, we ask how much would a rational buyer pay for (and for how much would a rational seller sell) a business interest. That presumes a hypothetical sale at time zero. Equation (A7-11) is the formula appropriate for quantifying sellers' transaction costs, because the buyer does not care about the seller's costs, which means he or she will not raise the price in order to cover the seller. However, the buyer does care that 10 years down the road, he or she will be a seller, not a buyer, and the new buyer will reduce the price to cover his or her transaction costs, and so on *ad infinitum*. Thus, we want to quantify the discounts due to transaction costs for the continuum of sellers beginning with the second sale, i.e., in year j. Equation (A7-11) accomplishes that.

Using an end-of-year Gordon model assumption instead of midyear cash flows leads to the identical equation, i.e., (A7-11) holds for both.

Buyer Discounts Begin with the First Transaction

An important variation of equation (A7-11) is to consider what happens if the first relevant transaction cost takes place at time zero instead of $t = j$, which is appropriate for quantifying the discount component due to buyers' transaction costs. With this assumption, we would modify the above analysis by inserting a $(1 - z)$ in front of the first series of bracketed terms in equation (A7-1) and increasing the exponent of all the other $(1 - z)$ terms by one. All the other equations are identical, with the $(1 - z)$ term added. Thus, the buyers' equivalent formula of equation (A7-8) is:

$$\text{NPV}_{\text{TC}} = (1 - z) \frac{\sqrt{1 + r}}{r - g} \left\{ \frac{1 - x^{10}}{1 - (1 - z)x^{10}} \right\}$$

NPV with buyers' transaction costs removed   (A7-8a)

Obviously, equation (A7-8a) is lower than equation (A7-8), because the first relevant cost occurs 10 years earlier. The generalized discount formula equivalent of equation (A7-11) for the buyer scenario is:

$$D = 1 - \frac{(1 - z)(1 - x^j)}{1 - (1 - z)x^j}$$

generalized discount, formula—buyers' transactions costs

(A7-11a)

We demonstrate the accuracy of equations (A7-11) and (A7-11a), which are excerpted from here and renumbered in the chapter as equations (7-9) and (7-9a), in Tables 7-12 and 7-13 in the body of the chapter.

NPV of Cash Flows with Finite Transactions Costs Removed[78]

The previous formulas for calculating the present value of the discount for buyers' and sellers' transactions costs are appropriate for business valuations. However, for calculating that component of DLOM for limited life entities such as limited partnerships whose document specifies a termination date, the formulas are inexact, although they are often good approximations. In this section we develop the formulas for components #3A and #3B of DLOM for limited life entities.[79] This section is very mathematical and will have practical significance for most readers only when

---

78. This section is written by R. K. Hiatt.
79. Even in limited partnerships, it is necessary to question whether the LP is likely to renew, i.e., extend its life. If so, then the perpetuity formulas (A7-11) and (A7-11a) may be appropriate.

the life of the entity is short (under 30 years) and the growth rate is close to the discount rate. Some readers may want to skip this section, perhaps noting the final equations, (A7-23) and (A7-24). Consider this section as reference material.

Let's assume a fractional interest in an entity, such as a limited partnership, with a life of 25 years that sells for every $j = 10$ years. Thus, after the initial hypothetical sale, there will be $s = 2$ sales[80] of the fractional interest before dissolution of the entity. Let's define n as the number of years to the last sale before dissolution. We begin by repeating equations (A7-1) and (A7-2) as (A7-12) and (A7-13), with the difference that the last incremental transaction cost occurs at $n = 20$ years instead of going on perpetually.

$$\text{NPV}_{\text{TC}} = \left[\frac{1}{(1+r)^{0.5}} + \frac{(1+g)}{(1+r)^{1.5}} + \cdots + \frac{(1+g)^9}{(1+r)^{9.5}} \right]$$
$$+ (1-z) \left[\frac{(1+g)^{10}}{(1+r)^{10.5}} + \cdots + \frac{(1+g)^{19}}{(1+r)^{19.5}} \right]$$
$$+ (1-z)^2 \left[\frac{(1+g)^{20}}{(1+r)^{20.5}} + \cdots \right] \tag{A7-12}$$

$$\frac{1+g}{1+r} \text{NPV}_{\text{TC}} = \left[\frac{1+g}{(1+r)^{1.5}} + \cdots + \frac{(1+g)^{10}}{(1+r)^{10.5}} \right]$$
$$+ (1-z) \left[\frac{(1+g)^{11}}{(1+r)^{11.5}} + \cdots + \frac{(1+g)^{20}}{(1+r)^{20.5}} \right]$$
$$+ (1-z)^2 \left[\frac{(1+g)^{21}}{(1+r)^{21.5}} + \cdots \right] \tag{A7-13}$$

Subtracting equation (A7-13) from equation (A7-12), we get:

$$\left[1 - \frac{1+g}{1+r} \right] \text{NPV}_{\text{TC}} = \left[\frac{1}{(1+r)^{0.5}} - \frac{(1+g)^{10}}{(1+r)^{10.5}} \right]$$
$$+ (1-z) \left[\frac{(1+g)^{10}}{(1+r)^{10.5}} - \frac{(1+g)^{20}}{(1+r)^{20.5}} \right]$$
$$+ (1-z)^2 \left[\frac{(1+g)^{20}}{(1+r)^{20.5}} \right] \tag{A7-14}$$

Note that the final term "should have" a subtraction of $(1+g)^\infty / (1+r)^{\infty+0.5}$, but that equals zero for $g < r$. Therefore, we leave that term out. Again, the first term of the equation reduces to $(r-g)/(1+r)$. We then multiply both sides by its inverse:

$$\text{NPV}_{\text{TC}} = \frac{1+r}{r-g} \left\{ \left[\frac{1}{(1+r)^{0.5}} - \frac{(1+g)^{10}}{(1+r)^{10.5}} \right] \right.$$
$$+ (1-z) \left[\frac{(1+g)^{10}}{(1+r)^{10.5}} - \frac{(1+g)^{20}}{(1+r)^{20.5}} \right]$$
$$\left. + (1-z)^2 \left[\frac{(1+g)^{20}}{(1+r)^{20.5}} \right] \right\} \tag{A7-15}$$

---

80. It is important not to include the initial hypothetical sale in the computation of s.

PART 3   Adjusting for Control and Marketability

As before, we divide the first term on the right-hand side of the equation by $\sqrt{1 + r}$ and multiply all terms inside the brackets by the same. This has the same effect as reducing the exponents in the denominators by 0.5 years.

$$NPV_{TC} = \frac{\sqrt{1 + r}}{r - g} \left\{ \left[1 - \left(\frac{1 + g}{1 + r} \right)^{10} \right] \right.$$
$$+ (1 - z) \left[\left(\frac{1 + g}{1 + r} \right)^{10} - \left(\frac{1 + g}{1 + r} \right)^{20} \right]$$
$$\left. + (1 - z)^2 \left[\left(\frac{1 + g}{1 + r} \right)^{20} \right] \right\} \tag{A7-16}$$

Letting $y = 1 - z$ and $x = (1 + g)/(1 + r)$, equation (A7-16) becomes:

$$NPV_{TC} = \frac{\sqrt{1 + r}}{r - g} [(1 - x^{10}) + y(x^{10} - x^{20}) + y^2 x^{20}] \tag{A7-17}$$

$$NPV_{TC} = \frac{\sqrt{1 + r}}{r - g} [(1 + yx^{10} + y^2 x^{20}) - (x^{10} + yx^{20})] \tag{A7-18}$$

Within the square brackets in equation (A7-18), there are two sets of terms set off in parentheses. Each of them is a finite geometric sequence. The first sequence solves to

$$\frac{1 - y^3 x^{30}}{1 - yx^{10}}$$

and the second sequence solves to

$$\frac{x^{10} - y^2 x^{30}}{1 - yx^{10}}$$

They both have the same denominator, so we can combine them. Thus, equation (A7-18) simplifies to:

$$NPV_{TC} = \frac{\sqrt{1 + r}}{r - g} \left[\frac{1 - x^{10} + y^2 x^{30} - y^3 x^{30}}{1 - yx^{10}} \right] \tag{A7-19}$$

Note that if we eliminate the two right-hand terms in the square brackets in the numerator, equation (A7-10) reduces to equation (A7-8). We can now factor the two right-hand terms and simplify to:

$$NPV_{TC} = \frac{\sqrt{1 + r}}{r - g} \left[\frac{1 - x^{10} + y^2 x^{30}(1 - y)}{1 - yx^{10}} \right]$$
$$= \frac{\sqrt{1 + r}}{r - g} \left[\frac{1 - x^{10} + zy^2 x^{30}}{1 - yx^{10}} \right]$$
$$= \frac{\sqrt{1 + r}}{r - g} \left[\frac{1 - x^{10} + z(1 - z)^2 x^{30}}{1 - (1 - z)x^{10}} \right] \tag{A7-20}$$

Since $j = 10$, $s = 2$, $n = 20$, and $n + j = 30$, we can now generalize this equation to:

$$NPV_{TC} = \frac{\sqrt{1 + r}}{r - g} \left[\frac{1 - x^j + z(1 - z)^s x^{n+j}}{1 - (1 - z)x^j} \right] \tag{A7-21}$$

As before, the discount component is $D = 1 - \text{NPV}_{\text{TC}}/\text{NPV}$. This comes to:

$$D = 1 - \frac{\dfrac{\sqrt{1 + r}}{r - g} \left[\dfrac{1 - x^j + z(1 - z)^s x^{n+j}}{1 - (1 - z)x^j} \right]}{\dfrac{\sqrt{1 + r}}{r - g}} \qquad \text{(A7-22)}$$

Canceling terms, this simplifies to:

$$D = 1 - \frac{1 - x^j + z(1 - z)^s x^{n+j}}{1 - (1 - z)x^j} \qquad \text{(A7-23)}$$

discount component—sellers' costs—finite life

Note that as the life of the entity (or the interest in the entity) that we are valuing goes to infinity, $n \to \infty$, so $x^{n+j} \to 0$ and (A7-23) reduces to equation (A7-11).

The equivalent expression for buyers' costs is:

$$D = 1 - \frac{(1 - z)[1 - x^j + z(1 - z)^s x^{n+j}]}{1 - (1 - z)x^j}$$

discount component—buyers' costs—finite life   (A7-24)

Summary of Mathematical Analysis in Remainder of Appendix

The remainder of the appendix is devoted to calculating partial derivatives necessary to evaluate the behavior of the discount formula (A7-11). The partial derivatives of D with respect to its underlying independent variables, g, r, z, and j, give us the slope of the discount as a function of each variable. The purpose in doing so is to see how D behaves as the independent variables change.

It turns out that D is a monotonic function with respect to each of its independent variables. That is analytically convenient, as it means that an increase in any one of independent variables always affects D in the same direction. For example, if D is monotonically increasing in g, that means that an increase in g will always lead to an increase in D, and a decrease in g leads to a decrease in D. If D is monotonically increasing, there is no value of g such that an increase in g leads either to no change in D or a decrease in D.

The results that we develop in the remainder of the appendix are that the discount, D, is monotonically increasing with g with z and decreasing with r and j. The practical reader will probably want to stop here.

MATHEMATICAL ANALYSIS OF THE DISCOUNT— CALCULATING PARTIAL DERIVATIVES

We can compute an alternative form of equation (A7-11) by multiplying the numerator by -1 and changing the minus sign before the fraction to a plus sign. This will ease the computations of the partial derivatives of the expression.

$$D = 1 + \frac{x^j - 1}{1 - (1 - z)x^j} \qquad \text{(A7-25)}$$

$$\frac{\partial D}{\partial x} = \frac{\{[1 - (1 - z)x^j]jx^{j-1}\} - \{(x^j - 1)[-(1 - z)jx^{j-1}]\}}{[1 - (1 - z)x^j]^2} \qquad \text{(A7-26)}$$

Factoring out jx^{j-1}, we get:

$$\frac{\partial D}{\partial x} = \frac{jx^{j-1}\{[1 - (1 - z)x^j] + (x^j - 1)(1 - z)\}}{[1 - (1 - z)x^j]^2} \qquad \text{(A7-27)}$$

$$\frac{\partial D}{\partial x} = \frac{jx^{j-1}[1 - (1 - z)x^j + (1 - z)x^j - (1 - z)]}{[1 - (1 - z)x^j]^2} \qquad \text{(A7-28)}$$

Note that $-(1 - z)x^j$ and $(1 - z)x^j$ cancel out in the numerator. Also, the $1 - (1 - z) = z$. This simplifies to:

$$\frac{\partial D}{\partial x} = \frac{jx^{j-1}z}{[1 - (1 - z)x^j]^2} > 0 \qquad \text{(A7-29)}$$

Since j, x, and z are all positive, the numerator is positive. Since the denominator is squared, it is also positive. Therefore, the entire expression is positive. The means that the discount is monotonically increasing in x.

We begin equation (A7-30) with a repetition of the definition of x in order to compute its partial derivatives.

$$x = \frac{1 + g}{1 + r} \qquad \text{(A7-30)}$$

Differentiating equation (A7-30) with respect to g, we get:

$$\frac{\partial x}{\partial g} = \frac{(1 + r)(1)}{(1 + r)^2} = \frac{1}{1 + r} > 0 \qquad \text{(A7-31)}$$

Differentiating equation (A7-30) with respect to r, we get:

$$\frac{\partial x}{\partial r} = \frac{-(1 + g)(1)}{(1 + r)^2} = -\frac{(1 + g)}{(1 + r)^2} < 0 \qquad \text{(A7-32)}$$

Using the chain rule, the partial derivative of D with respect to g is the partial derivative of D with respect to x multiplied by the partial derivative of x with respect to g, or:

$$\frac{\partial D}{\partial g} = \frac{\partial D}{\partial x}\frac{\partial x}{\partial g} > 0 \qquad \text{(A7-33)}$$

The first term on the right-hand side of the equation is positive by equation (A7-29), and the second term is positive by equation (A7-31). Therefore, the entire expression is positive and thus the discount is monotonically increasing in g. Using the chain rule again with respect to r, we get:

$$\frac{\partial D}{\partial r} = \frac{\partial D}{\partial x}\frac{\partial x}{\partial r} < 0 \qquad \text{(A7-34)}$$

Thus, the discount is monotonically decreasing in r. Now we make an algebraic substitution to simplify the expression for D in order to facilitate calculating other partial derivatives.

$$\text{Let } y = 1 - z \qquad (A7\text{-}35)$$

$$\frac{dy}{dz} = -1 \qquad (A7\text{-}36)$$

Substituting equation (A7-35) into equation (A7-25), we get:

$$D = 1 + \frac{x^j - 1}{1 - yx^j} \qquad (A7\text{-}37)$$

$$\frac{\partial D}{\partial y} = \frac{(1 - x^j)(-x^j)}{(1 - yx^j)^2} = \frac{x^j(x^j - 1)}{(1 - yx^j)^2} \qquad (A7\text{-}38)$$

$$\frac{\partial D}{\partial z} = \frac{\partial D}{\partial y}\frac{dy}{dz} = \frac{x^j(x^j - 1)(-1)}{[1 - (1 - z)x^j]^2} > 0 \qquad (A7\text{-}39)$$

The denominator of (A7-39), being squared, is positive. The numerator is also positive, as x^j is positive and less than one, which means that $x^j - 1$ is negative, which when multiplied by -1 results in a positive number. Thus, the entire partial derivative is positive, which means that D is monotonically increasing in z, the transaction costs. This result is intuitive, as it makes sense that the greater the transaction costs, the greater the discount.

Differentiating equation (A7-37) with respect to j, the average number of years between sales, we get:

$$\frac{\partial D}{\partial j} = \frac{(1 - yx^j)x^j \ln x - (x^j - 1)(-y)x^j \ln x}{(1 - yx^j)^2} \qquad (A7\text{-}40)$$

Factoring out $x^j \ln x$, we get:

$$\frac{\partial D}{\partial j} = \frac{x^j \ln x(1 - yx^j + yx^j - y)}{(1 - yx^j)^2} = \frac{x^j \ln x(1 - y)}{(1 - yx^j)^2} \qquad (A7\text{-}41)$$

$$\frac{\partial D}{\partial j} = \frac{x^j z \ln x}{[1 - (1 - z)x^j]^2} < 0 \qquad (A7\text{-}42)$$

The denominator is positive. The numerator is negative; since $x < 1$, $\ln x < 0$. Thus, the discount is monotonically decreasing in j, the average years between sale. That is intuitive, as the less frequently business sell, the smaller the discount should be.

Summary of Comparative Statics

Summarizing, the discount for periodic transaction costs is related in the following ways to its independent variables:

Variable	Varies with Discount	Monotonically
r	Negatively	Decreasing
g	Positively	Increasing
z	Positively	Increasing
j	Negatively	Decreasing

CHAPTER 8

Sample Restricted Stock Discount Study

ENCO, INC.

As of AUGUST 11, 1997

The information contained in this report is confidential. Neither all nor any part of the contents shall be conveyed to the public without the prior written consent and approval of Abrams Valuation Group (AVG). AVG's opinion of value in this report is valid only for the stated purpose and date of the appraisal.

Note: all names are fictional

Note: Because this sample report is in a book, there are slight changes in the table numbering and appearance of the report to accommodate the book format.

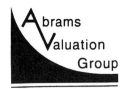

Abrams Valuation Group

Uniquely Applying Original Valuation Theory

Letter of Opinion

November 18, 1998

Mr. Robert Smith
2633 Elm Way
La Jolla, CA 92037

Dear Mr. Smith:

In accordance with your instructions, we have made a determination of the Discount for Lack of Marketability (DLOM) necessary to calculate the fair market value (FMV) of the common stock that you received in ENCO, Inc. ("ENCO," or "the Company") as of August 11, 1997, the date that you sold your company, Smith Metals, to ENCO. The stock is restricted according to SEC Rule 144, and it becomes marketable one year after the date of your sale. ENCO trades on Nasdaq, and the closing price of its freely trading shares on August 11, 1997 was 2 3/8, or $2.375.

It is our understanding that this appraisal will be used for income tax purposes. The DLOM and related FMV, as determined within our report, shall not be used for other purposes or dates without our written consent, as they can be misleading and dangerous.

The definition of fair market value is:

The price at which property [in this case, the capital stock of the Company] *would change hands between a willing seller and a willing buyer, when neither is under compulsion to buy and when both have reasonable knowledge of the relevant facts.*[1]

The scope of our engagement included discussions with you and Len Storm, Esq., Vice President and Legal Secretary of ENCO, as to the securities laws that apply, as he understands them. Per your instructions, we assume Len Storm's understanding of the timing of your ability to sell your ENCO stock to be correct. If his information were incorrect, that would cause a change in the related DLOM.

Based upon our investigation and analysis and subject to the attached report and Statement of Limiting Conditions, it is our opinion that the restricted stock discount (the DLOM) is **20.5%**. The closing price of ENCO, Inc. common stock on August 11, 1997, was $2.375 per share.[2] The

---

1. American Society of Appraisers Business Valuation Standards. Also, the wording is virtually identical in Reg. § 1.170A-1(c)(2) (income tax, charitable contributions of property); see Reg. §§ 20.2031-1(b) (second sentence) (estate tax), 25.2512-1 (second sentence) (gift tax).
2. Source: American Online, Prophet Line.

20.5% discount is $0.486 per share, leaving the fair market value of the restricted stock on that date at $1.889 per share (see Table 8-3 of the report for those calculations).

We retain a copy of this letter in our files, together with field data from which it was prepared. We consider these records confidential, and we do not permit access to them by anyone without your authorization.

USPAP (Uniform Standards of Professional Appraisal Practice) Certification:

I certify that to the best of my knowledge and belief:

- The statements of fact contained in this report are true and correct, the reported analyses, opinions and conclusions are limited only by the reported conditions, and they are our personal, unbiased professional analyses, opinions, and conclusions.
- We have no present or prospective interest in the property that is the subject of this report, and we have no personal interest or bias with respect to the parties involved.
- Our compensation is not contingent on an action or event resulting from the analyses, opinions, conclusions in or use of this report.
- Our analyses, opinions, and conclusions were developed and this report has been prepared in conformity with the Uniform Standards of Professional Appraisal Practice and the Business Valuation Standards of the American Society of Appraisers.
- No one has provided significant professional assistance to the person signing this report.
- I have passed the USPAP examination and am certified through the year 2001. I am an Accredited Senior Appraiser with the American Society of Appraisers, with certification current to the year 2000.

Sincerely yours,

Jay B. Abrams, ASA, CPA, MBA

INTRODUCTION

    Background

    Stock Ownership

    Purpose of the Appraisal

    No Economic Outlook Section

    Sources of Data

VALUATION

    Commentary to Table 8-1: Regression Analysis of Management
      Planning Data

      Previous Restricted Stock Studies

      Change in SEC Rule 144

      The Data

    Commentary to Table 8-1A: Revenue and Earnings Stability

    Commentary to Table 8-1B: Price Stability

    Valuation Using Options Pricing Theory

      Options Theory

      Black–Scholes Put Option Formula

      Chaffe's Article: Put Options to Calculate DLOM of Restricted
        Stock

      Commentary to Table 8-2: Black-Scholes Calculation of DLOM for
        ENCO, Inc.

      Commentary to Table 8-2A: Annualized Standard Deviation of
        Continuously Compounded Returns

      Commentary to Table 8-3: Final Calculation of Discount

    Conclusion of Discount for Lack of Marketability

ASSUMPTIONS AND LIMITING CONDITIONS

APPRAISER'S QUALIFICATIONS

INTRODUCTION

Background

On August 11, 1997, Robert Smith sold his company, Smith Metals, LLC, to ENCO, Inc. ("ENCO," or "the Company") and received 500,000 shares of ENCO Common Stock that is subject to the greater of two sets of restrictions in transfer:

1. The sales contract with ENCO: According to Section 2.12(b)(v), Robert Smith must wait one year to sell his ENCO stock.

2. In accordance with SEC Rule 144, Robert Smith must wait one year to begin selling his stock, at which point he can make quarterly sales equal to the greater of:

   (a) Rule 144 (e)(1)(i): 1% of the outstanding shares. With 112.5 million shares outstanding at the valuation date (the date of sale), 1% is 1.125 million shares.

   (b) Rule 144 (e)(1)(ii): The average weekly trading volume for the four weeks preceding the date of sale. The average weekly trading volume for the month preceding the sale was 900,000 shares. Thus, (2)(a) predominates, and 1.125 million is the maximum sale per quarter according to Rule 144 after the one-year waiting period.

The sale did not qualify as a tax-free reorganization, and you need the fair market value of the ENCO stock to compute your capital gains tax.

Stock Ownership

ENCO is publicly traded on Nasdaq with a ticker symbol of ENCO. Through the sale of Smith Metals, Robert Smith acquired less than 1% of ENCO's stock.

Purpose of the Appraisal

The purpose of this appraisal is to calculate the discount for lack of marketability (DLOM) needed to ascertain the fair market value for income tax purposes of the 500,000 shares of ENCO stock owned by Robert Smith. Your instructions are that we are to assume the market price is the fair market value of the unrestricted stock—a reasonable assumption—and that the only calculation necessary to produce the fair market value of the restricted stock is the DLOM.

The term *fair market value* is defined as "the amount at which property [in this case, the capital stock of the Company] would change hands between a willing buyer and a willing seller, when the former is not under any compulsion to buy and the latter is not under any compulsion to sell, and when both parties have reasonable knowledge of relevant facts."[3]

---

3. American Society of Appraisers Business Valuation Standards. Also, the wording is virtually identical in Reg. § 1.170A-1(c)(2) (income tax, charitable contributions of property); see Reg. §§ 20.2031-1(b) (second sentence) (estate tax), 25.2512-1 (second sentence) (gift tax).

No Economic Outlook Section

The Economic Outlook, a standard section in business valuations, is irrelevant in this study. This section would be relevant in valuing ENCO stock, but that is not our assignment. The same is true of a History of the Company section. Thus, we proceed to the Valuation section.

Sources of Data

1. Financial statements sent by Len Storm, Esq., Vice President and Legal Secretary of ENCO.
2. Copy of ENCO stock certificate issued to Robert Smith including copies of the '33 Act legend and contractual legend.
3. One-year secondary market Treasury Bill rate as of 8/11/97 from the Federal Reserve Bank of St. Louis, internet web site http://www.stls.frb.org.
4. America Online, Prophet Line stock quotes.
5. Restricted stock transaction data from Management Planning, Inc., Princeton, New Jersey.

VALUATION

We use two valuation methodologies in calculating the restricted stock discount. The first is based on our own statistical analysis using multiple regression of data collected by Management Planning, Inc.[4] The second involves using a Black–Scholes put option as a proxy for the discount.

Commentary to Table 8-1: Regression Analysis of Management Planning Data

Previous Restricted Stock Studies

There have been 10 studies of sales of restricted stocks.[5] In the first nine studies the authors did not publish the underlying data and merely presented their analysis and summary of the data. Additionally, only the Hall/Polacek study contains data beyond 1988, theirs going through 1992. The Management Planning Study contains data on trades from 1980–1996. Thus, it is superior to the other studies in two ways: the detail of the data exists, and the data are more current. Therefore, we use the Management Planning study exclusively.

Change in SEC Rule 144

On April 29, 1997, SEC Rule 144 changed from a two-year holding period to a one-year holding period for limited sales of stock. We should expect the shortening of the period of restriction to decrease the discount. The latest Management Planning data contain four observations with ex-

---

4. Published in Mercer (1997), chap. 12. Also, MPI provided us with four additional data points and some data corrections.
5. See Mercer, p. 69 for a summary of the results of the first nine studies.

PART 3   Adjusting for Control and Marketability

pected holding periods of less than two years, which will enable us to statistically infer the effect of the change in Rule 144 on DLOM.

The Data

Table 8-1 is two pages long. The first one and one-quarter pages contain data on 53 sales of restricted stock between 1980–1996. Column A is numbered 1 through 53 to indicate the sale number. Column C, our dependent (Y) variable, is the restricted stock discount for each transaction.

Columns D through J are our seven statistically significant independent variables, which we have labeled X_1, X_2, . . . X_7. Below is a description of the independent variables:

#	Independent Variable
1	Revenues squared.
2	Shares sold—$: the post-discount dollar value of the traded restricted shares.
3	Market capitalization = price per share times shares outstanding summed for all classes of stock.
4	Earnings stability: the unadjusted R^2 of the regression of net income as a function of time, with time measured as years 1, 2, 3, . . . We calculate this in Table 8-1A, regression #1.
5	Revenue stability: the unadjusted R^2 of the regression of revenue as a function of time, with time measured as years 1, 2, 3, . . . We calculate this in Table 8-1A, regression #2.
6	Average years to sell: the weighted average years to sell by a nonaffiliate, based on SEC Rule 144.
7	Price stability: This ratio is calculated by dividing the standard deviation of the stock price by the mean of the stock price. Management Planning used the end-of-month stock prices for the 12 months prior to the valuation date.

We regressed 30 other independent variables included in the Management Planning study, and all were statistically insignificant. We restrict our commentary to the seven independent variables that were statistically significant at the 95% level.

Table 8-1, page 2 contains the regression statistics. Adjusted R^2 is 59.47% (C66), a reasonable though not stunning result for such an analysis. That means the regression model accounts for 59.47% of the variation in the restricted stock discounts. The other 40.53% of variation in the discounts that remains unexplained are due to two possible sources: other significant independent variables of which we (and Management Planning) do not know and random variation.

The standard error of the y-estimate is 8.7% (C67 rounded). We can form approximate 95% confidence intervals around the y-estimate by adding and subtracting two standard errors, or 17.4%.

Cell C77 contains the y-intercept, and C78 through C84 contain the regression coefficients for the independent variables. E77 to E84 contains the t-statistics. Only the y-intercept itself is not significant at the 95% confidence level. The earnings stability and market capitalization variables are significant at the 98% level,[6] and all the other variables are significant at the 99+% confidence level.

---

6. The statistical significance is one minus the P-value, which is in F79 through F86.

TABLE 8-1

Abrams Valuation Group Regression of Management Planning, Inc. Data [1]

		C	D	E	F	G	H	I	J
		Y	X_1	X_2	X_3	X_4	X_5	X_6	X_7
		Discount	Rev^2	Shares Sold-$	Mkt Cap	Earn Stab	Rev Stabil	Avg Yrs To Sell	Price Stability [2]
6	Air Express Int'l	0.0%	8.58E+16	$4,998,000	25,760,000	0.08	0.22	2.84	12.0
7	AirTran Corp	19.4%	1.55E+16	$9,998,000	63,477,000	0.90	0.94	2.64	12.0
8	Anaren Microwave, Inc.	34.2%	6.90E+13	$1,250,000	13,517,000	0.24	0.78	2.64	28.6
9	Angeles Corp	19.6%	7.99E+14	$1,800,000	16,242,000	0.08	0.82	2.13	8.4
10	AW Computer Systems, Inc.	57.3%	1.82E+13	$1,843,000	11,698,000	0.00	0.00	2.91	22.6
11	Besicorp Group, Inc.	57.6%	1.57E+13	$1,500,000	63,145,000	0.03	0.75	2.13	98.6
12	Bioplasty, Inc,	31.1%	6.20E+13	$11,550,000	43,478,000	0.38	0.62	2.85	44.9
13	Blyth Holdings, Inc.	31.4%	8.62E+13	$4,452,000	98,053,000	0.04	0.64	2.13	58.6
14	Byers Communications Systems, Inc.	22.5%	4.49E+14	$5,007,000	14,027,000	0.90	0.79	2.92	6.6
15	Centennial Technologies, Inc.	2.8%	6.75E+13	$656,000	27,045,000	0.94	0.87	2.13	35.0
16	Chantal Pharm. Corp.	44.8%	5.21E+13	$4,900,000	149,286,000	0.70	0.23	2.13	51.0
17	Choice Drug Delivery Systems, Inc.	28.8%	6.19E+14	$3,375,000	21,233,000	0.29	0.89	2.86	23.6
18	Crystal Oil Co.	24.1%	7.47E+16	$24,990,000	686,475,000	0.42	0.57	2.50	28.5
19	Cucos, Inc.	18.8%	4.63E+13	$2,003,000	12,579,000	0.77	0.87	2.84	20.4
20	Davox Corp.	46.3%	1.14E+15	$999,000	18,942,000	0.01	0.65	2.72	24.6
21	Del Electronics Corp.	41.0%	4.21E+13	$394,000	3,406,000	0.08	0.10	2.84	4.0
22	Edmark Corp	16.0%	3.56E+13	$2,000,000	12,275,000	0.57	0.92	2.84	10.5
23	Electro Nucleonics	24.8%	1.22E+15	$1,055,000	38,435,000	0.68	0.97	2.13	21.4
24	Esmor Correctional Svces, Inc.	32.6%	5.89E+14	$3,852,000	50,692,000	0.95	0.90	2.64	34.0
25	Gendex Corp	16.7%	2.97E+15	$5,000,000	55,005,000	0.99	0.71	2.69	11.5
26	Harken Oil & Gas, Inc.	30.4%	7.55E+13	$1,999,000	27,223,000	0.13	0.88	2.75	19.0
27	ICN Paramaceuticals, Inc.	10.5%	1.50E+15	$9,400,000	78,834,000	0.11	0.87	2.25	23.9
28	Ion Laser Technology, Inc.	41.1%	1.02E+13	$975,000	10,046,000	0.71	0.92	2.82	22.0
29	Max & Erma's Restaurants, Inc.	12.7%	1.87E+15	$1,192,000	31,080,000	0.87	0.87	2.25	18.8
30	Medco Containment Svces, Inc.	15.5%	5.42E+15	$99,994,000	561,890,000	0.84	0.89	2.85	12.8
31	Newport Pharm. Int'l, Inc.	37.8%	1.10E+14	$5,950,000	101,259,000	0.00	0.87	2.00	30.2
32	Noble Roman's Inc.	17.2%	8.29E+13	$1,251,000	11,422,000	0.06	0.47	2.79	17.0
33	No. American Holding Corp.	30.4%	1.35E+14	$3,000,000	79,730,000	0.63	0.84	2.50	22.1
34	No. Hills Electronics, Inc.	36.6%	1.15E+13	$3,675,000	21,812,000	0.81	0.79	2.83	52.7
35	Photographic Sciences Corp	49.5%	2.70E+14	$5,000,000	44,113,000	0.06	0.76	2.86	27.2
36	Presidential Life Corp	15.9%	4.37E+16	$38,063,000	246,787,000	0.00	0.00	2.83	17.0
37	Pride Petroleum Svces, Inc.	24.5%	4.34E+15	$21,500,000	74,028,000	0.31	0.26	2.83	18.0
38	Quadrex Corp.	39.4%	1.10E+15	$5,000,000	71,016,000	0.41	0.66	2.50	44.2
39	Quality Care, Inc.	34.4%	7.97E+14	$3,150,000	19,689,000	0.68	0.74	2.88	7.0
40	Ragen Precision Industries, Inc.	15.3%	8.85E+14	$2,000,000	22,653,000	0.61	0.75	2.25	26.0
41	REN Corp-USA	17.9%	2.85E+15	$53,625,000	151,074,000	0.02	0.88	2.92	19.8
42	REN Corp-USA	29.3%	2.85E+15	$12,003,000	163,749,000	0.02	0.88	2.72	36.1
43	Rentrak Corp.	32.5%	1.15E+15	$20,650,000	61,482,000	0.60	0.70	2.92	30.0
44	Ryan's Family Steak Houses, Inc.	8.7%	1.02E+15	$5,250,000	159,390,000	0.90	0.87	2.13	13.6
45	Ryan's Family Steak Houses, Inc.	5.2%	1.02E+15	$7,250,000	110,160,000	0.90	0.90	2.58	14.4

46	41	Sahlen & Assoc., Inc.	27.5%	3.02E+15	$6,057,000	42,955,000	0.54	0.81	2.72	26.1
47	42	Starrett Housing Corp.	44.8%	1.11E+16	$3,000,000	95,291,000	0.02	0.01	2.50	12.4
48	43	Sudbury Holdings, Inc.	46.5%	1.39E+16	$22,325,000	33,431,000	0.65	0.17	2.96	26.6
49	44	Superior Care, Inc.	41.9%	1.32E+15	$5,660,000	50,403,000	0.21	0.93	2.77	42.2
50	45	Sym-Tek Systems, Inc.	31.6%	4.03E+14		20,550,000	0.34	0.92	2.58	13.4
51	46	Telepictures Corp.	11.6%	5.50E+15	$15,250,000	106,849,000	0.81	0.86	2.72	6.6
52	47	Velo-Bind, Inc.	19.5%	5.51E+14	$2,325,000	18,509,000	0.65	0.85	2.81	14.5
53	48	Western Digital Corp.	47.3%	4.24E+14	$7,825,000	50,417,000	0.00	0.32	2.64	22.7
54	49	50-Off Stores, Inc.	12.5%	6.10E+15	$5,670,000	43,024,000	0.80	0.87	2.38	23.7
55	50	ARC Capital	18.8%	3.76E+14	$2,275,000	18,846,000	0.03	0.74	1.63	35.0
56	51	Dense Pac Microsystems, Inc.	23.1%	3.24E+14	$4,500,000	108,862,000	0.08	0.70	1.17	42.4
57	52	Nobel Education Dynamics, Inc.	19.3%	1.95E+15	$12,000,000	60,913,000	0.34	0.76	1.74	32.1
58	53	Unimed Pharmaceuticals	15.8%	5.49E+13	$8,400,000	44,681,000	0.09	0.74	1.90	21.0
59		Mean	**27.1%**	**5.65E+15**	**$9,223,226**	**$78,621,472**	**0.42**	**0.69**	**2.54**	**25.4**
60		Standard deviation	**13.7%**				**0.35**	**0.27**	**0.39**	**16.1**

61

Management Planning Study: Summary Output of Regression

63 **Regression Statistics**

64	Multiple R	0.8058
65	R square	0.6493
66	Adjusted R square	0.5947
67	Standard error	0.0873
68	Observations	53

T A B L E 8-1 *(continued)*

Abrams Valuation Group Regression of Management Planning, Inc. Data [1]

	A	B	C	D	E	F	G	H	I	J
70	ANOVA									
71			df	SS	MS	F	Significance F			
72			Regression	7	0.6354	0.0908	11.9009	0.0000		
73			Residual	45	0.3432	0.0076				
74			Total	52	0.9786					
76			Coefficients	Standard Error	t Stat	P-value	Lower 95%	Upper 95%		
77			Intercept	−0.0673	0.1082	−0.6221	0.5370	−0.2854	0.1507	
78			Rev2	−4.629E − 18	9.913E − 19	−4.6698	0.0000	−6.626E − 18	−2.633E − 18	
79			Shares sold-$	−3.619E − 09	1.199E − 09	−3.0169	0.0042	−6.035E − 09	−1.203E − 09	
80			Mkt cap	4.789E − 10	1.790E − 10	2.6754	0.0104	1.184E − 10	8.394E − 10	
81			Earn stab	−0.1038	0.0402	−2.5831	0.0131	−0.1848	−0.0229	
82			Rev stabil	−0.1824	0.0531	−3.4315	0.0013	−0.2894	−0.0753	
83			Avg yrs to sell	0.1722	0.0362	4.7569	0.0000	0.0993	0.2451	
84			Price stability [2]	0.0037	0.0008	4.3909	0.0001	0.0020	0.0053	
86			Management Planning Study: Applying Regression Results to Company Data							
88			Y	X_1	X_2	X_3	X_4	X_5	X_6	X_7
89			Discount	Rev^2	Shares Sold-$	Mkt Cap	Earn Stab	Rev Stabil	Avg Yrs To Sell	Price Stability [1]
90			ENCO parameters	Constant-NA	5.90E+14	933,311	267,187,500	0.12	0.54	1.0000	27.01
91			Coefficients C77 to C84	−0.0673	−4.629E − 18	−3.619E − 09	4.789E − 10	−0.1038	−0.1824	0.1722	0.0037
92			=row 90* row 91	−0.0673	−0.0027	−0.0034	0.1280	−0.0125	−0.0988	0.1722	0.0986
93			Restricted stock discount (sum of row 94)	**21.41%**							

[1] *Source:* Management Planning, Inc. Princeton NJ (except for "Avg Yrs To Sell" and "Rev2" which we derived from their data).
[2] See Table 8-1B for the calculation of Price Stability.

We transpose the results in C77 though C84 into row 91. Row 90 contains the ENCO parameters for each variable. The shares sold − $ variable actually depends on the restricted stock discount, the dependent variable, and the latter also depends on the former. Therefore, we must derive ENCO's input for this independent variable through an iterative process. With the aid of a spreadsheet program, the task is simple. We input the numbers of shares sold times the Share price times one minus the restricted stock discount, or 500,000*$2.375*(1-C93) for ENCO's shares sold − $ value and activate the iterative capability of the spreadsheet program. For columns D through J, we multiply row 90 × row 91 = row 92, which is the regression determined influence of each independent variable on the discount. C91 is the y-intercept, which equals C92 and does not get multiplied like the independent variables do.

The sum of all the values in Row 92 is 21.41% and appears in C93. This is the final answer according to this valuation approach.

Commentary to Table 8-1A: Revenue and Earnings Stability

Table 8-1A contains two regression analyses. Regression #1, starting at row 19, is net income as a function of time (measured in years). Regression #2, starting at row 40, is revenue as a function of time, also measured in years. The R^2 is 0.12 (B23) and 0.54 (B44) for regressions #1 and #2, respectively. We transfer these amounts to Table 8-1, cells G90 and H90, respectively.

Commentary to Table 8-1B: Price Stability

Table 8-1B contains the calculation of price stability. Cells B5 through B16 show the month-end stock prices for ENCO from August 30, 1996, through July 31, 1997. The standard deviation of these prices is 0.84 (B17), and the arithmetic mean of the stock prices is 3.11 (B18). Dividing the standard deviation by the mean and multiplying by 100 produces Management Planning, Inc.'s measure of price stability, which is 27 (B19).

Valuation Using Options Pricing Theory

Options Theory

The economic theory on which we rely is options pricing theory. The paradigm options pricing model is the Black–Scholes Options pricing model (Black–Scholes, or BSOPM), developed by University of Chicago Professors Fisher Black and Myron Scholes, the latter of whom received the Nobel Prize in Economics for developing the model (Black had died in the meantime).

The Black–Scholes model is based on a heat exchange equation in physics. (It is truly a wonder that an equation developed in the physical world would be the one to explain the value of stock options.)

A call option is a contract enabling one to buy a specific number of shares of a company at a specific price and time. For example, one might buy an option to purchase 100 shares of IBM at $100 per share on a

T A B L E 8-1A

Calculation of Revenue and Earnings Stability (R^2)

	A	B	C	D	E	F	G
4	**Year**	**Year**	**Revenues**	**Net Income**			
5	1987	1	160,150	(1,079,123)			
6	1988	2	654,008	(1,403,474)			
7	1989	3	377,568	(1,531,562)			
8	1990	4	1,589,000	(1,243,000)			
9	1991	5	16,915,000	(1,303,000)			
10	1992	6	8,022,200	2,282,000			
11	1993	7	6,540,228	(14,486,000)			
12	1994	8	7,022,000	1,757,000			
13	1995	9	3,562,232	283,000			
14	1996	10	19,960,514	4,719,000			
15	1997	11	24,280,000	6,813,000			
17	**Regression Analysis**						
19	**Regression #1: SUMMARY OUTPUT: ENCO Net Income = f(Year)**						
21	**Regression Statistics**						
22	Multiple R	0.35					
23	R square	0.12					
24	Adjusted R square	0.02					
25	Standard error	5354052					
26	Observations	11					
28	**ANOVA**						
29		**df**	**SS**	**MS**	**F**	**Significance F**	
30	Regression	1	3.518E+13	3.518E+13	1.227	0.2966	
31	Residual	9	2.580E+14	2.867E+13			
32	Total	10	2.932E+14				
34		**Coefficients**	**Standard Error**	**t Stat**	**P-value**	**Lower 95%**	**Upper 95%**
35	Intercept	−3865352	3462304	−1.12	0.29	−11697634	3966929
36	Year	565556	510489	1.11	0.30	−589251	1720363
40	**Regression #2: SUMMARY OUTPUT: ENCO Revenues = f(Year)**						
42	**Regression Statistics**						
43	Multiple R	0.736					
44	R square	0.542					
45	Adjusted R square	0.491					
46	Standard error	6074120					
47	Observations	11					
49	**ANOVA**						
50		**df**	**SS**	**MS**	**F**	**Significance F**	
51	Regression	1	3.93E+14	3.93E+14	10.65	10.0098	
52	Residual	9	3.32E+14	3.69E+13			
53	Total	10	7.25E+14				
55		**Coefficients**	**Standard Error**	**t Stat**	**P-value**	**Lower 95%**	**Upper 95%**
56	Intercept	−3756247228	1153657477	−3.3	0.01	−6366003741	−1146490715
57	Year [2]	1889732	579145	3.3	0.01	579615	3199849

[1] Data source: Financial Statements sent by Len Storm, Esq., Vice President and Legal Secretary of ENCO.

Calculation of Price Stability

	A	B
4	**Date**	**Closing Price**
5	8/30/96	4.3750
6	9/30/96	3.7500
7	10/31/96	3.7500
8	11/29/96	3.1250
9	12/31/96	2.8750
10	1/31/97	4.0625
11	2/28/97	3.8750
12	3/31/97	2.8750
13	4/30/97	2.1250
14	5/30/97	2.1875
15	6/30/97	2.3750
16	7/31/97	1.9375
17	Std dev	0.84
18	Mean price	3.11
19	Price stability	27.01

specific date. A European option is such that one can buy only on that date, while an American option allows one to buy anytime up to and including that date. The original Black–Scholes model works on the assumption of a European option. A put option is the opposite of a call. It enables one to sell the stock at a specific price and time. Let us examine a put option.

Suppose IBM were selling today at $100 per share.[7] What would be the value of the ability to sell 100 shares of IBM on the last day of this year at $100 per share? If the stock price in a year were greater than $100, the value would be zero. If the price were less than or equal to $100, it would be $100 minus the actual stock price, multiplied by the number of shares.[8] There are two ways to cash out on the put option: you can buy the stock at its new lower market value and then sell it for $100 to the writer of the option, or you can sell the option itself.

The problem is that we do not know what the price of the stock will be. Black–Scholes assumes a normal probability distribution (the bell-shaped curve) of prices on the expiration date of the option. The bell-shaped curve is symmetrical and peaks in the center, which is the statistical mean, median, and mode, these being three different types of averages, which are not identical for asymmetric distributions.[9]

If we assume the center of the distribution is the exercise price, then the Black–Scholes calculated value of a put option is the area under the left half of the bell-shaped curve multiplied by the profit at each price,

---

7. We have not researched IBM's actual price. We use $100 per share for ease of illustration.

8. We are ignoring transactions costs and, for the moment only, the time value of money.

9. Technically it is the natural logarithm of prices that is normally distributed, but for a more intuitive explanation, we speak in terms of prices rather than log prices.

with some present value adjustments. In other words, it is the statistical probability of each point on the curve times the profit at each point.

All normal distributions are measured by two and only two parameters: the mean and the standard deviation. The mean is the average, and the standard deviation is a statistical measure of the width of the curve. In a normal distribution, one standard deviation on either side of the mean creates includes 68% confidence interval, and two standard deviations on either side includes 95% of the entire population.

Let's assume the mean expected stock price at the expiration of the option is $100 per share. If the standard deviation is $1 per share, then there is a 68% probability that the stock value will be between $99 and $101 and a 95% probability that the stock value at expiration will be between $98 and $102. That would be a tight distribution and would look like a tall, thin bell-shaped curve. There would only be a 5% probability that the price would be below $98 or above $102. Since the distribution is symmetric, that means a 2½% probability of being below $98 and a 2½% probability of being above $102. The chances of hitting a jackpot on this stock are very low.

Now let's assume the standard deviation is $20 per share, or 20% of the price. Now there is a 95% probability the price will be within $40 per share (two standard deviations) of $100, or between $60 and $140. The probability of hitting the jackpot is much higher.

We now have the background to understand how the stock volatility is the main determinant of the value of the option. The more volatile the stock, the shorter and fatter is the normal curve and the greater is the probability of making a lot of money on the investment. If your stock ends up on the right side of the curve, it does not matter how far up it went—you will choose to not exercise the option and you lose only the price of the option itself. In contrast to owning the stock itself, as an option holder it matters not at all whether the stock ends up at $100 per share or $140 per share—your loss is the same. Only the left side matters. Therefore, a put option on a volatile stock is much more valuable than one on a stable stock.

Black–Scholes Put Option Formula

The Black–Scholes options pricing model has the following forbidding formula:

$$P = EN(-d_2)e^{-Rft} - SN(-d_1)$$

where:

S = stock price
$N(\ )$ = cumulative normal density function
E = exercise price
Rf = risk-free rate, i.e., treasury rate of the same term as the option
t = time remaining to expiration of the option
d_1 = [ln(S/E) + (R_f + 0.5 × variance) × t]/[std dev × $t^{0.5}$]
d_2 = d_1 − [std dev × $t^{0.5}$]

Chaffe's Article: Put Options to Calculate DLOM of Restricted Stock

David Chaffe (Chaffe 1973, p. 182) wrote a brilliant article in which he reasoned that buying a hypothetical put option on Section 144 restricted stock would "buy" marketability, and the cost of that put option is an excellent measure of the discount for lack of marketability of restricted stock.

Commentary to Table 8-2: Black–Scholes Calculation of DLOM for ENCO, Inc.

Table 8-2 is the Black–Scholes put option calculation of the restricted stock discount. We begin in row 5 with S, the stock price on the valuation date of August 11, 1997, of $2.375. We then assume that E, the exercise price, is identical (row 6).

Row 7 is the time in years from the valuation date to marketability. According to SEC Rule 144, Robert Smith has a one-year period of restriction before he can sell all of his ENCO shares.

Row 8 shows the one year treasury bill rate as of August 11, 1997, which was 5.32% (see note 1, Table 8-2 for the data source). Row 9 is the square of row 10. Row 10 contains the annualized standard deviation of ENCO's continuously compounded returns, which we calculate in Table 8-2A to be 0.57.

Rows 11 and 12 are the calculation of the two Black–Scholes parameters, d_1 and d_2, the formulas of which appear in notes [2] and [3] of Table 8-2. Rows 13 and 14 are the cumulative normal density functions for $-d_1$ and $-d_2$.[10] For example, look at cell B13, which is $N(-0.380) =$

T A B L E 8-2

Black–Scholes Call and Put Options

	A	B
5	S = stk price on valuation date	$2.375
6	E = exercise price	$2.375
7	t = time To expiration (yrs)	1.0
8	R_f = risk-free rate [1]	5.32%
9	var = variance	0.33
10	std dev = standard deviation (Table 8-2A, C35)	0.57
11	d_1 = 1st Black–Scholes Parameter [2]	0.380
12	d_2 = 2nd Black-Scholes Parameter [3]	(0.194)
13	$N(-d_1)$ = cum normal density function	0.3521
14	$N(-d_2)$ = cum normal density function	0.5771
15	$P = [E * N(-d_2)*e^{-Rft} - S * N(-d_1)]$ [4]	$0.46
16	P/S	**19.51%**

[1] *Source:* 1 year secondary market Treasury Bill rate as of 8/11/97 from the Federal Reserve Bank of St. Louis, internet web site http://www.stls.frb.org

[2] $d_1 = [\ln(S/E) + (Rf + .5 * \text{variance}) * t] / [\text{std dev} * \text{SQRT}(t)]$, where variance is expressed as an annual term.

[3] $d_2 = d_1 - [\text{std dev} * \text{SQRT}(t)]$, where std dev is expressed in annual terms.

[4] The put option formula can be found in *Options Futures and Other Derivatives*, 3rd Ed. by John C. Hull, Prentice Hall, 1997, pp. 241 and 242. The formula is for a European style put option.

---

10. We use d_1 and d_2 to calculate call option values and their negatives to calculate put option values.

0.3521. This requires some explanation. The cumulative normal table from which the 0.3521 came assumes the normal distribution has been standardized to a mean of zero and standard deviation of 1.[11] This means that there is a 35.21% probability that our variable is less than or equal to 0.380 standard deviations below the mean. In cell B14, $N(-d_2) = N(0.194) = 0.5771$, which means there is a 57.71% probability of being less than or equal to 0.194 standard deviations above the mean. For perspective, it is useful to note that since the normal distribution is symmetric, $N(0) = 0.5000$, i.e., there is a 50% probability of being less than or equal to the mean, which implies there is a 50% probability of being above the mean.

In row 15 we calculate the value of the put option, which is $0.46 (B15) for the one-year option. In row 16 we calculate the ratio of the fair market values of the put option to the stock price on the valuation date. That ratio is our calculation of the restricted stock discount using Black–Scholes. Thus, our calculation of the restricted stock discount is 19.51% (B16) for the one-year period of restriction.

Commentary to Table 8-2A: Annualized Standard Deviation of Continuously Compounded Returns

In Table 8-2A we calculate the annualized standard deviation of continuously compounded returns for use in Table 8-2. Column A shows the date, Column B shows the closing price, and Columns C and D show the continuously compounded returns.

We calculated continuously compounded returns over 10 trading days intervals for ENCO stock. In column C we start with the 1/23/97 closing price and in column D we start with the 1/30/97 closing price. For example, the 10-trading-day return from 1/23/97 (A5) to 2/6/97 (A7) is calculated as follows:

$$\text{return} = \text{Ln}(B7/B5) = \text{Ln}(3.75/4.25) = -0.12516 \text{ (cell C7)}$$

In cells C33 and D33 we get two measures of standard deviation of 0.09414 and 0.13500 respectively. To get the annualized standard deviation we must multiply each interval standard deviation by the square root of the number of intervals which would occur in a year. The equation is as follows:

$$\sigma_{\text{annualized}} = \sigma_{\text{interval returns}} \times \text{SQRT (\# of interval returns in sample period}$$

$$\times \text{ 365 days/days in sample period)}$$

For example, the sample period in column C is the time period from the close of trading on 1/23/97 to the close of trading on 7/31/97 or 189 days, and the number of calculated returns is 13. Therefore the annualized standard deviation of returns is:

$$\sigma_{\text{annualized}} = 0.09414 \times \text{SQRT}(13 \times 365/189) = 0.47169 \text{ (cell C34)}$$

Similarly, the annualized standard deviation of returns in column D is

---

11. One standardizes a normal distribution by subtracting the mean from each value and dividing by the standard deviation.

Standard Deviation of Continuously Compounded Returns

	A	B	C	D
4	Date	Closing Price	Interval Returns	
5	1/23/97	4.2500		
6	1/30/97	4.1250		
7	2/6/97	3.7500	−0.12516	
8	2/13/97	3.6250		−0.12921
9	2/21/97	3.2500	−0.14310	
10	2/28/97	3.8750		0.06669
11	3/7/97	3.7500	0.14310	
12	3/14/97	3.3750		−0.13815
13	3/21/97	3.2500	−0.14310	
14	3/31/97	2.8750		−0.16034
15	4/7/97	2.7500	−0.16705	
16	4/14/97	2.7500		−0.04445
17	4/21/97	2.7500	0.00000	
18	4/28/97	2.1875		−0.22884
19	5/5/97	2.7500	0.00000	
20	5/12/97	2.6250		0.18232
21	5/19/97	2.3125	−0.17327	
22	5/27/97	2.0625		−0.24116
23	6/3/97	2.0625	−0.11441	
24	6/10/97	2.2500		0.08701
25	6/17/97	2.1250	0.02985	
26	6/24/97	2.3750		0.05407
27	7/2/97	2.0625	−0.02985	
28	7/10/97	2.1875		−0.08224
29	7/17/97	1.9375	−0.06252	
30	7/24/97	2.1250		−0.02899
31	7/31/97	1.9375	0.00000	
32	8/7/97	2.3750		0.11123
33	**Interval std deviation**		0.09414	0.13500
34	**Annualized std deviation**		0.47169	0.67644
35	**Average of 2 std deviations**		0.57406	

0.67644 (D34), while the average of the two is 0.57406 (C35), which transfers to Table 8-2 cell B10.

The reason that we use 10-day intervals in our calculation instead of daily intervals is that the bid ask spread on the stock may create apparent volatility that is not really present. This is because the quoted closing prices are from the last trade. In Nasdaq trading, when one sells to a dealer it is at the bid price, but when one buys it is at the ask price. If the last price of the day is switching randomly from a bid to an ask price and vice versa, this can cause us to measure an apparent volatility that is not really there. By using 10-day intervals, we reduce any measurement effect caused by the spread.

Commentary to Table 8-3: Final Calculation of Discount

Table 8-3 is our final calculation of the restricted stock discount. We use a weighted average of the two valuation approaches discussed earlier in the report.

According to the multiple regression analysis in Table 8-1, cell C93, the discount should be 21.41%. We show that in Table 8-3 in cell C6. In

Final Calculation of Discount

	A	B	C	D	E
4					Weighted
5	Method	Source Table	Discount	Weight	Discount
6	Multiple regression analysis	8-1, C93	21.41%	50%	10.7%
7	Black-Scholes put option	8-2, B16	19.51%	50%	9.8%
8	Total			100%	**20.5%**
10	Freely trading closing price, 8/11/97 [1]				$ 2.375
11	Less discount for lack of marketability-20.5%				$ (0.486)
12	Fair market value of restricted stock				$ 1.889
13	Number of shares				500,000
14	FMV of restricted shares (rounded)				$945,000

Source: America Online, Prophet Line.

C7 we show the Black–Scholes calculation of 19.51%, which we calculated in Table 8-2, B16. We weight the two approaches equally, which results in a discount of 20.5% (E8). The closing price of ENCO, Inc. common stock on August 11, 1997, was $2.375 (E10) per share.[12] The 20.5% discount is $0.486 (E11) per share, leaving the fair market value of the restricted stock on that date at $1.889 per share (E12). Multiplying that by 500,000 shares (E13), the fair market value of the ENCO stock received by Robert Smith is $945,000 (E14).

Conclusion of Discount for Lack of Marketability

It is our opinion, subject to this report and the statement of limiting conditions, that the proper discount to fair market value of the restricted shares from the traded price of ENCO, Inc. stock on August 11, 1997, is **20.5%**. Assuming the closing price of ENCO stock on that date of $2.375 per share is the fair market value of the freely trading shares, the discount of 20.5% is **$0.486** per share, leaving a fair market value of the 500,000 shares of restricted stock of **$1.889** per share, or $945,000 (E14) for Robert Smith.

ASSUMPTIONS AND LIMITING CONDITIONS

In accordance with recognized professional ethics, the fee for this service is not contingent upon our conclusion of value, and neither Abrams Valuation Group nor any of its employees has a present or intended interest in the Company.

Per your instructions, we have relied upon Robert Smith's information as to shares outstanding and other relevant information. We have been accepted this information without verification as being correct. The same is true as to the dates of marketability, though our information came from Len Storm, Vice President and Legal Secretary of ENCO, Inc.

---

12. Source: America Online, Prophet Line.

The conclusions are based on our analysis and discussions with Robert Smith. We did not make any site visit, as we deemed that unnecessary. We further assume that present ENCO Management would continue to maintain the character and integrity of the enterprise through any sale, reorganization, or diminution of the owners' participation or equity interest. We know of no significant pending legal action against the Company of which the market is unaware;[13] nor do we know of any other "skeleton in the closet," and we assume none is or will be occurring. If this did happen, then might change the value of the Company and Robert Smith's underlying stock.

Our opinion of the discount for lack of marketability in this report is valid only for the stated purpose and only at the date of the appraisal. It is our understanding that this opinion will be used for income tax purposes. The fair market value, as determined within our report, shall not be used for other purposes or dates.

Though some similarities exist between value as set forth for this purpose and others, it would be incorrect to use the price per share as determined within our report for any other purposes due to specific timing, performance, and marketability issues that arise in evaluating the fair market value of a company. Accordingly, any such use of the value as determined within this report for other purposes would be inaccurate and possibly misleading and no such use shall be made without written permission from Abrams Valuation Group.

Our determination of fair market value as reported herein does not represent investment advice of any kind to any person and does not constitute a recommendation as to the purchase or sale of shares of the Company or as to any our course of action.

Future services regarding the subject matter of this report, including, but not limited to, testimony or attendance in court shall not be required of Abrams Valuation Group unless previous arrangements have been made in writing.

This report may only be presented to persons whose use is relevant to its purpose, and only the entire report can be so conveyed. Giving part of this report for someone to read can lead to dangerous misunderstanding and is prohibited.

Neither all nor any part of the contents of this report shall be conveyed to the public through advertising, public relations, news, sales, mail, direct transmittal, or other media without the prior written consent and approval of Abrams Valuation Group.

APPRAISER'S QUALIFICATIONS

Jay B. Abrams, ASA, CPA, MBA, author and inventor, is a nationally recognized consultant within the valuation field.

Mr. Abrams lectured at the June 1996 Toronto International Conference of the American Society of Appraisers, the organization from which

---

13. By the efficient markets hypothesis, if the market knows about a lawsuit or even a potential lawsuit, the stock price will reflect that. Here we are saying we know of no insider relevant information that would change the market price if the public knew about that.

he holds the professional designation of Accredited Senior Appraiser (ASA) in Business Valuation. He has lectured for the National Association of Certified Valuation Analysis and the Anthony Robbins' Financial Mastery Seminar.

Mr. Abrams has provided services to clients representing a variety of organizations from small entrepreneurs to Columbia Pictures, Dr. Pepper, Purex Corporation, and other Fortune 1000 firms in the area of intangibles, including goodwill, customer lists, licensing agreements, contracts, and business enterprise and capital stock appraisals for numerous purposes, including the following:

- Employee stock ownership plans (ESOPs).
- Estate planning, estate and gift taxes.
- Income taxes and charitable contributions.
- Mergers and acquisitions and sales.
- Divestitures.
- Warrants and stock options.
- Shareholder buy/sell agreements.
- Blocks of publicly traded securities.
- Private placements and public offerings.
- Restricted securities.
- Recapitalization and reorganizations.
- Debt and equity financing.
- Company dissolutions.
- Litigation settlement.

Additionally, Mr. Abrams has prepared and given expert testimony in the capital stock and business enterprise valuation areas in various courts of law.

Mr. Abrams' valuation experience encompasses a wide array of industries and assignments, for mergers/acquisitions, sales and leaseback, litigation support, leveraged buyouts, and stockholder agreements. Mr. Abrams was Vice-President of Pacific Corporate Valuation, Inc. in charge of the valuation practice, and he was a Project Manager at Arthur D. Little Valuation, Inc. He was a cofounder and president of Raycom, a radio communications firm, and prior to this was an auditor with Arthur Andersen & Company. Mr. Abrams received his MBA from the University of Chicago in finance and marketing, where he also pursued graduate studies in economics.

Mr. Abrams invented and published the Abrams Table of Equity Premia and has published an article quantifying the discount for lack of marketability. He invented several formulas for valuing leveraged ESOPs, as well as the Abrams Table of Accounting Transposition Errors, used for troubleshooting such errors. He also wrote software to automatically generate a table of potential sources of error.

Mr. Abrams' writings include:

- *Quantitative Business Valuation*, McGraw-Hill, November 2000.
- "ESOPs: Measuring and Apportioning the Dilution," *Valuation*, June 1997.

- "Discount Rates as a Function of Log Size and Valuation Error Measurement," *The Valuation Examiner*, February/March, 1997.
- "An Iterative Valuation Approach," *Business Valuation Review*, March 1995.
- "A Breakthrough in Calculating Reliable Discount Rates," *Valuation*, August, 1994.
- "Discount for Lack of Marketability: A Theoretical Model," *Business Valuation Review*, September 1994.
- "Cash Flow: A Mathematical Derivation," *Valuation*, March 1994.
- "An Iterative Procedure to Value Leveraged ESOPs," *Valuation*, January 1993.
- "How to Quickly Find and Fix Accounting Transposition Errors," *The Practical Accountant*, June 1992.
- Coauthor of "Valuation of Companies for ESOP Purposes," Chapter 8 *in Employee Stock Ownership Plans* by Robert W. Smiley, Jr. and Ronald J. Gilbert, Prentice Hall/Rosenfeld Launer Publications, New York, 1989.
- "The Annuity Discount Factor: Generalization, Analysis of Special Cases, and Relationship to the Gordon Model and Fixed-Rate Loan Amortization," unpublished.

CHAPTER 9

Sample Appraisal Report

2.80% AND 2.25% MEMBER INTERESTS IN ABC COMPANY, LLC

As of DECEMBER 25, 1999 and JANUARY 3, 2000

The information contained in this report is confidential. No part or all of the contents can be conveyed to the public without the prior written consent and approval of Abrams Valuation Group (AVG). AVG's opinion of value in this report is valid only for the stated purpose and date of the appraisal.

All names in this sample report are fictional.

Note: Because this sample report is in a book, there are slight changes in the table numbering and appearance of the report to accommodate the book format.

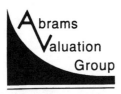

Abrams
Valuation
Group

Uniquely Applying Original Valuation Theory

January 4, 2000

Mr. Bradley J. Jones
Manager
ABC Company, LLC
PO Box 99214
San Diego, CA 92169

Dear Mr. Jones:

On January 6, 1999, ABC Company, LLC ("ABC," or "the LLC"), a California Limited Liability Company, was established for purposes of investing in real estate and other assets. On December 25, 1999, Tina M. Smith made four gifts of member interests of 2.80% in the LLC to the other existing members, who are her children. On January 3, 2000, Mrs. Smith made four gifts of 2.25% member interests.

In accordance with your instructions, we have performed a Complete Appraisal, documented in a Self-Contained Report, to calculate the discounts for lack of control and lack of marketability (collectively, "the Fractional Interest Discount") for the four 2.80% and 2.25% member interest gifts for gift tax purposes.

Our opinion of the Fractional Interest Discount will be effective from December 25, 1999, through January 3, 2000, for gift tax purposes. The fractional interest discounts, as determined within our report, shall not be used for other purposes or dates without our written consent, as they may be misleading and dangerous.

The term fair market value is defined as follows: "the amount at which property [in this case, the member interests in the LLC] would change hands between a willing buyer and a willing seller, when the former is not under any compulsion to buy and the latter is not under any compulsion to sell, and when both parties have reasonable knowledge of relevant facts."[1]

The scope of our engagement did not include a physical visit to the properties or your offices, nor a separate valuation of the former.

For the fair market value of the properties, we relied on the appraisals by ABC Real Estate Appraisals as of December 1998 and the estimate of fair market value for the Dutch Flat property by Bradley Jones. All information regarding the LLC was provided by Bradley Jones and the LLC's attorney, David Hollander, Esq., and its accountant, David Sofer,

---

1. American Society of Appraisers Business Valuation Standards. Also, the wording is virtually identical in Reg. § 1.170A-1(c)(2) (income tax, charitable contributions of property); see Reg. §§ 20.2031-1(b) (second sentence) (estate tax), 25.2512-1 (second sentence) (gift tax).

CPA. This information has been accepted, without additional verification, as correctly reflecting the financial statements and value and nature of the underlying assets, and is your responsibility.

In our opinion, based upon our investigation and analysis and subject to the attached report and Statement of Limiting Conditions, the appropriate fractional interest discount for the subject 2.80% and 2.25% member interests is **48%**. The fair market value of each 2.80% interest is **$20,000**, and the fair market value of each 2.25% interest is **$16,250.**

We retain a copy of this letter in our files, together with the field data from which it was prepared. We consider these records confidential, and we do not permit access to them by anyone without your authorization.

USPAP (Uniform Standards and Principals of Appraisal Practice) Certification:

I certify that to the best of my knowledge and belief that

- The statements of fact contained in this report are true and correct, the reported analyses, opinions and conclusions are limited only by the reported conditions, and they are our personal, unbiased, professional analyses, opinions, and conclusions.
- We have no present or prospective interest in the property that is the subject of this report, and we have no personal interest or bias with respect to the parties involved.
- Our compensation is not contingent on an action or event resulting from the analyses, opinions, conclusions in this report or the use thereof.
- Our analyses, opinions, and conclusions were developed, and this report has been prepared, in conformity with the Uniform Standards of Professional Appraisal Practice and the Business Valuation Standards of the American Society of Appraisers.
- No one has provided significant professional assistance to me.
- I have passed the USPAP examination and am certified through 2001. Additionally, I am an Accredited Senior Appraiser (ASA) with the American Society of Appraisers. My certification is current through the year 2000.

Sincerely yours,

Jay B. Abrams, ASA, CPA, MBA

BIBLIOGRAPHY

Chaffe, B. H., III. 1993. "Option Pricing as a Discount for Lack of Marketability in Private Company Valuations," *Business Valuation Review* (December).
Mercer, Z. Christopher. 1997. *Quantifying Marketability Discounts.* Memphis, Tenn.: Peabody.

INTRODUCTION
  Purpose of the Report
  Valuation of Considerations
  Sources of Data
HISTORY AND DESCRIPTION OF THE LLC
  Significant Terms and Legal Issues
  Conclusion
ECONOMIC OUTLOOK
  Economic Growth
  Inflation
  Interest Rates
  State and Local Economics
  Summary
FINANCIAL REVIEW
  Commentary to Table 9-2: FMV Balance Sheets
  Commentary to Table 9-3: Income Statements
  Commentary to Table 9-4: Cash Distributions
VALUATION
  Valuation Approaches
  Selection of Valuation Approach
  Economic Components Approach
  Commentary to Table 9-5: Calculations of Combined Discounts
    Section 1: The Combined Discounts
    Section 2: Discount for Lack of Control
  Commentary to Table 9-5A: Delay-to-Sale
  Commentary to Table 9-5C: Calculation of DLOM
    Buyer's Monospony Power
    Transactions Costs
    Final DLOM
  Commentary to Table 9-6: Partnership Profiles Approach—1999
    Comparability of Partnership Profiles to the Subject Interest
    Statistical Methodology
    Regression Results of Partnership Profiles Database
    Commentary to Table 9-6A: Correlation Matrix
    Applying the Regression Equation
    Adjustments to the Discount
  Commentary to Table 9-7: Private Fractional Interest Sales
    Comparability to the Subject Interest
    Statistical Methodology
    Regression Results of Partnership Profiles Database
  Commentary to Table 9-8: Final Calculation of Fractional Interest
  Discounts
    2.80% Member Interest

    Final Calculation of FMV of Fractional Interests

    Conclusion

STATEMENT OF LIMITING CONDITIONS

APPRAISER'S QUALIFICATIONS

APPENDIX: TAX COURT'S OPINION FOR DISCOUNT FOR LACK OF
  MARKETABILITY

INTRODUCTION

THE COURT'S 10 FACTORS

APPLICATION OF THE COURT'S 10 FACTORS TO THE VALUATION

INTRODUCTION

Purpose of the Report

On January 6, 1999, ABC Company, LLC ("ABC," or "the LLC"), a California Limited Liability Company, was established for purposes of investing in real estate and other assets. On December 25, 1999, Tina M. Smith made fours gifts of member interests of 2.80% in the LLC to the other existing members, who are her children. Mrs. Smith also made four gifts of 2.25% member interests on January 3, 2000.

The purpose of this valuation is to determine the correct discounts for lack of control and lack of marketability (collectively, "the Fractional Interest Discount") for the four member interest gifts each of 2.80% and 2.25%. Our opinion of the Fractional Interest Discount will be effective from December 25, 1999 through January 3, 2000 for gift tax purposes. The Fractional Interest Discount, as determined within our report, shall not be used for other purposes or dates without our written consent, as they may be misleading and dangerous.

The term *fair market value* is defined as "the amount at which property [in this case, the member interests in the LLC] would change hands between a willing buyer and a willing seller, when the former is not under any compulsion to buy and the latter is not under any compulsion to sell, and when both parties have reasonable knowledge of relevant facts."[2]

Valuation Considerations

The valuation of closely held securities requires consideration of all relevant factors that may influence the market price. The factors recognized by tax courts, the Internal Revenue Service, and professional investors generally include the following:

- The nature and history of the business enterprise.
- The outlook of the economy and the specific industry.
- The book value and financial condition of the business.
- The earnings capacity of the business.
- The dividend paying capacity of the business.
- The nature and value of the tangible and intangible assets (goodwill) of the business.
- The market price of securities of publicly traded corporations engaged in the same or similar lines of business.
- The marketability, or lack thereof, of the securities.
- The existence, if any, of a control premium with regard to the block of securities being valued.
- Sales of the stock (or partnership or LLC interest) and the size of the block of the stock to be valued.

---

2. American Society of Appraisers Business Valuation Standards. Also, the wording is virtually identical in Reg. § 1.170A-1(c)(2) (income tax, charitable contributions of property); see Reg. §§ 20.2031-1(b) (second sentence) (estate tax), 25.2512-1 (second sentence) (gift tax).

These considerations are outlined and described in Revenue Ruling 59-60, 1959-1 CB 237, as modified by Revenue Ruling 65-193, 1965-2 CB 370, and Revenue Ruling 77-287, IRB 1977-33. Although Revenue Ruling 59-60 specifically addresses itself to stock valuations for gift and estate tax purposes, the principles set forth may be applied to a wide spectrum of valuation problems, including those related to stockholder buy/sell agreements, mergers and acquisitions, Employee Stock Ownership Plans, corporate reorganizations, marital dissolutions, and bankruptcies. This report will discuss these factors and address other items relevant to the member interests to determine their effect upon the fair market value of the LLC interests.

Sources of Data

1. Survey of Professional Forecasters" Federal Reserve Bank of Philadelphia, November 19, 1999. Internet site http://www.phil.frb.org/files/spf/survq499.html.
2. Operating Agreement of the LLC.
3. ABC Real Estate Appraisals.
4. Conversations with Bradley Jones.
5. LLC's balance sheet and income statement.
6. Mrs. Tina Smith's Federal Tax Returns from 1997 and 1998.
7. Survey of Professional Forecasters, www.phil.frb.org/files/spf/survq499.html.
8. Houlihan Lokey Howard & Zukin, *Mergerstat Review—1999*, p. 23.
9. Cost of Capital Quarterly—1999, SIC Code #6798 (REITs), Ibbotson Associates.
10. Management Planning, Inc. restricted stock data.
11. Partnership Profiles, Inc. secondary limited partnership data.
12. Jones, Roach & Caringella private sale data.

HISTORY AND DESCRIPTION OF THE LLC

Tina M. Smith and her four children, listed below in Table 9-1, founded the LLC on January 6, 1999. Mrs. Smith owned several properties, which she contributed to the LLC. The original capital contributions and member interests are as appears above in Table 9-1.

All four 5% members are children of Tina Smith. According to Bradley Jones, the member interests are the same as of the valuation date, even though there have been additional contributions.

Significant Terms and Legal Issues

The LLC is governed by its Operating Agreement dated January 6, 1999. According to the Operating Agreement, the LLC is to be dissolved on December 31, 2030, unless the term is extended by amendment to the Operating Agreement or it is dissolved earlier.

TABLE 9-1

Member Interests at Inception on 1/6/96

Member	Initial Capital Contribution	%
Tina M. Smith[a]	$200,000	80%
Bradley J. Jones	10,000	5%
David R. Jones	10,000	5%
Larry T. Smith	10,000	5%
Lisa C. Dubliner	10,000	5%
Total	**$240,000**	**100%**

Source: Exhibit A, Operating Agreement of the LLC.
[a] As Trustee under the Tina M. Smith Revocable Living Trust, and amendments thereto, 9/11/90.

Section 11 of the Operating Agreement specifies a three-month right of first refusal (ROFR) in which its other members have to buy out a member who wants to sell.

Bradley J. Jones is the Manager of the LLC and has the right to bind it legally. However, his authority is subject to the Management Committee.

Conclusion

The LLC's ROFR is a moderate impairment of marketability and, therefore, fair market value. This happens because buyers are averse to investing their time in the due diligence process when they can be so easily outbid by having their bid matched by insiders who have legal preference. To be slightly conservative, we do not make an explicit adjustment for this in our final calculation of the fractional interest discount.

ECONOMIC OUTLOOK

Economic Growth

Forty-three forecasters surveyed by the Federal Reserve Bank of Philadelphia expect that the U.S. economy will expand at an annual rate of 3.7% in 1999's fourth quarter and at an annual rate of 3.1% in 2000. The forecasters see growth slipping a bit in the first quarter of 2000, to 2.3%, but rebounding from that rate over the following three quarters. Unemployment is expected to average 4.3% in 2000.[3]

Inflation

Expectations for inflation, measured by the Consumer Price Index, over the next 10 years are 2.50%. The expected inflation for 2000 is 2.50%.[4] For the purposes of this valuation, we forecast annual inflation at 3%.

---

3. "Survey of Professional Forecasters" Federal Reserve Bank of Philadelphia, November 19, 1999. Internet site http://www.phil.frb.org/files/spf/survq499.html.

4. *Ibid.*

PART 3   Adjusting for Control and Marketability

Interest Rates

Three-month Treasury Bills are expected to average 5.1% in 2000, while the yield on 10-year Treasury Bonds is expected to average 6.1.[5]

State and Local Economics

State and local economics are not sufficiently relevant to warrant research in this report, as they are fully considered in the valuation of the real estate.

Summary

The economic forecast for the United States appears moderately positive, with modest growth and low inflation.

FINANCIAL REVIEW

Commentary to Table 9-2: FMV Balance Sheets

Table 9-2 consists of a historical balance sheet of the LLC in column B and a fair market value balance sheet in column C, both dated December 25, 1999, the valuation date. The source of the historical 1999 balance sheet and income statement is the LLC's internally generated statements as of December 14, 1999.

Bradley Jones stated that he expects no other income, expenses, or payments for the remainder of 1999, with one exception. The LLC will pay his accrued salary of $1,600 on December 15. Additionally, there would be another payment of his salary at the end of December, which is after the December 25, 1999, valuation date. Technically, we should accrue another ten days of his salary to the valuation date, but the difference is immaterial. Thus, we show an accrual of $3,200 for his entire December salary in row 20.

The only difference between the amounts in columns B and C is that we substitute the appraised fair market values for the properties in column C in place of the cost basis in column B. The historical balance sheet is not relevant to the valuation analysis, and we present it in order to be complete.

All fair market values of properties are appraised by ABC Real Estate Appraisals, with the exception of Dover Field (Row 15), which is 2.77 acres of land and one studio. Bradley Jones estimates its fair market value at $40,000.

The fair market value of the properties are $1,387,000 (C16), which is approximately $667,000 above their cost basis. The net asset value, or fair market value of the equity, is $1,389,185 (B22).

---

5. *Ibid.*

TABLE 9-2

Balance Sheets 12/25/99 [1]

	A	B	C
		Historical	**FMV [2]**
4	**Assets:**		
5	Cash	**11,234**	**11,234**
6	Computer equipment-net	**1,251**	**1,251**
7	Real estate:		
8	4627-35 Bass St.		370,000
9	88 Apple Road, Julian		95,000
10	000 Pumpkin Patch [3]		40,000
11	37830 & 37848 Geese Rd., Ranchita		135,000
12	4463-65 Grape St.		215,000
13	852 Brown Ave.		300,000
14	1351 Kansas St. (80% owned by LLC) [4]		192,000
15	Dover Field		40,000
16	Total real estate [5]	**719,254**	**1,387,000**
17	Total assets	**731,739**	**1,399,485**
18	**Liabilities**		
19	Security deposits	7,100	7,100
20	Accrued manager's salary payable	3,200	3,200
21	Total liabilities	**10,300**	**10,300**
22	Total capital	721,439	1,389,185
23	Total liabilities & capital	**731,739**	**1,399,485**

[1] The source of the historical balance sheet (and income statement) is the LLC's internally drafted statement as of 12/14/99. Bradley Jones expects no other income, expenses, or payments through the end of the year, with the exception of his own salary of $3,200 per month. Technically, we should accrue that salary through 12/25/99. However, to facilitate the income statement analysis for an entire year, it is preferable to accrue his salary through 12/31/99. The difference of six days of salary is immaterial to the valuation.

[2] All properties appraised by ABC Real Estate Appraisals as of 12/30/98 or 12/3/98, except for Dover Field, which is 2.77 acres of land, plus one studio. Bradley Jones, LLC Manager, estimates its FMV at $40,000. All other assets and liabilities are per the LLC's 12/14/99 Balance Sheet.

[3] This is vacant land.

[4] Four gifts of 5% each = 20% Tenants-in-Common interests were already gifted to Bradley Jones, David R. Jones, Larry T. Smith, and Lisa C. Dubliner. This is 80% of the appraised FMV.

[5] The historical numbers consist of the following:

Total buildings	494,005
Less accumulated depreciation-bldgs	(116,310)
Buildings-net	377,695
Construction in progress (Brown Ave.)	44,864
Land	296,695
Total real estate	**719,254**

Bradley Jones reports that ABC Real Estate Appraisals told him verbally that the appropriate FMV for the Brown Ave. property, which is the one with the construction-in-progress, is still the $300,000 at which it was appraised in 1998.

Commentary to Table 9-3: Income Statements

Table 9-3 presents income statement data for three years. Column B contains a complete income statement for 1999. January 6, 1999, was the inception of the LLC, so the income statement excludes January 1 through January 5, when the properties were still owned by Tina M. Smith as an individual. Additionally, the 1997 and 1998 income data, which appear in columns D and C, respectively, are partial data taken from Mrs. Smith's tax returns—specifically from Schedule E.

Row 32 shows net income as appears on the LLC's income statement and Mrs. Smith's tax returns. Net income was $27,733, $17,843, and $28,696 in 1997–1999, respectively (D32, C32, and B32).

Next, it is necessary to subtract salary for Bradley Jones's services to the properties. In 1997 and 1998 he was part-time and managed only one

TABLE 9-3

Income Statements [1]

	A	B	C	D
4		1999	1998	1997
5	Rental income	82,170		
6	Late fees	50		
7	Total income	**82,220**		
8	**Expenses:**			
9	Fire equipment maintenance	29		
10	Auto	2,905		
11	Bank charges	64		
12	Dues & subscriptions	72		
13	Equipment rental	396		
14	Franchise fees	800		
15	Insurance	5,284		
16	Landscaping	1,535		
17	Licenses and permits	623		
18	Postage and delivery	241		
19	Accounting	1,380		
20	Consulting	1,750		
21	Legal	1,500		
22	Property taxes	10,576		
23	Repairs	17,854		
24	Supplies	6,169		
25	Telephone	505		
26	Gas & electric	430		
27	Water	1,502		
28	Rounding error	−1		
29	Total expenses	**53,614**		
30	Net operating income	**28,606**		
31	Interest income	90		
32	Net income before adjustments [2]	**28,696**	17,843	27,733
33	Less management salary [3]	−38,400	−2,443	−2,708
34	Adjusted net income [4]	**−9,704**	**15,400**	**25,025**
35	1997–1999 average net income	**30,721**		
36	1997–1999 total net income	**10,240**		

[1] *Sources:* The LLC's 12/14/99 Income Statement provided by Bradley Jones and Schedule E's from Tina Smith's 1997–1998 tax returns.

[2] This amount equals net income on the LLC's income statement.

[3] In 1999, Bradley Jones made $3,200 per month, which is arm's-length. His salary was recorded as a draw against earnings, but it should be charged as an expense. In earlier years, Mrs. Smith paid an outside property manager. Bradley managed one of her properties, without pay. In 1997-1998, we subtract the same amount paid to the property manager as Bradley's arm's-length salary in those years.

[4] This income statement is 1/1/99 to 12/14/99. Bradley Jones expects no more income or expense for the remainder of 1999, with the exception of his own salary, which we have accrued.

of the properties, and he was unpaid. For those two years we subtracted the same amount as Mrs. Smith paid her outside property manager—approximately $2,400 to $2,700 (C33 and D33). In 1999, Mr. Jones worked full-time for the LLC, and we subtract his actual (and arm's-length) salary of $38,400 (B33), which on the LLC's income statement was charged as a draw against profits.

We subtract row 33 from row 32 to arrive at adjusted net income in row 34. Adjusted net loss was −$9,704 (B34) in 1999. In 1997 and 1998 adjusted net income was $25,025 and $15,400 (D34 and C34). Total adjusted net income for the three years was $30,721 (B35), and the three-year average was $10,240 (B36).

Commentary to Table 9-4: Cash Distributions

In Table 9-4, we calculate the margins from net income and property appreciation as well as cash distributions. We use the first two items in our calculations in Table 9-5C, and we use the latter in Table 9-6.

We begin with adjusted net income of −$9,704 (B5, from Table 9-3, B34) for 1999 only and $10,240 (C5, from Table 9-3, B36) for the average of 1997–1999. We then divide that by the net asset value of $1,389,185 (Row 6, from Table 9-2, C22) to arrive at the net income margins of −0.70% and 0.74% (Row 7).

We assume property appreciation at 2.5% for inflation[6] and 0.5%—a reasonable estimate—for real growth, totaling 3.00% (row 8). Adding rows 6 and 7, which are net income margins and property appreciation, we come to a forecast total returns from the property of 2.30% and 3.74% (row 9).

Bradley Jones expects to retain 25% (row 10) of income for reinvestment, which leaves one minus 25%, or 75% (row 11) for cash distributions. Finally, we multiply the net income margins in row 7 by the expected distributions of available income in row 11 to calculate expected distributions in row 12. As the 1999 amount is negative, we use only the 1997–1999 average of 0.55% in C12 as our forecast of distributions. Again, we will use this forecast in Table 9-6 to calculate the fractional interest discount using the Partnership Profiles approach.

VALUATION

Valuation Approaches

We have considered the following basic approaches in calculating the fractional interest discount:

TABLE 9-4

Cash Distributions

	A	B	C
4		**1999**	**1997–1999 Avg**
5	Adjusted net income (Table 9-3: B34, B36)	−9,704	10,240
6	Net asset value (Table 9-2, C22)	1,389,185	1,389,185
7	Net income margin	**−0.70%**	**0.74%**
8	Property appreciation [1]	3.00%	3.00%
9	Total returns	**2.30%**	**3.74%**
10	Retention percentage [2]	25.00%	25.00%
11	Expected distributions = 1-retention %	75.00%	75.00%
12	Expected distributions	**−0.52%**	**0.55%**

[1] Assumed at CPI expected inflation of 2.5% (Survey of Professional Forecasters, www.phil.frb.org/files/spf/survq499.html), plus real growth of 0.5%
[2] Bradley Jones expects the LLC to retain 25% of net income for future growth.

---

6. CPI expected inflation from Survey of Professional Forecasters, www.phil.frb.org/files/spf/survq499.html.

- Economic components approach.
- Partnership profiles database approach.
- Market approach—sales of unregistered private fractional interests.
- Quantitative marketability discount model.

Selection of Valuation Approach

We have selected the Economic components approach, the Partnership Profiles database approach, and the market approach—sales of unregistered Private Fractional Interests as the appropriate ones for valuing the member interests. These first two are more accurate and objective than the QMDM, which was ineffective in its ability to model restricted stock discounts.[7] The third provides us with a market benchmark.

Economic Components Approach

In this valuation approach we quantify the underlying economic components that make up the discount for lack of marketability (DLOM) and for lack of control (DLOC). Chapter 7 of *Quantitative Business Valuation: A Mathematical Approach for Today's Professionals,* by Jay B. Abrams, ASA, CPA, MBA, is the theoretical basis for this approach. We will refer to this as "the chapter." Much of the wording of this section is in the context of valuing corporate stock, as that is the context of the chapter, but the logic also applies to valuing interests in limited partnerships, general partnerships, TICs, and LLCs.

DLOC is relatively simple and has no subcomponents. However, DLOM is more complicated. Abrams identifies four components of the discount for lack of marketability in the chapter: Delay-to-sale, monopsony power, and incremental transaction costs for both the buyer and the seller. The first component, delay-to-sale, is the economic impact of the incremental time that it would take to sell the subject property (in this case, the various member interests) beyond the time that it would normally take to sell the underlying property from which we draw our comparisons, i.e., a 100% interest in the property. The second component is the monopsony power to the few buyers of small businesses (or other illiquid investments). The third and fourth components are differentials in transaction costs for both the buyer and seller between purchasing a fractional interest compared to a 100% interest.

Table 9-5, section 1 shows the calculation of the combined discount (DLOM + DLOC) for the 2.80% member interests according to the economic components approach. In Table 9-5, section 2 we calculate the discount for lack of control. The calculation of the discount for lack of marketability is contained in Tables 9-5A, 9-5B, and 9-5C.

---

7. See Chapter 7 of Jay Abrams' book *Valuing Businesses: Advanced Techniques For Practitioners,* McGraw-Hill, to be published in November 2000.

TABLE 9-5

Economic Components Approach: 2.80% Member Interest

	A	B	C	D	E	F	G
5	Section 1: Combined Discounts						
7	Pure	Percent					
8	Discount	Remaining					
9	31.3%	68.7%	Discount-lack of marketability (Table 9-5C, D14)				
10	26.0%	74.0%	Discount-lack of control (E20)				
11		50.8%	Total % remaining = 68.7% * 74.0%				
12		**49.2%**	Discount = 1 − total % remaining				
15	Section 2: Discount-Lack of Control						
17	Average premium (= P) for control [1]				40.7%		
18	Discount-minority interest = P/(1 + P)				28.9%		
19	Adjustment: for 2.80% member interest-subtract 10% [2]				90%		
20	Discount-lack of control				**26.0%**		

[1] *Source:* Mergerstat-1999, page 23. There is new research in Chapter 7 of Abrams' book *Quantitative Business Valuation: A Mathematical Approach for Today's Professionals* which suggests that control premiums for private firms probably should be on the order of 21 to 28% above the marketable minority level. This would imply a lower discount for lack of control. However, in private firms the possibility of wealth transfer from minority interests to control interests could very well increase DLOC. In Chapter 7, Abrams also cited international voting rights premia (VRP) as high as 82 percent and an American outlier VRP 42 percent that might indicate the value of control to be higher than 28 percent. Taking these data into consideration, we use the Mergerstat acquisition premium to arrive at our DLOC.

[2] A 2.80% Member Interest should have more influence than a typical minority interest in the stock market. We quantify this by reducing the discount for lack of control by 10%, leaving 90% of the discount for lack of control.

Commentary to Table 9-5: Calculation of Combined Discounts

Section 1: The Combined Discounts

In this section we show the combined effects of both discounts: for lack of marketability and lack of control. Cell A9 contains the DLOM of 31.3% from Table 9-5C, D14. Cell A10 contains the DLOC of 26.0%, calculated in Section 2. The remaining value after the DLOM is 1 − 31.3% = 68.7% (B9). The remaining value after the DLOC is 1 − 26.0% = 74.0% (B10). Multiplying the two remaining values produces a total remaining value of 68.7% × 74.0% = 50.8% (B11). The combined discount is 1 − 50.8% = 49.2% (B14) for the 2.80% member interest.

Section 2: Discount for Lack of Control[8]

Minority interests typically have no cash flow from their investments. The control owners are able to divert corporate funds to themselves in the form of high salaries, perks, etc., which give them cash flow without generating corporate taxes. Closely held business owners of C corporations generally do not declare dividends, which are not tax-deductible as are salaries, bonuses, and perks. Minority shareholders have no cash flow

---

8. The following paragraph is introducing valuation theory that is necessary, even though it is couched in terms of minority share ownership in C corporations, which is not the current assignment. We will modify the conclusions that arise from this discussion as appropriate for this valuation assignment.

from excess salaries and receive no dividends. The only way to get cash flow is to pray for the company to sell, and even then the control shareholder can sell his shares without taking the minority shareholders along. Also, the minority shareholder cannot generally force the sale of the firm to achieve liquidity, with an important exception discussed below. The position of a minority shareholder in a closely held company is usually quite weak and vulnerable.

The standard valuation industry calculation of the minority interest discount begins with measuring control premiums in acquisitions of publicly held firms. Such acquisitions generally take place at substantial premiums. There is a value to control, and buyers pay for it.

On the contrary, there is negative value to a lack of control, and buyers will discount value because of it. If we assume a 40% premium, that means a company trading at $100 per share before being acquired will be acquired at $140 per share, or a $40 per share or 40 per cent premium. The other perspective is to say that there is a $40 discount for minority interest from the control price of $140, i.e., the discount for lack of control (DLOC). DLOC is then $40/140, or 28.6%. A more general formula to calculate the minority interest discount is DLOC = $P/(1 + P)$, where P is the control premium in percentage.

The average control premium paid in 1998 was 40.7%[9] (E17), which implies a discount for lack of control of 28.9% (E18).

A 2.80% member interest has more influence over policy than a typical minority interest in the stock market. Because of the 2.80% member interest's greater control, we reduce the discount for lack of control by 10%, leaving 90% (E19) of the minority interest discount. Multiplying 28.9% × 90% = 26.0% (E20), the discount for lack of control, which we transfer to A10.

Commentary to Table 9-5A: Delay-to-Sale

Table 9-5A displays our calculation of the first of four components of DLOM, the delay-to-sale. The chapter discusses how stock in privately held firms is illiquid. Most firms of substance require a year or more to sell. We begin the calculation by making a comparison of owning a private firm to holding restricted securities of a publicly traded firm.

There have been many studies that consistently find that the sellers of restricted securities, who can choose to wait for two years[10] and sell

9. Houlihan Lokey Howard & Zukin, *Mergerstat Review—1999*, p. 23. There is new research in Chapter 7 of Abrams' book *Quantitative Business Valuation: A Mathematical Approach for Today's Professionals* which suggests that control premiums for private firms probably should be on the order of 21–28% above the marketable minority level. This would imply a lower discount for lack of control. However, in private firms the possibility of wealth transfer from minority interests to control interests could very well increase DLOC. In Chapter 7, Abrams also cites international voting rights premia (VRP) as high as 82% and an American outlier VRP 42% that might indicate the value of control to be higher than 28%. Taking these data into consideration, we use the Mergerstat acquisition premium to arrive at our DLOC.

10. The SEC changed Rule 144 on April 29, 1997 to require only a one year instead of a two year waiting period to sell restricted securities for nonaffiliate owners. The studies we refer to were conducted prior to April 29, 1997, and therefore measure the discount taken at the time of sale instead of waiting two years.

Calculation of Component #1: Delay to Sale [1]

	A	B	C	D
5		**Coefficients**	**Subject Co. Data**	**Discount**
6	Intercept	0.1292	NA	12.9%
7	Revenues^2 (Table 9-3, B7)^2	$-5.39E - 18$	$6.76E + 09$	0.0%
8	Value of block-post-discount [2]	$-4.39E - 09$	$ 30,351	0.0%
9	FMV-100% interest in property (Table 9-2, C22) [3]	$6.10E - 10$	$1,389,185	0.1%
10	Earnings stability (Table 9-5B, B40)	-0.1381	0.1124	-1.6%
11	Revenue stability (Table 9-5B, B21)	-0.1800	0.1749	-3.1%
12	Average years to sell [4]	0.1368	1.0000	13.7%
13	**Total discount (transfer to Table 9-5C, B9)**			**22.0%**
15	Block size in percent	2.80%		

[1] This table is identical to Table 7-5, Regression #2 from Abrams' book, with only subject's data changed.

[2] Equal to fractional interest of FMV * (1-discount for delay to sale).

[3] In the restricted stock study, this was a marketable minority interest value. Due to the limitations of the data available, we must use the FMV of the whole property, which is a control value.

[4] We normally assume it takes one year to sell such illiquid, fractional interests. A 3-month right of first refusal would tend to make this interest somewhat more difficult than most to sell. However, we take a conservative approach and assume it has no further impact. Thus, we remain with a one-year delay to sale.

all or part of their securities according to Rule 144 at the prevailing market price, sell privately at an average discount of 35% (Pratt et al. 1996, chap. 15). However, if a business takes one year on average to sell, what is the discount? Furthermore, should every business be discounted equally for an equal delay-to-sale, or do other business characteristics influence the delay-to-sale discount?

To answer these questions, Jay Abrams developed an original equation for the delay-to-sale discount. The equation was derived by performing regression analysis on the data from the Management Planning Study. The Management Planning Study, presented as an entire chapter in Mercer (1997), contains data on 49 restricted stock trades from 1980-1995. An additional four restricted stock sales in 1996, obtained from Management Planning, were added to the analysis.[11] Abrams tested 37 independent variables included in or derived from the Management Planning study. Only the following 7 independent variables were statistically significant at the 95% level.

#	Independent Variable
1	Revenues squared.
2	Shares sold $-$ $: This is the post-discount dollar value of the transaction.
3	Market capitalization = price per share times shares outstanding summed for all classes of stock.
4	Earnings stability: the unadjusted R^2 of the regression of net income as a function of time, with time measured as years 1, 2, 3, . . . This is calculated in *Quantitative Business Valuation: A Mathematical Approach for Today's Professionals* in Table 7-5, regression #1.
5	Revenue stability: the unadjusted R^2 of the regression of revenue as a function of time, with time measured as years 1, 2, 3, . . . This is calculated in *Quantitative Business Valuation: A Mathematical Approach for Today's Professionals* in Table 7-5, regression #2.

---

11. In addition, Management Planning provided a few small corrections to the original data.

PART 3 Adjusting for Control and Marketability

#	Independent Variable
6	Average years to sell: This is the weighted average years to sell by a nonaffiliate, based on SEC Rule 144.
7	Price stability: this ratio is calculated by dividing the standard deviation of the stock price by the mean of the stock price. The end-of-month stock prices for the 12 months prior to the valuation date are used.

The regression has an adjusted R^2 of 59%. This means that 59% of the variation in restricted stock discounts is explained by the regression model. The subject of this report does not have the data necessary to calculate the Price stability variable. Therefore, we need to use a modified version of the regression which excludes price stability. We also rename variables #2 and #3 "value of block—post-discount" and "FMV-100% interest in the LLC" to better suit the context of this application. The adjusted R^2 of this alternate regression is 43%. The coefficients of the regression equation appear in column B.

In order to employ Abrams' equation, we must determine the parameters for the LLC. Column C contains the LLC's parameters. Cell C7 contains the square of the LLC's 1999 revenue, $6.76 billion, shown as 6.76E+09.

The value of block—post-discount variable actually depends on the final delay-to-sale discount, the dependent variable. Therefore, we must derive the LLC's input for this independent variable through an iterative process. With the aid of a spreadsheet program, the task is simple. We input the FMV of equity, $1,389,185, which comes from Table 9-2, C22, times the percentage interest times one minus the delay-to-sale discount, or $1,389,185 \times 2.80\% \times (1 - D13) = \$30,351$ (C8) for the LLC's value of block—post-discount and activate the iterative capability of the spreadsheet program.

For the FMV-100% interest in the LLC (C9), we simply input the FMV of the LLC's equity, $1,389,185 from Table 9-2, C22.

To determine the LLC's earnings and revenue stability, we perform a regression analysis of the LLC's earnings as a function of time and its revenue as a function of time. The results of the regressions are in Table 9-5B. The R^2 of the earnings regression (Table 9-5B, B40) is the earnings stability of 0.1124 in C10. The R^2 of the revenue regression (Table 9-5B, B21) is the revenue stability of 0.1749 in C11.

Due to the circumstances of the subject member interests, one who desires to sell such a member interest could easily search for several years to find a buyer. We assume a one-year incremental delay to sale, which is a conservative estimate (C12).

To calculate the actual discount for delay to sale, we multiply the coefficients in column B by the LLC's parameters in Column C. Then, we add together the y-intercept value and the products of the coefficients and the parameters, which yields a delay to sale discount of 22.0% (D13). This figure is inserted in Table 9-5C, cell B9.

Commentary to Table 9-5C: Calculation of DLOM

Table 9-5C is our calculation of DLOM. Component 1 was discussed in our commentary to Table 9-5A. Therefore we begin with a discussion of

TABLE 9-5B

Earnings and Revenue Stability

	A	B	C	D
4	Year	Year	Revenue	Income
5	1	1989	$89,044	$1,165
6	2	1990	$79,646	$8,033
7	3	1991	$89,894	$(34,588)
8	4	1992	$90,645	$(25,486)
9	5	1993	$73,825	$(24,984)
10	6	1994	$70,739	$19,203
11	7	1995	$61,853	$(18,186)
12	8	1996	$70,476	$6,916
13	9	1997	$82,054	$25,025
14	10	1998	$75,147	$15,400
15	11	1999	$82,220	$(9,704)

17 SUMMARY OUTPUT-REVENUE REGRESSION

19 **Regression Statistics**

20 Multiple R	0.418245668
21 R square	**0.174929439**
22 Adjusted R square	0.083254932
23 Standard error	8831.270953
24 Observations	11

26 ANOVA

27	df	SS	MS	F	Significance F
28 Regression	1	148819808.3	148819808.3	1.908157952	0.200494368
29 Residual	9	701922119.9	77991346.65		
30 Total	10	850741928.2			

32	Coefficients	Standard Error	t Stat	P-value	Lower 95%	Upper 95%	Lower 95.0%	Upper 95.0%
33 Intercept	85664.6	5710.916139	15.00015022	$1.128E-07$	72745.6003	98583.5997	72745.6	98583.6
34 Year	-1163.145455	842.0286469	-1.381360906	0.200494368	-3067.948041	741.6571321	-3067.95	741.6571

36	SUMMARY OUTPUT-EARNINGS REGRESSION								
38	**Regression Statistics**								
39	Multiple R	0.335265099							
40	R square	**0.112402687**							
41	Adjusted R square	0.013780763							
42	Standard error	20145.2116							
43	Observations	11							
45	ANOVA								
46		df	SS	MS	F	Significance F			
47	Regression	1	462537437.2	462537437.2	1.139733262	0.313506838			
48	Residual	9	3652465953	405829550.4					
49	Total	10	4115003391						
51		Coefficients	Standard Error	t Stat	P-value	Lower 95%	Upper 95%	Lower 95.0%	Upper 95.0%
52	Intercept	−15685.85455	13027.29977	−1.204075658	0.259270779	−45155.67649	13783.9674	−45155.7	13783.97
53	Year	2050.581818	1920.770561	1.067582906	0.313506838	−2294.506377	6395.670013	−2294.51	6395.67

Calculation of DLOM: 2.80% Member Interest

	A	B	C	D	E	F	G
4	Section 1: Calculation of the Discount For Lack of Marketability						
6				= 1 − Col. [C]			
7		Pure Discount	PV of Perpetual	Remaining			
8	Component	= z [1]	Discount [2]	Value			
9	1	22.0%	22.0%	78.0%	Delay to sale-1 yr (Table 9-5A, D13)		
10	2	9.0%	9.0%	91.0%	Buyer's monopsony power-thin markets		
11	3A	2.0%	3.2%	96.8%	Transactions costs-buyers [3]		
12	3B	0.0%	0.0%	100.0%	Transactions costs-sellers [4]		
13	Percent remaining			68.7%	Total % remaining = components 1 × 2 × 3A × 3B		
14	Final discount			**31.3%**	Discount = 1 − Total % Remaining		
16	Section 2: Assumptions and Intermediate Calculations:						
18	Discount rate = r [5]				**13.38%**		
19	Constant growth rate = g [6]				**3.18%**		
20	Intermediate calculation: x = (1 + g)/(1 + r)				**0.9101**		
21	Avg # years between sales = j				**10**		

[1] Pure Discounts: For Component #1, Table 9-5A, cell D13; For Component #2, 9% per Schwert article. For Components #3A and #3B, see notes [3] and [4] below.

[2] Formula For Sellers' Discount: $1 − (1 − x^j)/(1 − (1 − z)^*x^j)$, per equation [7-9], used for Component #3B. Formula For Buyers' Discount: $1 − (1 − z)^*(1 − x^j)/(1 − (1 − z)^*x^j)$, per equation [7-9a], used for Component #3A. Components #1 and #2 simply transfer the pure discount.

[3] We assume 2% incremental costs for the buyer, who would have to perform due diligence on the other member interests in addition to due diligence on the property itself.

[4] Our survey of brokers dealing with fractional LP interests found that brokerage fees for interests in LPs is similar to the standard 6% real estate commission. Therefore, we assume that there are no incremental costs for the seller.

[5] Per Cost of Capital Quarterly-1999, SIC Code 6798 (REITs), 10 Yr Avg. Small Composite returns = 10.38%. We add 3% for the incremental risk of a small operation with very low profits.

[6] This equals the total returns minus expected distributions, Table 9-4, C9 minus C12.

Component 2, buyer's monopsony power, and Components 3A and 3B, buyers' and sellers' transactions costs.

Buyer's Monopsony Power

The control stockholders of privately held firms have no guarantee at all that they can sell their firms. The market for privately held businesses is very thin. Most small and medium-sized firms are unlikely to attract more than a small handful of buyers—and even then probably not more than one or two every several months—while the seller of publicly traded stock has millions of potential buyers. Just as a monopolist is a single seller who can drive up price by withholding production, a single buyer—a monopsonist—can drive price down by withholding purchase.

The presence of 100 or even 10 interested buyers is likely to drive the selling price of a business to its theoretical maximum, i.e., "the right price." The absence of enough buyers may confer monopsony power to the few who are interested. Therefore, a small, unexciting business will have an additional component to the discount for lack of marketability because of the additional bargaining power accruing to the buyers in thin markets.

It is easy to think that component 2 might already be included in component 1, i.e., they both derive from the long time it takes to sell an illiquid asset. To demonstrate that they are indeed distinct components and that we are not double counting, it is helpful to consider the hypothetical case of a very exciting privately held firm that has just discovered the cure for cancer. Such a firm would have no lack of interested buyers, yet it still is very unlikely to be sold in less than one year. In that year other things could happen. Congress could pass legislation regulating the medical breakthrough, and the value could decrease significantly. Therefore, it would still be necessary to have a significant discount for component 1, while component 2 would be zero. It may not take longer to sell the corner dry cleaning store, but the first firm is virtually guaranteed to be able to sell at the highest price after its required marketing time, whereas the dry cleaning store will have the additional uncertainty of sale. Also, its few buyers would have more negotiating power than the buyers of the firm with the cure for cancer.

The results from Schwert, described in Chapter 7 of *Quantitative Business Valuation: A Mathematical Approach for Today's Professionals*, are relevant here.[12] He found that the presence of multiple bidders for control of publicly-held companies on average led to increased premiums of 12.2% compared to takeovers without competitive bidding. Based on the regression in Table 4 of his article, we assumed a typical deal configuration that would apply to a privately-held firm.[13] The premium without an auction was 21.5%. Adding 12.2%, the premium with an auction was 33.7%. To calculate the discount for lack of competition, we go in the other direction, i.e., 12.2% divided by one + 33.7% = 0.122/1.337 = 9.1%, or approximately 9%. This is a useful benchmark for the second component of DLOM. We have inserted it in Table 9-5C, B10.

It is quite possible that the buyer's monopsony power for any subject interest should be larger or smaller than 9%, depending on the facts and circumstances of the situation. We are using Schwert's measure of the effect of multiple versus single bidders as a conservative estimate for component 2. It may possibly have a downward bias because the markets for the underlying minority interests in the same firms is very deep. So it is only the market for *control* of publicly held firms that is thin. The market for privately held firms is thin for whole firms and razor thin for minority interests. A 9% buyer's monopsony power discount (B10) for the subject interest is a conservative assumption.

Transactions Costs

Transactions costs for both the buyer and the seller include: legal, accounting, and appraisal fees, the opportunity cost of internal management spending its time on the sale rather than on other company business, and investment banking (or, for small sales, business broker) fees. The appraisal fees are for two main categories: the pre-transaction deal appraisal to help buyer and/or seller establish the right price, and post-transaction, tax-based appraisal for allocation of purchase price and/or valuation of in-process R&D.

We are only interested in incremental transactions costs that occur as a result of a fractional interest transaction. The buyer of a 2.80% member interest would not only have to perform due diligence on the LLC itself,

---

12. G. William Schwert, "Markup Pricing in Mergers and Acquisitions." *Journal of Financial Economics 41* (1996): 153–192.
13. We assume a successful purchase, a tender offer, and a cash deal.

but also on the other members. Thus, the buyer would experience additional due diligence costs, which we estimate at 2% (B11). For the seller, we assume a zero incremental brokerage cost (B12).

Transactions costs are different than the first two components of DLOM. For Components 3A and 3B we need to explicitly calculate the present value of the occurrence of transactions costs every time the interest sells. The reason is that, unlike the first two components, transactions costs are actually out-of-pocket costs that leave the system. They are paid to attorneys, accountants, appraisers, and investment bankers or business brokers. Additionally, the internal management of both the buyer and the seller must spend significant time on the project to make it happen, and they often have to spend time on failed acquisitions before being successful.

We need to distinguish between the buyer's transactions costs and the seller's costs. This is because the buyer's transactions costs are always relevant, whereas the seller's transactions costs for the immediate transaction reduce the net proceeds to the seller but do not reduce FMV. However, before the buyers are willing to buy, they should be saying, "It's true, I don't care about the sellers' costs. That's their problem. However, 10 years or so down the road when it's my turn to be the seller, I do care about that." To the extent that sellers' costs exceed the brokerage cost of selling publicly-traded stock, in 10 years my buyer will pay me less because of those costs, and therefore I must pay my sellers less because of my costs as a seller in Year 10. Additionally, the process goes on forever, because in Year 20, my buyer becomes a seller and faces the same problem." Thus, we need to quantify the present value of periodic buyer's transactions costs through an infinity of time beginning with the immediate sale and sellers' transactions costs that begin with the second sale of the business. With the following two formulas, we can adjust the sellers' and buyers' transactions costs to present value and calculate the resulting discount as follows:

Formula for NPV of buyers' costs

$$D_{3A} = 1 - \frac{(1 - z)(1 - x^J)}{1 - (1 - z)x^J}, \text{ where } x = \frac{1 + g}{1 + r}$$

Formula for NPV of sellers' costs

$$D_{3B} = 1 - \frac{1 - x^j}{1 - (1 - z)x^j}$$

In the above equations, D is the discount for transactions costs, g is the growth rate of the business, r is the discount rate of the business, j is the average number of years between transactions, and $g < r, \Rightarrow 0 < x < 1$. The derivation of these two equations appears in the Mathematical Appendix to Chapter 7 of *Quantitative Business Valuation: A Mathematical Approach for Today's Professionals*. An analysis of partial derivatives in the Mathematical Appendix shows that the discount, i.e., DLOM, always increases with increases in growth (g) and transactions costs (z) and always decreases with increases in the discount rate (r) and the average number of years between sales (j). The converse is true as well. Decreases in the independent variables have the opposite effect of increases on DLOM.

To apply these equations to the LLC, we must determine a discount rate, a growth rate, and an average number of years between sales. Our assumptions for these variables are in section 2 of Table 9-5C. We assume a 13.38% discount rate (E18). We derive the discount rate by adding the following components:

1. The 10-year average rate of return on investment for a small composite of Real Estate Investment Trusts of 10.38%;[14] plus

2. A 3% premium for incremental risk of a small operation with very low profits, based on professional judgment.

The expected growth rate for the LLC is the expected total returns minus expected distributions, or Table 9-4, cell C9 minus C12, or 3.74% − 0.55% = 3.18% (Table 9-5C, E19).[15]

The present value of the 2% pure discount for buyers' incremental transactions costs is 3.2% (C11), and it is zero (C12) for the sellers' zero incremental transactions costs. As we explained above, there is no need to adjust the first two DLOM components.

Final DLOM
To calculate the final DLOM, we must first compute the value remaining after each discount. The remaining values after the four discounts are 100% − 22% = 78% (D9), 100% − 9.0% = 91% (D10), 100% − 3.2% = 96.8% (D11), and 100% − 0% = 100.0% (D12). The total remaining value is the product of the remaining values of all the components of DLOM, 78.0% × 91.0% × 96.8% × 100.0% = 68.7% (D13). Subtracting the total remaining value from one yields a total DLOM of 31.3% (D14). We insert this figure in Table 9-5, cell A9.

Commentary to Table 9-6: Partnership Profiles Approach—1999[16]

The May/June 1999 edition of *The Partnership Spectrum*, a statistical compendium published by Partnership Profiles, Inc., contains a wealth of data about trades in the secondary limited partnership market, including the average discount at which each partnership sold from its valuation. Table 9-6B shows the partnerships and their related discounts.

Comparability of Partnership Profiles to the Subject Interest
The member interests are fairly comparable to the LP interests in the Partnership Profiles database. An ideal database to value the member interests would be one that contained information on the selling prices, discounts from underlying net asset value, and other relevant factors that could affect discounts for member interests of a size and nature similar to the subject of our valuation. This would be an "apples-to apples" comparison. Because of the differences between the member interests we are

---

14. *Cost of Capital Quarterly*—1999, SIC Code #6798 (REITs), Ibbotson Associates.
15. There is an apparent, but not real, rounding error.
16. The author regrets that because this section contains so many statistical concepts and so much necessary statistical jargon, it is difficult reading (refer to Partnership Profiles, Inc. website at partnershipprofiles.com).

valuing and the Partnership Profiles LP interests, we make adjustments to the calculated discount as discussed later.

Statistical Methodology

We performed extensive multiple regression analysis of the database. As independent variables, we tested regular (Ryields) and special distribution yields (Syields) for 1992–1998, in simple form as well as quadratic, natural logarithms, and inverses; cumulative cash distributions as a percentage of 1998 FMV; unrealized capital gains; leverage; FMV; property type; triple/net leases; and independent versus General Partner appraisal. Logarithms and reciprocals of zero have been converted to logarithms and reciprocals of 0.001. We removed all variables with statistical significance under 95% and repeated the regression.[17]

Regression Results of Partnership Profiles Database

The top of Table 9-6 shows the overall regression results. R^2 and adjusted R^2 are 70.4% (B8) and 69.4% (B9), respectively.[18] This means that the regression model explains 69.4% of the variation in the discounts.

The standard error of the y-estimate is 7.96% (B10). We can form an approximate 95% confidence interval around the regression estimate by adding and subtracting two standard errors, or approximately $\pm 15.9\%$.

There are three independent variables in the final regression:

1. **Leverage:** The ratio of debt to the December 31, 1998, market value of assets (Debt/MVA98).
2. 1998 regular yield (Ryld98),[19]
3. A dummy variable for triple-net leases (TNL).

The regression equation is:

$$\text{Average Discount} = 0.387 + (0.115 \times \text{Leverage}) - (2.296 \times 1998 \text{ Yield})$$
$$- (0.073 \times \text{TNL})$$

The y-intercept and the x-coefficients appear in cells B20 to B23. The y-intercept of 0.387 means that when all the independent variables have a zero value, then the average discount from net asset value is 38.7%. All three independent variables are zero when the LP has no leverage, cash distributions, or triple-net leases.

The signs of the x-coefficients are important. The positive sign to the leverage variable means that increased financial leverage increases the discount from net asset value. This is intuitively appealing, as leveraged

---

17. The statistical significance level is the degree of confidence that we have that the coefficient of the independent variable is not really zero. A 90% significance level, e.g., means we are 90% certain that the coefficient of that variable is really not zero instead of the measure that we obtained from the regression.
18. The adjusted R^2 is a downward adjustment to remove the effects of irrelevant variables randomly increasing R^2.
19. This variable excludes special distributions. Also, the database did show first quarter 1999 distributions for many of the partnerships and second quarter distributions for some, but using sporadic data such as this would cloud our results. Therefore, we used distributions for the first prior full year, 1998, which all partnerships reported.

TABLE 9-6

Regression Analysis of Partnership Profiles Database—1999 [1]

	A	B	C	D	E	F	G
4	SUMMARY OUTPUT						
6	**Regression Statistics**						
7	Multiple R	0.839306575					
8	R square	0.704435526					
9	Adjusted R square	0.693752473					
10	Standard error	0.079631408					
11	Observations	87					
13	ANOVA						
14		df	SS	MS	F	Significance F	
15	Regression	3	1.254399586	0.41813	65.93953	6.66022E-22	
16	Residual	83	0.526316376	0.00634			
17	Total	86	1.780715963				
19		Coefficients	Std Error	t Stat	P-value	Lower 95%	Upper 95%
20	Intercept	0.387231995	0.023	16.5698	7.73E-28	0.340750627	0.433713
21	Debt/MVA98	0.115269034	0.043	2.66025	0.00937	0.029086922	0.201451
22	RYld98	−2.29555895	0.320	−7.17703	2.75E-10	−2.931724028	−1.659394
23	TNL	−0.07286963	0.022	−3.35275	0.001207	−0.116098278	−0.029641
26	**Variable**	**X-Coefficient**	**Client Data**	**Regress**			
27	Debt/MVA98 (B33)	0.115269034	0.0%	0.0%			
28	RYld98 (Table 9-4, C12)	−2.29555895	0.005528601	−1.3%			
29	TNL	−0.07286963	0	0.0%			
30	Subtotal			−1.3%			
31	Intercept			38.7%			
32	Discount before adjustments			37.5%			
33	Adjustments:						
34	No public registration [2]			15.0%			
35	Increased influence [3]			−5.0%			
36	Total adjustments			**10.0%**			
37	Discount			**47.5%**			
39	**Calculation of Debt/MVA98**						
40	Debt	0					
41	MVA98 (market value of assets-1998) [4]	1,389,185					
42	Debt/MVA98	0.0%					

[1] Based on the data in Table 9-6B.
[2] The Partnership Profiles LPs are publicly registered, which is not true of the Member interests. Thus, the latter should bear a larger discount for that factor.
[3] The Partnership Profiles Limited Partners have no influence over the Partnership, while the subject Member interests do. We decrease the discount to account for that difference.
[4] Table 9-2, C22.

firms are riskier than equity-financed firms, and the higher the risk, the higher the discount. The negative signs to the other two variables—yield and triple-net lease—mean that investors consider LPs with higher cash yields and triple-net leases to be lower risk, which is also true. Thus, our regression results make intuitive sense. Also, higher cash yields make up for some of the disadvantage of lack of marketability.

The yields were significant in nonlinear forms, that is, natural logarithms, denoted as ln, and inverses. Additionally, the cumulative yield since inception was also statistically significant. While these additional independent variables did add to the adjusted R^2 and lowered the standard error of the y-estimate, they did not dramatically improve the regression results, and it is far easier and more practical to work with a much simpler equation.

Commentary to Table 9-6A: Correlation Matrix

Table 9-6A is a correlation matrix. Looking down column B, we can see that the average discount is strongly negatively correlated to yields (B7–B10), the restaurant dummy variable (B15), and triple-net leases (B19). This means that high cash distributions to LPs drive down discounts, which is intuitive.

Triple-net leases (TNL) also result in lower discounts, which is also intuitive, because TNL landlords have far less operating risk than other landlords. The correlation of discounts to restaurants is really an indirect relationship, because there is a strong positive correlation of 82% (L19) between TNL and restaurants. In other words, it means that most restaurants are on a TNL.

The average discount is strongly positively related only to leverage (Debt/MVA98) (B6). Looking down column C, we can see that leverage is strongly negatively related to yields. This also makes sense, as highly leveraged partnerships have to worry about making their debt payments before they consider making cash distributions.

It is significant that the yields across time are highly correlated. For example, the 1998 yields are 78%, 81%, and 75% correlated to the 1997, 1996, and 1995 yields, respectively, as can be seen in cells D8 through D10.

By using the 1998 yield as the only yield appearing as an independent variable in the regression equation, we still indirectly pick up the earlier yields because they are so highly correlated. Using only one year's yield has the additional benefit of removing the problem of multicollinearity. When the subject interest 1998 and earlier yields are uncorrelated, then it is necessary to use a more long-run value for the 1998 yields. For example, if 1998 yields are extraordinarily high (low) and expected to decrease (increase) in the future, then it is appropriate to eliminate the extraordinary part of the subject interest's yield and only use that portion which one would reasonably expect to continue in the future with normal growth.

Applying the Regression Equation

We apply the above regression equation to the LLC in Table 9-6, Rows 26 to 32. First, we repeat the regression x-coefficients from B21 to B23 in B27 to B29. The LLC's data are in C27 to C29. The triple-net-lease dummy variable equals zero, as the LLC's properties are not subject to TNLs. We multiply the x-coefficients in B27 to B29 by the LLC's data in C27 to C29 to come to the regression results for the LLC in D27 to D29, which we subtotal in D30 as -1.3%. We then repeat the y-intercept of 38.7% from B20 in D31 and add that to the subtotal, to come to a discount before adjustments of 37.5% (D32).

T A B L E   9-6A

Correlation Matrix

	A	B	C	D	E	F	G	H	I	J	K	L	M	N	O	P	Q
4		Avg Disc	Debt/MVA98	RYld98	RYld97	RYld96	RYld95	C	MF	R	MH	RST	Combo	Parking	Eq Dist	TNL	Indep
5	Avg disc	1.00															
6	Debt/MVA98	0.61	1.00														
7	RYld98	−0.80	−0.61	1.00													
8	RYld97	−0.64	−0.42	0.78	1.00												
9	RYld96	−0.68	−0.48	0.81	0.76	1.00											
10	RYld95	−0.65	−0.47	0.75	0.72	0.88	1.00										
11	C	0.07	0.12	0.00	−0.11	−0.15	−0.15	1.00									
12	MF	0.00	0.28	0.04	0.14	0.12	0.04	−0.19	1.00								
13	R	0.01	−0.06	0.01	−0.02	0.02	0.01	−0.08	−0.14	1.00							
14	MH	0.16	0.13	−0.07	−0.04	−0.01	−0.04	−0.09	−0.16	−0.07	1.00						
15	RST	−0.52	−0.35	0.40	0.34	0.43	0.41	−0.15	−0.28	−0.12	−0.13	1.00					
16	Combo	0.20	0.02	−0.21	−0.18	−0.26	−0.15	−0.20	−0.36	−0.15	−0.17	−0.29	1.00				
17	Parking	−0.09	−0.09	0.01	0.01	0.02	0.02	−0.05	−0.09	−0.04	−0.04	−0.07	−0.09	1.00			
18	Eq dist	0.14	−0.05	−0.09	−0.09	−0.21	−0.11	0.04	0.14	0.08	0.31	−0.42	0.29	0.17	1.00		
19	TNL	−0.51	−0.22	0.43	0.36	0.46	0.44	0.09	−0.34	−0.03	−0.16	0.82	−0.24	−0.09	−0.51	1.00	
20	Indep	−0.20	−0.37	0.30	0.16	0.16	0.20	0.27	−0.43	0.07	−0.07	0.40	−0.16	−0.14	−0.11	0.47	1.00

Partnership Profiles Database: Price-to-Value Discounts—1999

5	A Name	B Avg Disc
6	Aetna Real Estate Associates	23%
7	ChrisKen Partners Cash Income	28%
8	Consolidated Capital Inst. Props. 1	28%
9	Consolidated Capital Inst. Props. 2	35%
10	First Capital Inst. Real Estate 4	21%
11	HCW Pension Real Estate Fund	29%
12	I.R.E. Pension Investors II	40%
13	John Hancock Realty Income Fund II	12%
14	Murray Income Properties I	25%
15	Murray Income Properties II	25%
16	Rancon Income Fund I	39%
17	Realty Parking Properties I	8%
18	Realty Parking Properties II	28%
19	Wells Real Estate Fund II-A	8%
20	Wells Real Estate Fund III-A	31%
21	Wells Real Estate Fund IV-A	38%
22	Wells Real Estate Fund VI-A	26%
23	Wells Real Estate Fund VII-A	25%
24	Wells Real Estate Fund VIII-A	24%
25	Wells Real Estate Fund IX-A	24%
26	Wells Real Estate Fund X-A	20%
27	Windsor Park Properties 6	15%
28	Angeles Income Properties II	30%
29	Angeles Opportunity Properties	37%
30	Angeles Partners XII	34%
31	ChrisKen Growth & Income II	16%
32	Consolidated Capital Inst. Props. 3	25%
33	Consolidated Capital Properties III	28%
34	Davidson Growth Plus	41%
35	Davidson Income Real Estate	38%
36	Multi-Benefit Realty Fund '87-1 (A units)	29%
37	Nooney Income Fund II	42%
38	Shelter Properties VII	35%
39	Uniprop Man. Hous. Com. Inc. Fund I	45%
40	Uniprop Man. Hous. Com. Inc. Fund II	41%
41	Windsor Park Properties 3	38%
42	Windsor Park Properties 5	27%
43	Windsor Park Properties 7	46%
44	Angeles Income Properties III	42%
45	Angeles Income Properties IV	42%
46	Angeles Income Properties 6	29%
47	Angeles Partners IX	36%
48	Angeles Partners XI	25%
49	Consolidated Capital Properties V	52%
50	Davidson Diversified Real Estate I	62%

Adjustments to the Discount

For Lack of Public Registration. The Partnership Profiles database consists exclusively of firms that are publicly registered, though privately traded. The lack of public registration of the member interests renders them less marketable than the Partnership Profiles database. Therefore we must increase the fractional interest discount for that factor. We assume that a 15% increase is reasonable (D34).

Partnership Profiles Database: Price-to-Value Discounts—1999

5	A Name	B Avg Disc
51	Davidson Diversified Real Estate II	61%
52	Davidson Diversified Real Estate III	38%
53	First Capital Income Properties XI	41%
54	First Capital Income & Growth Fund XII	44%
55	First Dearborn Income Properties	58%
56	Multi-Benefit Realty Fund '87-1 (B units)	57%
57	InLand Capital Fund	47%
58	Inland Land Appreciation Fund I	45%
59	Inland Land Appreciation Fund II	48%
60	Scottsdale Land Trust	46%
61	CNL Income Fund III	9%
62	CNL Income Fund V	9%
63	CNL Income Fund VI	15%
64	CNL Income Fund VII	11%
65	CNL Income Fund VIII	16%
66	CNL Income Fund IX	11%
67	CNL Income Fund X	12%
68	CNL Income Fund XI	17%
69	CNL Income Fund XII	13%
70	CNL Income Fund XIII	15%
71	CNL Income Fund XIV	8%
72	CNL Income Fund XV	6%
73	CNL Income Fund XVI	14%
74	CNL Income Fund XVIII	7%
75	Carey Institutional Properties	28%
76	Corporate Property Associates 10	16%
77	Corporate Realty Income Fund I	27%
78	DiVall Income Properties 3	12%
79	DiVall Insured Income Properties 2	1%
80	John Hancock Realty Income Fund III	12%
81	Net 1 LP	23%
82	Net 2 LP	28%
83	Capital Mortgage Plus	23%
84	Capital Source LP	15%
85	Capital Source LP II	22%
86	Krupp Government Income Trust	10%
87	Krupp Government Income Trust II	15%
88	Krupp Insured Mortgage LP	9%
89	Krupp Insured Plus LP	15%
90	Krupp Insured Plus II	11%
91	Krupp Insured Plus III	2%
92	Paine Webber Insured Mortgage 1-B	21%
93	**Max**	**61.7%**
94	**Min**	**0.8%**
95	**Mean**	**26.8%**
96	**Std deviation**	**14.4%**

For Additional Influence of Private versus Public Interest. The member interests should have more influence than the small LP interests from which we calculated the regression coefficients, and they actually do have a vote. We reduce the discount by 5% in D35.

The adjustments for lack of public registration and additional influence are both reasonable estimates. In total, our net adjustments are 10%

(D36). Adding D32 and D36, the total discount for the LLC interest is 47.5% (D37).

Benchmarks for Net Effect of the Adjustments. The x-coefficients for the dummy variables can give us a feel for how the discount might vary if Partnership Profiles had data available on trades of LLCs with assets more similar to our subject. The coefficient for the triple-net lease dummy variable is 7.2%. In earlier years, typical coefficients for other dummy variables have ranged from -5–12%. Therefore, the net adjustment for no public registration and increased influence of 10% appears reasonable.

There is another way to benchmark the net adjustments. According to Jay Abrams' conversations with brokers who sell LP interests, shifting from selling a publicly registered LP interest to a private LP interest adds approximately 7–10 months in the selling time, which is 58–83% of one year. If we multiply that by the "Average Years to Sell" x-coefficient of 0.1368 in Abrams' book[20], we get an increase in discount of 8–11%. In the book, there was another regression[21], and the "Average Years to Sell" x-coefficient for that one was 0.1722. Using that instead of the 0.1368 leads to estimates of the net adjustment of 10–14%. Furthermore, it is reasonable to assume that the decrease in discount from the "increased influence" factor in the private LP is offset by the increase in the discount for the additional monopsony power to the buyer of the private LP interest. Thus, 8% to 14% is a reasonable range for net adjustments.

Commentary to Table 9-7: Private Fractional Interest Sales

Robert Jones, a real estate appraiser with the firm Jones, Roach & Caringella in San Diego, provided us with actual transaction data for illiquid fractional interests in real estate. Table 9-7 shows the detail and our analysis of the interests and their related discounts.

Comparability to the Subject Interest

The member interests are very comparable to the fractional interests in Table 9-7. The main difference is that the subject member interest represents ownership in several properties, not just one.

Statistical Methodology

We performed simple and multiple regression analysis of the database. As independent variables, we tested the transaction amount (Price), the percentage interest (Size), the FMV of the entire property, and dummy variables for the time period of the transaction (pre-1990) and whether the interest was a GP interest in a general partnership. We did not have yield data.

---

20. Table 7-5, p. 240, cell B54. In other words, the regression in the book shows that for each year of inability to sell, restricted stocks experience a discount of 13.68%.

21. Applicable when the subject company has been publicly traded for at least six months, and thus historical stock prices are available to calculate the "Price Stability" variable. See Table 7-5, p. 239, cell B26.

Regression Results of Partnership Profiles Database

The bottom of Table 9-7 shows the overall regression results. R^2 and adjusted R^2 are 49.0% (C37) and 41.7% (C38), respectively.[22] This means that the regression model explains 41.7% of the variation in the discounts.

The standard error of the y-estimate is 10.07% (B10). We can form an approximate 95% confidence interval around the regression estimate by adding and subtracting two standard errors, or approximately ±20.1%.

The dummy variable for whether the transaction was pre-1990 or not is the only variable in the final regression:

The regression equation is:

$$\text{Average Discount} = 0.4679 - 0.1846 \times \text{pre-1990}$$

The y-intercept and the x-coefficient appear in cells B43 to B44. The y-intercept of 0.4679 means that when all the independent variables have a zero value, or in this case when the transaction occurs after the end of the 1980s, then the average discount from net asset value is 46.79%, or 46.8% rounded.

One should not place great weight on the regression equation above. It was derived from a small data set, and the explanatory variable for yield is missing. It is nevertheless relevant evidence of the fractional interest discount in real-world transactions.

Commentary to Table 9-8: Final Calculation of Fractional Interest Discounts

2.80% Member Interest

To calculate the final discount, we weight the first two valuation approaches equally at 45% each, as both approaches appear equally important, valid, and reliable. The third approach we weight only 10% because of the small and incomplete data set from which its regression model was derived. The 49.2% (C8) discount calculated using the economic components approach comes from Table 9-5, B12, the 47.5% (C9) discount using the Partnership Profiles Regression comes from Table 9-6, D37, and the 46.8% (C10) discount comes from Table 9-6, C43.[23] The weighted average of the three discounts is 48.2% (E11), which we round to 48% in E12.

Final Calculation of FMV of Fractional Interests

Gifts Transferred on December 25, 1999. To calculate the FMV of the 2.80% fractional interests gifted on December 25, 1999, we calculate the dollar value of a 100% fractional interest discount, $1,389,185 × 48% = $666,809 (B18 × B19 = B20). Note that B18 is the FMV of the equity before discounts, which comes from Table 9-2, C22.

Next we subtract this discount from the FMV of equity to determine the FMV of a 100% Fractional Interest, $1,389,185 − $666,809 = $722,376

---

22. The adjusted R^2 is a downward adjustment to remove the effects of irrelevant variables randomly increasing R^2.

23. As this is not a pre-1990 valuation, the regression estimate for the discount is equal to the intercept coefficient.

T A B L E 9-7

Private Fractional Interest Sales [1]

	A	B	C	D	E	F	G	H	I	J	K
4							Pro-Rata				
5				Date	Size	FMV-100%	Value	Price	Discount	Pre 1990	GP
6	1	Linda Vista Rd., S Diego [2] [3]	GP	1/1/1984	6.7%	NA	NA	NA	20.0%	1	1
7	2	Eighth Ave., S. Diego	TIC	9/1/1985	66.7%	60,000	40,000	27,000	32.5%	1	0
8	3	Fifth Ave., S. Diego [2] [4]	GP	4/1/1988	33.3%	3,000,000	1,000,000	675,000	32.5%	1	1
9	4	West 61st St., Los Angeles	TIC	10/1/1996	33.3%	90,000	30,000	10,000	66.7%	0	0
10	5	Garden Grove Ave., Reseda	TIC	10/1/1996	25.0%	145,000	36,250	22,000	39.3%	0	0
11	6	K St., S. Diego	TIC	2/1/1998	20.0%	325,000	65,000	36,000	44.6%	0	0
12	7	So. Calif. [5]	LP	7/1/1998	2.5%	5,460,000	136,500	75,000	45.1%	0	0
13	8	So. Calif. [5]	LP	7/1/1998	0.5%	14,800,000	74,000	37,000	50.0%	0	0
14	9	Brant St., S. Diego	TIC	6/1/1999	50.0%	1,680,000	840,000	545,000	35.1%	0	0

[1] Source of data: Jones, Roach & Caringella, Real Estate Appraisers, S. Diego.

[2] These are interests in General Partnerships, not GP interests in Limited Partnerships.

[3] The seller reportedly would not hypothecate her interest for a required construction loan and offered to sell her interest to another partner who would. This indicates that the seller may have have had unusual leverage, which may have reduced the discount.

[4] We have reduced the nominal selling price of $750,000 by 10% to account for the "very beneficial financing" provided to the buyer by the seller. Exact details of the financing agreement are unknown.

[5] The seller had tried to sell his interest on the open market and had offers at a 75% discount from pro rata value. He then sold his interest to the GP, who had tried to discourage the sale. It is quite possible that the GP did not extract the full market discount and that the full discount was actually 75%. This is because the GP is in the business of forming partnerships, not taking advantage of limited partners.

REGRESSION RESULTS [6]

35	Regression Statistics	
36	Multiple R	0.7000
37	R square	0.4900
38	Adjusted R square	0.4171
39	Standard error	0.1007
40	Observations	9

42		Coeff	Std Error	t Stat	P-value	Lower 95%	Upper 95%
43	Intercept	0.4679	0.0411	11.3857	0.0000	0.3708	0.5651
44	Pre 1990	-0.1846	0.0712	-2.5933	0.0358	-0.3529	-0.0163

[6] We found that with the constraints of the available data, the best explanatory variable for discounts was the time of the transaction, where the time is categorized pre-1990 or post-1990. This might best be explained by investors' increased perception of risk due to the real estate crash in 1990. Had it been available, we would expect that using yield as a second independent variable would have significantly increased the explanatory power of the regression.

Final Calculation of Fractional Interest Discount

	A	B	C	D	E
4	**2.80% Member Interest**				
6			**Indication**		**Wtd Avg**
7		**Table**	**of Discount**	**Weight**	**Discount**
8	Economic components approach	9-5, B12	49.2%	45.0%	22.1%
9	Regression of partnership profiles database	9-6, D37	47.5%	45.0%	21.4%
10	Regression of private fractional interest data [1]	V-3, C43	46.8%	10.0%	4.7%
11	Total			100.0%	48.2%
12	**Round to**				**48%**
14	Final Calculation of FMV of Fractional Interests				
16	**Date of gift**	**12/25/99**	**1/3/00**		
17	**Fractional interest**	**2.80%**	**2.25%**		
18	FMV of equity (Table 9-2, C22)	$1,389,185	$1,389,185		
19	Fractional interest discount-% (E11)	48%	48%		
20	Fractional interest account-$	$ 666,809	$ 666,809		
21	100% fractional interest FMV of equity	$ 722,376	$ 722,376		
22	FMV of 2.80% and 2.25% member interests	$ 20,227	$ 16,253		
23	**Rounded FMV of 2.80% and 2.25% member interests**	**$ 20,000**	**$ 16,250**		

Note: Mrs. Smith intends to make four gifts of $16,250 on approximately 1/3/2000. We have ignored second-order effects of gifting a smaller interest (2.25% vs. 2.80%) in Table 9-5A, B15, as it has no impact on the final calculation. Thus, in our opinion, a 2.25% interest gifted on 1/3/2000 has a FMV of $16,250.

[1] As this is not a pre-1990 valuation, the regression estimate for the discount is equal to the intercept coefficient. We do not weight this valuation method heavily, due to the relatively little data that were available for the regression.

(B18 − B20 = B21). Finally, we multiply the FMV of a 100% fractional interest by the 2.80% interest to calculate the FMV of the 2.80% member interest, $722,376 × 2.80% = $20,227 (B21 × B17 = B22), which we round to $20,000 in B23.

Gifts Transferred on January 3, 2000. Mrs. Smith also made four gifts of 2.25% LP interests on January 3, 2000, which we value in column C. We multiply the $722,376 (C21 = B21) 100% fractional interest fair market value of the equity by a 2.25% member interest in C17 to arrive at a fair market value of $16,253 (C22), which we round to $16,250 (C23).

The calculations in Table 9-5A depend on the size of the interests in cell B15. However, the change from a 2.80% member interest to a 2.25% member interest is so small that it actually has no impact. Thus, we use the same fractional interest discount of 48% for the January 3, 2000 gifts.

Conclusion

In our opinion, subject to this report and the Statement of Limiting Conditions, the appropriate fractional interest discount for a **2.80%** and **2.25%** member interests in the LLC as of December 25, 1999 through January 3, 2000 is **48%,** which amounts to fair market values of **$20,000** and **$16,250,** respectively.

STATEMENT OF LIMITING CONDITIONS

In accordance with recognized professional ethics, the fee for this service is not contingent upon our conclusion of fractional interest discount, and neither Abrams Valuation Group nor any of its employees has a present or intended interest in the subject interest.

We have relied upon financial information provided by Bradley Jones and David Sofer, CPA, and have accepted it as correct without further verification. We assume there are no material transactions between December 14, 1999, the date of the LLC's financial statements, and December 25, 1999, and January 3, 2000, the dates of the gifts. For use of this report in the year 2000, we assume there are no material changes in property values and that there are no material changes in the equity of the LLC or its member interests.

All other information used in this report is from sources we deem reliable. We have accurately reflected such information in this report; however, we make no representation as to our sources' accuracy or completeness and have accepted their information without further verification.

We have not made a physical visit to the properties. We assume that the present owners would continue to maintain the character and integrity of the property through any sale, reorganization, or diminution of the owners' participation or equity interest. We also assume there are no present or future "skeletons in the closet," e.g., environmental problems with the property, litigation, and so on.

Our opinion of the fractional interest discount in this report is valid only for the stated purpose and only for the effective dates of the appraisal. It is our understanding that this opinion will be used for gift tax purposes. The fractional interest discount shall not be used for other purposes and cannot even be used for the same purposes and time frame for different size member interests, as they could be misleading and dangerous. Though some similarities exist between the fractional interest discount for this purpose and others, it would be incorrect to use the discount as determined in our report for any other purposes. Specific timing, performance, and marketability issues that arise in evaluating the fair market value of the properties and related ownership interests could change the results. Accordingly, any such use of the fractional interest discount as determined in this report for other purposes or effective dates may be inaccurate and misleading, and no such use shall be made without our written consent.

Our determination of the fractional interest discount does not represent investment advice of any kind to any person and does not constitute a recommendation as to the purchase or sale of shares of the property or related interests or regarding any other course of action.

Future services regarding the subject matter of this report, including, but not limited to, testimony or attendance in court shall not be required of Abrams Valuation Group unless previous arrangements have been made in writing.

No part or all of the contents of this report shall be conveyed to the public through advertising, public relations, news, sales, mail, direct transmittal, or other media without the prior written consent and approval of Abrams Valuation Group. This report may only be distributed in its entirety to those directly involved with the purpose of this study. All other users are to be considered unintended users.

This report may not be distributed in part, as only a thorough reading of this report can accurately convey the logic contained within. Excerpts taken out of context can be dangerously misleading and are therefore forbidden without the written consent of Abrams Valuation Group.

APPRAISER'S QUALIFICATIONS

Jay B. Abrams, ASA, CPA, MBA, author and inventor, is a nationally recognized valuation economist.

Mr. Abrams lectured at the June 1996 Toronto International Conference of the American Society of Appraisers, the organization from which he holds the professional designation of Accredited Senior Appraiser (ASA) in Business Valuation. He has lectured for the National Association of Certified Valuation Analysts and the Anthony Robbins' Financial Mastery Seminar.

Mr. Abrams has provided services to clients representing a variety of organizations from small entrepreneurs to Columbia Pictures, Dr. Pepper, Purex Corporation, and other Fortune 1000 firms in the area of intangibles, including goodwill, customer lists, licensing agreements, contracts, and business enterprise and capital stock appraisals for numerous purposes, including the following:

- Employee stock ownership plans (ESOPs).
- Estate planning, estate and gift taxes.
- Income taxes and charitable contributions.
- Mergers and acquisitions and sales.
- Divestitures.
- Warrants and stock options.
- Shareholder buy/sell agreements.
- Blocks of publicly traded securities.
- Private placements and public offerings.
- Restricted securities.
- Recapitalization and reorganizations.
- Debt and equity financing.
- Company dissolutions.
- Litigation settlement.

Additionally, Mr. Abrams has prepared and given expert testimony in the capital stock and business enterprise valuation areas in various courts of law.

Mr. Abrams' valuation experience encompasses a wide array of industries and assignments, for mergers/acquisitions, sales and leaseback, litigation support, leveraged buyouts, and stockholder agreements. Mr. Abrams was Vice-President of Pacific Corporate Valuation, Inc. in charge of the valuation practice, and he was a Project Manager at Arthur D. Little

Valuation, Inc. He was a cofounder and president of Raycom, a radio communications firm, and prior to this was an auditor with Arthur Andersen & Company. Mr. Abrams received his MBA from the University of Chicago in finance and marketing, where he also pursued graduate studies in economics.

Mr. Abrams invented and published the Abrams Table of Equity Premia and has published an article quantifying the discount for lack of marketability. He invented several formulas for valuing leveraged ESOPs, as well as the Abrams Table of Accounting Transposition Errors, used for troubleshooting such errors. He also wrote software to automatically generate a table of potential sources of error.

Mr. Abrams' writings include:

- *Quantitative Business Valuation: A Mathematical Approach for Today's Professionals*, McGraw-Hill, November 2000.
- "ESOPs: Measuring and Apportioning the Dilution," *Valuation*, June 1997.
- "Discount Rates as a Function of Log Size and Valuation Error Measurement," *The Valuation Examiner*, February/March, 1997.
- "An Iterative Valuation Approach," *Business Valuation Review*, March 1995.
- "A Breakthrough in Calculating Reliable Discount Rates," *Valuation*, August, 1994.
- "Discount for Lack of Marketability: A Theoretical Model," *Business Valuation Review*, September, 1994.
- "Cash Flow: A Mathematical Derivation," *Valuation*, March 1994.
- "An Iterative Procedure To Value Leveraged ESOPs," *Valuation*, January 1993.
- "How to Quickly Find and Fix Accounting Transposition Errors," *The Practical Accountant*, June 1992.
- Coauthor of "Valuation of Companies for ESOP Purposes," Chapter 8 *in Employee Stock Ownership Plans* by Robert W. Smiley, Jr. and Ronald J. Gilbert, Prentice Hall/Rosenfeld Launer Publications, New York, 1989.
- "The Annuity Discount Factor: Generalization, Analysis of Special Cases, and Relationship to the Gordon Model and Fixed-Rate Loan Amortization," unpublished.

BIBLIOGRAPHY

Mercer, Z. Christopher. 1997. *Quantifying Marketability Discounts*. Memphis, Tenn.: Peabody.

Pratt, Shannon P., Robert F. Reilly, and Robert P. Schweihs. 1996. *Valuing a Business*, 3d ed. Burr Ridge, Ill.: McGraw-Hill.

APPENDIX

Tax Court's Opinion for Discount for Lack of Marketability[24]

INTRODUCTION

The U.S. Tax Court outlined a list of 10 nonexclusive factors that in the Court's opinion affect discount for lack of marketability (DLOM). We first present its list and then we comment on each item as to how we considered it in our analysis.

THE COURT'S TEN FACTORS

The Court's 10 factors are:

1. The value of the subject corporation's privately traded securities vis-à-vis its publicly traded securities (or, if the subject corporation does not have stock that is traded both publicly and privately, the cost of a similar corporation's public and private stock). These are known as "Letter Stock" or restricted securities, the restrictions arising from Section 144 of the Securities Exchange Commission Rules.
2. An analysis of the subject corporation's financial statements.
3. The corporation's dividend-paying capacity, its history of paying dividends, and the amount of its prior dividends.
4. The nature of the corporation, its history, its position in the industry, and its economic outlook.
5. The corporation's management.
6. The degree of control transferred with the block of stock to be valued.
7. Any restriction on the transferability of the corporation's stock.
8. The period of time for which an investor must hold the subject stock to realize a sufficient profit.
9. The corporation's redemption policy.
10. The cost of effectuating a public offering of the stock to be valued, e.g., legal, accounting, and underwriting fees[25]

The Court in general had the right idea. It created a list of criteria with which to judge the difference in marketability between the source of the valuation data and the asset to which we are applying the data.

---

24. *Bernard Mandelbaum, et al. v. Commissioner*, TCM, CCH Dec. 50, 687(M), 1995-254.
25. See *Estate of Gilford v. Commissioner* [Dec. 43,622], 88 T.C. 38, 60 (1987); Northern Trust Co. v. Commissioner [Dec. 43,261], 87 T.C. 349, 383-389 (1986); see also Rev. Rul. 77287, 1977-2 C.B. 319 (valuation of restricted securities).

APPLICATION OF THE COURT'S 10 FACTORS TO THE VALUATION

In this section we will address the factors in the Tax Court's opinion and demonstrate how we have incorporated those factors into our analysis of the discount for lack of marketability (DLOM), which, combined with the discount for lack of control (DLOC), forms the fractional interest discount. The following analysis applies regardless of the form of the subject entity, whether it is a common stock interest in a corporation, Limited or General Partnership interest, LLC interest, etc. We use the terms *the entity* and *the subject interest* to maintain generality.

1. We estimate the letter stock discount in the delay-to-sale component of the economic components approach. We do this either by a regression analysis or a Black–Scholes put option calculation, depending on the availability of data.

2. Our analysis of the entity's financial statements is incorporated into the calculation of DLOM in the calculation of transactions costs, expected growth rates, the discount rate, and the delay-to-sale component of the economic components approach.

3. We incorporate the dividends (distributions) into the analysis in the Partnership Profiles (PP) approach. This is the single most important factor in the regression model. Dividends or distributions are also incorporated indirectly into the calculation of DLOM through their effect on the growth rate and, therefore, the transactions costs.

4. The nature of the entity and its history, industry position, composition of assets, and economic outlook are factors that are very significant in the valuation of the underlying assets. The comments to item 2 apply here as well.

5. Management can be significant in determining the fractional interest discount because of two factors: its dividend policy, which is already considered in 3, and more importantly, its potential for making decisions that favor one group of owners over another or withholding bad news from any ownership group. Owners of private interests generally have more influence with their management than the LPs in the Partnership Profiles database would with theirs. We consider this factor in the adjustment for increased influence in Partnership Profiles approach.

6. The degree of control of the block of stock is, strangely enough, significant in calculating DLOM. The reason why that appears strange is that the degree of control has its own discount—the DLOC—for lack of control. Why then does the degree of control influence the DLOM? The reason is found in the above-mentioned book, Chapter 7 in *Quantitative Business Valuation: A Mathematical Approach for Today's Professionals*. We calculate control premiums and discount for lack of control by looking at control premiums paid for marketable minority interests in the stock market. But control matters less in publicly held firms

than in privately held firms because the former generally have both current cash flow in the form of dividends and instant marketability in the ability to cash out in three days. Furthermore, management of publicly held firms are generally managing to maximize the per-share values of the minority shareholders. With privately held firms, control shareholders often divert wealth from minority shareholders (similarly general partners in LPs and managing members in LLCs can divert wealth from limited partners and other members). It is rare to see dividends in closely held corporations, and there is generally no ability to cash out. Therefore, there is an interactive effect in being both a minority shareholder (or LP/ minority interest member) and owning an interest in a private firm. The whole is worse than the sum of the two parts. As in 5 above, we have considered this in the adjustment for increased influence in the Partnership Profiles approach.

7. The marketability of private interests is limited, since there is no formal market for such interests. We consider this limitation in the economic components approach in the following ways: (a) in the calculation of the delay-to-sale component; and (b) in accounting for the buyer's monopsony power (component 2). In the Partnership Profiles approach, we implicitly considered the lack of marketability in selecting the discount for lack of public registration.

8. We incorporate time horizons into the delay-to-sale component in the economic components approach and the adjustment for lack of public registration in the Partnership Profiles approach. We also incorporate time horizons in another fashion in the selection of the variable j—the average years between sales—in the economic components approach.

9. The entity's redemption policy is relevant in determining one's ability to cash out of an investment. The subject entity does not provide a redemption option.

10. The cost of undergoing an initial public offering is about 15–18% for a small firm. There is a possibility that an IPO might lower the discount by making the subject interest more marketable. However, the cost of the IPO and the subsequent regulatory administrative costs would be prohibitive in the case, and we don't need to account for the IPO possibility here.

PART FOUR

Putting It All Together

Part 4 of this book consists of Chapters 10 and 11. Chapter 10 empirically tests the log size and economic components models by reconciling price to cash flow (P/CF) multiples calculated using these models with P/CF multiples for groups of firms of different sizes in the Institute of Business Appraisers' (IBA) database. The results provide weak support for the two models, but missing data make it impossible to provide strong support. There is simply too much data we need that does not exist in the IBA database or any other one of which I am aware.

In Chapter 11 we look at two issues. In the first half of the chapter we calculate 95% confidence intervals around our valuation estimate using the log size model (both for all 72 years of New York Stock Exchange data and for the past 60 years), assuming we forecast cash flows and adjust for control and marketability perfectly. The importance of this is to understand how much statistical uncertainty there is in our valuation estimates.

The second half of Chapter 11 is concerned with measuring the valuation errors that arise from errors in forecasting cash flow and growth rates and calculating discount rates. We look at the effects of both relative and absolute errors and show how the majority of these errors affect the valuation of large firms more than small firms.

Whereas Part 3 of this book consists of practical, hands-on, "how-to" chapters, Part 4 does not. It can be skipped by the time-pressed reader. Nevertheless, for one who wants to be well educated and familiar with important theoretical and empirical issues in valuation, these chapters are important.

Empirical Testing of Abrams' Valuation Theory[1]

INTRODUCTION
Steps in the Valuation Process

Applying a Valuation Model to the Steps

TABLE 10-1: LOG SIZE FOR 1938–1986

TABLE 10-2: RECONCILIATION TO THE IBA DATABASE

Part 1: IBA P/CF Multiples

Part 2: Log Size P/CF Multiples

Conclusion

CALCULATION OF DLOM

Table 10-4: Computation of the Delay-to-Sale Component–$25,000 Firm

Table 10-5: Calculation of Transactions Costs

Table 10-6: Calculation of DLOM

Table 10-6A–10-6F: Calculations of DLOM for Larger Firms

Calculation of DLOM for Large Firms

INTERPRETATION OF THE ERROR

CONCLUSION

1. I offer my profound thanks to Mr. Raymond Miles for his considerable help. Without his vitally important research, this article would be impossible. Also, Professor Haim Mendelson of Stanford University provided extremely helpful comments.

INTRODUCTION

Many appraisers have long believed that when small businesses sell, they are priced very differently than large businesses and that the rules governing their valuation are totally different. I, too, held this opinion at one time, but this chapter is evidence—though not proof—that it is not true.

A skeptic could level the charge that the log size discount rate equation is based on a mathematical relationship that exists between returns and size of New York Stock Exchange (NYSE) firms, but it may not apply to the universe of small and medium privately held firms. Additionally, the calculations of the transactions costs component of the discount for lack of marketability (DLOM) is based on interviews, then quantified in an equation and extrapolated downwards for small firms. Thus, it's nice in theory, but does it really work in practice?

The purpose of this chapter is to subject the log size and economic components models to empirical testing to see whether they do a good job of explaining real world transactions of smaller businesses. Our primary data comes from an article published by Raymond Miles (Miles 1992) ("the article") about the relationship of size to price earnings (PE) multiples in the Institute of Business Appraisers' (IBA) database.

Steps in the Valuation Process

Using a simple discounted cash flow model as the valuation paradigm, valuation consists of four steps:

1. Forecast cash flows.
2. Discount to net present value.
3. Adjust for marketability or lack thereof.
4. Adjust for degree of control.

Applying a Valuation Model to the Steps

The sales described in the article are all $1 million or less. It is a reasonable assumption that the vast majority of the small firms in the IBA transactional database are mature. The number of high-growth startup firms in that database is likely to be small. Therefore, it is reasonable to assume a constant growth rate to perpetuity. Using a Gordon model to apply to the next year's forecast cash flows should give us a fairly accurate FMV on a marketable minority level. Using a midyear assumption, the formula is:

$$FMV = CF_{t+1} \frac{\sqrt{1 + r}}{r - g}$$

where r is the discount rate, which we will estimate using the log size model, and g is the constant growth rate, which we will estimate. That takes care of the first two valuation steps.

We will use the economic components model from Chapter 7 for our calculations of DLOM. We assume a control premium of 25%, which is the approximate midpoint of the 21–28% range estimated in Chapter 7.

There are only two major principals in steps 2 and 3 of business valuation: risk and marketability, which are both functions of size. Thus, size is the overriding principle in steps 2 and 3 of the valuation process, and step 1 determines size. If value depends only on the forecast cash flows, risk, and marketability, and the latter two are in turn dependent on size, then in essence value depends only on size (and possibly control). That statement sounds like a tautology, but it is not.

This chapter is an attempt to identify the fewest, most basic principles underlying the inexact science of valuation. The remainder of this chapter covers the calculations that test the log size model and DLOM calculations.

TABLE 10-1: LOG SIZE FOR 1938–1986

In Table 10-1 we develop the log size equation for the years 1938–1986. We use 1938 as the starting year to eliminate the highly volatile Roaring Twenties and Depression years 1926–1937. The reason we stop at 1986 has to do with the IBA database. The article is based on sales from 1982–1991.[2] We take 1986 as the midpoint of that range and calculate our log size equation from 1938–1986.

Cells B7–B16 and C7–C16 contain the mean and standard deviation of returns for the 10 deciles for the period 1938–1986. We need to be able to regress the returns against 1986 average market capitalization for each decile. Unfortunately, those values are unavailable and we must estimate them.

D7–D16 contain the market capitalization for the average firm in each decile for 1994, the earliest year for which decile breakdowns are available. E7–E16 are the 1986 year-end index values in Ibbotson's Table 7-4. F7–F16 are the 1994 year-end index values, with our estimate of income returns removed.[3]

Column G is our estimate of 1986 average market capitalization per firm for each decile. We calculate it as Column D × Column E ÷ Column F. Thus, the average firm size in decile #1 for 1986 is $7.3 billion (G7), and for decile #10 it is $32.49 million (G16).

Rows 18–35 contain our regression analysis of arithmetic mean returns as a function of the logarithm of the market capitalization—exactly

---

2. A footnote in the article states that in relation to Figure 1 (and I confirmed this with the author, Raymond Miles), those dates apply to the rest of the article.
3. SBBI, Table 7-4, approximate income returns have been removed from the 1994 values. The adjustment was derived by comparing the large company stock total return indices with the capital appreciation indices for 1994 and 1986 per SBBI Tables B-1 and B-2. It was found that 77.4% of the total return was due to capital appreciation. There were no capital appreciation indices for small company stocks. We removed $1 - 77.4\% = 22.6\%$ of the gain in the decile index values for deciles #1 through #5, 22.6%/2 = 11.3% for deciles #6 through #8, and made no adjustment for #9 and #10. Larger stocks tend to pay larger dividends.

Log Size Equation for 1938–1986 NYSE Data by Decile and Statistical Analysis: 1938–1986

	A	B	C	D	E	F	G	H
					Year-End Index Values [1]		[D] × [E]/[F]	Ln [G]
	Decile	Mean	Std Dev	94 Mkt Cap	1986	1994	1986 Mkt Cap	Ln(Mkt Cap)
7	1	11.8%	15.8%	14,847,774,614	198.868	404.436	7,300,897,357	22.7113
8	2	14.0%	18.3%	3,860,097,544	434.686	920.740	1,822,371,137	21.3234
9	3	15.0%	19.7%	2,025,154,234	550.313	1,248.528	892,625,877	20.6097
10	4	15.8%	22.0%	1,211,090,551	637.197	1,352.924	570,396,575	20.1618
11	5	16.7%	23.0%	820,667,228	856.893	1,979.698	355,217,881	19.6882
12	6	17.1%	23.8%	510,553,019	809.891	1,809.071	228,566,124	19.2473
13	7	17.6%	26.4%	339,831,804	786.298	1,688.878	158,216,901	18.8795
14	8	19.0%	28.5%	208,098,608	1,122.906	2,010.048	116,253,534	18.5713
15	9	19.7%	29.9%	99,534,481	1,586.521	2,455.980	64,297,569	17.9790
16	10	22.7%	38.0%	33,746,259	6,407.216	6,654.508	32,492,195	17.2965

SUMMARY OUTPUT

Regression Statistics

Multiple R	0.9806
R square	0.9617
Adjusted R square	0.9569
Standard error	0.0064
Observations	10

ANOVA

	df	SS	MS	F	Significance F
Regression	1	0.0082	0.0082	200.6663	0.0000
Residual	8	0.0003	0.0000		
Total	9	0.0085			

	Coefficients	Standard Error	t Stat	P-value	Lower 95%	Upper 95%
Intercept	0.5352	(0.0186)	20.6710	0.0000	0.4755	0.5949
Ln(Mkt Cap)	0.0259	(0.0013)	(14.1657)	0.0000	(0.0216)	(0.0156)

[1] SBBI, Table 7-3*, approximate income returns have been removed from the 1994 values. The adjustment was derived by comparing the large company stock total return indices with the capital appreciation indices for 1994 and 1986 per SBBI Tables B-1 and B-2. It was found that 77.4% of the total return was due to capital appreciation. There were no capital appreciation indices for small company stocks. We removed (1–77.4%) of the gain in the decile index values for deciles 1 through 5, [(1–77.4%)/2] for deciles 6 through 8, and made no adjustment for 9 and 10. Larger stocks tend to pay larger dividends.
*Used with permission. © 1998 Ibbotson Associates, Inc. All rights reserved. [Certain portions of this work were derived from copyrighted works of Roger G. Ibbotson and Rex Sinquefield.] Source: © CRSP University of Chicago. Used with permission. All rights reserved.

the same as Table 4-1, regression #2. The regression equation is: $r = 0.5352 - 0.0186 \ln \text{FMV}$.[4] We use this regression equation in Table 10-2.

TABLE 10-2: RECONCILIATION TO THE IBA DATABASE

Table 10-2 is the main table in this chapter. All other tables provide details that flow into this table.

The purpose of the table is to perform two series of calculations, which make up part 1 and part 2 of the table, respectively. The first series calculates adjusted price to cash flow (P/CF) multiples for each size category of IBA database results described in the article. The second series is to calculate theoretical P/CF multiples using the log size equation and the DLOM methodology in Chapter 7. Ultimately we compare them, and they match reasonably well.

Unfortunately, there are much data that we do not have, which will force us to make estimates. There are so many estimates in the following analysis, that we will not be able to make strong conclusions. It would be easy to manipulate the results in Table 10-2 to support different points of view. Nevertheless, it is important to proceed with the table, as we will still gain valuable insights. Additionally, it points out the deficiencies in the information set available. This is not a criticism of the IBA database. All of the other transactional databases of which I am aware suffer from the same problems. This analysis highlights the type of information that would be ideal to have in order to come to stronger conclusions.

Part 1: IBA *P*/CF Multiples

We begin in row 6. The mean selling prices in row 6 are the means of the corresponding range of selling prices reported in the article. Thus, B6 = $25,000, which is the mean selling price for firms in the $0 to $50,000 category. At the high end, H6 = $750,000, which is the mean price in the $500,000 to $1 million sales price category.

Row 7 is the mean P/E multiple reported in the article. Note that the P/E multiple constantly rises as the mean selling price rises. Figure 10-1 shows this relationship clearly. Row 8 is owner's discretionary income, which is row 6 divided by row 7, i.e., $P \div P/E = E$, where P is price and E is earnings.

The IBA's definition of owner's discretionary income is net income before income taxes and owner's salary. It does not conform to the arm's-length income that appraisers use in valuing businesses. Therefore, we subtract our estimate of an arm's-length salary for owners, which we do in row 9. This is an educated guess, but Raymond Miles felt my estimates were reasonable.

In row 10, we add back personal expenses charged to the business. Unfortunately, no one has any data on this. I have asked many accountants for their estimates, and their answers vary wildly. Ultimately, I decided to estimate this at 10% (cell B33) of owner's discretionary income (row 8).

---

4. For public firms, this is market capitalization, i.e., price per share × number of shares.

TABLE 10-2

Reconciliation to IBA Database

	A	B	C	D	E	F	G	H	I
									Avg
4	**Part 1: IBA P/CF Multiples**								
6	Mean selling price: Illiquid 100% Int	25,000	75,000	125,000	175,000	225,000	375,000	750,000	
7	Mean P/E ratio	1.66	2.11	2.44	2.74	3.06	3.44	4.26	
8	Owner's discretionary inc = [6]/[7]	15,060	35,545	51,230	63,869	73,529	109,012	176,056	
9	Arm's length salary	22,500	25,000	30,000	35,000	40,000	50,000	75,000	
10	Personal exp charged to bus—assume B33* [8]	1,506	3,555	5,123	6,387	7,353	10,901	17,606	
11	Adjusted net income = [8] − [9] + [10]	(5,934)	14,100	26,352	35,255	40,882	69,913	118,662	
12	Effective corp. inc tax rate	0%	0%	0%	0%	0%	0%	0%	
13	Adjusted inc taxes	0	0	0	0	0	0	0	
14	Adj net inc after tax	(5,934)	14,100	26,352	35,255	40,882	69,913	118,662	
15	Cash flow/net income (assumed)	95%	95%	95%	95%	95%	95%	95%	
16	Adj cash flow after tax = [14] * [15]	(5,637)	13,395	25,035	33,493	38,838	66,417	112,729	
17	Avg disc to cash equiv value (Table 10-3)	6.7%	6.7%	6.7%	6.7%	6.7%	6.7%	6.7%	
18	Adj sell price [illiq 100% int] = {1 − [17]}*[6]	23,317	69,951	116,585	163,220	209,854	349,756	699,512	
19	Adjusted price/cash flow multiple = [18]/[16]	NM	5.2	4.7	4.9	5.4	5.3	6.2	
21	**Part 2: Log Size P/CF Multiples**								
22	Control prem-% (1982–1991 Avg) [note 1]	25%	25%	25%	25%	25%	25%	25%	
23	DLOM-% (Tables 10-6, 10-6A, 10-6B, etc.)	9.9%	10.1%	10.2%	10.2%	10.5%	12.4%	18.6%	
24	Adj sell price (mkt min) = [18]/{(1 + [22])*(1 − [23])}	20,704	62,221	103,838	145,440	187,511	319,458	687,614	
25	Discount rate = r = .5352 − .0186 ln (FMV$_{Mkt\ Min}$)	35.0%	33.0%	32.0%	31.4%	30.9%	29.9%	28.5%	
26	Growth rate = g (assumed)	2.0%	2.5%	3.0%	4.0%	4.5%	5.0%	6.0%	
27	Theoretical P/CF = (1 + g)*SQRT(1 + r)/(r − g)	3.6	3.9	4.1	4.4	4.5	4.8	5.3	
28	P/CF-Illiquid control = [27]*(1 + [22])*(1 − [23])	4.0	4.4	4.6	4.9	5.1	5.3	5.4	
29	Error {1 − [28]/[19]}	NM	16.5%	1.7%	-0.2%	6.3%	0.2%	12.5%	
30	Absolute error [note 2]	NM	16.5%	1.7%	0.2%	6.3%	0.2%	12.5%	4.1%
31	Squared error [note 2]		2.7%	0.0%	0.0%	0.4%	0.0%	1.6%	4.2%
33	Personal exp = % of Owner's discretionary inc	10%							0.4%

35	**Sensitivity Analysis: How the error varies with personal exp**	Cell B33	Error
37		2%	17.3%
38		4%	14.0%
39		6%	10.7%
40		8%	7.4%
41		10%	4.1%

[1] Approximate midpoint of the 21% to 28% control premium estimated in Chapter 7

[2] The averages are for the last 5 columns only, as the sales under $100,000 are mostly likely asset-based, not income based.

P/E Ratio as a Function of Size (From the IBA Database)

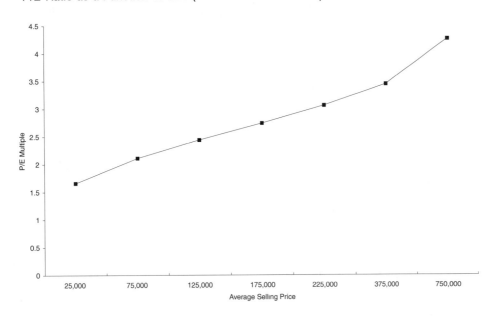

Row 11 is adjusted net income, which is row 8 − row 9 + row 10. Row 12 is an estimate of the effective corporate income tax rate. This is a judgment call. An accountant convinced me that even for the $1 million sales, the owner's discretionary income is low enough that it would not be taxed at all. Any excess remaining over salary would be taken out of taxable income as a bonus. I acceded to his opinion, though this point is arguable—especially for the higher dollar sales. It is true that what counts here is not who the seller is, but who the buyer is. A large corporation buying a small firm would still impute corporate taxes at the maximum rate; however, only the last category is at all likely to be bought by a large firm, and even then, most buyers of $0.5 to $1 million firms are probably single individuals. Therefore, it makes sense to go with no corporate taxes, with a possible reservation in our minds about the last column.

With this zero income taxes assumption, row 13 equals zero and row 14, adjusted income after taxes, equals row 11.

Next we need to convert from net income to cash flow. Again, the information does not exist, so we need to make reasonable assumptions. For most businesses, cash flow lags behind net income. Most of these are small businesses that sold for fairly small dollar amounts, which means that expected growth—another important missing piece of information—must be low, on average. The lower the growth, the less strain on cash flow. We assume cash flow is 95% of adjusted net income. It would be reasonable to assume this ratio is smaller for the higher value businesses, which presumably have higher growth. We do not vary our cash flow ratio, as none of these are likely to be very high-growth businesses. Thus, all cells in row 15 equal 95%. In row 16 we multiply row 14 by row 15 to calculate adjusted after-tax cash flow.

The next step in adjusting the IBA multiples is to reduce the nominal selling price to a cash-equivalent selling price, which we calculate in Table

10-3. Exhibit 33-3 in Pratt (Pratt 1993) shows a summary of sale data from Bizcomps. Businesses selling for less than $100,000 have a 60% average cash down, and businesses selling for more than $500,000 have an average 58% cash down. Using a 60% cash down, we assume the seller finances the 40% (Table 10-3, B11) balance for 7 years, which is 84 months (B8, C8) at 8% (B5) with a market rate of 14% (C5).

The annuity discount factor (ADF), the formula for which is

$$\text{ADF} = \frac{1 - [1/(1 + r)^n]}{r}$$

is 53.3618 (C9) at the market rate of interest and 64.15926 (B9) at the nominal rate. One minus the ratio of two equals the discount to cash equivalent value if the loan is 100% financed, or

$$1 - \frac{53.3618}{64.15926} = 16.8\%$$

(B10). We multiply this by the 40% financed (B11) to calculate the average discount to cash equivalent value of 6.7% (B12), which we transfer back to Table 10-2, row 17.

Multiplying the mean selling price in row 6 by one minus the discount to cash equivalent value in row 17 leads to an adjusted mean selling price in row 18. For example, $25,000 \times (1 - 6.7\%) = \$23,317$ [B6 $\times$ (1 − B17) = B18].

Finally, we divide row 18 by row 16 to calculate the adjusted price to cash flow (P/CF) multiple for the IBA database. In general, the P/CF multiple rises as price rises, although not always. There is no meaningful P/CF multiple in B19, because adjusted cash flow in B16 is negative. The P/CF multiples begin in C19 at 5.2 for a mean selling price of $75,000, then decline to 4.7 (D19) for a mean selling price of $125,000, and rise steadily to 6.2 (H19) for a mean selling price of $750,000. The only exception is that the P/CF is greater at 5.4 for the $225,000 selling price than at 5.3 for the $375,000 selling price. The first anomaly is probably not significant, because many, if not most, firms selling under $100,000 are

T A B L E 10-3

Proof of Discount Calculation

	A	B	C
4		Nominal	Market
5	r	8%	14%
6	i = r/12	0.6667%	1.1667%
7	Yrs	7	7
8	n = Yrs *12	84	84
9	ADF @ 14%, 84 mos.	64.15926114	53.36176
10	Discount on total prin	16.8%	
11	% financed	40%	
12	Discount on % financed	**6.7%**	

priced based on their assets rather than their earnings capacity. The second anomaly, from P/CF of 5.4 to 5.3, is a very small reversal of the general pattern of rising P/CF multiples in the IBA database.

Part 2: Log Size *P*/CF Multiples

In this section of Table 10-2 we will calculate "theoretical" P/CF multiples based on the log size model and the DLOM calculations in Chapter 7. The term *theoretical* is somewhat of a misnomer, as the calculation of both the log size equation and DLOM is empirically based. Nevertheless, we use the term for convenience.

Before we can apply the log size equation from Table 10-1, we need a marketable minority interest FMV, while the adjusted selling price (FMV) in row 18 is a illiquid control value. Therefore, we need to divide row 18 by one plus the control premium times one minus DLOM, which we do in row 24. We assume a control premium of 25% (row 22), which is the approximate midpoint of the 21–28% range of control premiums discussed in Chapter 7.

The calculation of DLOM is unique for each size category and appears in Tables 10-6 and 10-6A–10-6F. We will cover those tables later. In the meantime, DLOM rises steadily from 9.9% (B23) for the $25,000 mean selling price to 18.6% (H23) for the $750,000 mean selling price category.

Row 24, the marketable minority FMV, is row 18 ÷ [(1 + row 22) × (1 − row 23)]. The marketable minority values are all lower than the illiquid control values, as the control premium is much greater in magnitude than DLOM.

We calculate the log size discount rate in row 25 using the regression equation from Table 10-1. It ranges from a high of 35.2% (B25) for the smallest category to a low of 28.7% (H25) for the largest category.

Next we estimate the constant growth rates that the buyers and sellers collectively implicitly forecast when they agreed on prices. It is unfortunate that none of the transactional databases that are publicly available contain even historical growth rates, let alone forecast growth rates. Therefore, we must make another estimate. We estimate growth rates to rise from 2% (B26) to 6% (H26), growing at 0.5% for each category, except the last one going from 5% to 6%. It is logical that buyers will pay more for faster growing firms.

In row 27 we calculate a midyear Gordon model:

$$(1 + g) \frac{\sqrt{1 + r}}{r - g}$$

with r and g coming from rows 25 and 26, respectively.[5] This is a marketable minority interest P/CF multiple when cash flow is expressed as the trailing year's cash flow. In row 28 we convert this to an illiquid control P/CF by doing the reverse of the procedure we performed in row

---

5. The purpose of the $(1 + g)$ term is correct for the fact that we are applying it to each dollar of prior year's cash flow and not to the customary next year's cash flow.

24—we multiply by one plus the control premium and one minus DLOM, i.e., $P/\text{CF}_{\text{Illiq Control}} = P/\text{CF}_{\text{MM}} \times (1 + \text{CP}) \times (1 - \text{DLOM}) = \text{row } 27 \times (1 + \text{row } 22) \times (1 - \text{row } 23)$.

In row 29 we calculate the error, which is one minus the ratio of row 28 divided by row 19, or one minus the ratio of the forecast log size-based P/CF to the IBA's adjusted P/CF. Row 30 is the absolute value of the errors in row 29. The absolute values of the errors are most extreme for the low and high values of the mean selling price, with a 16.5% (C30) absolute error for the $75,000 mean selling price and a 12.5% (H30) absolute error for the $750,000 selling price, with small absolute errors in between ranging around 0.2–6.3%. The mean error is 4.1% (I29).[6]

Conclusion

The mean absolute error is 4.2% (I30). Rounding this to 4%, that is a very respectable result. It is evidence supporting the log size model in Chapter 4 and control premium and economic components model of DLOM in Chapter 7.

Nevertheless, as mentioned before, there are too much missing data and resulting guesswork to come to solid conclusions. The estimates are all reasonable, but one could make different reasonable estimates and come to very different results. Thus, this analysis is worthwhile evidence, but it proves nothing.

In the remainder of the chapter we will describe the DLOM calculations in Tables 10-4, 10-6, and their variations as 10-4A, 10-6A, etc.

CALCULATION OF DLOM

As discussed in Chapter 7, there are three components in the economic components model to the calculation of DLOM. Components #1 and #3, the delay to sale and transactions costs components, require unique analysis for each IBA size category. Therefore, we have one spreadsheet for each of the two components for each IBA size category. Tables 10-4 and 10-6 are the calculations of components #1 and #3, respectively, for the $25,000 mean selling price firm. Additionally, Table 10-6 contains the DLOM calculations. We will describe these tables in detail. Tables 10-4A and 10-6A are identical to Tables 10-4 and 10-6, the only difference being that these are calculations for the $75,000 mean selling price firms. This series continues all the way through Tables 10-4F and 10-6F for the $750,000 mean selling price IBA category. Table 10-5 contains the calculations of the buyer and seller transactions costs for all size categories.

Table 10-4: Computation of the Delay-to-Sale Component—$25,000 Firm

Table 10-4 is identical to Table 7-10, except that we are customizing the calculation for this IBA category of firm. We begin by inserting the selling

---

6. This excludes the $75,000 mean selling price errors, as that is likely due to the sale being priced on an asset rather than an income basis. We also exclude this category in the other measures of mean error.

Calculation of Component #1—Delay to Sale—$25,000 Firm [1]

	A	B	C	D
4		**Coefficients**	**Co. Data**	**Discount**
5	Intercept	0.1342	NA	13.4%
6	Revenues^2	−5.33E − 18	5.625E + 09	0.0%
7	Value of block-post-discount [2]	−4.26E − 09	$ 25,000	0.0%
8	FMV-marketable minority 100% interest	5.97E − 10	**$ 25,000**	0.0%
9	Earnings stability [3]	−0.1376	0.4200	−5.8%
10	Revenue stability [3]	−0.1789	0.6900	−12.3%
11	Average years to sell	0.1339	0.2500	3.3%
12	**Total Discount [4]**			**0.0%**
14	Value of block-pre-discount [5]	$ 25,000		
16	Selling price	$ 25,000		
17	Adjusted net income	$ (5,934)		
18	Assumed pre-tax margin	NA		
19	Sales	$ 75,000		
20	Sales^2	5.625E+09		

[1] Based on Abrams regression of Management Planning, Inc. data-Regression #2, Table 7-10

[2] Equal to Pre-Discount Shares Sold in dollars * (1-Discount). B7 equals B14 only when the discount = 0%.

[3] Earnings and Revenue stability are assumed at the averages from Table 7-5, G60 and H60, respectively, for all FMVs. In the Management Planning data, a correlation analysis revealed that firm size and the stability measures are uncorrelated. Therefore, we assume the same levels for all FMVs.

[4] Total Discount = max(discount, 0), because Disc < 0 indicates the model is outside of its range of reasonability.

[5] In our regression of the Management Planning, Inc. data, this was a marketable minority interest value. This is an illiquid control value and is higher by 12% to 25% than the marketable minority value. The regression coefficient relating to market capitalization in B8 is so small that the difference is immaterial, and it is easier to work with the value available.

price in B16 and adjusted net income in B17. For the larger IBA categories, net income (owner's discretionary income) is positive, and we divide that by an assumed pretax margin of 5% in B18 to estimate sales in B19. We cannot do that for the $25,000 sales category only, because of net losses. We estimate sales at three times the selling price, or $75,000 (B19). The square of sales is then 5.625×10^9, which is calculated in B20 and transferred to C6.[7]

We insert the $25,000 mean selling price in C8, C14, and C16. Here we are calculating the value of 100% of the stock, so the block value and the value of the entire firm will be identical, which is not true in the restricted stock calculations in Table 7-10.[8]

Cell C7 is the post-discount value of the block. However, both C7 and C14 equal $25,000. This is because the discount calculation came to zero (D12). Normally, C7 would be lower than C14.

A correlation analysis of the Management Planning data, not shown in the book, revealed that firm size and earnings and revenue stability are uncorrelated. Thus, we use the averages from Table 7-5, G60 and H60 of 0.42 (C9) and 0.69 (C10), respectively.

---

7. The calculations in B16 to B20 did not appear in Table 7-10, as they were unnecessary there.

8. Technically, we should be using the marketable minority FMV rather than the illiquid control FMV in Table 10-4 (and its variants 10-4A, etc.), cell C14 (which also affects C7 and C8). However, we do not yet know the marketable minority FMV, as that is the point of the exercise. To even attempt to calculate it would require multiple iterations, which would greatly complicate the analysis and add nothing, as the regression coefficients in B7 and B8 are so small that the difference is immaterial. Therefore, we use the illiquid control values.

Finally we assume that a $25,000 firm takes only three months, or 0.25 (C11) years to sell. Summing D5 through D11 actually results in a slightly negative discount, which does not make sense. Therefore, we use a spreadsheet formula to calculate D12 as the maximum of the sum of D5:D11 and zero. The delay to sale component is zero for all size categories except $375,000 and $750,000. The calculations of component #1 of DLOM for those two categories appear in Tables 10-4E and 10-4F. The main reason for this is that we assume is takes either 0.25 years or 0.33 years to sell firms under the $375,000 category, while we assume that it takes 0.5 years and 1.0 years to sell in the $375,000 and $750,000 categories, respectively (Tables 10-4E and 10-F, C11). The resulting discounts are still small in magnitude. In Table 10-4E, D12, we calculate component #1 as 1.9%, and in Table 10-4F, D12, we calculate component #1 as 8.4%.

Though we did not elect to do so here, it would be a reasonable approach to rely on our findings in Chapter 7 that the regression analysis does not work well for delays to sale of much less than a year. That being the case, it would make sense to use a different model—even something so simple as a present value—to calculate the delay to sale component for under one year. For example, if we assume a 25% discount rate, a three-month delay to sale implies a 5% discount as component #1, and a four-month delay to sale implies a 7% discount as component #1. It is important to recognize that not all models work well across all ranges of data, and sometimes circumstances force us to use different models. For simplicity in this analysis, we did not elect to use another model.

Table 10-5: Calculation of Transactions Costs

Table 10-5 contains our calculations of transactions costs for both buyer and seller for all of the IBA size categories. Column A denotes whether the transactions costs are for buyer or sellers. Column B is the mean selling price of the IBA study. Column C is the base 10 logarithm of column B.

Columns D and F contain, respectively, the x-coefficient and the constant from the regression in Table 7-11. In column E we multiply column C by column D. We add columns E and F together to obtain column G, which is the regression forecast of all transactions costs except for the business broker (or investment banker). Column H contains the business broker fees, which we assume at 10% for sellers and zero for buyers. Finally, column I is the grand total forecast of transactions costs for buyers and sellers by size category. Note that both buyer and seller transactions costs decline as firm size grows.

While the $10 million firm in rows 20 and 21 are outside of the scope of the IBA study, we use them later on in our own analysis to extrapolate the results that we derive from our analysis of the IBA study.

Table 10-6: Calculation of DLOM

Table 10-6 is exactly the same format and logic as Table 7-14, which we already described in Chapter 7. B9 through B12 contain the pure discounts for the four economic components. B9, the pure discount for com-

T A B L E 10-5

Calculation of Transaction Costs for Firms of All Sizes in the IBA Study

	A	B	C	D	E	F	G	H	I
5		FMV	log$_{10}$ FMV	X-Coeff.	log FMV × Coeff.	Regr. Constant	Forecast Subtotal	Bus. Broker	Forecast Total
6	Buyer	$ 25,000	4.39794	−0.01727	−0.07596	0.15310	**7.7%**	0.0%	**7.7%**
7	Seller	$ 25,000	4.39794	−0.01599	−0.07034	0.14139	**7.1%**	10.0%	**17.1%**
8	Buyer	$ 75,000	4.87506	−0.01727	−0.08420	0.15310	**6.9%**	0.0%	**6.9%**
9	Seller	$ 75,000	4.87506	−0.01599	−0.07797	0.14139	**6.3%**	10.0%	**16.3%**
10	Buyer	$ 125,000	5.09691	−0.01727	−0.08804	0.15310	**6.5%**	0.0%	**6.5%**
11	Seller	$ 125,000	5.09691	−0.01599	−0.08152	0.14139	**6.0%**	10.0%	**16.0%**
12	Buyer	$ 175,000	5.24304	−0.01727	−0.09056	0.15310	**6.3%**	0.0%	**6.3%**
13	Seller	$ 175,000	5.24304	−0.01599	−0.08386	0.14139	**5.8%**	10.0%	**15.8%**
14	Buyer	$ 225,000	5.35218	−0.01727	−0.09245	0.15310	**6.1%**	0.0%	**6.1%**
15	Seller	$ 225,000	5.35218	−0.01599	−0.08561	0.14139	**5.6%**	10.0%	**15.6%**
16	Buyer	$ 375,000	5.57403	−0.01727	−0.09628	0.15310	**5.7%**	0.0%	**5.7%**
17	Seller	$ 375,000	5.57403	−0.01599	−0.08915	0.14139	**5.2%**	10.0%	**15.2%**
18	Buyer	$ 750,000	5.87506	−0.01727	−0.10148	0.15310	**5.2%**	0.0%	**5.2%**
19	Seller	$ 750,000	5.87506	−0.01599	−0.09397	0.14139	**4.7%**	10.0%	**14.7%**
20	Buyer	$10,000,000	7.00000	−0.01727	−0.12091	0.15310	**3.2%**	0.0%	**3.2%**
21	Seller	$10,000,000	7.00000	−0.01599	−0.11196	0.14139	**2.9%**	2.0%	**4.9%**

Note: Regression constants and x-coefficients come from Table 7-11. The $10 million firm, using a Lehman Bros. Formula, has a 2% investment banker fee instead of a 10% business broker's fee.

369

TABLE 10-6

Calculation of DLOM

	A	B	C	D	E	F	G
4	Section 1: Calculation of the Discount For Lack of Marketability						
6				= 1 − Col. [C]			
7		Pure Discount	PV of Perpetual	Remaining			
8	Component	= z [1]	Discount [2]	Value			
9	1	0.0%	0.0%	100.0%	Delay to sale		
10	2	9.0%	9.0%	91.0%	Buyer's monopsony power—thin markets		
11	3A	5.7%	6.1%	93.9%	Transactions costs—buyers		
12	3B	15.1%	1.0%	99.0%	Transactions costs—sellers		
13	Percent remaining			90.1%	Total % remaining = components 1 × 2 × 3A × 3B		
14	**Final discount**			**9.9%**	Discount = 1 − total % remaining		
16	Section 2: Assumptions and Intermediate Calculations:						
18	FMV-equity of co. (before discounts)				$ 25,000		
19	Discount rate = r [3]				34.7%		
20	Constant growth rate = g				2.0%		
21	Intermediate calculation: x = (1 + g)/(1 + r)				0.7574		
22	Avg # years between sales = j				10		

[1] Pure Discounts: For Component #1, Table 10-4, cell D12; For Component #2, 9% per Schwert article. For Component #3A and #3B, Table 10-5, cells I6 and I7 − 2% for public brokerage costs.

[2] PV of Perpetual Discount Formula: $1 − (1 − x^j)/((1 − (1 − z)*x^j))$, per equation [7-9], used for Component #3B.

PV of Perpetual Discount Formula: $1 − (1 − z)*(1 − x^j)/((1 − (1 − z)*x^j))$, per equation [7-9a], used for Component #3A.

Components #1 and #2 simply transfer the pure discount.

[3] The formula is: 0.5352 − (.0186 ln FMV), based on Table 10-1, B34 and B35.

ponent #1, equals zero, and that comes from our calculation in Table 10-4, D12. B10, the pure discount for component #2, equals 9%. That is the same as it was in Table 7-14, and it comes from the Schwert article. Components 3A and 3B come from Table 10-5, cells I6 and I7, respectively, less a 2% brokerage cost for publicly traded stock. These two components are equal to 5.7% (B11) and 15.1% (B12), respectively.

As in Table 7-12, the first two components transfer from B9 and B10 to C9 and C10 directly. However, as discussed in the commentary to Table 7-12, transactions costs "leave the system" with every sale. Thus, we must present value a perpetuity of transactions costs that occur every $j = 10$ years. We do so using the formulas in note [2] to the spreadsheet, which are equations (7–9) and (7–9a) from Chapter 7. The present value of all buyers' transactions costs is 6.1% (C11), and the present value of all sellers' transactions costs is 1.0% (C12). The final calculation of DLOM is 11.9% (D14)

Tables 10-6A–10-6F: Calculations of DLOM for Larger Firms

Tables 10-6A–10-6F are structured and calculated identically to Table 10-6. There are five differences in the parameters, the first four of which tend to increase DLOM as firm size increases, and the last to decrease DLOM as firm size increases.

Calculation of Component #1—Delay to Sale—$75,000 Firm [1]

	A	B	C	D
4		Coefficients	Co. Data	Discount
5	Intercept	0.1342	NA	13.4%
6	Revenues^2	−5.33E − 18	7.952E + 10	0.0%
7	Value of block-post-discount [2]	−4.26E − 09	$ 75,000	0.0%
8	FMV-marketable minority 100% interest	5.97E − 10	**$ 75,000**	0.0%
9	Earnings stability (assumed)	−0.1376	0.4200	−5.8%
10	Revenue stability (assumed)	−0.1789	0.6900	−12.3%
11	Average years to sell	0.1339	0.2500	3.3%
12	**Total Discount [4]**			**0.0%**
14	Value of block-pre-discount [5]	$ 75,000		
16	Selling price	$ 75,000		
17	Adjusted net income	$ 14,100		
18	Assumed pre-tax margin	5%		
19	Sales	$281,991		
20	Sales^2	7.95E + 10		

[1] Based on Abrams regression of Management Planning, Inc. data-Regression #2, Table 7-10
[2] Equal to Pre-Discount Shares Sold in dollars * (1-Discount). B7 equals B14 only when the discount = 0%.
[3] Earnings and Revenue stability are assumed at the averages from Table 7-5, G60 and H60, respectively, for all FMVs. In the Management Planning data, a correlation analysis revealed that firm size and the stability measures are uncorrelated. Therefore, we assume the same levels for all FMVs.
[4] Total Discount = max(discount, 0), because Disc < 0 indicates the model is outside of its range of reasonability.
[5] In our regression of the Management Planning, Inc. data, this was a marketable minority interest value. This is an illiquid control value and is higher by 12% to 25% than the marketable minority value. The regression coefficient relating to market capitalization in B8 is so small that the difference is immaterial, and it is easier to work with the value available.

Calculation of Component #1—Delay to Sale—$125,000 Firm [1]

	A	B	C	D
4		Coefficients	Co. Data	Discount
5	Intercept	0.1342	NA	13.4%
6	Revenues^2 [2]	−5.33E − 18	2.778E + 11	0.0%
7	Value of block-post-discount [2]	−4.26E − 09	$125,000	0.0%
8	FMV-marketable minority 100% interest	5.97E − 10	**$125,000**	0.0%
9	Earnings stability (assumed)	−0.1376	0.4200	−5.8%
10	Revenue stability (assumed)	−0.1789	0.6900	−12.3%
11	Average years to sell	0.1339	0.3330	4.5%
12	**Total Discount [4]**			**0.0%**
14	Value of block-pre-discount [5]	$125,000		
16	Selling price	$125,000		
17	Adjusted net income	$ 26,352		
18	Assumed pre-tax margin	5%		
19	Sales	$527,049		
20	Sales^2	2.78E + 11		

[1] Based on Abrams regression of Management Planning, Inc. data-Regression #2, Table 7-10
[2] Equal to Pre-Discount Shares Sold in dollars * (1-Discount). B7 equals B14 only when the discount = 0%.
[3] Earnings and Revenue stability are assumed at the averages from Table 7-5, G60 and H60, respectively, for all FMVs. In the Management Planning data, a correlation analysis revealed that firm size and the stability measures are uncorrelated. Therefore, we assume the same levels for all FMVs.
[4] Total Discount = max(discount, 0), because Disc < 0 indicates the model is outside of its range of reasonability.
[5] In our regression of the Management Planning, Inc. data, this was a marketable minority interest value. This is an illiquid control value and is higher by 12% to 25% than the marketable minority value. The regression coefficient relating to market capitalization in B8 is so small that the difference is immaterial, and it is easier to work with the value available.

Calculation of Component #1—Delay to Sale—$175,000 Firm [1]

	A	B	C	D
4		**Coefficients**	**Co. Data**	**Discount**
5	Intercept	0.1342	NA	13.4%
6	Revenues^2 [2]	−5.33E − 18	4.972E + 11	0.0%
7	Value of block-post-discount [2]	−4.26E − 09	$175,000	0.0%
8	FMV-marketable minority 100% interest	5.97E − 10	**$175,000**	0.0%
9	Earnings stability (assumed)	−0.1376	0.4200	−5.8%
10	Revenue stability (assumed)	−0.1789	0.6900	−12.3%
11	Average years to sell	0.1339	0.3330	4.5%
12	**Total Discount [4]**			**0.0%**
14	Value of block-pre-discount [5]	$175,000		
16	Selling price	$175,000		
17	Adjusted net income	$ 35,255		
18	Assumed pre-tax margin	5%		
19	Sales	$705,109		
20	Sales^2	4.97E + 11		

[1] Based on Abrams regression of Management Planning, Inc. data-Regression #2, Table 7-10

[2] Equal to Pre-Discount Shares Sold in dollars * (1-Discount). B7 equals B14 only when the discount = 0%.

[3] Earnings and Revenue stability are assumed at the averages from Table 7-5, G60 and H60, respectively, for all FMVs. In the Management Planning data, a correlation analysis revealed that firm size and the stability measures are uncorrelated. Therefore, we assume the same levels for all FMVs.

[4] Total Discount = max(discount, 0), because Disc < 0 indicates the model is outside of its range of reasonability.

[5] In our regression of the Management Planning, Inc. data, this was a marketable minority interest value. This is an illiquid control value and is higher by 12% to 25% than the marketable minority value. The regression coefficient relating to market capitalization in B8 is so small that the difference is immaterial, and it is easier to work with the value available.

Calculation of Component #1—Delay to Sale—$225,000 Firm [1]

	A	B	C	D
4		**Coefficients**	**Co. Data**	**Discount**
5	Intercept	0.1342	NA	13.4%
6	Revenues^2 [2]	−5.33E − 18	6.685E + 11	0.0%
7	Value of block-post-discount [2]	−4.26E − 09	$225,000	−0.1%
8	FMV-marketable minority 100% interest	5.97E − 10	**$225,000**	0.0%
9	Earnings stability (assumed)	−0.1376	0.4200	−5.8%
10	Revenue stability (assumed)	−0.1789	0.6900	−12.3%
11	Average years to sell	0.1339	0.3330	4.5%
12	**Total Discount [4]**			**0.0%**
14	Value of block-pre-discount [5]	$225,000		
16	Selling price	$225,000		
17	Adjusted net income	$ 40,882		
18	Assumed pre-tax margin	5%		
19	Sales	$817,647		
20	Sales^2	6.69E + 11		

[1] Based on Abrams regression of Management Planning, Inc. data-Regression #2, Table 7-10

[2] Equal to Pre-Discount Shares Sold in dollars * (1-Discount). B7 equals B14 only when the discount = 0%.

[3] Earnings and Revenue stability are assumed at the averages from Table 7-5, G60 and H60, respectively, for all FMVs. In the Management Planning data, a correlation analysis revealed that firm size and the stability measures are uncorrelated. Therefore, we assume the same levels for all FMVs.

[4] Total Discount = max(discount, 0), because Disc < 0 indicates the model is outside of its range of reasonability.

[5] In our regression of the Management Planning, Inc. data, this was a marketable minority interest value. This is an illiquid control value and is higher by 12% to 25% than the marketable minority value. The regression coefficient relating to market capitalization in B8 is so small that the difference is immaterial, and it is easier to work with the value available.

Calculation of Component #1—Delay to Sale—$375,000 Firm [1]

	A	B	C	D
4		Coefficients	Co. Data	Discount
5	Intercept	0.1342	NA	13.4%
6	Revenues^2 [2]	−5.33E − 18	1.955E + 12	0.0%
7	Value of block-post-discount [2]	−4.26E − 09	$368,041	−0.2%
8	FMV-marketable minority 100% interest	5.97E − 10	**$375,000**	0.0%
9	Earnings stability (assumed)	−0.1376	0.4200	−5.8%
10	Revenue stability (assumed)	−0.1789	0.6900	−12.3%
11	Average years to sell	0.1339	0.5000	6.7%
12	**Total Discount [4]**			**1.9%**
14	Value of block-pre-discount [5]	$375,000		
16	Selling price	$375,000		
17	Adjusted net income	$ 69,913		
18	Assumed pre-tax margin	5%		
19	Sales	$1,398,256		
20	Sales^2	1.96E + 12		

[1] Based on Abrams regression of Management Planning, Inc. data-Regression #2, Table 7-10

[2] Equal to Pre-Discount Shares Sold in dollars * (1-Discount). B7 equals B14 only when the discount = 0%.

[3] Earnings and Revenue stability are assumed at the averages from Table 7-5, G60 and H60, respectively, for all FMVs. In the Management Planning data, a correlation analysis revealed that firm size and the stability measures are uncorrelated. Therefore, we assume the same levels for all FMVs.

[4] Total Discount = max(discount, 0), because Disc < 0 indicates the model is outside of its range of reasonability.

[5] In our regression of the Management Planning, Inc. data, this was a marketable minority interest value. This is an illiquid control value and is higher by 12% to 25% than the marketable minority value. The regression coefficient relating to market capitalization in B8 is so small that the difference is immaterial, and it is easier to work with the value available.

Calculation of Component #1—Delay to Sale—$750,000 Firm [1]

	A	B	C	D
4		Coefficients	Co. Data	Discount
5	Intercept	0.1342	NA	13.4%
6	Revenues^2 [2]	−5.33E − 18	1.955E + 12	0.0%
7	Value of block-post-discount [2]	−4.26E − 09	$686,724	−0.3%
8	FMV-marketable minority 100% interest	5.97E − 10	**$750,000**	0.0%
9	Earnings stability (assumed)	−0.1376	0.4200	−5.8%
10	Revenue stability (assumed)	−0.1789	0.6900	−12.3%
11	Average years to sell	0.1339	1.0000	13.7%
12	**Total Discount [4]**			**8.4%**
14	Value of block-pre-discount [5]	$ 750,000		
16	Selling price	$ 750,000		
17	Adjusted net income	$ 69,913		
18	Assumed pre-tax margin	5%		
19	Sales	$1,398,256		
20	Sales^2	1.96E + 12		

[1] Based on Abrams regression of Management Planning, Inc. data-Regression #2, Table 7-10

[2] Equal to Pre-Discount Shares Sold in dollars * (1-Discount). B7 equals B14 only when the discount = 0%.

[3] Earnings and Revenue stability are assumed at the averages from Table 7-5, G60 and H60, respectively, for all FMVs. In the Management Planning data, a correlation analysis revealed that firm size and the stability measures are uncorrelated. Therefore, we assume the same levels for all FMVs.

[4] Total Discount = max(discount, 0), because Disc < 0 indicates the model is outside of its range of reasonability.

[5] In our regression of the Management Planning, Inc. data, this was a marketable minority interest value. This is an illiquid control value and is higher by 12% to 25% than the marketable minority value. The regression coefficient relating to market capitalization in B8 is so small that the difference is immaterial, and it is easier to work with the value available.

TABLE 10-4G

Calculation of Component #1—Delay to Sale—$10 Million Firm [1]

		A	B	C	D
4			**Coefficients**	**Co. Data**	**Discount**
5	Intercept		0.1342	NA	13.4%
6	Revenues^2 [2]		−5.33E − 18	2.560E + 14	−0.1%
7	Value of block-post-discount [2]		−4.26E − 09	$ 9,489,650	−4.0%
8	FMV-marketable minority 100% interest		5.97E − 10	$10,000,000	0.6%
9	Earnings stability (assumed)		−0.1376	0.4200	−5.8%
10	Revenue stability (assumed)		−0.1789	0.6900	−12.3%
11	Average years to sell		0.1339	1.0000	13.4%
12	**Total Discount [4]**				**5.1%**
14	Value of block-pre-discount [5]	$10,000,000			
16	Selling price	$10,000,000			
17	Divide by P/E multiple assumed at 12.5 = net inc	$ 800,000			
18	Assumed pre-tax margin	5%			
19	Sales	$16,000,000			
20	Sales^2	2.56E + 14			

[1] Based on Abrams regression of Management Planning, Inc. data-Regression #2, Table 7-10

[2] Equal to Pre-Discount Shares Sold in dollars * (1-Discount). B7 equals B14 only when the discount = 0%.

[3] Earnings and Revenue stability are assumed at the averages from Table 7-5, G60 and H60, respectively, for all FMVs. In the Management Planning data, a correlation analysis revealed that firm size and the stability measures are uncorrelated. Therefore, we assume the same levels for all FMVs.

[4] Total Discount = max(discount, 0), because Disc < 0 indicates the model is outside of its range of reasonability.

[5] In our regression of the Management Planning, Inc. data, this was a marketable minority interest value. This is an illiquid control value and is higher by 12% to 25% than the marketable minority value. The regression coefficient relating to market capitalization in B8 is so small that the difference is immaterial, and it is easier to work with the value available.

TABLE 10-6A

Calculation of DLOM

	A	B	C	D	E	F	G
4	**Section 1: Calculation of the Discount For Lack of Marketability**						
6				= 1 − Col. [C]			
7		**Pure Discount**	**PV of Perpetual**	**Remaining**			
8	**Component**	**= z [1]**	**Discount [2]**	**Value**			
9	1	0.0%	0.0%	100.0%	Delay to sale		
10	2	9.0%	9.0%	91.0%	Buyer's monopsony power—thin markets		
11	3A	4.9%	5.3%	94.7%	Transactions costs—buyers		
12	3B	14.3%	1.2%	98.8%	Transactions costs—sellers		
13	Percent remaining			89.9%	Total % remaining = components 1 × 2 × 3A × 3B		
14	**Final discount**			**10.1%**	Discount = 1 − total % remaining		
16	**Section 2: Assumptions and Intermediate Calculations:**						
18	FMV-equity of co. (before discounts)			$ 75,000			
19	Discount rate = r [3]			32.6%			
20	Constant growth rate = g (Table 10-2, row 24)			2.5%			
21	Intermediate calculation: x = (1 + g)/(1 + r)			0.7728			
22	Avg # years between sales = j			10			

[1] Pure Discounts: For Component #1, Table 10-4, cell D12; For Component #2, 9% per Schwert article. For Component #3A and #3B, Table 10-5, cells I8 and I9 − 2% for public brokerage costs.

[2] PV of Perpetual Discount Formula: $1 - (1 - x^{\hat{}}j)/((1 - (1 - z)^*x^{\hat{}}j))$, per equation [7-9], used for Component #3B.

PV of Perpetual Discount Formula: $1 - (1 - z)^*(1 - x^{\hat{}}j)/((1 - (1 - z)^*x^{\hat{}}j))$, per equation [7-9a], used for Component #3A.

Components #1 and #2 simply transfer the pure discount.

[3] The formula is: 0.5352 − (.0186 ln FMV), based on Table 10-1, B34 and B35.

Calculation of DLOM

	A	B	C	D	E	F	G
4	Section 1: Calculation of the Discount For Lack of Marketability						
6				= 1 − Col. [C]			
7		**Pure Discount**	**PV of Perpetual**	**Remaining**			
8	**Component**	**= z [1]**	**Discount [2]**	**Value**			
9	1	0.0%	0.0%	100.0%	Delay to sale		
10	2	9.0%	9.0%	91.0%	Buyer's monopsony power—thin markets		
11	3A	4.5%	4.9%	95.1%	Transactions costs—buyers		
12	3B	14.0%	1.3%	98.7%	Transactions costs—sellers		
13	Percent remaining			89.8%	Total % remaining = components 1 × 2 × 3A × 3B		
14	**Final discount**			**10.2%**	Discount = 1 − total % remaining		
16	Section 2: Assumptions and Intermediate Calculations:						
18	FMV-equity of co. (before discounts)			**$ 125,000**			
19	Discount rate = r [3]			**31.7%**			
20	Constant growth rate = g (Table 11-2, row 24)			**3.0%**			
21	Intermediate calculation: x = (1 + g)/(1 + r)			**0.7822**			
22	Avg # years between sales = j			**10**			

[1] Pure Discounts: For Component #1, Table 10-4, cell D12; For Component #2, 9% per Schwert article. For Component #3A and #3B, Table 10-5, cells I10 and I11 − 2% for public brokerage costs.
[2] PV of Perpetual Discount Formula: $1 - (1 - x^j)/((1 - (1 - z)^* x^j))$, per equation [7-9], used for Component #3B.
PV of Perpetual Discount Formula: $1 - (1 - z)^*(1 - x^j)/((1 - (1 - z)^* x^j))$, per equation [7-9a], used for Component #3A.
Components #1 and #2 simply transfer the pure discount.
[3] The formula is: 0.5352 − (.0186 ln FMV), based on Table 10-1, B34 and B35.

Calculation of DLOM

	A	B	C	D	E	F	G
4	Section 1: Calculation of the Discount For Lack of Marketability						
6				= 1 − Col. [C]			
7		**Pure Discount**	**PV of Perpetual**	**Remaining**			
8	**Component**	**= z [1]**	**Discount [2]**	**Value**			
9	1	0.0%	0.0%	100.0%	Delay to sale		
10	2	9.0%	9.0%	91.0%	Buyer's monopsony power—thin markets		
11	3A	4.3%	4.7%	95.3%	Transactions costs—buyers		
12	3B	13.8%	1.3%	98.7%	Transactions costs—sellers		
13	Percent remaining			89.8%	Total % remaining = components 1 × 2 × 3A × 3B		
14	**Final discount**			**10.2%**	Discount = 1 − total % remaining		
16	Section 2: Assumptions and Intermediate Calculations:						
18	FMV-equity of co. (before discounts)			**$ 175,000**			
19	Discount rate = r [3]			**31.0%**			
20	Constant growth rate = g (Table 10-2, row 24)			**3.0%**			
21	Intermediate calculation: x = (1 + g)/(1 + r)			**0.7860**			
22	Avg # years between sales = j			**10**			

[1] Pure Discounts: For Component #1, Table 10-4, cell D12; For Component #2, 9% per Schwert article. For Component #3A and #3B, Table 10-5, cells I12 and I13 − 2% for public brokerage costs.
[2] PV of Perpetual Discount Formula: $1 - (1 - x^j)/((1 - (1 - z)^* x^j))$, per equation [7-9], used for Component #3B.
PV of Perpetual Discount Formula: $1 - (1 - z)^*(1 - x^j)/((1 - (1 - z)^* x^j))$, per equation [7-9a], used for Component #3A.
Components #1 and #2 simply transfer the pure discount.
[3] The formula is: 0.5352 − (.0186 ln FMV), based on Table 10-1, B34 and B35.

Calculation of DLOM

	A	B	C	D	E	F	G
4	Section 1: Calculation of the Discount For Lack of Marketability						
6				= 1 − Col. [C]			
7		Pure Discount	PV of Perpetual	Remaining			
8	Component	= z [1]	Discount [2]	Value			
9	1	0.0%	0.0%	100.0%	Delay to sale		
10	2	9.0%	9.0%	91.0%	Buyer's monopsony power—thin markets		
11	3A	4.1%	4.5%	95.5%	Transactions costs—buyers		
12	3B	13.6%	1.6%	98.4%	Transactions costs—sellers		
13	Percent remaining			89.5%	Total % remaining = components 1 × 2 × 3A × 3B		
14	**Final discount**			**10.5%**	Discount = 1 − total % remaining		
16	Section 2: Assumptions and Intermediate Calculations:						
18	FMV-equity of co. (before discounts)			$ 225,000			
19	Discount rate = r [3]			30.6%			
20	Constant growth rate = g (Table 10-2, row 24)			4.5%			
21	Intermediate calculation: x = (1 + g)/(1 + r)			0.8003			
22	Avg # years between sales = j			10			

[1] Pure Discounts: For Component #1, Table 10-4, cell D12; For Component #2, 9% per Schwert article. For Component #3A and #3B, Table 10-5, cells I4 and I5 − 2% for public brokerage costs.
[2] PV of Perpetual Discount Formula: $1 - (1 - x^\wedge j)/((1 - (1 - z)^*x^\wedge j))$, per equation [7-9], used for Component #3B.
PV of Perpetual Discount Formula: $1 - (1 - z)^*(1 - x^\wedge j)/((1 - (1 - z)^*x^\wedge j))$, per equation [7-9a], used for Component #3A.
Components #1 and #2 simply transfer the pure discount.
[3] The formula is: 0.5352 − (.0186 ln FMV), based on Table 10-1, B34 and B35.

Calculation of DLOM

	A	B	C	D	E	F	G
4	Section 1: Calculation of the Discount For Lack of Marketability						
6				= 1 − Col. [C]			
7		Pure Discount	PV of Perpetual	Remaining			
8	Component	= z [1]	Discount [2]	Value			
9	1	1.9%	1.9%	98.1%	Delay to sale		
10	2	9.0%	9.0%	91.0%	Buyer's monopsony power—thin markets		
11	3A	4.7%	5.3%	94.7%	Transactions costs—buyers		
12	3B	14.2%	1.9%	98.1%	Transactions costs—sellers		
13	Percent remaining			87.6%	Total % remaining = components 1 × 2 × 3A × 3B		
14	Final discount			**12.4%**	Discount = 1 − total % remaining		
16	Section 2: Assumptions and Intermediate Calculations:						
18	FMV-equity of co. (before discounts)			$ 375,000			
19	Discount rate = r [3]			29.6%			
20	Constant growth rate = g (Table 11-2, row 24)			5.0%			
21	Intermediate calculation: x = (1 + g)/(1 + r)			0.8100			
22	Avg # years between sales = j			10			

[1] Pure Discounts: For Component #1, Table 10-4, cell D12; For Component #2, 9% per Schwert article. For Component #3A and #3B, Table 10-5, cells I6 and I7 − 1% for public brokerage costs.
[2] PV of Perpetual Discount Formula: $1 - (1 - x^\wedge j)/((1 - (1 - z)^*x^\wedge j))$, per equation [7-9], used for Component #3B.
PV of Perpetual Discount Formula: $1 - (1 - z)^*(1 - x^\wedge j)/((1 - (1 - z)^*x^\wedge j))$, per equation [7-9a], used for Component #3A.
Components #1 and #2 simply transfer the pure discount.
[3] The formula is: 0.5352 − (.0186 ln FMV), based on Table 10-1, B34 and B35.

Calculation of DLOM

	A	B	C	D	E	F	G
4	**Section 1: Calculation of the Discount For Lack of Marketability**						
6				= 1 − Col. [C]			
7		Pure Discount	PV of Perpetual	Remaining			
8	Component	= z [1]	Discount [2]	Value			
9	1	8.4%	8.4%	91.6%	Delay to sale		
10	2	9.0%	9.0%	91.0%	Buyer's monopsony power—thin markets		
11	3A	4.2%	4.8%	95.2%	Transactions costs—buyers		
12	3B	13.7%	2.3%	97.7%	Transactions costs—sellers		
13	Percent remaining			81.4%	Total % remaining = components 1 × 2 × 3A × 3B		
14	**Final discount**			**18.6%**	Discount = 1 − total % remaining		
16	**Section 2: Assumptions and Intermediate Calculations:**						
18	FMV-equity of co. (before discounts)			$ 750,000			
19	Discount rate = r [3]			28.3%			
20	Constant growth rate = g (Table 11-2, row 24)			6.0%			
21	Intermediate calculation: x = (1 + g)/(1 + r)			0.8259			
22	Avg # years between sales = j			10			

[1] Pure Discounts: For Component #1, Table 10-4, cell D12; For Component #2, 9% per Schwert article. For Component #3A and #3B, Table 10-5, cells I8 and I9 − 2% for public brokerage costs.
[2] PV of Perpetual Discount Formula: $1 - (1 - x^j)/((1 - (1 - z)*x^j))$, per equation [7-9], used for Component #3B.
PV of Perpetual Discount Formula: $1 - (1 - z)*(1 - x^j)/((1 - (1 - z)*x^j))$, per equation [7-9a], used for Component #3A.
Components #1 and #2 simply transfer the pure discount.
[3] The formula is: 0.5352 − (.0186 ln FMV), based on Table 10-1, B34 and B35.

Calculation of DLOM

	A	B	C	D	E	F	G
4	**Section 1: Calculation of the Discount For Lack of Marketability**						
6				= 1 − Col. [C]			
7		Pure Discount	PV of Perpetual	Remaining			
8	Component	= z [1]	Discount [2]	Value			
9	1	5.1%	5.1%	94.9%	Delay to sale		
10	2	9.0%	9.0%	91.0%	Buyer's monopsony power—thin markets		
11	3A	2.7%	3.6%	96.4%	Transactions costs—buyers		
12	3B	4.4%	1.5%	98.5%	Transactions costs—sellers		
13	Percent remaining			85.0%	Total % remaining = components 1 × 2 × 3A × 3B		
14	**Final discount**			**15.0%**	Discount = 1 − total % remaining		
16	**Section 2: Assumptions and Intermediate Calculations:**						
18	FMV-equity of co. (before discounts)			$10,000,000			
19	Discount rate = r [3]			23.5%			
20	Constant growth rate = g (Table 10-2, row 24)			8.0%			
21	Intermediate calculation: x = (1 + g)/(1 + r)			0.8743			
22	Avg # years between sales = j			10			

[1] Pure Discounts: For Component #1, Table 10-4, cell D12; For Component #2, 9% per Schwert article. For Component #3A and #3B, Table 10-5, cells I20 and I21 − 2% for public brokerage costs.
[2] PV of Perpetual Discount Formula: $1 - (1 - x^j)/((1 - (1 - z)*x^j))$, per equation [7-9], used for Component #3B.
PV of Perpetual Discount Formula: $1 - (1 - z)*(1 - x^j)/((1 - (1 - z)*x^j))$, per equation [7-9a], used for Component #3A.
Components #1 and #2 simply transfer the pure discount.
[3] The formula is: 0.5352 − (.0186 ln FMV), based on Table 10-1, B34 and B35.

1. As firm size increases, our assumed growth rate, g, increases. By our analysis of the partial derivatives in the Mathematical Appendix to Chapter 7, that causes an increase in DLOM.

2. As firm size increases, the log size discount rate, r, decreases. By our analysis of the partial derivatives in the Mathematical Appendix to Chapter 7, that also causes an increase in DLOM.

3. As mentioned earlier, for firm sizes under $375,000, we assumed the delay to sale to be 0.33 years or less, which lead to a zero discount for component #1. For the $375,000 and $750,000 firms, we assumed a one-half-year and one-year delay to sale, which led to a component #1 pure discount of 1.9% (Table 10-6E, B9) and 8.4% (Table 10-6F, B9), respectively. The latter accounts for the vast majority of the much higher DLOM for the $750,000 mean selling price firms. Had that been zero, like all of the others except the $375,000 firm, DLOM for the $750,000 firms would have been 13.1%—much closer to DLOM for the smaller firms.

4. We assumed a 1% broker's fee for publicly traded stocks for the $375,000 and $750,000 firms, while we assumed a 2% fee for the firms under that size. This increased the pure discount for components #3A and #3B by 1% for those two size categories, and therefore increased DLOM.

5. Transactions costs decrease as size increases. Buyers' transactions costs are 7.7% (Table 10-5, I6) for $25,000 firms and 5.2% for $750,000 firms (I18), for a difference of 2.5%. Sellers' transactions costs are 17.1% (I7) for $25,000 firms and 14.7% (I19) for $750,000 firms, for a difference of 2.4%.

Items 1 through 4 above cause DLOM to increase with size, while item 5 causes DLOM to decrease with size. Looking at Table 10-2, it is clear that the first four items dominate, which causes DLOM to increase with size. This is not a result that I would have predicted before. I would have thought that overall, DLOM decreases with size.

As mentioned earlier in this chapter, had we used a different model, it would have been possible to assign a pure discount for the delay to sale of perhaps 3–5% using another model. This would have narrowed the differences between DLOM for the small firms and the large ones, but we would still have come to the counterintuitive conclusion that DLOM increases with firm size.

Calculation of DLOM for Large Firms

The preceding result begs the question of what happens to DLOM beyond the realm of small firms. To answer this question, we extend our analysis to Tables 10-4G and 10-6G.

Table 10-4G is otherwise identical to its predecessor, Table 10-4F. Since we do not have the benefit of the IBA data at this size level, we have to forecast sales in a different fashion. The calculation of component #1 is still not sensitive at this level to the square of revenues, so we can afford to be imprecise. Assuming an average P/E multiple of 12.5, we divide the assumed $10 million selling price by the P/E multiple to arrive at net income of $800,000. Dividing that by an assumed pretax margin of 5% leads to sales of $16 million (B19), which is 2.56×10^{14} (B20, transferred to C6) when squared. That contributes only –0.1% (D6) to the calculation of the pure discount from the delay to sale component (it was 0.0% in Table 10-4F, D6).

The really significant difference in the calculation comes from cell D7, which is -4.0% in Table 10-4G and zero in Table 10-4F. The final calculation of component #1 is 5.1% (D12) for the $10 million firm, compared to 8.4% for the $750,000 firm. Thus it seems that component #1 rises sharply somewhere between $375,000 and $750,000 firms, but then begins to decline as the size effect dominates and causes transactions costs to decline, while not adding any additional time to sell the firm.

Table 10-6G is our calculation of DLOM for the $10 million firm. Comparing it to Table 10-6F, the DLOM calculation for the $750,000 firm, the final result is 15.0% (Table 10-6G, D14) versus 20.4% (Table 10-6F, D14). Thus, it appears that DLOM should continue to decline with size. Thus it appears that DLOM rises with size up to about $1 million in selling price and declines thereafter. Another factor we did not consider here that also would contribute to a declining DLOM with size is that the number of interested buyers would tend to increase with larger size, which should lower component #2—buyer's monopsony power—below the 9% from the Schwert article cited in Chapter 7.

INTERPRETATION OF THE ERROR

As mentioned earlier, the magnitude of the error in Table 10-2 is fairly small. The five right columns average a 0.4% error (I29) and a 4.2% (I30) mean absolute error. We can interpret this as a victory for the log size and economic components models—and I do interpret it that way, to some degree. However, the many assumptions that we had to make render our calculations too speculative for us to place much confidence in them. They are evidence that we are probably not way off the mark, but certainly fall short of proving that we are right.

An assumption not specifically discussed yet is the assumption that the simple means of Raymond Miles's categories is the actual mean of the transactions in each category. Perhaps the mean of transactions in the $500,000 to $1 million category is really $900,000, not $750,000. Our results would be inaccurate to that extent and that would be another source of error in reconciling between the IBA P/E multiples and my P/CF multiples. It does appear, though, that Table 10-2 provides some evidence of the reasonableness of the log size and economic components models.

Amihud and Mendelson (1986) show that there is a clientele effect in investing in publicly held securities. Investors with longer investment horizons can amortize their transactions costs, which are primarily the bid–ask spread and secondarily the broker's fees,[9] over a longer period, thus reducing the transactions cost per period. Investors will thus select

---

9. Because broker's fees are relatively insignificant in publicly held securities, we will ignore them in this analysis. That is not true of business broker's fees for selling privately held firms.

their investments by their investment horizons, and each security will have two components to its return: that of a zero bid–ask spread asset and a component that rewards the investor for the illiquidity that he is taking on in the form of the bid–ask spread.

Thus, investors with shorter investment horizons will choose securities with low bid–ask spreads, which also have smaller gross returns, and investors with longer time horizons will choose securities with larger bid–ask spreads and larger gross returns. Their net returns will be higher on average than those of short-term investors because the long-term investor's securities choices will have higher gross returns to compensate them for the high bid–ask spread, which they amortize over a sufficiently long investment horizon to reduce its impact on net returns. A short-term investment in a high bid–ask spread stock would lose the benefit of the higher gross return by losing the bid–ask spread in the sale with little time over which to amortize the spread.

Investors in privately held firms usually have a very long time horizon, and the transactions costs are considerable compared to the bid–ask spreads of NYSE firms. In the economic components model I assumed investors in privately held firms have the same estimate of j, the average time between sales, in addition to the other variables, growth (g), discount rate, (r), and buyers' and sellers' transactions costs, z. There may be size-based, systematic differences in investor time horizons; if so, that would be a source of error in Table 10-2.

Sufficiently long time horizons may also predispose the buyer to forgo some of the DLOM he or she is entitled to. If DLOM should be, say, 25%, what is the likelihood of the buyer caving in and settling for 20% instead? If time horizons are $j = 10$ years, then the buyer amortizes the 5% "loss" over 10 years, which equals 0.5% per year. If $j = 20$, then the loss is only 0.25% per year. Thus, long time horizons should tend to reduce DLOM, and that is not a part of the economic components model—at least not yet. It would require further research to determine if there are systematic relationships between firm size and buyers' time horizons.

CONCLUSION

It does seem, then, that we are on our way as a profession to developing a "unified valuation theory," one with one or two major principles that govern all valuation situations. Of course, there are numerous subprinciples and details, but we are moving in the direction of a true science when we can see the underlying principles that unify all the various phenomena in our discipline.

Of course, if one asks if valuation is a science or an art, the answer is valuation is an art that sits on top of a science. A good scientist has to be a good artist, and valuation art without science is reckless fortune telling.

BIBLIOGRAPHY

Amihud, Yakov, and Haim Mendelson. 1986. "Asset Pricing and the Bid–Ask Spread." *Journal of Financial Economics* 17:223–249.

Miles, Raymond C. 1992. "Price/Earnings Ratios and Company Size Data for Small Businesses." *Business Valuation Review* (September): 135–139.

Pratt, Shannon P. 1993. *Valuing Small Businesses and Professional Practices,* 2d ed. Burr Ridge, Ill.: McGraw-Hill.

CHAPTER 11

Measuring Valuation Uncertainty and Error

INTRODUCTION
  Differences Between Uncertainty and Error
  Sources of Uncertainty and Error
MEASURING VALUATION UNCERTAINTY
  Table 11-1: 95% Confidence Intervals
    Valuing the Huge Firm
    Valuation Errors in the Others Size Firms
    The Exact 95% Confidence Intervals
    Table 11-2: 60-Year Log Size Model
  Summary of Valuation Implications of Statistical Uncertainity in the
    Discount Rate
MEASURING THE EFFECTS OF VALUATION ERROR
  Defining Absolute and Relative Error
  The Valuation Model
  Dollar Effects of Absolute Errors in Forecastng Year 1 Cash Flow
  Relative Effects of Absolute Errors in Forecasting Year 1 Cash Flow
  Absolute and Relative Effects of Relative Errors in Forecasting Year 1
    Cash Flow
  Absolute Errors in Forecasting Growth and the Discount Rate
    Definitions
    The Mathematics
    Example Using the Error Formula
    Relative Effects of Absolute Error in r and g
    Example of Relative Valuation Error
    Valuation Effects on Large Versus Small Firms
    Relative Effect of Relative Error in Forecasting Growth and
      Discount Rates
    Tables 11-4–12-4b: Examples Showing Effects on Large vs. Small
      Firms
  Table 11-5: Summary of Effects of Valuation Errors
SUMMARY AND CONCLUSIONS

INTRODUCTION

This chapter describes the impact of various sources of valuation uncertainty and error on valuing large and small firms. It will also provide the reader with a greater understanding of where our analysis is most vulnerable to the effects of errors and demonstrate where appraisers need to focus the majority of their efforts.

Differences between Uncertainty and Error

It is worthwhile to explain the differences between uncertainty and error. I developed the log size equation in Chapter 4 by regression analysis. Because the R^2 is less than 100%, size does not explain all of the differences in historical rates of return. Unknown variables and/or random variation explain the rest. When we calculate a 95% confidence interval, it means that we are 95% sure that the true value of the dependent variable is within the interval and 5% sure it is outside of the interval. That is the uncertainty. One does not need to make an error to have uncertainty in the valuation.

Let's suppose that for a firm of a particular size, the regression-determined discount rate is 20% and the 95% confidence interval is between 18% and 23%. It may be that the true and unobservable discount rate is also 20%, in which case we have uncertainty, but not error. On the other hand, if the true discount rate is anything other than 20%, then we have both uncertainty and error—even though we have used the model correctly. Since the true discount rate is unobservable and unknowable for privately held firms, we will never be certain that our model will calculate the correct discount rate—even when we use it properly. If one makes a mistake in using the model, that is what we mean by appraiser error. For the remainder of this chapter, we will use the simpler term, *error,* to mean appraiser-generated error. The first part of the chapter deals with valuation uncertainty, and the second part deals with valuation error.

Sources of Uncertainty and Error

We need only look at the valuation process in order to see the various sources of valuation uncertainty and error. As mentioned in the Introduction to this book, the overall valuation process is:

- Forecast cash flows.
- Discount cash flows to present value.
- Calculate valuation premiums and discounts for degree of control and marketability.

Uncertainty is always present, and error can creep into our results at each stage of the valuation process.

MEASURING VALUATION UNCERTAINTY

In forecasting cash flows, even when regression analysis is a valid tool for forecasting both sales and costs and expenses, it is common to have fairly wide 95% confidence intervals around our sales forecasts, as we discovered in Chapter 2. Thus, we usually have a substantial degree of uncertainty surrounding the sales forecast and a typically smaller, though material, degree of uncertainty around the forecast of fixed and variable costs. As each company's results are unique, we will not focus on a quantitative measure of uncertainty around our forecast of cash flows in this chapter.[1] Instead, we will focus on quantitative measures of uncertainty around the discount rate, as that is generic.

For illustration, we use a midyear Gordon Model formula, $(\sqrt{1 + r})/(r - g)$, as our valuation formula. Although a Gordon model is appropriate for most firms near or at maturity, this method is inapplicable to startups and other high-growth firms, as it presupposes that the company being valued has constant perpetual growth.

Table 11-1: 95% Confidence Intervals

Table 11-1 contains calculations of 95% confidence intervals around the valuation that results from our calculation of discount rate. We use the 72-year regression equation for the log size model. It is the relevant time frame for comparison with CAPM, since the CAPM results in the SBBI 1998 Yearbook (Ibbotson Associates 1998) are for 72 years.[2] Later, in Table 11-2, we examine the 60-year log size model for comparison. For purposes of this exercise, we will assume the forecast cash flows and perpetual growth rate are correct, so we can isolate the impact of the statistical uncertainty of the discount rate.

The exact procedure for calculating the 95% confidence intervals is mathematically complex and would strain the patience of most readers. Therefore, we will use a simpler approximation in our explanation and merely present the final results of the exact calculation in row 42.

Valuing the Huge Firm

Because the log size model produces a mathematical relationship between return and size, our exploration of 95% confidence intervals around a valuation result necessitates separate calculations for different-size firms. We begin with the largest firms and work our way down.

In Table 11-1, cell B5 we show last year's cash flow as $300 million. Using the log size model, the discount rate is 13%[3] (B6), and we assume a perpetual growth rate of 8% (B7). We apply the perpetual growth rate to calculate cash flows for the first forecast year. Thus, forecast cash flow = $300 million × 1.08 = $324 million (B8).

In B12 we repeat the 13% discount rate. Next we form a 95% confidence interval around the 13% rate in the following manner. Regression

---

1. In the second part of the chapter we will explore the valuation impact of appraiser error in forecasting cash flows.
2. While Chapter 4 was updated to include the Ibbotson 1999 SBBI Yearbook results, this chapter has not. Therefore, this chapter does not contain the 1998 stock market results, which were very poor for the log size model. As noted in Chapter 4, large firms outperformed small firms. Therefore, the confidence intervals calculated in this chapter would be wider if we were to include the 1998 results, which are reported in the 1999 SBBI Yearbook.
3. Calculation of the log size discount rate is in rows 35–38. The regression equation in these rows is based on the 1998 SBBI Yearbook and therefore does not match the equation in Table 4-1.

#2 in Table 4-1 has 10 observations. The number of degrees freedom is $n - k - 1$, where n is the number of observations and k is the number of independent variables; thus we have eight degrees of freedom. Using a t-distribution with eight degrees of freedom, we add and subtract 2.306 standard errors to form a 95% confidence interval. The standard error of the log size equation through SBBI 1998 was 0.76% (B48), which when multiplied by 2.306 equals 1.75%. The upper bound of the discount rate calculated by log size is 13% + 1.75% = 14.75% (B11), and the lower bound is 13% − 1.75% = 11.25% (B13).[4]

For purposes of comparison, we assume that CAPM also arrives at a 13% discount rate (B16). We multiply the CAPM standard error of 2.42% (B49) by 2.306 standard errors, yielding ±5.58% for our 95% confidence interval. In cell B15 we add 5.58% to the 12% discount rate, and in cell B17 we subtract 5.58% from the 12% rate, arriving at upper and lower bounds of 18.58% and 7.42%, respectively.

Rows 19 to 21 show the calculations of the midyear Gordon model multiples $(GM) = (\sqrt{1 + r})/(r + g)$. For $r = 13\% \pm 1.75\%$ and $g = 8\%$, $GM = 21.2603$ (B20), which we multiply by the $324 million cash flow (B8) to come to an FMV (ignoring discounts and premiums) of $6.89 billion (B24).

We repeat the process using 14.75%, the upper bound of the 95% confidence interval for the discount rate (B11) in the GM formula, to come to a lower bound of the GM of 15.8640 (B19). Similarly, using a discount rate of 11.25% (the lower bound of the confidence interval, B13) the corresponding upper bound GM formula is 32.4791 (B21). The FMVs associated with the lower and upper bound GMMs are $5.14 billion (B23) and $10.52 billion (B25), or 74.6% (C23) and 152.8% (C25), respectively, of our best estimate of $6.89 billion.

Cell C39 shows the average size of the 95% confidence interval around the valuation estimate. It is 39%, which is equal to $\frac{1}{2} \times [(1 - 74.6\%) + (152.8\% - 1)]$. It is not literally true that the 95% confidence interval is the same above and below the estimate, but it is easier to speak in terms of a single number.

Row 28 shows the Gordon model multiple using a CAPM discount rate, which we assume is identical to the log size model discount rate. Using the CAPM upper and lower bound discount rates in B15 and B17, the lower and upper bounds of the 95% confidence interval for the CAPM Gordon model are 10.2920 (B27) and −178.5324 (B29), respectively. Obviously, the latter is an explosive, nonsense result, and the average 95% confidence interval is infinite in this case.

---

4. This is an approximation. The exact formula is:

$$Y_0 = \hat{\mu}_0 \pm t_{0.025} s \sqrt{\frac{1}{n} + \frac{x_0^2}{\sum_i x_i^2} + 1}$$

where $\hat{\mu}_0$ is the regression-determined discount rate for our subject company, x_i are the deviations of the natural logarithm of each decile's market capitalization from the mean log of the 10 Ibbotson decile average market capitalizations, $t_{0.025}$ is the two-tailed, 95% t-statistic, s is the standard error of the y-estimate as calculated by the regression, $n = 10$, the number of deciles in the regression sample, and x_0 is the deviation of the log of the FMV of the subject company from the mean of the regression sample.

Part 4   Putting It All Together

We obtain the same estimate of FMV for CAPM as the log size model (B32, B24), but look at the lower bound estimate in B31. It is $3.33 billion (rounded), or 48.4% (C31) of the best estimate, versus 74.6% (C23) for the same in the log size model. The CAPM standard error being more than three times larger creates a huge confidence interval and often leads to explosive results for very large firms.

Valuation Error in the Other-Size Firms

The remaining columns in Table 11-1 have the same formulas and logic as columns B and C. The only difference is that the size of the firm varies, which implies a different discount rate and therefore different 95% confidence intervals. In column D we assume the large firm had cash flows of $15 million last year (D5), which will grow at 7% (D7). We see that the log size model has an average 95% confidence interval of $\pm 14\%$ (E39) and CAPM has an average 95% confidence interval of $\pm 56\%$ (E40).

Columns F and H are successively smaller firms. Note how the minimum valuation uncertainty declines with firm size.

The approximate 95% confidence intervals for log size are 39%, 14%, 9%, and 7% (row 39) for the huge, large, medium, and small firm, respectively. The CAPM confidence intervals also decline with firm size, but are much larger than the log size confidence intervals. For example, the CAPM small firm 95% confidence interval is $\pm 23\%$ (I40)—much larger than the 7% (I39) interval for the Log Size Model.

The Exact 95% Confidence Intervals

As mentioned earlier, rows 39 and 40 are a simplified approximation of the 95% confidence intervals around the discount rates, used to minimize the complexity of an already intricate series of calculations and related explanations.

Row 42 contains the exact 95% confidence intervals for log size. Note that the exact 95% confidence intervals are larger than their approximations in Rows 39 to 40. There are no actual 95% confidence intervals for CAPM.[5]

Aside from the direct effect of size on the calculation of the discount rate, there is a secondary, indirect effect of size on the confidence intervals. All other things being equal, confidence intervals are at their minimum at the mean of the data set, which is over $4 billion for the NYSE, and increase the further we move away from the mean. The huge firm in column B—and to a lesser extent the large firm in column D—are close to the mean of the NYSE market capitalization. Therefore, we have two opposing forces operating on the confidence intervals. The mathematics of the log size equation and Gordon model multiple are such that the smaller the firm, the smaller the confidence interval for the FMV. However, the smaller firms are far below the mean of the NYSE sample, so that tends to increase the actual 95% confidence interval.

Thus, the direct effect and the indirect effect on the confidence intervals work in opposite directions. Jumping ahead of ourselves for a mo-

---

5. The reason for this is that the CAPM calculations in the SBBI Yearbook are not a pure regression, because the y-intercept is forced to the risk-free rate.

ment, that explains the result in Table 11-2 (which is virtually identical to Table 11-1 using the 60-year log size regression equation instead of the 72-year equation) that the exact log size confidence interval for the small firm is ±3%, while it is ±2% for the medium firm. If the SBBI Yearbook compiled similar information for Nasdaq companies, this secondary effect would be far less, and it is almost certain that the small firm 95% confidence interval would be smaller than the medium firm confidence interval.

Table 11-2: 60-Year Log Size Model

As mentioned above, Table 11-2 is identical to Table 11-1 except that it uses the 60-year log size equation instead of the 72-year equation. In this case we have a much smaller standard error of 0.14% (B35). There is no comparison to CAPM, because no corresponding data is available. Note that the actual 95% confidence intervals dramatically reduce to ±5% of value for the huge firm (C29) and ±2–3% of value for the other size firms (E29, G29, and I29).

At this point, we remember that there are more sources of uncertainty than the discount rate, and even with the log size model itself there remain questions concerning the underlying data set. I eliminated the first 12 years of data for reasons that I and others consider valid. Nevertheless, that adds an additional layer of uncertainty to the results that we cannot quantify.

Summary of Valuation Implications of Statistical Uncertainty in the Discount Rate

The 95% confidence intervals are very sensitive to our choice of model and data set. Using the log size model, we see that under the best of circumstances of using the past 60 years of NYSE data, the huge firms ($5 billion in FMV in our example, corresponding to CRSP Decile #2) have a ±5% (Table 11-2, C29) 95% confidence interval arising just from the statistical uncertainty in calculating the discount rate. All other-size firms have 95% confidence intervals of ±2–3% around the estimate (Table 11-2, row 29). If one holds the opinion that using all 72 years of NYSE data is appropriate—which I do not—then the confidence intervals are wider, with ±45% (Table 11-1, C42) for the billion dollar firms and ±13% (G42, I42) to 17% (E42) minimum intervals for small to medium firms. Actually, the confidence intervals around the valuation are not symmetric, as the assumption of a symmetric t-distribution around the discount rate results in an asymmetric 95% confidence interval around the FMV, with a larger range of probable error on the high side than the low side.

Huge firms tend to have larger confidence intervals because they are closer to the edge, where the growth rate approaches the discount rate.[6] Small to medium firms are farther from the edge and have smaller confidence intervals. The CAPM confidence intervals are much larger than the log size intervals.

---

6. Smaller firms with very high expected growth will also be close to the edge, although not as close as large firms with the same high growth rate.

TABLE 11-1

95% Confidence Intervals

	A	B	C	D	E	F	G	H	I
4		**Huge Firm**		**Large Firm**		**Med. Firm**		**Small Firm**	
5	Cash flow-CF$_{t-1}$	300,000,000		15,000,000		1,000,000		100,000	
6	r (assume correct)	13%		19%		24%		28%	
7	g = constant growth rate	8%		7%		5%		5%	
8	Cash Flow$_t$	324,000,000		16,050,000		1,050,000		105,000	
9	Discount rate range								
10	Log size model								
11	Upper bound [2]	14.75%		20.75%		25.75%		29.75%	
12	As calculated [1]	13.00%		19.00%		24.00%		28.00%	
13	Lower bound [2]	11.25%		17.25%		22.25%		26.25%	
14	CAPM								
15	Upper bound	18.58%		24.58%		29.58%		33.58%	
16	As calculated [1]	13.00%		19.00%		24.00%		28.00%	
17	Lower bound	7.42%		13.42%		18.42%		22.42%	
18	Gordon model-log size								
19	Lower bound [3]	15.8640		7.9903		5.4036		4.6019	
20	Gordon-mid [3]	21.2603		9.0906		5.8608		4.9190	
21	Upper bound [3]	32.4791		10.5666		6.4105		5.2882	
22	FMV-log size model								
23	Lower bound [4]	5,139,936,455	74.6%	128,244,770	87.9%	5,673,826	92.2%	483,200	93.6%
24	Gordon-mid [4]	6,888,334,487	100.0%	145,904,025	100.0%	6,153,845	100.0%	516,495	100.0%
25	Upper bound [4]	10,523,225,754	152.8%	169,594,333	116.2%	6,731,077	109.4%	555,257	107.5%
26	Gordon model-CAPM								
27	Lower bound	10.2920		6.3488		4.6310		4.0439	
28	Gordon-mid	21.2603		9.0906		5.8608		4.9190	
29	Upper bound	−178.5354	Explodes	16.5899		8.1092		6.3517	
30	FMV-CAPM								
31	FMV-lower	3,334,607,119	48.4%	101,898,640	69.8%	4,862,595	79.0%	424,611	82.2%
32	FMV-mid	6,888,334,487	100.0%	145,904,025	100.0%	6,153,845	100.0%	516,495	100.0%
33	FMV-upper	NA	NA	266,268,022	182.5%	8,514,618	138.4%	666,929	129.1%
34	Verify discount rate [5]								
35	Add constant	47.62%		47.62%		47.62%		47.62%	
36	−1.518% * ln (FMV)	−34.39%		−28.54%		−23.73%		−19.97%	
37	Discount rate	13.23%		19.08%		23.89%		27.65%	
38	Rounded	**13%**		**19%**		**24%**		**28%**	
39	Approx 95% conf. int. − log size +/− [6]		39%		14%		9%		7%
40	Approx 95% conf. int. − CAPM +/− [6]		Explodes		56%		30%		23%
42	Actual 95% conf. int. − log size +/− [7]		45%		17%		13%		13%

When we add differences in valuation methods and models and all the other sources of uncertainty and errors in valuation, it is indeed not at all surprising that professional appraisers can vary widely in their results.

MEASURING THE EFFECTS OF VALUATION ERROR

Up to now, we have focused on calculating the confidence intervals around the discount rate to measure valuation uncertainty. This uncertainty is generic to all businesses. It was also briefly mentioned that we

95% Confidence Intervals

	A		B	C	D	E	F	G	H	I
4			**Huge Firm**		**Large Firm**		**Med. Firm**		**Small Firm**	
44	Assumptions:									
46	Log size constant		47.62%							
47	Log size X coefficient		−1.518%							
48	Standard error-log size		0.76%							
49	Standard error-CAPM		2.42%							

Notes:

[1] We assume both the Log Size Model & CAPM arrive at the same discount rate.

[2] The lower and upper bounds of the discount rate are 2.306 standard errors below and above the discount rate estimated by the model. In a t-Distribution with 8 degrees of freedom, 2.306 standard errors approximately yields a 95% confidence interval. See footnote [7] for the exact formula.

[3] This is the Gordon Model with a midyear assumption. The multiple = SQRT(1 + r)/(r − g), where r is the discount rate and g is the perpetual growth rate. We use the lower and upper bounds of r to calculate our ranges. See footnote [7] for the exact calculation of the confidence intervals.

[4] FMV = Forecast Cash Flow-Next Year = CF_{t+1} × Gordon Multiples

[5] Log Size equation uses data through SBBI 1998 and therefore does not match Table 4-1 exactly.

[6] For simplicity of explanation, this is an approximate 95% confidence interval and is 2.306 standard errors above and below the forecast discount rate, with its effect on the valuation. See footnote [7] for the exact confidence interval.

[7] These are the actual confidence intervals using the exact formula:

$$Y_0 = \hat{\mu}_0 \pm t_{0.025}s \sqrt{\frac{1}{n} + \frac{x_0^2}{\sum x_i^2} + 1} \,,$$

where the $\hat{\mu}_0$ is the regression-determined discount rate, $t_{0.025}$ is the two-tailed 95% confidence level t-statistic, s is the standard error of the regression (0.76% for Log Size), and x_i is the deviation of ln(mkt cap) of each decile from the mean ln(mkt cap) of the Ibbotson deciles. The actual confidence intervals are calculated only for the Log Size Model. CAPM is not a pure regression, as its y-intercept is forced to the risk-free rate, and therefore the error term is a mixture of random error and systematic error resulting from forcing the y-intercept.

can calculate the 95% confidence intervals around our forecast of sales, cost of sales, and expenses, though that process is unique to each firm. All of these come under the category of uncertainty. One need not make errors to remain uncertain about the valuation.

In the second part of this chapter we will consider the impact on the valuation of the appraiser making various types of errors in the valuation process. We can make some qualitative and quantitative observations using comparative static analysis common in economics.

The practical reader in a hurry may wish to skip to the conclusion section, as the analysis in the remainder of the chapter does not provide any tools that one may use directly in a valuation. However:

1. The conclusions are important in suggesting how we should allocate our time in a valuation.
2. The analysis is helpful in understanding the sensitivity of the valuation conclusion to the different variables (forecast cash flow, discount rate, and growth rate) and errors one may make in forecasting or calculating them.

Defining Absolute and Relative Error

We will be considering errors from two different viewpoints:

- By variable—we will consider errors in forecasting cash flow, discount rate, and growth rate.

TABLE 11-2

95% Confidence Intervals—60-Year Log Size Model

	A	B	C	D	E	F	G	H	I
4		**Huge Firm**		**Large Firm**		**Med. Firm**		**Small Firm**	
5	Cash flow-CF$_{t-1}$	300,000,000		15,000,000		1,000,000		100,000	
6	r (assume correct)	15%		19%		23%		26%	
7	g = constant growth rate	8%		7%		5%		5%	
8	Cash flow$_t$	324,000,000		16,050,000		1,050,000		105,000	
9	Discount rate range								
10	Log size model								
11	Upper bound [2]	15.32%		19.32%		23.32%		26.32%	
12	As calculated [1]	15.00%		19.00%		23.00%		26.00%	
13	Lower bound [2]	14.68%		18.68%		22.68%		25.68%	
14	Gordon model-log size								
15	Lower bound [3]	14.6649		8.8644		6.0608		5.2710	
16	Gordon-mid [3]	15.3197		9.0906		6.1614		5.3452	
17	Upper bound [3]	16.0379		9.3292		6.2657		5.4217	
18	FMV-log size model								
19	Lower bound [4]	4,751,416,807	95.7%	142,274,156	97.5%	6,363,826	98.4%	553.459	98.6%
20	Gordon-mid [4]	4,963,589,879	100.0%	145,904,025	100.0%	6,469,480	100.0%	561,249	100.0%
21	Upper bound [4]	5,196,269,792	104.7%	149,734,328	102.6%	6,578,981	101.7%	569,281	101.4%
22	Verify discount rate								
23	Log size constant	41.72%		41.72%		41.72%		41.72%	
24	−1.204% * ln (FMV)	−26.88%		−22.63%		−18.88%		−15.94%	
25	Discount rate	14.84%		19.09%		22.84%		25.78%	
26	Rounded	**15%**		**19%**		**23%**		**26%**	
27	Min 95% conf. int. − log size +/−		4%		3%		2%		1%
29	Actual 95% conf. int. − log size +/−		5%		3%		2%		3%
31	Assumptions:								
33	Log size constant	**41.72%**							
34	Log size X coefficient	**−1.204%**							
35	Standard errors-log size	**0.14%**							

- By type of error, i.e., absolute versus relative errors. The following examples illustrate the differences between the two:
  - Forecasting cash flow: If the correct cash flow forecast should have been $1 million dollars and the appraiser incorrectly forecast it as $1.1 million, the absolute error is $100,000 and the relative error in the forecast is 10%.
  - Forecasting discount and growth rates: If the correct forecast of the discount rate is 20% and the appraiser incorrectly forecast it as 22%, his absolute forecasting error is 2% and his relative error is 10%.

We also will measure the *valuation effects* of the errors in absolute and relative terms.

- Absolute valuation error: We measure the absolute error of the valuation in dollars. Even if the absolute error is measured in percentages, e.g., if we forecast growth too high by 2% in absolute terms, it causes an absolute valuation error that we measure in dollars. For example, a 2% absolute error in the discount rate might lead to a $1 million overvaluation of the firm.

- Relative valuation error: The relative valuation error is the absolute valuation error divided by the correct valuation. This is measured in percentages. For example, if the value should have been $5 million and it was incorrectly stated as $6 million, there is a 16.7% overvaluation.

The Valuation Model

We use the simplest valuation model in equation (11-1), the end-of-year Gordon model, where V is the value, r is the discount rate, and g is the constant perpetual growth rate.

$$V = \frac{CF}{r - g} = CF \frac{1}{r - g} \quad \text{Gordon model end-of-year assumption}^7 \quad (11\text{-}1)$$

Dollar Effects of Absolute Errors in Forecasting Year 1 Cash Flow

We now assume the appraiser makes an absolute (dollar) error in forecasting Year 1 cash flows. Instead of forecasting cash flows correctly as CF_1, he or she instead forecasts it as CF_2. We define a positive forecast error as $CF_2 - CF_1 = \Delta CF > 0$. If the appraiser forecasts cash flow too low, then $CF_1 < CF_2$, and $\Delta CF < 0$.

Assuming there are no errors in calculating the discount rate and forecasting growth, the valuation error, ΔV, is equal to:

$$\Delta V = CF_2 - CF_1 = \left[CF_2 \frac{1}{r - g} - CF_1 \frac{1}{r - g} \right]$$

$$= (CF_2 - CF_1) \frac{1}{r - g} \quad (11\text{-}2)$$

Substituting $\Delta CF = CF_2 - CF_1$ into equation (11-2), we get:

$$\Delta V = \Delta CF \frac{1}{r - g} \quad (11\text{-}3)$$

valuation error when r and g are correct and CF is incorrect

We see that for each $1 increase (decrease) in cash flow, i.e., $\Delta CF = 1$, the value increases (decreases) by $1/(r - g)$.[8] Assuming equivalent growth rates in cash flow, large firms will experience a larger increase in value in absolute dollars than small firms for each additional dollar of

---

7. For simplicity, for the remainder of this chapter we will stick to this simple equation and ignore the more proper log size expression for r, the discount rate, where $r = a + b \ln V$.
8. It would be $\sqrt{1 + r}/(r - g)$ for the more accurate midyear formula. Other differences when using the midyear formula appear in subsequent footnotes.

cash flow. The reason is that r is smaller for large firms according to the log size model.[9]

If we overestimate cash flows by \$1, where $r = 0.15$, and $g = 0.09$, then value increases by $1/(0.15 - 0.09) = 1/0.06 = \$16.67$. For a small firm with $r = 0.27$ and $g = 0.05$, $1/(r - g) = 1/0.22$, implying an increase in value of \$4.55. If we overestimate cash flows by \$100,000, i.e., $\Delta CF = \$100,000$, we will overestimate the value of the large firm by \$1.67 million ($\$100,000 \times 16.67$) and the small firm by \$455,000 ($\$100,000 \times 4.55$). Here again, we find that larger firms and high-growth firms will tend to have larger valuation errors in absolute dollars; however, it turns out that the opposite is true in relative terms.

Relative Effects of Absolute Errors in Forecasting Year 1 Cash Flow

Let's look at the relative error in the valuation ("the relative effect") due to the absolute error in the cash flow forecast. It is equal to the valuation error in dollars divided by the correct valuation. If we denote the relative valuation error as $\%\Delta V$, it is equal to:

$$\%\Delta V = \frac{\Delta V}{V} \quad \text{relative valuation error} \tag{11-4}$$

We calculate equation (11-4) as (11-3) divided by (11-1):

$$\% \text{ error} = \frac{\Delta V}{V} = \frac{\Delta CF/(r - g)}{CF/(r - g)} = \frac{\Delta CF}{CF} \tag{11-5}$$

relative valuation error from absolute error in CF

For any given error in cash flow, ΔCF, the relative valuation error is greater for small firms than large firms, because the numerators are the same and the denominator in equation (11-5) is smaller for small firms than large firms.

For example, suppose the cash flow should be \$100,000 for a small firm and \$1 million for a large firm. Instead, the appraiser forecasts cash flow \$10,000 too high. The valuation error for the small firm is $\$10,000/\$100,000 = 10\%$, whereas it is $\$10,000/\$1,000,000 = 1\%$ for the large firm.[10]

Absolute and Relative Effects of Relative Errors in Forecasting Year 1 Cash Flow

It is easy to confuse this section with the previous one, where we considered the valuation effect in relative terms of an absolute error in dollars in forecasting cash flows. In this section, we will consider an across-the-

---

9. According to CAPM, small beta firms would be more affected than large beta firms. However, there is a strong correlation between beta and firm size (see Table 4-1, regression #3), which leads us back to the same result.
10. This formula is identical using the midyear Gordon model, as the $\sqrt{1 + r}$ appears in both numerators in equation (11-5) and cancel out.

board relative (percentage) error in forecasting cash flows. If we say the error is 10%, then we incorrectly forecast the small firm's cash flow as $110,000 and the large firm's cash flow as $11 million. Both errors are 10% of the correct cash flow, so the errors are identical in relative terms, but in absolute dollars the small firm error is $10,000 and the large firm error is $1 million. To make the analysis as general as possible, we will use a variable error of $k\%$ in our discussion.

A $k\%$ error in forecasting cash flows for both a large firm and a small firm increases value in both cases by $k\%$,[11] as shown in equations (11-6) through (11-8) below. Let V_1 = the correct FMV, which is equation (11-6) below, and V_2 = the erroneous FMV, with a $k\%$ error in forecasting cash flows, which is shown in equation (11-7). The relative (percentage) valuation error will be $V_2/V_1 - 1$, which we show in equation (11-8).

$$V_1 = CF \frac{1}{r - g} \qquad (11\text{-}6)$$

In equation (11-6), V_1 is the correct value, which we obtain by multiplying the correct cash flow, CF, by the end-of-year Gordon model multiple. Equation (11-7) shows the effect of overestimating cash flows by $k\%$. The overvaluation, V_2, equals:

$$V_2 = (1 + k)CF \frac{1}{r - g} = (1 + k)V_1 \qquad (11\text{-}7)$$

$$\%\Delta V = \frac{V_2}{V_1} - 1 = k \qquad (11\text{-}8)$$

relative effect of relative error in forecasting cash flow

Equation (11-8) shows that there is a $k\%$ error in value resulting from a $k\%$ error in forecasting Year 1 cash flow, regardless of the initial firm size.[12] Of course, the error in dollars will differ. If the percentage error is large, there is a second-order effect in the log size model, as a $k\%$ overestimate of cash flows not only leads to a $k\%$ overvaluation, as we just discussed, but also will cause a decrease in the discount rate, which leads to additional overvaluation. It is also worth noting that an undervaluation works the same way. Just change k to 0.9 for a 10% undervaluation instead of 1.1 for a 10% overvaluation, and the conclusions are the same.

Absolute Errors in Forecasting Growth and the Discount Rate

A fundamental difference between these two variables and cash flow is that value is nonlinear in r and g, whereas it is linear in cash flow. We will develop a formula to quantify the valuation error for any absolute

---

11. Strictly speaking, the error is really k, not $k\%$. However, the description flows better using the percent sign after the k.
12. Again, this formula is the same with the midyear Gordon model, as the square root term cancels out.

Part 4   Putting It All Together

error in calculating the discount rate or the growth rate, assuming cash flow is forecast correctly.

Definitions
First we begin with some definitions. Let:

V_1 = the correct value

V_2 = the erroneous value

r_1 = the correct discount rate

r_2 = the erroneous discount rate

g_1 = the correct growth rate

g_2 = the erroneous growth rate[13]

CF = cash flow, which we will assume to be correct in this section

Δ = the change in any value, which in our context means the error

We will consider a positive error to be when the erroneous value, discount rate, or growth rate is higher than the correct value. For example, if g_1 = 5% and g_2 = 6%, then $\Delta g = g_2 - g_1$ = 1%; if g_1 = 6% and g_2 = 5%, then Δg = −1%.

The Mathematics
The correct valuation, according to the end-of-year Gordon model, is:

$$V_1 = \frac{CF}{r_1 - g_1} \quad \text{the correct value} \qquad (11\text{-}9)$$

The erroneous value is:

$$V_2 = \frac{CF}{r_2 - g_2} \quad \text{the erroneous value} \qquad (11\text{-}10)$$

The error, $\Delta V = V_2 - V_1$, equals:

$$\Delta V = \frac{CF}{r_2 - g_2} - \frac{CF}{r_1 - g_1} = CF\left(\frac{1}{r_2 - g_2} - \frac{1}{r_1 - g_1}\right) \qquad (11\text{-}11)$$

In order to have a common denominator, we multiply the first term in round brackets by $(r_1 - g_1)/(r_1 - g_1)$ and we multiply the second term in round brackets by $(r_2 - g_2)/(r_2 - g_2)$.

$$\Delta V = CF\left[\frac{(r_1 - g_1) - (r_2 - g_2)}{(r_1 - g_1)(r_2 - g_2)}\right] \qquad (11\text{-}12)$$

Rearranging the terms in the numerator, we get:

$$\Delta V = CF\left[\frac{(r_1 - r_2) - (g_1 - g_2)}{(r_1 - g_1)(r_2 - g_2)}\right] \qquad (11\text{-}13)$$

Changing signs in the numerator:

---

13. Actually, only one of the two variables—r_2 or g_2—need be erroneous. The other one can be correct, which would make it equal to its r_1 or g_1 counterpart.

$$\Delta V = CF \left[\frac{-(r_2 - r_1) + (g_2 - g_1)}{(r_1 - g_1)(r_2 - g_2)} \right] \qquad (11\text{-}14)$$

which simplifies to:

$$\Delta V = CF \left[\frac{-\Delta r + \Delta g}{(r_1 - g_1)(r_2 - g_2)} \right] \qquad (11\text{-}15)$$

absolute effect of absolute error in r or g[14]

Example Using the Error Formula

Let's use an example to demonstrate the error formula. Suppose cash flow is forecast next year at $100,000 and that the correct discount and growth rate are 20% and 5%, respectively. The Gordon model multiple is $1/(0.25 - 0.05) = 5$, which leads to a valuation before discounts of $500,000. Instead, the appraiser makes an error and uses a zero growth rate. His erroneous Gordon model multiple will be $1/(0.25 - 0) = 4$, leading to a $400,000 valuation. The appraiser's error is an undervaluation of $400,000 $- $500,000 = -$100,000.

Using equation (11-15),

$$\Delta V = \$100,000 \left[\frac{0 - 0.05}{(0.25 - 0.05)(0.25 - 0)} \right] = 100,000 \left[\frac{-0.05}{0.2 \times 0.25} \right]$$

$$= 100,000 \times \frac{-0.05}{0.05} = -\$100,000$$

Relative Effects of Absolute Error in r and g

The relative valuation error, as before, is the valuation error in dollars divided by the correct valuation, or:

$$\% \text{ Error} = \frac{\Delta V}{V} = \frac{CF(-\Delta r + \Delta g)/(r_1 - g_1)(r_2 - g_2)}{CF/(r_1 - g_1)} \qquad (11\text{-}16)$$

$$\% \text{ Error} = \frac{\Delta V}{V} = \frac{-\Delta r + \Delta g}{r_2 - g_2} \qquad (11\text{-}17)$$

relative effects of absolute error in r and g[15]

---

14. When $\Delta r = 0$, then the formula using the midyear Gordon model is identical to equation (11-15), with the addition of the term $\sqrt{1 + r}$ after the CF, but before the square brackets. When there is an error in the discount rate, the error formula using the midyear Gordon model is

$$CF \left[\frac{(r_1 - g_1)\sqrt{1 + r_2} - (r_2 - g_2)\sqrt{1 + r_1}}{(r_1 - g_1)(r_2 - g_2)} \right]$$

The partial derivative for g is similar to the discrete equation for change:

$$\frac{\partial V}{\partial g} = \frac{CF}{(r - g)^2}$$

Since it is a partial derivative, we hold r constant, which means $\Delta r = 0$, and instead of having $r_2 - g_2$, we double up on $r_1 - g_1$, which we can simplify to $r - g$. Again, these formulas are correct only when CF is forecast correctly.

15. This formula would be identical using the midyear Gordon model, as the $\sqrt{1 + r}$ would appear in both numerators in equation (11-16) and cancel out.

Part 4 Putting It All Together

Example of Relative Valuation Error

From the previous example, the relative valuation error is

$$\frac{\$400,000}{\$500,000} - 1 = -20\%$$

a 20% undervaluation. Using equation (11-17), the relative error is

$$\frac{0 - 0.05}{0.25 - 0} = -\frac{0.05}{0.25} = -20\%$$

which agrees with the previous calculation and demonstrates the accuracy of equation (11-17). It is important to be precise with the deltas, as it is easy to confuse the sign. In equation (11-17) the numerator is $-\Delta r + \Delta g$. It is easy to think that since there is a plus sign in front of Δg, we should use a positive 0.05 instead of -0.05. This is incorrect, as we are assuming that the appraiser's error in the growth rate itself is negative, i.e., the erroneous growth rate minus the correct growth rate, $(V_2 - V_1)$ $= 0 - 0.05 = -0.05$.

Valuation Effects on Large Versus Small Firms

Next we look at the question of whether large or small firms are more affected by identical errors in absolute terms in the discount or growth rate. The numerator of equation (11-17) will be the same regardless of size. The denominator, however, will vary with size. Holding g_2 constant, r_2 will be smaller for large firms, as will $r_2 - g_2$. Thus, the relative error, as quantified in equation (11-17), will be larger for large firms than small firms, assuming equal growth rates.[16]

Table 11-3 demonstrates the above conclusion. Columns B through D show valuation calculations for the huge firm, as in Table 11-1. Historical cash flow was $300 million (B6), and we assume a constant 8% (B7) growth rate as being correct, which leads to forecast cash flow of $324 million (B8). Using the log size model, we get a discount rate of 15% (B9), as shown in cells B14–B17. In B10, we calculate an end-of-year Gordon model multiple of 14.2857, which differs from Table 11-1, where we were using a midyear multiple. Multiplying row 8 by row 10 produces a value of $4.63 billion (B11).

Column C contains the erroneous valuation, where the appraiser uses a 9% growth rate (C7) instead of the correct 8% growth rate in B7. That leads to a valuation of $5.45 billion (C11). The valuation error is $821.4 million (D11), which is C11 − B11. Dividing the $821.4 million error by the correct valuation of $4.63 million, the valuation error is 17.7% (D12). We repeat the identical procedure with the small firm in columns E–G using the same growth and discount rate as the huge firm, and the valuation error is 6.9% (G12). This demonstrates the accuracy of our conclusion from equation (11-17) that equal absolute errors in the growth rate

---

16. As before, this is theoretically not true in CAPM, which should be independent of size. However, in reality, β is correlated to size.

Absolute Errors in Forecasting Growth Rates

	A	B	C	D	E	F	G
		Huge Firm			Small Firm		
4							
5		Correct	Erroneous	Error	Correct	Erroneous	Error
6	Cash flow-CF_{t-1}	300,000,000	300,000,000		100,000	100,000	
7	g = growth rate	8%	9%		8%	9%	
8	Cash flow$_t$	324,000,000	327,000,000		108,000	109,000	
9	Discount rate	15.0%	15.0%		26.0%	26.0%	
10	Gordon multiple-end year	14.2857	16.6667		5.5556	5.8824	
11	FMV	4,628,571,429	5,450,000,000	821,428,571	600,000	641,176	41,176
12	Percentage error			17.7%			6.9%
13	Verify discount rate						
14	−0.01204 * ln(FMV)	−26.80%	−26.99%		−16.02%	−16.10%	
15	Add constant	41.72%	41.72%		41.72%	41.72%	
16	Discount rate	14.92%	14.73%		25.70%	25.62%	
17	Rounded	15%	15%		26%	26%	

or discount rate cause larger relative valuation errors for large firms than small firms.

Let's now compare the magnitude of the effects of an error in calculating cash flow versus discount or growth rates. From equation (11-8), a 1% relative error in forecasting cash flows leads to a 1% valuation error. From equation (11-17), a 1% absolute error in forecasting growth leads to a valuation error of $0.01/(r_2 - g_2)$. Using typical values for the denominator, the valuation error will most likely be in the range of 4–20% for each 1% error in forecasting growth (or error in the discount rate). *This means we need to pay relatively more attention to forecasting growth rates and discount rates than we do to producing the first year's forecast of cash flows, and the larger the firm, the more care we should be taking in the analysis.*

Also, it is clear from (11-15) and (11-17) that it is the net error in both r and g that drives the valuation error, not the error in either one individually. Using the end-of-year Gordon model, equal errors in r and g cancel each other out. With the more accurate midyear formula, errors in g have slightly more impact on the value than errors in r, as an error in r has opposite effects in the numerator and denominator.

Relative Effect of Relative Error in Forecasting Growth and Discount Rates

We can investigate the impact of a $k\%$ relative error in estimating g by restating the Gordon model in equation (11-18) below with the altered growth rate $(1 + k)g$. We denote the correct value as V_1 and the incorrect value as V_2.

$$V_2 = \frac{CF}{r - (1 + k)g} \tag{11-18}$$

The ratio of the incorrect to the correct value is V_2/V_1, or:

$$\frac{V_2}{V_1} = \frac{r - g}{r - (1 + k)g} \qquad (11\text{-}19)$$

The relative error in value resulting from a *relative* error in forecasting growth will be $(V_2/V_1) - 1$, or:

$$\% \text{ Error} = \frac{r - g}{r - (1 + k)g} - 1 \qquad (11\text{-}20)$$

relative error in value from relative error in growth

Thus, if both a large and small firm have the same growth rate, then the lower discount rate of the large firm will lead to larger relative valuation errors in the large firm than the small firm. Note that for $k = 0$, (11-20) = 0, as it should. When k is negative, which means we forecast growth too low, the result is the same—the under-valuation is greater for large firms than small firms.

A relative error in forecasting the discount rate shifts the $(1 + k)$ in front of the r in (11-20) instead of being in front of the g. The formula is:

$$\% \text{ Error} = \frac{r - g}{(1 + k)r - g} - 1 \qquad (11\text{-}21)$$

relative error in value from relative error in r

Tables 11-4 through 11-4B: Examples Showing Effects on Large Versus Small Firms

Table 11-4 shows the calculations for $k = 10\%$ (B38) relative error in forecasting growth. Rows 5–6 contain the discount rate and growth rate for a huge firm in column B and a small firm in column C, respectively. The end-of-year Gordon model multiples are 50 (B7) and 5.5556 (C7) for the huge and the small firm, respectively. Multiplying the Gordon model multiples by the forecast cash flows in row 8 results in the correct values, V_1, in row 9 of $15 billion and $555,556, respectively.

Now let's see what happens if we forecast growth too high by 10% for each firm. Row 10 shows the erroneously high growth rate of 9.9%. Row 11 contains the new Gordon model multiples, and row 12 shows V_2, the incorrect values we obtain with the high growth rates. Row 13 shows the ratio of the incorrect to the correct valuation, i.e., V_2/V_1, and Row 14 shows the relative error, $(V_2/V_1) - 1 = 81.82\%$ for the huge firm and 5.26% for the small firm.

Rows 20–36 are a sensitivity analysis that show the relative valuation errors for various combinations of r and g using equation (11-20), with $k = 10\%$. Note that the bolded cells in F20 and F36 match the results in row 14, confirming the accuracy of the error formula. This verifies our observation from analysis of equation (11-20) that equal relative errors in forecasting growth will create much larger relative valuation errors for large firms than small firms, holding growth constant. All we need do is notice that the relative errors in the sensitivity analysis decline as we move down each column, and as small firms have higher discount rates, the lower cells represent the smaller firms.

TABLE 11-4

Percent Valuation Error for 10% Relative Error in Growth

	A	B	C	D	E	F	G
4	**Description**	**Huge Firm**	**Small Firm**				
5	r	11%	27%				
6	g	9%	9%				
7	Gordon model	50.0000	5.5556				
8	Cash flow	300,000,000	100,000				
9	V_1	15,000,000,000	555,556				
10	(1 + PctError)*g	9.90%	9.90%				
11	Gordon model 2	90.9091	5.8480				
12	V_2	27,272,727,273	584,795				
13	V_2/V_1	1.8182	1.0526				
14	$(V_2/V_1) - 1$	81.82%	5.26%				
16	**Sensitivity Analysis: Valuation Error for Combinations of r and g**						
18				**Growth rate = g**			
19	**Discount Rate = r**	5%	6%	7%	8%	9%	10%
20	11%	9.09%	13.64%	21.21%	36.36%	**81.82%**	NA
21	12%	7.69%	11.11%	16.28%	25.00%	42.86%	100.00%
22	13%	6.67%	9.38%	13.21%	19.05%	29.03%	50.00%
23	14%	5.88%	8.11%	11.11%	15.38%	21.95%	33.33%
24	15%	5.26%	7.14%	9.59%	12.90%	17.65%	25.00%
25	16%	4.76%	6.38%	8.43%	11.11%	14.75%	20.00%
26	17%	4.35%	5.77%	7.53%	9.76%	12.68%	16.67%
27	18%	4.00%	5.26%	6.80%	8.70%	11.11%	14.29%
28	19%	3.70%	4.84%	6.19%	7.84%	9.89%	12.50%
29	20%	3.45%	4.48%	5.69%	7.14%	8.91%	11.11%
30	21%	3.23%	4.17%	5.26%	6.56%	8.11%	10.00%
31	22%	3.03%	3.90%	4.90%	6.06%	7.44%	9.09%
32	23%	2.86%	3.66%	4.58%	5.63%	6.87%	8.33%
33	24%	2.70%	3.45%	4.29%	5.26%	6.38%	7.69%
34	25%	2.56%	3.26%	4.05%	4.94%	5.96%	7.14%
35	26%	2.44%	3.09%	3.83%	4.65%	5.59%	6.67%
36	**27%**	2.33%	2.94%	3.63%	4.40%	**5.26%**	6.25%
38	Relative Error in g	**10%**					

Formula in B20: (which copies to the other cells in the sensitivity analysis) = (($A20 − B$19)/($A20 − ((1 + $PctError)*B$19))) − 1

Table 11-4A is identical to Table 11-4, with the one exception that the growth rate is a negative 10% instead of a positive 10%. Table 11-4A demonstrates that, assuming identical real growth rates, forecasting growth too low also affects large firms more than small firms.

Table 11-4B is also identical to Table 11-4, except that it measures the relative valuation error arising from relative errors in calculating the discount rate. Table 11-4B uses equation (11-21) instead of equation (11-20) to calculate the error. It demonstrates that relative errors in forecasting the discount rate affect the valuation of large firms more than the valuation of small firms, assuming identical real growth rates.

Table 11-5: Summary of Effects of Valuation Errors

Table 11-5 summarizes the effects of the valuation errors. Each cell in the table contains three items:

Percent Valuation Error for −10% Relative Error in Growth

	A	B	C	D	E	F	G
4	**Description**	**Huge Firm**	**Small Firm**				
5	r	11%	27%				
6	g	9%	9%				
7	Gordon model	50.0000	5.5556				
8	Cash Flow	300,000,000	100,000				
9	V_1	15,000,000,000	555,556				
10	(1 + PctError)*g	8.10%	8.10%				
11	Gordon model 2	34.4828	5.2910				
12	V_2	10,344,827,586	529,101				
13	V_2/V_1	0.6897	0.9524				
14	$(V_2/V_1) - 1$	**−31.03%**	**−4.76%**				
16	**Sensitivity Analysis: Valuation Error for Combinations of r and g**						
18					**Growth rate = g**		
19	**Discount Rate = r**	5%	6%	7%	8%	**9%**	10%
20	11%	−7.69%	−10.71%	−14.89%	−21.05%	**−31.03%**	NA
21	12%	−6.67%	−9.09%	−12.28%	−16.67%	−23.08%	−33.33%
22	13%	−5.88%	−7.89%	−10.45%	−13.79%	−18.37%	−25.00%
23	14%	−5.26%	−6.98%	−9.09%	−11.76%	−15.25%	−20.00%
24	15%	−4.76%	−6.25%	−8.05%	−10.26%	−13.04%	−16.67%
25	16%	−4.35%	−5.66%	−7.22%	−9.09%	−11.39%	−14.29%
26	17%	−4.00%	−5.17%	−6.54%	−8.16%	−10.11%	−12.50%
27	18%	−3.70%	−4.76%	−5.98%	−7.41%	−9.09%	−11.11%
28	19%	−3.45%	−4.41%	−5.51%	−6.78%	−8.26%	−10.00%
29	20%	−3.23%	−4.11%	−5.11%	−6.25%	−7.56%	−9.09%
30	21%	−3.03%	−3.85%	−4.76%	−5.80%	−6.98%	−8.33%
31	22%	−2.86%	−3.61%	−4.46%	−5.41%	−6.47%	−7.69%
32	23%	−2.70%	−3.41%	−4.19%	−5.06%	−6.04%	−7.14%
33	24%	−2.56%	−3.23%	−3.95%	−4.76%	−5.66%	−6.67%
34	25%	−2.44%	−3.06%	−3.74%	−4.49%	−5.33%	−6.25%
35	26%	−2.33%	−2.91%	−3.55%	−4.26%	−5.03%	−5.88%
36	**27%**	−2.22%	−2.78%	−3.38%	−4.04%	**−4.76%**	−5.56%
38	Relative Error in g	**−10.0%**					

Formula in B20: (which copies to the other cells in the sensitivity analysis) = (($A20 − B$19)/($A20 − ((1 + $PctError)*B$19))) − 1

1. The formula for the valuation error.
2. The equation number containing the error formula.
3. Whether the error is larger for large firms, small firms, or there is no difference.

The upper half of the table shows the valuation effects of absolute errors in forecasting the variables (cash flow, discount rate, and growth rate), and the lower half of the table shows the valuation effects of relative errors in forecasting the variables.

In 10 of the 12 cells in the table that contain error formulas, the valuation errors are greater for large firms than for small firms. Only equation (11-5), which is the relative valuation error resulting from a dollar error in forecasting cash flows, affects small firms more than large firms. Equation (11-8), the relative valuation error resulting from a relative error in forecasting cash flows, affects both small and large firms alike. It

Percent Valuation Error for 10% Relative Error in Discount Rate

	A	B	C	D	E	F	G
4	**Description**	**Huge Firm**	**Small Firm**				
5	r	11%	27%				
6	g	9%	9%				
7	Gordon model	50.0000	5.5556				
8	Cash Flow	300,000,000	100,000				
9	V_1	15,000,000,000	555,556				
10	(1 + PctError)*g	12.10%	29.70%				
11	Gordon model 2	32.2581	4.8309				
12	V_2	9,677,419,355	483,092				
13	V_2/V_1	**0.6452**	**0.8696**				
14	$(V_2/V_1) - 1$	**−35.48%**	**−13.04%**				
16	**Sensitivity Analysis: Valuation Error for Combinations of r and g**						
18		**Growth rate = g**					
19	**Discount Rate = r**	**5%**	**6%**	**7%**	**8%**	**9%**	**10%**
20	11%	−15.49%	−18.03%	−21.57%	−26.83%	**−35.48%**	−52.38%
21	12%	−14.63%	−16.67%	−19.35%	−23.08%	−28.57%	−37.50%
22	13%	−13.98%	−15.66%	−17.81%	−20.63%	−24.53%	−30.23%
23	14%	−13.46%	−14.89%	−16.67%	−18.92%	−21.88%	−25.93%
24	15%	−13.04%	−14.29%	−15.79%	−17.65%	−20.00%	−23.08%
25	16%	−12.70%	−13.79%	−15.09%	−16.67%	−18.60%	−21.05%
26	17%	−12.41%	−13.39%	−14.53%	−15.89%	−17.53%	−19.54%
27	18%	−12.16%	−13.04%	−14.06%	−15.25%	−16.67%	−18.37%
28	19%	−11.95%	−12.75%	−13.67%	−14.73%	−15.97%	−17.43%
29	20%	−11.76%	−12.50%	−13.33%	−14.29%	−15.38%	−16.67%
30	21%	−11.60%	−12.28%	−13.04%	−13.91%	−14.89%	−16.03%
31	22%	−11.46%	−12.09%	−12.79%	−13.58%	−14.47%	−15.49%
32	23%	−11.33%	−11.92%	−12.57%	−13.29%	−14.11%	−15.03%
33	24%	−11.21%	−11.76%	−12.37%	−13.04%	−13.79%	−14.63%
34	25%	−11.11%	−11.63%	−12.20%	−12.82%	−13.51%	−14.29%
35	26%	−11.02%	−11.50%	−12.04%	−12.62%	−13.27%	−13.98%
36	**27%**	−10.93%	−11.39%	−11.89%	−12.44%	**−13.04%**	−13.71%
38	Relative Error in g	**10%**					

Formula in B20: (which copies to the other cells in the sensitivity analysis) = (($A20 − B$19)/($A20 − ((1 + $PctError)*B$19))) − 1

is not surprising that the only two exceptions to the greater impact of valuation errors being on large firms comes from cash flows, as value is linear in cash flows. The nonlinear relationship of value to discount rate and growth rate causes errors in those two variables to impact the valuation of large firms far more than small firms and to impact the value of both more than errors in cash flow.

Errors in forecasting growth have the greatest impact on value. Value is positively related to forecast growth. Errors in forecasting discount rates are a close second in effect,[17] though opposite in sign. Value is negatively related to discount rate. Errors in forecasting the first year's cash flow by far have the *least* impact on value.

---

17. Again, this result comes from using the midyear Gordon model, not the end-of-year formula.

TABLE 11-5

Summary of Effects of Valuation Errors

Valuation Effects of Absolute Errors in the Variables [1]			
Valuation Error	**Cash Flow**	**Discount Rate = r**	**Growth Rate = g**
Absolute ($)	$\Delta V = \Delta CF \dfrac{1}{(r-g)}$ (11-3) Large firms	$\Delta V = CF\left[\dfrac{-\Delta r + \Delta g}{(r_1 - g_1)(r_2 - g_2)}\right]$ (11-15) Large firms	$\Delta V = CF\left[\dfrac{-\Delta r - \Delta g}{(r_1 - g_1)(r_2 - g_2)}\right]$ (11-15) Large firms
Relative (%)	$\dfrac{\Delta V}{V} = \dfrac{\Delta CF}{CF}$ (11-5) Small firms	$\dfrac{\Delta V}{V} = \dfrac{-\Delta r + \Delta g}{(r_2 - g_2)}$ (11-17) Note [3] Large firms	$\dfrac{\Delta V}{V} = \dfrac{-\Delta r + \Delta g}{(r_2 - g_2)}$ (11-17) Note [3] Large firms

Valuation Effects of Relative Errors in the Variables [1]			
Valuation Error	**Cash Flow**	**Discount Rate = r**	**Growth Rate = g**
Absolute ($)	$\Delta V = kV_1$ Note [2] Large firms	Note [4] NA Large firms	Note [4] NA Large firms
Relative (%)	$\dfrac{V_2}{V_1} - 1 = k$ (11-8) No difference	$\%Error = \dfrac{r-g}{(1+k)r - g} - 1$ (11-21) Large firms	$\%Error = \dfrac{r-g}{r - (1+k)g} - 1$ (11-20) Large firms

[1] Each cell shows the formula for the valuation error, the equation number in the chapter for the formula, and whether the valuation error is larger for large firms, small firms, or there is no difference.

[2] This formula is not explicitly calculated in the chapter. We can calculate it as: $V_2 - V_1 = [(1 + k)V_1 - V_1] = kV_1$.

[3] While there is no difference in the magnitude of valuation errors arising from an error in r or g when we measure value by the end-of-year Gordon model, when we use the midyear Gordon model, errors in g have slightly more impact than errors in r (and much more impact than errors in cash flow).

[4] Omitted because these expressions are complex and add little to understanding the topic.

Another issue in valuation error in using the log size model is that while an initial error in calculating the discount rate is self-correcting using an iterative method, an error in calculating cash flows or the growth rate not only causes its own error, but also will distort the calculation of the discount rate. For example, overestimating growth, g, will cause an overvaluation, which will lower the discount rate beyond its proper level, which will in turn cause a second order overvaluation. We did not see this in our comparative static analysis, because for simplicity we were working with the Gordon model multiple in the form of equation (11-1). We allowed r to be an apparently independent variable instead of using its more proper, but complicated log size form of $r = a + b \ln V$. Thus, the proper Gordon model using a log size discount rate is: .

$$V = CF \times \frac{1}{a + b \ln V - g}$$

The secondary valuation error caused by a faulty forecast of cash flows or growth rate will be minimal because the discount rate, as calculated using the log size model, is fairly insensitive to the error in the estimate of value. As mentioned earlier, on the surface, this would not be a source of error using CAPM, as the discount rate in CAPM does not depend on the magnitude of the subject company's cash flows. However, that is not really true, as CAPM betas are correlated to size.

SUMMARY AND CONCLUSIONS

We discussed valuation uncertainty in the first part of this chapter and valuation error in the second part. Using the past 60 years of NYSE data, the actual 95% confidence intervals around the valuation estimate for our statistical uncertainty in calculating the discount rate range from ±5% for huge firms down to ±2–3% for firms of other sizes, as calculated in Tables 11-1 and 11-2. Using all 72 years of NYSE data leads to much larger confidence intervals, and using CAPM leads to even much larger confidence intervals. Additionally, we could calculate the 95% confidence intervals around the sales and expense forecast.

Errors in forecasting the growth rate and calculating the discount rate cause much larger valuation errors than errors in forecasting the first year's cash flow. Thus, the bottom line conclusion from our analysis is that we need to be most careful in forecasting growth and discount rates because they have the most profound effect on the valuation. Usually we spend the majority of our efforts forecasting cash flows, and it might be tempting to some appraisers to accord insufficient analytic effort to the growth forecast and/or the discount rate calculation. Hopefully, the results in this chapter show that that is a bad idea.

In this chapter we have not specifically addressed uncertainty and errors in calculating valuation discounts, but one must obviously realize that they, too, add to the overall uncertainty that we have in rendering an opinion of value. There is material in Chapter 7 relating to uncertainty in calculating restricted stock discounts, which forms part of our overall uncertainty in calculating the discount for lack of marketability.

After analysis of just the uncertainty alone in the valuation—not even considering the possibility that somewhere we have made an actual error—a healthy humility about our final valuation conclusions is appropriate.

BIBLIOGRAPHY

Ibbotson and Associates. 1998. *Stocks, Bonds, Bills and Inflation: 1998 Yearbook*. Chicago: The Associates.

Special Topics

INTRODUCTION

Part 5, which consists of Chapters 12, 13, and 14, deals with topics that do not fit into any other part of the book. All three are practical "how-to" chapters.

Chapter 12 concerns valuing startups. The chapter discusses three topics. The first is the "First Chicago" approach, which is a weighted average, multiscenario approach to valuing startups. It has the benefit of breaking down the vast range of possibilities into discrete scenarios that are more credible than attempting to model all possibilities in a single scenario. Whereas almost all of this book is my own original work, the First Chicago Approach and the related section on the venture capital approach are based on a series of articles by Brad Fowler. It is important to understand the multiscenario approach, not only for its own sake in valuing simple start-ups but also as a preparation to understand the decision tree approach in the debt restructuring study.

Chapter 12 also provides an example—again based on Fowler's work—of using a venture capital valuation approach. While this is technically a different valuation approach, we will consider it as essentially the same topic as the First Chicago approach.

The second topic in Chapter 12 is the presentation of the essential parts of an actual debt restructuring study I did for a client. It is an example of using an original adaptation of decision tree logic for incorporating the effects of probabilistic milestones into a spreadsheet for the valuation. In this study the viability of the subject company, the probability of obtaining venture capital financing, its ability to survive on its own without venture capital financing, and its value depend on the outcome of four different sales milestones. The logic and structure of this analysis work well for other types of milestones, such as technological (e.g., successful development) and administrative (e.g., obtaining Food and Drug Administration approval).

The third topic in Chapter 12 is presenting an exponentially declining sales growth model[1] to semiautomate the process of modeling different

---

[1] I thank R. K. Hiatt for developing this.

sales growth patterns. This is a great time saver in valuing startups using a top-down approach.[2] Typically, sales grow rapidly in the early years, then more slowly, eventually coming to an expected constant growth rate. Rather than manually insert every year's sales growth, the appraiser can instantly change the entire sales growth pattern over n years by changing the contents of four spreadsheet cells. Furthermore, it makes extensive sensitivity analysis, normally a cumbersome procedure, trivial.

ESOP valuation has generated a number of lawsuits. One of the sore points of ESOP valuation that has led to litigation is the dilution in value that the ESOP experiences after the sale. Selling stock to an ESOP that does not have the cash to pay for the stock always causes a dilution in value to the shareholders the instant the transaction takes place. Of course, it takes time for the bad news to become known, as usually the next valuation takes place one year later. Employees may be angry, feeling that they (through the ESOP) paid too much for the owner's stock. They may feel someone has pulled a fast one. This can endanger the life and health of the business.

In Chapter 13 we develop formulas to calculate the post-transaction fair market value (FMV) *before* doing the transaction. This enables the appraiser to provide accurate information to the ESOP trustee that will enable both sides to enter the transaction with both eyes open. It also demystifies the dilution in value and provides an accurate benchmark with which to measure future performance. The chapter also provides precise formulas with which the appraiser can perform the financial engineering necessary to enable the owner to reduce his or her transaction price in order to share some or all of the ESOP's dilution. While this is not common, sometimes there are benevolent owners who are sufficiently well off and concerned about their employees to do that.

In general, this is a very mathematical chapter. For those readers who prefer to minimize the amount of mathematics they must read, we have included Appendix 13-B, a shortcut chapter.

Chapter 14 is a short, simple chapter that makes use of results in Chapter 13. When partners or shareholders buy out one another, as a first approximation there is no impact to the fair market value per share. This is certainly true when the buyer has the cash to pay to the seller.

However, when the buyer does not have the cash and the company itself takes out a loan to finance the purchase, secondary effects occur that can be significant. Post-transaction, the firm will be more highly leveraged, which increases the discount rate. We use the dilution formulas from Chapter 13 to provide a benchmark lower limit of fair market value per share. The appraiser can then employ traditional discounted cash flow analysis to value the firm. The result is likely to be a post-transaction fair market value per share that is lower than the pre-transaction per share value.

---

[2] This is in contrast to the bottom-up approach, where the appraiser inserts a series of assumptions to enable one to forecast sales. This might include line items such as market size, market share for the subject company, etc.

CHAPTER 12

Valuing Startups

ISSUES UNIQUE TO STARTUPS

ORGANIZATION OF THE CHAPTER

FIRST CHICAGO APPROACH

    Discounting Cash Flow Is Preferable to Net Income

    Capital Structure Changes

    Venture Capital Rates of Return

    Table 12-1: Example of the First Chicago Approach

    Advantages of the First Chicago Approach

    Discounts for Lack of Marketability and Control

VENTURE CAPITAL VALUATION APPROACH

    Venture Capital Rates of Return

    Summary of the VC Approach

DEBT RESTRUCTURING STUDY

    Backgound

    Key Events

    Decision Trees and Spreadsheet Calculations

    Table 12-3: Statistical Calculation of FMV

        Organization

        Section 1A: Venture Capital Scenario

            Probability of VC Financing after Sale #1

            Probability of VC Financing after Sale #2

            Generalizing to Probability of VC Financing after Sale #k

            Explanation of Table 12-3, Section 1A

        Section 1B: The Bootstrap Scenario Assuming Debt Restructuring with Parent

        Section 2: No-Restructure Scenario

        Section 3: FMVs per Share under Various Restructure Scenarios

            Venture Capital Scenario

            No-Restructure Scenario

Conclusion
Section 4: Year 2000 Investor Percentage Taken
EXPONENTIALLY DECLINING SALES GROWTH MODEL

ISSUES UNIQUE TO STARTUPS

A number of issues fairly unique to valuing startups arise chiefly from the uncertainty associated with new ventures. This uncertainty usually necessitates a more complex, multiple scenario analysis known as the First Chicago approach and requires more creativity on the part of the appraiser than other, more routine assignments.[3] In this chapter we also present a much shorter, easier valuation method for startups, known as the venture capital pricing approach.

Many new ventures have sequential events (milestones) that may or may not occur, and the valuation depends upon the probabilities of the occurrence of these milestones. Often, in order for event n to occur, event $(n - 1)$ must occur—but it may or may not. When valuing such firms, we often combine the First Chicago approach with decision tree analysis to arrive at a credible fair market value. This is a much more complex task than the First Chicago approach by itself. The most common types of milestones are sales, financing, technical, and regulatory, the latter two being universal in the valuation of pharmaceutical and biotechnology firms.

Another issue is that startups typically have a pattern of rapid sales growth followed by declining sales growth rates, finally reaching some steady state growth rate. Performing sensitivity analysis can be cumbersome when the appraiser manually enters sales growth rates under a number of different scenarios.

ORGANIZATION OF THE CHAPTER

This chapter addresses these issues in three parts. Part 1 consists of the First Chicago approach of forecasting multiple scenarios, each with its own discounted cash flow analysis. We produce a conditional FMV for each scenario and then calculate a weighted average FMV based on VC industry research that specifies the probabilities of each scenario coming to fruition. We also include the venture capital pricing approach in Part 1, as it is short and simple.

Part 2 consists of using a very sophisticated decision tree analysis to value an early stage firm for the purpose of deciding whether or not to restructure its debt (the "debt restructuring study"). The success or failure of the firm depends on the outcome of a sequence of four events which will impact the decision. This came from an actual valuation assignment.

Part 3 consists of a mathematical technique to streamline the process of forecasting sales for a startup. We call the technique the exponentially declining sales growth model. This model enables the user to generate a realistic, exponentially declining sales pattern over the life of the product/service with ease and greatly simplifies and facilitates sensitivity analysis, as it eliminates or at least greatly reduces the need to manually insert sales growth percentages in spreadsheets.

---

[3] Two more sophisticated approaches are using Monte Carlo simulation and real options, which are excellent solutions but beyond the scope of this chapter.

FIRST CHICAGO APPROACH

Startups are much riskier ventures than mature businesses. Because of a lack of sales history and often a lack of market information, a number of widely varying scenarios are plausible, and the range of outcomes is much wider and more unpredictable than that of mature businesses.

In a DCF analysis the forecast cash flows are supposed to be the weighted average cash flows, with the appraiser having considered the full range of possible outcomes. However, it is difficult to do this with such a wide range of possible outcomes. Instead, typically the appraiser, investment banker, or venture capitalist uses the usually optimistic forecast of the client—perhaps downplayed somewhat—and discounts that to present value at a very high rate, around 50–75%.

Thus, a more traditional single-scenario DCF analysis to calculate fair market value is not only more difficult to perform, but it is also far more subject to criticism by parties with different interests. Short of using Monte Carlo simulation—a complex approach requiring specialized software that is warranted only in a limited number of assignments with very sophisticated clients—it is virtually impossible to portray the cash flows accurately in a single scenario. Instead, the best solution is to use a multi-scenario approach known as the First Chicago approach. I name the typical scenarios: very optimistic (the grand slam home run), optimistic (the home run), conservative (the single), and pessimistic (the strikeout).

According to James Plummer (Plummer 1987), Stanley C. Golder (Golder 1986) was the originator of the First Chicago approach, named after First Chicago Ventures, a spinoff of First Chicago Bank's Equity Group. In 1980 he founded the venture firm Golder, Thoma, and Cressey. James Plummer actually gave the name to the First Chicago approach. Bradley Fowler wrote the original literature on the First Chicago approach (Fowler 1989, 1990, 1996).

Discounting Cash Flow Is Preferable to Net Income

While discounting forecast cash flow is always preferable to discounting forecast net income, it is even more important to use cash flow in valuing startups than it is in mature firms. This is because cash is far more likely to run out in a startup than in a mature firm. When that happens, the firm is forced either to take on new investment, which dilutes existing shareholders' ownership in the company, or go out of business. In both cases, using a discounted future net income approach will lead to a serious overvaluation.

When budget is a consideration, it is possible to discount forecast net income instead of cash flow. However, it is critical that the appraiser at least do some due diligence to ascertain that the subject company will not run out of cash.

Capital Structure Changes

Startups tend to have somewhat frequent changes in capital structure. Investment often occurs in several traunches. These changes can involve replacing debt with common or preferred equity and new investment in equity. This complicates the value calculations because one must be very careful about whose equity he or she is measuring. Each round of investment dilutes existing equity, and it is easy to measure the wrong equity portion if one is not careful.

Venture Capital Rates of Return

Venture capitalists price companies by determining the present value of cash flow or future earnings. One method of valuation is to discount an optimistic forecast of FMV at the required rate of return. Required rates of return for VC vary directly with the stage of the company, with startups being the riskiest, hence requiring rates of return of 50–75% (Plummer 1987).

Fowler cites (Fowler 1990) a survey published by Venture Economics covering 200 companies which indicated that 40% of VC investments lost money, 30% proceeded sideways or were classified as "the living dead," 20% returned 2–5 times invested capital, 8% returned 5–10 times, and 2% returned greater than 10 times the investment. In a follow-up article (Fowler 1996) he refers to comments made by Professor Stewart Myers of MIT in his November 1995 address to the American Society of Appraisers confirming that 70–80% of VC investments are failures, whereas 20–30% are big winners. In addition, Professor Myers observed that the overall IRR for successful VC partnerships was approximately 25%.[4]

The 25% rate of return is consistent with a more recent *Wall Street Journal* article (Pacelle 1999) which cites Venture Economics as a source that venture capital firms returned an average 27.4% over the past 5 years, although they returned only 15.1% over the past 20 years. From this, we can calculate the first 15 years' (roughly 1979–1993) compound average return as 11.27%.[5] That is a very low return for VC firms. It is comparable to NYSE decile #1 firm long-run returns. I would attribute that low return to two factors. That period:

1. Was the infancy of the VC industry, and the early entrants faced a steep learning curve.
2. Included two severe recessions.

It is not reasonable to expect VC investors to be happy with a 15% return long run. The five-year average of 27.4% is more in line with the risk undertaken.

As to batting averages, a reasonable synthesis of this information is that 2% of VC investments are grand slams, 8% are home runs, 20% are moderately successful, and 70% are worthless or close to it.

---

[4] He also mentioned that the average VC project return was 1%. He said the difference in returns is due to the skewness in the distribution that comes from the venture capitalists quickly identifying and pulling the plug on the losers, i.e., they do not continue to fund the bad projects. Thus, the bad projects have the least investment.

[5] The equation is: $(1 + r_{15})(1.274)^5 = 1.151^{20}$, which solves to $r_{15} = 11.27\%$.

Table 12-1: Example of the First Chicago Approach

In Table 12-1 we use these percentages for weighting the four different scenarios, very optimistic, optimistic, conservative, and pessimistic, respectively.

Initially we perform discounted cash flow calculations to determine the conditional FMV of the subject company under the different scenarios. Typical venture capital rates of return include the discount for lack of marketability (DLOM) and discount for lack of control (DLOC). This tends to obscure the discount rate, DLOM, and DLOC. The appropriate discount rate using the First Chicago approach begins with the average success rate of approximately 25% reported by Professor Myers.

The 25%, however, is a geometric average rate of return. We should estimate an increment to add in order to estimate the arithmetic rate of return.[6] In Table 5-4 we show arithmetic and geometric mean rates of return from log size model regressions of the 1938–1997 New York Stock Exchange data for different size firms.

For a firm of $1 million FMV, the regression forecast arithmetic and geometric returns, rounded to the nearest percent, are 25% and 18%, respectively, for a differential of 7%. For a firm of $25 million FMV, the regression forecast arithmetic and geometric returns, rounded to the nearest percent, are 21% and 16%, respectively, for a differential of 5%. We can add the size-based differential to estimate the arithmetic average rate of return to use for our discount rate. For most size ranges the result comes to approximately 30%.[7]

Column B of Table 12-1 lists the conditional FMVs obtained from discounted cash flow analyses using different sets of assumptions. In the very optimistic scenario we forecast outstanding performance of the company, with a resulting FMV of $130,000,000 (B6). Cells B7 and B8 display the FMVs arising from optimistic and conservative forecasts, respectively. In the pessimistic scenario we assume the company fails completely, resulting in zero value. When valuing a general partnership interest, which

TABLE 12-1

First Chicago Method

	A	B	C	D
5		**Conditional FMV [1]**	**Probability [2]**	**Wtd FMV**
6	Very optimistic scenario	$130,000,000	2%	$2,600,000
7	Optimistic scenario	50,000,000	8%	4,000,000
8	Conservative scenario	10,000,000	20%	2,000,000
9	Pessimistic scenario [1]	0	70%	—
10	Weighted average FMV		100%	$8,600,000

Notes:
[1] Individual discounted cash flow analyses are the source for the numbers in this column
[2] Based on the VC rates discussed in the chapter

---

[6] I confirmed this in a telephone conversation with Professor Myers.
[7] Fowler's article did not address this adjustment.

has unlimited liability, the appraiser should consider the possibility of negative value.

Column C lists the probability associated with each scenario. These are derived directly from the empirical probabilities of VC success discussed above. We calculate the weighted FMV in column D by multiplying the conditional FMV in column B by its associated probability in column C and summing the results. Thus, in this example the weighted average FMV is $8,600,000 (D10).

Advantages of the First Chicago Approach

The major advantages of the First Chicago approach are:

1. It reduces the uncertainty associated with a single FMV by allowing for several scenarios representing differing levels of success of the company.
2. It breaks down the huge range of potential outcomes into "bite-size" chunks, i.e., the individual scenarios, that are credible and plausible when performed carefully.
3. It makes the appraiser's probability distribution of outcomes explicit. In doing so, it has two additional advantages: (a) If the client agrees with the conditional FMVs of each scenario but for some reason feels the probabilities are not representative of the subject company's chances, it is an easy exercise for the client to weight the probabilities differently and adjust the valuation him or herself. This is particularly important when the assignment is to provide existing shareholders with information to negotiate with funding sources. If both sides accept the scenario valuations, it is usually easy for them to come to terms by agreeing on the probabilities of the outcomes, which they can easily do without the appraiser; and (b) it protects the appraiser. When the appraiser shows a final weighting of the conditional FMVs multiplied by their probabilities to calculate the FMV and the appraiser shows the probability of total failure as, say, 70%, it can protect the appraiser from a disgruntled investor in the event the company fails. The appraiser has clearly communicated the high probability of investors losing all their money, despite the fact that the FMV may be very high—and, we hope, is—due to the large values in the upper 30% of probable outcomes.

Therefore, the First Chicago approach is normally the preferred method of valuation of startups. It is also useful in valuing existing firms that are facing radically different outcomes that are hard to forecast. For example, I used it recently to assist warring shareholders who wanted one side to buy out the other in a four-year-old company. The firm was profitable and had grown rapidly, but there were several major uncertainties that were impossible to credibly consider with accuracy in a single DCF scenario. The uncertainties were as follows:

1. There was much customer turnover in the prior year, despite healthy growth.

2. If one of the shareholders left, sales might suffer greatly for two or three years and even endanger the company.

3. There were regulatory issues that could have had a dramatic impact on the company.

4. Profit margins were highly variable in the past four years and could have been affected by regulation.

Collectively, these uncertainties made a single scenario forecast of sales growth and profitability very difficult. Despite considerable partisanship by the shareholders, who often actively lobbied for changes in the DCF analyses, the First Chicago approach enabled us to credibly model the different paths the Company could take and quantify the valuation implications of that. Ultimately, we presented them with the valuation of the different scenarios and our estimates of the probabilities, and the weighted average of the product of the two constituted our estimate of FMV. We also explained that they could change their subjective weighting of probabilities of outcomes, thus changing the FMV. Ultimately, they worked out an arrangement without any further need for our help.

Discounts for Lack of Marketability and Control

Finally, venture capitalists typically have more control and possibly marketability than most other investors. When valuing the interests of other investors, the appraiser must add the incremental discounts for lack of control and marketability that apply to the specific interests, i.e., an arm's-length investor would typically require a higher rate of return on smaller interests than the 30% that the VC expects.

VENTURE CAPITAL VALUATION APPROACH

In this approach the appraiser estimates net earnings at cash-out time, often at Year 5 or 6. He or she then estimates a P/E multiple and multiplies the two to estimate the cash out.

In Table 12-2 we use Fowler's (Fowler 1989) numbers, with minor changes in the presentation. Fowler assumed Year 5 net income of $1,936,167 and multiplied it by a P/E multiple of 12 to calculate the Year 5 cash out at $23.2 million (B5), rounded.

TABLE 12-2

VC Pricing Approach [1]

	A	B
5	Assumed cash out-5 yrs @ 12 × earnings	$23,200,000
6	Present value factor-5 years @ 45% ROI	0.1560
7	Present value-rounded	**$ 3,619,000**

[1] *Source:* Bradley Fowler, What Do Venture Capital "Pricing Methods Tell About Valuation of Closely Held Firms?" Business Valuation Review, June 1989, page 77.

He then used a 45% rate of return to discount cash flows, based on industry statistics he presented in the article, which we repeat below in the next section. The present value factor at 45% for five years is 0.156, and the present value of the Company is then $3,619,000 (B7, rounded).

Venture Capital Rates of Return

Fowler (1989) cited rates of return from two different studies. Plummer (1990) found that the required rates of return (ROR), which included discounts for lack of control (DLOC) and discounts for lack of marketability (DLOM), were:

Stage of Development of Co.	Required Rate of Return
Seed capital stage	50–75%
1st stage	40%–60%
2nd stage	35%–50%
3rd stage	30%–50%
4th stage	30%–40%

Morris (1988, p. 55) writes that VCs are looking for the following rates of return:

Stage of Development of Co.	Required Rate of Return
Seed capital stage	50%+
2nd stage	30–40%

Summary of the VC Approach

The VC approach is a valid valuation approach, though certainly less analytically precise than the First Chicago approach. Nevertheless, it is used by venture capitalists, and it serves as a "quick-and-dirty" valuation method, on the one hand, and as a useful alternative approach, on the other.

This concludes Part 1 of this chapter. Part 2 is a complex decision tree analysis combined with multiscenario valuation.

DEBT RESTRUCTURING STUDY

Early-stage technology-based companies often find themselves in financial hot water. They incur large expenses for years during the development of a new product. Consequently, they run short of funds and often require the infusion of venture capital, which may or may not occur. In the following example—which is based on an actual assignment, with names and numbers changed—the Subject Company has several possible events that can impact the probability of obtaining venture capital as well as surviving as a firm without venture capital, i.e., bootstrapping to success.

Background

The Company and its former parent ("the parent") share a nearly identical set of shareholders—well over 100. The president is the major shareholder of the firm, with effective, but not absolute control. The parent had lent the Company $1 million to get started as a spinoff, but the debt would be coming due in four years, and the Company has no way of paying it off.

The parent proposed the following restructuring of the debt:

1. The parent would convert the debt into $400,000 of convertible preferred stock—and part of the valuation exercise was to determine how many shares of preferred stock that would be. There would be no preferred dividends, but the parent would have a liquidation preference.

2. The president would have to relinquish a certain number of his shares in the parent back to the parent, which had a ready buyer for the shares.

In return for relinquishing his shares to the parent, the president wants the Company to issue 1.3 million new shares to him. The board of directors wants an independent appraisal to determine whether the transaction is favorable to the other shareholders. This example, however, is typical of the types of decisions faced by startup firms in their quest for adequate funding. More importantly, the statistical approach we use in this valuation is applicable to the valuation of many startups, regardless of industry.

Key Events

The company president, Mr. Smith, has identified a sequence of four key events that could occur, and each one of them increases the Company's ability to obtain venture capital financing as well as to successfully bootstrap the firm without VC financing. The events are sequentially dependent, i.e., event #1 is necessary, but not sufficient for event #2 to occur. Events #1, #2, and #3 must occur in order for #4 to occur. These events are:

1. Event #1: The Company sells its product to company #1. The conditional probability of this event occurring is 75% (Table 12-3, cell B11).

2. Event #2: The Company sells its product to company #2. The conditional probability of this happening, assuming event #1 occurs, is 90% (B12).

3. Event #3: The Company sells its product to company #3, which has a 60% (B13) conditional probability, i.e., assuming event #2 occurs.

4. Event #4: The Company sells its product to company #4. If the Company sells its product to company #3, then it has an 80% (B14) probability of selling it to company #4.

While these four events are all potential sales, the statistical process involved in this analysis is generic. The four events could just as easily be a mixture of technology milestones, rounds of financing, regulatory, sales, and other events.

Decision Trees and Spreadsheet Calculations

Our analysis begins as decision trees, which appear in Figures 12-1 and 12-2. However, careful analysis leads to our being able to generalize the decision tree calculations mathematically and transform them into expressions that we can calculate in a spreadsheet. This has tremendous computational advantage, which is not very apparent in a four-milestone analysis. Increase the number of milestones to 20, and the decision tree becomes very unwieldy to present, let alone to calculate, while the spreadsheet is easy. The discussions over the next few pages ultimately culminate in the development of equations (12-3) through (12-6). The equations provide the blueprint for the structure of the calculations in Table 12-3.

Table 12-3: Statistical Calculation of FMV

Table 12-3 is a statistical calculation of the FMV of the common shares of the Company owned by the existing minority shareholders, based on the probabilities of the different events occurring and the results of DCF analyses of several different scenario outcomes.

Organization

The table is divided into three sections. In the first two sections, 1A and 1B, the Company does restructure its debt with the parent. Section 1A is the calculation of the probability-weighted contribution to the FMV of the current shareholders' shares when the Company is successful in obtaining venture capital. Several possible combinations of events can lead to this outcome, and we identify the probabilities and payoffs of each combination in order to calculate the FMV of the common stock owned by the existing minority shareholders. Section 1B is the probability-weighted equivalent of section 1A when the Company is not successful in obtaining venture capital and instead attempts to bootstrap its way to success. The total of sections 1A and 1B is the FMV of current shareholders' shares, assuming the Company restructures the debt.

Section 2 is an analysis of the combination of events in which the Company does not restructure its debt with the parent. Section 3 is a summary of the FMVs under the different scenarios and contains calculations of the per share values. This is the bottom line of the valuation assignment.

Section 1A: Venture Capital Scenario

In section 1A the primary task is to determine the probability of receiving venture capital funding. Once we have accomplished that, it is simple to determine the contribution to FMV from the VC scenario.

Figure 12-1 is a diagram of the decision tree for section 1A. We begin by noting that there is a 75% probability of making sale #1 and a 25% probability of not making sale #1, in which case the Company fails. We denote the former as $P(1) = 75\%$ and the latter as $P(-1) = 25\%$. We

T A B L E 12-3

Statistical Calculation of Fair Market Value

Section 1A: Weighted Average Values Assuming Venture Capital Scenario & Debt Restructure With Parent

	A	B	C	D	E	F	G	H	I	J
Formula			Cum. Product [B]		[1 − [D]]	Cumulative Product [E]	[C] × [D] × [F$_{n-1}$]	1 − VC%	[G] × B18 × [H]	[1 − Min] × [I]
Event		Conditional Probability of Sale	Cumulative Joint Probability of Sale	Venture Cap Conditional Probability	Prob No VC = 1 − VC Cond. Probability	Cum. no VC	Prob of VC	Current Shareholders % Own	Current Shareholders FMV − Control	Current Shareholders FMV − Minor
#1: Company makes sale #1		75.000%	75.000%	50.000%	50.000%	50.000%	37.500%	50.000%	$18,750,000	$14,062,500
#2: Company makes sale #2		90.000%	67.500%	60.000%	40.000%	20.000%	20.250%	60.000%	$12,150,000	$9,112,500
#3: Company makes sale #3		60.000%	40.500%	70.000%	30.000%	6.000%	5.670%	70.000%	$3,969,000	$2,976,750
#4: Company makes sale #4		80.000%	32.400%	100.000%	0.000%	0.000%	1.944%	85.000%	$1,652,400	$1,239,300
Totals							**63.364%**		**$36,521,400**	**$27,391,050**

Assumptions

FMV − VC scenario	$100,000,000
Minority interest discount (assumed)	25%

Section 1B: Bootstrap Scenario Assuming Debt Restructuring With Parent

	A	B	C	D	E	F	G	H	I	J	K
Formula			Cum. Product [B]		1 − [D]	Cum. Prod. [E]		P[Sili, −(i + 1)] × {1 − [B$_{t+1}$]}×[G]; [C] × [F]	Note [1]	[H] × [I]	[1 − Min] × [J]
Event		Conditional Probability	Cumulative Joint Probability	Venture Cap Conditional Probability	Prob No VC = 1 − VC Cond. Probability	Cum. No VC	Bootstrap Conditional Probability	Prob of Survival/ No − VC	Conditional FMV	Wtd Avg FMV = FMV − Control	Current Shareholders FMV − Minor
#1: Company makes sale #1		75.000%	75.000%	50.000%	50.000%	50.000%	30.000%	1.125%	15,286,460	171,973	$128,980
#2: Company makes sale #2		90.000%	67.500%	60.000%	40.000%	20.000%	35.000%	1.890%	15,464,845	292,286	219,214
#3: Company makes sale #3		60.000%	40.500%	70.000%	30.000%	6.000%	75.000%	0.365%	15,732,422	57,345	43,009
#4: Company makes sale #4		80.000%	32.400%	100.000%	0.000%	0.000%	90.000%	0.000%	16,000,000	0	0
Totals								**3.380%**		**$521,603**	**$391,202**

Section 2: No Debt Restructure With Parent

37	#1: Company makes sale #1	75.000%	75.000%	100.000%	0.000%	100.000%	30.000%	2.250%	7,286,460	$163,945	$122,959
38	#3: Company makes sale #2	90.000%	67.500%	100.000%	0.000%	100.000%	35.000%	9.450%	7,464,845	705,428	529,071
39	#3: Company makes sale #3	60.000%	40.500%	100.000%	0.000%	100.000%	75.000%	6.075%	7,732,422	469,745	352,308
40	#4: Company makes sale #4	80.000%	32.400%	100.000%	0.000%	100.000%	90.000%	29.160%	8,000,000	2,332,800	1,749,600
41	Totals							46.935%		$3,671,918	$2,753,938

	Assumptions	Restructure	No Restructure
43			
44	= Adjusted FMV – bootstrap	$16,000,000	$8,000,000
45	Minority interest discount (assumed)	25.0%	

Section 3: Calculation of FMV per Share (row 49)

		Restructure			No Restructure: Investor % = 33.33%
52		Venture Capital	Bootstrap	Total	
53	Sec 1: venture capital scenario	$27,391,050	$391,202	$27,782,252	$2,753,938
54	Calculation of fully diluted shares:				
55	Original shares	1,000,000	1,000,000		1,000,000
56	Options:				
57	200,000 @ $0.50 per share [2]	200,000	200,000		200,000
58	66,667 shares @ $0.75 per share	66,667	0		0
59	100,000 shares @ $1.00 per share	100,000	0		0
60	Preferred stock conversion [3]	9,624	0		0
61	Total option shares	376,290	200,000		200,000
62	Original shares plus options	1,376,290	1,200,000		1,200,000
63	Proposed issuance to president	1,300,000	1,300,000		0
64	Shares to outside investors [4]	0	0		600,000
65	Fully-diluted shares [5]	2,676,290	2,500,000		1,800,000
66	Fully-diluted FMV/share–post transaction	$10.235	$0.156	$10.391	$1.530

419

T A B L E 12-3 *(continued)*

Statistical Calculation of Fair Market Value

	A	B	C	D	E	F	G	H	I	J	K
68	**Section 4: 2000 Investor Percentage Taken**										
70		**Control FMVs**									
71	t2000 FMV-40% disc rate—control basis	$8,000,000									
72	Less: minority interest discount-% (assumed)	−25.0%									
73	Less: minority interest discount-$	($2,000,000)									
74	2000 FMV-40% discount rate—minority basis	$6,000,000									
75	Percentage required for $2 million investment	33.3%									

Preferred stock-stated value	$400,000
FMV per share of common	$10.391
Multiply by 4	$41.56
Convert to # common shares	**9,624**

Notes:

[1] Column I Calculations: Beginning with FMV for Event #4, we subtract $750,000 for not reaching each of Events #4 and #3 and $500,000 for not reaching Event #2. All previous numbers are tax effected and present valued.

[2] Only the 200,000 shares are applicable in all scenarios. The remaining options apply only to the V.C. Scenario

[3] Assume 4 to 1 Preferred-to-Common conversion ratio, per CFO, as follows:

[4] In the Bootstrap-No Restructure Scenario, the Company falls $1 million short of cash and owes $1 million to the parent. We assume it will have to take on $2M investment for 33% of the stock. See Section 4.

[5] Actually, fully-diluted shares will be more, as will FMV when VC shares are included. In Section 1A, Columns H and I, we calculated the FMV of the current shareholders' shares, which is simpler than using actual FMV and wtd avg shares

FIGURE 12-1

Decision Tree for Venture Capital Funding

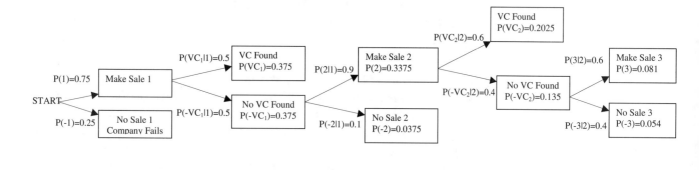

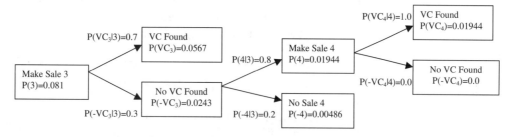

Many of the probabilities in this figure appear in Table 12-3, Section 1A, Columns B, D, and G.
Also P(-VC$_1$|1) is equivalent to [1-P(VC$_1$|1)] in the text and P(-2|1)=[1-P(2|1)] etc.

denote the conditional probabilities of subsequent sales as $P(j|j - 1)$, where j is the sale number. For example, $P(2|1)$ is the conditional probability of making sale #2, given that the Company already made sale #1. The probability of making sale #2 is the probability of making sale #1 multiplied by the conditional probability of making sale #2, given that the Company makes sale #1, or: $P(2) = P(1) \times P(2|1) = 0.75 \times 0.9 = 0.675$. Also note that $P(1)$ is the same as $P(1|0)$ since there is no sale zero.

Probability of VC Financing After Sale #1. If the Company makes sale #1, there is a 50% conditional probability of receiving VC funding at that time. We denote that event as VC$_1$, which means receiving VC funding after sale #1 but before sale #2 is attempted,[8] and we denote its conditional probability of occurrence as $P(VC_1|1)$, i.e., the probability of VC funding after sale #1, given that sale #1 occurs. The probability of receiving VC funding after the first sale is the conditional probability of the first sale occurring times the conditional probability of VC funding, given the sale.[9] The statistical statement is: $P(VC_1) = P(1) \times P(VC_1|1)$, where $P(1)$ is the probability of making sale #1. Thus $P(VC_1) = 0.75 \times 0.5 = 0.375$.

We denote the conditional probability of failure to obtain VC funding after sale #1 as $P(-VC_1|1) = 1 - P(VC_1|1) = 0.5$. Thus the absolute prob-

---

[8] From now on, when we say "after sale i," we also mean "but before the Company attempts sale $i + 1$."

[9] For the first sale, the conditional probability and the absolute probabilities are identical.

ability of not receiving VC financing after sale #1 is $P(-VC_1) = P(1) \times P(-VC_1|1) = 0.75 \times 0.5 = 0.375$, which is the same result as $P(VC_1)$. This occurs because the conditional probability of obtaining venture capital, given that the Company makes the first sale, is 50%. At any other probability, $P(VC_1|1) \neq P(-VC_1|1)$. These statements generalize for sale i, $i = 1, 2, 3, 4$.

Probability of VC Financing after Sale #2. Let's move on to the next step in our analysis: sale #2 and the probability of VC funding after it. If the Company receives VC after sale #1, we have already quantified that above. Our task in this iteration is to quantify the probability of VC funding if it did not come after sale #1 but does come after sale #2. Thus, the chain of events we are quantifying in this round is: sale #1 $\rightarrow -VC_1$ $\rightarrow$ sale #2 $\rightarrow VC_2$, i.e., the Company makes sale #1, doesn't receive venture capital, makes sale #2, then receives venture capital.

The probability of obtaining VC funding after sale #2 is:

$$P(VC_2) = P(1) \times [1 - P(VC_1|1)] \times P(2|1) \times P(VC_2|2)$$
$$= 0.75 \times (1 - 0.5) \times 0.9 \times 0.6 = 0.2025 \qquad (12\text{-}1)$$

Note that the conditional probability of VC financing, given that the Company makes sale #2, $P(VC_2|2) = 0.6$, compared to 0.5 after sale #1. In general, it makes sense that the conditional probability of receiving VC financing rises with each new key sale.

We can rearrange equation (12-1) as:

$$P(VC_2) = P(1) \times P(2|1) \times [1 - P(VC_1|1)] \times P(VC_2|2) \qquad (12\text{-}2)$$

In other words, the probability of obtaining VC financing after sale #2 is the cumulative joint probability of making both sale #1 and sale #2 times the conditional probability of not obtaining VC funding after sale #1 times the conditional probability of obtaining VC funding after sale #2.

Generalizing to Probability of VC Financing after Sale #k. We can generalize the probability of obtaining VC funding after sale #k as:[10]

$$P(VC_k) = \left(\prod_{i=1}^{k} P(i|i-1) \prod_{j=0}^{k-1} [1 - P(VC_j|j)] \right) P(VC_k|k) \qquad (12\text{-}3)$$

Equation (12-3) states that the probability of obtaining venture capital financing after sale #k is the cumulative joint probability of sale #k occurring times the cumulative joint probability of having been refused VC financing through sale #(k − 1) times the conditional probability of receiving VC financing after sale #k.

Finally, the total probability of obtaining VC financing is the sum of equation (12-3) across all n sales, where $n = 4$ in this example:

---

[10] Of course, $P(1|0) \equiv P(1)$, as the former has no meaning. Also, in the first iteration of equation (12-3), i.e., when $j = 0$, the term $P(VC_j|j)$ is the cumulative probability of receiving VC financing from sale #0, which is a zero probability. Thus $1 - P(VC_j|j)$ goes to 1.0, as it should.

PART 5 Special Topics

$$P(\text{VC}) = \sum_{k=1}^{n} \left[\prod_{i=1}^{k} P(i|i-1) \prod_{j=0}^{k-1} [1 - P(\text{VC}_j|j)] \right] P(\text{VC}_k|k) \quad (12\text{-}4)$$

Explanation of Table 12-3, Section 1A. Column A lists the sales events described above, and column B lists their associated conditional probabilities in cells B11–B14, i.e., $P(1) = 75\%$ (B11), $P(2|1) = 90\%$ (B12), etc. Column C is the cumulative joint probability, which is just the cumulation of the conditional probabilities. For example, the cumulative joint probability of making sale #4 is $P(1) \times P(2|1) \times P(3|2) \times P(4|3) = 75\% \times 90\% \times 60\% \times 80\% = 32.4\%$ (C14), where the conditional probabilities we multiply by each other are in cells B11–B14. Cells C11–C14 represent the term $\prod_{i=1}^{n} P(i|i-1)$ in equations (12-3) and (12-4).

Column D is the president's forecast of the conditional probability of obtaining venture capital financing. Each conditional probability is $P(\text{VC}_j|j)$, i.e., the probability of obtaining VC financing after sale #j, given that the Company makes sale #j, but before attempting sale #$j + 1$. Every subsequent sale increases the probability of obtaining venture capital beyond the level of the previous event. The conditional probability of VC financing rises from 50% (D11) after sale #1 to 60%, 70%, and 100% for sales #2, #3, and #4, respectively (D12–D14).

Column E, the conditional probability of not receiving VC financing after each sale, is one minus column D. Column F is the cumulative product of column E. It is the $\prod_{j=0}^{k-1} [1 - P(\text{VC}_j/j)]$ in equation (12-3) when we use the cumulation of the previous sale. For example, the probability of obtaining VC financing after the sale to company #4 is the cumulative joint probability of making sale #4, which is 32.4% (C14) $\times$ the cumulative joint probability of not having obtained VC financing after the first *three* sales, which is 6% (F13) $\times$ the conditional probability of making sale #4, which is 100% (D14) = 1.944% (G14).

Finally, the probability of obtaining VC financing, according to equation (12-4), is 65.364% (G15), the sum of column G. The FMV of the company, if it obtains VC financing, is $100 million (B18), which we determined with a DCF analysis.

Column H is one minus the percentage that Mr. Smith estimates the venture capital firm would take in the company's stock. After sale #1, he estimates the venture capitalist would take 50%, leaving 50% (H11) to the existing shareholders after the conditional transaction. If the Company makes the sale to company #2, it will be in a stronger bargaining position, and Mr. Smith estimates the venture capitalist would take 40% of the Company, leaving 60% (H12) to existing shareholders after the transaction. If the Company makes the sale to company #3, then he estimates the venture capitalist would take 30% of the Company, leaving 70% (H13) to the existing shareholders after the transaction. Finally, if the Company makes the sale to company #4, then he estimates the venture capitalist would take 15% of the Company, leaving 85% (H14) to the existing shareholders after the transaction.

Columns I and J are the FMVs of the current shareholders' shares on a control and minority basis resulting from obtaining venture capital financing. Later on, we will add in the current shareholders' FMV from bootstrapping the Company to come to a total current shareholders' FMV for the debt restructure option. Column I is the control value FMV and is obtained by multiplying the probability of obtaining VC financing in column G times the $100 million FMV of the Company if it receives VC financing (B18) times column H, the current shareholder ownership percentages. Column J is the FMV on a minority interest basis, which is column I times one minus the minority interest discount of 25.0% (B19), the magnitude of which is an arbitrary assumption in this analysis. The total FMVs of current shareholder shares are $36,521,400 (I15) and $27,391,050 (J15) on a control and minority basis, respectively.

The final equation describing the FMV is:[11]

$$\text{FMV (VC)} = \left\{ \sum_{k=1}^{n} \left(\prod_{i=1}^{k} P(i|i-1) \prod_{j=0}^{k-1} [1 - P(\text{VC}_j/j)] \right) \right.$$

$$\left. P(\text{VC}_k|k) \times \text{SH}\%_k \right\} \times \$100 \text{ million} \qquad (12\text{-}5)$$

In words, the contribution to FMV from the VC scenario is the sum of the probabilities of obtaining VC, which we quantified in equation (12-4), times the $100 million FMV of the company, assuming it is VC financed.

Section 1B: The Bootstrap Scenario Assuming Debt Restructuring with Parent

Bootstrapping occurs when the Company fails to attract venture capital but still manages to stay in business. The bootstrap scenario includes both success and failure at its attempts to bootstrap. Figure 12-2 shows the decision tree for the bootstrap scenario.

The pattern of events is that in each iteration, the Company can make the sale or not make the sale. After each sale, it might get VC financing or it might not. In section 1B we are not interested in the nodes on the decision tree where the Company receives VC financing, as we have already quantified that in section 1A. Thus, we do not show those nodes. Nevertheless, it is important to account for the probabilities of obtaining VC financing because if we don't, we will be double-counting that portion of the time that the Company could finance through a VC or bootstrap successfully. The Company can't do both at the same time. Thus, we remove the statistical probability of overlap. We accomplish that by multiplying all probabilities by $[1 - P(\text{VC}_i|i)]$ for all relevant i, where i is the sale number (also the iteration number).

If the Company does not make the sale, then it has a probability of survival and failure. We denote the survival after its last sale as Sj, where j is the sale number. The conditional probability of survival after its last sale is $P[Sj|j, -(j+1)]$. For example, if the company makes sale #3, does not make sale #4, and survives, we denote that as S3, and its conditional

---

[11] The term SH% is the percentage ownership of the current shareholders after VC financing.

FIGURE 12-2

Decision Tree for Bootstrapping Assuming Debt Restructure and No Venture Capital

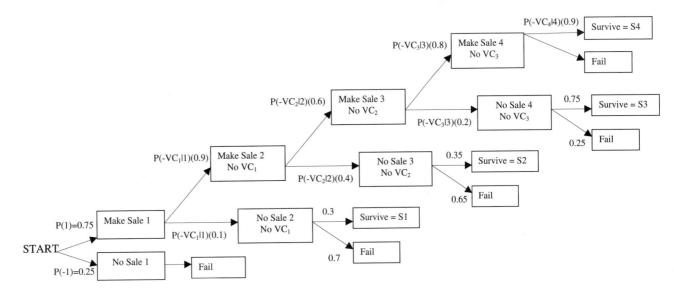

Note: P(-VC$_1$|1) is equivalent to [1-P(VC$_1$|1)] in the text.

probability of occurrence is $P(S3|3, -4)$, which reads, "the probability of Company long-term survival, given that it made sale #3, but does not make sale #4." If the Company makes the next sale, then we repeat the iteration, incrementing the sale number.

Without going through all of the step-by-step analysis we did for the VC scenario, the FMV of the bootstrap scenario is:

$$\text{FMV (Bootstrap)} = \sum_{j=1}^{n} \left[\prod_{i=1}^{j} P(i|i-1)[1 - P(\text{VC}_i|i)] \right] \tag{12-6}$$
$$(1 - P(j+1|j))P[Sj|j, -(j+1)]\text{FMV }(Sj)$$

Let's use the first iteration as an example. The probability of making sale #1 is 0.75. There is a 0.5 probability of obtaining VC financing if the company makes sale #1, so there is also a 0.5 probability of not obtaining VC financing, i.e., $[1 - P(\text{VC}_i|i)] = 0.5$. In order to terminate at S1, the company must make sale #1 and fail to make sale #2, which means we multiply by $[1 - P(2|1)]$, which is equal to one minus the conditional probability of making sale #2 = 1 − 0.9 (B30) = 0.1. The probability of survival if the Company makes sale #1 but stops there is 0.30 (G29). Thus, $P(S1) = P(1) \times [1 - P(\text{VC}_1|1)] \times [1 - P(2|1)] \times P(S1|1, -2) = 0.75 \times (1 - 0.5) \times (1 - 0.9) \times 0.3 = 1.125\%$ (H29).[12]

Column I is the conditional FMV of the company at each respective event level. This is different than in section 1, where the FMV is the same

---

[12] Note that for the last milestone, $1 - P(n+1|n)$ must be equal to 1, since the probability of making the $(n+1)$st sale is zero.

regardless of stage. The reason is that in section 1 the sole objective is obtaining venture capital funding, which will enable the Company to sell to the world. The lost profits on the key sales not made is immaterial compared to the $100 million FMV. In contrast, in section 1B each sale is significant relative to the total value and adds to the value of the company.[13]

In section 1B we begin with a conditional FMV of $16,000,000 (B44, repeated in I32). That value contains an implicit assumption that the Company makes it to event #4, the sale to Company #4. At each level before that, we subtract the net present value of the after-tax profits[14] from the sale that does not occur, i.e., we work our way backwards up this column. We assume pretax profits of $750,000 for the sales in events #3 and #4 and $500,000 for event #2. The numbers are then tax effected and discounted to present value. If the Company does not make it to event #1, this model assumes the Company fails entirely and has a zero value.

Column J is the contribution to the FMV of the Company on a control basis coming from the bootstrap scenario and is simply column H times column I, which totals $521,603 (J33).

Column K is the same value as column J, except that it is a minority interest conditional FMV. The discount for minority interest is 25%, which appears in B45. On a minority interest basis, the bootstrap scenario FMV is $391,202 (K33).

Section 2: No Restructure Scenario

The final scenario is the no-restructure with parent scenario. Section 2 is identical to section 1B, except:

1. Column F, the probability of not obtaining venture capital financing, is 100% by definition for all four events in section 2, since the president informs us that a VC will not finance the Company as long as it still has the parent's debt on the books.
2. Column I is calculated identically to section 1B, except that the baseline FMV as calculated by DCF analysis is $8 million (C44, repeated in I40) for the no-restructure scenario instead of $16 million (B44, repeated in I32).

Columns J and K in section 2B are the same as in Section 2A, except that there are no values originating from the venture capital scenario that have to be removed.

Section 3: FMVs per Share under Various Restructure Scenarios

In section 3 we calculate the fully diluted FMV per share post-transaction under the various scenarios.

---

[13] The sales actually do affect the values in section 1, but their impact is immaterial relative to the much larger total value, which is not true in the bootstrap scenarios.
[14] To be more precise, we would also include the related cash flow effects.

Venture Capital Scenario. The conditional FMV of the Company on a minority interest basis from the venture capital scenario is $27,391,050 (B53, transferred from J15). The Company currently has 1,000,000 shares of common stock outstanding, as appears in B55, C55, and F55. Rows 57–59 show employee stock options. Row 57 shows outstanding options for 200,000 shares at $0.50 per share. These options are in the money, and we assume they will be exercised. That would result in $100,000 being paid to the Company, which is included in the DCF analysis and is therefore already incorporated into the $27,391,050 value. These 200,000 additional shares are taken into account in all of the valuation scenarios.

Rows 58 and 59, however, are for options that are granted but could only be exercised if the Company does the restructure and obtains VC financing.[15] Mr. Johnson says that if the Company does obtain VC financing, it will issue 66,667 options with a $0.75 exercise price this year (B58) and 100,000 options (B59) at a $1.00 per share exercise price next year. Again, the cash inflows from exercise of the options are already included in the DCF analysis.

In the restructure scenario the parent receives $400,000 of preferred stock, which can be converted to common if the Company goes public or gets acquired. Otherwise, it only serves to increase the liquidation preference, as preferred dividends will never be paid. Therefore, the dividends, which are not tax deductible, do not appear in any of the cash flows. We presume in the venture capital scenario that the probability of going public or being acquired is significant and that preferred will convert. According to Mr. Johnson, a reasonable conversion ratio is 4 to 1. In note 3 to section 3 the $400,000 is divided by four times the fully diluted FMV of $10.391 per share (D66, repeated in footnote [3]) or $41.56 per share, resulting in an estimated conversion to common shares of 9,624 (footnote [3], transferred to B60). This calculation is a simultaneous equation and requires the use of multiple iterations on the spreadsheet. The number of converted shares depends on the fair market value per common share, but the FMV per common share depends on the number of preferred shares.

The total option shares are 376,290 (B61), including the assumed conversion of preferred in the venture capital scenario. In B63 we show the proposed issuance of 1.3 million shares to the president. Adding the 1,000,000 original shares, 376,290 option granted shares, and the 1.3 million new shares, we come to 2,676,290 (B65) fully diluted shares in the venture capital scenario. Dividing the $27,391,050 FMV by 2,676,290 shares, we arrive at the FMV per share of $10.235 (B66) for the venture capital scenario.

Next we consider the bootstrap portion of the restructure scenario. We begin with the $391,202 (K33) FMV as calculated in section 1B and repeat it in C53. Again, this is the portion of bootstrap value from which venture capital is excluded.

In this scenario the fully diluted shares are the same as in the venture capital scenario, except that the 66,667, 100,000 and 9,624 shares in rows

---

[15] The Company cannot obtain VC financing without restructuring its debt.

58–60 are zero in this case. There are 1,200,000 shares (C62) in this scenario before issuing the 1.3 million, and 2,500,000 (C65) shares after doing so. Dividing $391,202 by 2,500,000 shares, we come to a FMV of this scenario of $0.156 (C66) per share. Adding the per share values together, we come to $10.235 + $0.156 = $10.391 (B66 + C66 = D66) as the weighted average conditional FMV of the restructure scenario.

No-Restructure Scenario. The name of this scenario is somewhat of a misnomer. It means that the Company does not restructure its debt with the parent. At the onset of this assignment there was no way to know this, but restructuring of debt would eventually be required. The discounted cash flow analysis leads to the conclusion that the Company is unlikely to be able to generate enough cash to pay off the parent's note by its due date of December 31, 2000[16]—even though the forecast shows profits. Therefore, the Company has two choices: become insolvent and undergo liquidation or restructure later, and undergo a distress sale of equity approximately one year before the note becomes due.

The second choice obviously leads to a higher value for the shareholders, as it preserves the cash flows, even though some of them will be diverted to the new investor. Accordingly, we ran a DCF analysis to the fiscal year ending closest to the due date of the note. That value is $8,000,000 and appears in C44.

The subtotal number of shares is 1,200,000 (F62) before the new investor. Since there is no restructure with the parent in this scenario, the shares issued to the president is zero here (F63). In section 4 we calculate that the new investor will demand one-third of the Company posttransaction (see description below). That implies the investor will demand 600,000 shares (F64), which will bring the total shares to 1,800,000 (F65). Dividing $2,753,938 (K41, repeated in F53) by 1,800,000 shares leads to a value of $1.530 (F66) per share for the no-restructure scenario (this should more appropriately be called "restructure later").

Conclusion

Thus, the restructure is preferable by a FMV per share of $10.391 − $1.530 = $8.861 per share (= D66 − F66).

Section 4: Year 2000 Investor Percentage

A future restructure would be a more distressed one than the current one. The discounted cash flow analysis indicates that the Company would be short of cash to pay off the note. With two years gone by, the Company is more likely to lose the possibility of becoming the market leader and more likely to be an also ran. Also, it would be a far more highly leveraged firm without the restructure. Therefore, it would be a higher-risk firm in the year 2000, which dictates using a higher discount rate than the other scenarios. The result is a value of $8,000,000 (C44, repeated as B71) before the minority interest discount.

---

[16] The analysis was done in 1996.

Subtracting the $2 million (B73) minority interest discount leaves us with an FMV of $6 million (B74). In the DCF we determined the Company would need a $2 million investment by a new investor, who would require taking one-third (B75) of the Company. This percentage is used in section 3, F52 in the no-restructure calculations, as discussed above.

EXPONENTIALLY DECLINING SALES GROWTH MODEL

When forecasting yearly sales for a startup, the appraiser ideally has a bottom-up forecast based on a combination of market data and reasonable assumptions. Sometimes those data are not available to us, and even when they are available, it is often beneficial to use a top-down approach based on reasonable assumptions of sales growth rates. In this section we present a model for forecasting sales of a startup or early-stage company that semiautomates the process of forecasting sales and can easily be manipulated for sensitivity analysis. The other choice is to insert sales growth rates manually for, say, 10 years, print out the spreadsheet with that scenario, change all 10 growth rates, and repeat the process for valuation of multiple scenarios. Life is too short.

One such sales model that has intuitive appeal is the exponentially declining sales growth rate model, presented in Table 12-4. In the model we have a peak growth rate (P), which decays with a decay rate constant (k) to a final growth rate (G). The mathematics may look a little difficult, but it is not necessary to understand the math in order to benefit from using the model.

The top of Table 12-4 is a list of the parameters of the model. In the example the final sales growth rate (G) is set at 6% (E6), and the additional growth rate (A) is calculated to be 294% (E7). The additional growth rate (A) is the difference between the peak growth rate (P), which is set at 300% (E8), and the final sales growth rate of 6%. Next we have the decay rate constant (k), which is set at 0.50 (E9). The larger the decay rate constant, the faster the sales growth rate will decline to the final growth rate. Finally, we have Year 1 forecast sales of 100 (E10). All the variables are specified by the model user with the exception of the additional growth rate (A), which depends on P and G.

Example #1 shows the forecast sales growth rates (row 17) and sales (row 18) using the previously specified variables for a case where the sales growth rate declines after Year 2. We have no sales growth rate in Year 1 because we assume there are no prior year sales. The expression for the sales growth rate $= G + Ae^{-k(t-2)}$, for all t greater than or equal to 2, where t is expressed in years. For Year 2 the sales growth rate is $G + Ae^{-k(2-2)} = G + A = 6\% + 294\% = 300\%$ (C17), which is our specified peak growth rate P. Year 3 growth is $G + Ae^{-k(3-2)} = 6\% + (294\% \times e^{-0.5 \times 1}) = 184\%$ (D17). Year 4 growth is $G + Ae^{-k(4-2)} = 6\% + 294\% \times e^{-0.5 \times 2} = 114\%$ (E17), etc. To calculate yearly sales, we simply multiply the previous year sales by one plus the forecast growth rate.

Example #1A is identical to example #1, except that we have changed the decay rate constant (k) from 0.50 to 0.30. Notice how reducing k slows the decay in the sales growth rate. In example #2 we present a case of the peak growth rate (P) occurring in a general future year f, where we

TABLE 12-4

Sales Model with Exponentially Declining Growth Rate Assumption

	A	B	C	D	E	F	G	H	I	J	K
5	**Variable Name**			**Symbol**	**Value**	**Specified/Calculated**					
6	Final growth rate			**G**	6%	Specified					
7	Additional growth rate			**A**	294%	Calculated					
8	Peak growth rate			**P**	**300%**	Specified					
9	Decay rate			**k**	0.50	Specified					
10	First year's sales			**Sales1**	100	Specified					
13	**Example # 1 - Sales growth rate declines after year 2**										
14	Yearly growth = $G + Ae^{-k(t-2)}$ for all t greater than or equal to 2										
16	**Year**	**1**	**2**	**3**	**4**	**5**	**6**	**7**	**8**	**9**	**10**
17	Growth	N/A	300%	184%	114%	72%	46%	30%	21%	15%	11%
18	Sales	100	400	1,137	2,436	4,179	6,093	7,929	9,566	10,989	12,240
21	**Example # 1A - Changing the decay rate (k) from 0.50 to 0.30 slows the decline in the sales growth rate**										
23	Year	1	2	3	4	5	6	7	8	9	10
24	Growth	N/A	300%	224%	167%	126%	95%	72%	55%	42%	33%
25	Sales	100	400	1,295	3,463	7,810	15,194	26,072	40,307	57,237	75,937
28	**Example # 2 - Sales growth rate declines after future year f**										
29	Sales growth rate = $G + Ae^{-k(t-f)}$, for all t greater than or equal to f, where sales growth rate declines after future year f and										
30	the peak sales growth (P) occurs in year f. Growth through year f is to be specified by model user. The following is an										
31	example with year f = 4, and decay rate k = 0.5										
33	Year	1	2	3	4	5	6	7	8	9	10
34	Growth	N/A	100%	200%	300%	184%	114%	72%	46%	30%	21%
35	Sales	100	200	600	2,400	6,824	14,613	25,077	36,559	47,575	57,393

Formula in Cell C17: = G + A*EXP(−k*(C16 − 2))

FIGURE 12-3

Sales Forecast (Decay Rate = 0.5)

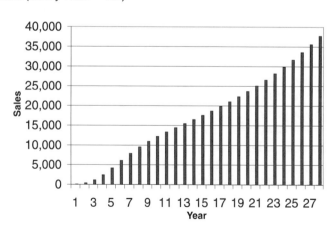

Sales Forecast (Decay Rate = 0.3)

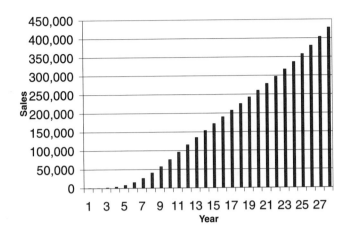

have chosen the future year to be Year 4. The model user specifies the growth rates prior to Year f (we have chosen 100% and 200% in Years 2 and 3, respectively). The growth rates for year f and later are $G + Ae^{-k(t-f)}$. As you can see, the growth rates from Years 4 through 10 in this example are identical to the growth rates from Years 2 through 8 in example #1.

Figures 12-3 and 12-3A are graphs that show the sales forecasts from examples #1 and #1A extended to 28 years. The slower decay rate of 0.3 in Figure 12-3A (versus 0.5 in Figure 12-3) leads to much faster growth. After 28 years, sales are close to $450,000 versus $38,000. Changing one single parameter can give the analyst a great deal of control over the sales forecast. When sensitivity analysis is important, we can control the decline in sales growth simply by using different numbers in cell E9, the decay rate. This is not only a nice time saver, but it can lead to more accurate forecasts, as many phenomena in life have exponential decay (or growth), e.g., the decay of radiation, population of bacteria, etc.

BIBLIOGRAPHY

Fowler, Bradley A. 1989. "What Do Venture Capital Pricing Methods Tell About Valuation of Closely Held Firms?" *Business Valuation Review* (June): 73–79.

———. 1990. "Valuation of Venture Capital Portfolio Companies—and Other Moving Targets." *Business Valuation Review* (March): 13–17.

———. 1996. "Venture Capital Rates of Return Revisited." *Business Valuation Review* (March): 13–16.

Golder, Stanley C. 1986. "Structuring and Pricing the Financing." In *Pratt's Guide to Venture Capital Sources*, 10th ed., ed. Stanley E. Pratt and Jane K. Morris. Wellesley Hills, Mass.: Venture Economics.

Morris, Jane K. 1988. In *Pratt's Guide to Venture Capital Sources*, 12th ed., ed. Jane K. Morris. Wellesley Hills, Mass.: Venture Economics.

Pacelle, Mitchell. 1999. "Venture Firms Dethroning Buyout Kings." *Wall Street Journal*, 7, June 1999. p, C1.

Plummer, James L. 1987. *QED Report on Venture Capital Financial Analysis*. Palo Alto, Calif.: QED Research, Inc. [See especially 2-7–2-10 and 6-2–6-13.]

Pratt, Stanley E. and Jane K. Morris, *Guide to Venture Capital Sources*, Venture Economics, 1986.

CHAPTER 13

ESOPs: Measuring and Apportioning Dilution[1]

INTRODUCTION
   What Can Be Skipped
DEFINITIONS OF DILUTION
   Dilution to the ESOP (Type 1 Dilution)
   Dilution to the Selling Owner (Type 2 Dilution)
   Defining Terms
TABLE 13-1: CALCULATION OF LIFETIME ESOP COSTS
THE DIRECT APPROACH
   FMV Equations—All Dilution to the ESOP (Type 1 Dilution; No Type 2 Dilution)
   Table 13-2, Sections 1 and 2: Post-transaction FMV with All Dilution to the ESOP
   The Post-transaction Value Is a Parabola
   FMV Equations—All Dilution to the Owner (Type 2 Dilution)
   Table 13-2, Section 3: FMV Calculations—All Dilution to the Seller
   Sharing the Dilution
   Equation to Calculate Type 2 Dilution
   Tables 13-3 and 13-3A: Adjusting Dilution to Desired Levels
   Table 13-3B: Summary of Dilution Tradeoffs
THE ITERATIVE APPROACH
   Iteration #1
   Iteration #2
   Iteration #3
   Iteration #n
SUMMARY

---

1. Adapted and reprinted with permission from *Valuation* (June 1997): 3–25 and (January 1993): 76–103, American Society of Appraisers, Herndon, Virginia.

Advantages of Results

Function of ESOP Loan

Common Sense Is Required

To Whom Should the Dilution Belong?

    Definitions

    The Mathematics of the Post-transaction Fair Market Value Balance Sheet

    Analyzing a Simple Sale

    Dilution to Non-selling Owners

    Legal issues

    Charity

APPENDIX A: MATHEMATICAL APPENDIX

APPENDIX B: SHORTER VERSION OF CHAPTER 13

This chapter is the result of further thought and research on my treatment of valuing ESOPs (Abrams 1993 and 1997). It not only simplifies those articles, but it goes far beyond them. Reading them is not necessary for understanding this chapter.

INTRODUCTION

Leveraged ESOPs have confused many firms due to their failure to understand the phenomenon of dilution and inability to quantify it. Many ESOPs have soured because employees paid appraised fair market value of the stock being sold to the ESOP, only to watch the fair market value significantly decline at the next valuation because the ESOP loan was not included in the pre-transaction fair market value. As a result, employees have felt cheated. Lawsuits have sometimes followed, further lowering the value of the firm and the ESOP.

There are several types of problems relating to the dilution phenomenon:

1. The technical problem of defining and measuring the dilution in value to the ESOP *before* it happens.
2. The business problem of getting the ESOP Trustee, participants, and selling owner(s) to agree on how to share the dilution.
3. The technical problem of how to engineer the price to accomplish the desired goals in 2.
4. The problem of how to communicate each of the foregoing to all of the participants so that all parties can enter the transaction with both eyes open and come away feeling the transaction was win–win instead of win–lose.

This chapter provides the analytical solutions to problems 1 and 3 that are necessary for resolving the business and communication problems of 2 and 4. The appraiser will be able to include the dilution in his or her initial valuation report so that employees will not be negatively surprised when the value drops at the next annual valuation. Additionally, the appraiser can provide the technical expertise to enable the parties to share the dilution, solving problem 3. Both parties will then be fully informed beforehand, facilitating a win–win transaction.

What Can Be Skipped

This chapter contains much tedious algebra. For readers who wish to skip all of the mathematics and optional sections and simply get the bottom line can read the "quick-and-dirty" version of this chapter in Appendix B. The section on the iterative approach can be safely skipped, as it enhances the understanding of dilution but contains no additional formulas of practical significance.

DEFINITIONS OF DILUTION

Two potential parties can experience dilution in stock values in ESOP transactions: the ESOP and the owner. The dilution that each experiences differs and can be easily confused.

Additionally, each party can experience two types of dilution: absolute and relative. Absolute dilution is defined in the section immediately below. Relative dilution is more complicated because we can calculate dilution relative to more than one base. Several formulas can be developed to calculate relative dilution, but they are beyond the scope of this book. Thus, for the remainder of this chapter, *dilution* will mean absolute dilution.

Dilution to the ESOP (Type 1 Dilution)

We define type 1 dilution as the payment to the selling owner less the post-transaction fair market value of the ESOP. This can be stated either in dollars or as a percentage of the pre-transaction value of the firm. By law, the ESOP may not pay more than fair market value to the company or to a large shareholder, though it is nowhere defined in the applicable statute whether this is pre- or post-transaction value. Case law and Department of Labor proposed regulations indicate that the pre-transaction value should be used.[2]

Dilution to the Selling Owner (Type 2 Dilution)

We define Type 2 dilution as the difference in the pre-transaction fair market value of the shares sold and the price paid to the seller. Again, this can be in dollars or as a percentage of the firm's pre-transaction value. Since it is standard industry practice for the ESOP to pay the owner the pre-transaction price, Type 2 Dilution is virtually unknown. Those sellers who wish to reduce or eliminate dilution to the ESOP can choose to sell for less than the pre-transaction fair market value.

When the ESOP bears all of the dilution, we have only type 1 dilution. When the owner removes all dilution from the ESOP by absorbing it himself, then the selling price and post-transaction values are equal and we have only type 2 dilution. If the owner absorbs only part of the dilution from the ESOP, then the dilution is shared, and we have both type 1 and type 2 dilution.

As we will show in Table 13-3B and the Mathematical Appendix, when the seller takes on a specific level of type 2 dilution, the decrease in type 1 dilution is greater than the corresponding increase in type 2 dilution.

The seller also should consider the effects of dilution on his or her remaining stock in the firm, but that is beyond the scope of this book.

Defining Terms

We first define some of terms appearing in the various equations.
Let:

p = percentage of firm sold to the ESOP, assumed at 30%

t = combined federal and state corporate income tax rate, assumed at 40%

---

2. *Donovan v. Cunningham*, 716 F.2d 1467. 29 CFR 2510.3-18(b).

r = the annual loan interest rate, assumed at 10%

i = the monthly loan interest rate = $r/12 = 0.8333\%$ monthly

V_{1B} = the pre-transaction value of 100% of the stock of the firm after discounts and premiums at the firm level but before those at the ESOP level,[3] assumed at \$1,000,000, as shown in Table 13-2. The B subscript means before considering the lifetime cost of initiating and maintaining the ESOP (see E, e, and V_{jA} below). V_{1B} does not consider the cost of the loan. This differs from V_{jB}, as described below.

V_{1A} = Same as V_{1B}, except this is the pre-transaction value after deducting the lifetime cost of initiating and maintaining the ESOP (see E, e, and V_{jA} below) but before considering the loan. Note this differs from V_{jA}, where $j > 1$, where we do subtract the cost of the ESOP loan as of iteration $j - 1$.

V_{jB} = the value of the firm at the jth iteration before deducting the lifetime ESOP costs (see E below) but after subtracting the net present value of the ESOP loan (see NPLV) as calculated in iteration $j - 1$ (for $j > 1$).

V_{jA} = the value of the firm at the jth iteration after deducting the lifetime ESOP costs (see immediately below) and the ESOP loan as of the $(j - 1)$st iteration.

V_n = the final post-transaction value of the firm, i.e., at the nth iteration

E = the lifetime costs of initiating and running the ESOP. These are generally legal fees, appraisal fees, ESOP administration fees, and internal administration costs. We assume initial costs of \$20,000 and annual costs of \$10,000 growing at 6% each year. Table 13-1 shows a sample calculation of the lifetime costs of the ESOP as \$40,000.[4]

e = lifetime ESOP costs as a percentage of the pre-transaction value = E/V_{1B} = \$40,000/\$1 million = 4%.

D_E = one minus net Discounts (or plus net premiums) at the ESOP level. This factor converts the fair market value of the entire firm on an illiquid control level (V_{1B}) to a fair market value (on a 100% basis) at the ESOP's level of marketability and control ($D_E V_{1B}$). If we assume that the ESOP provides complete marketability (which normally one should not, but we are doing so here for didactic purposes), then to calculate D_E we must merely reverse out the control premium that was applied to the entire firm (in the calculation of V_{1B}), which we will assume was 43%, and reverse out the discount for lack of marketability that was applied, which we will assume was 29%.[5] The result is: $D_E = [1/(1 + 43\%)] \times [1/(1 - 29\%)] = 0.7 \times 1.4 = 0.98$. In other words, the net effect of reversing out the assumed discount and premium is a 2% net

---

3. In Abrams (1993) the discounts and premiums at the firm level are a separate variable. This treatment is equally as accurate and is simpler.
4. How to calculate the pre-transaction value of the firm is outside the scope of this article.
5. These are arbitrary assumptions chosen for mathematical ease.

discount. It could also be a net premium if the minority discount were less or the premium for marketability were higher. Also, if we were to assume that the ESOP shares were not at a marketable minority level, other adjustments would be required.

L_j = the amount of the ESOP Loan in iteration j, which equals the payment to the owner. That equals the FMV of the firm in iteration j multiplied by pD_E, the percentage of the firm being sold to the ESOP, multiplied again by the factor for discounts or premiums at the ESOP level. Mathematically, $L_j = pD_E \, V_{jA}$. Note: this definition only applies in the Iterative Approach where we are eliminating type 1 dilution.

$NPVL_j$ = the after-tax, net present value of the ESOP loan as calculated in iteration j. The formula is $NPVL_j = (1 - t)L_j$, as explained below.

n = The number of iterations

D_1 = type 1 dilution (dilution to the ESOP)

D_2 = type 2 dilution (dilution to the seller)

FMV = fair market value

TABLE 13-1: CALCULATION OF LIFETIME ESOP COSTS

We begin by calculating the lifetime cost of the ESOP, including the legal, appraisal, and administration costs, which are collectively referred to throughout this chapter as the administration costs or as the lifetime ESOP costs.

The estimated annual operating costs of the ESOP in Table 13-1 are $10,000 pretax (B5), or $6,000 after-tax (B6). We assume an annual required rate of return of 25% (B7). Let's further assume ESOP administration costs will rise by 5% a year (B8). We can then calculate the lifetime value of the annual cost by multiplying the first year's cost by a Gordon Model multiple (GM) using an end-of-year assumption. The GM formula is $1/(r - g)$, or $1/(0.25 - 0.05) = 5.000$ (B9). Multiplying 5.000 by $6,000, we obtain a value of $30,000 (B10).

TABLE 13-1

Calculation of Lifetime ESOP Costs

	A	B
5	Pre-tax annual ESOP costs	$10,000
6	After-tax annual ESOP costs = (1 − t) * pre-tax	6,000
7	Required rate of return = r	25%
8	Perpetual growth of ESOP costs = g	5%
9	Gordon model multiple (end year) = 1/(r − g)	5.000
10	Capitalized annual costs	**30,000**
11	Initial outlay-pre-tax	20,000
12	Initial outlay-after-tax = (1 − t) * pre-tax	12,000
13	Lifetime ESOP costs	42,000
14	Lifetime ESOP costs-rounded to (used in Table 13-2, B9)	**$40,000**

We next calculate the immediate costs of initiating the ESOP at time zero, which we will assume are $20,000 (B11), or $12,000 after-tax (B12). Adding $30,000 plus 12,000, we arrive at a lifetime cost of $42,000 for running the ESOP (B13), which for simplicity we round off to $40,000 (B14), or 4% of the pre-transaction value of $1 million.[6] Adopting the previous definitions, $E = \$40,000$ and $e = 4\%$.

The previous example presumes that the ESOP is not replacing another pension plan. If the ESOP is replacing another pension plan, then it is only the incremental lifetime cost of the ESOP that we would calculate here.

THE DIRECT APPROACH

Using the direct approach, we calculate all valuation formulas directly through algebraic substitution. We will develop post-transaction valuation formulas for the following situations:

1. All dilution remains with the ESOP.
2. All dilution goes to the owner.
3. The ESOP and the owner share the dilution.

We will begin with 1. The owner will be paid pre-transaction price, leaving the ESOP with all of the dilution in value. The following series of equations will enable us to quantify the dilution. All values are stated as a fraction of each $1 of pre-transaction value.

FMV Equations—All Dilution to the ESOP (Type 1 Dilution; No Type 2 Dilution)

$$1 \quad \text{pre-transaction value} \tag{13-1}$$

We pay the owner the $p\%$ he or she sells to the ESOP reduced or increased by D_E, the net discounts or premiums at the ESOP level. For every $1 of pre-transaction value, the payment to the owner is thus:

$$pD_E \quad \text{paid to owner in cash = ESOP loan} \tag{13-1a}$$

$$tpD_E \quad \text{tax savings on ESOP loan} \tag{13-1b}$$

The after-tax cost of the loan is the amount paid to the owner less the tax savings of the loan, or equations (13-1a) and (13-1b).

$$(1 - t)pD_E \quad \text{after-tax cost of the ESOP loan} \tag{13-1c}$$

$$e \quad \text{after-tax lifetime cost of the ESOP} \tag{13-1d}$$

When we subtract (13-1c) plus (13-1d) from (13-1), we obtain the remaining value of the firm:

---

6. For simplicity, we do not add a control premium and deduct a discount for lack of marketability at the firm level and then reverse that procedure at the ESOP level, as I did in Abrams (1993).

$$1 - (1 - t)pD_E - e \quad \text{post-transaction value of the firm} \quad (13\text{-}1e)$$

Since the ESOP owns $p\%$ of the firm, the post-transaction value of the ESOP is $p \times D_E \times (13\text{-}1e)$:

$$pD_E - (1 - t)p^2D_E^2 - pD_E e \quad \text{post-transaction value of the ESOP}$$

$$(13\text{-}1f)$$

The dilution to the ESOP (type 1 dilution) is the amount paid to the owner minus the value of the ESOP's $p\%$ of the firm, or $(13\text{-}1a)$ − $(13\text{-}1f)$:

$$pD_E - [pD_E - (1 - t)p^2D_E^2 - pD_E e]$$
$$= (1 - t)p^2 D_E^2 + pD_E e \quad \text{dilution to ESOP} \quad (13\text{-}1g)$$

Table 13-2, Sections 1 and 2: Post-transaction FMV with All Dilution to the ESOP

Now that we have established the formulas for calculating the FMV of the firm when all dilution goes to the ESOP, let's look at a concrete example in Table 13-2. The table consists of three sections. Section 1, rows 5–10, is the operating parameters of the model. Section 2 shows the calculation of the post-transaction values of the firm, ESOP, and the dilution to the ESOP according to equations (13-1e), (13-1f), and (13-1g), respectively, in rows 12–18. Rows 21–26 prove the accuracy of the results, as explained below.

Section 3 shows the calculation of the post-transaction values of the firm and the ESOP when there is no dilution to the ESOP. We will cover that part of the table later. In the meantime, let's review the numerical example in section 2.

B13 contains the results of applying equation (13-1e) using section 1 parameters to calculate the post-transaction value of the firm, which is $0.783600 per $1 of pre-transaction value. We multiply the $0.783600 by the $1 million pre-transaction value (B5) to calculate the post-transaction value of the firm = $783,100 (B14). The post-transaction value of the ESOP according to equation (13-1f) is $0.230378[7] (B15) × $1 million pre-transaction value (B5) = $230,378 (B16).

We calculate dilution to the ESOP according to equation (13-1g) as $(1 - 0.4) \times 0.3^2 \times 0.98^2 + 0.3 \times 0.98 \times 0.04 = 0.063622$ (B17). When we multiply the dilution as a percentage by the pre-transaction value of $1 million, we get dilution of $63,622 (B18, B26).

We now prove these results and the formulas in rows 21–26. The payment to the owner is $300,000 × 0.98 (net of ESOP discounts/premiums) = $294,000 (B22). The ESOP takes out a $294,000 loan to pay the owner, which the company will have to pay. The after-tax cost of the loan is $(1 - t)$ multiplied by the amount of the loan, or 0.6 × $294,000 = $176,400 (B23). Subtracting the after tax cost of the loan and the $40,000 lifetime ESOP costs from the pre-transaction value, we come to a post-

---

7. Which itself is equal to $pD_E \times$ the post-transaction value of the firm, or B6 × B7 × B14.

FMV Calculations: Firm, ESOP, and Dilution

	A	B	C
4	**Section 1: Parameters**		
5	V_{1B} = pre-transaction value	$1,000,000	
6	p = percentage of stock sold to ESOP	30%	
7	D_E = net ESOP discounts/premiums	98%	
8	t = tax rate	40%	
9	E = ESOP costs (lifetime costs capitalized; Table 13-1, B14)	$40,000	
10	e = ESOP costs/pre-transaction value = E/V_{1B}	4%	
12	**Section 2: All Dilution To ESOP**		
13	$(1 - e) - (1 - t) pD_E$ = post-trans FMV-firm (equation [13-1e])	0.783600	
14	Multiply by pre-trans FMV = B5*B13 = B24	**$783,600**	
15	$pD_E - (1 - t)p^2D_E^2 - pD_E e$ = post-trans FMV-ESOP (equation [13-1f])	0.230378	
16	Multiply by pre-trans FMV = B5*B15 = B25	**$230,378**	
17	$(1 - t)p^2D_E^2 + pD_E e$ = dilution to the ESOP (equation [13-1g])	0.063622	
18	Multiply by pre-trans FMV = B5*B17 = B26	**$63,622**	
20	**Proof of Section 2 Calculations:**		
21	Pre-trans FMV = B5	**$1,000,000**	
22	Payment to owner = B6*B7*B21	294,000	
23	After tax cost of loan = (1 - B8) * B22	176,400	
24	Post-trans FMV-firm = B21 - B23 - B9 = B14	783,600	
25	Post-transaction FMV of ESOP = B6*B7*B24 = B16	230,378	
26	Dilution to the ESOP = B22 - B25 = B18	**$63,622**	
28	**Section 3: All Dilution To Seller**	**Multiple**	**× V_{1B} = FMV**
29	$V_n = (1 - e)/[1 + (1 - t)pD_E]$ = post-trans FMV—firm = B40 (equation [13-3n])	0.816049	**$816,049**
30	$L_n = p * D_E * V_n$ = post-trans FMV-ESOP (equation [13-3j])	0.239918	**$239,918**
31	Dilution to seller = (B6*B7) - B30 = (equation [13-3o])		5.4082%
32	Dilution to seller = B5*C31		**$54,082**
33	Dilution to seller = B22 - C30		**$54,082**
35	**Proof of Calculation in C29:**		
36	Pre-trans FMV = B5	**$1,000,000**	
37	Payment to owner = C30	239,918	
38	Tax shield = t * B37	95,967	
39	After tax cost of ESOP loan = B37 - B38	143,951	
40	Post-trans FMV-firm = B36 - B39 - B9 = C29	**$816,049**	

transaction value of the firm of $783,600 (B24), which is identical to the value obtained by direct calculation using formula (13-1e) in B14. The post-transaction value of the ESOP is $pD_E \times$ post-transaction FMV—firm, or $0.3 \times 0.98 \times \$783,600 = \$230,378$ (B25, B16). The dilution to the ESOP is the payment to the owner minus the post-transaction value of the ESOP, or $294,000 (B22) − $230,378 (B25) = $63,622 (B26, B18). We have now proved the direct calculations in rows 14, 16, and 18.

The Post-Transaction Value is a Parabola

Equation (13-1f), the formula for the post-transaction value of the ESOP, is a parabola. We can see this more easily by rewriting (13-1f) as

$$V = -D_E^2(1 - t)p^2 + D_E(1 - e)p$$

where V is the post-transaction value of the ESOP. Figure 13-1 shows this function graphically. The straight line, pD_E, is a slight modification of a simple 45° line $y = x$ (or in this case $V = p$), except multiplied by $D_E = 98\%$. This line is the payment to the owner when the ESOP bears all of the dilution. The vertical distance of the parabola (equation [13-1f]) from the straight line is the dilution of the ESOP, defined by equation (13-1g), which is itself a parabola. Figure 13-1 should actually stop where $p = 100\%$, but it has been extended merely to show the completion of the parabola, since there is no economic meaning for $p > 100\%$.

We can calculate the high point of the parabola, which is the maximum post-transaction value of the ESOP, by taking the first partial derivative of equation (13-1f) with respect to p and setting the equation to zero:

$$\frac{\partial V}{\partial p} = -2(1 - t)D_E^2 p + D_E(1 - e) = 0 \qquad (13\text{-}2)$$

This solves to

$$p = \frac{(1 - e)}{2(1 - t)D_E} \qquad (13\text{-}1f)$$

or $p = 81.63265\%$. Substituting this number into equation (13-1f) gives us the maximum value of the ESOP of $V = 38.4\%$.[8] This means that if the owner sells any greater portion than 81.63265% of the firm to the ESOP,

FIGURE 13-1

Post-Transaction Value of the ESOP Vs. % Sold

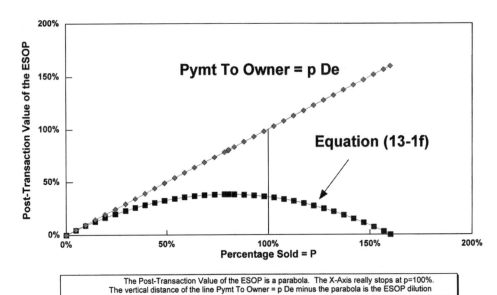

The Post-Transaction Value of the ESOP is a parabola. The X-Axis really stops at p=100%. The vertical distance of the line Pymt To Owner = p De minus the parabola is the ESOP dilution

---

8. We can verify this is a maximum rather than minimum value by taking the second partial derivative, $\partial^2 V / \partial p^2 = -2(1 - t)D_E^2 < 0$, which confirms the maximum.

PART 5 Special Topics

he actually *decreases* the value of the ESOP, assuming a 40% tax rate and no outside capital infusions into the sale. The lower the tax rate, the more the parabola shifts to the left of the vertical line, until at $t = 0$, where most of the parabola is completed before the line.[9]

FMV Equations—All Dilution to the Owner (Type 2 Dilution)

Let's now assume that instead of paying the owner pD_E, the ESOP pays him some unspecified amount, x. Accordingly, we rederive (13-1)–(13-1g) with that single change and label our new equations (13-3)–(13-3j).

$$1 \quad \text{pre-transaction value} \qquad (13\text{-}3)$$

$$x \quad \text{paid to owner in cash} = \text{ESOP loan} \qquad (13\text{-}3\text{a})$$

$$tx \quad \text{tax savings on ESOP loan} \qquad (13\text{-}3\text{b})$$

$$(1 - t)x \quad \text{after-tax cost of the ESOP loan} \qquad (13\text{-}3\text{c})$$

$$e \quad \text{after-tax ESOP cost} \qquad (13\text{-}3\text{d})$$

When we subtract (13-3c) plus (13-3d) from (13-3), we come to the remaining value of the firm of:

$$(1 - e) - (1 - t)x \quad \text{post-transaction value of the firm} \quad (13\text{-}3\text{e})$$

Since the ESOP owns $p\%$ of the firm and the ESOP bears its net discount, the post-transaction value of the ESOP is $p \times D_E \times (13\text{-}3\text{e})$, or:

$$pD_E(1 - e) - (1 - t)pD_Ex \quad \text{post-transaction value of the ESOP} \quad (13\text{-}3\text{f})$$

We can eliminate dilution to the ESOP entirely by specifying that the payment to the owner, x, equals the post-transaction value of the ESOP (13-3f), or:

$$x = pD_E(1 - e) - (1 - t)pD_Ex \qquad (13\text{-}3\text{g})$$

Moving the right term to the left side,

$$x + (1 - t)pD_Ex = pD_E(1 - e) \qquad (13\text{-}3\text{h})$$

Factoring out x,

$$x[1 + (1 - t)pD_E] = pD_E(1 - e) \qquad (13\text{-}3\text{i})$$

Dividing through by $1 + (1 - t)pD_E$,

$$x = \frac{pD_E(1 - e)}{1 + (1 - t)pD_E}$$

post-transaction FMV of ESOP, all dilution to owner   (13-3j)

---

9. This is because equation (13-1f) becomes $V = -D_E^2 p^2 + D_E(1 - e)p$. Given our D_E and e, V is then approximately equal to $-0.92\ (p^2 - p)$. If $t = 0$, $e = 0$, and there were no discounts and premiums at the ESOP level, i.e., $D_E = 1$, then the owner would be paid p, the post-transaction value of the firm would be $1 - p$, and the post-transaction value of the ESOP would be $p(1 - p)$, or $-p^2 + p$. This parabola would finish at $p = 1$. The maximum post-transaction ESOP value would be 25% at $p = 50\%$.

Substituting equation (13-3j) into the x term in (13-3e), the post-transaction value of the firm is:

$$(1 - e) - (1 - t) \frac{pD_E(1 - e)}{1 + (1 - t)pD_E} \qquad (13\text{-}3k)$$

Factoring out the $(1 - e)$ from both terms, we get:

$$(1 - e)\left[1 - \frac{(1 - t)pD_E}{1 + (1 - tpD_E)}\right] \qquad (13\text{-}3l)$$

Rewriting the 1 in the brackets as

$$\frac{1 + (1 - t)pD_E}{1 + (1 - t)pD_E}$$

we obtain:

$$(1 - e)\frac{1 + (1 - t)pD_E - (1 - t)pD_E}{1 + (1 - t)pD_E} \qquad (13\text{-}3m)$$

The numerator simplifies to 1, which enables us to simplify the entire expression to:

$$\frac{1 - e}{1 + (1 - t)pD_E} \quad \text{post-transaction value of the firm—}$$

$$\text{type 1 dilution} = 0 \qquad (13\text{-}3n)$$

The dilution to the seller is the pre-transaction FMV of shares sold minus the price paid, or:

$$pD_E - \frac{1 - e}{1 + (1 - t)pD_E} \qquad (13\text{-}3o)$$

Table 13-2, Section 3: FMV Calculations— All Dilution to the Seller

In section 3 we quantify the engineered price that eliminates all dilution to the ESOP, which according to equation (13-3n) is:

$$\$1 \text{ million} \times \frac{(1 - 0.04)}{[1 + (0.6) \times (0.3) \times (0.98)]}$$

$$= \$1 \text{ million} \times 0.816049 \text{ (B29)} = \$816,049 \text{ (C29)}$$

Similarly, the value of the ESOP is: $0.3 \times 0.98 \times 0.816049 \times \$1,000,000$ = \$239,918 (C30) which is also the same amount that the owner is paid in cash. We can prove this correct as follows:

1. The ESOP borrows \$239,918 (B37) to pay the owner and takes out a loan for the same amount, which the firm pays.
2. The firm gets a tax deduction, which has a net present value of its marginal tax rate multiplied by the principal of the ESOP loan, or 40% × \$239,918, or \$95,967 (B38), which after being subtracted from the payment to the owner leaves an after-tax cost of the payment to the owner (which is the identical to the after-tax cost of the ESOP loan) of \$143,951 (B39).

PART 5   Special Topics

3. We subtract the after-tax cost of the ESOP loan of \$143,951 and the \$40,000 lifetime ESOP costs from the pre-transaction value of \$1 million to arrive at the final value of the firm of \$816,049 (B40). This is the same result as the direct calculation by formula in B29, which proves (13-3n). Multiplying by pD_E (0.3 × 0.98 = 0.297) would lead to the same result as in B30, which proves the accuracy of (13-3j).

We can also prove the dilution formulas in section 3. The seller experiences dilution equal to the normative price he or she would have received if he or she were not willing to reduce the sales price, i.e., \$294,000 (B22) less the engineered selling price of \$239,918 (C30), or \$54,082 (C33). This is the same result as using a direct calculation from equation (13-3o) of 5.4082% (C31) × the pre-transaction price of \$1 million = \$54,082 (C32).

The net result of this approach is that the owner has shifted the entire dilution from the ESOP to himself. Thus, the ESOP no longer experiences any dilution in value. While this action is very noble on the part of the owner, in reality few owners are willing and able to do so.

Sharing the Dilution

The direct approach also allows us to address the question of how to share the dilution. If the owner does not wish to place all the dilution on the ESOP or absorb it personally, he or she can assign a portion to both parties. By subtracting the post-transaction value of the ESOP (13-3f) from the cash to the owner (13-3a), we obtain the amount of dilution. We can then specify that this dilution should be equal to a fraction k of the default dilution, i.e., the dilution to the ESOP when the ESOP bears all of the dilution. In our nomenclature, the post-transaction value of the ESOP − dilution to the ESOP = k × (default dilution to the ESOP). Therefore,

$$k = \frac{\text{Actual Dilution to ESOP}}{\text{Default Dilution to ESOP}}, \text{ or}$$

$$k = \text{the \% dilution remaining with the ESOP}$$

The reduction in dilution to the ESOP is $(1 - k)$. For example, if $k = 33\%$, the ESOP bears 33% of the dilution; the reduction in the amount of dilution borne by ESOP is 67% (from the default figure of 100%).

The formula used to calculate the payment to the owner when dilution is shared by both parties is:

$$x - [pD_E(1 - e) - (1 - t)pD_E x] = k[(1 - t)p^2 D_E^2 + pD_E e] \quad (13\text{-}4)$$

Collecting terms, we get:

$$x[1 + (1 - t)pD_E] = pD_E(1 - e) + k[(1 - t)p^2 D_E^2 + pD_E e]$$

Dividing both sides by $[1 + (1 - t)pD_E]$, we solve to:

$$x = \frac{pD_E(1 - e) + k[(1 - t)p^2 D_E^2 + pD_E e]}{1 + (1 - t)pD_E} \quad (13\text{-}4a)$$

In other words, equation (13-4a) is the formula for the amount of payment to the owner when the ESOP retains the fraction k of the default dilution. If we let $k = 0$, (13-4a) reduces to (13-3j), the post-transaction FMV of the ESOP when all dilution goes to the owner. When $k = 1$, (13-4a) reduces to (13-1a), the payment to the owner when all dilution goes to the ESOP.

Equation to Calculate Type 2 Dilution

Type 2 dilution is equal to pD_E, the pre-transaction selling price adjusted for control and marketability, minus the engineered selling price, x. Substituting equation (13-4a) for x, we get:

$$D_2 = pD_E - \frac{pD_E(1 - e) + k[(1 - t)p^2D_E^2 + pD_E e]}{1 + (1 - t)pD_E} \qquad (13\text{-}4b)$$

Tables 13-3 and 13-3A: Adjusting Dilution to Desired Levels

Table 13-3 is a numerical example using equation (13-4a). We let $p = 30\%$ (B5), $D_E = 98\%$ (B6), $k = 2/3$ (B7), $t = 40\%$ (B8), and $e = 4\%$ (B9). B10 is the calculation of x, the payment to the seller—as in equation (13-4a)—which is 27.6%. B11 is the value of the ESOP post-transaction, which we calculate according to equation (13-3f),[10] at 23.36%. Subtracting the post-transaction value of the ESOP from the payment to the owner (27.60% − 23.36%) = 4.24% (B12) gives us the amount of type 1 dilution.

The default type 1 dilution, where the ESOP bears all of the dilution, would be $(1 - t)p^2D_E^2 + pD_E e$, according to equation (13-1g), or 6.36% (B13). Finally, we calculate the actual dilution divided by the default dilution, or 4.24%/6.36% to arrive at a ratio of 66.67% (B14), or 2/3, which is the same as k, which proves the accuracy of equation (13-4a). By des-

T A B L E 13-3

Adjusting Dilution to Desired Levels

	A	B
5	p = percentage sold to ESOP	30.00%
6	D_E = net discounts at the ESOP level	98.00%
7	k = Arbitrary fraction of remaining dilution to ESOP	**66.67%**
8	t = tax rate	40.00%
9	e = % ESOP costs	4.00%
10	x = % to owner = $pD_E(1 - e) + k[(1 - t)(p^2D_E^2 + pD_E e)]/[1 + (1 - t)pD_E]$ (equation [13-4a])	27.60%
11	ESOP post-trans = $pD_E[1 - e - (1 - t)x]$ (equation [13-3f])	23.36%
12	Actual dilution to ESOP = B10 − B11	4.24%
13	Default dilution to ESOP : $(1 - t)D_E^2 p^2 + pD_E e$ (equation [13-1g])	6.36%
14	Actual/default dilution: [12]/[13] = k = [7]	66.67%
15	Dilution to owner = (B5*B6) − B10	**1.80%**
16	Dilution to owner = $p^*D_E - ((p^*D_E)^*(1 - e) + k^*((1 - t)^*D_E^{2*}p^2 + p^*D_E^*e))/(1 + (1 - t)^*p^*D_E)$	**1.80%**

10. With pD_E factored out.

Adjusting Dilution to Desired Levels—All Dilution to Owner

	A	B
5	p = percentage sold to ESOP	30.00%
6	D_E = net discounts at the ESOP level	98.00%
7	k = Arbitrary fraction of remaining dilution to ESOP	**0.00%**
8	t = tax rate	40.00%
9	e = % ESOP costs	4.00%
10	x = % to owner = $pD_E(1 - e) + k[(1 - t)(p^2D_E^2 + pD_Ee)]/1 + (1 - t)pD_E$ (equation [13-4a])	23.99%
11	ESOP post-trans = $pD_E[1 - e - (1 - t)x]$ (equation [13-3f])	23.99%
12	Actual dilution to ESOP = [10] − [11]	0.00%
13	Default dilution to ESOP : $(1 - t)D_E^2p^2 + pD_Ee$ (equation [13-1g])	6.36%
14	Actual/default dilution: [12]/[13] = k = [3]	0.00%
15	Dilution to owner = (B5*B6) − B10	5.41%
16	Dilution to owner = $p*D_E - ((p*D_E)*(1 - e) + k*((1 - t)*D_E^2*p^2 + p*D_E*e))/(1 + (1 - t)*p*D_E)$	5.41%

ignating the desired level of dilution to be 2/3 of the original dilution, we have reduced the dilution by 1/3, or (1 − k).

If we desire dilution to the ESOP to be zero, then we substitute k = 0 in (13-4a), and the equation reduces to

$$x = \frac{pD_E(1 - e)}{[1 + (1 - t)pD_E]}$$

which is identical to equation (13-3j), the post-transaction value of the ESOP when the owner bears all of the dilution. You can see that in Table 13-3A, which is identical to Table 13-3 except that we have let k = 0 (B7), which leads to the zero dilution, as seen in B14.

Type 2 dilution appears in Table 13-3, rows 15 and 16. The owner is paid 27.6% (B10) of the pre-transaction value for 30% of the stock of the company. He normally would have been paid 29.4% of the pre-transaction value (B5 × B6 = 0.3 × 0.98 = 29.4%). Type 2 dilution is 29.4% − 27.60% = 1.80% (B15). In B16 we calculate type 2 dilution directly using equation (13-4b). Both calculations produce identical results, confirming the accuracy of (13-4b). In Table 13-3A, where we let k = 0, type 2 dilution is 5.41% (B15 and B16).

T A B L E 13-3B

Summary of Dilution Tradeoffs

	A	B	C	D	E
5		Scenario: Assignment of Dilution			
6		100% to	2/3 to		100% to
7	Dilution Type	ESOP	ESOP	Difference	Owner
8	1 (ESOP)	6.36%	4.24%	2.12%	0.00%
9	2 (seller)	0.00%	1.80%	−1.80%	5.41%
10	Source table	13-2	13-3		13-3A

Table 13-3B: Summary of Dilution Tradeoffs

In Table 13-3B we summarize the dilution options that we have seen in Tables 13-2, 13-3, and 13-3A to get a feel for the tradeoffs between type 1 and type 2 dilution. In Table 13-2, where we allowed the ESOP to bear all dilution, the ESOP experienced dilution of 6.36%. In Table 13-3, by apportioning one-third of the dilution to him or herself, the seller reduced type 1 dilution by 6.36% − 4.24% = 2.12% (Table 13-3B, D8) and undertook type 2 dilution of 1.80% (D9). The result is that the ESOP bears dilution of 4.24% (C8) and the owner bears 1.8% (C9). In Table 13-3A we allowed the seller to bear all dilution rather than the ESOP. The seller thereby eliminated the 6.36% type 1 dilution and accepted 5.41% type 2 dilution.

Judging by the results seen in Table 13-3B, it appears that when the seller takes on a specific level of type 2 dilution, the decrease in type 1 dilution is greater than the corresponding increase in type 2 dilution. This turns out to be correct in all cases, as proven in the Appendix A, the Mathematical Appendix.

As mentioned in the introduction, the reader may wish to skip to the conclusion section. The following material aids in understanding dilution, but it does not contain any new formulas of practical significance.

THE ITERATIVE APPROACH

We now proceed to develop formulas to measure the engineered value per share that, when paid by the ESOP, will eliminate dilution to the ESOP. We accomplish this by performing several iterations of calculations. Using iteration, we will calculate the payment to the owner, which becomes the ESOP loan, and the post-transaction fair market values of the firm and the ESOP.

In our first iteration the seller pays the ESOP the pre-transaction FMV without regard for the ESOP loan. The existence of the ESOP loan then causes the post-transaction values of the firm and the ESOP to decline, which means the post-transaction value of the ESOP is lower than the pre-transaction value paid to the owner.

In our second iteration we calculate an engineered payment to the owner that will attempt to equal the post-transaction value at the end of the first iteration. In the second iteration the payment to the owner is less than the pre-transaction price because we have considered the ESOP loan from the first iteration in our second iteration valuation. Because the payment is lower in this iteration, the ESOP loan is lower than it is in the first iteration. We follow through with several iterations until we arrive at a steady-state value, where the engineered payment to the owner exactly equals the post-transaction value of the ESOP. This enables us to eliminate all type 1 dilution to the ESOP and shift it to the owner as type 2 dilution.

Iteration #1

We denote the pre-transaction value of the firm before considering the lifetime ESOP administration cost as V_{1B}.

$$V_{1B} = \text{pre-transaction value} \qquad (13\text{-}5)$$

The value of the firm after deducting the lifetime ESOP costs but before considering the ESOP loan is:[11]

$$V_{1A} = V_{1B} - E = V_{1B} - V_{1B}e = V_{1B}(1 - e) \qquad (13\text{-}5a)$$

The owner sells $p\%$ of the stock to the ESOP, so the ESOP would pay p times the value of the firm. However, we also need to adjust the payment for the degree of marketability and control of the ESOP. Therefore, the ESOP pays the owner V_{1A} multiplied by $p \times D_E$, or:

$$L_1 = pD_EV_{1A} = pD_EV_{1B}(1 - e) \qquad (13\text{-}5b)$$

Our next step is to compute the net present value of the loan. In this chapter we greatly simplify this procedure over the more complex calculation in my original article (Abrams 1993).[12]

The net present value of the payments of any loan discounted at the loan rate is the principal of the loan. Since both the interest and principal payments on ESOP loans are tax deductible, the after-tax cost of the ESOP loan is simply the principal of the loan multiplied by one minus the tax rate.[13] Therefore:

$$\text{NPVL}_1 = (1 - t)pD_EV_{1B}(1 - e) \qquad (13\text{-}5c)$$

Iteration #2

We have now finished the first iteration and are ready to begin iteration #2. We begin by subtracting equation (13-5c), the net present value of the ESOP loan, from the pre-transaction value, or:

$$
\begin{aligned}
V_{2B} &= V_{1B} - (1 - t)pD_EV_{1B}(1 - e) \\
&= V_{1B}[1 - pD_E(1 - t)(1 - e)] \qquad (13\text{-}6)
\end{aligned}
$$

We again subtract the lifetime ESOP costs to arrive at V_{2A}.

$$V_{2A} = V_{2B} - E \qquad (13\text{-}6a)$$

$$V_{2A} = V_{1B}[1 - pD_E(1 - t)(1 - e)] - V_{1B}e \qquad (13\text{-}6b)$$

Factoring out the V_{1B}, we get:

---

11. V_{1A} is the only iteration of V_{jA} where we do not consider the cost of the loan. For $j > 1$, we do consider the after-tax cost of the ESOP loan.
12. You do not need to read that article to understand this chapter.
13. One might speculate that perhaps the appraiser should discount the loan by a rate other than the nominal rate of the loan. To do so would implicitly be saying that the firm is at a suboptimal D/E (debt/equity) ratio before the ESOP loan and that increasing debt lowers the overall cost of capital. This is closer to a matter of faith than science, as there are those that argue on each side of the fence. The opposite side of the fence is covered by two Nobel Prize winners, Merton Miller and Franco Modigliani (MM), in a seminal article (Miller and Modigliani 1958). MM's famous Proposition I states that in perfect capital markets, i.e., in the absence of taxes and transactions costs, one cannot raise the value of the firm with debt. They acknowledge a secondary tax effect of debt, which I use here literally and no further, i.e., adding debt increases the value of the equity only to the extent of the tax shield. Also, even if there is an optimal D/E ratio and the subject company is below it, it does not need an ESOP to borrow to achieve the optimal ratio.

$$V_{2A} = V_{1B}[(1 - e) - pD_E(1 - t)(1 - e)] \qquad (13\text{-}6c)$$

Factoring out the $(1 - e)$, we then come to the post-transaction value of the firm in iteration #2 of:

$$V_{2A} = V_{1B}(1 - e)[1 - pD_E(1 - t)] \qquad (13\text{-}6d)$$

It is important to recognize that we are not double-counting E, i.e., subtracting it twice. In equation (13-6) we calculate the value of the firm as its pre-transaction value minus the net present value of the loan against the firm. The latter is indirectly affected by E, but in each new iteration, we must subtract E directly in order to count it in the post-transaction value.

The post-transaction value of the ESOP loan in iteration #2 is $p \times D_E \times$ (13-6d), or:

$$L_2 = pD_E V_{1B}(1 - e)[1 - pD_E(1 - t)] \qquad (13\text{-}6e)$$

The net present value of the loan is:

$$\text{NPVL}_2 = (1 - t)pD_E V_{1B}(1 - e)[1 - (1 - t)pD_E] \qquad (13\text{-}6f)$$

Iteration #3

We now begin the third iteration of value. The third iteration FMV before lifetime ESOP costs is $V_{1B} - \text{NPVL}_2$, or:

$$V_{3B} = V_{1B} - (1 - t)pD_E V_{1B}(1 - e)[1 - (1 - t)pD_E] \qquad (13\text{-}7)$$

Factoring out V_{1B}, we have:

$$V_{3B} = V_{1B}\{1 - pD_E(1 - t)(1 - e)[1 - (1 - t)pD_E]\} \qquad (13\text{-}7a)$$

Multiplying terms, we get:

$$V_{3B} = V_{1B}[1 - pD_E(1 - t)(1 - e) + p^2D_E^2(1 - t)^2(1 - e)] \qquad (13\text{-}7b)$$

$$V_{3A} = V_{3B} - E \qquad (13\text{-}7c)$$

$$V_{3A} = V_{1B}[1 - pD_E(1 - t)(1 - e) + p^2D_E^2(1 - t)^2(1 - e) - e] \qquad (13\text{-}7d)$$

Moving the e at the right immediately after the 1:

$$V_{3A} = V_{1B}[(1 - e) - pD_E(1 - t)(1 - e) \\ + p^2D_E^2(1 - t)^2(1 - e)] \qquad (13\text{-}7e)$$

Factoring out the $(1 - e)$:

$$V_{3A} = V_{1B}(1 - e)[1 - pD_E(1 - t) + p^2D_E^2(1 - t)] \qquad (13\text{-}7f)$$

Note that the 1 in the square brackets $= p^0 D_E^0(1 - t)^0$

Iteration #n

Continuing this pattern, it is clear that the nth iteration leads to the following formula:

$$V_{nA} = V_{1B}(1 - e) \sum_{j=0}^{n-1} (-1)^j p^j D_E^j(1 - t)^j \qquad (13\text{-}8)$$

This is an oscillating geometric sequence,[14] which leads to the following solutions. The ultimate post-transaction value of the firm is:

$$V_{nA} = V_{1B} \frac{1 - e}{1 - [- pD_E(1 - t)]}$$

or, dropping the subscript A and simplifying: (13-8a)
post-transaction value of the firm—
with type 1 dilution = 0[15]

$$V_n = V_{1B} \frac{1 - e}{1 + (1 - t)pD_E} \qquad (13\text{-}9)$$

Note that this is the same equation as (13-3n). We arrive at the same result from two different approaches.

The post-transaction value of the ESOP is $p \times D_E \times$ the value of the firm, or:

$$L_n = V_{1B} \frac{pD_E(1 - e)}{1 + (1 - t)pD_E}$$

post-transaction value of the ESOP—
with type 1 dilution = 0 (13-10)

This is the same solution as equation (13-3j), after multiplying by V_{1B}. The iterative approach solutions in equations (13-9) and (13-10) confirm the direct approach solutions of equations (13-3n) and (13-3j).

SUMMARY

In this chapter we developed formulas to calculate the post-transaction values of the firm, ESOP, and the payment to the owner, both pre-transaction and post-transaction, as well as the related dilution. We also derived formulas for eliminating the dilution in both scenarios, as well as for specifying any desired level of dilution. Additionally, we explored the trade-offs between type 1 and type 2 dilution.

Advantages of Results

The big advantages of these results are:

1. If the owner insists on being paid at the pre-transaction value, as most will, the appraiser can now immediately calculate the dilutive effects on the value of the ESOP and report that in the initial valuation report.[16] Therefore, the employees will be

---

14. For the geometric sequence to work, $|pD_E(1 - t)| < 1|$, which will almost always be the case.
15. The reason the e term is in the numerator and not the denominator like the other terms is that the lifetime cost of the ESOP is fixed, i.e., it does not vary as a proportion of the value of the firm (or the ESOP), as that changes in each iteration.
16. Many ESOP trustees prefer this information to remain as supplementary information outside of the report.

entering the transaction with both eyes open and will not be disgruntled or suspicious as to why the value, on average, declines at the next valuation. This will also provide a real benchmark to assess the impact of the ESOP itself on profitability.

2. For owners who are willing to eliminate the dilution to the ESOP or at least reduce it, this chapter provides the formulas to do so and the ability to calculate the trade-offs between type 1 and type 2 dilution.

Function of ESOP Loan

An important byproduct of this analysis is that it answers the question of what is the function of the ESOP loan. Obviously it functions as a financing vehicle, but suppose you were advising a very cash rich firm that could fund the payment to the owner in cash. Is there any other function of the ESOP loan? The answer is yes. The ESOP loan can increase the value of the firm in two ways:

1. It can be used to shield income at the firm's highest income tax rate. To the extent that the ESOP payment is large enough to cause pre-tax income to drop to lower tax brackets, that portion shields income at lower than the marginal rate and lowers the value of the firm and the ESOP.

2. If the ESOP payment in the first year is larger than pre-tax income, the firm cannot make immediate use of the entire tax deduction in the first year. The unused deduction will remain as a carryover, but it will suffer from a present value effect.

Common Sense Is Required

A certain amount of common sense is required in applying these formulas. In extreme transactions such as those approaching a 100% sale to the ESOP, we need to realize that not only can tax rates change, but payments on the ESOP loan may entirely eliminate net income and reduce the present value of the tax benefit of the ESOP loan payments. In addition, the viability of the firm itself may be seriously in question, and it is likely that the appraiser will have to increase the discount rate for a post-transaction valuation. Therefore, one must use these formulas with at least two dashes of common sense.

To Whom Should the Dilution Belong?

Appraisers almost unanimously consider the pre-transaction value appropriate, yet there has been considerable controversy on this topic. The problem is the apparent financial sleight of hand that occurs when the post-transaction value of the firm and the ESOP precipitously declines immediately after doing the transaction. On the surface, it somehow seems unfair to the ESOP. In this section we will explore that question.

Definitions

Let's begin to address this issue by assessing the post-transaction fair market value balance sheet. We will use the following definitions:

Pre-Transaction	Post-Transaction
A_1 = assets	A_2 = assets = A_1 (assets have not changed)
L_1 = liabilities	L_2 = liabilities
C_1 = capital	C_2 = capital

Note that the subscript 1 refers to pre-transaction and the subscript 2 refers to post-transaction.

The Mathematics of the Post-Transaction Fair Market Value Balance Sheet

The nonmathematical reader may wish to skip or skim this section. It is more theoretical and does not result in any usable formulas.

The fundamental accounting equation representing the pre-transaction balance sheet is:

$$A_1 = L_1 + C_1 \quad \text{pre-transaction FMV balance sheet} \qquad (13\text{-}11)$$

Assuming the ESOP bears all of the dilution, after the sale liabilities increase and capital decreases by the sum of the after-tax cost of the ESOP loan and the lifetime ESOP costs,[17] or:

$$C_1 \times [(13\text{-}1c) + (13\text{-}1d)]$$

$$\text{increase in liabilities and decrease in debt} \qquad (13\text{-}12)$$

As noted in the definitions, assets have not changed. Only liabilities and capital have changed.[18] Thus the post-transaction balance sheet is:

$$A_2 = \{L_1 + C_1[(1 - t)pD_E + e]\} + \{C_1 - C_1[(1 - t)pD_E + e]\} \quad (13\text{-}13)$$

The first term in braces equals L_2, the post-transaction liabilities, and the second term in braces equals C_2, the post-transaction capital. Note that $A_2 = A_1$. Equation (13-13) simplifies to:

$$A_2 = \{L_1 + C_1[(1 - t)pD_E + e]\} + \{C_1[1 - (1 - t)pD_E + e]\}$$

$$\text{post-transaction balance sheet} \qquad (13\text{-}14)$$

Equation (13-14) gives us an algebraic expression for the post-transaction fair market value balance sheet when the ESOP bears all of the dilution.

Analyzing a Simple Sale

Only two aspects relevant to this discussion are unique about a sale to an ESOP: (1) tax deductibility of the loan principal, and (2) forgiveness of the ESOP's debt. Let's analyze a simple sale to a non-ESOP buyer and later to an ESOP buyer. For simplicity we will ignore tax benefits of all loans throughout this example.

---

17. Again, these should only be the incremental costs if the ESOP is replacing another pension plan.
18. For simplicity, we are assuming the company hasn't yet paid any of the ESOP's lifetime costs. If it has, then that amount is a reduction in assets rather than an increase in liabilities. Additionally, the tax shield on the ESOP loan could have been treated as an asset rather than a contraliability, as we have done for simplicity. This is not intended to be an exhaustive treatise on ESOP accounting.

Suppose the fair market value of all assets is $10 million before and after the sale. Pre-transaction liabilities are zero, so capital is worth $10 million, pre-transaction. If a buyer pays the seller personally $5 million for one-half of the capital stock of the Company, the transaction does not impact the value of the firm—ignoring adjustments for control and marketability. If the buyer takes out a personal loan for the $5 million and pays the seller, there is also no impact on the value of the company. In both cases the buyer owns one-half of a $10 million firm, and it was a fair transaction.

If the corporation takes out the loan on behalf of the buyer but the buyer ultimately has to repay the corporation, then the real liability is to the buyer, not the corporation, and there is no impact on the value of the stock—it is still worth $5 million. The corporation is a mere conduit for the loan to the buyer.

What happens to the firm's value if the corporation takes out and eventually repays the loan? The assets are still worth $10 million post-transaction.[19] Now there are $5 million in liabilities, so the equity is worth $5 million. The buyer owns one-half of a firm worth $5 million, so his or her stock is only worth $2.5 million. Was the buyer hoodwinked?

The possible confusion over value clearly arises because it is the corporation itself that is taking out the loan to fund the buyer's purchase of stock, and the corporation—not the buyer—ultimately repays the loan. By having the corporation repay the loan, the other shareholder is forgiving his or her half of a $5 million loan and thus gifting $2.5 million to the buyer.[20] Thus, the "buyer" ultimately receives a gift of $2.5 million in the form of company stock. This is true whether the buyer is an individual or an ESOP.[21]

Dilution to Non-Selling Owners

When there are additional business owners who do not sell to the ESOP, they experience dilution of their interests without the benefit of getting paid. Conceptually, these owners have participated in giving the ESOP a gift by having the Company repay the debt on behalf of the ESOP.

To calculate the dilution to other owners, we begin with the post-transaction value of the firm in equation (13-1e) and repeat the equation as (13-1e*). Then we will calculate the equivalent equations for the non-selling owner as we did for the ESOP in equations (13-1f) and (13-1g), and we will relabel those equations by adding an asterisk.

$$1 - (1 - t)pD_E - e$$

post-transaction value of the firm (repeated)   (13-1e*)

If the nonselling shareholder owns the fraction q of the outstanding stock, then his or her post-transaction value is:

---

19. There is a second-order effect of the firm being more highly leveraged and thus riskier that may affect value (and which we are ignoring here). See Chapter 14.

20. The other half of the forgiveness is a wash—the buyer forgiving it to himself or herself.

21. This does not mean that an ESOP brings nothing to the table in a transaction. It does bring tax deductibility of the loan principal as well as the Section 1042 rollover.

$$q - q(1 - t)pD_E - qe$$

$$\text{post-transaction value of nonselling shareholder's stock} \quad \text{(13-1f*)}$$

Finally, we calculate dilution to the nonselling shareholder as his or her pre-transaction value of q minus the pre-transaction value in equation (13-1f*), or:

$$q[(1 - t)pD_E + e]$$

$$\text{dilution to nonselling shareholder's stock}[22] \quad \text{(13-1g*)}$$

The dilution formula (13-1g*) tells us that the dilution to the non-selling shareholder is simply his or her ownership, q, multiplied by the dilution in value to the firm itself, which is the sum of the after-tax cost of the ESOP loan and the lifetime costs. Here, because we are not multiplying by the ESOP's ownership modified for its unique marketability and control attributes, we do not get the squared terms that we did in equation (13-1f) and (13-1g).

It is also important to note that equations (13-1f*) and (13-1g*) do not account for any possible increase in value the owner might experience as a result of having greater relative control of the firm. For example, if there were two 50% owners pre-transaction and one sells 30% to the ESOP, post-transaction the remaining 50% owner has relatively more control than he or she had before the transaction. To the extent that we might ascribe additional value to that increase in relative control, we would adjust the valuation formulas. This would mitigate the dilution in equation (13-1g*).

Legal Issues

As mentioned above, appraisers almost unanimously consider the pre-transaction value appropriate. Also mentioned earlier in the chapter, case law and Department of Labor proposed regulations indicate the pre-transaction value is the one to be used. Nevertheless, there is ongoing controversy going back to *Farnum*, a case in which the Department of Labor withdrew before going to court, that the post-transaction value may the most appropriate price to pay the seller.

In the previous section we demonstrated that the ESOP is receiving a gift, not really paying anything for its stock. Therefore, there is no economic justification for reducing the payment to the owner below the pre-transaction fair market value, which is the price that the seller would receive from any other buyer. If the ESOP (or any party on its behalf) demands that it "pay" no more than post-transaction value, it is tantamount to saying, "The gift you are giving me is not big enough."

While the dilution may belong to the ESOP, it is nevertheless an important consideration in determining the fairness of the transaction for

---

22. One would also need to consider adjusting for each nonselling shareholder's control and marketability attributes. To do so, we would have to add a term in equation (13-1g*) immediately after the q. The term would be the owner's equivalent of D_E, except customized for his or her ownership attributes. The details of such a calculation are beyond the scope of this chapter.

purposes of a fairness opinion. If a bank loans $10 million to the ESOP for a 100% sale, with no recourse or personal guarantees of the owner, we may likely decide it is not a fair transaction to the ESOP and its participants. We would have serious questions about the ESOP's probability of becoming a long-range retirement program, given the huge debt load of the Company post-transaction.

Charity

While the dilution technically belongs to the ESOP, I consider it my duty to inform the seller of the dilution phenomenon and how it works. While affirming the seller's right to receive fair market value undiminished by dilution, I do mention that if the seller has any charitable motivations to his or her employees—which a minority do—then voluntarily accepting some of the dilution will leave the Company and the ESOP in better shape. Of course, in a partial sale it also leaves the remainder of the owner's stock at a higher value than it would have had with the ESOP bearing all of the dilution.

BIBLIOGRAPHY

Abrams, Jay B. 1993. "An Iterative Procedure to Value Leveraged ESOPs." *Valuation* (January): 71–103.
———. 1997. "ESOPs: Measuring and Apportioning Dilution." *Valuation* (June): 3–25.
Miller, Merton, and Franco Modigliani. 1958. "The Cost of Capital, Corporation Finance, and the Theory of Investment." *American Economic Review* 48: 61–97.

APPENDIX A: MATHEMATICAL APPENDIX

The purpose of this appendix is to perform comparative static analysis, as is commonly done in economics, on the equations for dilution in the body of the chapter in order to understand the tradeoffs between type 1 and type 2 dilution.

We use the same definitions in the appendix as in the chapter. Type 1 dilution is equal to the payment to the owner less the post-transaction value of the ESOP, or $x -$ (13-3f):

$$D_1 = x - [pD_E(1 - e) - (1 - t)pD_Ex] \qquad \text{(A13-1)}$$

Factoring out the x,

$$D_1 = x[1 + (1 - t)pD_E] - pD_E(1 - e) \qquad \text{(A13-2)}$$

We can investigate the impact on type 1 dilution for each $1 change in payment to the owner by taking the partial derivative of (A13-2) with respect to x.

$$\frac{\partial D_1}{\partial x} = 1 + (1 - t)pD_E > 1 \qquad \text{(A13-3)}$$

Equation (A13-3) tells us that each additional dollar paid to the owner increases dilution to the ESOP by more than $1.

A full payment to the owner (the default payment) is pD_E for $1 of pre-transaction value. We pay the owner x, and the difference of the two is D_2, the type 2 dilution.

$$D_2 = pD_E - x \qquad \text{(A13-4)}$$

We can investigate the impact on type 2 for each $1 change in payment to the owner by taking the partial derivative of (A13-4) with respect to x.

$$\frac{\partial D_2}{\partial x} = -1 \qquad \text{(A13-5)}$$

Type 2 dilution moves in an equal but opposite direction from the amount paid to the owner, which must be the case to make any sense. Together, equations (A13-3) and (A13-5) tell us that each additional dollar paid the owner increases the dilution to the ESOP more than it reduces the dilution to the owner. We can also see this by taking the absolute value of the ratio of the partial derivatives:

$$\frac{|\partial D_2 / \partial x|}{|\partial D_1 / \partial x|} = \frac{1}{1 + (1 - t)pD_E} < 1 \qquad \text{(A13-6)}$$

Significance of the Results

Equation (A13-6) demonstrates that for every $1 of payment forgone by the owner, the dilution incurred by the owner will always be less than the dilution eliminated to the ESOP. The reason for this is that every $1 the owner forgoes in payment costs him $1 in type 2 dilution, yet it saves the ESOP:

1. The $1, plus
2. It reduces the ESOP loan by pD_E and saves the ESOP the after-tax cost of the lowered amount of the loan, or $(1 - t)pD_E$.

There appears to be some charity factor inherent in the mathematics.

Finally, we have not dealt with the fact that by the owner taking on some or all of the dilution from the ESOP loan, he or she increases the value of his or her $(1 - p)$ share of the remaining stock by reducing the dilution to it. Such an analysis has no impact on the valuation of the ESOP, but it should be considered in the decision to initiate an ESOP.

APPENDIX B: SHORTER VERSION OF CHAPTER 13

This appendix provides a bare-bones version of Chapter 13, removing all mathematical analysis and optional sections of the iterative approach and all of the second part of the chapter. The reader can then see the bottom line of the chapter without struggling through the voluminous mathematics. It will also serve as a refresher for those who have already read the chapter.

INTRODUCTION

Leveraged ESOPs have confused many firms due to their failure to understand the phenomenon of dilution and inability to quantify it. Many ESOPs have soured because employees paid appraised fair market value of the stock being sold to the ESOP, only to watch the fair market value significantly decline at the next valuation because the ESOP loan was not included in the pre-transaction fair market value. As a result, employees have felt cheated. Lawsuits have sometimes followed, further lowering the value of the firm and the ESOP.

There are several types of problems relating to the dilution phenomenon:

1. The technical problem of defining and measuring the dilution in value to the ESOP *before* it happens.
2. The business problem of getting the ESOP Trustee, participants, and selling owner(s) to agree on how to share the dilution.
3. The technical problem of how to engineer the price to accomplish the desired goals in 2.
4. The problem of how to communicate each of the foregoing to all of the participants so that all parties can enter the transaction with both eyes open and come away feeling the transaction was win–win instead of win–lose.

This chapter provides the analytical solutions to problems 1 and 3 that are necessary for resolving the business and communication problems of 2 and 4. The appraiser will be able to include the dilution in his or her initial valuation report so that employees will not be negatively surprised when the value drops at the next annual valuation. Additionally, the appraiser can provide the technical expertise to enable the parties to share the dilution, solving problem 3. Both parties will then be fully informed beforehand, facilitating a win–win transaction.

DEFINITIONS OF DILUTION

Two potential parties can experience dilution in stock values in ESOP transactions: the ESOP and the owner. The dilution that each experiences differs and can be easily confused.

Additionally, each party can experience two types of dilution: absolute and relative. Absolute dilution is defined in the section immediately below. Relative dilution is more complicated because we can calculate dilution relative to more than one base. Several formulas can be developed to calculate relative dilution, but they are beyond the scope of this book. Thus, for the remainder of this chapter, *dilution* will mean absolute dilution.

Dilution to the ESOP (Type 1 Dilution)

We define type 1 dilution as the payment to the selling owner less the post-transaction fair market value of the ESOP. This can be stated either in dollars or as a percentage of the pre-transaction value of the firm. By law, the ESOP may not pay more than fair market value to the company or to a large shareholder, though it is nowhere defined in the applicable statute whether this is pre- or post-transaction value. Case law and Department of Labor proposed regulations indicate that the pre-transaction value should be used.[23]

Dilution to the Selling Owner (Type 2 Dilution)

We define Type 2 dilution as the difference in the pre-transaction fair market value of the shares sold and the price paid to the seller. Again, this can be in dollars or as a percentage of the firm's pre-transaction value. Since it is standard industry practice for the ESOP to pay the owner the pre-transaction price, Type 2 Dilution is virtually unknown. Those sellers who wish to reduce or eliminate dilution to the ESOP can choose to sell for less than the pre-transaction fair market value.

When the ESOP bears all of the dilution, we have only type 1 dilution. When the owner removes all dilution from the ESOP by absorbing it himself, then the selling price and post-transaction values are equal and we have only type 2 dilution. If the owner absorbs only part of the dilution from the ESOP, then the dilution is shared, and we have both type 1 and type 2 dilution.

As we will show in Table 13-3B and the Mathematical Appendix, when the seller takes on a specific level of type 2 dilution, the decrease in type 1 dilution is greater than the corresponding increase in type 2 dilution.

The seller also should consider the effects of dilution on his or her remaining stock in the firm, but that is beyond the scope of this book.

Defining Terms

We first define some of terms appearing in the various equations.
Let:

p = percentage of firm sold to the ESOP, assumed at 30%

t = combined federal and state corporate income tax rate, assumed at 40%

r = the annual loan interest rate, assumed at 10%

i = the monthly loan interest rate = $r/12$ = 0.8333% monthly

E = the lifetime costs of initiating and running the ESOP. These are generally legal fees, appraisal fees, ESOP administration fees, and internal administration costs. We assume initial costs of $20,000 and annual costs of $10,000 growing at 6% each year. Table 13-1 shows a sample calculation of the lifetime costs of the ESOP as $40,000.[24]

e = lifetime ESOP costs as a percentage of the pre-transaction value = E/V_{1B} = $40,000/$1 million = 4%.

D_E = one minus net Discounts (or plus net premiums) at the ESOP level. This factor converts the fair market value of the entire firm

---

23. *Donovan v. Cunningham,* 716 F.2d 1467. 29 CFR 2510.3-18(b).
24. How to calculate the pre-transaction value of the firm is outside the scope of this article.

on an illiquid control level (V_{1B}) to a fair market value (on a 100% basis) at the ESOP's level of marketability and control ($D_E V_{1B}$). If we assume that the ESOP provides complete marketability (which normally one should not, but we are doing so here for didactic purposes), then to calculate D_E we must merely reverse out the control premium that was applied to the entire firm (in the calculation of V_{1B}), which we will assume was 43%, and reverse out the discount for lack of marketability that was applied, which we will assume was 29%.[25] The result is: $D_E = [1/(1 + 43\%)] \times [1/(1 - 29\%)] = 0.7 \times 1.4 = 0.98$. In other words, the net effect of reversing out the assumed discount and premium is a 2% net discount. It could also be a net premium if the minority discount were less or the premium for marketability were higher. Also, if we were to assume that the ESOP shares were not at a marketable minority level, other adjustments would be required.

D_1 = type 1 dilution (dilution to the ESOP)

D_2 = type 2 dilution (dilution to the seller)

FMV = fair market value

TABLE 13-1: CALCULATION OF LIFETIME ESOP COSTS

We begin by calculating the lifetime cost of the ESOP, including the legal, appraisal, and administration costs, which are collectively referred to throughout this chapter as the administration costs or as the lifetime ESOP costs.

The estimated annual operating costs of the ESOP in Table 13-1 are $10,000 pretax (B5), or $6,000 after-tax (B6). We assume an annual required rate of return of 25% (B7). Let's further assume ESOP administration costs will rise by 5% a year (B8). We can then calculate the lifetime value of the annual cost by multiplying the first year's cost by a Gordon model multiple (GM) using an end-of-year assumption. The GM formula is $1/(r - g)$, or $1/(0.25 - 0.05) = 5.000$ (B9). Multiplying 5.000 by $6,000, we obtain a value of $30,000 (B10).

We next calculate the immediate costs of initiating the ESOP at time zero, which we will assume are $20,000 (B11), or $12,000 after-tax (B12). Adding $30,000 plus 12,000, we arrive at a lifetime cost of $42,000 for running the ESOP (B13), which for simplicity we round off to $40,000 (B14), or 4% of the pre-transaction value of $1 million.[26] Adopting the previous definitions, $E = \$40,000$ and $e = 4\%$.

The previous example presumes that the ESOP is not replacing another pension plan. If the ESOP is replacing another pension plan, then it is only the incremental lifetime cost of the ESOP that we would calculate here.

---

25. These are arbitrary assumptions chosen for mathematical ease.

26. For simplicity, we do not add a control premium and deduct a discount for lack of marketability at the firm level and then reverse that procedure at the ESOP level, as I did in Abrams (1993).

THE DIRECT APPROACH

Using the direct approach, we calculate all valuation formulas directly through algebraic substitution. We will develop post-transaction valuation formulas for the following situations:

1. All dilution remains with the ESOP.
2. All dilution goes to the owner.
3. The ESOP and the owner share the dilution.

We will begin with 1. The owner will be paid pre-transaction price, leaving the ESOP with all of the dilution in value. The following series of equations will enable us to quantify the dilution. All values are stated as a fraction of each $1 of pre-transaction value.

FMV Equations—All Dilution to the ESOP (Type 1 Dilution; No Type 2 Dilution)

$$1 \quad \text{pre-transaction value} \qquad \text{(A13-7)}$$

We pay the owner the $p\%$ he or she sells to the ESOP reduced or increased by D_E, the net discounts or premiums at the ESOP level. For every $1 of pre-transaction value, the payment to the owner is thus:

$$pD_E \quad \text{paid to owner in cash} = \text{ESOP loan} \qquad \text{(A13-7a)}$$

$$tpD_E \quad \text{tax savings on ESOP loan} \qquad \text{(A13-7b)}$$

The after-tax cost of the loan is the amount paid to the owner less the tax savings of the loan, or equations (A13-7a) and (A13-7b).

$$(1 - t)pD_E \quad \text{after-tax cost of the ESOP loan} \qquad \text{(A13-7c)}$$

$$e \quad \text{after-tax lifetime cost of the ESOP} \qquad \text{(A13-7d)}$$

When we subtract (A13-7c) plus (A13-7d) from (A13-7), we obtain the remaining value of the firm:

$$1 - (1 - t)pD_E - e \quad \text{post-transaction value of the firm} \qquad \text{(A13-7e)}$$

Since the ESOP owns $p\%$ of the firm, the post-transaction value of the ESOP is $p \times D_E \times$ (A13-7e):

$$pD_E - (1 - t)p^2 D_E^2 - pD_E e$$
$$\text{post-transaction value of the ESOP} \qquad \text{(A13-7f)}$$

The dilution to the ESOP (type 1 dilution) is the amount paid to the owner minus the value of the ESOP's $p\%$ of the firm, or (A13-7a) − (A13-7f):

$$pD_E - [pD_E - (1 - t)p^2 D_E^2 - pD_E e]$$
$$= (1 - t)p^2 D_E^2 + pD_E e \quad \text{dilution to ESOP} \qquad \text{(A13-7g)}$$

Table 13-2, Sections 1 and 2: Post-transaction FMV with All Dilution to the ESOP

Now that we have established the formulas for calculating the FMV of the firm when all dilution goes to the ESOP, let's look at a concrete example in Table 13-2. The table consists of three sections. Section 1, rows 5–10, is the operating parameters of the model. Section 2 shows the calculation of the post-transaction values of the firm, ESOP, and the dilution to the ESOP according to equations (A13-7e), (A13-7f), and (A13-7g), respectively, in rows 12–18. Rows 21–26 prove the accuracy of the results, as explained below.

Section 3 shows the calculation of the post-transaction values of the firm and the ESOP when there is no dilution to the ESOP. We will cover that part of the table later. In the meantime, let's review the numerical example in section 2.

B13 contains the results of applying equation (A13-7e) using section 1 parameters to calculate the post-transaction value of the firm, which is $0.783600 per $1 of pre-transaction value. We multiply the $0.783600 by the $1 million pre-transaction value (B5) to calculate the post-transaction value of the firm = $783,100 (B14). The post-transaction value of the ESOP according to equation (A13-7f) is $0.230378[27] (B15) × $1 million pre-transaction value (B5) = $230,378 (B16).

We calculate dilution to the ESOP according to equation (A13-7g) as $(1 - 0.4) \times 0.3^2 \times 0.98^2 + 0.3 \times 0.98 \times 0.04 = 0.063622$ (B17). When we multiply the dilution as a percentage by the pre-transaction value of $1 million, we get dilution of $63,622 (B18, B26).

We now prove these results and the formulas in rows 21–26. The payment to the owner is $1 million × 30% × 0.98 (net of ESOP discounts/premiums) = $294,000 (B22). The ESOP takes out a $294,000 loan to pay the owner, which the company will have to pay. The after-tax cost of the loan is $(1 - t)$ multiplied by the amount of the loan, or 0.6 × $294,000 = $176,400 (B23). Subtracting the after tax cost of the loan and the $40,000 lifetime ESOP costs from the pre-transaction value, we come to a post-transaction value of the firm of $783,600 (B24), which is identical to the value obtained by direct calculation using formula (A13-7e) in B14. The post-transaction value of the ESOP is pD_E × post-transaction FMV—firm, or 0.3 × 0.98 × $783,600 = $230,378 (B25, B16). The dilution to the ESOP is the payment to the owner minus the post-transaction value of the ESOP, or $294,000 (B22) − $230,378 (B25) = $63,622 (B26, B18). We have now proved the direct calculations in rows 14, 16, and 18.

The Post-transaction Value Is a Parabola

Equation (A13-7f), the formula for the post-transaction value of the ESOP, is a parabola. We can see this more easily by rewriting (A13-7f) as

$$V = -D_E^2(1 - t)p^2 + D_E(1 - e)p$$

where V is the post-transaction value of the ESOP. Figure 13-1 shows this

---

27. Which itself is equal to pD_E × the post-transaction value of the firm, or B6 × B7 × B14.

function graphically. The straight line, pD_E, is a slight modification of a simple 45° line $y = x$ (or in this case $V = p$), except multiplied by $D_E = 98\%$. This line is the payment to the owner when the ESOP bears all of the dilution. The vertical distance of the parabola (equation [13-1f]) from the straight line is the dilution of the ESOP, defined by equation (A13-7g), which is itself a parabola. Figure 13-1 should actually stop where $p = 100\%$, but it has been extended merely to show the completion of the parabola, since there is no economic meaning for $p > 100\%$.

We can calculate the high point of the parabola, which is the maximum post-transaction value of the ESOP, by taking the first partial derivative of equation (A13-7f) with respect to p and setting the equation to zero. This solves to

$$p = \frac{(1 - e)}{2(1 - t)D_e}$$

or $p = 81.63265\%$. Substituting this number into equation (A13-7f) gives us the maximum value of the ESOP of $V = 38.4\%$.[28] This means that if the owner sells any greater portion than 81.63265% of the firm to the ESOP, he actually *decreases* the value of the ESOP, assuming a 40% tax rate and no outside capital infusions into the sale. The lower the tax rate, the more the parabola shifts to the left of the vertical line, until at $t = 0$, where most of the parabola is completed before the line.[29]

FMV Equations—All Dilution to the Owner (Type 2 Dilution)

Let's now assume that instead of paying the owner pD_E, the ESOP pays him some unspecified amount, x. Accordingly, we rederive (A13-7)–(A13-7g) with that single change and label our new equations (A13-8)–(A13-8j).

1	pre-transaction value	(A13-8)
x	paid to owner in cash = ESOP loan	(A13-8a)
tx	tax savings on ESOP loan	(A13-8b)
$(1 - t)x$	after-tax cost of the ESOP loan	(A13-8c)
e	after-tax ESOP cost	(A13-8d)

When we subtract (A13-8c) plus (A13-8d) from (A13-8), we come to the remaining value of the firm of:

---

28. We can verify this is a maximum rather than minimum value by taking the second partial derivative, $\partial^2 V / \partial p^2 = -2(1 - t)D_E^2 < 0$, which confirms the maximum.
29. This is because equation (13-1f) becomes $V = -D_E^2 p^2 + D_E(1 - e)p$. Given our D_E and e, V is then approximately equal to $-0.92(p^2 - p)$. If $t = 0$, $e = 0$, and there were no discounts and premiums at the ESOP level, i.e., $D_E = 1$, then the owner would be paid p, the post-transaction value of the firm would be $1 - p$, and the post-transaction value of the ESOP would be $p(1 - p)$, or $-p^2 + p$. This parabola would finish at $p = 1$. The maximum post-transaction ESOP value would be 25% at $p = 50\%$.

$$(1 - e) - (1 - t)x \quad \text{post-transaction value of the firm} \quad \text{(A13-8e)}$$

Since the ESOP owns $p\%$ of the firm and the ESOP bears its net discount, the post-transaction value of the ESOP is $p \times D_E x$ (A13-8e), or:

$$pD_E(1 - e) - (1 - t)pD_E x$$

$$\text{post-transaction value of the ESOP} \quad \text{(A13-8f)}$$

We can eliminate dilution to the ESOP entirely by specifying that the payment to the owner, x, equals the post-transaction value of the ESOP (A13-8f), or:

$$x = pD_E(1 - e) - (1 - t)pD_E x \quad \text{(A13-8g)}$$

which solves to:

$$x = \frac{pD_E (1 - e)}{1 + (1 - t)pD_E}$$

$$\text{post-transaction FMV of ESOP, all dilution to owner} \quad \text{(A13-8j)}$$

Substituting equation (A13-8j) into the x term in equation (A13-8e), the post-transaction value of the firm is:

$$\frac{1 - e}{1 + (1 - t)pD_E} \quad \text{post-transaction value of the firm---}$$

$$\text{type 1 dilution} = 0 \quad \text{(A13-8n)}$$

The dilution to the seller is the pre-transaction FMV of shares sold minus the price paid, or:

$$pD_E - \frac{1 - e}{1 + (1 - t)pD_E} \quad \text{(A13-8o)}$$

Table 13-2, Section 3: FMV Calculations—All Dilution to the Seller

In section 3 we quantify the engineered price that eliminates all dilution to the ESOP, which according to equation (A13-8n) is:

$$\$1 \text{ million} \times \frac{(1 - 0.04)}{[1 + (0.6) \times (0.3) \times (0.98)]}$$

$$= \$1 \text{ million} \times 0.816049 \text{ (B29)} = \$816,049 \text{ (C29)}$$

Similarly, the value of the ESOP is: $0.3 \times 0.98 \times 0.816049 \times \$1,000,000 = \$239,918$ (C30) which is also the same amount that the owner is paid in cash. We can prove this correct as follows:

1. The ESOP borrows $239,918 (B37) to pay the owner and takes out a loan for the same amount, which the firm pays.

2. The firm gets a tax deduction, which has a net present value of its marginal tax rate multiplied by the principal of the ESOP loan, or 40% × $239,918, or $95,967 (B38), which after being subtracted from the payment to the owner leaves an after-tax

cost of the payment to the owner (which is identical to the after-tax cost of the ESOP loan) of $143,951 (B39).

3. We subtract the after-tax cost of the ESOP loan of $143,951 and the $40,000 lifetime ESOP costs from the pre-transaction value of $1 million to arrive at the final value of the firm of $816,049 (B40). This is the same result as the direct calculation by formula in B29, which proves (A13-8n). Multiplying by pD_E (0.3 × 0.98 = 0.297) would lead to the same result as in B30, which proves the accuracy of (A13-8j).

We can also prove the dilution formulas in section 3. The seller experiences dilution equal to the normative price he or she would have received if he or she were not willing to reduce the sales price, i.e., $294,000 (B22) less the engineered selling price of $239,918 (C30), or $54,082 (C33). This is the same result as using a direct calculation from equation (A13-8o) of 5.4082% (C31) × the pre-transaction price of $1 million = $54,082 (C32).

The net result of this approach is that the owner has shifted the entire dilution from the ESOP to himself. Thus, the ESOP no longer experiences any dilution in value. While this action is very noble on the part of the owner, in reality few owners are willing and able to do so.

Sharing the Dilution

The direct approach also allows us to address the question of how to share the dilution. If the owner does not wish to place all the dilution on the ESOP or absorb it personally, he or she can assign a portion to both parties. By subtracting the post-transaction value of the ESOP (A13-8f) from the cash to the owner (A13-8a), we obtain the amount of dilution. We can then specify that this dilution should be equal to a fraction k of the default dilution, i.e., the dilution to the ESOP when the ESOP bears all of the dilution. In our nomenclature, the post-transaction value of the ESOP − dilution to the ESOP = k × (default dilution to the ESOP). Therefore,

$$k = \frac{\text{Actual Dilution to ESOP}}{\text{Default Dilution to ESOP}},$$

or k = the % dilution remaining with the ESOP

The reduction in dilution to the ESOP is $(1 - k)$. For example, if k = 33%, the ESOP bears 33% of the dilution; the reduction in the amount of dilution borne by ESOP is 67% (from the default figure of 100%).

The formula used to calculate the payment to the owner when dilution is shared by both parties is:

$$x - [pD_E(1 - e) - (1 - t)pD_E x] = k[(1 - t)p^2 D_E^2 + pD_E e] \quad \text{(A13-9)}$$

which solves to:

$$x = \frac{pD_E(1 - e) + k[(1 - t)p^2 D_E^2 + pD_E e]}{1 + (1 - t)pD_E} \quad \text{(A13-9a)}$$

In other words, equation (A13-8a) is the formula for the amount of payment to the owner when the ESOP retains the fraction k of the default dilution. If we let $k = 0$, (A13-8a) reduces to (A13-8j), the post-transaction FMV of the ESOP when all dilution goes to the owner. When $k = 1$, (A13-9a) reduces to (A13-7a), the payment to the owner when all dilution goes to the ESOP.

Equation to Calculate Type 2 Dilution

Type 2 dilution is equal to pD_E, the pre-transaction selling price adjusted for control and marketability, minus the engineered selling price, x. Substituting equation (A13-9a) for x, we get:

$$D_2 = pD_E - \frac{pD_E(1 - e) + k[(1 - t)p^2 D_E^2 + pD_E e]}{1 + (1 - t)pD_E} \quad \text{(A13-9b)}$$

Tables 13-3 and 13-3A: Adjusting Dilution to Desired Levels

Table 13-3 is a numerical example using equation (A13-9a). We let $p = 30\%$ (B5), $D_E = 98\%$ (B6), $k = 2/3$ (B7), $t = 40\%$ (B8), and $e = 4\%$ (B9). B10 is the calculation of x, the payment to the seller—as in equation (A13-9a)—which is 27.6%. B11 is the value of the ESOP post-transaction, which we calculate according to equation (A13-8f),[30] at 23.36%. Subtracting the post-transaction value of the ESOP from the payment to the owner (27.60% − 23.36%) = 4.24% (B12) gives us the amount of type 1 dilution.

The default type 1 dilution, where the ESOP bears all of the dilution, would be $(1 - t)p^2D_E^2 + pD_E e$, according to equation (A13-7g), or 6.36% (B13). Finally, we calculate the actual dilution divided by the default dilution, or 4.24%/6.36% to arrive at a ratio of 66.67% (B14), or 2/3, which is the same as k, which proves the accuracy of equation (A13-9a). By designating the desired level of dilution to be 2/3 of the original dilution, we have reduced the dilution by 1/3, or $(1 - k)$.

If we desire dilution to the ESOP to be zero, then we substitute $k = 0$ in equation (A13-9a), and the equation reduces to

$$x = \frac{pD_E(1 - e)}{[1 + (1 - t)pD_E]}$$

which is identical to equation (A13-8j), the post-transaction value of the ESOP when the owner bears all of the dilution. You can see that in Table 13-3A, which is identical to Table 13-3 except that we have let $k = 0$ (B7), which leads to the zero dilution, as seen in B14.

Type 2 dilution appears in Table 13-3, rows 15 and 16. The owner is paid 27.6% (B10) of the pre-transaction value for 30% of the stock of the company. He normally would have been paid 29.4% of the pre-transaction value (B5 × B6 = 0.3 × 0.98 = 29.4%). Type 2 dilution is 29.4% − 27.60% = 1.80% (B15). In B16 we calculate type 2 dilution directly using equation

---

30. With pD_E factored out.

(A13-9b). Both calculations produce identical results, confirming the accuracy of (A13-9b). In Table 13-3A, where we let $k = 0$, type 2 dilution is 5.41% (B15 and B16).

Table 13-3B: Summary of Dilution Tradeoffs

In Table 13-3B we summarize the dilution options that we have seen in Tables 13-2, 13-3, and 13-3A to get a feel for the tradeoffs between type 1 and type 2 dilution. In Table 13-2, where we allowed the ESOP to bear all dilution, the ESOP experienced dilution of 6.36%. In Table 13-3, by apportioning one-third of the dilution to him or herself, the seller reduced type 1 dilution by 6.36% − 4.24% = 2.12% (Table 13-3B, D8) and undertook type 2 dilution of 1.80% (D9). The result is that the ESOP bears dilution of 4.24% (C8) and the owner bears 1.8% (C9). In Table 13-3A we allowed the seller to bear all dilution rather than the ESOP. The seller thereby eliminated the 6.36% Type 1 dilution and accepted 5.41% type 2 dilution.

Judging by the results seen in Table 13-3B, it appears that when the seller takes on a specific level of type 2 dilution, the decrease in type 1 dilution is greater than the corresponding increase in type 2 dilution. This turns out to be correct in all cases, as proven in Appendix A, the Mathematical Appendix.

SUMMARY

In this mini-chapter we developed formulas to calculate the post-transaction values of the firm, ESOP, and the payment to the owner, both pre-transaction and post-transaction, as well as the related dilution. We also derived formulas for eliminating the dilution as well as for specifying any desired level of dilution. Additionally, we explored the trade-offs between type 1 and type 2 dilution.

Advantages of Results

The big advantages of these results are:

1. If the owner insists on being paid at the pre-transaction value, as most will, the appraiser can now immediately calculate the dilutive effects on the value of the ESOP and report that in the initial valuation report.[31] Therefore, the employees will be entering the transaction with both eyes open and will not be disgruntled and/or suspicious as to why the value, on average, declines at the next valuation. This will also provide a real benchmark to assess the impact of the ESOP itself on profitability.

---

31. Many ESOP trustees prefer this information to remain as supplementary information outside of the report.

2. For owners who are willing to eliminate the dilution to the ESOP or at least reduce it, this chapter provides the formulas to do so and the ability to calculate the trade-offs between type 1 and type 2 dilution.

Function of ESOP Loan

An important byproduct of this analysis is that it answers the question of what is the function of the ESOP loan. Obviously it functions as a financing vehicle, but suppose you were advising a very cash rich firm that could fund the payment to the owner in cash. Is there any other function of the ESOP loan? The answer is yes. The ESOP loan can increase the value of the firm in two ways:

1. It can be used to shield income at the firm's highest income tax rate. To the extent that the ESOP payment is large enough to cause pre-tax income to drop to lower tax brackets, then that portion shields income at lower than the marginal rate and lowers the value of the firm and the ESOP.
2. If the ESOP payment in the first year is larger than pre-tax income, the firm cannot make immediate use of the entire tax deduction in the first year. The unused deduction will remain as a carryover, but it will suffer from a present value effect.

Common Sense Is Required

A certain amount of common sense is required in applying these formulas. In extreme transactions such as those approaching a 100% sale to the ESOP, we need to realize that not only can tax rates change, but payments on the ESOP loan may entirely eliminate net income and reduce the present value of the tax benefit of the ESOP loan payments. In addition, the viability of the firm itself may be seriously in question, and it is likely that the appraiser will have to increase the discount rate for a post-transaction valuation. Therefore, one must use these formulas with at least two dashes of common sense.

To Whom Should the Dilution Belong?

Appraisers almost unanimously consider the pre-transaction value appropriate, yet there has been considerable controversy on this topic. The problem is the apparent financial sleight of hand that occurs when the post-transaction value of the firm and the ESOP precipitously declines immediately after doing the transaction. On the surface, it somehow seems unfair to the ESOP. In this section we will explore that question.

Analyzing a Simple Sale

Only two aspects relevant to this discussion are unique about a sale to an ESOP: (1) tax deductibility of the loan principal, and (2) forgiveness of the ESOP's debt. Let's analyze a simple sale to a non-ESOP buyer and later to an ESOP buyer. For simplicity we will ignore tax benefits of all loans throughout this example.

Suppose the fair market value of all assets is $10 million before and after the sale. Pre-transaction liabilities are zero, so capital is worth $10 million, pre-transaction. If a buyer pays the seller personally $5 million for one-half of the capital stock of the Company, the transaction does not impact the value of the firm—ignoring adjustments for control and marketability. If the buyer takes out a personal loan for the $5 million and pays the seller, there is also no impact on the value of the company. In both cases the buyer owns one-half of a $10 million firm, and it was a fair transaction.

If the corporation takes out the loan on behalf of the buyer but the buyer ultimately has to repay the corporation, then the real liability is to the buyer, not the corporation, and there is no impact on the value of the stock—it is still worth $5 million. The corporation is a mere conduit for the loan to the buyer.

What happens to the firm's value if the corporation takes out and eventually repays the loan? The assets are still worth $10 million post-transaction.[32] Now there are $5 million in liabilities, so the equity is worth $5 million. The buyer owns one-half of a firm worth $5 million, so his or her stock is only worth $2.5 million. Was the buyer hoodwinked?

The possible confusion over value clearly arises because it is the corporation itself that is taking out the loan to fund the buyer's purchase of stock, and the corporation—not the buyer—ultimately repays the loan. By having the corporation repay the loan, the other shareholder is forgiving his or her half of a $5 million loan and thus gifting $2.5 million to the buyer.[33] Thus, the "buyer" ultimately receives a gift of $2.5 million in the form of company stock. This is true whether the buyer is an individual or an ESOP.[34]

Dilution to Nonselling Owners

When there are additional business owners who do not sell to the ESOP, they experience dilution of their interests without the benefit of getting paid. Conceptually, these owners have participated in giving the ESOP a gift by having the Company repay the debt on behalf of the ESOP.

Assuming the nonselling owner has the fraction q of the outstanding stock of the firm, his or her dilution is equal to:

$$q[(1 - t)\, pD_E - e]$$

dilution to nonselling shareholder's stock[35]   (A13-1g*)

The dilution formula (A13-1g*) tells us that the dilution to the nonselling shareholder is simply his or her ownership, q, multiplied by the

---

32. There is a second-order effect of the firm being more highly leveraged and thus riskier that may affect value (and which we are ignoring here). See Chapter 14.

33. The other half of the forgiveness is a wash—the buyer forgiving it to himself or herself.

34. This does not mean that an ESOP brings nothing to the table in a transaction. It does bring tax deductibility of the loan principal as well as the Section 1042 rollover.

35. One would also need to consider adjusting for each nonselling shareholder's control and marketability attributes. To do so, we would have to add a term in equation (13-1g*) immediately after the q. The term would be the owner's equivalent of D_E, except customized for his or her ownership attributes. The details of such a calculation are beyond the scope of this chapter.

dilution in value to the firm itself, which is the sum of the after-tax cost of the ESOP loan and the lifetime costs.

It is also important to note that equation (A13-1g*) does not account for any possible increase in value the owner might experience as a result of having greater relative control of the firm. For example, if there were two 50% owners pre-transaction and one sells 30% to the ESOP, post-transaction the remaining 50% owner has relatively more control than he or she had before the transaction. To the extent that we might ascribe additional value to that increase in relative control, we would adjust the valuation formulas. This would mitigate the dilution in equation (A13-1g*).

Legal Issues

As mentioned above, appraisers almost unanimously consider the pre-transaction value appropriate. Also mentioned earlier in the chapter, case law and Department of Labor proposed regulations indicate the pre-transaction value is the one to be used. Nevertheless, there is ongoing controversy going back to *Farnum*, a case in which the Department of Labor withdrew before going to court, that the post-transaction value may be the most appropriate price to pay the seller.

In the previous section we demonstrated that the ESOP is receiving a gift, not really paying anything for its stock. Therefore, there is no economic justification for reducing the payment to the owner below the pre-transaction fair market value, which is the price that the seller would receive from any other buyer. If the ESOP (or any party on its behalf) demands that it "pay" no more than post-transaction value, it is tantamount to saying, "The gift you are giving me is not big enough."

While the dilution may belong to the ESOP, it is nevertheless an important consideration in determining the fairness of the transaction for purposes of a fairness opinion. If a bank loans $10 million to the ESOP for a 100% sale, with no recourse or personal guarantees of the owner, we may likely decide it is not a fair transaction to the ESOP and its participants. We would have serious questions about the ESOP's probability of becoming a long-range retirement program, given the huge debt load of the Company post-transaction.

Charity

While the dilution technically belongs to the ESOP, I consider it my duty to inform the seller of the dilution phenomenon and how it works. While affirming the seller's right to receive fair market value undiminished by dilution, I do mention that if the seller has any charitable motivations to his or her employees—which a minority do—then voluntarily accepting some of the dilution will leave the Company and the ESOP in better shape. Of course, in a partial sale it also leaves the remainder of the owner's stock at a higher value than it would have had with the ESOP bearing all of the dilution.

CHAPTER 14

Buyouts of Partners and Shareholders

INTRODUCTION

AN EXAMPLE OF A BUYOUT

  The Solution

    First-Order Impact of Buyout on Post-transaction Valuation

    Secondary Impact of Buyout on Post-transaction Valuation

    ESOP Dilution Formula as a Benchmark

EVALUATING THE BENCHMARKS

INTRODUCTION

Buying out a partner or shareholder is intellectually related to the problem of measuring dilution in employee stock ownership plans (ESOPs), which is covered in the previous chapter. There is no substantive difference in the post-transaction effects of buying out partners versus shareholders, so for ease of exposition we will use the term *partners* to cover both situations.

AN EXAMPLE OF A BUYOUT

Suppose you have already valued the drapery manufacturer owned by the Roth family, the Drapes of Roth. Its FMV on an illiquid minority interest basis is $1 million pre-buyout. There are four partners, each with a 25% share of the business: I. M. Roth, U. R. Roth, Izzy Roth, and B. Roth. There are 1 million shares issued and outstanding, so the per share FMV is $1 million FMV/1 million shares = $1.00 per share. The problem is the impact on the post-transaction FMV if the three other Roths become wroth with Izzy Roth and want to buy him out.

The Solution

The solution to the problem first depends whether the three Roths have enough money to buy out Izzy with their personal assets. If so, then there is no impact on the value of the firm. If not then the firm typically will take out a loan to buy out Izzy.[1]

First-Order Impact of Buyout on Post-transaction Valuation

To a first approximation, there should be no impact on the FMV per share. For simplicity of discussion, we ignore the subtleties of differentials in the discount for lack of control of 25% versus 33 1/3% interests, although in actuality the appraiser must consider that issue. The FMV of the firm has declined by the amount of the loan to $750,000. The shareholders bought 250,000 shares, leaving $750,000 shares. Our first approximation of the post-transaction value is $750,000/750,000 shares = $1.00 per share, or no change.

Secondary Impact of Buyout on Post-transaction Valuation

The $250,000 has increased the debt-to-equity ratio of the firm. The firm has increased its financial risk, which raises the overall risk of the firm.[2] It is probably appropriate to raise the discount rate 1–2% to reflect the additional risk and rerun the pre-transaction discounted cash flows to come to a potential post-transaction valuation. Suppose that value is $0.92

---

1. It is possible for the shareholders to take out the loan individually and the firm would pay it indirectly by bonusing out sufficiently large salaries to cover the personally loans above and beyond their normal draw. This has no impact on the solution, as both the direct and indirect approaches will come to the same result.
2. In the context of the capital asset pricing model, the stock beta rises with additional financial leverage.

per share. Is that reasonable? What if the tentative post-transaction value were $0.78 per share? Is that reasonable?

ESOP Dilution Formula as a Benchmark

A benchmark would be very helpful to determine reasonability. Let's set up a hypothetical ESOP with tax attributes similar to the partner to be bought out. A loan to fund this purchase would have no tax advantages. While the interest is tax deductible, the firm does not need to engage in this buyout transaction in order to achieve its optimal debt to equity ratio in order to have the minimum possible weighted average cost of capital (WACC). The firm can borrow optimally without a buyout. Therefore, it is reasonable to consider the after-tax cost of the loan to be the same as its pre-tax amount, which is the payment to the partner.

The following is a listing and calculation of the various values pertinent to this transaction. All values are a fraction of a starting pre-transaction value of $1.

$$1 \quad \text{pre-buyout FMV} \qquad \qquad (14\text{-}1)$$

$$x \quad \text{payment to the partner} \qquad \qquad (14\text{-}2)$$

$$1 - x \quad \text{post-transaction FMV—Firm} \qquad \qquad (14\text{-}3)$$

The hypothetical ESOP owns p% of the firm, where p is the portion of the partnership bought from the selling partner. Its post-transaction value is:

$$p(1 - x) \quad \text{post-transaction FMV—Hypothetical ESOP} \qquad (14\text{-}4)$$

The first four formulas tell us that for every $1 of pre-transaction value, the company pays the selling partner x, which leaves a post-transaction value of the firm of $1 - x$ and post-transaction of the ESOP's interest in the partnership of $p(1 - x)$.

The company should pay the partner the amount that equates the payment to the partner with the post-transaction value of the hypothetical ESOP, or:

$$x = p(1 - x) \quad \text{Payment = Post-Trans. FMV- Hypothetical ESOP} \quad (14\text{-}5)$$

Collecting terms,

$$x + px = p \qquad \qquad (14\text{-}5a)$$

$$x(1 + p) = p \qquad \qquad (14\text{-}5b)$$

Dividing through by $1 + p$, we come to a final solution of:

$$x = \frac{p}{1 + p} \qquad \qquad (14\text{-}6)$$

Note that equation (14-6) is identical to equation (13-3j) when $e = 0$, $t = 0$, and $D_E = 1$. This makes sense for the following reasons:

1. This is a buyout of a partner. The ESOP is hypothetical only. There are no lifetime ESOP costs, which means $e = 0$.

2. There are no tax benefits of the loan to buy out the partner. Therefore, tax savings on the hypothetical ESOP loan are zero and $t = 0$.

3. There are no ESOP level marketability attributes of marketability and control in the buyout of the partner, therefore $D_E = 1$.[3]

Substituting $p = 25\%$ into equation (14-6), $x = 20\%$. Let's check the results.

1. The Company pays 20% of the pre-transaction value to the partner
2. The post-transaction value is the remaining 80%.
3. There are three real partners remaining plus the hypothetical ESOP, for a total of four partners
4. Each remaining partner has a ¼ share of the 80%, or 20%, which is equal to the payment to the first partner. This demonstrates that equation (14-6) works.

Thus, for every $1.00 of pre-transaction value, this hypothetical ESOP benchmark leaves us with $0.80 per share post-transaction value.

EVALUATING THE BENCHMARKS

If the transaction would not increase financial risk, the post-transaction value of the firm would be the same as the pre-transaction value, or $1.00 per share. Incorporating the leverage into the valuation, we have results of $0.92 per share and $0.78 per share using two different additions to the discount rate in our discounted cash flow analysis. Our hypothetical ESOP benchmark value is $0.80 per share. What is reasonable?

It is clear that the post-transaction value cannot be more than the pre-transaction value, so the latter is a ceiling value. It is also clear that the hypothetical ESOP approach is a floor value, because the ESOP really does not exist and the 250,000 shares are really not outstanding. The hypothetical ESOP approach assumes the shares are outstanding. Therefore, the post-transaction value must be higher than the hypothetical ESOP value.

Now we know the post-transaction value of the firm should be less than $1.00 per share and greater than $0.80 per share. The $0.92 per share post-transaction value looks quite reasonable, while the $.78 per share value is obviously wrong. If we had added 1% to the discount rate to arrive at the $0.92 per share and 2% to the discount rate to produce the $0.78 per share result, the 1% addition would appear to be the right one.

---

3. However, this is where the differences mentioned earlier, i.e., differences in the discount for lack of control of a 25% partner versus a 1/3 partner, would come into play.

Glossary

ADF (annuity discount factor)   the present value of a finite stream of cash flows for every beginning $1 of cash flow. See Chapter 3.

control premium   the additional value inherent in the control interest as contrasted to a minority interest, which reflects its power of control[1]

CARs (cumulative abnormal returns)   a measure used in academic finance articles to measure the excess returns an investor would have received over a particular time period if he or she were invested in a particular stock. This is typically used in control and takeover studies, where stockholders are paid a premium for being taken over. Starting some time period before the takeover (often five days before the first announced bid, but sometimes a longer period), the researchers calculate the actual daily stock returns for the target firm and subtract out the expected market returns (usually calculated using the firm's beta and applying it to overall market movements during the time period under observation). The excess actual return over the capital asset pricing model-determined expected return market is called an "abnormal return." The cumulation of the daily abnormal returns over the time period under observation is the CAR. The term CAR(−5, 0) means the CAR calculated from five days before the announcement to the day of announcement. The CAR(−1, 0) is a control premium, although Mergerstat generally uses the stock price five days before announcement rather than one day before announcement as the denominator in its control premium calculation. However, the CAR for any period other than (−1, 0) is not mathematically equivalent to a control premium.

DLOC (discount for lack of control)   an amount or percentage deducted from a pro rata share of the value of 100% of an equity interest in a business, to reflect the absence of some or all of the powers of control.[2]

DLOM (discount for lack of marketability)   an amount or percentage deducted from an equity interest to reflect lack of marketability.[3]

---

1. Business Valuation Standards, Definitions, American Society of Appraisers.
2. Ibid.
3. Ibid.

economic components model Abrams' model for calculating DLOM based on the interaction of discounts from four economic components. This model consists of four components: the measure of the economic impact of the delay-to-sale, monopsony power to buyers, and incremental transactions costs to both buyers and sellers. See the second half of Chapter 7.

discount rate the rate of return on investment that would be required by a prudent investor to invest in an asset with a specific level risk. Also, a rate of return used to convert a monetary sum, payable or receivable in the future, into present value.[4]

fractional interest discount the combined discounts for lack of control and marketability.

g the constant growth rate in cash flows or net income used in the ADF, Gordon model, or present value factor.

Gordon model present value of a perpetuity with growth. The end-of-year Gordon model formula is $1/(r - g)$, and the midyear formula is $\sqrt{1 + r}/(r - g)$. See Chapter 3.

log size model Abrams' model to calculate discount rates as a function of the logarithm of the value of the firm. See Chapter 4.

markup the period after an announcement of a takeover bid in which stock prices typically rise until a merger or acquisition is made (or until it falls through).

Ordinary least squares (OLS) regression analysis a statistical technique that minimizes the sum of the squared deviations between a dependent variable and one or more independent variables and provides the user with a *y*-intercept and *x*-coefficients, as well as feedback such as R^2 (explained variation/total variation) *t*-statistics, *p*-values, etc. See Chapter 2.

NPV (net present value of cash flows) Same as PV, but usually includes a subtraction for an initial cash outlay.

PPF (periodic perpetuity factor) a generalization formula invented by Abrams that is the present value of regular but noncontiguous cash flows that have constant growth to perpetuity. The end-of-year PPF is equal to:

$$PPF = \frac{(1 + r)^b}{(1 + r)^j - (1 + g)^j}$$

and the midyear PPF is equal to

$$PPF = \frac{\sqrt{1 + r}\,(1 + r)^b}{(1 + r)^j - (1 + g)^j}$$

where *r* is the discount rate, *b* is the number of years (before) since the last occurrence of the cash flow, and *j* is the number of years between cash flows. See Chapter 3.

PV (present value of cash flows) the value in today's dollars of cash flows that occur in different time periods.

---

4. Ibid.

present value factor equal to the formula $1/(1 + r)^n$, where n is the number of years from the valuation date to the cash flow and r is the discount rate. For business valuation, n should usually be midyear, i.e., $n = 0.5, 1.5, \ldots$

QMDM (quantitative marketability discount model) model for calculating DLOM for minority interests.[5]

r the discount rate

runup the period before a formal announcement of a takeover bid in which one or more bidders are either preparing to make an announcement or speculating that someone else will.

---

5. Z. Christopher, Mercer, *Quantifying Marketability Discounts: Developing and Supporting Marketability Discounts in the Appraisal of Closely Held Business Interests* (Memphis, Tenn: Peabody, 1997)

Index

Amihud, Y., 232, 282, 379, 381
Andersson, Thomas, 219, 283
Annin, Michael, 148, 155

Banz, Rolf, 119, 155
Barca, F., 220, 282
Bergstrom, C., 282
Berkovitch, E., 221, 282
Bhattacharyya, Gouri K., 22, 52
Black, Fisher, 303
Black-Scholes options pricing model (BSOPM),
    192, 235, 246, 251–254, 256, 281, 303, 305–306
Black-Scholes put option, 233, 243–246, 298, 306
Boatwright, David, 258n
Bolotsky, Michael J., 198, 200–206, 230–231, 282
Bradley, M.A., 210, 220, 224–225, 233, 282
Brealey, R.A., 175, 177

Center for Research in Security Prices (CRSP),
    162n
Chaffe, David B.H., 241–242, 251, 282, 307, 317
Copeland, Tom, 176
Crow, Matthew R., 249

Desai, A., 210, 220, 224–225, 233, 282

Eckbo, B.E., 220–221, 282
Einhorn, Hillel J., 250, 282
Ellsberg, Daniel, 250, 282
Euler's constant, 49, 51
Excel, 2, 44, 51, 115, 124, 136

Fagan, Timothy J., 214, 217, 283
Fama, Eugene F., 119, 146, 155
Fama-French Cost of Equity Model, 147–148
Fowler, Bradley, 405, 410–411, 414–415, 431
Franks, J.R., 221, 282

Freeman, Neill, 233–234, 283
French, Kenneth R., 119, 146, 155

Gilbert, Gregory A., 146, 155, 167
Glass, Carla, 208, 224, 226
Golder, Stanley C., 410, 431
Gordon, M.J., 59, 90n
Gordon model, 25, 50, 59–60, 63–79, 87–90, 93–
    97, 140, 153, 157, 175–176, 207, 230, 263–264,
    287, 385–387, 392, 394, 396, 398–399, 403
Grabowski, Roger, 113, 119, 126, 144, 146, 148–
    151, 155, 166, 241
Gregory, Gordon, 258n
Guideline Company Method, 46–52, 59, 114,
    153, 167–168

Hall, Lance, 236, 298
Hamada, R.S., 183, 190
Harris, Ellie G., 222, 282
Harrison, Paul, 113, 131, 133–135, 155
Hayes, Richard, 134, 155
Hiatt, R.K., 246n, 262n, 287n, 405n
Hogarth, Robin M., 250, 282
Horner, M.R., 220, 282
Houlihan Lokey Howard & Zukin (HLHZ)
    studies, 198, 206, 210, 212–213, 217, 226, 329n
Hull, John C., 241n

Ibbotson & Associates, 120, 134, 147n, 148, 155,
    162, 170, 176–177, 385, 387, 404
Ibbotson, Roger G., 139n, 147, 151, 154–155, 207
Indro Daniel C., 175, 177
Institute of Business Appraisers (IBA), 272–273

Jacobs, Bruce I., 119, 152–153, 155, 167
Jankowske, Wayne C., 200–201, 204–206, 231,
    282
Johnson, Bruce A., 274, 276, 282
Johnson, Richard A., 22, 52

Joyce, Allyn A., 170, 177
Julius, J. Michael, 249

Kahneman, Daniel, 247, 284
Kaplan, Paul D., 147, 155
Kasper, Larry J., 88n, 222, 234–235, 281–282
Kasper bid-ask spread model, 191, 222, 234–235
Kasper discounted time to market model, 232
Kim, E.H., 210, 220, 224–225, 233, 282
King, David, 113, 119, 126, 144, 146, 148–151, 155, 166, 241, 282
Koller, Tim, 176

Lang, L.H.P., 221, 282
Lease, Ronald C., 210, 212, 214, 217, 219, 227, 231, 280
Lee, Wayne Y., 175, 177
Lerch, Mary Ann, 282
Levy, H., 220, 283
Levy, Kenneth N., 119, 152–153, 155, 167
Lotus, 2, 44–45, 124, 136

Maher, Maria, 219, 283
Management Planning, Inc., 235–241, 250–251, 255–256, 273–275, 279, 298–303, 330
Maquieira, Carlos P., 210, 220–221, 224–227, 283
McCarter, Mary M., 208, 224, 226, 282
McConnell, John J., 210, 212, 213–214, 217, 219, 227, 231, 282–283
Megginson, William L., 210, 212–214, 219–221, 224–227, 283
Mendelson, Haim, 232, 282, 379, 381
Menyah, Kojo, 210, 222, 235, 281
Mercer, Z. Christopher, 59, 90n, 191–192, 197, 200–203, 206–209, 224–226, 232–235, 248–249, 252, 273–281, 283, 317, 350, 477n
Mercer Quantitative Marketability Discount Model (QMDM), 2, 59, 89, 191, 232–234, 248–249, 273–281, 477
Mergerstat Review, 198, 201, 203, 209n, 225, 233–234
Meyers, Roy H., 235n
Mikkelson, Wayne H., 210, 212–214, 217, 219, 227, 231, 282
Miles, Raymond, 272, 359n, 379, 381
Miller, Merton, 449n
Modigliani, Franco, 449n
Morris, Jane K., 431
Much, Paul J., 214, 283
Murrin, Jack, 176
Myers, Stewart C., 175–177, 411

Nail, Lance, 210, 220–221, 224–227, 283
Nath, Eric 200–204, 206–209, 227, 283
Narayanan, M. P., 221, 282

Neal, L., 134, 155
Newton, Isaac, 156

Obenshain, Douglas, 258n

Pacelle, Mitchell, 411, 431
Paudyal, Krishna, 210, 222, 235, 283
Peterson, James D., 147, 155
Phillips, John R., 233–234, 283
Plummer, James L., 410, 431
Polacek, Tim, 236, 298
Pratt, Shannon P., 18, 19, 42, 46, 52, 207, 235, 253, 283, 350, 364, 381
Pratt, Stanley E., 431

Reilly, Robert F., 18, 19, 42, 46, 52, 235, 251, 253, 283
Roach, George P., 206, 221, 224–225, 283
Roll, Richard, 210, 283
Rothschild, Baron, 134n
Rydqvist, K., 220, 279, 282–283

Schilt, James H., 281
Schweihs, Robert P., 18, 19, 42, 46, 52, 235, 251, 253, 283
Schwert, G. William, 151–152, 155, 192, 209–211, 220–222, 235, 255, 269, 283, 335n
Scholes, Myron, 303
Scott, William Jr., 140n
Seguin, Paul J., 151–152, 155
Shannon, Donald, 3
Shapiro, E., 59, 90n
Sharpe-Lintner model, 146
Simpson, David W., 283
Solomon, King, 134
Stern, Joel, 281
Stillman, R., 220, 283
Stoll, H.R., 223, 283
Stulz, R., 282

Thomas, George B. Jr., 155–156
Tversky, Amos, 247, 284
Twain, Mark, 170

Vander Linden, Eric, 207, 284

Walkling, R.A., 280
Watson, John Jr., 236n, 255n
Williams, J.B., 59n, 90n
Wonnacott, Thomas H., 22, 52
Wonnacott, Ronald J., 22, 52

Zingales, L., 220, 284
Zukin, James H., 207, 284

About the Author

Jay B. Abrams, ASA, CPA, MBA, a nationally known authority in valuing privately held businesses, has published numerous seminal articles.

Mr. Abrams is the principal of Abrams Valuation Group in La Jolla, California, a firm that specializes in business valuation. He was a Project Manager at Arthur D. Little Valuation, Inc. in Los Angeles, California, where he performed the valuations of Columbia Pictures, Dr. Pepper, Purex, MCO Geothermal, VSA, and many other large firms.

Mr. Abrams has several inventions to his name, many of which are discussed in this work. In 1992 he published the solution to a 500-year-old problem—how to pinpoint an accounting transposition error.

Mr. Abrams has an MBA in finance from the University of Chicago, where he also took graduate courses in the Department of Economics. He received his B.S. in Business Administration from California State University, Northridge, where he received the Arthur Young Outstanding Accounting Student Award in 1972.

Mr. Abrams has spoken in a variety of different professional and public forums about valuing privately held businesses, including the 1998 Conference of the National Association of Valuation Analysts; the 1996 International Conference of the American Society of Appraisers, in Toronto; Anthony Robbins' Mastery University; and the National Center for Employee Ownership Annual Conference. He has taught business valuation as continuing legal education and at the University of California at San Diego Extension.

Mr. Abrams lives in San Diego, California, with his wife and five children.